San Francisco

timeout.com/sanfrancisco

PENGUIN BOOKS

Published by the Penguin Group
Penguin Books Ltd, 80 Strand, London WC2R ORL, England
Penguin Books USA Inc., 375 Hudson Street, New York, New York 10014, USA
Penguin Books Australia Ltd, 250 Camberwell Road, Camberwell, Victoria 3124, Australia
Penguin Books Canada Ltd, 10 Alcorn Avenue, Toronto, Ontario, Canada M4V 3B2
Penguin Books (NZ) Ltd, cnr Rosedale and Airborne Roads, Albany, Auckland, New Zealand

Penguin Books Ltd, Registered Offices: 80 Strand, London WC2R 0RL, England

First edition 1996
Second edition 1998
Third edition 2000
Fourth edition 2002
Fifth edition 2004

10 9 8 7 6 5 4 3 2 1

Colour reprographics by Icon, Crowne House, 56-58 Southwark Street, London SE1 1UN
Printed and bound by Cayfosa-Quebecor, Ctra. de Caldes, Km 3 08 130 Sta, Perpètua de Mogoda, Barcelona, Spain

Edited and designed by
Time Out Guides Limited
Universal House
251 Tottenham Court Road
London W1T 7AB
Tel + 44 (0)20 7813 3000
Fax + 44 (0)20 7813 6001
Email guides@timeout.com
www.timeout.com

Editorial

Editor Simon Coppock
Deputy Editor Jessica Eveleigh
Consultant Editor Bonnie Wach
Listings Editors Elise Proulx, Kristen Salvatore
Proofreader Tamsin Shelton
Indexer Jonathan Cox

Editorial/Managing Director Peter Fiennes
Series Editor Ruth Jarvis
Deputy Series Editor Lesley McCave
Guides Co-ordinator Anna Norman
Accountant Sarah Bostock

Design

Art Director Mandy Martin
Acting Art Director Scott Moore
Acting Art Editor Tracey Ridgewell
Acting Senior Designer Astrid Kogler
Designer Sam Lands
Junior Designer Oliver Knight
Digital Imaging Dan Conway
Ad Make-up Charlotte Blythe

Picture Desk

Picture Editor Jael Marschner
Deputy Picture Editor Kit Burnet
Picture Researchers Alex Ortiz, Ivy Lahon
Picture Desk Assistant Laura Lord

Advertising

Sales Director Mark Phillips
International Sales Manager Ross Canadé
International Sales Executive James Tuson
Advertising Sales (San Francisco) Robin Bleiweiss
Advertising Assistant Lucy Butler

Marketing

Marketing Manager Mandy Martinez
US Publicity & Marketing Associate Rosella Albanese

Production

Guides Production Director Mark Lamond
Production Controller Samantha Furniss

Time Out Group

Chairman Tony Elliott
Managing Director Mike Hardwick
Group Financial Director Richard Waterlow
Group Commercial Director Lesley Gill
Group Marketing Director Christine Cort
Group General Manager Nichola Coulthard
Group Art Director John Oakey
Online Managing Director David Pepper
Group Production Director Steve Proctor
Group IT Director Simon Chappell

Contributors

Introduction Bonnie Wach. **History** Michael Ansaldo (*Queen Califia* Julia Bloch; *The I-Hotel* Mike Arago). **San Francisco Today** Bonnie Wach. **Architecture** Erin Cullerton. **Literary San Francisco** Kristin Palm. **Where to Stay** Amy Weaver; *additional reviews* Jake Bumgardner, Simon Coppock (*Death beds* Jessica Eveleigh). **Sightseeing: Introduction** Simon Coppock. **Downtown & SoMa** Anna Mantzaris. **North Beach & Around** Michael Ansaldo (*Dead Beat with a Martini* Jake Bumgardner; *Barbary Lane* Simon Coppock). **Mission & Castro** Genanne Walsh. **Haight, Western Addition & Hayes Valley** Amy Weaver (*Denizens of iniquity* Heather Bradley; *Robert Crumb* Matt Markovich). **Pacific Heights to Golden Gate Bridge** Matt Markovich. **Richmond, Sunset & Golden Gate Park** Matt Markovich; *Golden Gate Park* Amy Weaver (*Free parking* Amy Weaver). **East Bay** Laura Paskell-Brown. **Restaurants & Cafés** Rob Farmer; *additional reviews* Bonnie Wach (*Later than breakfast* Matt Markovich). **Bars** Matt Markovich; *additional reviews* Simon Coppock, Matt Markovich (*Bookshops, Thrift, fleas & second-hand* Kristin Palm; *Vinyl junkies* Ken Taylor). **Festivals & Events** Kristen Salvatore (*Our Lady of Guadalupe* Simon Coppock). **Children** Elise Proulx. **Film** Mike Arago. **Galleries** Erin Cullerton (*Art for artists' sake* Jessica Eveleigh). **Music & Nightlife** Kimberly Chun; *Classical & Opera* Amy Weaver (*Real contemporary* Amy Weaver; *The party principles* Steve Robles). **Queer San Francisco** Genanne Walsh. **Sport & Fitness** Jake Bumgardner (*Shark Attack!* Lena Katz). **Theatre & Dance** Anna Mantzaris. **Trips Out of Town: Introduction** Jonathan Cox. **Heading North & Heading South** Lena Katz (*All points north, Shore thing* Jessica Eveleigh). **Wine Country** Rob Farmer. **Heading East** Laura Paskell-Brown. **Directory** Elise Proulx; *Further reference* Simon Coppock (*Sun, wind & fog* Kristen Salvatore; *Wi-Fi…why not?* Matt Markovich). **Additional editing** Jonathan Cox. **Additional checking** Matt Markovich, Anna Mantzaris.

Maps JS Graphics (john@jsgraphics.co.uk), Mapworld (MapworldUK@aol.com) and Reineck & Reineck (reineck@reineckandreinceck.com).

Photography by Jon Perugia, except p6, p29 Hulton Getty; p14 Time Life; p76, p94, p194 Corbis; p235 Getty News & Sport; p265 Raye Santos/Yosemite Park; p263, p268 Alamy.
The following pictures were provided by featured establishments/artists: p62, p246.

The Editor would like to thank: Cath Phillips, the staff at the San Francisco Convention & Visitors Bureau and all who have contributed to previous editions of this guide.

Contents

Introduction   2

In Context   5
History   6
San Francisco Today   17
Architecture   21
Literary San Francisco   26

Where to Stay   31
Where to Stay   32

Sightseeing   53
Introduction   54
Downtown & SoMa   56
North Beach & Around   73
The Mission & the Castro   85
Haight, Western Addition &
   Hayes Valley   91
Pacific Heights to the
   Golden Gate Bridge   96
Richmond, Sunset &
   Golden Gate Park   104
The East Bay   111

Eat, Drink, Shop   115
Restaurants   116
Cafés   141
Bars   148
Shops & Services   159

Arts & Entertainment   187
Festivals & Events   188
Children   195
Film   199
Galleries   204
Music   209
Nightlife   219
Queer San Francisco   224
Sport & Fitness   234
Theatre & Dance   244

Trips Out of Town   249
Introduction   250
Heading North   251
Wine Country   256
Heading East   263
Heading South   267

Directory   273
Getting Around   274
Resources A-Z   280
Further Reference   292
Index   294

Maps   301
BART & Muni Map   302
Trips Out of Town   304
City Overview   305
San Francisco by Area   306
San Francisco Street Maps   308
Street Index   316

Introduction

For all its world-class attractions, acclaimed restaurants and historic landmarks, San Francisco is at heart just a small town strapped into big-city shoes. Spend any amount of time in one area and don't be surprised if you start bumping into familiar faces. Surrounded on three sides by water, San Francisco's petite frame – it's only seven miles (11 kilometres) square – nonetheless encompasses 43 hills, more than two dozen neighbourhoods, three-quarters of a million people, 120,000 dogs and 225,000 cars.

The advantages of compact geography are fairly obvious – especially to travellers who like to walk. In an afternoon, you can stroll the glorious span of the Golden Gate Bridge, swing by a nudist beach, trade barks with a bevy of boisterous sea lions, sip a fine espresso and practise Italian in a café, have an ancient herbalist mix you up a love potion in Chinatown, ride a cable car over Nob Hill – and be back at your downtown hotel in time for a glorious supper.

The city's quirky personality is perhaps less apparent than its steep slopes, but if you forgo the car and stick to the myriad public transport options, you'll soon discover San Francisco's nooks, crannies and quixotic charms, as well as coming to understand its many nicknames: Paris of the Pacific, Baghdad by the Bay, Athens of the West, bawdy, naughty Frisco town. It's Brigadoon too, emerging shimmering from the mists on a foggy morning like a fairytale castle, revealing vistas that will make you catch your breath as you hurriedly reach for the camera.

Suck it all in – from high-tech SoMa to Tenderloin lowlifes, from the beauty of the bridges to the beastliness of the traffic, from the damp chill of the fog to that eye-wateringly hot plate of Hunan chicken – and you'll soon be feeling at one with the place. This city's spirit of openness and hell-bent pursuit of pleasure have been irresistible to idealists, explorers and entrepreneurs for centuries. You can't help but have a good time.

ABOUT THE TIME OUT CITY GUIDES

Time Out San Francisco is one of the expanding series of *Time Out* guides, produced by the people behind London and New York's successful listings magazines. Our guides are all written and updated by resident experts who have striven to provide you with all the most up-to-date information you'll need to explore the city or read up on its background, whether you're a local or a first-time visitor.

THE LOWDOWN ON THE LISTINGS

Above all, we've tried to make this book as useful as possible. Addresses, telephone numbers, websites, transport information, opening times, admission prices and credit card details have all been included in the listings. And, as far as possible, we've given details of facilities, services and events, all checked and correct as we went to press. However, owners and managers can change their arrangements at any time, and they often do. Before you go out of your way, we'd advise you to telephone and check opening times, ticket prices and other particulars.

While every effort has been made to ensure the accuracy of the information contained in this guide, the publishers cannot accept responsibility for any errors it may contain.

PRICES AND PAYMENT

We have noted where venues such as shops, hotels, restaurants, museums, attractions and the like accept the following credit cards: American Express (AmEx), Diners Club (DC), Discover (Disc), MasterCard (MC) and Visa (V). Many will also accept travellers' cheques, along with other credit cards (Carte Blanche, for example).

The prices we've supplied should be treated as guidelines, not gospel. If you find that prices vary wildly from those we've quoted, please write and let us know. We aim to give the best and most up-to-date advice, so we always want to know if you've been badly treated or overcharged.

THE LIE OF THE LAND

San Francisco is made up a series of distinct neighbourhoods, each with its own quirks and characteristics (and often its own climate). Although the names of these neighbourhoods are pretty much fixed – North Beach, Pacific Heights, the Castro, the Mission, Russian Hill, Civic Center, the Tenderloin and so on – the boundaries that separate them are occasionally fuzzy. We have used the most commonly accepted demarcations – see page 306 for a map of the

various areas – but you may find slightly different boundaries in other tourist literature and on other maps. Consult the introduction to the Sightseeing section – on page 54 – for a brief but detailed breakdown of these various city neighbourhoods.

Most of the city's street layout is fairly easy to understand, based as it is on the grid system common to so many US towns. When listing an address for a venue, we have given the street address plus the nearest cross street or streets, to make it easier to identify. The public transport system is comprehensive and efficient and will take you pretty much wherever you want to go within San Francisco; for more details, see page 275. You will only need a car if you are planning a journey outside the city to places ill-served by public transport, such as the wineries of Napa and Sonoma Valleys. Our Trips Out of Town section starts on page 249. For information on driving and car rental, see page 277.

TELEPHONE NUMBERS

There are various telephone area codes that serve the Bay Area: 415 for San Francisco and Marin County, 510 for Berkeley and Oakland, 650 for the peninsula cities and 707 for Napa and Sonoma Counties. Phone numbers throughout the guide are listed as if you're dialling from within San Francisco.

Advertisers

We would like to stress that no establishment has been included in this guide because it has advertised in any of our publications and no payment of any kind has influenced any review. The opinions given in this book are those of *Time Out* writers and entirely independent.

If you're dialling from outside your area code, you'll have to add an initial 1 (1-415, 1-510 and so on). All 1-800 and 1-888 numbers can be dialled free of charge within the US, but few of them are free from the UK. For more on telephones and codes, see page 286.

ESSENTIAL INFORMATION

For all the practical information you might need for visiting San Francisco, including visa and customs information, advice on facilities and access for the disabled, emergency telephone numbers and local transport, turn to the Directory chapter at the back of the guide. It starts on page 273.

MAPS

Wherever possible, a map reference is provided for every venue listed in the guide, indicating the page and grid reference at which it can be found on our detailed street maps of San Francisco. There is also a map showing the different neighbourhoods within San Francisco, overview maps of the city and the wider Bay Area, and a transport map showing the BART and Muni system in downtown San Francisco. The maps section starts on page 301.

LET US KNOW WHAT YOU THINK

We hope you enjoy *Time Out San Francisco*, and we'd like to know what you think of it. We welcome tips for places that you consider we should include in future editions and take note of your criticism of our choices. There's a reader's reply card at the back of this book for your feedback, or you can email us at sanfranciscoguide@timeout.com.

There is an online version of this guide, and guides to over 45 international cities, at **www.timeout.com**.

In Context

History	**6**
San Francisco Today	**17**
Architecture	**21**
Literary San Francisco	**26**

Features

SF heroes Queen Califia	11
The I-Hotel	12
Dog days	18
Inside out	24
The Grotto	28

Protests at City Hall.
See p10.

NO
CHINESE
CHEAP LABOR
FOR US

History

Through earthquakes and fire, boom and bust, San Francisco's powers of reinvention remain strong.

When excavation began in 1969 for BART's Civic Center station, workers uncovered the body of a young woman. Experts dated the remains to approximately 2,950 BC, the city's earliest known burial – and a glimpse into the rich indigenous culture of the Bay Area.

During the last Ice Age 15,000 years ago, nomadic tribes migrated across the Bering Strait from Asia and eventually settled along the shores of the Bay. Ringed by reeds and hills covered with pastures, the Bay Area sustained more than 10,000 Northern Californian Indians of different tribes, later collectively dubbed Costanoans ('coast dwellers') by the Spanish.

Despite its current name, the San Francisco Bay is an estuary, mixing the cold Pacific Ocean with the San Joaquin and Sacramento rivers, whose flows originate from the fresh snowmelt of the Sierra Nevada. The Bay reached its present size about 100,000 years ago when melting glaciers flooded the world's oceans. Rising sea water flowed inland through the Golden Gate, the point where prominent coastal hills jostling around two peninsulas almost meet. This estuary protects three natural islands: Alcatraz, Angel and Yerba Buena.

The people who inhabited these areas were the Ohlone. They apparently lived in harmony both with their Miwok neighbours and the land, which provided them with rich pickings of game, fish, shellfish, fruit and nuts – a land of 'inexpressible fertility' in the words of a later French explorer. The Ohlone and their neighbours lived a successful hunter-gatherer existence – 'dancing on the brink of the world', as an Ohlone song went – until their disastrous introduction to 'civilisation' with the arrival of Spanish missionaries. Their previous rare contacts with Europeans had been friendly and travellers had been impressed by the welcome the Costanoans gave them. But the Spanish brought with them the dubious gifts of Christianity, hard labour and diseases like smallpox, which annihilated half the native population of California in a matter of 75 years.

Because the Ohlone and other local tribes had no tradition of recording their history, orally or otherwise, their destruction has largely been ignored. *The Ohlone Way* by Malcolm Margolin is an attempt to trace the lost culture of those Northern Californian Indians.

THEY CAME, THEY SAW
Looking at the Golden Gate today, it's not hard to imagine how early navigators missed the mile-wide opening. The Bay and its Indians

were hidden from view by 'stynkinge fogges' (as Drake later complained), which prevented numerous explorers over a period of 200 years from discovering the harbour entrance.

An early series of Spanish missions, sent up the coast by Hernán Cortés, notorious conqueror of Mexico and the Aztecs, never got as far as Upper California. In 1542, under the flag of Cortés's successor, Antonio de Mendoza, Portuguese explorer Juan Rodríguez Cabrillo became the first European to visit the area. Inspired by a popular 16th-century novel, the Spanish named their new-found California (see p11 **SF heroes: Queen Califia**). Cabrillo passed the Bay's entrance on his way north and on his way back again, but failed to discover its large natural harbour.

An Englishman got even closer, yet still managed to miss it. In 1579, during a foraging and spoiling mission in the name of the Virgin Queen, Elizabeth I, the then-unknighted Francis Drake landed in Miwok Indian territory just north of the Bay. With one ship, the *Golden Hind*, and a crew in dire need of rest and recreation, he put in for a six-week berth on the Marin coastline, probably near Point Reyes. Long before the Pilgrims landed at Plymouth Rock or the English settled Cupid's Cove at Newfoundland, Drake claimed California for Elizabeth I as 'Nova Albion' or 'New Britain'.

It would take another 190 years for a white man to set eyes on the Bay. Spurred on by the pressure of British colonial ambitions in America, the Spanish sent northbound missions to stake out their own territories, intent on converting the *bestias* and claiming land for the Spanish crown. In 1595 Portuguese explorer Sebastian Rodríguez Cermeno, sailing under the Spanish flag, was shipwrecked just north of the Golden Gate at what is now known as Drake's Bay. Before he made his way back to Mexico in a small boat saved from the ship, he named the protected cove Bahia de San Francisco. In 1769 the 'sacred expedition' of Gaspar de Pórtola, a Spanish aristocrat who would later become the first governor of California, and the Franciscan priest Father Junipero Serra, set off with 60 men on a gruelling march across the Mexican desert to establish a mission at San Diego. The expedition then worked its way north to Monterey, building missions and baptising Indians as they went. During the expedition, an advance party discovered the unexpectedly long bay 100 miles (160km) further up the coast. Mistaking it for Cermeno's cove, they called it Bahia de San Francisco. But since the expedition's brief was only to claim Monterey, the party returned to San Diego.

It was not until August 1775 that the *San Carlos*, a Spanish supply vessel, became the first ship to sail into the Bay. Meanwhile, a mission set off to establish a safer land route to what would eventually become San Francisco. Roughly concurrent with the signing of the American Declaration of Independence, Captain Juan Bautista de Anza led an advance party to the southern point of the Golden Gate, which he declared a perfect location for a Spanish military garrison, or *presidio*. Three miles (4.8km) inland to the south-east, a suitable site was found for a mission. Before the year was out, the *presidio* was erected and the mission – named Misión San Francisco de Asis after the holy order operating in Upper California, but popularly known as Mission Dolores – was established by the indefatigable Serra.

FOLLOW THE BEAR

Over time, a combination of favouritism, authoritarianism and religious fervour helped sow the seeds of resentment and resistance in all the territories colonised by Spain. The country's hold on its American empires first began to crumble in Mexico, which declared itself a republic in 1821. The Mexican annexation of California in the same year opened up the area to foreign settlers, among them American pioneers such as fur trapper Jedediah Smith, who in 1828 became the first white American to reach California over the Sierra Nevada mountain range. His feat might have been the more impressive, but the sedate arrival by whaler ship of an Englishman had more lasting impact. Captain William Richardson, who in 1835 built the first dwelling on the site of the future San Francisco, is credited with giving San Francisco its first name: Yerba Buena, named after the sweet mint (literally 'good herb') the Spanish used for tea.

That same year, the United States tried unsuccessfully to buy the whole of the Bay Area from the Mexicans. In the long run, however, they got California for free: the declaration of independence of the territory of Texas, and its subsequent annexation by the US, triggered the Mexican-American war in June 1846. The resulting Guadalupe-Hidalgo Treaty of 1848 officially granted the Union all the land from Texas to California and the Rio Grande to Oregon. But before the treaty could be nailed down, a few hotheads decided to 'liberate' the territory from Mexico themselves.

The short-lived Mexican rule of California coincided with the era of idealistic frontiersmen like Kit Carson and a certain Captain John Fremont. In June 1846 Fremont convinced a motley crew to take over the abandoned *presidio* to the north of Yerba Buena in Sonoma, proclaiming his new state the 'Bear Flag Republic' after the ragged banner he raised

What Londoners take when they go out.

over Sonoma's square (the design was eventually adopted as California's state flag). Fremont also christened the mouth of San Francisco Bay the 'Golden Gate', after Istanbul's Golden Horn. A few weeks after the Bear Flaggers annexed Sonoma, the US Navy captured Yerba Buena without a struggle and the whole of California became US territory.

The infant Yerba Buena was just a sleepy trading post of 500 people. The newly appointed mayor, Lieutenant Washington A Bartlett, officially renamed it 'San Francisco' on 30 January 1847. But, unbeknown to its residents, the tiny settlement was about to change beyond all recognition.

ALL THAT GLITTERS

In the early 1840s the Swiss-born John Sutter was running New Helvetia, a large ranch in California's Central Valley, and he encouraged American citizens to settle the land. One such homesteader was James Marshall. Just as he was finishing construction on a water-powered mill on the American River near Sacramento, Marshall discovered gold in a sawmill ditch. Sutter and Marshall attempted to keep their findings secret, but when newspaper publisher Sam Brannan dramatically waved a bottle of gold dust in San Francisco's town square, gold fever went global. The 1849 Gold Rush was on.

The news of riches brought in droves of drifters and fortune-seekers. Their fever was fanned by people like Brannan, whose *California Star* newspaper told of men digging up a fortune in an hour. (Brannan was also to become California's first millionaire by selling goods he had hoarded to prospectors. Pure coincidence.) Many never made it: by land, the journey meant months of exposure to blizzards, mountains, deserts and hostile tribes; by sea, they faced disease, starvation or brutal weather. Still, more than 90,000 prospectors appeared in California in the first two years after gold was discovered. More than 300,000 had arrived in the state by 1854 – or one out of every 90 people then living in the US. Though they called themselves the Argonauts, after the mythical sailors who accompanied Jason in search of the Golden Fleece, locals named them after the year the Rush began: the Forty-Niners.

In many ways, they besieged San Francisco. The port town they arrived in was one without structure, government or even a distinct name – to many it was still 'Yerba Buena'. They found more hardship than gold: on their way through San Francisco to the mines, predatory merchants fleeced them; when they returned, broke, they were left to grub mean existences from the city streets, seeking refuge in brothels, gambling dens and bars.

Within two years of Sutter's discovery, nearly 100,000 men had passed through the city; the population grew from 600 in 1848 to 25,000 in 1849, swelling the tiny community into a giant, muddy campsite. Despite a huge fire that levelled the settlement on Christmas Eve in 1849, a new town rose up to take its place and the population exploded.

This brave new San Francisco was not a place for the faint-hearted. Lawlessness and arson ruled; frontier justice was commonplace. Writers Mark Twain and Bret Harte and, later, Robert Louis Stevenson, Oscar Wilde and Anthony Trollope all travelled to the area to report on its lurid reputation, describing a boomtown full of violence and vice.

'Whipped into a fury, vigilantes lynched their first victim in June 1851.'

The opening of a post office marked the city's first optimistic stab at improving links with the rest of the continent. John White Geary, appointed postmaster by President James Knox Polk, rented a room at the corner of Montgomery and Washington Streets, where he marked out a series of squares for each letter of the alphabet and began filing letters. This crude set-up was San Francisco's first postal system. Then, in April 1850 – the year that California became the Union's 31st state – San Francisco's city charter was approved and the city elected Geary its first mayor. In order to furnish the city with proper streets, Geary established a council, which later bought the ship *Euphemia* to serve as San Francisco's first jail. It proved a sound investment. The council's first concern was to impose law and order on San Francisco's massive squatter town. Gangs of hoodlums controlled certain districts: the Ducks, led by Australian convicts, lived at a spot known as Sydney Town. Together with New York toughs the Hounds, they roamed Telegraph Hill, raping and pillaging the more orderly community of Chilean merchants who occupied Little Chile. Eventually, enraged, right-minded citizens decided to take the law into their own hands. Whipped into a fury by rabble-rousing Sam Brannan, vigilantes lynched their first victim, John Jenkins, at Portsmouth Square in June 1851. They strung up three more thieves during the following weeks – and the other Ducks and Hounds wisely cut out for the Sierras.

Though their frontier justice temporarily curbed the area's excesses, Mayor Geary understandably viewed the vigilantes as part of the problem, not the solution. But his crusade against lawlessness was hardly helped when riverbed gold started running dry. By 1853 boom had turned to bust and the resulting depression set a cyclical pattern oft-repeated through the city's history. By the mid 1860s San Francisco was bankrupt.

Henry Comstock's 1859 discovery of a rich blue vein of silver (the 'Comstock Lode') in western Nevada triggered a second invasion by fortune-seekers: the Silver Rush. This time, though, the ore's nature demanded more elaborate methods of extraction, with high yields going to a small number of companies and tycoons rather than individual prospectors. Before the supply had been exhausted, silver barons had made enough money to transform San Francisco, establishing a neighbourhood of nouveaux riches atop Nob (a name adapted from the word 'nabob') Hill. By 1870 the city was no longer just a raucous boom-and-bust town. If the nabobs took the moral and geographical high ground, those on the waterfront were busy legitimising their reputation as occupants of the 'Barbary Coast'. Naïve newcomers and drunken sailors were seen as fair game by gamblers and hoods waiting to 'shanghai' them (shanghai, like 'hoodlum', is a San Francisco expression), as were the immigrant women who found themselves trapped into a life of prostitution or slavery. At one low point, the female population numbered just 22; many a madam made fortune enough to buy her way on to Nob Hill.

The seeds of San Francisco's present-day multiculturalism were sown during this period, when a deluge of immigrants poured in from all over the world. French immigrants vying with Italians to make the best bread started baking sourdough in North Beach. A young German garment-maker named Levi Strauss started using rivets to strengthen the jeans he made for miners. In Chinatown criminal *tongs*, Mafia-like gangs, controlled the opium dens and other rackets; a Chinese immigrant, Wah Lee, opened the city's first laundry. The building in the 1860s of the transcontinental railroad, which employed thousands of Chinese labourers at low pay rates, led to further expansion of Chinatown. Despite their usefulness as cheap labour, the Chinese became the targets of racist anti-immigrant activity; indeed, proscriptive anti-Chinese legislation persisted until 1938.

Even in those days entertainment was high on the agenda for San Franciscans. In 1853 the city boasted five theatres and some 600 saloons and taverns serving 42,000 customers. Locals downed seven bottles of champagne for every bottle swallowed in Boston (San Francisco still leads the US in alcohol consumption per capita). Lola Montez, entertainer to European monarchs and thieves, arrived on a paddle-steamer from Panama in 1853 and her 'spider dance' became an instant hit at the American Theater.

San Francisco's relative isolation from the rest of the continent meant the city was hardly affected by the Civil War that devastated the American South in the early 1860s. The rest of the country seemed remote; sometimes mail took six months to arrive. Communications were slowly improving, however. Telegraph wires were being strung across the continent and where telegraph poles ran out, the Pony Express picked up messages, relaying up to 75 riders across the West to the Pacific coast. By the mid 1860s the telegraph pole had all but rendered the Pony Express obsolete; the transcontinental railroad was its *coup de grâce*.

The completion of the Central Pacific Railroad in 1869 was the signal for runaway consumption in the city. The biggest spenders were the 'Big Four', Charles Crocker, Collis P Huntington, Mark Hopkins and Leland Stanford, millionaires who were the powerful and influential principal investors behind the Central Pacific. They were highly adept at making money and brutally competitive. Their eagerness to impress the West with their flamboyantly successful business practices manifested itself in the mansions they built on Nob Hill. By 1871 121 businessmen controlled $146 million, according to one newspaper – but others got in on the act. In particular, four Irishmen – the 'Bonanza Kings': James Flood, William O'Brien, James Fair and John Mackay – made the ascent to Nob Hill despite starting out as rough-hewn miners and bartenders chipping out their fortunes from the Comstock Lode.

A Scottish-Irish banker, William Ralston, opened the Bank of California on Sansome Street in 1864. Partnered by a Prussian engineer called Adolph Sutro (later famous for building the first Cliff House and the Sutro Baths), Ralston was determined to extract every last ounce of silver from the Comstock's Sun Mountain. Unfortunately, he did so too quickly: the ore ran out before he could recoup his investment. Ralston's bank collapsed. Smiling to the last in an effort to calm his investors, Ralston drowned himself. He left behind the luxurious Palace Hotel and a lasting contribution towards San Francisco's new civic pride: Golden Gate Park. Ralston's company provided the water for designer William Hammon Hall's audacious project, which transformed a barren area of sand dunes into a magnificent expanse of trees, flowers and lakes.

THE BIG ONE

The city continued to grow, and by 1900 its population had reached more than a third of a million, making it the ninth-largest city in the

SF heroes Queen Califia

Ask an average Californian – even one as well informed and intellectually curious as your typical San Franciscan – where their state's name comes from and you're unlikely to get a confident answer. They might guess it originated with California's early Spanish settlers, but few realise it comes from the mighty, mythical Amazon Queen Califia.

Queen Califia first appeared in *Las sergas de Esplandián* (*The Exploits of Esplandián*), a 1510 novel by Garcia Ordóñez de Montalvo, who describes an idyllic island ruled by a passionate and virtuous queen: 'Know ye that at the right hand of the Indies there is an island named California, very close to that part of the Terrestrial Paradise, which was inhabited by black women, without a single man among them, and that they lived in the manner of Amazons.'

Like any good Amazon, Califia possessed the powers of the earth, moon and water. She was brave and noble as any male leader (in the 16th century this was high praise indeed). And Montalvo doesn't stop there. In his account, Califia commands mighty troops of women warriors and a force of 500 griffins, mythical monsters with the head and wings of an eagle and the body and tail of a lion. None of which, unfortunately, was enough to protect her from being captured, converted to Christianity and roped into an arranged marriage to a Spanish knight. Sound familiar? It could be argued that the story foreshadows California's entire colonial history.

No matter. When Cortés, having sailed up the west coast of Mexico, landed at the tip of the Golden State in 1535, he was still so enamoured of the fictional queen that he and his entourage believed they had discovered the 'land at the right hand of the Indies' and dubbed it California. California is the only US state to have been named after a mythological character, and its namesake is depicted in a stunning 1926 mural (*pictured*) that adorns the Room of the Dons in the historical Mark Hopkins Inter-Continental Hotel in San Francisco's Nob Hill district.

Some argue 'California' is derived from the Greek, while others believe it simply comes from the Spanish word *calif* (or 'caliph'), derived from the Arabic name *Khalifah*, which means 'successor'. Literary types point out that Montalvo was probably also aware of the association between Califia and Kali, the Indian goddess of creation and destruction.

Of course the tale of Cortés's fabulous error has detractors. Some historians argue that the idea of the Spanish explorer naming this part of the New World after a fictional queen is as romanticised as Montalvo's vision of a matriarchal paradise. But take one look at the Mark Hopkins mural, and you'll understand one reason California – and San Francisco in particular – is a haven for queens.

Union. But on 18 April 1906, shortly after 5am, dogs began howling and horses whinnying – noises that, along with glasses tinkling and windows rattling, marked the unnerving moments before an earthquake.

When the quake hit – a rending in the tectonic plates 25 miles (40km) beneath the ocean bed that triggered the shifting of billions of tons of rock – it generated more energy than all the explosives used in World War II. The rip snaked inland, tearing a gash now known as the San Andreas Fault down the coastline. Cliffs appeared from nowhere, cracks yawned, ancient redwoods toppled and part of the newly built City Hall tumbled down. A second tremor struck, ripping the walls out of buildings. A ghastly pause followed, then people ran into the streets in their nightclothes.

Tragically, one of the earthquake's many victims was a man the city badly needed just

The I-Hotel

On the corner of Jackson and Kearny Streets, where the Financial District meets Chinatown, there was this gigantic hole. All around it real estate prices were rocketing, but for more than 25 years this hole – almost a whole block long – remained. Known in better times as 'Manilatown', the surrounding area had been the thriving hub of San Francisco's Filipino community, and the intersection at 848 Kearny Street was the site of the International Hotel (or 'I-Hotel'), home to elderly Filipinos and Chinese for more than 50 years. Until, that is, the summer of 1977.

When the first Filipino immigrants (men respectfully known as 'Manong') came to San Francisco in the early part of the 20th century, they were denied the right to own property or businesses. Most Manongs were forced to undertake menial labour and live in residential hotels, like the I-Hotel. But time passed, mores changed and Filipino-Americans became homeowners and business and community leaders. Soon the Bay Area was home to the largest population of Filipinos outside the Philippines. Many of the Manong, however, remained in their single hotel rooms. By the late 1960s the I-Hotel was one of the last such residential hotels in Manilatown – with $45-a-month rent meaning few of the tenants had any plans to leave. Property developers, enamoured of Manilatown's position at the edge of the ever-expanding Financial District, decided to evict the tenants and demolish the hotel for a parking lot.

What the developers didn't count on was there being any resistance. In what is seen by many as the opening salvo of Asian-American activism, the eviction order brought college students out to protest next to grandfathers and community leaders, demanding that the Manong be permitted to live out the rest of their lives in dignity. After years of legal wrangling, final eviction orders came through and, at midnight on 4 August 1977, the police arrived in full riot gear. Thousands of protesters opposed baton-wielding officers, while Sheriff Richard Hongisto hacked down hotel doors with an axe so the residents could be hauled out. By 3am more than 50 elderly Filipino- and Chinese-Americans had been forcibly removed from their tiny rooms and thrown on to the street. The hotel was duly demolished and it seemed that the story of the I-Hotel had reached an end.

Then a curious thing happened. Shown live on television news, the sorry events attracted such opprobrium that the city felt obliged to block new construction. Sympathetic politicos and seminal documentary *The Fall of the I-*

then: Fire Chief Dennis Sullivan. He was found in the rubble of the firehouse and died some days later. The fire brigade seemed lost without him. The second tremor had destroyed the city alarms and disrupted the water pipes feeding the fire hydrants, leaving the famous firefighters of the West absolutely helpless.

The fire that followed the earthquake compounded the damage. It spread until Mayor Eugene Schmitz and General Frederick Funston, in desparation, blew up the mansions along Van Ness Avenue, creating a firebreak.

The earthquake and three-day inferno were initially thought to have accounted for 700 dead, but military records now reveal that the figure probably ran to several thousand. A quarter of a million people were left homeless and thousands of acres of buildings were destroyed; on Schmitz's orders, anyone suspected of looting in the ensuing chaos was shot dead. On the third day of the catastrophe the wind changed direction, bringing rain. By 21 April the fire was out.

Before the ashes cooled, citizens set about rebuilding. Within ten years San Francisco had risen from the ruins. Some claimed that in the rush to rebuild, city planners passed up the chance to replace its grid street system with a more sensible one that followed the area's natural contours. But there's no doubt that San Francisco was reborn as a cleaner, more attractive city – within three years of the fire, it could boast half of the nation's concrete and steel buildings. Such statistical pride was not out of keeping with the 'boosterism' that accelerated San Francisco's post-Gold Rush growth into a large, modern city. The most potent symbol of restored civic pride was the new City Hall, whose construction was secured by an $8-million city bond. Completed in 1915, it rose some 16 feet (five metres) higher than its model, the Capitol building in Washington, DC.

Between 1913 and 1915 two waterways were opened that would prove critical to California's economic vitality. In 1913 the Los Angeles aqueduct was completed, beginning the

Hotel (1983), created from his own footage by filmmaker Curtis Choy, kept up the pressure. But it was not until 2003 that a suitable plan for the site emerged: an alliance between the Roman Catholic Archdiocese of San Francisco, the Chinatown Community Center and other groups was forged to build a new International Hotel complex. It would house a Chinese-language school, affordable senior housing and a community centre/museum.

In the summer of 2003, with great fanfare, the groundbreaking took place on the new site (*pictured*). In commemoration of the struggles surrounding the I-Hotel, bricks from the original building will be used in the new. Along with the hotel's original brass plaque.

transformation of a sleepy Southern California cowtown into the urban sprawl of modern LA. Then, in 1915, the Panama Canal's opening considerably shortened shipping times between the Atlantic and Pacific coasts, an achievement celebrated in San Francisco by the Panama-Pacific Exposition. Not even the outbreak of World War I in Europe could dampen the city's high spirits. Their optimism was well founded: the war provided a boost to California's mining and manufacturing industries. But, as elsewhere in America, the good times were quickly swallowed up in the world depression signalled by the Wall Street Crash of 1929.

It hit San Francisco port especially badly – half the workforce was laid off. On 9 May 1934, under the leadership of Harry Bridges, the International Longshoremen's Association declared a coastwide strike. Other unions, including the powerful Teamsters, came out in sympathy, shutting down West Coast ports for three months. Blackleg workers managed to break through the picket on 5 July – Bloody

Thursday – but with disastrous results. As violence escalated, police opened fire, killing two strikers and wounding 30. A general strike was called for 14 July, when 150,000 people stopped work and brought San Francisco to a standstill for three days. The strike fizzled out when its leaders couldn't agree on how to end the stalemate, but the action wasn't completely futile: the longshoremen won a wage increase and control of the hiring halls.

At the same time, San Francisco managed an extraordinary amount of construction. In 1932 the Opera House was completed; in 1933 the island of Alcatraz was transferred from the army to the Federal Bureau of Prisons, which set about building a high-security lock-up for 'incorrigible' convicts. The San Francisco Museum of Modern Art, the first West Coast museum to exclusively feature 20th-century works, opened in 1935. The same decade saw the completion of San Francisco–Oakland Bay Bridge, and six months before work started on the Golden Gate Bridge's revolutionary design.

The beautiful people have their **Summer of Love**. *See p15*.

In 1939 the city hosted another fair on man-made Treasure Island. The Golden Gate International Exposition was described as a 'pageant of the Pacific'; those who went were dubbed 'the Thirty-Niners' by local wits. Nobody knew at the time, but this was to be San Francisco's last big celebration for a while: in 1941 the Japanese attacked Pearl Harbor and America entered World War II.

World War II changed the city almost as much as the Gold Rush or the Great Quake. More than 1.5 million men and thousands of tons of material were shipped out to the Pacific from the Presidio, Travis Air Force Base and Treasure Island. Between 1941 and 1945 almost the entire Pacific war effort passed under the Golden Gate. The massed ranks of troops and some half a million civilian workers flooding San Francisco turned the city into a milling party town hell-bent on sending its boys into battle with smiles on their faces.

Towards the end of the war in Europe, in April 1945, representatives of 50 nations met at the San Francisco Opera House to draft the United Nations Charter. It was signed on 26 June 1945 and formally ratified in October at the General Organisation of the United Nations in London. Many people felt that San Francisco was the ideal location for its headquarters, but the British and French thought it too far to travel. To the city's great disappointment, the UN moved to New York.

BEATNIK BLUES AND HIPPIE HIGHS

The immediate post-war period was coloured by the return of the demobilised GIs. One such was poet Lawrence Ferlinghetti. While studying at the Sorbonne in the early 1950s, Ferlinghetti

had discovered Penguin paperbacks, which inspired him to open his tiny, wedge-shaped bookshop at 261 Columbus Avenue. Called City Lights, this shop became a mecca for the bohemians later dubbed 'the Beat Generation' by Jack Kerouac.

The Beat Generation reflected the angst and ambition of a post-war generation attempting to escape both the shadow of the Bomb and the rampant consumerism of ultra-conformist 1950s America. In Kerouac's definition, Beat could stand for beatific or being beat – exhausted. The condition is best explained in his novel *On the Road*, which charts the coast-to-coast odysseys of San Francisco-based Beat saint Neal Cassady (thinly disguised as Dean Moriarty), poet Allen Ginsberg and Kerouac himself (named Sal Paradise).

'The emergence of the Beat Generation made North Beach the literary centre of San Francisco and nurtured a new vision that would spread far beyond its bounds,' reflected Lawrence Ferlinghetti, 40 years on. 'The Beats prefigured the New Left evolution and the impulse for change that swept eastward from San Francisco.' The attention of the world might have been on the beret-clad artists and poets populating North Beach cafés, but an event in Anaheim, 500 miles (800km) to the south, was more reflective of mainstream America: Disneyland opened in 1955.

Despite the imaginary perfect world portrayed by Disney, the media exposure received by Kerouac and Ginsberg established the Bay Area as a centre for the burgeoning counter-culture, generating mainstream American suspicions that San Francisco was the fruit-and-nut capital of the US. Their fears were about to be confirmed by the hippie explosion of the 1960s. The Beats and hippies might have shared a love of marijuana and a common distaste for 'the system', but Kerouac – now an embittered alcoholic – abhorred what he saw as the hippies' anti-Americanism. (It was, in fact, the Beats who coined the term 'hippie' to refer to those they saw as second-rate, lightweight hipsters.) Kerouac's distaste for these new bohemians was shared by John Steinbeck, winner of the 1962 Nobel Prize for Literature, who shied away from the recognition he received in the streets.

The original Beats had no interest in political action, but the newer generation embraced it. A sit-in protest against a closed session of the House of Representatives Un-American Activities Committee (HUAC) at the City Hall in 1961 drew protesters from San Francisco State University and the University of California's Berkeley campus. It quickly degenerated into a riot, establishing the pattern for later protests and police responses. In 1964 Berkeley students returning from a summer of Civil Rights protests in the South, butted heads with university officials over the right to use campus facilities for their campaigns. The conflict signalled the beginning of the 'free speech movement', led by student activist Mario Savio, also marking the split between the politically conscious and those who chose to opt out of the system altogether. America's escalating involvement in the Vietnam War added urgency to the voices of dissent; Berkeley students remained at the forefront of protests on campuses around the country.

The availability of LSD, its popularity boosted in San Francisco by such events as the Human Be-in organised by Allen Ginsberg in 1967 and the Acid Tests overseen by Owsley Stanley and the Grateful Dead, drew an estimated 8,000 hippies from across America. Some 5,000 stayed, occupying the cheap Victorian houses around the Haight-Ashbury district (dubbed 'the Hashbury') not far from Golden Gate Park. The San Franciscan laissez-faire attitude combined with the sun, drugs and acid-induced psychedelic music explosion to give rise to the famous Summer of Love. By 1968, however, the spread of hard drugs, notably heroin, had taken the shine off the hippie movement; the fatal stabbing by Hell's Angels of a Rolling Stones fan at the Altamont Speedway during their 1969 concert there seemed to confirm darker times were ahead.

Like its drugs, the city's politics were getting harder. Members of the Black Panther movement, a radical black organisation founded across the Bay in Oakland by Huey Newton and Bobby Seale, asked themselves why they

should ship out to shoot the Vietnamese when the real enemy was at home. Around Oakland the Panthers took to exercising the American right to bear arms. Gunfights inevitably followed: in April 1968 Panther leader Eldridge Cleaver was wounded and 17-year-old Bobby Hutton killed in a shoot-out with Oakland police. By the early 1970s the Black Panther movement had petered out, its leaders either dead, imprisoned or, like Cleaver, on the run. The kidnapping in 1974 of Patty Hearst, heir to the Hearst newspaper fortune, was perhaps the point at which the 1960s revolution turned into deadly farce. When she was captured along with the other members of the tiny Symbionese Liberation Army, Hearst seemed to have been brainwashed into joining the cause.

Despite the violence that characterised the student and anti-war protests, black radicalism and failed revolutions, the enduring memory of 1960s San Francisco is as the host city to the Summer of Love. The psychedelic blasts of the Grateful Dead, Big Brother and the Holding Company, Janis Joplin, Country Joe and the Fish, Jefferson Airplane and Quicksilver Messenger Service defined both the San Francisco sound and counter-cultural attitude. Jann Wenner, a Berkeley student, founded *Rolling Stone* magazine in 1967 to explain and advance the cause, helping to invent New Journalism in the process.

THE RAINBOW REVOLUTION

San Francisco's radical baton was taken up in the 1970s by the gay liberation movement. Local activists insisted that gay traditions had always existed in the city, first among the Ohlone and later during the 1849 Gold Rush when women in the West were more scarce than gold. Early groups like the Daughters of Bilitis, the Mattachine Society and the Society for Individual Rights (SIR) had paved the way for more radical new political movements. In 1977 gay activists made successful forays into mainstream politics: SIR's Jim Foster became the first openly gay delegate at a Democratic Convention and Harvey Milk was elected to the city's Board of Supervisors.

Then, on 28 November 1978, Dan White entered City Hall and shot and killed Milk and Mayor George Moscone. White was a former policeman from a working-class background, who had run for supervisor as an angry, young, blue-collar populist – and won. But he suffered poor mental health and had to resign under the strain of office. He quickly changed his mind and asked Mayor Moscone to reinstate him. Milk, who held the deciding vote, persuaded the mayor not to let the unstable White back in, with catastrophic consequences. White turned himself in after the killings; in the poorly prosecuted court case, the jury returned two verdicts of voluntary manslaughter. White was sentenced to seven years. His 'Twinkie Defense' was notorious: his attorney argued that White's junk-food diet (especially the eponymous chocolate bars) had led to diminished mental capacity at the time of the murder.

The killings had stunned San Francisco and the verdict outraged the populace: White's sentence prompted one journalist to wonder why the jury had not posthumously convicted Milk of 'unlawful interference with a bullet fired from the gun of a former police officer'. Gay men and women responded by storming City Hall and hurling rocks through the windows. The disturbance escalated into a full-blown battle, known as the White Night Riot. Dan White committed suicide not long after his release from prison.

'Silicon Valley's economic boom rejuvenated the city and reshaped its skyline.'

Gay life and politics changed radically and irrevocably with the onset of the HIV virus, which tore the gay community apart and caused controversy when the bathhouses (symbol of gay liberation and promiscuity) were closed in panic over the spread of the disease. Gay radicals branded *Chronicle* writer Randy Shilts a 'fascist Nazi, traitor and homophobe' when he criticised bathhouse owners who refused to post safe-sex warnings, but his book *And the Band Played On* is still the definitive account of the period.

Since its identification, some 18,000 San Franciscans have died of AIDS. The levelling-out of numbers of new cases and the dangerous misperception that the epidemic is ebbing have endangered fundraising efforts, but the city remains home to the most efficient volunteers in the country. Medical preventionists continue to make inroads into all sexually active communities; caretakers have taken charge of housing, food and legal problems for the roughly two per cent of the city who have been diagnosed as HIV-positive. As sufferers live longer thanks to new drugs, the city continues to need more resources to assist them.

COLLAPSE AND RECOVERY

Because of its location on the San Andreas Fault, San Francisco has always lived in anticipation of a major earthquake to rival the 1906 disaster. One came in October 1989. The Loma Prieta earthquake, named after the ridge of mountains at its epicentre, registered 7.1 on the Richter scale (the 1906 quake was an estimated 7.8). Part of the West Oakland Freeway collapsed, crushing drivers; the Marina district was devastated by fires; and 50 feet (15 metres) of the Bay Bridge's upper deck collapsed. In only 15 seconds more than 19,000 homes were damaged or destroyed, 62 people killed and 12,000 were displaced. It was the nation's most costly natural disaster.

As the 1990s progressed, changes in the city reflected those in the world beyond. The end of the Cold War meant cuts in military spending, and the Presidio – operated as a US military base for almost 150 years – was closed in 1994. As part of the Base Closure and Realignment act, the land transferred to the National Park Service. The collapse of the Soviet Union also brought in a wave of Russian immigrants, many of them settling in the already ethnically diverse Richmond District.

San Francisco also experienced a remarkable renaissance. Its proximity to Silicon Valley's economic boom rejuvenated the city's business structure and reshaped the skyline. In the wake of the Loma Prieta earthquake, the Embarcadero Freeway was torn down and the city's historic bayside boulevard transformed into a palm-tree-lined haven for walkers, joggers, in-line skaters and cyclists. Numerous major projects were brought to completion and others begun: in 1995 the San Francisco Museum of Modern Art moved into a new building in burgeoning SoMa and voters passed a bond allowing for the restoration of City Hall, while Pac Bell Park (now SBC Park), the first privately funded Major League Baseball park in nearly 40 years, opened for the 2000 season. The Yerba Buena Center and Zeum children's museum also opened their doors during this time.

As the 20th century rolled into the 21st, San Francisco was suffering from many of the same social problems as plague other major US cities. Homelessness was particularly severe, with up to 14,000 destitute men and women sleeping without nightly shelter. The problem was compounded by the late '90s internet boom, which brought workers from around the world into an increasingly tight housing market, causing gentrification of working-class neighbourhoods and threatening to homogenise the city. But by the end of the decade, fortunes had turned, rents began to drop and the city was reinventing itself again. San Francisco maintains its best-of-the-West-Coast reputation for magnificent food, stylish design, charming architecture and a multicultural, ideas-driven population. In 1889 Rudyard Kipling described San Francisco as a 'mad city inhabited for the most part by perfectly insane people'. 'It's hard to leave,' he concluded.

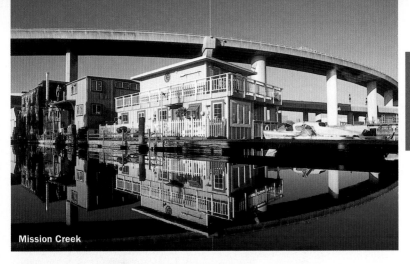

Mission Creek

San Francisco Today

Recovering from the last Big Thing or gearing up for the next? In San Francisco, the future is now.

If there was one sound that captured the mood of San Francisco today, it would have to be a big exhale. Whether a collective sigh of relief, the last wind blowing through the billowing sails of an ill-fated internet venture, or a breath of resignation that things are back to something resembling normal is anyone's guess.

It's clear in the years following the 1990s dot-com boom and bust that the energy is different: the pace has slowed, and among the survivors – hardcore San Franciscans, not the breed of carpetbaggers and fair-weather fans that were spawned in the dot-com age – there's a sense of new-found optimism.

To be sure, casualties of dot-com warfare are everywhere. Not since the Gold Rush of 1849 has the landscape been so dramatically and forcibly changed by economic fortunes. The most visible signs are the scads of brand new loft complexes that still lie relatively vacant in the South of Market (SoMa) district – the cash-rich entrepreneurs who fuelled and financed them vanished like worthless stocks. But the lasting effects of the internet revolution are evident as well. Only a few years ago, areas

like Dogpatch and the Mission/SoMa corridor felt like artificial residential communities dreamt up by developers trying to recoup their investment. They have now metamorphosed into bona fide neighbourhoods, with crowded restaurants and coffee shops, upscale grocery stores, dry cleaners, hairdressers – even pre-schools.

The question remains, especially when it comes to complexes of such immense scope as Mission Bay (13,068,000 square feet/1,214,057 square metres of office, residential, research and retail facilities that won't be completed for another 20 years), if we build it, will they come? Judging by the well-heeled crowds shopping for morel mushrooms and baby fennel at the newly ensconced Ferry Plaza Farmers' Market (*see p65* **Foodie frenzy**), investors have every reason to be optimistic. The gorgeous new market hall, a one-stop shop for locally grown organic produce, seafood, artisan cheeses and myriad other gourmet goodies, is perhaps San Francisco's first post-bust success story.

In this culinary capital, one sure sign that things are looking up is the opening of a spate of new restaurants. Yet even these have taken

Dog days

It's a running joke these days that the term 'breeder' (formerly a derogatory jibe by gays aimed at straight couples with children) now once again refers to the person who provided the pedigree for your Pomeranian.

In this town, dogs are the new children, and the children better watch out. From the Castro and Noe Valley to posh Pacific Heights and the edgy Western Addition, a bow-wow boom has taken hold – one that is vocal, forthright and not afraid to bare its political teeth.

With an estimated 120,000-plus dogs in San Francisco, concerns such as where you can let Rover run unleashed have become make-or-break issues for political candidates and owners, armed with 'I have a dog and I vote' bumper stickers and some disposable

on a more humble, egalitarian mantle, sporting names like Town Hall and Public as opposed to the more self-aggrandising names of the last few years – Gary Danko, Roy's, Paragon.

The tourism trade, San Francisco's bread and butter, seems to be climbing ever so slightly out of the abyss caused by 9/11, SARS and the Iraq war. While occupancy rates are still down, three major hotels – the Omni, St Regis and the Argonaut – have opened or are about to open in the tourist epicentres of downtown and Fisherman's Wharf. At least one more will follow them: Joie de Vivre's 200-room Hotel Vitale is due to open on the Embarcadero in spring 2005.

The arts, a sector never neglected by the local culturati even in lean times, looks to have a banner year in 2005, with no fewer than four important museums opening. The Mexican

Museum designed by famed Mexican architect Ricardo Legorreta, the Jewish Museum, housed in a historic Willis Polk substation, and the Museum of the African Diaspora will all occupy prominent sites in the Yerba Buena arts district. Meanwhile, the de Young, one of the city's two fine arts museums, is scheduled to make a dramatic debut in its new building, designed by renowned Swiss architects Herzog and de Meuron, in Golden Gate Park. Across the concourse, the Academy of Sciences, is receiving a similar overhaul over the next four years.

Even the retail market is showing signs of life. After years of delays, New York's mega fashion emporium Bloomingdale's finally broke ground at the site of an old department store next to the San Francisco Shopping Centre on Market Street. When complete, it will be the largest retail centre on the West Coast.

income, are rapidly becoming one of the city's most influential forces. They're fuelling a mini-business boom in the form of dog-walking services, gourmet canine treats and pampered pet accoutrements. There's even a literary magazine for enlightened dog lovers.

For travellers with four-legged companions, San Francisco may well be the best town in America. The city's pooch-friendly hotels are numerous: the Kimpton Group, one of the city's most upscale boutique hotel chains, allows small dogs at nearly all its 14 properties; and places like the **Hotel Monaco** (see p38) are offering pet-pampering packages with in-room treats, towels and dog-walking services.

Although the high-profile death of Diane Whipple, a school teacher mauled by a neighbour's dog, and the high-flying but short-lived career of Pets.com (the golden puppy of the dot-com glory days) put San Francisco pet owners in the national spotlight, it is, literally, the more pedestrian concerns – pooper-scooper laws, whether dogs should be allowed in the same fields as children, who has right of way in city parks – that preoccupy residents nowadays.

Stand around Alta Plaza Park in Pacific Heights or just about any playground in Noe Valley and you'll most likely be privy to heated discussions. Yet most acknowledge the canine population explosion with the same bemused indifference they did the rise of the hippies, raves and dot-commies. The city may indeed be going to the dogs, but this too shall pass.

I have a dog and I vote.

POLITICS AS UNUSUAL

Economic unrest invariably leads to times of political unrest, and so it was for the unhappy legions of disenfranchised and disillusioned twentysomethings who lost their jobs during the dot-com bust. In 2003 these people – energetic, angry and with a lot of free time on their hands – created one of the liveliest mayoral elections in recent history. The mayoral race might have been overshadowed in the international news by the election of Arnold Schwarzenegger as California's governor, but in these parts, the neck-and-neck contest between mayoral dark horse Matt Gonzalez, a Green Party candidate, and Establishment-endorsed frontrunner Gavin Newsom was the only story. The 36-year-old Democratic Party candidate Newsom prevailed in what some labelled a battle of brains versus beauty – by most

accounts, the cuter candidate won. Either way, veteran politico Willie Brown and the Old Guard are out of the picture and the well-oiled City Hall machinery looks to get squeakier over the next four years. (On the Governator matter, by the way, locals will happily point out that it wasn't them who voted Arnie into office.)

One of the most contentious issues facing San Francisco, and the hot-button platform issue that cast Newsom into the spotlight, was his proposal to solve the city's rampant homeless problem with 'care not cash', undoing decades of policies that have routinely given indigents financial support. Newsom's plan to offer rehabilitation treatment and social services, not money, is being lauded by some and lambasted by others; the latter by residents who fear it's a conservative swing away from San Francisco's traditionally tolerant, liberal core.

Homeless: life on the street. *See p19.*

At the other end of the spectrum, the home-buying market continues to defy all predictions, enjoying record-breaking sales and driving prices – already at stratospheric levels – into the realm of science fiction. Who's buying these homes and how they're paying for them is a mystery to local residents. As is the name of San Francisco's magnificent baseball stadium. It opened to much fanfare and neon in 2000 as Pacific Bell Park. Now, through the miracle of modern corporate mergers and acquisitions, it is to be known as SBC Park. For at least the next 15 minutes. The name change unleashed a tide of angry letters to newspaper editors, but hasn't affected ticket sales. Fans still flock to see their beloved Giants, hoping the homerun phenomenon Barry Bonds will finally bring a World Series Championship to the City by the Bay.

Thankfully for non-homeowners, the brutal rental market of the last few years has subsided. Apartments and flats, which had less than one per cent vacancy during the height of the dot-com era, are now fairly abundant, and rents have dropped significantly – although they're still among the highest in the nation.

The job exodus doesn't seem to have offered up much relief for San Francisco's two biggest headaches: parking and traffic. You're still likely to sit bumper-to-bumper almost any time of day on the Golden Gate Bridge (affectionately known as the 'Car-Strangled Spanner'), and construction of a new span on the San Francisco-Oakland Bay Bridge and the Carquinez Bridge have made travelling to the East Bay a ritual of grinding teeth. Meanwhile, the city's vigilant 'meter maids' make parking on city streets an expensive proposition. Forget to drop a quarter in the meter and you can expect to pay a minimum penalty of $35.

The only bright spot for commuters in the new millennium thus far has been the long-awaited opening of a BART train route to the airport – making it accessible via public transport for the first time, and taking the bite out of the standard $30 taxi fare.

GETTING CONNECTED

Regardless of the limping tech market, San Francisco remains a society that socialises, communicates, job-hunts, shops for gifts and groceries – even romances – via the internet. Nowhere is this better illustrated than on Craigslist.com. Started by entrepreneur Craig Newmark in 1995 as a small community online bulletin board, it is today, along with Google, as pervasive in San Francisco parlance as BART trains and double low-fat lattes. Craigslist is a clearing-house of help wanted ads, items for sale, apartment rentals, outreach programmes, Missed Connections ('you were the girl wearing the red beret. I was the guy who spilled your Martini.') and general community chit-chat for a generation weaned in the Digital Age (*see p62* **SF heroes: Craig Newmark**).

Catch a few minutes of this constantly revolving electronic conversation at an internet café and you begin to understand why San Francisco is a city perpetually poised on the brink of the next Big Thing – a place where change is not only possible, it's inevitable. Whether it comes in the form of an earthquake or an internet revolution, a political upheaval or a peace movement, it is this sense of renewal and reinvention that keeps San Franciscans optimistic, and keeps this city – for all its foibles – from ever becoming boring.

Architecture

There's a new heart under the old skin of SF architecture.

San Francisco's love for its architectural past is no secret, but with more architects and designers per capita than any other US city, its built environment is a visual melting pot of the old and the new. While the city's rolling topography and quirky, 19th-century architecture captivate most visitors, a recent building boom (ushered in by the city's last mayor, Willie Brown) has had celebrity architects proposing bolder statements and treating historic structures all over town to modern renovations. San Francisco will always be a prickly city to build in – thanks to a rigid planning department, its small size and a heroically opinionated populace – but one thing's for sure: the mini metropolis won't be left behind in the 21st century.

FRAGILE FOUNDATIONS
The oldest building in the city is the **Mission Dolores**, whose thick adobe walls and painted hammer beams represent the early European settlement of Yerba Buena. Founded in 1776 and completed in 1791, the simple chapel sits north of a cemetery where Indians, outlaws and the city's first Irish and Hispanic mayors are buried. Mission Dolores was one of 21 missions built in California by the Spanish; only two others, at Carmel and Monterey, rival it for authentic atmosphere. Along with a

portion of the original walls of the Officers' Club in the Presidio, the Mission is the only piece of colonial architecture to have out lived the city's steep progress from a hamlet to a metropolis.

The town inhabited by the Forty-Niners (or 'Argonauts', as the Gold Rush immigrants were called) suffered a series of fires. Tiny Portsmouth Square in present-day Chinatown marked the heart of the early outpost, but was completely levelled by two blazes; the surrounding streets all perished in the fire that followed the 1906 earthquake. The best buildings to have survived from the Gold Rush era are in the **Jackson Square Historical District** (best viewed on Jackson between Montgomery and Sansome Streets).

WEST-COAST VICTORIANA
A sudden burst of 19th-century prosperity quickly filled San Francisco's once-empty sloping streets with what have become its signature Victorian terraced houses. Built by middle-class tradesmen in the Mission and Lower Haight districts, and by rich merchants in Presidio Heights and around Alamo Square, these famous **'Painted Ladies'** provide the city's most characteristic architectural face. One of the most popular views of the city is framed by a row of six

painted Victorians along Steiner Street between Hayes and Grove Streets ('Postcard Row'); these are only the most-photographed examples of more than 14,000 versions of the city's architectural vernacular, some of which surpass them in fancifulness.

Built of wooden frames decorated with mass-produced ornamentation, San Francisco's Victorians come in four distinct styles: Gothic Revival, Italianate, Stick-Eastlake and Queen Anne. The earliest Gothic Revival houses have pointed arches over their windows and were often painted white, rather than the bright colours of the later styles. The Italianate style, with tall cornices, neo-classical elements and add-on porches, are best exemplified in the Lower Haight, notably on Grove Street near Webster Street. Other examples can be found at 1900 Sacramento Street (near Lafayette Park) and at the Lilienthal-Pratt House, built in 1876 at 1818 California Street.

The Italianate was succeeded by the Stick-Eastlake style, named after furniture designer Charles Eastlake and characterised by square bay windows framed with angular, carved ornamentation. The 'Sticks' are the most common among Victorian houses left in the city; a shining example is the over-the-top extravaganza at 1057 Steiner Street, on the corner of Golden Gate Avenue. Finally, with its turrets, towers and curvaceous corner bay windows, the so-called Queen Anne style is amply demonstrated by the Wormser-Coleman House in Pacific Heights (1834 California Street, at Franklin Street). The most extravagant example is the **Haas-Lilienthal House**, built in 1886 by Bavarian grocer William Haas. He treated himself to a home with 28 rooms and six bathrooms. The house has been turned into a museum and is one of the few Victorians open to the public.

OPULENCE AND INTRIGUE

Another example of the ostentation that was part and parcel of San Francisco's booming late 19th-century lifestyle can be seen at the **Palace Hotel**, whose guests have included everyone from Rudyard Kipling to visiting European royalty. Opened in 1875, it epitomised local entrepreneur Billy Ralston's dreams – and his inability to resist Italian marble and solid gold dinner services, still on display in the lobby. Locals mourned the original building after it burned down in the 1906 fire, but the city rebuilt it, glassing in the atrium for elegant dining and adding fashionable art deco murals in the bar. It is still wonderful, combining echoes of Old Vienna and a Prohibition-era speakeasy.

Engineer Adolph Sutro was Ralston's friend and his equal in ambition. He eventually came to own most of the western side of the city, including the sandy wasteland on San Francisco's westernmost edge. This he had bought in 1881 for his **Sutro Baths**. Annexed by the new Golden Gate Park, Sutro's therapeutic baths were the most elaborate in the Western world. Much in need of repair by the 1960s and badly burned in a fire, the baths were sold to developers for high-rise apartments that were never built. They are now unofficially the city's favourite ruins. The adjoining **Cliff House** hotel and saloon burned to the ground twice: the rebuilt eight-storey 'castle' was destroyed again in 1907, then went through further incarnations before opening as a bar and restaurant.

Closer to the downtown area, San Francisco's 'Big Four' businessmen – Mark Hopkins, Leland Stanford, Collis P Huntington and Charles Crocker – made their architectural mark in the late 19th century by building grand edifices. Their mining investments funded railroads and public transport, banks and businesses, and their baronial mansions on Nob Hill, victims of the 1906 fire, now mark the sites of top luxury hotels. These include the Mark Hopkins Inter-Continental Hotel (1 Nob Hill, at California and Mason Streets) and the Stouffer Renaissance Court Hotel (905 California Street).

The **Crocker Mansion**, a Queen Anne manor built in 1888, filled half the block now occupied by Grace Cathedral. Directly across from the cathedral is the Flood Mansion, a brilliant example of the grandeur of the homes that once perched on Nob Hill. The 42-room sandstone marvel was built in 1886 by silver baron James C Flood. It now houses a private club. Another surviving house that has not been turned into a hotel is the **Spreckels Mansion**, an impressive Beaux Arts building. Built in 1912 for sugar baron Adolph Spreckels, it is now owned by mega-selling novelist Danielle Steel. It is not open to the public.

The city also has more than its share of architectural curiosities, among them the **Columbarium**. Built in 1898, this neo-classical temple holds the ashes of thousands of San Franciscans and is decorated with mosaic tiling and elaborate urns in imaginatively bedecked niches.

Oriental promise meets occidental vulgarity at the Vedanta Temple (2963 Webster Street), an eccentricity built in 1905 for the Hindu Vedanta Society. Its bizarre mix of styles includes a Russian Orthodox onion-shaped dome, a Hindu cupola, castle-like crenellations and Moorish arches. It is open to the public for Friday night services. You can also visit the Octagon House. Built in 1861 during a city-wide craze for the health-giving properties of eight-sided buildings, the house is one of just two octagonal buildings left. Furnished in early colonial style, the upper floors have been fully restored, with a central staircase leading to a domed skylight.

CIVIC ART

When the growing city began to burst at its peninsula seams, a ferry network evolved to carry passengers to and from the Bay Area cities. In 1896 the **Ferry Building** (recently renovated and reopened; *see p24* **Inside out**) was built on the Embarcadero as a symbol of civic pride for the young city, its clocktower inspired by the Moorish campanile of Seville Cathedral. After the 1906 earthquake a passion for engineering spurred an interest in Chicago architect Daniel Burnham's 'City Beautiful' project. This resulted in a proposal for a heroic new Civic Center planted below a terraced Telegraph Hill, enlaced with tree-lined boulevards that would trace the city's contours.

The plan was the result of Burnham's two-year consultations with leading city architects Bernard Maybeck and Willis Polk, and countered the city's impractical grid street pattern – but it never came to fruition. Under Mayor 'Sunny Jim' Rolph, the main thrust of the 1915 Civic Center complex came from public contests, many won by Arthur Brown, architect of the mighty-domed City Hall. Other Civic Center buildings erected at this time include the former main library (now the redeveloped Asian Art Museum; *see p24* **Inside out**), the War Memorial Opera House and the Bill Graham Civic Auditorium. All reflect the imperial, Parisian Beaux Arts style, sometimes described as French Renaissance or classical baroque. The buildings were distinguished by their grandiose proportions and their ornamentation, as well as their theatrical halls and stairways.

It was largely Rolph's idea to host the huge Panama-Pacific Exposition in 1915, for which he commissioned Bernard Maybeck to build the **Palace of Fine Arts** and its myriad pavilions. Originally made of wood and plaster, the Palace is the only building that remains from the Exposition (it was rebuilt of reinforced concrete in the 1960s). At around the same time, Julia Morgan, another Arts and Crafts architect, was at work on much of the East Bay and on the extravagant Hearst Castle – home of San Francisco newspaper magnate William Randolph Hearst – located south down the coast at San Simeon.

Passionate rebuilding continued during the Depression, resulting in the opening of the San Francisco-Oakland Bay Bridge (1936), Golden Gate Bridge (1937) and a slew of Works Progress Administration buildings, such as Coit Tower and the prison on Alcatraz island. The WPA, introduced as part of President Roosevelt's New Deal job-creation scheme, had a hand in everything from murals by Mexican artist Diego Rivera to the organisation of community archives. The best examples from this period include the 1932 Herbst Theatre, with murals by Frank Brangwyn, the 1930 Pacific Coast Stock Exchange, with its Rivera mural, and the Rincon Annex Post Office Building (now part of the Rincon Center). The Rincon, built in 1940 to include Anton Refregier's murals, is a fine example of steel-trimmed marble.

> ## 'At first unpopular, the Transamerica Pyramid now has few detractors, becoming for many a symbol for the city itself.'

While Frank Lloyd Wright's **Marin Civic Center**, completed after his death in 1972 and located north of the city in San Rafael, is his most stunning civic work (the film *Gattaca* was filmed there), the only Frank Lloyd Wright building in the city is the Folk Art International. Wright designed the building in 1948 as a prototype Guggenheim; it now houses a tribal and folk art gallery, and is open to the public.

ROLLING OUT THE NEW

Pietro Belluschi and Pier Luigi Nervi's **St Mary's Cathedral**, a 255-foot-high (78-metre) concrete structure supporting a cross-shaped, stained-glass ceiling, is a 1970s symbol of anti-quake defiance (nicknamed St Maytag, because it resembles a giant washing machine agitator). Also built in 1972, the 853-foot (260-metre) **Transamerica Pyramid** is one of San Francisco's best-known buildings, the $34-million, seismic-proofed structure boasts an internal suspension system, which served to succesfully protect its 48 storeys and 212-foot (65-metre) spire in the 1989 quake. At first unpopular, the pyramid now has few detractors, instead becoming to many a symbol for the city itself, even featuring in the Beach Blanket Babylon revue – a sure sign of civic affection.

The new **Main Library**, designed by Cathy Simon of architects Pei Cobb Freed, is a marriage of Beaux Arts and more recent styles.

Inside out

San Francisco may be loved worldwide for its unsurpassable beauty, but it's the city's unsung European likeness that makes it truly unique. A mere seven by seven miles (11 by 11km), San Francisco – like most small European cities – has nary any room to build. On top of this, the city's famously ornery planning department doesn't help matters.

So how does anything new get built? Sadly for the modernists, not very easily. The ones that do make it past the planning department's chopping block must first suffer tedious design reviews and – true to San Francisco spirit – exasperating rounds of public debate. Swiss architects Herzog & de Meuron's winning design for the new **MH de Young Memorial Museum** was one such victim. By the time the cutting-edge, sweeping glass and steel design was accepted, three years had passed and countless websites had sprung up in opposition.

That's why adaptive reuse, the rehabilitation and reuse of historic buildings and landmarks – effectively rebuilding them from the inside out – is so common in San Francisco. Not only does it appease the planning department and legitimise the efforts of the San Francisco Redevelopment Agency, it also provides a solution to the city's pesky size constraints.

One of San Francisco's earliest examples is architect Joseph Esherick's renovation of **The Cannery** (1968), located on Fisherman's Wharf. Originally owned by Del Monte, it was once the largest peach cannery in the world. Esherick was given free reign to gut and entirely rebuild the interior; the result is three energetic levels of shopping space.

More recent examples of adaptive reuse have focused on breathing new life into San Francisco's cultural centres. Located in the former main library (originally designed by George Kelham in 1915), the much-touted **Asian Art Museum** (2003; *pictured*) was designed by the master of adaptive reuse: Italian architect Gae Aulenti (best known for her transformation of Paris's Musée d'Orsay). While Aulenti preserved the original rococo foyer and grand hall, her use of glass-topped courtyards creates a spectacularly modern experience. Inside the newly renovated **Ferry Building** (2003), the original Great Nave – the steel-framed structure's famous 660-foot-long (20-metre) sky-lit, two-storey interior – has been impeccably restored, accommodating everything from office space and shops to the ever-popular Ferry Plaza Farmers' Market (*see p65* **Foodie frenzy**). Even Daniel Libeskind's proposed **Jewish Museum** (2006) will not rise anew. Instead, the quixotic design calls for gold-toned extensions clad in stainless steel that will jut out of Willis Polk's original power station.

As though even more were needed to prove that San Francisco is a town that likes its modern architecture to look old,

One side links the building to the more contemporary Marshall Plaza, while the other echoes the old library to the north with grandiose, neo-classical columns. The dramatic interior centres around a five-storey atrium beneath a domed skylight designed to let natural light filter throughout the building.

Recent architectural activity, much of it to do with the opening of new museums, has centred in and around the hip SoMa arts district. **SFMOMA**, designed by Mario Botta and opened in 1995, features a series of stepped boxes and a signature squared circle facing west. Nearby, the new Jewish Museum (due to open in 2006) is architect Daniel Libeskind's strikingly contemporary update of a former substation originally created by Willis Polk in 1907. Within the same block, architect Ricardo Legorreta's new Mexican Museum, a sophisticated, layered box made of red stone, also opens in 2006.

West of SFMOMA, Yerba Buena's Esplanade Gardens is a beautiful urban park, framed by museums, theatres and shops, and replete with lush greenery, fountains, sculptures, cafés and the Metreon, a hyper-modern urban mall owned by Sony. It is also home to San Francisco's first Design Museum. Directly opposite the Metreon, Moscone West, the Moscone Convention Centre's latest addition, is a stunning all-glass structure, incorporating a graphic display screen designed by New York artists/architects Elizabeth Diller and Ricardo Scofidio.

Elsewhere across town, the city's beloved **MH de Young Memorial Museum** will in 2005 move into a new home on its current site in Golden Gate Park. The ultra-modern design, by Swiss architects Herzog & de Meuron (creators of London's Tate Modern), caused serious controversy when it was first unveiled. Angular in shape, it will have a helix-like viewing tower that rises high above the park (*see above*

Fisher-Friedman's Oriental Warehouse, which is located at Delancey and Brannan Streets and was once home to Pacific Mail Steamship Company Warehouse, is San Francisco's most breathtaking residential example. All that remains of the 1867 landmark building is the original brick façade, beautifully restored to act as a skin to the newer warehouse, and upscale, modern lofts, within. Even more remarkable, though, is filmmaker George Lucas's new headquarters in the Presidio – the **Letterman Digital Arts Center**. The huge 111,320-square-yard (93,078-square-metre) campus opens in 2005 and – believe it or not – it will mimic every aspect of the surrounding historic buildings, right down to the details of the gabled porches of the old officers' quarters.

Inside out). Just nearby, the **California Academy of Sciences** will close its doors between 2004 and 2008, while world-renowned architect Renzo Piano (famous for the Centre Pompidou in Paris) gives it a modern facelift that will include a living 'green' roof. The city's recent museum explosion will also result in a new International Women's Museum, due to open in 2008: plans have been drawn up for a state-of-the-art complex inside Pier 26, along the historic waterfront. Last but not least, Golden Gate Park's oldest building, the **San Francisco Conservatory of Flowers**, recently reopened after severe wind damage caused it to close in 1995. The Conservatory's whimsical Victorian design, modelled after London's Kew Gardens, received a full-scale seismic upgrade.

Other new additions to the skyline include Cesar Pelli's JP Morgan Chase Building (Mission and First Streets) and the latest iteration of San Francisco's 140-year-old **Union Square**, while among several pending projects making waves in the community and among the stuffy members of the city's planning department are Thom Mayne's radical proposal for the new Federal Building at Seventh and Mission Streets (opening in 2005), and a new Mission Bay Residential Block by flamboyant Miami-based firm Arquitectonica (creators of New York's ostentatious Westin Hotel). Of course, no city would be complete without an Ian Schrager hotel, and San Francisco has its own. Notwithstanding the Clift being declared bankrupt in 2003, it soldiers on: the well-heeled visitor can still enjoy Philippe Starck's eye-catching redesign. Meanwhile, such far less interesting and garishly large structures as the new Four Seasons Hotel on Market Street get built with little scrutiny. But such is the life of buildings in San Francisco, where temperament, design and ideas change as frequently as the hills go up and down.

Literary San Francisco

There's nothing's black and white about the city's still-thriving lexical love affair.

You've been puffing up that endless hill and suddenly the fog lifts – the ocean! – and the poetry wells up in your soul. Or some old drunk rolls up, offers to sell you his story for a buck: 'Kerouac was writing 'bout me, you know.' With its wealth of characters and soothing Left Coast liberalism, the atmospheric foghorns and alleys and views – well, no wonder San Francisco is a mecca for writers. It was ever thus: from Mark Twain and Bret Harte arriving in the 1860s to report on the Gold Rush to Tom Wolfe writing about a mass of youth on their own kind of quest a full century later. From Dashiell Hammett and Jack London to Gertrude Stein, William Saroyan and Danielle Steel, some of the country's best-known writers have called the city home, and the supply of new novelists, poets and performers just ain't drying up.

ARRIVALS AND DEPARTURES

Journalist and budding fiction writer **Mark Twain** worked in SF in the 1860s, constructing his literary persona and leaving for New York once *The Celebrated Jumping Frog of Calaveras County* hit the big time in 1867. Like most San

Francisco writers, Twain came to create himself and went East when he was ready. Twain, **Bret Harte** and **Ambrose Bierce** built on a foundation of journalistic irony and muckraking that gave the West an independent literary culture in the 1860s and 1870s. Nowhere was that spirit more evident than at the Bohemian Club, an outgrowth of raucous newsman breakfasts hosted by *San Francisco Chronicle* writer James Bowan.

An ailing **Robert Louis Stevenson** arrived in the city in 1879 in pursuit of his darling, Fanny Osbourne. He lived at 868 Bush Street while Osbourne was in Oakland waiting for a divorce: the two finally married in 1880. Stevenson then wrote about San Francisco in *The Wrecker* and about his Napa Valley honeymoon in *The Silverado Squatters*. His house is in St Helena in Napa Valley; Robert Louis Stevenson State Park is nearby.

Jack London is one of the Bay Area's few successful native writers. As an adolescent, London's seafaring jobs included a stint as an oyster pirate in the Bay. His working-class background fostered socialist ideals – in tandem with an unpalatable doctrine of white supremacy. He headed north in 1897 for the Yukon Gold Rush and began publishing stories in 1899. Famous for *The Call of the Wild* and *The Sea Wolf*, he spent his latter years in the part of northern Sonoma Valley known as the Valley of the Moon – also the name of one of his novels. The Jack London Museum, Wolf House and the writer's grave can be found in the Jack London State Historic Park in Glen Ellen. Oakland's Jack London Square bears little resemblance to the waterfront of the author's youth, but the cabin he occupied in the Yukon was relocated here in 1970.

Like London, **Gertrude Stein** was raised in Oakland. She made her literary name among the expat modernists and artistic avant-garde of early 20th-century Paris, hosting a salon with San Francisco-born secretary and partner Alice B Toklas. A return to the West Coast elicited one of Stein's famously gnomic utterances: 'There is no there there.'

DETECTIVE GAMES

Dashiell Hammett came to San Francisco in 1921. Beginning in 1923, Hammett wrote and published 11 of his 'Continental Op' stories in *Black Mask*, stories set in the city and written while the tubercular Hammett was living at 620 Eddy Street. In 1926 he went to work for the Albert Samuels jewellery company at 985 Market. Shortly afterwards, he collapsed. He went on disability pay, moved to the countryside and became a full-time writer. Living at 891 Post Street, he wrote the series of novels – *Red Harvest* and *The Dain Curse*, *The Maltese Falcon* and *The Glass Key* – that established the hard-boiled detective novel as *the* American genre. *The Maltese Falcon* fixed Hammett as a money-spinner for Hollywood producers; he was saved from drinking himself to death in LA by the onset of World War II. Blacklisted as a Communist in the 1950s, Hammett was jailed for refusing to testify during the McCarthy trials. He disappeared from public life until the playwright Lillian Hellman resurrected him.

The US is still uncomfortable over how it treated Hammett, which may explain why his commemorative plaque (on Burrit Alley, off Bush Street) acknowledges *The Maltese Falcon* and its protagonist Sam Spade, not their creator. Hammett's and Spade's entwined lives are detailed in *The Literary World of San Francisco* (City Lights, 1985) by Don Herron and Nancy Peters. Don Herron's *The Dashiell Hammett Tour* (City Lights, 1991) details the walking tour he conducts. Both

books are out of print, which is a good excuse to browse through the city's wondrous second-hand bookshops (we've listed our favourites, *see p164* **The best: Bookshops**).

BEAT DOWN TO YOUR SOUL

Jack Kerouac came to the city in 1947, drawn here by charismatic Neal Cassady, at the end of the trip that was to make him famous a decade later with the publication of *On the Road*. Kerouac had typed the book on a single continuous scroll over three weeks, subsequently editing the manuscript into more conventional paragraphs in 1952; it then only took another five years to become an overnight bestseller. (The original scroll manuscript was sold in May 2001 to a private collector for a record-breaking $2.4 million.) *San Francisco Blues* was written in the Cameo Hotel in what was then skid row on Third Street, an area later bulldozed to make way for the Moscone Center. *The Subterraneans*, written in 1953, is set in North Beach, but is actually a New York story transposed to protect the characters.

'The poem's central image is the Moloch-face of the Drake Hotel on Powell Street, as observed by a Ginsberg high on peyote.'

For more revelatory accounts of San Francisco, readers should look to *The Dharma Bums* and *Desolation Angels*, which vividly report on the Beat milieu and the epochal Six Gallery reading (*see p97* **Go! Go! Gone**). Famous as the reading at which unknown poet **Allen Ginsberg** read the first part of his soon-notorious poem *Howl*, the six poets included and were introduced by literary guru Kenneth Rexroth, then the city's leading literary figure. An irascible pacifist, Rexroth worked tirelessly to keep Japanese Californians out of internment camps in the war era, and his translations of Chinese and Japanese poets have contributed largely to a wider readership for these works. His salon at 250 Scott Street was the centre of what was later called the **San Francisco Poetry Renaissance**.

Allen Ginsberg himself had come to San Francisco to (in his own words) 'find the Whitman self-reliance to indulge a celebration of self'. Here he came to terms with his homosexuality, met his lover Peter Orlovsky and began writing *Howl*. The central image of the poem is the Moloch-face of the Drake Hotel on Powell Street, as observed by a Ginsberg high on peyote.

The Grotto

Writer? Lonely? Living in an ivory tower? Well, get over it and get over here. Not only does the city have a long history of producing esteemed writers, it also has one of supporting communities of local wordsmiths. For a start, there's the 19th-century Bohemian Club, whose luminaries included Ambrose Bierce, Ina Coolbrith, Joaquin Miller and Prentice Mulford. Or the gang of writers who coalesced around Beat poet Allen Ginsberg in the wake of Six Gallery reading (*see p97* **Go! Go! Gone**), along with the hundreds of young people who flocked to North Beach over the next decade looking to become writers by osmosis.

Those looking for an emblem of this ferment of poetic community-building should look no further than **Jack Spicer**. In the late 1950s Spicer edited the mimeographed periodical *J* from contributions left in a box in the Place, a bar at 1546 Grant Avenue. This unorthodox approach ensured the mag was alive to the literature of the moment, fostering a community of new writers who had previously felt isolated.

This creative milieu has been extended into the new millennium by the **San Francisco Writers' Grotto** (www.sfgrotto.org), which was started in a Victorian on Market Street in 1994 by three friends: Ethan Canin, Po Bronson and Ethan Watters. It has since flourished into a 22-member collective, and is now housed in a former cat and dog hospital in SoMa. Elves at work in the Grotto come in all shapes of literary size from the ennobled (Bronson and Watters; Canin has since

moved on) to the up-and-coming (Vendela Vida and Mary Roach) to the little-known (no names necessary but these spaces are being jealously watched).

These artists-in-residence are prone to dropping their status as Grotto members into their professional biogs as if it's an alternative Pulitzer. While its offices are small, the Grotto is just as selective as the prize judges: 'It's impossible to over-emphasise the care you should take in choosing the people with whom you will spend so much time,' Watters warns in an essay encouraging the proliferation of Grotto-like spaces.

In contrast to the rowdily spontaneous Beats, the denizens of Grottoland have decidedly 21st-century concerns: debates are more likely to centre on who's collecting money for the DSL bill than for the jug of wine or benzedrine inhalers, and networking is most definitely the order of the day. Yet the Grotto has not deserted its community. It hosts a number of public events, all of which are must-attend functions for SF's literary stargazers, particularly the reading nights at the library and see-and-be-seen aftermath parties back at the Grotto. It also hosts – a beautifully San Franciscan touch, this – brunches for visiting authors who might otherwise find themselves adrift in the city.

And should anyone consider such extreme literary socialising strange, consider this: eating, drinking, talking about books... what's not to like?

Lawrence Ferlinghetti, one-time Poet Laureate of the city and owner of City Lights Booksellers & Publishers, published the now-legendary black-and-white pocket-sized edition of *Howl and Other Poems*. A subsequent obscenity trial targetting Ferlinghetti and *Howl* catapulted the Beats to public attention and began the breakdown of the American obscenity laws in the 1960s.

The Beat scene was centred on North Beach. Gino & Carlo's bar still stands at 548 Green Street (between Columbus and Grant Avenues). Vesuvio is where Kerouac drank away his chance of meeting Henry Miller. It is located across Jack Kerouac Alley from City Lights. A Beat tour leaves from the store every Saturday at noon.

FURTHER TALES OF THE CITY

The Haight-Ashbury scene doesn't seem to have much of a literary monument – perhaps this is because (to quote Tom Wolfe) if you can remember it, you weren't really there. **Ken Kesey** and the reborn Neal Cassady began their trips festivals at the Longshoreman's Hall on Fisherman's Wharf, and the scene moved through the Avalon Ballroom on Polk Street and the Fillmore on Geary, to the Haight. *The Electric Kool-Aid Acid Test* by **Tom Wolfe** is the best account of this voyage, along with Emmet Grogan's memoir of the Diggers, *Ringolevio*. Kesey and Robert Stone, who wrote about the era's psychic fallout in *Dog Soldiers*, were both products of Pulitzer Prize-winning novelist Wallace Stegner's writing programme at Stanford University.

The Castro hasn't produced its literary testament yet, although A Different Light bookstore is one of the best sources for queer fiction. Before his death, Randy Shilts produced an account of the coming of AIDS in *And the Band Played On*, as well as a biography of Harvey Milk, but Armistead Maupin, the city's most flamboyant author to embrace queer themes, sets his *Tales of the City* series outside the internationally recognised gay district: on Macondray Lane on Russian Hill.

WORD UP: EGGERS ET AL

Easily the most name-dropped author in San Francisco today is **Dave Eggers**. The author of the sleeper success *A Heartbreaking Work of Staggering Genius*, Eggers moved to the Bay Area in his early twenties, after the death of his parents, to raise his youngest brother. His experiences form the basis of his book. Eggers has been at the forefront of a burgeoning fiction renaissance, headquartered at 826 Valencia. Combining a youth literacy centre with a publishing house, 826 is home to Eggers' literary journal *McSweeney's* and a pompous, self-regarding and generally excellent periodical called *The Believer*. Eggers himself can be caught at events sponsored by the San Francisco Writers' Grotto (*see p28* **The Grotto**).

As if to prove the literary bug bites all who settle here, filmmaker **Francis Ford Coppola** (who lives in Wine Country north of the city) has also founded a popular journal. His *Zoetrope: All Story* has published such names as Neil LaButte, Eric Bogosian, Abbas Kiarostami, as well as the Godfather himself. Like the Grotto, *Zoetrope* sponsors several see-and-be-seen events throughout the year, many at Coppola's Café Niebaum-Coppola in North Beach.

For the poetically inclined, the DIY momentum that spawned numerous small presses and reading series during the Beats heyday is still going strong. At the core is San Francisco State University's **San Francisco Poetry Center** (1600 Holloway Avenue, 338 2227, www.sfsu.edu). Dedicated by WH Auden in 1954, it sponsors a wide variety of readings. Building on SFPC's success and the incredible poetic diversity of the city are the 20-year-old poetry series at Small Press Traffic (California College of the Arts, 1111 Eighth Street) and the New College of California (777 Valencia Street).

The published word is buoyed by the many readings, festivals and poetry slams held daily across the city and East Bay. An outgrowth of the Beat 'happenings' of the 1960s, the city's slam and spoken word scene remains vital: long-time slammers **Beth Lisick**, **Justin Chin** and **Beau Sia** are still performers to watch. Poetry and performance crossover at Kearny Street

Workshop, a vibrant home for Asian-American writers, which hosts readings at its home base at the South of Market Cultural Center (934 Brannan Street, 552 2131, www.somarts.org). Also keep an eye out for YouthSpeaks, a spoken word workshop for younger writers.

Each distinctive scene intersects every September at Litquake, a four-day festival that brings diverse genres together in a celebration of the city's rich literary offerings. Novelist and Pulitzer-winner **Michael Chabon**, international sensation **Isabelle Allende** and children's author **Lemony Snicket** are all festival-goers.

Still harbouring doubts that literature is in the blood of Bay Area locals? The small North Bay town of **Bolinas**, a long-standing and exclusive enclave of artists and writers, recently held an official ballot to declare themselves official lovers of nature. The proposal read (in part): 'to like to eat the blueberries to like the bears is not hatred to hotels and motor boats.' Practically on a par with Walt Whitman.

Gertrude Stein.
See p27.

In Context

Where to Stay

Where to Stay 32

Features

The best Hotels 33
Chain gang 34
Death beds 48

Where to Stay

Warm-hearted and quirkily comfortable, San Francisco's hotels are so comfortable you never want to get out of bed.

For the ultimate in luxury, you can't beat the **Four Seasons Hotel & Residences**. *See p34.*

There are so many places to stay in San Francisco that narrowing it down can be tough. When you can choose between a peace-and-love Victorian guesthouse in Haight-Ashbury, a wood-burning fireplace and view of the Pacific Ocean, a Japanese tatami room with a deep soaking tub or the priceless convenience of a basic room in Union Square, how does one decide? Fortunately, there are good options for every taste and budget, from the over-the-top luxury palaces and discreet hideaways preferred by business executives and celebrities to rudimentary backpacker hostels.

Most hotels are concentrated in the downtown area – Union Square, the Tenderloin, Nob Hill and SoMa – and a good deal of them are forgettable corporate institutions. However, here is also where you'll find most of the glitziest places and even a few cosy bed and breakfast inns that feel miles away from the city. If you're the type who wants style and atmosphere without the hefty rates, you're in luck. San Francisco has lots of moderately priced but happening digs, often in restored

older properties. Two hotel groups in particular, **Kimpton** and **Joie de Vivre**, make a business of doing just that – sprucing up fading beauties and giving them some personality, as well as stocking them with amenities that satisfy today's savvy travellers. Some of the most popular places – the Monaco (*see p38*), Phoenix (*see p41*) and Triton (*see p35*) – are on their rosters, alongside plenty of lesser-known, more modest gems. For those whose budgets are tighter than the taxman, we've listed some hostels too (*see p52*).

Since the last edition of this guide, San Francisco's hotels have been suffering from low occupancy rates due to a combination of the nation's continuing economic woes and the fallout of 9/11 – even pricey places were giving rooms away for a song, often unadvertised. Many in the business also admit that online booking services like hotels.com have forced them to keep their rates competitive. In any case, rates in this edition are mostly lower than in the last, but as we went to press they were beginning to creep up again in line with improving occupancy rates. We await further developments with interest, but the opening of the St Regis (due in autumn 2004) and Joie de Vivre's Hotel Vitale (early 2005) suggests some see grounds for optimism.

If you don't want to arrange your own lodgings, try **San Francisco Reservations** (1-800 677 1570, 1-510 628 4450, fax 1-510 628 9025/www.hotelres.com). It deals with more than 300 hotels, often at preferential rates, and there's no booking fee. Do ask about its hotel packages: it sometimes offers discount admission to museums and other promotions.

PRICES AND SERVICES

The price for a basic double room with private bath, phone and TV (and often continental breakfast) is around $79 to $130 a night. If you're willing to go really basic, you can find the same for about $59 a night. For anything luxurious you'll fork out considerably more. This price doesn't include the 14 per cent **room tax**. Hotels often have lower rates on their websites, and be sure to ask about specials when you call (it's not uncommon to get a better deal if you call the hotel directly, rather than going through the central booking agency). When making a reservation, be prepared to hold at least one night with a credit card – and find out about cancellation policies, so you don't get stuck paying for a room you can't use.

Be warned that if you're using the **telephone** in your room, most hotels add a surcharge for every phone call. Even local calls (usually free in the US) can cost 50¢, the same price you'd pay to use a public phone; any number, even those that are 'toll-free', can incur hefty hotel fees. Always ask before you dial. Unless otherwise stated, all the hotels listed have telephones in the rooms.

Parking fees range from free to around $20 per night, sometimes a good deal more. The city has recently instituted a 14 per cent tax on parking, so the quoted prices may go up.

All hotels are required by law to provide accommodation for disabled visitors and, thanks to California's strict anti-smoking policies, all hotels have no-smoking rooms – many are no-smoking throughout. The law also prohibits smoking in public spaces, which means hotel restaurants, lobbies and so forth.

Union Square

This area is San Francisco's most popular hotel zone, but the northern edge of the Tenderloin (*see p38*) also has great options, all of which are close to the shopping and transport hub of Union Square.

Deluxe

Campton Place Hotel

340 Stockton Street, CA 94108, at Post Street (1-800 235 4300/781 5555/fax 955 5536/ www.camptonplace.com). BART Powell/Muni Metro F, J, K, L, M, N/bus 2, 3, 4, 30, 38, 45, 76/ cable car Powell-Hyde or Powell-Mason. **Rates** single $335-$470; double $445; suite $550-$1,800. **Credit** AmEx, DC, MC, V. **Map** p311 G3.

It's been more than 20 years since the former Drake-Wiltshire Hotel gave itself a hefty $18-million facelift and reopened as the Campton Place. Ever since, it has attracted a very discreet, and wealthy, following. The hotel, which neatly packs 110 rooms into a small space, offers exceptional service, including valet-assisted packing and unpacking. Small dogs are allowed to stay with their owners; staff will even walk them if you're too busy. The hotel's elegant restaurant is excellent for a romantic evening.

The best Hotels

To be ridiculously trendy

This week it's the **Clift Hotel** (*see p38*), of course. Although last week it was the **W Hotel** (*see p42*).

For a room with a view

The **Mandarin Oriental** (*see p37*) may be the third-tallest building in town, but the **Hotel Cosmo** (*see p37*) and the **Fisherman's Wharf Youth Hostel** (*see p52*) offer equally breathtaking vistas at affordable prices.

For a counter-culture trip

Ask for Allen Ginsberg's room at the **Hotel Bohème** (*see p42*) or the Flower Power Suite at the **Red Victorian** (*see p49*).

For bathtime luxury

Try a clawfooted tub at the **Archbishop's Mansion** (*see p49*) or soak in a deep Japanese tub at the **Radisson Miyako** (*see p50*).

To be hip and ecologically aware

The **Hotel Triton** (*see p35*) strikes the perfect balance between comfort and conscience.

To be pampered like royalty

The **Four Seasons** (*see p34*) and **Ritz-Carlton San Francisco** (*see p45*). At your service.

Hotel services Air-conditioning. Babysitting. Bar. Business services. Concierge. Conference facilities. Gym. Laundry. Limousine service. Parking ($15; valet parking $35). Restaurant. Safe. **Room services** *Dataport. Fax. Hi-fi. Iron. Minibar. Room service (24hr). Turndown. TV: cable (VCR available).*

Four Seasons Hotel & Residences

757 Market Street, CA 94103, between Third & Fourth Streets (633 3000/www.fourseasons.com). BART Powell/Muni Metro F, J, K, L, M, N/ bus 30, 38, 45, 76/cable car Powell-Hyde or Powell-Mason. **Rates** *single/double $469-$600; suite $800-$4,900.* **Credit** *AmEx, DC, Disc, MC, V.* **Map** p311 G/H4.

Open since late 2001, this ultra-exclusive 36-storey hotel imposes itself on an ugly but convenient stretch of Market Street. With 277 rooms and suites, 142 residential condos, high-end shops and an upscale restaurant, it feels like its own universe. As you might expect, the hotel understands the

Chain gang

If you're in town during high season without a place to lay your head, a central reservation hotline for the familiar chain hotels may be your only friend. At least in San Francisco the chains often have a bit of character. Room rates were unpredictable when we went to press, so the price bands below are for guidance only.

Deluxe ($150 and over)

Crowne Plaza 1-888 218 0808/ www.crowneplaza.com
Hyatt 1-800 233 1234/www.hyatt.com
Marriott 1-800 932 2198/ www.marriott.com
Starwood (Sheraton) 1-888 625 5144/ www.starwood.com/sheraton

Mid-range ($100-$150)

Best Western 1-800 780 7234/ www.bestwestern.com
Hilton 1-800 774 1500/www.hilton.com
Holiday Inn 1-800 465 4329/ www.holiday-inn.com
Travelodge 1-800 578 7878/ www.travelodge.com

Budget (under $100)

Howard Johnson 1-800 446 4656/ www.hojo.com
Ramada 1-800 272 6232/ www.ramada.com
Super 8 1-800 800 8000/ www.super8.com

needs of business travellers, with staff at the in-house tech centre on hand to provide support. Once guests are through working, they can make the most of the two-storey health club, with its indoor pool and jacuzzi.

Hotel services Air-conditioning. Babysitting. Bar. Beauty salon. Business centre. Concierge. Conference facilities. Gym. Laundry. Limousine service. Parking ($35). Pool. Restaurant. Spa. **Room services** *CD player. Dataport. Minibar. Room service (24hr). Safe. Turndown. TV: cable (VCR available).*

Hotel Nikko

222 Mason Street, CA 94102, at O'Farrell Street (1-800 645 5687/394 1111/fax 394 1106/ www.hotelnikkosf.com). BART Powell/Muni Metro F, J, K, L, M, N/bus 27, 38/cable car Powell-Hyde or Powell-Mason. **Rates** *single/double $139-$350; suite $500-$2,000.* **Credit** *AmEx, DC, Disc, MC, V.* **Map** p310 G4.

The minute you walk into the Nikko's vast, white marble lobby you begin to relax. Part of the Japan Airlines hotel chain, the 25-storey hotel is, as you would expect, incredibly popular with Japanese visitors. Recently refurbished, the 533 rooms and 22 suites are large and bright, furnished with luxurious fabrics, light wood furniture and lush green plants. The design is clean, tranquil and elegant – modern but with Asian touches. Suites on the Nikko Club floors offer stunning views and use of a private lounge with laptops and refreshments. Amenities include an indoor swimming pool, gym and sauna, and the acclaimed Anzu sushi bar and steak house.

Hotel services Air-conditioning. Bar. Beauty salon. Business services. Concierge. Conference facilities. Gym. Jacuzzi. Laundry. Limousine service. Parking ($39). Pool. Restaurant. Safe. **Room services** *CD player. Dataport. Fax. Iron. Minibar. Room service (24hr). Safe. Turndown. TV: cable.*

Mid-range

Hotel Diva

440 Geary Street, CA 94102, at Mason Street (1-800 553 1900/885 0200/fax 346 6613/ www.hoteldiva.com). BART Powell/Muni Metro F, J, K, L, M, N/bus 2, 3, 4, 38, 76/cable car Powell-Hyde or Powell-Mason. **Rates** *single/double $99-$149; suite $250-$450.* **Credit** *AmEx, DC, Disc, MC, V.* **Map** p310 G4.

A block from Union Square in the heart of the city's Theatre District, the Diva is stylish but a bit sterile. Its owners – who also run the Metropolis (*see p35*) – have given the 114 rooms and suites a modern maritime feel, with white walls, pools of cobalt carpet and sculptured steel headboards fashioned into waves. Some rooms are rather dark and poky; those ending in 08 and 12 are the biggest.

Hotel services Air-conditioning. Business centre. Concierge. Conference facilities. Gym. Laundry. Parking ($30). Safe. **Room services** *CD player. Dataport. Games console. Iron. Room service (11am-midnight). Safe. TV: cable/pay movies/VCR.*

The **Hotel Rex**, named after local pacifist poet Kenneth Rexroth.

Hotel Metropolis

*25 Mason Street, CA 94102, at Turk Street
(1-800 553 1900/775 4600/fax 775 4606/www.
hotelmetropolis.com). BART Powell/Muni Metro
F, J, K, L, M, N/bus 27, 31/cable car Powell-Hyde
or Powell-Mason.* **Rates** single/double $89-$149.
Credit AmEx, DC, Disc, MC, V. **Map** p310 G4.

With its four-elements decor, this the Metropolis is
eco-friendly ying meets mid-priced yang. Each floor
is colour-coded in shades of olive green (earth), taupe
(wind), yellow (fire) and aquamarine (water). The 105
rooms and five suites have nicely understated furnishings – one of the suites, specially designed for
kids, has bunk beds, a chalkboard and toys, including the all-important Nintendo. There's a small
library and a lovely painted ceiling in the lobby.
Cable TV and better-than-average toiletries complete
the comfortable picture. From the tenth floor, where
some rooms have balconies, there are splendid
views over Potrero Hill to the Oakland hills beyond.
Hotel services *Business centre. Gym. Laundry.
Parking ($29). Safe.* **Room services** *Dataport
(2nd floor). Games console. Iron. TV: cable.*

Hotel Rex

*562 Sutter Street, CA 94102, between Powell
& Mason Streets (1-800 433 4434/fax 433 3695/
www.thehotelrex.com).* **Rates** single $129-$149;
double $149-$249; suite $269-$339. **Credit** AmEx,
DC, Disc, MC, V. **Map** p310 G3.

Named after Kenneth Rexroth, MC for the fabled Six
Gallery reading (*see p97* **Go! Go! Gone**), the recently renovated Rex is one of the city's most appealing
small hotels, reminiscent of a 20th-century salon.
The Rex does a genial job of celebrating San
Francisco's literary history – there are books scattered throughout, and the walls are adorned with
caricatures of writers with local ties, Allen Ginsberg,
Dashiell Hammett and Gertrude Stein among them.
The hotel caters to living authors too – publishers
often put their clients up here. The Rex's 'business
centre' is full of antique typewriters alongside
modern amenities. There's also the matchbox-sized
bistro Café Andrée. Named after Rexroth's wife, it
was at one time the hotel's bookshop.
Hotel services *Babysitting. Bar. Business centre.
Concierge. Laundry. Parking (valet parking $30).
Restaurant. Safe.* **Room services** *CD player.
Dataport. Minibar. TV: cable/pay movies.*

Hotel Triton

*342 Grant Avenue, CA 94108, at Bush Street (1-800
800 1299/394 0500/www.hoteltriton.com). Bus 2, 3,
4, 15, 30, 45, 76.* **Rates** single/double $149-$299;
suite $299-$359. **Credit** AmEx, DC, Disc, MC, V.
Map p311 G3.

This avant-garde hotel and local artists' showcase
is right next to the ornate Chinatown gate. It's
popular with celebrities and musicians – the Red Hot
Chili Peppers stay here, and Woody Harrelson is
a fan of the hotel's two-dozen EcoRooms. Soon,
he'll be able to feel good about staying in any of
the 140 rooms here, since the Triton's goal is to be
a totally green hotel by the end of 2004 – think
organic cotton sheets and 'Earthly Beds' made
entirely of recycled materials. Also on the hotel's

eclectic menu are on-site yoga classes, nightly tarot readings and free wine and beer in the lobby, along with some unusual room choices, such as small 'Zen Dens' with incense, books on Buddhism, and daybeds. There are also suites designed by hoary rockers Jerry Garcia, Carlos Santana and, wait for it, Graham Nash.
Hotel services *Air-conditioning. Business centre. Concierge. Conference facilities. Gym (24hr). Laundry. Parking ($33). Restaurant. Safe.* **Room services** *Dataport. Fax. Hi-fi. Iron. Minibar. Room service (7am-9pm). TV: cable (VCR – suites only).*

Orchard Hotel

665 Bush Street, CA 94108, between Stockton & Powell Streets (1-888 717 2881/362 8878/fax 362 8088/www.theorchardhotel.com). Bus 2, 3, 4, 30, 45, 76/cable car Powell-Hyde or Powell-Mason. **Rates** single/double $209-$289; suite $289-$369. **Credit** AmEx, DC, Disc, MC, V. **Map** p311 G3.
One of San Franciso's newer boutique hotels, the ten-storey Orchard offers 96 rooms and nine suites that are rather bland in design, but pristine and very comfortable. Perks include Aveda toiletries, a free newspaper and continental breakfast. The wine list at the Solea restaurant and wine bar is an oenophile's delight. It is a bit of a steep hike up from the hotel to Bush Street, but the Powell cable car line is only steps away. The hotel is no-smoking throughout.
Hotel services *Air-conditioning. Babysitting. Bar. Business services. Concierge. Conference facilities. Gym. Laundry. Limousine service. Parking ($30). Restaurant. Safe.* **Room services** *CD player. Dataport. DVD. Iron. Minibar. Room service (7am-10.30pm). Turndown. TV: cable.*

The Serrano

405 Taylor Street, CA 94102, at O'Farrell Street (1-877 294 9709/885 2500/fax 474 4879/www. serranohotel.com). Bus 27, 38/cable car Powell-Hyde or Powell-Mason. **Rates** single/double $149-$259; suite $229-$349. **Credit** AmEx, DC, Disc, MC, V. **Map** p310 G4.
This sister property to the more lavish and expensive Monaco (*see p38*) sits right next door, just blocks from Union Square and in the heart of the Theatre District. The 17-storey Spanish Revival building has a Moorish-style lobby – lots of jewel-tones, rich dark woods and high, elaborately painted ceilings – but the rooms are cosy, with buttery yellow damask walls, cherrywood furniture and warm red striped curtains. The upper floors have good city views. Pet-friendly and kid-friendly, the Serrano has a game library and guests are invited, when they check in, to play a round of blackjack for prizes. Ponzu, the hotel's hip Asian-fusion restaurant, is a great place for dinner too.
Hotel services *Bar. Business centre. Concierge. Conference facilities. Laundry. Parking ($35). Restaurant.* **Room services** *Dataport. Games console. Iron. Minibar. Room service (7-10am, 5-10pm Mon-Fri; 8-11am, 5-10pm Sat, Sun). Safe. Shoeshine. TV: cable/pay movies.*

Also recommended

Hotel Union Square *114 Powell Street, CA 94102, between Ellis & O'Farrell Streets (1-800 553 1900/397 3000/fax 399 1874/www.hotelunion square.com).* **Rates** single/double $99-$149; suite $200-$295.
Stratford Hotel *242 Powell Street, CA 94102, at Geary Street (1-888 554 6835/397 7080/fax 397 7087).* **Rates** single $69; double $79-$99.

Budget

Hotel Cosmo

761 Post Street, CA 94109, at Jones Street (1-800 794 6011/673 6040/reservations 1-800 252 7466/fax 563 6739/www.hotel-cosmo.com). Bus 2, 3, 4, 27, 76. **Rates** single/double $89-$159; suite $139-$199. **Credit** AmEx, DC, Disc, MC, V. **Map** p310 G4.
Discover the latest trendy hotel before everyone else does. Formerly the Hotel Bedford (the first Kimpton property), the newly renovated Cosmo is fashioning itself as a hangout for the artsy crowd, with monthly art openings and a lobby filled with local works. But the buzz hasn't quite caught on – perhaps because the 17-storey hotel feels a little big to pull it off. At the time of writing the hotel was still undergoing a facelift, with half of the rooms in the Bedford's frilly decor, half in the more interesting new design, a study in '50s art moderne. Though the 1929 building has plenty of deco charm, the lavender and silver colour scheme (even the façade is purple) is a bit much. Still, the corner suites, with stunning views, are one of the best bargains in town.
Hotel services *Bar. Business Centre. Conference Facilities. Laundry. Parking ($25). Patio.* **Room services** *Games console. Iron. TV: cable.*

Financial District

Deluxe

Mandarin Oriental

222 Sansome Street, CA 94104, between Pine & California Streets (1-800 622 0404/276 9888/fax 433 0289/www.mandarinoriental.com). BART Montgomery/Muni Metro F, J, K, L, M, N/bus 10, 15, 41/cable car California. **Rates** single/double $475-$725; suite $1,400-$3,000. **Credit** AmEx, DC, Disc, MC, V. **Map** p311 H3.
Few hotels in the world can boast such extraordinary views nor such a decadent means of enjoying them as the Mandarin Oriental. Its lobby is on the ground floor of the 48-storey First Interstate Building (the city's third-tallest building) and all of its 158 rooms, including four suites, are on the top 11 floors, affording breathtaking vistas of the city and Bay. The rooms contain blond wood furnishings and Asian artwork, and are decked out in sumptous fabrics. All of them have binoculars and some, more importantly, have glass bathtubs beside the windows. If that isn't enough, the Mandarin was recently voted top hotel in the city for customer service.

Hotel services *Air-conditioning. Bar. Business centre. Concierge. Conference facilities. Gym. Laundry. Limousine service. Parking ($34). Restaurants (2).* **Shoeshine. Room services** *CD player. Dataport. Iron. Minibar. Room service (24hr). Safe. Turndown. TV: cable.*

Also recommended

Hyatt Regency *5 Embarcadero Center, CA 94111, at California Street (1-800 233 1234/788 1234/ fax 398 2567/http://sanfrancisco.hyatt.com).* **Rates** single $155-$299; double $180-$324; suite $255-$399. **Park Hyatt** *333 Battery Street, CA 94111, at Clay Street (1-800 492 8822/392 1234/fax 421 2433/ http://sanfrancisco.hyatt.com).* **Rates** single $235-$345; double $235-$370; suite $470-$4,000.

Tenderloin

Deluxe

Adagio Hotel

550 Geary Street, CA 94102, between Taylor & Jones Streets (775 5000/fax 775 9388/www.thehotel adagio.com). Bus 27, 38. **Rates** single/double $139-$209; suite $795-$895. **Credit** AmEx, DC, Disc, MC, V. **Map** p310 G4.

In June 2003 the Shannon Court reopened as the Adagio, having been extensively remodelled. It's been welcoming travellers under different names – El Cortez before the Shannon Court – since 1929, but its current incarnation must be the best yet. The decor combines muted colours and arty photos, making the hotel feel comfortable as well as chic, smart without being too business-like. Having Pascal Rigo's Cortez (*see p119*) as the hotel bar and breakfast room is no minor recommendation either, and Aveda bathroom products, ethernet link-up and unobtrusive but super-slick room service (returning from a leisurely break-fast downstairs we found the beds already made) complete the sense of being rather well looked after. **Hotel services** *Babysitting. Bar. Business centre. Concierge. Conference facilities. Gym. Laundry. Limousine service. Parking ($29). Restaurant.* **Room services** *CD player. Dataport. Games console. Minibar. Room service (6.30am-10pm). TV: cable/pay movies.*

Clift Hotel

495 Geary Street, CA 94102, at Taylor Street (1-800 652 5438/775 4700/fax 441 4621/ www.clifthotel.com). Bus 2, 3, 4, 27, 38, 76. **Rates** single/double $325-$385; suite $950-$2,025. **Credit** AmEx, DC, Disc, MC, V. **Map** p310 G4.

Since its post-renovation reopening in 2001, the Clift – long one of the city's beloved landmarks – has staked out its new place as the city's trendiest hotel. Another love child of hotel impresario Ian Schrager and designer Philippe Starck, the Clift is imposing in its grandeur before you even step inside. The building seems impenetrable, the only street-level sign that you've arrived being rakish doormen guarding the sleek glass entryway. Inside is a design fantasy-land set in a cavernous, dramatic space. The

Clift's over-the-top decor, not to mention its attitude, might not add up to everyone's idea of a welcome, but, fortunately, the 373 rooms and suites are less intense, with soft, relaxing colour schemes, comfy sleigh beds and elegant floor-to-ceiling mirrors. Non-residents love drinks in the Redwood (*see p151*) or splurging on dinner at Asia de Cuba (*see p119*). **Hotel services** *Air-conditioning. Babysitting. Bar. Business services. Concierge. Conference facilities. Garden. Gym. Laundry. Limousine service. Parking ($40). Restaurant. Safe. Spa.* **Room services** *CD player. Dataport. DVD. Iron. Minibar. Room service (24hr). Safe. Turndown. TV: cable/web TV.*

Hotel Monaco

501 Geary Street, CA 94102, at Taylor Street (1-866 622 5284/292 0100/fax 292 0111/www.monaco-sf.com). Bus 2, 3, 4, 27, 38, 76. **Rates** single/double $179-$369; suite $229-$489. **Credit** AmEx, DC, Disc, MC, V. **Map** p310 G4.

This Beaux Arts building, built in 1910, underwent a $24-million facelift in 1995; now few hotels can match it for sheer, larger-than-life, romantic indulgence. There are hand-painted ceiling domes and grandiose, art nouveau murals in the common areas, while the rooms have canopy-draped beds surrounded by a jumble of vibrant patterns. (Be warned: the cheaper rooms can be a bit small.) The sumptuous Grand Café next door has the feel of a Parisian train station in the '20s, somewhat contradicted by the three-storey bunny sculpture. Rates include free morning coffee and afternoon tea, wine and cheese receptions with neck massages, and tarot readings. **Hotel services** *Air-conditioning. Bar. Business services. Concierge. Conference facilities. Gym. Laundry. Limousine service. Parking ($35). Restaurant. Safe. Spa.* **Room services** *CD player. Dataport. Fax. Games console. Iron. Room service (24hr). Safe. Shoeshine. Turndown. TV: cable/web TV. Whirlpool tubs.*

Mid-range

Hotel Bijou

111 Mason Street, CA 94102, at Eddy Street (1-800 771 1022/771 1200/fax 346 3196/ www.hotelbijou.com). Muni Metro F, J, K, L, M, N/bus 27, 31. **Rates** single/double $79-$149. **Credit** AmEx, DC, Disc, MC, V. **Map** p311 G4.

Cinephiles will love this cleverly executed homage to '30s movie houses, and if you're happy in the edgy neighbourhood, you'll appreciate the hotel's proximity to Market Street. The walls are covered in black-and-white images of old cinema marquees and local film schedules are posted on a board each day. There's also a 'film hotline' giving locations of movie shoots going on about town. All 65 of the comfortably stylish rooms are named after a movie shot in the city, but there's nothing to distinguish *Vertigo* from *Mrs Doubtfire* besides the film still on the wall. Best of all, there's a mini-theatre with real vintage cinema seating (albeit in front of a television, not a big screen) where guests can enjoy nightly viewings.

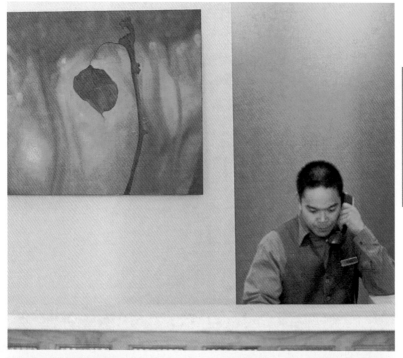

Pamper yourself at the sleek, slick **Adagio Hotel**. *See p38.*

*Hotel services Business services. Concierge.
Conference facilities. Continental breakfast. Laundry.
Parking (valet parking $21).* **Room services**
Dataport. TV: cable.

Phoenix Hotel

*601 Eddy Street, CA 94109, at Larkin Street
(1-800 248 9466/776 1380/fax 885 3109/
www.thephoenixhotel.com). Bus 19, 31.*
Rates single/double $99-$149; suite $149-$209.
Credit AmEx, DC, Disc, MC, V. **Map** p310 F4.
What do Johnny Depp, Pearl Jam and the late John
F Kennedy Jr have in common? They've all stayed
at the funky Phoenix, one of San Francisco's glam
pads – located, oddly enough, in one of the city's
least glitzy neighbourhoods. The 44 rooms have a
tropical style, with bamboo furniture and herbiage
helping to create the feel of an oasis. The adjoining
Bambuddha restaurant and cocktail lounge (*see
p219*) serves exotic Asian-themed cocktails and
Asian tapas to guests basking poolside.
Hotel services *Bar. Concierge. Garden. Parking
(free). Pool. Safe.* **Room services** *Dataport. TV: cable.*

Also recommended

Savoy Hotel *580 Geary Street, CA 94102,
between Jones & Taylor Streets (1-800 227 4223/
441 2700/fax 441 4123/http://thesavoyhotel.com).*
Rates single/double $99-$169; suite $149-$169.

Budget

The **Adelaide Hostel** (*see p52*) also has
private rooms, six of them en suite.

The Andrews

*624 Post Street, CA 94109, between Jones &
Taylor Streets (1-800 926 3739/fax 928 6919/
www.andrewshotel.com). Bus 2, 3, 4, 27, 38, 76.*
Rates single/double $89-$165; suite $139-$175.
Credit AmEx, MC, V. **Map** p310 G3/4.
This is one of those interesting old-school San
Francisco hotels that resonates with history, character and, dare one say it, soul. It's hard to believe
such a respectable-looking place was originally
erected in 1905 as the opulent Sultan Turkish Baths
(the Queen Anne structure was made into a hotel two
decades later). Sadly, there's nary a sauna or a hot
tub to be found today, but, for the price, it would be
hard to find a cosier and more convenient spot. From
the grandfather clock in the lobby to the old cage
elevator to the musty hallways and small, comfortable (if a tad old-fashioned) rooms, it feels like the set
of a classic film noir. Walls are on the thin side.
Hotel services *Bar. Concierge. Parking ($25).
Restaurant. Safe.* **Room services** *Dataport. Iron.
Minibar. Room service (5.30-10pm). TV: cable/VCR.*

Halcyon Hotel

*649 Jones Street, CA 94102, between Post & Geary
Streets (1-800 627 2396/929 8033/fax 441 8033/
www.bradyacres.com). Bus 2, 3, 4, 27, 38, 76.*
Rates single/double $85; family room $95-$115;
weekly rates $510-$650.* **Credit** AmEx, DC, Disc,
MC, V. **Map** p310 G4.

This pleasant and popular *pension* has 25 comfortably furnished 'efficiency studio' rooms with well-
stocked kitchenettes (microwaves, no cookers),
private baths with clawfoot tubs, unlimited local
calls, on-site laundry (free soap) and lots of extra
touches to make a traveller, especially one who has
been on the move a lot, breathe a sigh of relief.
Though the weekly rates quoted above are official,
check the website for specials – a room for a week
can sometimes cost as little as $350 per person.
Hotel services *Business services. Laundry.*
Room services *Dataport. Safe. TV: cable.*

Civic Center

Mid-range

The Inn at the Opera

*333 Fulton Street, CA 94102, at Franklin Street
(1-800 590 0157/863 8400/fax 861 0821/
www.innattheopera.com). Bus 5, 21, 47, 49.*
Rates single/double $129-$145; suite $175-$275.
Credit AmEx, Disc, DC, MC, V. **Map** p314 F4/5.
Opposite the opera house, and a block from City
Hall, this attractive hotel is well located for those
who plan to partake of lots of culture during their
stay. It's also on the brink of Hayes Valley, one of
the city's best shopping districts. The Inn can't be
bettered for opera buffs – visiting stars stay here
(including Luciano Pavarotti) and there are framed
portraits of opera composers on the walls, sheet
music lining some bureau drawers and impressive
sound systems in every room, tuned to a classical
station. The 30 rooms and 18 suites are all handsome
and fairly spacious, most have kitchenettes; own-
made cookies await guests on arrival. The hotel
restaurant is popular for pre- and post-performance
dinners. The Inn attracts an older crowd.
Hotel services *Bar. Business services. Concierge.
Restaurant. Parking ($22).* **Room services**
*Dataport. Room service (7am-10am, 5-10pm).
Turndown. TV: cable/VCR.*

SoMa

Deluxe

Palace Hotel

*2 New Montgomery Street, CA 94105, at Market
Street (1-800 325 3589/512 1111/fax 243 8062/
www.sfpalace.com). BART Montgomery/Muni Metro
F, J, K, L, M, N/bus 2, 3, 4, 5, 9, 10, 15, 21, 30, 45,
71.* **Rates** single/double $499-$559; suite $775-$4,400.
Credit AmEx, DC, Disc, MC, V. **Map** p311 H3.
Long one of the world's grandest hotels, the Palace
has welcomed in the past such famous guests as
Winston Churchill, Thomas Edison and Franklin D
Roosevelt; a $160-million restoration in 1991 made
sure the dignitaries kept coming. Today the Palace
dining rooms are absolutely breathtaking, the 80,000
panes of stained glass in the Garden Court's ceiling
dome simply spectacular and the hotel's covered

swimming pool by far the finest in the city. No matter, then, that the 553 rooms are really rather modest. If you aren't staying, make a point of visiting for afternoon tea. *See also p48* **Death beds.**
Hotel services *Air-conditioning. Babysitting. Bar. Business centre. Concierge. Conference facilities. Gym. Laundry. Limousine service. Parking ($30). Pool. Restaurants (3). Safe. Sauna. Shoeshine. Spa.* **Room services** *Dataport. Iron. Minibar. Room service (24hr). Safe. Turndown. TV: cable/web TV/pay movies.*

W Hotel
181 Third Street, CA 94103, at Howard Street (1-800 946 8357/777 5300/fax 817 7823/www. whotels.com). BART Montgomery/bus 9, 14, 15, 30, 45, 76. **Rates** single/double $199-$449; suite $1,000-$1,800. **Credit** AmEx, DC, Disc, MC, V. **Map** p311 H4.
This may no longer be the very trendiest hotel in town, but it's still a stylish spot to drop your bags. The sparse elegance of its minimalist decor, the hip dance music playing throughout and the laptop-toting after-work crowd sauntering through for cocktails in the bar (*see p152*) all seem to flow seamlessly out of the brilliance of its location next to SFMOMA. The 423 rooms are as artistically modern as the lobby, and are loaded with all the latest gadgets: CD players, 27-inch TVs, wireless keyboards, high-speed internet access and goose-down duvets. Some rooms have views over Yerba Buena Gardens.
Hotel services *Air-conditioning. Bars (2). Business services. Concierge. Conference facilities. Gym. Laundry. Parking ($40). Pool. Restaurants (2). Safe.* **Room services** *CD player. Dataport. Fax. Internet. Iron. Minibar. Room service (24hr). TV: cable/web TV/VCR.*

Mid-range

The Mosser
54 Fourth Street, CA 94103, between Mission & Market Streets (986 4400/fax 495 7653). BART Powell/Muni Metro F, J, K, L, M, N/bus 9, 30, 45. **Rates** single/double $99-$179; suite $189-$249. **Credit** AmEx, DC, Disc, MC, V. **Map** p311 H4.
The Mosser is an affordable choice for those seeking a stylish location in SoMa. On the premises of the former Victorian Mosser (actually built in 1911, technically making it an Edwardian structure), the property was extensively updated in 2001 by the designer of the W (*see above*). Many of the quirky details were left untouched – an ornate stained-glass window in the lobby, antique phone booths, a painfully slow cage elevator – making a stay here a slightly Gothic experience. Rooms are small and a bit dark, hidden down labyrinthine hallways, and some have shared baths. Still, there's plenty of cool amenities to satisfy the young cosmopolitan guests: good linens, the latest gadgets, soothing colours. There's also Anabelle's Bistro next door.
Hotel services *Babysitting. Bar. Business services. Concierge. Parking (valet parking $27). Restaurant.* **Room services** *Dataport. Games console. Iron. TV: pay movies/web TV.*

Budget

Bay Bridge Inn
966 Harrison Street, CA 94107, between Fifth & Sixth Streets (397 0657/fax 495 5117/ www.baybridgeinn.com). Bus 12, 27, 42. **Rates** single $65-$135; double $70-$150. **Credit** AmEx, Disc, MC, V. **Map** p315 H5.
There's no reason why you would want to spend a lot of time at the Bay Bridge Inn. Still, the 22 plain motel-style rooms are cheap and clean. They're also convenient for the Moscone Convention Center and for the 11th Street nightclub corridor.
Hotel services *Air-conditioning. Business services. Limousine service. Parking (free). Safe.* **Room services** *Dataport. Iron. Jacuzzi. TV: cable.*

Chinatown

Budget

Grant Plaza Hotel
465 Grant Avenue, CA 94108, at Pine Street (1-800 472 6899/434 3883/fax 434 3886/ www.grantplaza.com). Bus 15, 30, 45/cable car California. **Rates** single $59-$79; double $69-$105. **Credit** AmEx, DC, Disc, MC, V. **Map** p311 G3.
As long as you're not planning to drive anywhere (Grant Plaza is in the middle of crowded Chinatown) you're unlikely to find a better deal anywhere in the city. There are 72 immaculately clean (if small) rooms, complete with contemporary furnishings, private bath, TV and phone. You can also split the larger rooms four ways, which works out at less than hostel rates. The corner rooms on the higher floors are the largest and brightest.
Hotel services *Concierge. Parking ($17.50). Safe.* **Room services** *Dataport. TV: cable.*

North Beach

Mid-range

Hotel Bohème
444 Columbus Avenue, CA 94133, between Vallejo & Green Streets (433 9111/fax 362 6292/ www.hotelboheme.com). Bus 15, 30, 39, 41, 45. **Rates** single/double $149-$175. **Credit** AmEx, DC, Disc, MC, V. **Map** p311 G2.
Want to immerse yourself in North Beach and its Beat history? This charming hotel – opened after the earthquake by an Italian immigrant family and reopened as the Bohème in 1995 – positively brims with it. The ochre walls are lined with photos of the smoky '50s jazz era, fragments of poetry turn up everywhere and, if you're lucky, you can sleep in Allen Ginsberg's room (No.204), a small queen (naturally) facing Columbus Avenue. In his last years he was often seen here in the bay window, tapping away on his laptop. The 16 rooms here are tiny, but the Bohème is surrounded by cafés and restaurants,

The **Clift Hotel**. *See p38.*

with City Lights (*see p165*) just across the street. Light sleepers should ask for a room that doesn't face the bustle of Columbus Avenue.
Hotel services *Business services. Complimentary afternoon sherry. Concierge. Parking ($31). Safe.*
Room services *Dataport. TV: cable.*

Washington Square Inn
1660 Stockton Street, CA 94133, at Filbert Street (1-800 388 0220/981 4220/fax 397 7242). Bus 15, 30, 39, 41, 45/cable car Powell-Mason. **Rates** single/double $145-$245. **Credit** AmEx, DC, Disc, MC, V. **Map** p311 G2.
This convivial inn is in a quiet section of North Beach, by one of the city's prettiest urban parks and an easy stroll to the local shops and restaurants. The interior is lovely, with large gilt mirrors and pots of exotic orchids, and each of the 15 rooms is decorated with French antiques and lush fabrics. Service is also excellent: guests are offered tea, wine and hors d'oeuvres every afternoon. Rates include continental breakfast.
Hotel services *Laundry. Parking (valet parking $25). Safe.* **Room services** *Room service (7.30am-midnight). Turndown. TV: cable.*

Budget

San Remo Hotel
2337 Mason Street, CA 94133, at Chestnut Street (1-800 352 7366/776 8688/fax 776 2811/www.san remohotel.com). Bus 15, 30, 39/cable car Powell-Mason. **Rates** single $55-$75; double $65-$85; penthouse $155-$175. **Credit** AmEx, DC, MC, V. **Map** p310 G2.
Originally a boarding house for dockworkers displaced in the 1906 fire, this meticulously restored Italianate Edwardian is now home to one of the city's best bargains. Though the rooms are small and the spotless shower rooms shared (there's also one bath), you'd be hard-pressed to find finer accommodation at this price. The 63 rooms have brass or cast-iron beds, wicker furniture and antique armoires – but no telephone or TV. Ask for a room on the upper floor facing Mason Street or, if the penthouse is free, book it: you'll never want to leave.
Hotel services *Bar. Business services. Concierge. Conference facilities. Laundry (self-service). Parking ($10-$14). Restaurant. Safe.*

Fisherman's Wharf

Deluxe

Argonaut Hotel
495 Jefferson Street, CA 94109, at Hyde Street (1-800 790 1415/563 0800/fax 563 2800/ www.argonauthotel.com). Muni Metro F/bus 10, 30, 47/cable car Powell-Hyde. **Rates** single/double $169-$229; suite $489-$629. **Credit** AmEx, DC, Disc, MC, V. **Map** p310 F1.
In August 2003 the early 20th-century fruit-packing Haslett Warehouse reopened as SF's newest luxury hotel, directly opposite Hyde Street Pier. The blue-

Beat central: **Hotel Bohème**. *See p42.*

and-yellow maritime decor is clearly aimed at the kids, but there's a classy lobby with its enclosed fire, stripped wood and bare bricks nicely offset by chirpy nautical props. The 252 carefully furnished rooms have all mod cons (ethernet, CD/DVD player, games console), but it's in the suites that the hotel excels itself: hot tub with a seaview, tripod telescope in the lounge by the dining table. Staff are helpful and friendly to a fault, though the pith-helmeted doormen take some getting used to. Breakfast is served in the Blue Mermaid (*see p128*) on the ground floor. If you want a sea view, ask for a north-facing room on the third floor or above.

Hotel services *Babysitting. Bar. Business centre. Concierge. Conference facilities. Gym. Laundry. Parking (valet parking $32). Restaurant.* **Room services** *CD/DVD player. Dataport. Games console. Iron. Minibar. Safe. TV: pay movies/web TV.*

Mid-range

Best Western Tuscan Inn

425 North Point Street, CA 94133, at Mason Street (1-800 648 4626/561 1100/fax 561 1199/ www.tuscaninn.com). Muni Metro F/bus 10, 15, 30, 39, 47/cable car Powell-Mason. **Rates** *single $99-$169; double $101-$179; suite $179-$229.* **Credit** AmEx, DC, Disc, MC, V. **Map** p310 G1.

It doesn't look like much from the outside, but the Best Western has a lot going for it. There's the inviting lobby (at its best for afternoon wine-tasting when the fireplace takes the chill right out of you) and the comfortable, tastefully decorated rooms. There's also the excellent restaurant Café Pescatore. A good choice if you want to be near Pier 39 – and proximity to the cable car turnaround means there's an easy escape from all the touristy madness.

Hotel services *Air-conditioning. Bar. Concierge. Conference facilities. Laundry. Parking ($26). Restaurant. Safe.* **Room services** *Dataport. Games console. Iron. Minibar. Room service (7am-1am). Turndown. TV: cable.*

The Wharf Inn

2601 Mason Street, CA 94133, at Beach Street (1-800 548 9918/673 7411/fax 776 2181/ www.wharfinn.com). Muni Metro F/bus 15, 39, 47/ cable car Powell-Mason. **Rates** *single/double $99-$299; suite $299-$399.* **Credit** AmEx, DC, Disc, MC, V. **Map** p310 G1.

This updated motel – part of a chain – is right in the thick of Fisherman's Wharf. But besides the location, what sets it apart is the friendly, personal service and the fact that most rooms have balconies, some overlooking Pier 39. The 51 rooms and three suites (one is a two-bedroom 'penthouse' with two furnished decks) were recently redecorated to a playful '60s-retro beach-motel theme, all golds and mossy greens. Rooms come with the standard amenities and there's always fresh coffee in the lobby.

Hotel services *Business services. Concierge. Limousine service. Parking (free). Safe.* **Room services** *Dataport. Iron. TV: cable (limited).*

Nob Hill

Deluxe

Huntington Hotel

1075 California Street, CA 94108, at Taylor Street (1-800 227 4683/474 5400/fax 474 6227/www.huntingtonhotel.com). Bus 1/cable car California. **Rates** *single $295-$440; double $320-$465; suite $490-$1,120.* **Credit** AmEx, DC, Disc, MC, V. **Map** p310 G3.

Family-owned and operated, the Huntington exemplifies understated luxury. The hotel is perched high on Nob Hill next to Grace Cathedral, with the 137 charming, well-appointed rooms and 32 suites offering incredible views of the city. What could be better than a swim in the pool overlooking Union Square or an indulgent treatment at the lush Nob Hill Spa (345 2888)? The California cable car line goes right past the door.

Hotel services *Air-conditioning. Bar. Concierge. Conference facilities. Gym. Laundry. Limousine service. Parking ($29). Pool. Restaurant. Safe. Spa.* **Room services** *Dataport. Fax. Minibar. Room service (6am-11.30pm). Turndown. TV: cable.*

Ritz-Carlton San Francisco

600 Stockton Street, CA 94108, at California Street (1-800 241 3333/296 7465/fax 291 0288/ www.ritzcarlton.com/hotels/san_francisco). Bus 1, 30, 45/cable car California. **Rates** *single/double $375-$495; suite $395-$5,200.* **Credit** AmEx, DC, Disc, MC, V. **Map** p311 G3.

Among the fine hotels on Nob Hill, it's the Ritz that gets all the attention. Deservedly so. After a four-year, multi-million-dollar renovation, the 1909 neo-classical landmark opened its doors as the Ritz-Carlton in 1991. It has been pampering its affluent guests ever since. Amenities at the 336-room hotel include an indoor spa with gym, swimming pool, whirlpool and sauna; the Dining Room (*see p131*), an award-winning French restaurant; daily piano performances in the Lobby Lounge; and an armada of valets to fulfil your every need. The rooms, while sumptuously appointed, are rather staid compared with the grandiose façade and lobby, but include all the luxury items you would expect. Club-level guests can use the elegant Club Lounge, with continuous food and drinks. Plebs can pop in for the Sunday Jazz Brunch, held on a sunken roof terrace surrounded by roses and bougainvillea.

Hotel services *Air-conditioning. Babysitting. Bar. Business centre. Concierge. Conference facilities. Garden. Gym. Laundry. Limousine service. Parking ($45). Pool. Restaurants (2). Safe. Shoeshine. Spa.* **Room services** *CD player. Dataport. Games console. Iron. Minibar. Room service (24hr). Safe. Turndown. TV: cable/pay movies.*

Also recommended

Fairmont Hotel & Tower *950 Mason Street, CA 94108, at California Street (1-800 527 4727/ 772 5000/fax 772 5013/www.fairmont.com).*

Don't be misled: staff are super-friendly at the **Argonaut Hotel**. *See p44.*

Rates single $149-$580; double $174-$545; suite $630-$8,000.
Mark Hopkins Inter-Continental *1 Nob Hill, CA 94108, at Mason Street (1-800 662 4455/ 392 3434/fax 421 3302).* **Rates** single/double $179-$490; suite $550-$3,500.
Renaissance Stanford Court Hotel *905 California Street, CA 94108, at Powell Street (1-800 227 4736/989 3500/fax 391 0513/ www.marriott.com).* **Rates** single/double $199-$229; suite $675-$875.

Mid-range

Executive Hotel Vintage Court

650 Bush Street, CA 94108, at Powell Street (1-800 654 1100/392 4666/fax 433 4065/ www.vintagecourt.com). Bus 2, 3, 4, 30, 45, 76/ cable car Powell-Mason or Powell-Hyde. **Rates** single/double $199-$229; penthouse suite $329-$349. **Credit** AmEx, DC, Disc, MC, V. **Map** p311 G3.
Convenient for both Union Square and Chinatown but outside the city bustle, this elegant and relaxed hotel gives guests a taste of Wine Country. Each of its 107 rooms is named after a Californian winery, and there are daily tastings beside the lobby's grand marble fireplace (sometimes hosted by a local winemaker). The bathrooms are a little outmoded, but the bedrooms have been respectably redone – bay windows with venetian blinds, handsome writing desks, green-striped padded headboards. The penthouse Niebaum-Coppola Suite boasts Bay views, a jacuzzi, a wood-burning fireplace and a stained-glass window dating back to 1912. Masa's (*see p118*), the hotel's well-regarded French restaurant, serves some of the most coveted food in town; guests get priority for reservations.
Hotel services *Airport transfers. Business services. Babysitting. Bar. Complimentary continental breakfast, tea & coffee. Concierge. Conference facilities. Internet. Parking ($24;*

valet parking $32). Laundry. Restaurant.
Room services *Dataport. Games console. Iron. TV: pay movies (VCR available).*

White Swan Inn

845 Bush Street, CA 94108, between Taylor & Mason Streets (1-800 999 9570/775 1755/ fax 775 5717/www.jdvhospitality.com). Bus 2, 3, 4, 76/cable car Powell-Hyde or Powell-Mason. **Rates** single/double $139-$259; suite $229-$309. **Credit** AmEx, Disc, DC, MC, V. **Map** p310 G3.
One of a smattering of cosy, English-style bed and breakfasts on Bush Street, the stately White Swan boasts a cutesy theme, plates of fresh-baked cookies and a gas fireplace in all 26 rooms – plus a very nice big hearth in the downstairs parlour, where a full breakfast, afternoon tea and evening wine and cheese are served. If you don't mind a bit of fustiness, you'll be very happy here. Next door, sister property the Petite Auberge is a cheaper version of the Swan, with many of the same amenities.
Hotel services *Concierge. Conference facilities. Garden. Gym. Laundry. Parking ($30). Safe.*
Room services *Dataport. Iron. Room service (breakfast only). Turndown. TV: cable.*

Also recommended

Nob Hill Inn *1000 Pine Street, CA 94102, at Taylor Street (1-888 982 2632/673 6080/fax 673 6098).* **Rates** single/double $125-$165; suite $195-$275.

Budget

Ansonia Hotel

711 Post Street, CA 94109, between Leavenworth & Jones Streets (673 2670/www.ansoniahotel.com). Bus 2, 3, 4, 27, 76. **Rates** single $56-$66; double $66-$79; suite $105. **Credit** AmEx, MC, V. **Map** p310 G3.
Grandma's house is barely more comfortable and friendly than this bed and breakfast. It's a deceptively large place, with halls that feel like an Old

West hotel, a lobby that's like the sitting room of a railroad tycoon, and rooms that your great aunt would be totally at home in. With home-cooked breakfasts and dinners included, you can't beat the prices either. And it's only five minutes from Union Square and Market Street. There's an entrance around the block at 630 Geary; curiously, it's called the Abby Hotel on that side.

Hotel services *Business services. Complimentary breakfast. Laundry. Parking ($17). Safe boxes.* **Room services** *Fridge. Iron. TV.*

Commodore International Hotel

825 Sutter Street, CA 94109, between Jones & Leavenworth Streets (1-800 338 6848/923 6800/fax 923 6804/www.thecommodorehotel.com). Bus 2, 3, 4, 27, 76. **Rates** single/double $69-$159; suite $149-$225. **Credit** AmEx, DC, Disc, MC, V. **Map** p310 G3.

If you're looking for a reasonably priced hotel with lots of style and attitude, the Commodore could be for you. You might not get the hotel's theme at first,

but its resemblance to a '20s ocean liner starts to come clear after a while: the colourful lobby is a Lido Deck, complete with chaises longues; the stream-lined, very art deco Titanic Café off the lobby is full of nautical blues and yellows. All of the 110 spacious rooms have large bathtubs and big closets; you can also request one of the postmodern deco rooms with custom furnishings by local artists. The Red Room (*see p151*) bar is as popular as the hotel; drenched in hypnotic red, it is as decadent as the Lost Generation with stem cocktail glasses to match.

Hotel services *Bar. Concierge. Conference facilities. Laundry. Limousine service. Parking ($25). Restaurant (breakfast & lunch only). Safe.* **Room services** *Iron. TV: cable.*

Dakota Hotel

606 Post Street, CA 94109, at Taylor Street (931 7475/www.hotelsanfrancisco.com). Bus 2, 3, 4, 76/cable car Powell-Hyde or Powell-Mason. **Rates** single $55-$80; double $65-$80. **Credit** MC, V. **Map** p310 G3.

Death beds

While the majority of visitors to San Francisco sleep soundly and wake refreshed, some guests have never recovered from their stay in the city's luxury hotels – with a history of heart attacks and assassination attempts, mortality may be a factor when selecting a room.

SF hotel of choice for Queen Elizabeth II, Emperor Hirohito and a string of US Presidents since its opening in 1904, the **Westin St Francis** (335 Powell Street, 397 7000, www.westin.com) on Union Square has gained notoriety for more than one unhappy event. In 1950 singer Al Jolson died of a heart attack in suite 1221 while playing a game of gin rummy. He had stopped off in SF on his way to Hollywood, where he was due to feature on Bing Crosby's radio show. At 10pm on 24 October he sent his friend out to fetch him some bicarbonate of soda as he was feeling funny. But, before his friend could return, Jolson announced: 'It's looks like the end.' So it was. By coincidence Jolson met his end in the same room that, 29 years earlier, had seen the scandal of starlet Virginia Rappe's death, raped and crushed to death by gargantuan silent movie star Fatty Arbuckle. The Grim Reaper was also hovering in the lobby in September 1975, when former FBI agent Sara Jane Moore made a failed assassination attempt on President Gerald Ford outside the hotel – just 17 days after

26-year-old Lynette 'Squeaky' Fromme, a disciple of cult murderer Charles Manson, tried the same thing as Ford left the Senator Hotel in Sacramento.

It could be argued that the **Palace Hotel** (*see p41*) was unlucky even before its opening in 1875. The man who built it, William Ralston, committed suicide just weeks before the opening day, having run his financial empire into bankruptcy. Then President George F Harding fell under the malign spell. Considered the worst president the country has ever had (though many locals feel another has now usurped the accolade), Harding died in the Palace Hotel on 23 August 1923 under suspicious circumstances. Whether he died of anxiety (the President was on a public relations tour following the disaster of the so-called Tea Pot Dome oil scandal), heart attack, stroke or food poisoning is unclear, but there is supposition he was deliberately poisoned by his First Lady. Much speculation centred on a prediction from the psychic used by Harding's wife, which apparently stated the president would die in office. Rumours solidified with Mrs Harding's subsequent refusal to allow an autopsy. You'll find no reference to the pitiful affair at the Palace today, which should reassure those fearful of some kind of jinx: the dark deeds occurred at the hotel's original premises on Market Street, between New Montgomery and Third.

The sign on the door says 'Kick off your boots and stay awhile'. Once you've got past the typical lobby and *fin de siècle* elevator, you'll think you've been washed ashore in Corfu. The pink walls tease you all the way into comfy rooms, lit brightly by bay windows.
Hotel services *Business services. Concierge. Parking ($20).* **Room services** *Dataport. Iron. Room service (7.30am-4pm). TV: cable.*

Golden Gate Hotel

775 Bush Street, CA 94108, between Powell & Mason Streets (1-800 835 1118/392 3702/fax 392 6202/www.goldengatehotel.com). Bus 2, 3, 4, 76/ cable car Powell-Hyde or Powell-Mason. **Rates** single/double $85-$130. **Credit** AmEx, DC, MC, V. **Map** p310 G3.
The key word at this 1913 Edwardian hotel is cosy. With the fireplace in the tiny lobby and the walls of jumbled old photographs, this place has an agreeably lived-in feel. The 25 rooms have a comfortable mix of antiques and wicker furniture, and innkeepers John and Renate Kenaston take pride in maintaining the olde-worlde feel. Even the original birdcage lift is perfectly maintained. Request a room with a clawfoot tub if you enjoy a good soak, and don't be alarmed if hotel cat Captain Nemo wants to share your pillow – it's that kind of place. Free afternoon tea and cookies are served in the parlour. The hotel is no-smoking throughout.
Hotel services *Parking ($15). Safe.* **Room services** *Internet (wireless). TV: cable.*

Hotel Astoria

510 Bush Street, CA 94108, at Grant Avenue (434 8889). Bus 15, 30, 45. **Rates** single/double $50-$75. **Credit** MC, V. **Map** p311 G3.
The Astoria has two great assets: cleanliness and location. Spotless rooms will satisfy even the most finicky visitor and a spit in the wind takes you to Union Square, Chinatown (the gate is right outside), North Beach and the Embarcadero. Character and charm are all very well, but civilisation is built on practicality and location, location, location.
Hotel services *Business centre. Complimentary breakfast. Laundry. Parking ($20). Safe deposit box.* **Room services** *Gaming console. Iron. Safe. TV: cable.*

Also recommended

Grant Hotel *753 Bush Street, CA 94108, between Mason & Powell Streets (1-800 522 0979/421 7540/ fax 989 7719/www.granthotel.citysearch.com).* **Rates** single/double $55-$80.

Mission & Castro

There's not much accommodation in the vibrant Mission – and nothing we'd recommend. For places in the Castro (most of which welcome straight visitors) and some other options that cater specifically to a queer clientele, *see p225*. And the **Metro** (*see p50*) isn't far.

Haight-Ashbury

Mid-range

Stanyan Park Hotel

750 Stanyan Street, CA 94117, at Waller Street (751 1000/fax 668 5454/www.stanyanpark.com). Muni Metro N/bus 7, 33, 43, 66, 71. **Rates** single/double $130-$180; suite $259-$315. **Credit** AmEx, DC, Disc, MC, V. **Map** p313 C6.
This stately, three-storey Victorian building on the edge of Golden Gate Park has been accommodating travellers in style since 1904 – it's even on the National Register of Historic Places. Its 30 rooms are filled with authentic Victorian antiques, right down to the drapes and quilts. Large groups may be attracted to the six big suites with full kitchens, dining rooms and living spaces. Rates include breakfast and afternoon tea. No-smoking throughout.
Hotel services *Concierge. Parking ($12). Safe.* **Room services** *Dataport. TV: cable.*

Budget

The Red Victorian

1665 Haight Street, CA 94117, between Clayton & Cole Streets (864 1978/fax 863 3293/ www.redvic.com). Muni Metro N/bus 7, 33, 37, 43, 66, 71. **Rates** single/double $72-$126; suite $200. **Credit** AmEx, Disc, DC, MC, V. **Map** p313 C6.
Nothing comes as close to offering the quintessential Haight-Ashbury experience as a night at the unique Red Vic. Haight Street's only hotel offers 18 wildly decorated rooms, each with its own thematic twist – such as the rainbow-coloured Flower Child room and the tie-dyed Summer of Love room. Spend some time in owner Sami Sunchild's Peace & Arts Gallery and Meditation Room to really find yourself. Six of the rooms have private baths; the others share. A continental breakfast is included in the room price. Rooms don't have television, although you can request one, and the hotel is no-smoking throughout. Allergy sufferers should, however, be mindful of the hotel cat Mr Mouser, who stays downstairs.
Hotel services *Concierge. Parking ($12). Safe.* **Room services** *Dataport. Iron.*

Western Addition

Deluxe

Archbishop's Mansion

1000 Fulton Street, CA 94117, at Steiner Street (1-800 543 5820/563 7872/fax 885 3193). Bus 5, 22, 24. **Rates** single/double $165-$205; suite $235-$345. **Credit** AmEx, DC, Disc, MC, V. **Map** p313 E5.
Built for the Archbishop of San Francisco in 1904, this opulent French château is on historic Alamo Square Park, facing the row of 'Painted Ladies'.

Some visitors might find its *belle époque* style (chandeliers, heavy antiques and canopy beds) a bit much – it's certainly more magisterial than cosy. All ten rooms and five suites are named after an opera; the Don Giovanni suite has a hand-carved, cherub-laden four-poster bed, two fireplaces and a seven-headed shower (one to wash away each of the seven deadly sins, no kidding). Breakfast is included in the room price, as is afternoon wine and cheese.

Hotel services *Business services. Concierge. Conference facilities. Laundry. Parking (free). Safe.* **Room services** *CD player. Dataport. Iron. Room service (continental breakfast only). Snack bar. TV: cable/VCR.*

Radisson Miyako Hotel

1625 Post Street, CA 94115, at Laguna Street, Japantown (1-800 533 4567/922 3200/fax 921 0417). Bus 2, 3, 4, 22, 38. **Rates** single/double $89-$189; suite $189-$299. **Credit** AmEx, DC, Disc, MC, V. **Map** p310 E4.

It's no surprise that this pagoda-style corporate hotel, with its fountains and Zen gardens, is a favourite of Japanese business travellers. For those who want to experience a serene traditional Japanese tatami suite, but can't make it to Tokyo, the Miyako has two of them, complete with futons, sliding shoji screens and deep soaking tubs. Most of the 211 rooms and 17 suites are standard-issue Western style, but enlivened with Asian touches like Japanese bathing stools and tubs a foot deeper than the usual. Overlooking the Peace Pagoda, the Miyako is just steps away from dozens of good sushi restaurants, shops and a Japanese bathhouse. **Hotel services** *Air-conditioning. Business services. Conference facilities. Dry cleaning. Gym. Laundry. Massage. Parking ($13). Safe.* **Room services** *Dataports. Iron. TV: cable.*

Budget

Metro Hotel

319 Divisadero Street, CA 94117, between Oak & Page Streets (861 5364/fax 863 1970). Bus 6, 7, 22, 24, 66, 71. **Rates** single/double $66-$120. **Credit** AmEx, DC, Disc, MC, V. **Map** p313 E5.

Long a favourite of the just-out-of-college crowd wanting to put up visiting parents, the 22-room Metro is cheap, convenient and a good base for exploring neighbourhoods somewhat off the tourist track. Its location (technically in the Western Addition) feels more like the Haight, which is only two blocks away. The decor is basic, the walls a little thin and the street-side rooms noisy at night. All rooms have shower stalls only. Request one overlooking the charming back garden, which the hotel shares with the excellent French bistro next door. Around the corner is a bare-bones two-room studio apartment with kitchenette for around $100 a night.
Hotel services *Café. Garden.* **Room services** *TV.*

Mid-range

Hotel Drisco

2901 Pacific Avenue, CA 94115, at Broderick Street (1-800 634 7277/346 2880/fax 567 5537/www.hoteldrisco.com). Bus 3, 24. **Rates** single/double $185-$335; suite $245-$400. **Credit** AmEx, DC, Disc, MC, V. **Map** p309 D3.

Built as a luxury hotel in 1903, this place has been receiving famous and intellectual guests ever since; former president Dwight Eisenhower was a regular. Many of the guests are business travellers, so service is excellent, but the atmosphere can feel a little stiff. Remodelled a few years ago, it has 24 rooms and 19 suites, some with spectacular panoramic views. Parking is usually easy.
Hotel services *Business services. Concierge. Conference facilities. Gym. Laundry. Limousine service.* **Room services** *CD player. Dataport. Iron. Minibar. Safe. Turndown. TV: cable/VCR.*

Hotel Majestic

1500 Sutter Street, CA 94109, at Gough Street (1-800 869 8966/441 1100/fax 673 7331/www.thehotelmajestic.com). Bus 2, 3, 4, 38. **Rates** single/double $150-$175; suite $175-$275. **Credit** AmEx, DC, Disc, MC, V. **Map** p310 F4.

The Majestic was built as a railroad magnate's private residence in 1902, but it has been a hotel since 1904, which makes it the oldest in the city to have remained in continuous operation. Each of the 58 rooms and nine suites in this white five-storey Edwardian have canopied four-poster beds with quilts, a host of French Imperial and English antiques, and tons of Crabtree & Evelyn goodies. Many rooms have gas fireplaces, making the hotel a perennial on 'Most Romantic Lodgings' lists. Free wine and hors-d'oeuvres are served in the evening. **Hotel services** *Air-conditioning. Babysitting. Bar (with bar menu). Concierge. Conference facilities. Laundry. Parking ($19). Dining room (serves continental breakfast). Restaurant. Safe.* **Room services** *Dataport. Iron. Room service (24hr). Turndown. TV: cable.*

Jackson Court

2198 Jackson Street, CA 94115, at Buchanan Street (1-800 738 7477/929 7670/fax 929 1405/www.jacksoncourt.com). Bus 12, 24. **Rates** single/double $150-$175; suites $205-$225. **Credit** AmEx, MC, V. **Map** p309/10 E3.

Not many people have discovered this 19th-century brownstone mansion – a shame, because it's a superb B&B. Located on a calm residential stretch of Pacific Heights, Jackson Court is as quiet as a church. Each of the ten rooms has a private bath and is furnished with a soothing combination of antiques and tasteful contemporary pieces. Request the Library Room, with its brass bed and working fireplace. Rates include continental breakfast and afternoon tea.

The century-old **Hotel Drisco**. *See p50.*

Based in a two-storey Edwardian house, this B&B is a haven from bustling Union Street. The six rooms are furnished in traditional style, with canopied or brass beds, feather duvets and fresh flowers. All have private bathrooms, some with jacuzzi tubs. Alternatively, you could opt for the private Carriage House behind the Inn, which has the delight of its own garden. An extended continental breakfast can be taken in the parlour, in your room or on a terrace overlooking the hotel garden. Evening pampering is available in the form of hors d'oeuvres and cocktails, included in the room price. **Hotel services** *Concierge. Garden. Parking ($15). Safe.* **Room services** *Dataport. Hi-fi. Iron. TV: cable.*

Also recommended

Cow Hollow Motor Inn & Suites *2190 Lombard Street, CA 94123, at Steiner Street (921 5800/ fax 922 8515/www.cowhollowmotorinn.com).* **Rates** single/double $79-$135; suite $225-$275.

Marina

Budget

The **Fisherman's Wharf Youth Hostel** (*see p52*) has some private rooms.

Edward II Inn & Pub

3155 Scott Street, CA 94123, at Lombard Street (1-800 473 2846/922 3000/fax 931 5784/ www.edwardii.com). Bus 28, 30, 43, 76. **Rates** single/double $82.50-$120; suite $185-$235. **Credit** AmEx, MC, V. **Map** p309 D2.
While the Edward II may bill itself as an 'English country inn' it actually has a wide array of room styles catering to almost every whim and budget. You can choose from 25 rooms – some with shared baths – or seven suites and cottages, with kitchens, living rooms and whirlpool baths. All the rooms contain antique furnishings and fresh flowers. Complimentary breakfast and evening drinks are served in the adjoining pub. The inn's location is a little traffic-heavy, but it's near the shops and restaurants of Chestnut and Union Streets. **Hotel services** *Bar. Concierge. Parking ($12). Safe.* **Room services** *Dataport. Jacuzzi (suites only). Iron. TV: cable (VCR – suites only).*

Marina Inn

3110 Octavia Street, CA 94123, at Lombard Street (1-800 274 1420/928 1000/fax 928 5909/ www.marinainn.com). Bus 28, 30, 76. **Rates** single/double $65-$135. **Credit** AmEx, DC, MC, V. **Map** p309 E2.
Although this 1924, four-storey Victorian-style inn is located on one of the city's busiest streets, the 40 rooms are surprisingly quiet and stylishly furnished in soothing tones of yellow, green and rose, with pine fittings and four-poster beds. A continental breakfast is included in the price, as is afternoon sherry. **Hotel services** *Beauty salon. Café. Concierge. Safe.* **Room services** *Turndown. TV: cable.*

Hotel services *Concierge. Film library. Games room. Kitchen. Laundry. Parking (free).* **Room services** *Iron. Turndown. TV: cable/VCR.*

Cow Hollow

Mid-range

Hotel Del Sol

3100 Webster Street, CA 94123, at Greenwich Street (1-877 433 5765/921 5520/fax 931 4137/www.thehoteldelsol.com). Bus 22, 43, 76. **Rates** single/double $149-$199; suite $189-$199. **Credit** AmEx, DC, Disc, MC, V. **Map** p309/10 E2.
This funky '50s motor hotel – owned by the same group that runs the Phoenix (*see p41*) – has been transformed to reflect the playful West Coast spirit. Each of the 47 rooms and 11 suites is decorated with bright, splashy tropical colours, even the clock radios wake guests to the sound of rain or waves. The family suite has bunk beds, toys and games, and guests can go to the quirky Pillow Library to choose their own luxury pillows. Complimentary coffee, tea and muffins are served by the outdoor pool each morning. Added bonuses are free parking (a valuable commodity in this crowded neighbourhood) and the location, a few blocks from Chestnut and Union Streets. No smoking throughout. **Hotel services** *Air-conditioning. Business services. Laundry. Parking (free). Pool (outdoor, heated). Safe. Sauna.* **Room services** *Dataport. Iron. TV: cable/VCR.*

Union Street Inn

2229 Union Street, CA 94123, between Fillmore & Steiner Streets (346 0424/fax 922 8046/ www.unionstreetinn.com). Bus 22, 41, 45. **Rates** single/double $159-$289. **Credit** AmEx, MC, V. **Map** p309 E2/3.

Also recommended

Marina Motel *2576 Lombard Street, CA 94123, at Divisadero Street (1-800 346 6118/921 9406/ fax 921 0364/www.marinamotel.com).* **Rates** single $85-$99; double $99-$199.

Richmond

Budget

Seal Rock Inn

545 Point Lobos Avenue, CA 94121, at 48th Avenue (1-888 732 5762/752 8000/fax 752 6034/ www.sealrockinn.com). Bus 18, 38. **Rates** single $105-$133; double $115-$143; suite $132-$158. **Credit** AmEx, DC, MC, V.

Located next to Sutro Heights Park, this '60s motor-court lodge is the closest thing San Francisco has to a beach hotel: most of the 27 rooms in the boxy brown building have at least partial ocean views. They're also large and spotless, though the ageing furnishings in hues of beige, brown and grey won't win any interior-design awards. Most rooms on the third floor have wood-burning fireplaces – these book up early, but try to snag one if you can. There's free covered parking and a patio with heated out-door pool. When things quieten down at night, you can fall asleep to the sound of distant foghorns. **Hotel services** *Fax services. Parking (free). Patio. Pool (outdoor, heated). Restaurant.* **Room services** *Dataport. Iron. Refrigerator. TV: cable.*

Hostels

Budget-conscious travellers have almost 20 hostels to choose from in San Francisco and most of them are in good locations, from Union Square to Haight Street. The legendary Green Tortoise bus company even runs a guesthouse in North Beach. Go to **www.hostels.com/us.ca.sf.html** for a full listing of such establishments, both independent and internationally affiliated, or to **www.norcalhostels.org** for Hostelling International's three SF locations.

Adelaide Hostel

5 Isadora Duncan Court, CA 94102, off Taylor Street, between Post & Geary Streets, Tenderloin (1-877 359 1915/359 1915/fax 276 2366/ www.adelaidehostel.com). Bus 2, 3, 4, 27, 38, 76. **Rates** dormitory $20; single/double $55-$60. **Credit** AmEx, MC, V. **Map** p310 G4.

Students and European tourists on a tight budget will feel right at home in what was until 2003 a friendly old-fashioned *pension*, tucked into a quiet downtown alley. In early 2004 the owners expanded the 18 rooms to add six en suites and two 12-bed dormitories. Rooms have TVs, but no phones (there is a hotel payphone), and breakfast and internet use are free. **Hostel services** *Internet. Kitchen. Laundry. Safe.* **Room services** *Dataport. Iron. TV.*

Fisherman's Wharf Youth Hostel

Building 240, Fort Mason, CA 94123, at Bay & Franklin Streets, Marina (771 7277/ fax 771 1468/www.norcalhostels.org). Bus 10, 28, 30, 47, 49. **Rates** dormitories $22-$29; private rooms $67.50-$73.50. **Credit** MC, V. **Map** p310 E1.

Many San Franciscans would kill for the Bay view offered at this humble hostel. It's one of the most desirable locations in the city and, if you book at least 24 hours in advance, it's yours for less than $30 per night. Located in a historic Civil War building on National Park property, the hostel's dorm-style accommodation sleeps 170 in rooms of three to 24 people. In some hostels when you're not sleeping you'd prefer to be anywhere else, but here you'll want to hang out and enjoy the pool table, dining room, coffee bar and complimentary movies. There's even that rarest of San Francisco amenities: free parking. There's no curfew, and the café has free breakfast and a $3 dinner several nights a week. There's no smoking inside the building. **Hostel services** *Café. Internet. Kitchen. Laundry. Lockers. Payphone. Limited parking (free).*

HI Downtown

312 Mason Street, CA 94102, between Geary & O'Farrell Streets, Union Square (1-800 909 4776/788 5604/fax 788 3023/ www.hiayh.org). BART Powell/Muni Metro F, J, K, L, M, N/bus 27, 38/cable car Powell-Hyde or Powell-Mason. **Rates** $22-$29; private room $60. **Credit** MC, V. **Map** p310 G4.

Make your reservation at least five weeks in advance during the high season (June to September) to stay at this popular 260-bed hostel. It prides itself on its privacy and security, with guests accommodated in small two-, three-, four- or five-person single-sex rooms, each with its own lock and key (some of the larger rooms also have their own bathroom). Beds for walk-ins are available on a first-come, first-served basis: bring ID or you'll be turned away at the door. Smoking is not allowed on the premises. **Hostel services** *Internet. Kitchen. Lockers. Payphone. Safe. TV.*

HI San Francisco City Center

685 Ellis Street, CA 94109, between Larkin & Hyde Streets (1-800 909 4776 ext 62/474 5721/sfcitycenter@norcalhostels.org). Bus 19, 27, 31, 38. **Rates** $22-$24. **Credit** Disc, MC, V. **Map** p310 F4.

Hostelling International's newest San Francisco location has the advantage of convenience – its Civic Center/Tenderloin location may not be as postcard-perfect as the Fisherman's Wharf hostel, but it is close to everything. There are 262 beds in the 75 rooms of a restored seven-storey historic hotel, each with two to four beds, complete with private en suite baths – plus a spacious common area. **Hostel services** *Internet. Kitchen. Lockers. Storage. 24hr check-in & access.*

Sightseeing

Introduction	54
Downtown & SoMa	56
North Beach & Around	73
The Mission & the Castro	85
Haight, Western Addition & Hayes Valley	91
Pacific Heights to the Golden Gate Bridge	96
Richmond, Sunset & Golden Gate Park	104
The East Bay	<u>111</u>

Features

Top ten Sights	55
You're on cable	58
SF heroes Craig Newmark	62
Foodie frenzy	65
SF heroes Carol Doda	76
Walk 1 Dead Beat with a Martini	78
The Bird Man of Alcatraz	82
Barbary Lane	84
Walk 2 Sightseeing Mission	86
A touch of glass	89
Denizens of iniquity	93
SF heroes Robert Crumb	94
Go! Go! Gone	97
Salty batteries	100
Beaches City sands	103
Beaches Bare-faced cheeks	106
Walk 3 Free parking	108
Walk 4 The ice-cream's academic	112

Introduction

Indecently beautiful, blessed with exciting street life and world-class museums, San Francisco lacks no sightseeing virtue.

If there were a competition to design the world's most perfect city for visitors, San Francisco could well be the result. Bounded by the ocean on one side and a beautiful bay on two more, the city is squeezed into relatively small area – seven miles (11 kilometres) by seven – making it a dream for sightseers. Even when San Francisco's hills get too steep for your tired muscles, a comprehensive and efficient public transport system means you can almost always hop on a bus, train, street car or cable car.

San Francisco is a network of individualistic neighbourhoods, each with its own character – in many cases, neighbourhoods even have their own climates (*see p291* **Sun, wind & fog**). Most visitors spend their time in touristy, crowded and rather unappealing Fisherman's Wharf and Union Square. Our advice? Go instead where the locals go – North Beach and the Mission, say – or to only-in-San Francisco areas like the Castro and Haight-Ashbury. Or savour splendid views from Russian Hill and the palm-fringed Embarcadero. Or just start walking – your feet know where to take you.

THE NEIGHBOURHOODS

Arranged by area, our sightseeing chapters start at **Union Square**, where visitors are most likely to have procured a hotel or emerged from BART. From here, we explore the rest of downtown north of Market Street: the high-rise **Financial District**, the **Embarcadero**, the run-down **Tenderloin** and grand **Civic Center**. Then we go South of Market – into **SoMa** – centre of the dot-com boom then bust, and now home to the evolving museum district.

From downtown, we move north towards the water, to espresso-scented **North Beach**, vibrant **Chinatown**, **Fisherman's Wharf** and swanky **Russian Hill** and **Nob Hill**. We then leapfrog back south to the **Mission**, the city's Latino stronghold, its neighbour **Potrero Hill**, the city's queer heartland in the **Castro** and pretty **Noe Valley**. We next visit the central neighbourhoods: **Haight-Ashbury**, the sprawling **Western Addition** (including **Japantown** and the **Fillmore**) and upstart

> ▶ For more details on **public transport**, *see p274*; our **street maps** start on *p308*.

Hayes Valley. North from the Western Addition lie the upmarket trio of **Pacific Heights**, **Cow Hollow** and the **Marina**, the former military base of the **Presidio** and, of course, the **Golden Gate Bridge**. Then, tucked up against the Pacific, we visit the largely residential areas of **Richmond** and **Sunset**, with **Golden Gate Park** in between. Finally, we cross the Bay Bridge to the **East Bay** – a 20-minute ride by BART – to the People's Republic of **Berkeley** and ethnically diverse **Oakland**.

A few things about San Francisco never change: its relative safety (for danger zones, *see p287* **Safety & security**) and its topography. Lace up your walking shoes and remember: for every uphill there's a downslope.

BASIC NAVIGATION

As a rule of thumb, blocks in San Francisco work in units of 100 heading north or south away from **Market Street**, west from the **Embarcadero** or (for the numbered avenues) south from the **Presidio**. Thus 250 24th Avenue is the third block south of the Presidio; 375 Mason on the fourth block north of Market. Most street signs indicate whether you're heading towards larger or smaller numbers.

Tours

A shamelessly touristy bus tour can sometimes be perfect for a swift introduction to a new city: **Gray Line** (434 8697/www.graylinesanfrancisco. com) and **Golden Gate Tours** (788 5775/http:// new.enterit.com/Golden5775) are good options.

Fire Engine Tours & Adventures

333 7077/www.fireenginetours.com. **Tours** 1pm Mon, Wed-Sun; call for details of additional tours. **Cost** $30; $25 13-17s; $20 under-13s. **Credit** MC, V. The shiny red 1955 Mack fire engine whisks you from Beach Street, behind the Cannery, through the Presidio across the Golden Gate Bridge and back in 75 minutes. Wearing a fireman's coat. Book ahead.

49-Mile Scenic Drive

Guided by a series of blue-and-white seagull markers, car drivers are introduced to the most picturesque and historic parts of the city by this drive. Be aware, though, that the route can be traffic-snarled and confusing – make sure you get the $1 map from the Visitor Information Center (*see p290*) beforehand.

San Francisco Seaplane Tours

332 4843/www.seaplane.com. **Open** 9am-5pm daily.
Cost $129; $99 2-12s; $169 sunset Champagne tour.
Credit AmEx, MC, V.

Taking off from the water near Pier 39, this de
Havilland Beaver zooms round the Bay for half an
hour. There are flights from Sausalito too.

Spinnaker Sailing

543 7333/www.spinnaker-sailing.com. **Tours** *Sunset*
from 2hrs before sunset Wed, Fri, Sat. *Brunch* 11am-
2pm Sun. *Afternoon* 3-5pm Sun. **Cost** $25 sunset &
afternoon; $40 brunch. **Credit** AmEx, MC, V.

Dress warm for trips in this classic 78ft (24m)
square-rigged brigantine. The ship leaves from Pier
40 in South Beach Harbor. Book well in advance.

Walking

We've mapped good introductory walks to
North Beach (*see p78*), the Mission (*see p86*),
Golden Gate Park (*see p108*), Berkeley (*see
p112*) and the Marina (*see p197*), each with
approximate distance and walking times.
The times are only a rough guide and make
no allowance for the recommended stop-offs.
Some of the best guided and self-guided walks
are listed below; for more options call in at the
Visitor Information Center (*see p290*) or
check Sunday's *Chronicle*. It's also a good idea
to contact City Guides (557 4266/www.walking-
tours.com/cityguides) to find out about their
free tours. For walks around the Mission's
murals, *see p88*; to start exploring the city's
secret stairways, *see p84* **Barbary Lane**.

Barbary Coast Trail

This four-mile (six-kilometre) self-guided walk,
marked by bronze medallions showing a miner and
clipper ship, connects 20 sites, including a Barbary
Coast saloon and Hyde Street Pier's historic ships.
A concise guide to the route can be found at the
Visitor Information Center and various bookshops.

Chinatown Tour

981 8989/1-650 355 9657/www.wokwiz.com.
Tours 10am daily. **Cost** *Walk only* $28; $23 under-11s.
Walk & lunch $40; $35 under-11s. **Credit** MC, V.

The 2.5-hour Wok Wiz tour explores Chinatown's
culinary heritage through visits to herbalists, dim
sum restaurants and fortune cookie factories.

Cruisin' the Castro

550 8110/www.webcastro.com/castrotour. **Tours**
10am Tue-Sat. **Cost** $40 with lunch. **No credit cards.**

Lesbian raconteur Trevor Hailey runs the Castro's
most entertaining tour, pointing out historic queer
landmarks and tracing the origins of the gay community. The tour lasts four hours, including lunch.

Flower Power Walking Tour

863 1621. **Tours** 9.30am Tue, Sat. **Cost** $15.
No credit cards.

Top ten | Sights

Alcatraz
The wonderful audio tour makes for an
unforgettable visit. See p80.

Asian Art Museum
Gae Aulenti redesign is superb, the artefacts
amazing. See p68.

Cable cars
Ding-a-ling! The greatest, most atmospheric
ride in town. See p58 **You're on cable**.

Coit Tower
Beautiful views, stirring murals. See p80.

Ferry Plaza Farmers' Market
Join the locals doing what they love: buying,
eating and talking about food. See p63.

Golden Gate Bridge
One of the Seven Wonders of the
Engineering World. See p101.

Golden Gate Park
Lakes, windmills and the newly renovated
Conservatory of Flowers. See p107.

North Beach cafés
Sit down by the sidewalk with an espresso
and watch the world passing by. See p77.

SFMOMA
A stunningly housed, hugely varied
collection of modern art. See p70.

Sunset from the batteries
Bring a blanket and someone you love.
See p100 **Salty batteries**.

A 2.5-hour walk that relives 1967's Summer of Love,
exploring and celebrating the Haight's brief moment
at the forefront of global youth culture.

Pacific Heights Walking Tour

441 3000/www.sfheritage.org/events+tours.html.
Tours 12.30pm Sun. **Cost** $8; $5 under-12s. **No
credit cards.**

Starting at the Haas-Lilienthal House (*see p96*), this
tour spends a couple of hours among the area's
mansions, Victorian homes and classic row houses.

Dashiell Hammett Walking Tour

www.donherron.com. **Tours** *May, Sept* noon Sun;
call for other times. **Cost** $10. **No credit cards.**

For four hours you can walk in the footsteps of the
city's most famous thriller writer and see the places
he wrote about. Meet by the Main Library, at Fulton
and Larkin Streets; no reservations necessary.

Downtown & SoMa

Get your wallet ready, pack your heels in your handbag and put your culture goggles on.

Union Square.

Other neighbourhoods in San Francisco rely on quirkiness and charm, but Downtown runs on pure urban energy. With great shopping complemented by major museums (not least **SFMOMA**, *see p72*, and the splendid new **Asian Art Museum**, *see p68*), the sprawling area around Market Street is much more than just the adminstrative and financial heart of the city. Avoid the inevitable queues of tourists at the Powell Street cable car turnaround and the crowds milling around **Union Square** (*see below*) and make the effort to explore wider and deeper instead.

North of Market Street and east of Union Square, you'll find the city-slicker **Financial District** (*see p61*), with the gritty **Tenderloin** (*see p67*) and then the city's **Civic Center** (*see p68*) to the west. Sprawling along the south side of Market Street is **SoMa** (*see p70*), no longer the yuppie paradise it so recently was, but, with SFMOMA and SBC Park stadium, it's now a centre for both high-brow and popular culture. And all along the Bay shore, you'll find the elegant **Embarcadero** (*see p63*).

Around Union Square

In 1997 a $10,000 competition was launched to design a 'new Union Square' to replace the 1941 design by Timothy Pflueger (the Bay Area architect famous for cinemas, especially the glorious Castro Theatre, *see p230*). The winning design, plucked from more than 300 hopefuls, was eventually unveiled in July 2002 and, at a stroke, the flavour of the area was changed. Where the city's many homeless once congregated, Union Square is now a mecca for the legion of tourists and shoppers drawn to this hustling and bustling shopping district. With little greenery and few benches, April Phillips and Michael Fotheringham's $25-million design lacks the comfort of a truly populist urban space, but its wash of grey and pink granites and sleek silver banisters has found many supporters. Visitors perch on the oversized steps along the southern edge (designed for but never used by street performers) to get a little R&R between strenuous credit-card manoeuvres.

Not everything, of course, was made over. The square, which takes its name from pro-Union rallies held here on the eve of the Civil War, is anchored by a 97-foot (30-metre) Corinthian column that soars upwards from the middle of the square. Confusingly, this column has nothing to do with the Civil War: it celebrates Admiral Dewey's 1898 victory at Manila during the Spanish-American War, a monument to imperialism that might irk the locals if they actually knew what it commemorated. The monument, by Robert Aitken, was dedicated by President Theodore Roosevelt in 1903. In the square you'll find a kiosk containing the San Francisco's Parks Store and TIX Bay Area (*see p244*), a café and, at the Post and Stockton corner, the names of the city's mayors. Etched into granite along an odd vertical axis, they're too hard to read for any but the most determined history buff. During weekends the square is crowded with easels bearing iffy popular art.

On all four sides the square is surrounded by Northern California's premier shopping area, with upscale department stores (*see p160*) offering miles of clothing, jewellery, gifts and the rest. If the thought of all that stuff wears you out, get sustenance at the **Cheesecake Factory** (*see p141*) on the eighth floor of Macy's: if you don't mind waiting for up to an hour at prime dining times, you'll be blessed with a great view of the square from the balcony.

Fans of classic fiction should head west of Stockton to Burritt Alley. There, on a wall atop the Stockton Tunnel, brass plaques mark the location of the fictional murder that launches the byzantine plot of Dashiell Hammett's *The Maltese Falcon*. Scottish author Robert Louis Stevenson's San Francisco rooming house was just opposite at 608 Bush Street. Gumshoes and literary pilgrims congregate at **John's Grill** (63 Ellis Street, between Market and Powell Streets, 986 0069). Founded in 1908, this old-fashioned eaterie was frequented by both Hammett and his fictional alter ego Sam Spade. The obligatory Hammettiana adorns the walls.

Just east of Union Square, linking Stockton and Kearny Streets, **Maiden Lane** was a sinister alleyway 100 years ago. Now a chic shopping artery (gated by day to keep the cars out), this used to be where randy San Franciscans found the city's cheapest prostitutes. Far more salubrious is the exquisite **Folk Art International** (No.140, 392 9999), designed by Frank Lloyd Wright in 1948. The swooping circular interior, beautiful in itself, also has wonderful merchandise for sale: coffee-table books on South Seas art, say, or nandi masks from 17th-century India. You can probably window-shop the designer stores here without leaving the comfort of an outside table at **Mocca Café** (No.175): Chanel (No.155), Marc Jacobs (No.125) and Gump's (*see p160*) are hardly a wallet's throw away.

A walk on Powell Street is anything but music to the ears, but hearing the cable cars (*see p58* **You're on cable**) clatter past and vanish, only to realise that the cables are still humming under your feet, is a quintessential San Francisco experience. Revel too in the sheer silliness of the doormen of the **Sir Francis Drake Hotel** (No.450, 392 7755, www.sirfrancisdrake.com), standing to attention in English beefeater uniforms. At No.335, the glamorous **Westin St Francis Hotel** is where silent-era film star Fatty Arbuckle's lethal libido ignited Hollywood's first sex scandal in 1921 (*see p48* **Death beds**).

The **Powell Street** cable car turnaround, usually with a huge queue of waiting tourists, is at the foot of Market Street. (If you want to cut the waiting time, we've a spot of advice; *see p58* **You're on cable**.) Next to the Powell Street BART station entrance, at the lower level of Hallidie Plaza, you'll find the very helpful **Visitor Information Center** (*see p290*) – well worth popping in for maps and information, or to catch up on the email if you're suffering cyberspatial withdrawals.

On the opposite side of Market Street is the uninspiringly titled **San Francisco Centre** (*see p163*), a nine-storey complex with a graceful spiral escalator that leads directly down to an additional Powell Street BART entrance. Also nearby are Anthropologie, Gap, Urban Outfitters, Old Navy and scores of fashion big-wigs, not to mention the **Crocker Galleria** a few blocks east (*see p161*). It's virtually a ghost town at weekends, but the top-floor foodcourt is handy for cheap eats. Across the street from the Galleria is the historic **Mechanics' Institute** (*see p281*). Established in 1854, the Institute's library consists of over 160,000 books and is home to the oldest chess club in the country. But don't let the name fool you: the books aren't all about engineering, there's everything from philosophy to music here. Free tours are offered every Wednesday at noon.

Architectural landmarks in the vicinity include the triangular **Phelan Building**, on the north side of Market Street between Stockton and O'Farrell Streets. Built in 1908 by Mayor James Phelan as part of his famous post-quake reconstruction programme, it's still the largest of San Francisco's 'flat iron' structures (so-called because of their shape). How he would have felt about the giant CompUSA store on the bottom floor is not a matter of public record.

Sightseeing

You're on cable

When we think of landmarks, we usually think of them staying put. Indeed, the San Francisco cable car is the nation's only mobile landmark. If you visited the city between 1982 and 1984, you would have thought the city had gone the way of Los Angeles, New York or Chicago: no dinging, no slow climbs uphill, no clamouring for a seat (or at least a good place to hang on). Apart from those two years of rehabilitation, the city's most characteristic mode of transport has stayed on the ropes. In a good way.

Installed in 1873 by wily Scotsman Andrew Hallidie, the cable cars were an ingenious solution to San Francisco's eternal problem: how to get up those unforgiving hills. Nob Hill and Russian Hill, in particular, were tempting morsels of real estate, yet they remained mostly undeveloped. Horse-drawn carriages could barely make the climb, and Victorian gentlefolk were hardly willing to exhaust themselves clambering up and down on a daily basis. Enter Hallidie and his idea of introducing cable-drawn transport to the

city streets, a method he had first used hauling ore carts in California's gold mines. When, to everyone's amazement, his first cars worked flawlessly, imitators sprang up overnight. Soon more than 100 miles (160 kilometres) of tracks criss-crossed the city, operated by seven cable car companies.

It was not to last. Earthquakes, fires and the advent of automobiles and electric trolleys spelled doom for most of the cable car lines. By 1947 the city had proposed tearing up the last lines and replacing them with diesel buses, an idea nixed by the outraged citizenry – to everyone's relief nowadays. The federal government then declared the system a National Historic Landmark, which means the beloved cars are now here to stay. Only three lines survive today, covering a total of eight miles (13 kilometres): the Powell-Mason and Powell-Hyde lines, both of which depart from the Powell Street turnaround (the bottom of Powell at Market Street) and finally end up at Fisherman's Wharf; and the California line, which runs between

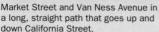

Sightseeing

Market Street and Van Ness Avenue in a long, straight path that goes up and down California Street.

Visitors are often surprised to learn that cable cars have no engine or other means of propulsion. All they need is a 'grip', a steel clamp that grabs on to a subterranean cable, running under the streets at a constant 9.5mph (15kmph). These cables never stop moving: you can hear them humming even when there are no cable cars in sight. Every car has two operators: a gripman, who works the cranks and levers that grab on to and release the underground cable; and a conductor, who takes fares and somehow manages to cram 90 or more passengers on to a single vehicle, many of them hanging off the running boards. Visit the **Cable Car Museum** (*see p84*) to inspect the system's inner workings. As well as Hallidie's original 1873 car, you'll get to see the immense winding turbines that power the cables. From the balcony you can watch the ten-foot (three-metre) wheels spinning, as gears and pulleys whirr.

TIPS AND TRICKS

First off, if you're expecting to see a criss-crossing network of cable cars dangling in the air above the city, think again. San Francisco cable cars remain firmly grounded, and are so-called because they are pulled by cables set in tracks on the street. While they're a legendary part of San Francisco, so is the hassle of waiting for one at the Powell Street turnaround. So don't. Instead, do what the locals do – walk up Powell a few blocks and board the car at O'Farrell or Union Square. If you aren't going anywhere in particular, the California Street line is rarely crowded, ideal for your first ride. The views aren't as good as on the Powell lines, but it's still a cable car, isn't it? When the trip is over you could step off at Grant Avenue to visit Chinatown. If you're tired of forking over the $3 fare, cable car rides are included in the price of one-, three- and seven-day Passports (*see p275*). Cars run every 12-15mins 6.30am-midnight. The Powell Street ticket booth is open from 8.30am until 8pm. For more information on travelling by cable car, *see p276*.

The Financial District

Still struggling with its uncertain economic future, San Franciscans are pretty divided over the status of the Financial District: is it where the few-and-far-between 'real' jobs can still be found, or just where working stiffs go to perish in cubicles? Neighbouring Union Square to the east, the **Financial District** is bounded by Market, Kearny and Jackson Streets, plus the Embarcadero to the east. It's been the business and banking hub of San Francisco and the American West for over a century and a half – as far back as the Gold Rush. Those interested in the area's museums and indoor sites must plan ahead; most places close at weekends and weekday opening tends to the nine-to-five norm.

The Financial District's northern edge is guarded by the **Transamerica Pyramid** (*see p63*) on Montgomery Street, San Francisco's tallest building. On the pyramid's east side, tiny **Redwood Park** is a cool refuge that lunching workers share with bronze frogs perpetually leaping from the pond. It's also pretty much the only spot within San Francisco where you can see California's famous redwood trees, albeit rather small ones. Samuel Clemens, aka Mark Twain, met a former firefighter named Tom Sawyer here: the building where they met is long gone, but Sawyer's childhood memories live on in Twain's classic novel. Across from the Transamerica, in front of the **California Pacific Bank**, a plaque marks another classic piece of vanished Americana – the Western Headquarters of Russell, Majors & Waddell, founders and operators of the Pony Express (1860-61) – while on nearby Commercial Street, in the city's former mint, the modest **Pacific Heritage Museum** (*see p63*) holds an art collection that's small, but worth discovering.

The **Bank of America** building (555 California Street, at Kearny Street) towers over the Financial District, both physically and psychologically. A bit shorter than the Transamerica, it's much more massive, with carnelian granite zig-zag walls often disappearing into the clouds above. It will be familiar to anyone who's seen the 1974 disaster epic *The Towering Inferno*, though the SFX folk added some extra storeys for effect. Unlike most other San Francisco skyscrapers, the Bank of America's top floor is open to the public. On the dizzying 52nd floor, the **Carnelian Room** (433 7500) is in private use during the day but, between 3pm and 11pm, metamorphoses into a cocktail lounge and upscale restaurant – and a favourite dating spot for San Franciscans.

At 465 California Street the **Merchant's Exchange** (421 7730) is no longer used to trade shares, but its historic spaces show the important role it once played in the financial life of the city. An impressive collection of William Coulter seascapes highlights the lavish trading hall, designed by Julia Morgan. Walk into the lobby to see a video about the building; any further explorations require an appointment.

To stoke up your gold fever, step along to 420 Montgomery to fawn over the gold nuggets and stagecoaches at the **Wells Fargo History Museum** (*see p63*). But beware the incessant chatter of large groups of kids: this is a favourite field-trip destination.

In February 2002 the grand **Omni Hotel** (500 California Street, 677 9494, www.omnisanfrancisco.com) opened at the corner of Montgomery and California, while the basement of the nearby Union Bank of California contains the **Museum of the Money of the American West** (400 California Street, at Sansome Street, 765 0400). The bank's doors and imposing columns may seem disproportionately massive in comparison to the museum's small Wild West collection, but the rare gold coins, three-dollar bills, nuggets and a notorious pair of pistols used in a fateful 1859 duel between two politicians make it worth a peek. The art-deco granite sculptures in front of the **Pacific Coast Stock Exchange** (*see p62*) are massive too, but not as impressive as the vibrant Diego Rivera mural inside. Sadly, access to the building is only available on a once-monthly guided tour – first Wednesday of the month.

Another artistic marvel, a huge Maxfield Parrish painting of the Pied Piper, can be found behind the bar at the lavish **Palace Hotel** (*see p41*) on Market Street, at New Montgomery Street. The well-heeled or recklessly indulgent can take afternoon tea in the Garden Court (2pm-4pm Tue-Sat, $28-$39), to the accompaniment of a harpist on Saturdays. Alteratively cheapskates can join the complimentary historic tour, which starts in the lobby (10am Tue, Sun, 2pm Thur).

Just a block to the west, at the intersection of Market, Kearny and Geary Streets, a select few centenarians meet annually at 5am on 18 April. The last survivors of the 1906 earthquake, they gather around ornate, lion-headed **Lotta's Fountain**, as they did all those years ago when families separated by the huge quake used the fountain as a message centre.

On the northern fringe of the Financial District, **Jackson Square Historical District** (bounded by Washington, Kearny and Sansome Streets and Pacific Avenue) is a last vestige of San Francisco's Barbary Coast, once a seething mass of low-life bars and 19th-century sex clubs, whose floor shows would have been hard for the most depraved modern sex tourist to stomach. Today these few blocks of 1850s-era brick buildings – housing upmarket antique shops and lovingly restored offices – are far from the waterfront, though they once stood on the very shoreline. Indeed, their foundations are made from the hulls of ships abandoned by eager gold-seekers.

Stroll along **Jackson Street** (between Sansome and Montgomery) and **Hotaling Street** to see the only neighbourhood left in San Francisco that pre-dates the ubiquitous Victorian style. It was spared during the 1906 quake and subsequent fire, not least because several of the buildings were liquor warehouses that had been built of stone to protect the precious booze. By the 1930s Jackson Square was popular with a number of bohemian artists and writers, including John Steinbeck and William Saroyan, who used to drink at 710 Montgomery Street, at the now long-vanished Black Cat Café. Local establishments popular

with after-work drinkers today include **Bix** (*see p148*), with its authentic late 1930s decor and brilliant Martinis.

Pacific Coast Stock Exchange

301 Pine Street, at Sansome Street (tours 285 0495). Bus 12, 15, 42/cable car California. **Open** *tours only* 3pm 1st Wed of mth. **Map** p309 H3.
While the Stock Exchange building is closed to the public, there is a free tour of sections of the classic art deco structure (booking essential). The Exchange was modernised in 1928 by architect Timothy Pflueger, who believed art should be an integral part of architecture. He commissioned sculptor Ralph Stackpole to create the two granite statues outside, which represent agriculture and industry (the twin sources of wealth), while above the entrance is a figure, called *Progress of Man*, with arms outstretched. The building's main attraction is on the tenth floor: Diego Rivera's 1930 mural *Allegory of California*. It's richly

SF heroes Craig Newmark

Don't call him a geek. Craig Newmark prefers to be called a nerd. The Craig behind Craigslist.org sports glasses and admits he used to wear a pocket protector. He finds books on molecular biology 'fun' and his mother writes nice things about him on the internet. Yet this self-proclaimed nerd has helped hook thousands of people up with dates, jobs and, yes, even sex.

Founded in San Francisco in 1995, Craigslist doesn't look like all that much. But in the Bay Area – and in 31 other cities – it is the first choice for posts seeking and offering roommates, apartments, jobs, activity partners and, um, casual encounters. Winning awards such as 'Best Chance for a Decent Date' and 'Best Geek Pickup Spot' (sorry, Craig… we meant 'Best Nerd Pickup Spot'), the list is now so beloved in San Francisco that it even spawned a 90-minute documentary by filmmaker Michael Ferris Gibson, as well as persistent rumours of a future sitcom. In a town where the term 'dot-com' is pretty much inseparable from 'crash', Craigslist is an extraordinary success.

'I was just telling a few friends about cool events,' Newmark says about the origins of his site. Originally from Morristown, New Jersey, Craig now works out of one of the city's trademark converted Victorians, spending his mornings with laptop, latte and *San Francisco Chronicle* in the local coffee shop. The staff all know him by name and other customers give him a friendly wave.

Which may help to explain why Craigslist keeps on growing among the bleached bones of so many other internet start-ups. Newmark himself says it has something to do with the website's lack of emphasis on making money. Put another way, Craigslist has made users the priority. 'I think social networking is really important,' he says. 'We all have this craving to connect.'

ironic that Rivera, a committed Communist, should have been allowed to create such a magnificent work within the very heart of capitalism; Stackpole, an old friend of Rivera, had recommended him for the job. The mural shows Bay Area industries, including aviation and oil, with Mother Earth in the centre and the emphasis firmly on workers rather than bosses.

Pacific Heritage Museum

608 Commercial Street, at Montgomery Street (399 1124). Bus 1, 5, 41, 42. **Open** 10am-4pm Tue-Sat. **Admission** free. **Map** p309 H3.
Once the city's mint, this structure is now a Bank of Canton. It's also a museum. Emphasising San Francisco's connections with the Pacific Rim, the museum features changing exhibits of contemporary artists from countries such as China, Taiwan, Japan and Thailand. Much of what is displayed here is on loan from private collections rarely seen elsewhere.

Transamerica Pyramid

600 Montgomery Street, between Clay & Washington Streets (983 4100). Bus 1, 10, 15, 41. **Map** p309 H3.
William Pereira's 853ft-tall (260m) building – the city's tallest – was completed in 1972, having provoked public outrage when its design was unveiled. But it's long since become an iconic spike on the city's skyline. Designed to be earthquake-proof, the pyramid sits on giant rollers that allow it to rock safely – it must work too, since the building wasn't damaged by the 1989 Loma Prieta quake. The current owners do not offer public access to the 27th-floor observation deck: only those with employee badges get inside. We know because we tried.

Wells Fargo History Museum

420 Montgomery Street, between California & Sacramento Streets (396 2619/www.wellsfargo history.com). Muni Metro F, J, K, L, M, N/bus 1, 12, 15, 41, 42. **Open** 9am-5pm Mon-Fri.
Admission free. **Map** p309 H3.
If you're in the area during business hours, pop into the headquarters of Wells Fargo, California's oldest bank. This collection of Gold Rush memorabilia also gives a history of banking in California. You'll find gold nuggets, an old telegraph machine and a Concord stagecoach, built in 1867, plus some interesting historical photos. Worth a quick stop.

The Embarcadero

During the working week, the Embarcadero can feel like an extension of the Financial District (*see p61*), but weekends are fun. A casual crowd mills about the Ferry Plaza Farmers' Market, while families take a scenic stroll with their kids and dogs in tow. Stretching along the waterfront from China Basin all the way up to Fisherman's Wharf (*see p80*), this waterfront strip was for years marred by the freeway. But the freeway was destroyed by the 1989 Loma Prieta quake and the Embarcadero re-emerged as a graceful, palm-lined boulevard.

At the foot of Market Street, the centrepiece of the Embarcadero is the rather stately **Ferry Building**, which divides even-numbered piers (to the south) from odd (to the north). Major renovations to this California Historic Civil Engineering Landmark, originally completed in 1898, were unveiled in 2003. Ten years in design and planning, the Ferry Building bustles every weekend with the unmissable **Ferry Plaza Farmers' Market** (*see p65* **Foodie frenzy**). The Ferry Building's 660-foot (201-metre) Grand Nave gets full to bursting with foodies, while daytrippers pile out of the back door to hop on ferries to Marin or the East Bay.

Opposite the Ferry Building stands **Justin Herman Plaza**, where you'll be confronted by Benecia-born artist Robert Arneson's bronze sculpture *Yin and Yang*. Looming behind it is the mysteriously dry fountain by French-Canadian artist Armand Vaillancourt, and at the foot of the Hyatt Regency (*see p38*) is Jean Dubuffet's *La Chiffonière*, a stainless-steel sculpture of a larger-than-life man. The phalanx of wafer-thin towers behind the plaza, at the foot of Sacramento, comprise the **Embarcadero Center** (*see p161*), a maze-like shopping/dining/theatre complex. For the artier end of celluloid production, check out the Embarcadero Landmark Theater (*see p200*).

Walk south from the Ferry Building along the Embarcadero to Howard and you'll see low cement walls where bronze starfish, turtles and octopi have 'washed up'. Nearby (and easy to miss) is the small sign that marks 'Herb Caen Way', named after the late and ever-popular *SF Chronicle* columnist. Lovers who come down this way may feel they've walked into their destiny: there's an immense Cupid's bow in gold, complete with a silver and red arrow. This is Claes Oldenburg and Coosje Van Bruggen's *Cupid's Span* (*see p207* **Public art**), installed in 2002 in a field of native grass.

This is also where you can snap one of the ultimate souvenir shots: it's the ideal view of the **Bay Bridge** (*see p64*). Continue south to **Red's Java House** (777 5626), a small and quirky snack shack that's been a favourite for coffee, beer and burgers since the 1920s. Between Brannan and Townsend Streets you'll come across a cement marker that says 'Great Seawall'. This is exactly what the Embarcadero was built to be. Work on the seawall started in 1878 and continued for nearly five decades.

Once you've had your fill of waterside views, head inland to the **Rincon Center** (*see p64*) at the intersection of Mission and Spear Streets. This former main post office, containing a number of impressive art pieces and historic murals, is clear of San Franciscans on the weekends except for the dim sum crowd at Yank Sing (*see p123*). Yank Sing also does

Sightseeing

takeaways next door, including a great 70-cent potsticker. The **Jewish Museum** (*see below*) is south of the Rincon Center, on Steuart Street.

Alternatively, you could head north. The Embarcadero becomes a long, gently curving promenade, extending all the way along the waterfront to the tomfooleries of Fisherman's Wharf (*see p80*). This stretch is favoured by cyclists, skateboarders and in-line skaters, as there are no street intersections to trouble them. Skaters meet at 9pm each Friday for the 'Midnight Rollers', a 12-mile (19-kilometre) skate through the city – and everyone's welcome to join them. Pier 7, a wide-open public pier jutting out into the Bay, offers lovely views of **Treasure Island** (*see below*). North again and a little inland, you'll find the offices of **Philo TV** at the intersection of Green and Sansome Streets. These occupy the former laboratory of boy-genius Philo T Farnsworth. On this spot in 1927 he invented the current system of TV transmission; there's even a plaque to prove it.

Bay Bridge

Linking downtown San Francisco with the East Bay (1-510 286 1148). Muni Metro N/bus 12/AC Transit bus A-Z across the bridge. **Toll** $2 westbound. **Map** p311 J3.

Heading east from Downtown, the San Francisco-Oakland Bay Bridge – better known simply as the Bay Bridge – is less famous than its sister span, but more useful day-to-day: it links San Francisco to a nationwide network of highways and railroads. Divided into two by dramatic Yerba Buena Island, the Bay Bridge is actually three separate bridges linked together: two suspension spans placed end to end on the west side of Yerba Buena, and a cantilever span on the east side. Combined, they make one of the world's longest bridges, more than eight miles (nearly 14km) across. Completed a year before the Golden Gate Bridge in 1936, the Bay Bridge was even more of an engineering challenge because of the much greater distances. The solution was to build a concrete pylon of inconceivably massive proportions in the middle of the Bay, and use it as an anchor point for two different suspension spans. Because much of it's hidden underwater, this central pylon draws little notice from the thousands who cross it each day, even though it remains one of the largest structures ever built in California – a solid concrete tower nearly as tall as the Transamerica Pyramid (*see p63*).

Designed by Charles H Purcell, the Bay Bridge has two levels, each with five lanes of traffic that cruise straight through Yerba Buena Island inside the largest vehicular tunnel on earth. Impressed? You will be when you emerge on the top deck heading west. It's a breathtaking way to enter the city. Part of its eastern upper level collapsed during the October 1989 earthquake. Engineers warned that 'the Big One' – the quake all Californians have been

expecting ever since Loma Prieta – could take out the entire eastern half of the bridge. The span is currently undergoing a very impressive retrofit, utilising aggressive new self-suspended bridge technology, which will result in a new span and a $50-million path for bicycles and pedestrians. The plan is due for completion in 2007. Meanwhile, a series of impressive cranes are in periodic operation along the northern side and constant roadworks cause somewhat less impressive traffic delays on the bridge.

Jewish Museum of San Francisco

121 Steuart Street, between Mission & Howard Streets (788 9990/www.jmsf.org). BART Embarcadero/Muni Metro N/bus 1, 12, 41. **Open** 10am-5pm Mon-Thur, Sun. **Admission** $5; $4 concessions; free under-12s. **No credit cards.** **Map** p311 J3.

Devoted to linking the art of the Jewish community with the community at large, the Jewish Museum runs educational programmes and shows works by students and established artists, many of them political or controversial in nature. The museum has a new home planned, next to Yerba Buena Gardens, in a Willis Polk power substation that dates back to 1907. It will be transformed by superstar architect Daniel Libeskind as his first US commission. The museum doesn't expect to be leaving Steuart Street for a few years yet, but has already joined collections with the Judah L Magnes Museum (*see p113*).

Rincon Center

101 Spear Street, at Mission Street (243 0473). BART Embarcadero/Muni Metro F/bus 1, 12, 14. **Open** 24hrs daily. **Map** p311 J3.

The lobby (facing Mission Street) of this art deco post office and residential/office tower has intriguing WPA-style murals. Painted in 1941 by the incorrigibly bad behaved Russian-born artist Anton Refregier, this luscious historical panorama includes many dark moments from California's past. The central atrium has a unique all-water sculpture dubbed *Rain Column*. Designed by Doug Hollis, the sculpture's more than 50 gallons (190l) of recycled water falls 85ft (26m) into a central pool every minute.

Treasure Island

Bus 108. **Map** p311 J3.

Flat-as-a-griddle Treasure Island, built on the shoals of neighbouring Yerba Buena Island, was man-made from boulders and sand as a site for 1939's Golden Gate International Exposition. After the fair closed, the plan was to turn the island into an airport, but with the outbreak of World War II it became a US naval station. Treasure Island was recently deeded back to the city and is now a sort of mid-bay suburb, with some lucky San Franciscans moving into the former military housing. Why lucky? The views are spectacular. Adjoining Yerba Buena Island is an important Coast Guard station. It's mostly closed to tourism though: you can drive on the island's one road, but there's nowhere to stop.

Foodie frenzy

Since 2002 the Ferry Plaza Farmers' Market has been one place you want to come to hungry. Over 8,000 square feet (743 square metres) of the newly renovated 1898 Ferry Building are given over to rows and rows of produce each Saturday, with white tents spilling out of the North and South arcades. Locals graze the aisles, feasting on toothpicks of aged goat's cheese, freshly baked bread slathered in flavoured olive oil and slices of organic persimmon, filling tote bags with goodies to take home. It's a meeting place too. Friends get together over wild mushrooms and scrambled eggs or just-made crab cakes, with chatty groups gathering at the communal tables and on outdoor benches to brunch while they watch the ferries come and go.

It took a decade for the market, sponsored by the Center for Urban Education about Sustainable Agriculture (CUESA), to find its permanent home. While it also opens on Tuesdays, Thursdays and Sundays, depending on the season (check www.cuesa.org), the best time to come is 8am to 2pm on a Saturday. For locals from all different backgrounds it's an essential part of the weekend routine: you'll see twentysomethings stocking up for the vegetable curry they're to cook back at their Victorian co-op, the stroller set buying roasted nuts and fresh seafood for dinner parties, and tourists dropping in as means of stretching their legs only to leave hours later with their arms full of bunches of sunflowers, freshly baked muffins and crisp, fresh apples.

There's a lot of hustle and bustle, which is all part of the fun, but does mean one should come prepared. Bring cash (there's only a small Bank of America ATM and you don't want to think about the queue) and make sure you've got small notes and coins; stallholders will appreciate the right change. Given the number of stalls, you should also consider your shopping approach. Some will head straight for the maps on the CUESA table and chart their course, others will be happy to wander where their taste buds lead them.

Even such tasty work can be arduous, so be sure to take a break at the indoor wine bar or shake off your shoes for a *gaiwan* tea presentation ($5 per person) at the tranquil **Imperial Tea Court** (*see p144*). Around $12 will get you a bowl of oyster stew at the frenetic **Hog Island Oyster Bar** (391 7117), and a mere $10 will get you a tasting of Tsar Nicoulai Caviar on a freshly baked mini-blini. You can then browse the Book Passage Store, grab a latte at **Peet's**, or sit back and enjoy spectacular views of the Bay with a spectacularly full stomach.

Search thousands of New York City restaurants and bars by name, neighborhood, category or keyword.

It's all at your fingertips with
Time Out New York's Eating & Drinking ONLINE.

Peace, brother. Out and about in the **Tenderloin**.

The Tenderloin

The Tenderloin is a far cry from the retail mecca of Union Square just a few blocks to the east. Home to a spirited and close-knit community, the area's bad reputation shouldn't put people off visiting the theatre district or checking out the Tenderloin's vibrant nightclubs and dive bars (*see p148* and *p219*). But hungry folk with their shopping carts, panhandling and crack addiction are still givens, so it's often best to hail a cab if you're here at night.

A five-minute walk from the Civic Center BART, aspiring chefs can be seen in their whites at the **California Culinary Academy** (*see below*). More characteristic of the area's reputation is **Mitchell Brothers O'Farrell Theatre** (895 O'Farrell Street, at Polk Street, 776 6686, www.ofarrell.com), the city's largest porn theatre. The outside wall sports a huge, photo-realist mural of marine life that has been used as a backdrop in many films and adverts. The porn palace was founded by brothers Artie and Jim Mitchell, who are as famous for their fratricidal relationship as for their pioneering introduction of professional business savvy to the previously slapdash world of adult entertainment. Founding their theatre on Independence Day in 1969, the Mitchells spent decades fighting US morality laws. Then it all went wrong: in 1991 Jim shot Artie to death. Jim's lawyers claimed he had accidentally

killed his brother in an attempt to get him off drugs and alcohol. The jury weren't impressed, and Jim went to San Quentin prison. He was released in 1997.

At 859 O'Farrell you'll find the **Great American Music Hall** (*see p216*). Said to be the oldest nightclub in San Francisco, there are rumours that a ghost haunts its glamorous interior. Appearances by such as Duke Ellington, Van Morrison and the Grateful Dead mean the place is now unimpeachably respectable, but in its less glorious past it was once a bordello.

Though the city is still struggling with the question of how to care for the large numbers of homeless in the Tenderloin (it was a key issue in the 2003 mayoral contest), various soup kitchens provide a partial solution. One pair of churches in particular share a long and compassionate history: **St Boniface Catholic Church**, as well as offering Mass in English, Spanish, Tagalog and Vietnamese, hosts dozens of benefit programmes and has a dining room that serves meals to the needy, as does the Free Meals programme at **Glide Memorial Church**, which started back in 1969.

California Culinary Academy (CCA)

625 Polk Street, at Turk Street (216 4329/ www.baychef.com). BART Civic Center/bus 19, 31. **Open** *Carème Room* 11.30am-1pm, 6-8pm Tue-Fri. **Map** p310/314 F4.

Founded in 1977, the Academy is large, scruffy and somewhat run-down, but gourmets will be delighted by the elegant Carème Room, where student-cooked meals are served to the public. The gift shop on the first floor has a small selection of kitchen gadgets and top-notch knife sets. Call in advance to reserve.

Glide Memorial United Methodist Church

330 Ellis Street, at Taylor Street (674 6000/ www.glide.org). BART Powell/Muni Metro F, J, K, L, M, N/bus 27, 31, 38. Map p310 G4.
Glide and the Reverend Cecil Williams are San Francisco icons, the Sunday services legendary. Each week without fail, the ecstatic gospel-singing drags an eclectic congregation to its feet. This is a Sunday morning must.

St Boniface Catholic Church

133 Golden Gate Avenue, at Leavenworth Street (863 7515). BART Civic Center/Muni Metro F, J, K, L, M, N/bus 5, 19, 31. Map p310/314 G4.
St Boniface's Romanesque interior, restored in the 1980s, includes some impeccable stencilling and a beautifully gilded apse topped by a four-storey cupola. You'll find the church is gated, so ring the buzzer to get in. Be sure to get there before 1.30pm during the week, when the church closes up for cleaning until the next morning.

Civic Center

San Francisco's Civic Center is a complex of imposing government buildings and immense performance halls, centred on the **Civic Center Plaza**, an expansive and well-tended lawn. Facing the plaza is the stunning Beaux Arts **City Hall** (*see p69*). Needing extensive retrofitting to repair damage from the 1989 earthquake and protect the structure against future seismic shocks, city planners decided to spend $300 million completely restoring the building to its original grandeur. The work took four years and was finally finished in 1999. (A scurrilous rumour suggests further repairs had to be made after sprinklers went off during the shooting of a Robin Williams movie.) Joe DiMaggio got hitched to Marilyn Monroe on the third floor of City Hall in 1954, although nobody knows in which office. It was also in City Hall, in 1978, that Dan White assassinated George Moscone and Harvey Milk (*see p15*). In fact, the City Hall is equal parts history lesson and architectural masterpiece.

In the south-east corner of Civic Center Plaza are the **Bill Graham Civic Auditorium** (*see p215*), named after the late, much-loved concert promoter, and the **Main Library** (*see p69*). The latter is a six-storey building that combines Beaux Arts elements with a healthy dash of modernism. North of the library is

United Nations Plaza, where a modest farmers' market operates on Wednesday and Sunday mornings under the approving gaze of Simón Bolívar, the great liberator of Central America. Among the pigeons and the homeless are 16 square markers that commemorate the 50th anniversary in 1995 of the founding of the United Nations in San Francisco, as well as Frank Happersberger's sprawling Pioneer Monument. Dedicated to the city in 1894, it was designed to chronicle the significant 'epochs in California history'. Another significant epoch was marked by the opening here of the terrific new **Asian Art Museum** (*see below*).

Across the four lanes of traffic on Van Ness Avenue is a trio of grand edifices. The multi-storey, curved glass façade of the **Louise M Davies Symphony Hall** (*see p210*) would be unforgettable even without the reclining Henry Moore bronzes in front. North of Grove Street is the **War Memorial Opera House** (*see p210*), which is directly behind City Hall and in many ways its companion piece, designed by the same architect (Arthur Brown) in the same style. Like its older sibling, the Opera House underwent a major retrofit and renovation after Loma Prieta. This is where the UN Charter was signed by 51 nations in June 1945. The last of the triumvirate of buildings is the **Veterans' Memorial Building** (Van Ness Avenue, at McAllister Street), a venerable workhorse used for everything from city offices and musical performances to museum exhibits and lectures. On its main floor it contains the diminutive **San Francisco Art Commission Gallery** (*see p205*), a free exhibition space that specialises in politically – or sociologically – driven art. Take the lift to the fourth floor and you'll find the **San Francisco Performing Arts Library and Museum** (*see p70*), which includes the brand new Costume Image Research Collection. The building also houses the beautiful **Herbst Theatre** (*see p244*).

Apart from A Clean Well-Lighted Place For Books (*see p165*) and Max's Opera Café (601 Van Ness, at McAllister Street, 771 7300), there's little to do in **Opera Plaza** apart from goggle at the buildings. You can check out Opera Plaza Cinemas (352 0810), but be sure to check which room your film is in – the screen in the 'screening room' is hardly bigger than a TV.

Asian Art Museum

200 Larkin Street, at Fulton Street (581 3500/ www.asianart.org). BART Civic Center/Muni Metro F, J, K, L, M, N/bus 5, 6, 7, 9, 19, 21, 66, 71. **Open** 10am-5pm Tue, Wed, Fri-Sun; 10am-9pm Thur. **Admission** $10; $6-$7 concessions. **Map** p314 F4.

Classic San Francisco: the Beaux Arts **City Hall**.

The Asian Art Museum once resided in Golden Gate Park (*see p104*), but in March 2003 reopened in the building that once contained the San Francisco Public Library. Extensively and beautifully redesigned by Gae Aulenti (the architect famous for the Musée d'Orsay conversion in Paris), the museum retains remnants of its previous role, including bookish quotes etched into the fabric of the building. It has one of the world's most comprehensive collections of Asian art, spanning 6,000 years of Asian history with over 15,000 displayed objects. Artefacts range from Japanese buddhas to sacred texts to items from the Ming dynasty. The café on the first floor serves American- and Asian-inspired dishes, and the gift shop is well-stocked with high-quality stationery, decorative items and a good selection of coffee-table books. Easily accessible by BART, the museum is now a bustle of activity every day of the week.

City Hall

1 Dr Carlton B Goodlett Place (Polk Street),
between McAllister & Grove Streets (554 4000/tours
554 6023). BART Civic Center/Muni Metro F, J, K,
L, M, N/bus 5, 21, 47, 49. **Open** 8am-8pm daily.
Admission free. **Map** p314 F4.
Built in 1915 to designs by Arthur Brown and John Bakewell, City Hall is the epitome of the Beaux Arts style seen across the whole Civic Center. It has lots of ornamental ironwork, elaborate plasterwork and a dome modelled on the one at St Peter's in Rome that is, in fact, 16ft (5m) higher than the one on the nation's capitol. The central rotunda is a magnificent space and the dome overlooks a five-storey colonnade, limestone and granite masonry, regal lighting and majestic marble floors. Dubbed 'the most significant interior space in the United States' by a New York architectural critic, the City Hall inspires a marked feeling of municipal awe.

Beneath its neo-classical exterior, the building hums with modern technology, and a system of rubber-and-steel 'base isolators' allows the structure to move a metre in any direction, protecting it from any future quakes. It contains 600 rooms, each letting in natural light, and houses the legislative and executive branches of both city and county government. Free tours are available daily, offering behind-the-scenes views of the Board of Supervisors' chambers (panelled in hand-carved Manchurian oak) and the mayor's office (weekdays only). The Museum of the City of San Francisco, housed in South Light Court, is disappointing, but souvenir-hunters will find the City Store, on the main floor in North Light Court, a thrill: SFPD mugs, bricks from Lombard Street, old street signs and city sweatshirts. There's a small café for the weary of feet, and the basement contains art sponsored by the San Francisco Arts Commission (*see p205*).

San Francisco Main Library

100 Larkin Street, between Grove & Hyde
Streets (library 557 4400/history room 557 4567/
www.sfpl.org). BART Civic Center/Muni Metro F, J,
K, L, M, N/bus 5, 19, 21, 26, 66, 71. **Open** *Library*
10am-6pm Mon, Sat; 9am-8pm Tue-Thur; noon-6pm
Fri; noon-5pm Sun. *History room* 10am-6pm Tue-
Thur, Sat; noon-6pm Fri; noon-5pm Sun. **Admission**
free; 3mth visitor's card $10. **Map** p314 F/G4.

Built in 1996 by the architectural firm Pei Cobb Freed, the main library is beautifully designed, although locals still complain about the institution's abundance of missing and lost books. Nonetheless, anyone who caught Nicholas Cage and Meg Ryan in the 1998 film *City of Angels* will recognise the airy interior. The San Francisco History Room occupies the top floor. It has changing exhibitions, a large photo archive and knowledgeable, friendly staff. The basement café is mediocre, but the small kiosk on the main floor has good bargains on local titles. 'Grotto Night' readings (*see p28* **The Grotto**) are held in the basement theatre every couple of months.

San Francisco Performing Arts Library & Museum

Fourth floor, Veterans' Memorial Building, 401 Van Ness Avenue, at McAllister Street, Civic Center (255 4800/www.sfpalm.org). Muni Metro F, J, K, L, M, N/ bus 5, 21, 47, 49. **Open** 11am-5pm Tue-Fri; 1-5pm Sat. **Admission** free. **Map** p314 F5.

Exhibitions here relate to every one of the performing arts, from puppet show to opera, but the principal attraction for scholars is the prodigious amount of resource material, amounting to thousands of books on design, fashion, music, theatre, opera and other art forms. PALM recently added the Costume Image Research Collection, which explores the history of Eastern and Western dress.

SoMa

Newcomers and tourists may take a minute to realise SoMa is a snappy acronym for what was once dowdy old 'South of Market' (the area south, logically enough, of Market Street). Nowadays the terms are interchangeable, depending on your mood, age and degree of attachment to the San Francisco of yore. Those referring to the neighbourhood's wild nightlife usually opt for the shorter, while shoppers and art-seekers tend to say they're going South of Market. (SFMOMA in SoMa? Bleurgh.) Either way, this neighbourhood, for most of its existence an industrial wasteland occupied mainly by warehouses and sweatshops, is now revitalised with a mega shopping centre, trendy nightspots and Yerba Buena Gardens. The dot-com bust has taken its toll, as evidenced by rows of live-work lofts for sale or rent, but the area's cultural life expands apace.

SoMa's showpiece is its **Yerba Buena Center for the Arts and Gardens Complex**. Bounded by Mission, Third, Folsom and Fourth Streets, this area was renovated as part of a city-funded revitalisation project in the 1980s and 1990s. It's a maze of attractions, gardens and businesses in a purpose-built complex that's half above ground and half below. **Esplanade Gardens** is an urban park with sculpture walks, shady trees and the *Revelations* waterfall, which was constructed in 1993 in memory of Martin Luther King Jr. A selection of Dr King's quotes are beautifully inscribed beneath the waterfall in many different languages. The **Yerba Buena Center for the Arts** (*see p247*) is an architectural beauty in itself. Filling the other half of the block (Fourth Street, from Howard to Mission Streets) is the **Metreon Center** (*see p161*). This four-storey 'entertainment destination' is a futuristic mall where 16 theatres (including a giant-screen IMAX) are augmented by high-tech shops, restaurants, video-game rooms and the country's only official Sony PlayStation store. The 270-foot (86-metre) lobby, which exits out into the Esplanade Gardens, contains amenities including ATM machines and public restrooms. The top floor is home to 'Where the Wild Things Are', an interactive tribute to renowned children's author and illustrator Maurice Sendak.

Across Third Street from Yerba Buena Gardens, you'll find the **San Francisco Museum of Modern Art** (**SFMOMA** to its legion of fans; *see p72*). There's also a top-quality museum shop (*see p180*) and a somewhat pricey café. Next to SFMOMA is the staggering St Regis Museum Tower. As we go to press, the **Museum of African Diaspora** (www.museumoftheafrican diaspora.org) is scheduled to open on the first three floors in autumn 2005. It will pair African oral storytelling traditions with new technology to re-examine the history and celebrate the culture of African-descended people. Also in 2005 the **Mexican Museum** (202 9700, www.mexicanmuseum.org), first located in the Mission District and then in Fort Mason (*see p98*), will celebrate its 30th anniversary by joining the thriving Yerba Buena cultural scene. Its new site will contain seven floors of Latino art, with a permanent collection of over 12,000 pieces that range from painting to textiles.

The vast **Moscone Convention Center**, a hive of exhibition halls, is named after assassinated mayor George Moscone, but is of little interest to casual visitors except for the Rooftop at Yerba Buena Gardens, ingeniously covering the top of the Moscone Center on the south side of Howard Street, which offers the hands-on, child-friendly attractions of **Zeum** (*see p196*), a art and technology centred aimed 8- to 18-year-olds. There's even the carousel, hand-carved by Charles Looff in 1906, that used to be at Playland at the Beach (a $2 ticket is good for two rides), and an ultra-cool interactive sculpture by Chico Macmurtrie: sit

on the middle pink bench and your weight
moves the metal figure up and down on top
of its globe (only attempt this before lunch).

Contrasting with all this modernity is
the high-ceilinged **St Patrick's Church**
(756 Mission Street, between Third and
Fourth Streets, 421 3730). Built in 1851,
St Patrick's ministered to the growing Irish
population brought to the city by the Gold
Rush. It was completely destroyed by the
1872 earthquake, but subsequently restored
to its original state. A San Francisco Musical
Lunch Break (777 3211, www.noontime
concerts.org) inside is a lovely diversion.
The **Cartoon Art Museum** (*see below*)
has opened its doors in place of the lamented
Friends of Photography/Ansel Adams Center,
just across the street from the free **California
Historical Society** (*see below*). The **Society
of California Pioneers** (*see p72*) is also
nearby. Several blocks south-west of Yerba
Buena, Folsom Street savours its gloriously
kinky reputation each autumn during the
annual **Folsom Street Fair** (*see p188*),
but the **Cake Gallery** (290 Ninth Street,
at Folsom Street, 861 2253) is a year-round
thrill: it's the only bakery in San Francisco
that sells pornographic cakes.

California Historical Society

*678 Mission Street, between Third & New
Montgomery Streets (357 1848/www.california
historicalsociety.org). BART Montgomery/
Muni Metro F, J, K, L, M, N/bus 9, 14, 15,
30.* **Open** noon-4.30pm Wed-Sat. **Admission**
$3; $1 concessions. **No credit cards.**
Map p311 H4.
The state's official historical group has focused its
efforts on assembling this impressive collection of
Californiana. The vaults hold half a million
photographs and thousands of books, magazines
and paintings, as well as an extensive Gold Rush
collection, which are presented as changing displays
on the state's history. The gift shop is the perfect for
that Golden State trivet, mug or totebag, but the
main reason to drop in is the tremendous bookshop.

Cartoon Art Museum

*655 Mission Street, between Third & New
Montgomery Streets (227 8666/www.cartoonart.org).
BART Montgomery/Muni Metro F, J, K, L, M,
N/bus 9, 14, 15, 30.* **Open** 11am-5pm Tue-Sun.
Admission $6; $4 concessions; $2 6-12s.
Map p311 H4.
The camera that was used to create the first anima-
tion for television (it was called Crusader Rabbit and
produced in 1949-51, tube trivia buffs) graces the
lobby of this new SoMa museum. Boasting over
5,000 pieces of cartoon and animation art, as well as
a research library, this is the only museum in the
Western US dedicated to the form. The first Tuesday
of each month is 'Pay What You Wish Day'.

SFMOMA. *See p72.*

San Francisco Museum of Modern Art (SFMOMA)

151 Third Street, between Mission & Howard Streets (357 4000/www.sfmoma.org). BART Powell or Montgomery/Muni Metro F, J, K, L, M, N/bus 9, 15, 30, 45, 76. **Open** *Memorial Day-Labor Day* 10am-6pm Mon, Tue, Fri-Sun; 10am-9pm Thur. *Labor Day-Memorial Day* 11am-6pm Mon, Tue, Fri-Sun; 11am-9pm Thur. **Admission** $10; $6-$7 concessions; free under-12s; half price 6-9pm Thur; free 1st Tue of mth. **Credit** *Café & shop only* AmEx, MC, V. **Map** p315 H4.
The second-largest US museum devoted to modern art (after MOMA in New York), SFMOMA opened with a flourish in 1995, reaping enthusiastic approval as much for its $60-million design as for any improvement to the collections. Swiss architect Mario Botta's red-brick building, with its huge, circular skylight, is as dramatic from the outside as within – and still feels brand new. The four floors of galleries that rise above the stark and stunning black marble reception area house an important permanent collection, with some 15,000 paintings, sculptures and works on paper, as well as thousands of photographs and a growing collection of works related to the media arts. The museum's range is formidable – from Jeff Koons to Anselm Kiefer, Magritte to Man Ray, Jasper Johns, Imogen Cunningham, Roy Lichtenstein, a characteristically geometric Piet Mondrian, a Marcel Duchamp urinal and one of Mark Rothko's luminous canvases. With an evident fondness for electronic and digital works, SFMOMA's director David Ross has made efforts to include Bay Area artists in most group shows. Don't miss the spectacular catwalk just beneath the sky-light, accessible from the top-floor galleries. Though not recommended for those who suffer from vertigo, it offers a stunning view of the striped marble below. Special exhibitions (such as the 2003 Chagall retrospective) have wrapped queues right around the building. The museum closes on Wednesdays.

Society of California Pioneers Seymour Pioneer Museum

300 Fourth Street, at Folsom Street (957 1849/www.californiapioneers.org). Bus 12, 15, 30, 45, 76. **Open** 10am-4pm Wed-Fri, 1st Sat of mth. *Library* prior appointment only (10am-noon, 1-4pm). **Admission** $3; $1 concessions. **No credit cards.** **Map** p311/315 H4.
Operated by descendants of the state's first settlers, this small museum has occasional intriguing displays on California history. There are also 19th-century paintings, sculpture and furniture.

Yerba Buena Center for the Arts

701 Mission Street, at Third Street (978 2787/www.yerbabuenaarts.org). BART Powell or Montgomery/Muni Metro F, J, K, L, M, N/bus 9, 15, 30, 45, 76. **Open** 11am-5pm Tue-Sun; 11am-8pm 1st Thur of mth. **Admission** $6; $3 concessions; free 1st Tue of mth. **Credit** AmEx, MC, V. **Map** p311 H4.
Last in the alphabet but first in the hearts of many, Yerba Buena Center is opposite SFMOMA and somewhat in its shadow, yet seems unintimidated, tugging at the modern art scene's shirt-tails with its scrappy

itinerary and great attitude. Housed in a futuristic-looking building designed by Fumihiko Maki, it contains four changing galleries and a 96-seat theatre. The museum's focus is on the new and the challenging – installation and video art, outsider art – and has included such diverse names as Henry Darger, Fred Thomaselli and Kumi Yamashita. It has now happily passed its tenth birthday.

South Park & South Beach

If there's any area that represents the phrase dot-com bust this is it. A few years ago, finding a clear space in the green oval of South Park took more time and moxie than snagging one of the coveted parking spaces. Now the 20-year-old BMW drivers have zoomed away, and you can take a picnic and spread out your biggest blanket without stepping on anyone's toes. This was San Francisco's first gated community, but suffered a string of misfortunes: while finding itself burnt to the ground early in the 20th century may have been careless, it was pure bad luck that the cable car was invented and encouraged the South Park millionaires to abscond to Nob Hill (*see p83*). South Park became an African-American enclave after World War II, then was neglected until the tornado of young men fluent in Java and html blew in during the 1990s. Now Multimedia Gulch has pretty much shut up shop as well, leaving South Park tranquil again, with the few dot-com survivors (*see p62* **SF heroes: Craig Newmark**) seeming much more, well, much more San Franciscan about things. Fashionistas in search of designer bargains will want to check out Jeremy's (*see p173*), where women's trousers are available in sizes 0 to 2. If funds don't permit you to get your fill there, try to catch one of the Isda & Co outlet (No.29, 512 1610) sample sales.

South-east of South Park, just south of the I-89, you'll find one of the city's oldest murals. Now somewhat faded, John Wehrle's dreamy seascape *Reflections* is on Fifth at Bryant. This is the beginning of **South Beach**. Near Pier 40 you'll find the recently renamed **SBC Park** stadium (*see p234*), which is home to the SF Giants and well liked, obviously, for the baseball, as well as its great views of the Bay. An intriguing architectural gem is just nearby: the **Francis 'Lefty' O'Doul Bridge** (Third Street, near Berry Street) is the city's only working drawbridge. A charming antique, it was designed by JB Strauss, who is better known for a much bigger span: the Golden Gate Bridge (*see p96*). The eponymous 'Lefty' was one of the all-time great baseball hitters. But the name O'Doul is a fabrication: Lefty's dad added the O' prefix to impress his future beloved's Irish parents. It worked too: that lady was to be Lefty's mother.

North Beach & Around

Chinese and Italians, bohos and tourists – everybody is drawn into the old heart of San Francisco.

No combination of neighbourhoods offers a greater cross-section of San Francisco life than those clustered around North Beach. From the century-old ethnic neighbourhoods of Chinatown and Little Italy to wealthy Nob Hill and the tacky tourism of Fisherman's Wharf, the mosaic of elements that makes this city one of the most colourful in the US can be found within just a few blocks. This district is also near the city's original port, making it the historic heart of the city all the way back to the Barbary Coast years. Compact, hilly and dense with attractions, this is probably the best part of San Francisco for walkers who like to pack a lot into a single outing. Make that cappuccino a double: you'll be needing the caffeine.

Chinatown

With its rows of curio shops, Chinatown initially feels like the worst of Western tourism, but venture into the back alleys and you'll find a little bit of the Far East alive and well. This contradiction is nothing new: Chinatown has been one of America's most-visited attractions since the 1920s, and a thriving, tightly knit community for 150 years. The 1849 Gold Rush and its promise of economic prosperity drew shiploads of Cantonese through the ports; famine and civil unrest across China in the ensuing decades gave the immigrants little incentive to return home. After the gold fields

dried up, many Chinese got construction jobs on the transcontinental railway. And like most new arrivals, they dreamed of striking it rich, despite severe anti-Chinese laws and an abundance of racist vigilantes in the late 19th century. The Chinese neighbourhood that arose in San Francisco had a well-deserved reputation for cheap whores, opium dens and all-hours gambling – activities that lured throngs of curious Caucasians – and, though the 1906 earthquake and fire devastated the district, the vice continued well into the 1920s.

In the aftermath of the quake, city fathers tried to appropriate what had become prime real estate, but the Chinese held fast and rebuilt their community. Even today, Chinatown's crowded streets and dark alleys, with laundry fluttering from fire escapes overhead, evokes an earlier era. Life carries on here as it has for more than a century. Nearly 100 restaurants serve exotic specialities ranging from duck's feet to taro-root dumplings, herbalists prepare natural remedies, and on special occasions lion-dancers gyrate to the sound of drums and firecrackers. While many of their wealthier countrymen now live in Richmond and Sunset, some 10,000 Chinese still live in the neighbourhood – one of the country's most densely populated – making Chinatown one of the largest Asian populations outside Asia.

A few blocks from Union Square, at Grant Avenue and Bush Street, the dragon-topped

A herbalist at work in **Chinatown.**

Chinatown Gate marks Chinatown's southern entrance. A gift from Taiwan in 1970, the green-tiled portal is a traditional village design, complete with quotation from Confucius urging passers-by to work for the common good.

Through the gate is **Grant Avenue**, Chinatown's main thoroughfare – and arguably the city's oldest. In the 1870s and 1880s, when Grant was called Dupont Street, it was patrolled and controlled by *tongs*, mutual-protection societies whose Mafia-style dealings sparked bitter, bloody battles over gambling and prostitution rackets. Today, however, the avenue is wholly commercial, with shops as far as the eye can see selling T-shirts, toys, ceramics, souvenirs and jewellery, the genuine mixed with junk. Streetlamps sculpted in the likeness of golden dragons line both sides of the street. These were created during the tourist boom of the 1920s at the prompting of the Chinese Chamber of Commerce. The buildings along Grant, on the other hand, have been built in undistinguished American styles, with a few exceptions. The **Ying On Labor Association** building (Nos.745-7) is a gaudy study in chinoiserie, while directly across the street the **Sai Gai Yat Bo Company** building (No.736) features antiquated ornate balconies and a pagoda-style roof. **Li Po** (*see p152*), named after the great drunken poet of the T'ang dynasty, is a bit more kitsch with its circular gold entrance. **Ten Ren Tea Company** (*see p179*), the city's largest tea retailer, offers free samples to help patrons choose from 40 varieties – not surprisingly, it's a favourite stop on most Chinatown guided tours. On the corner of California Street and Grant is the Roman Catholic **Old St Mary's Cathedral** (*see p77*), a sturdy 1854 edifice made of granite imported from China.

Half a block east of Grant Avenue, on the corner of Clay and Kearny Streets, you'll find **Portsmouth Square** (733 Kearny Street). It is named after the USS *Portsmouth*, which was Captain John B Montgomery's ship. It was he who first claimed San Francisco (then called Yerba Buena) from Mexico in 1946. In 1847 the first public school in California was built on the south-west corner of this plaza; the following year this was where Sam Brannan, owner of the city's first newspaper, the *California Star*, announced that gold had been discovered at Sutter's Mill. For these reasons, Portsmouth Square is considered by many the true birthplace of the city. Within a few years of Brannan's announcement, Chinese immigrants settled in the area for good, earning it unofficial designation as the 'Heart of Chinatown'; it was in Portsmouth Square that emergency shelter was set up for those residents displaced by the 1906 quake. Now the elderly congregate here to practise t'ai chi, argue politics and kibbitz over Chinese chess. Monuments include a copy of the Goddess of Liberty that figured in 1989's Tiananmen Square incident, and another, shaped like the galleon *Hispaniola*, dedicated to Robert Louis Stevenson, who used to sit here during his 1879 stint as a San Franciscan.

Linked to the square by a concrete footbridge, the **Chinese Culture Center** (*see p77*) is on the third floor of the Holiday Inn. At 743 Washington Street, the pagoda-like **Bank of Canton** is one of Chinatown's most photographed buildings. The offices of the *California Star* originally occupied the site, but the present structure was built in 1909 for the Chinese American Telephone Exchange. For four decades, multilingual phone operators routed calls throughout Chinatown by memory alone, as there was no phone directory for Chinese residents. The Bank of Canton restored the building in 1960.

Cameron House (920 Sacramento Street, at Stockton Street) is named after Donaldina Cameron, the New Zealand crusader who devoted her life to saving San Francisco's Chinese girls from prostitution and slavery. Now it provides family services to low-income Asian immigrants and residents. Though the organisation's mission has evolved, its home is just about the only place in the city where you can still see physical traces of the great 1906 fire: misshapen 'clinker' bricks, melted by the intense heat, protrude from the walls.

To the west of Grant Avenue, running the length of Chinatown, is **Stockton Street**. Bustling with locals speaking a range of Chinese dialects, its grocery stores attract throngs of customers but few tourists, and its live markets sport exotic delicacies and tanks swarming with fish, turtles and crabs. Stockton restaurants also have a more authentic feel than those on Grant Avenue – for many, this is the 'real' Chinatown.

One of the oldest religious structures in San Francisco is the **Kong Chow Temple**. Established in 1857, it was moved to its present home on the fourth floor of the **Chinatown Post Office** (855 Stockton Street, between Sacramento and Clay Streets) in 1977. Divination sticks, red satin banners, flowers and pyramids of oranges flank a fabulous altar from which a statue of the god Kuan Ti has a keen view of the Bay. It's said that President Harry Truman made an offering at the original location prior to his 1948 election. Nearby, the façade of the photogenic **Chinese Six Companies Building** (843 Stockton Street) sports ceramic carp, stone lions and coloured tiles.

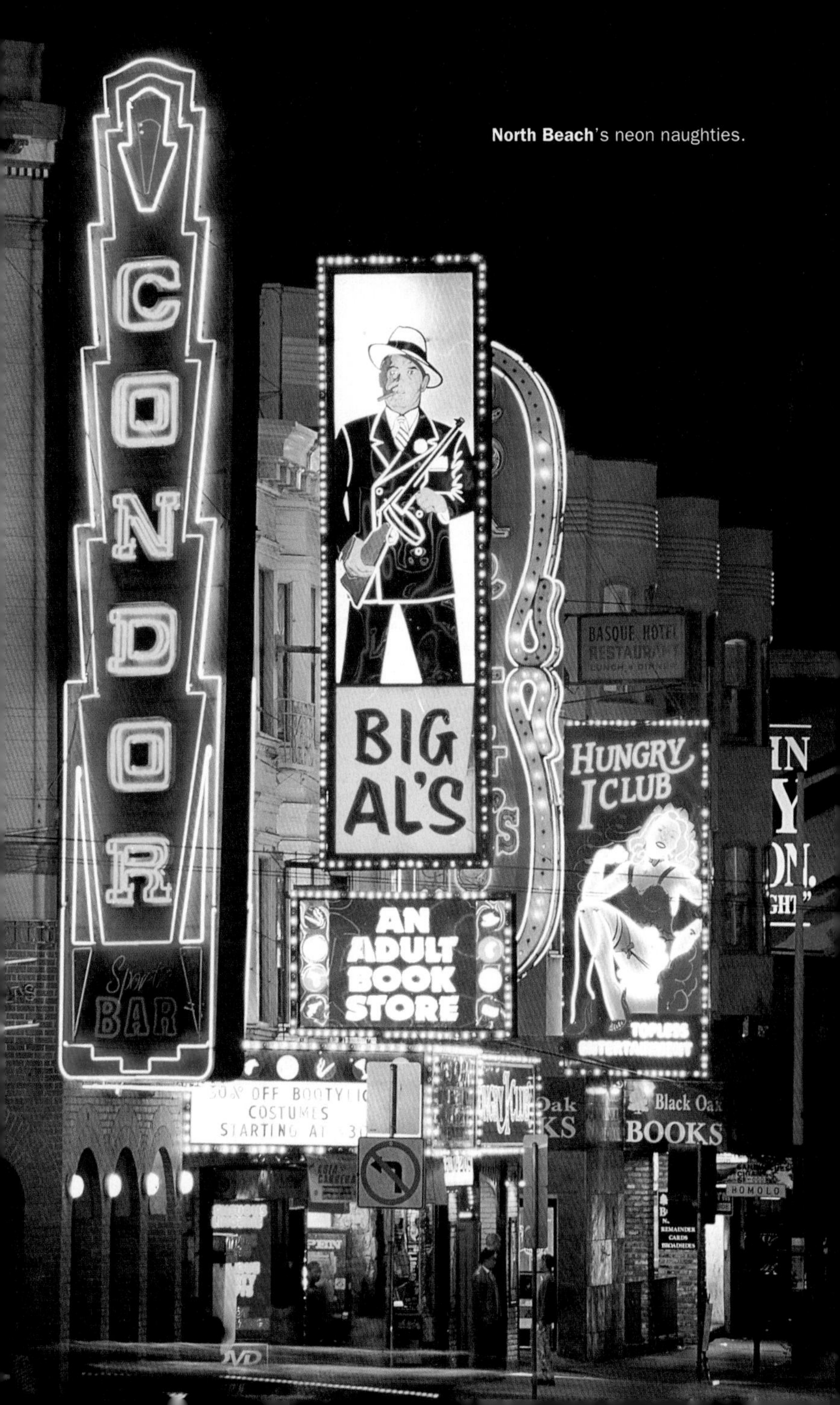

North Beach's neon naughties.

SF heroes Carol Doda

A pair of neon nipples once shone above the Condor Club's entrance like a beacon to visitors from less-liberated cities. Today the **Condor Club** (300 Columbus Avenue, at Broadway) caters to sports fans, but in the bar's museum the glowing boobs have been preserved, along with a few newspaper clips, as reminders that Carol Doda was once as big a tourist draw as the Golden Gate Bridge.

Forty years ago, Doda was just another cocktail waitress at the Condor Club – popular, it should be admitted, thanks to her impromptu dances on the club's piano, but just another waitress. Then Condor publicist Davey Rosenberg had an idea. He'd read about Austrian designer Rudy Gernreich's new topless bathing suit for women and sped to Joseph Magnin's department store to buy one for Doda, encouraging her to add it to her act.

On 19 June 1964, she did. Descending bare-breasted from the ceiling on a white baby grand piano, she twisted and frugged to the strains of 'Memphis, Tennessee'. It was a sensation. Within months, more than a dozen Broadway clubs had Doda clones, among them Yvonne D'Angers at the **Off Broadway**, Tara at **Big Al's** and Gaye Spiegelman (the 'Topless Mother of Eight') at the **El Cid**. The topless craze spread to restaurants, an ice-cream parlour and even a shoe-shine stand.

The Condor's marquee advertised its main attraction modestly enough: 'Miss Carol Doda, the Girl on the Piano'. Doda herself wanted to invest in something more spectacular. She underwent 20 weeks of silicone injections, swelling her 34-inch chest to a blouse-bursting 44-inches... then insured it with Lloyd's of London for $1.5 million.

Broadway was soon the city's hottest spot, but not everybody was charmed by the bacchanal. The traffic flow of 25,500-plus cars a day was a literal headache for locals, and Doda's notoriety frequently got her thrown out of 'respectable' North Beach establishments. Then, in 1965, the topless clubs were raided, with Doda herself among the 35 people arrested. With the help of controversial attorneys Melvin Belli and Patrick Hallinan, she was acquitted in less than 20 minutes. When similar legal strikes were made against New York topless dancers, Doda made an ambassadorial trip to the East Coast. On arrival she chastised the dancers: they had decided to compromise by wearing pasties. Doda's legal battles made her an unlikely anti-establishment hero. She appeared at UC Berkeley's Sproul Hall – the Bay Area home of the Free Speech Movement – in front of 20,000 ogling students, one of whom allegedly fell out of an oak tree.

Doda and the Condor Club continued to push the boundaries of free expression, going 'bottomless' in 1969 and surviving numerous legal actions through the 1970s, but by 1967 the tourist focus had shifted to Haight-Ashbury and Flower Power, and radical students were more interested in opposing the Vietnam War than protecting the human right to be naked in public. In 1986 Doda left the Condor to set up her own business in Cow Hollow. Always an entrepreneur – Harvard University named her 'Business Person of the Year' in 1974 – her new venture was the **Champagne & Lace Lingerie Boutique** (1850 Union Street, 776 6900), which she still runs to this day.

Perhaps the truest taste of Chinatown can be found in the alleys around Washington Street. Follow your nose to the **Golden Gate Fortune Cookie Factory** (56 Ross Alley, 781 3956), where you can watch cookies being made by hand. South of Washington, between Grant Avenue and Stockton Street, is picturesque **Waverly Place**, the scene in 1879 of a famous battle between two *tongs* over the ownership of an especially beautiful prostitute. There's also another ancient shrine, the **Tien Hau Temple** (125 Waverly Place). Another kind of history was made in quiet Spofford Alley, where between 1904 and 1910 Sun Yat-sen launched a revolution against the Manchu dynasty from the **Ghee Kung Tong Building** (36 Spofford Street). Wentworth Alley, east of Grant Avenue between Jackson and Washington Streets, is another untouristed backstreet.

Chinese American National Museum & Learning Center

965 Clay Street, between Stockton & Powell Streets (391 1188/www.chsa.org). Bus 1, 30, 45/cable car Powell-Hyde or Powell-Mason. **Open** 11am-4pm Tue-Fri; noon-4pm Sat, Sun. **Admission** $3; free 1st Thur of mth. **Credit** MC, V. **Map** p311 G3.
Formerly the Chinese Historical Society Museum, this new facility opened in November 2001 in improved digs at the historic Chinese YWCA building. Designed by renowned local architect Julia Morgan, the new building enabled the museum to continue its mission of promoting the understanding of Chinese history. Bilingual displays follow California's Chinese population from the frontier years to the Gold Rush, through the building of the railroads and the Barbary Coast opium dens. The expanded centre also serves as a learning resource for students, with books, videos and CD-Roms.

Chinese Culture Center

Third floor, Holiday Inn, 750 Kearny Street, at Portsmouth Square (986 1822). Bus 1, 15, 30, 45/cable car California. **Open** 10am-4pm Tue-Sun. **Admission** free. **Credit** MC, V. **Map** p311 H3.
The Center hosts a variety of events, including Asian-themed art exhibitions and performances, as well as workshops and walking tours. There's also an annual festival to celebrate Chinese New Year.

Old St Mary's Cathedral

660 California Street, at Grant Avenue (288 3800). Bus 1, 15, 30, 45/cable car California. **Open** 7am-4.30pm Mon-Fri; 10am-6.30pm Sat; 7am-2.30pm Sun. **Map** p311 G3.
Much early missionary work and the city's first English lessons for Chinese immigrants took place under this 19th-century building's foreboding clock tower: 'Son, observe the time and fly from evil', it warns. You can observe your time at lunchtime concerts staged in its daintily glorious interior.

North Beach

North and east of Columbus Avenue, North Beach nursed much of what made San Francisco famous: literature, coffee, jazz and sex. Originally home to the city's Italian community, it boasts many family-style restaurants. In the 1950s this European aura coupled with low rents attracted various bohemians, notably the Beats (*see p78* **Walk 1: Dead Beat with a Martini**). Legendary comedy clubs, and later punk venues, solidified North Beach's indelible stamp of hipness.

These days the mellow streets of North Beach, with their famously lambent light on sunny days, are still home to elderly Italians playing *bocce*, reading Neapolitan newspapers and nibbling *cannoli* in a dazzling array of coffee houses. The big, brash strip joints along Broadway are another tourist draw, whether locals like it or not: in fact, North Beach is as well known for its sex shows as for its literary heritage and lasagne.

Much of North Beach's history and many of its treasures lie along **Columbus Avenue**. Francis Ford Coppola has an office in **Columbus Tower**, the turreted green building on the corner of Columbus and Kearny. Long before he moved in, however, the structure was known as the Sentinel

Coit Tower.
See p80.

Sightseeing

Walk 1 Dead Beat with a Martini

Once a haven for seafarers, North Beach was almost completely destroyed in the 1906 earthquake and fire. It was repopulated with immigrant labourers, many of whom were Italian and stayed in the neighbourhood once they'd finished rebuilding it. Fantastic *ristorantes* and coffee shops sprang up everywhere, and in time the cheap *pensions* began to attract those most notorious of voluntary indigents: writers and musos.

Our walk starts on **Columbus Avenue**, where it intersects with Broadway heading east to west and Grant heading north and south. Here the literary spirits of North Beach are packed in so tightly you practically have to step into the road to avoid them. Especially if it's Saturday afternoon. First, have a peek into **Vesuvio** (No.255; *see p153*), whose surprisingly jaunty multi-coloured sign has welcomed poets and artists since it opened in 1948. Dylan Thomas couldn't resist when he was in town, nor can the dipsomaniacal poets and poetical dipsomaniacs of today. But we're not aiming to get liquored up just yet. To the right of Vesuvio is Jack Kerouac Alley – which, it is reasonable to suppose, was utilised by Allen Ginsberg and Kerouac himself for purposes other than writing – and on the opposite side of the alley the world-famous **City Lights** (No.261; *see p165*).

Cross Columbus heading east along Broadway. **Tosca** (No.242; *see p153*) can lay proud claim to having unceremoniously ejected Bob Dylan and entourage one boisterous evening, and it was at **Spec's** (12 William Saroyan Place; *see p153*) that famed *San Francisco Chronicle* columnist Herb Caen coined the derogatory term 'Beatnik' to describe the increasingly large

numbers of youths heading to North Beach in search of jazz, sex and poetry. Many of them found all three, but we're only interested in the former right now.

Head away from City Lights along the right-hand side of Broadway. Here the ghosts of great jazzmen past would gather to play another chorus were there not better music in heaven. At Nos.471-3 the **Jazz Workshop** once hosted the jazz A-list: Miles Davis, Cannonball Adderley, John Coltrane, Sonny Rollins and Ornette Coleman all raised their horns here – and it was also here that Lenny Bruce was first arrested for obscenity in 1961. Head up to Montgomery Street for a great view of the Bay Bridge, then cross over Broadway. Allen Ginsberg lived at 1010 Montgomery with Peter Orlovsky, probably conceiving his epochal poem *Howl* here. Were he still alive, Ginsberg would be rapidly

Building and was home to **Caesar's**, the restaurant credited with creating the salad of the same name. On its ground floor is elegant **Café Niebaum-Coppola** (291 1700), which sells its own brand of pasta alongside wines from the film director's Napa Valley vineyard. The focal point for the Beat movement, **City Lights** (*see p165*), is still owned by poet Lawrence Ferlinghetti and stays open until midnight daily. Next door, **Vesuvio** (*see p153*) is adorned with over-the-top murals.

Molinari Delicatessen (*see p179*), which has a cameo role in Armistead Maupin's *Babycakes*, sells olives, cheeses, salads, cold

cuts and own-made tortellini – perfect for enjoying *la dolce vita* in **Washington Square** to the north. Marking the heart of North Beach, this grassy rectangle is overlooked by the white stucco Romanesque **Church of St Peter and St Paul**, where Marilyn Monroe and local-hero Joe DiMaggio had their wedding photos taken. (Since both were divorced and Joe was a Catholic, they had actually got married in a civil ceremony at City Hall.) An 1879 statue of Benjamin Franklin stands in the park on a granite-encased time capsule scheduled for reopening in 2079. The park is a lovely place to watch people walk their dogs, approaching his eighties, so the old people's retirement home currently on the spot is not inappropriate, though one suspects few of the occupants would describe their lovers as Ginsberg described Orlovsky in 1972: 'a nice, clean-looking pecker, yellow hair, a youthful teeny little face, and a beautiful frank expression...'. Heading back along Broadway you'll pass the Green Tortoise Hostel at No.494. This was once the chic **El Matador**, where Frank Sinatra and Duke Ellington would perform for Marlon Brando's Hollywood set.

Enough of gone spectres. Turn right on to Kearny and you're facing more than 100 pretty steps. Locals call them the Kearny Steps, but actually the Macchiarini Steps. On sunny afternoons many people sit here with a book. From the top it's downhill (you'll be pleased to hear) for a break at **Caffe Trieste** (No.601; *see p145*). If it is Saturday you'll be treated to some opera, but any day of the week it's worth dropping in for an espresso and some bohemians. (An old fellow was practising his pliés when we were last in.) Francis Ford Coppola is alleged to have worked on *The Godfather* here, so don't be rude to anybody with a violin case. Drink up, and head back to Columbus.

Now make tracks east on Vallejo as far as Powell (resist the tempting cakes at Victoria Pastry Company as you cross Stockton) and take a right. Taking note of the amiable **North Star** (1560 Powell, at Green Street, 397 0577), continue to the end of the block where, on the right, you'll find **Capp's Corner** (1600 Powell Street, at Green Street, 989 2589). Drop in and put your name on the list (Saturday evenings are usually packed) and then, with the timetable in your head, go back

to the North Star. It's been here since 1882, but most regulars are too young to remember 1982. Relax into a Martini and work on building up an appetite. You'll need it for the heaped spaghetti with meatballs or osso bucco back at Capp's. Round off the meal with an espresso, and it's time to press on.

Turn right down Green Street, skipping the inevitable queue at Club Fugazi for **Beach Blanket Babylon** (*see p246*) – Green Street here is even called 'Beach Blanket Boulevard' in honour of the long-standing revue. If it's a sunny daytime, turn left and head up to Washington Square for a glorious mix of tatty old bohemians, wannabe alternative types and discreet Chinese ladies doing t'ai chi. But as it's evening, zig-zag across the intersection between Green, Columbus and Stockton, glancing (carefully) right at the Transamerica Pyramid (*see p61*) as you go. Stick on Green Street, passing Caffè Sport at No.574. When this was the **Cellar**, Kenneth Rexroth and ruth weiss read to improvised accompaniment here, a first foray into jazz poetry. Stop when you reach **Gino & Carlo's** (548 Green Street, 421 0896), easily recognisable by a puff of smokers out front and the four-deep mob surrounding the bar inside.

If you're not done with history yet, turn right on to Grant Avenue and head past the Grant & Green Saloon (No.1371), past the Lost & Found Saloon (No.1361), until you reach the plain old **Saloon** (No.1232; *see p212*). This is San Francisco's oldest bar, happily getting folks drunk since 1861. There's no smoky jazz, but it does have live blues. If you still fancy a Martini by the time you stumble out, it's way past time to hail the magic taxi home. **Distance** *about a mile (1.5 km).* **Time** *20min.*

play frisbee and kiss. At **Caffe Roma** (526 Columbus Avenue, 296 7942), coffee is roasted on the premises, while atmospheric **Mario's Bohemian Cigar Store** (*see p145*) sells delicious snacks – but no cigars.

Home to lap dancers and their fans, **Broadway** between Columbus Avenue and Montgomery Street is lined with nightclubs offering sexy floorshows, though there are far fewer now than in the swinging '60s. History was made at the **Condor Club** in 1964 by a buxom waitress called Carol Doda (*see p76* **SF heroes: Carol Doda**), while a new culture was forged in the **Mabuhay Gardens** at

443 Broadway (now the Velvet Lounge, a restaurant/nightclub), a world-famous punk mecca where the Dead Kennedys and Avengers got their start.

Two hotels sum up the area. **Hotel Bohème** (*see p42*) celebrates Beat heritage with framed photos of bohemian North Beach in the '50s and '60s, while the *pension*-like **San Remo Hotel** (*see p44*), a pretty Italianate Victorian, is ideal for soaking up the area's Italian ambience. **Telegraph Hill**, bordered by Grant Avenue and Green, Bay and Sansome Streets, was the site of the West Coast's first telegraph. The landmark **Coit Tower** (*see p80*) sits on top.

Coit Tower

*Peak of Telegraph Hill, at the end of Telegraph Hill
Boulevard (362 0808). Bus 39.* **Open** 10am-6pm
daily. **Admission** *Lift* $3.75. **Map** p311 G2.

This 210-foot-tall (64-metre) concrete turret, built by
City Hall architect Arthur Brown in 1933, was a gift
to the city from the eccentric Lillie Hitchcock Coit.
Snatched out of a life-threatening blaze when she
was just a child, Lillie was a lifelong fan of firemen
and her tower represents the nozzle of one of their,
er, hoses. Nor are the spectacular views from the top
the tower's only attraction. Wonderful murals were
created here under the supervision of Diego Rivera,
a series of socialist-realist images so subversive that,
when they were completed in 1934, the opening was
delayed and an errant hammer and sickle erased.

Fisherman's Wharf

Now that the commercial shipping and fishing
have moved elsewhere, Fisherman's Wharf –
roughly bounded by Jefferson, North Point and
Kearny Streets and Fort Mason – is a garish
and inexplicably popular tourist purgatory.
Daytrippers descend in thousands from the
terminus of the Powell-Hyde cable car line.
Except as a departure point for ferry trips to
Alcatraz (*see below*) and **Angel Island** (*see
p81*), the area is best avoided – unless you're
an unrepentant tourist or a masochist who
enjoys pointless souvenirs, pricey seafood and
lacklustre crowds wondering why they came.

Jefferson Street, the wharf's main drag, is
the ultimate tourist trap; the **Wax Museum**
(500 145 Jefferson Street, between Mason and
Taylor Streets, 1-800 439 4305) and **Ripley's
Believe It Or Not! Museum** (175 Jefferson
Street, at Taylor Street, 771 6188) are clichéd
seafront diversions, and sidewalk crab stalls
and seafood restaurants thrive. For the only
remaining glimpse of Fisherman's Wharf as it
once was, turn towards the water off Jefferson
and on to Leavenworth Street, then slip right
into **Fish Alley**. There you'll find real fishing
boats and real fishermen. Within shouting
distance of Jefferson, it feels like miles away.

At the eastern end, **Pier 39** is a sprawling
prefab array of seafront shops, attractions and
arcade games patently designed to separate you
from your money. Luckily, crowds of sea lions
barking and belching on nearby pontoons
provide a natural respite (their population
varies with the seasons). Offshore from H Dock
on Pier 39, **Forbes Island** (951 4900) is 700
tons (711,200 kilos) of man-made, engine-
propelled, floating lighthouse and restaurant.
Further west, at Pier 45, a World War II
submarine, the **USS Pampanito** (*see p81*),
has brought its ship-sinking days to an end
and opened its hull to the public.

A reminder of the area's former industrial
life is the **Cannery** (2801 Leavenworth Street,
enter on Jefferson or Beach Streets, 771 3112,
www.thecannery.com). Built in 1907 as a fruit-
canning factory, it's now another twee shopping
mall modelled on London's Covent Garden,
complete with street performers. Red-brick
Ghirardelli Square (at North Point and
Larkin Streets; *see p161*) dates to the 19th
century and housed, until the 1960s, a famous
chocolate factory. It is now a complex of shops
and restaurants. You can sort through any
tourist monstrosities you've acquired in the
central plaza, alongside the lovely Mermaid
Fountain by local artist Ruth Asawa.

The shores of **Aquatic Park** (between
Hyde Street and Van Ness Avenue) offer
one of the best strolls in the city, with a
panorama of the Golden Gate Bridge, Alcatraz,
windsurfers, sailing boats, wildly coloured
kites and dogs catching frisbees. Along the
Municipal Pier (accessible from the northern
end of Van Ness), fishermen try their luck;
at **Hyde Street Pier** (*see p81*) a fleet of
carefully restored historic ships, all of them
National Historic Landmarks, are docked
permanently. The pier is under the same
administration as the **San Francisco
Maritime National Historical Park
Museum Building** (*see p81*), opposite
Ghirardelli Square. A white art deco building
that looks like an ocean liner, it recaptures
West Coast whaling, steamboating and
perilous journeys 'around the Horn'.

The **Golden Gate Promenade** begins here,
continuing for three miles (five kilometres)
along the shoreline to **Fort Point** (*see p102*).
The entire waterfront from Aquatic Park to
Ocean Beach was incorporated into the Golden
Gate National Recreation Area in 1972, with
the authorities stopping Fisherman's Wharf-
style tourist kitsch spreading any further.

Alcatraz

*www.nps.gov/alcatraz. Blue & Gold ferry from
Pier 41, Embarcadero (Blue & Gold Ferry:
recorded information 773 1188/tickets 705 5555/
www.blueandgoldfleet.com).* **Tickets** with audio tour
$16; $8; without audio tour $11.50; after-dark tours
(4.20pm Thur-Sun) $23.50. **Credit** AmEx, Disc, MC,
V. **Map** p310 G1.

Alcatraz is Spanish for pelican, but to its inmates
it was simply 'the Rock'. The West Coast's first
lighthouse was built here in 1854, but it was soon
decided that the island's isolated setting made it
perfect for a prison. It became a military jail in
the 1870s, but it wasn't until it was converted into
a high-security federal penitentiary in 1934 that
the name Alcatraz became an international symbol
of punishment. Despite being in operation for
less than 30 years, Alcatraz remains fixed in the

Relive the golden days of sail aboard the ships at **Hyde Street Pier.**

imagination as the ultimate penal colony. (As do some of its inmates; *see p82* **The Bird Man of Alcatraz.**) Today its ominous prison buildings are no longer used, but the craggy outcrop lures well over a million visitors each year. The audio tour is quite brilliant.

Angel Island

897 0715/www.angel island.org. Blue & Gold ferry from Pier 41, Embarcadero (Blue & Gold Ferry: recorded information 773 1188/tickets 705 5555/ www.blueandgoldfleet.com). Open 8am-sunset daily. **Tickets** $10.50; $5.50-$9 concessions. **Credit** AmEx, Disc, MC, V. **Map** p310 G1.

There are two ferries during the week (10am, 11.30am) and three at weekends (9.45am, 11.30am, 2pm Sat, Sun), all arriving at the Ayala Cove visitors' centre, where there are maps, bikes to rent and all-important picnic tables. For more about Angel Island itself, *see p252.*

Hyde Street Pier

At the foot of Hyde Street (561 7100/ www.maritime.org). Muni Metro F/bus 19, 30, 42/cable car Powell-Hyde. **Open** 10am-5pm daily. **Admission** free ($5 for vessels). **No credit cards**. **Map** p310 F1.

Maritime fans, students of history and children will love the eight historic vessels permanently docked here. Typical of the ships that would have been common here in the 19th and early 20th centuries, they include the 1886 full-rigged *Balclutha*, built to carry grain from California to Europe; the *CA Thayer*, an 1895 sailing ship that carried timber along the West Coast; the *Alma*, an 1891 scow schooner that hauled cargo throughout the Bay Area; *Hercules*, a 1907 ocean tugboat; and the 1890 San Francisco commuter ferry *Eureka*.

Musée Mécanique

Pier 45, at the end of Taylor Street (346 2000/ www.museemecanique.citysearch.com). Bus 18, 38. **Open** 10am-7pm daily. **Admission** free. **Map** p310 F1.

Pack a pocketful of quarters before you visit the Musée Mécanique. This wonderful museum is actually an arcade housing over 170 old-fashioned coin-operated gizmos, ranging from fortune-telling machines to player pianos. Best of all is Laughing Sal, a somewhat scary relic from Whitney's Playland at the Beach, San Francisco's long-defunct coastside amusement park. She's an enormous mechanical figure with a crazy laugh that sends little kids running for their parents. Some of the machines date back to the 1880s.

San Francisco Maritime National Historical Park Museum Building

Beach Street, at Polk Street (556 3002/ www.maritime.org). Bus 19, 30, 32, 42, 47, 49/ cable car Powell-Hyde. **Open** 10am-5pm daily. **Admission** free. **Map** p310 F1.

This inelegantly named museum documents US maritime history with the aid of a mixture of photographs and ship models, including miniatures of passenger liners and US Navy ships. Its presentation is a little dated and is unlikely to thrill adults who don't already have an interest in the subject, but the interactive exhibits upstairs might distract the children for a half hour or so, and there's plenty of sea lore to learn if you're prepared to give it your attention.

USS Pampanito

Pier 45 (775 1943/www.maritime.org). Muni Metro F/bus 19, 30, 42/cable car Powell-Hyde. **Open** 9am-6pm Mon-Thur, Sun; 9am-9pm Fri, Sat. **Admission** $7; family ticket $20. **Credit** AmEx, MC, V. **Map** p310 F1.

The *Pampanito* is a World War II, Balao-class Fleet submarine with an impressive record: it made six patrols in the Pacific at the height of the war, sinking six Japanese ships and damaging four others. The vessel was recently restored to look much as it would have in its prime in 1945. The sub is still seaworthy too: in 1995 it sailed under the Golden Gate Bridge for the first time in 50 years.

The Bird Man of Alcatraz

Sightseeing

Alcatraz's status as one of San Francisco's top tourist attractions belies the fact that it was once the final stop for America's incorrigible criminals, Al Capone, 'Machine Gun' Kelly, 'Creepy' Karpis and Henry Young (the bank robber/murderer sanctified in the 1995 film *Murder in the First*) among them. But none of these exerts the same fascination as Robert Stroud.

Stroud is widely known as 'the Bird Man of Alcatraz', a brilliant but troubled man, benevolent bird lover and righteous foe of the inhumane prison regime. But this view of the man can be dated back pretty precisely to 1962 and Burt Lancaster gaining an Oscar nomination for his sympathetic performance as Stroud in *The Bird Man of Alcatraz*.

Stroud was indeed a man of uncommon intellect – in addition to writing two books on canaries and developing medicines for their various ailments, he taught himself several languages while in confinement – but the rest is pure Hollywood. Prone to violent outbursts, Stroud was accused of being a stool pigeon by fellow inmates, as well as a predatory homosexual. His nickname is a falsehood too: on Alcatraz he was not permitted to keep a single bird.

The 18-year-old Stroud had killed a bartender who allegedly refused to pay Stroud's prostitute girlfriend for services rendered. Shooting the barman execution-style, Stroud then coolly stole the $10 fee from the dead man's wallet. While serving his 12-year manslaughter sentence, Stroud stabbed a hospital orderly whom he believed had reported him for trying to extort narcotics. Following further complaints from fellow prisoners, he was transferred to Leavenworth Federal Penitentiary, where he continued to resist rehabilitation. In 1916 he murdered a guard – in front of 1,100 inmates in the prison mess hall – after learning that his brother had tried to visit on a non-designated day and been turned away. This time Stroud's sentence was first-degree murder; until his execution, Stroud would serve his time in solitary confinement. When his sentence was commuted in 1920 to life without parole, Stroud was still required to serve his time in solitary.

At Leavenworth Stroud discovered an injured bird in the recreation yard. The administration encouraged his sudden interest in ornithology, allowing him to breed and study some 300 birds in his two adjoining cells. Yet even this concession proved problematic. Stroud left carcasses of birds on which he had performed autopsies littering his workspace and laboured in his informal lab covered in bird excrement. He received so many letters from bird lovers that it was impossible to screen his mail, and the stacks of bird cages made searching

Russian Hill

Named after a group of wayward Russian sailors whose graves were discovered here in the 1840s, Russian Hill is a quiet, residential and very pricey neighbourhood roughly bordered by Larkin and North Point Streets, Columbus Avenue, Powell Street and Pacific Avenue. Its name is deceptive: it bears not the slightest trace of anything Russian today. Its most notorious landmark is the world's 'crookedest' (and perhaps most photographed) thoroughfare, **Lombard Street**, which snakes steeply down from Hyde Street to Leavenworth, packing nine hairpin bends into one brick-paved and over-landscaped block. In summer, tourists queue for the thrill of driving down its hazardous 27 per cent gradient at 5mph (8kph), much to the annoyance of local residents. Arrive early or late if you want to avoid the throng. For further thrills, test your skills behind the wheel on the steepest street in the city: Filbert Street between Hyde and Leavenworth descends at a whopping 31.5 per cent gradient.

Also on Russian Hill is the **San Francisco Art Institute** (*see p83*), housed in an attractive 1920s Spanish Revival building on Chestnut Street and containing a wonderful Diego Rivera mural. Struggle up Vallejo Street to take in the views from **Ina Coolbrith Park** at Taylor Street – it's less a park than a narrow ledge with benches; arrive early in the morning and you'll catch elderly Chinese practising t'ai chi here. Up from the park, the top of the **Vallejo Street Stairway**, designed by Willis Polk and surrounded on each side by landscaped gardens, is the apex of Russian Hill. Laura Ingalls Wilder, the author of *Little House on the Prairie*, used to live here (at 1019 Vallejo). Russian Hill is riven with quaint stairs and alleyways: if you don't mind the ups and downs, it's fun to prowl the neighbourhood for secret passages.

Sightseeing

his cell impossible. When he was transferred once more, guards were to discover the ever-resourceful Stroud had built an alcohol still out of some of his lab equipment.

In December 1942 Stroud was transferred to Alcatraz, where he was to spend the last 17 years of his life in 'deep lockdown' (you can enter his cell on tours of Alcatraz; *see*

p80). But the privileges he enjoyed at Leavenworth were not extended to him here: in short, no more birds. In 1959 the ailing Stroud was transferred to the Medical Center for Federal Prisoners in Missouri, where he died in 1963. *The Bird Man of Alcatraz* was on general release, but Stroud was never allowed to see it.

Landmark addresses in the district include **29 Russell Street**, off Hyde Street, where Jack Kerouac lived with Neal and Carolyn Cassady during his most creative period in the 1950s; and the **Feusier Octagon House**, one of the city's oldest dwellings, which is at 1067 Green Street near Leavenworth. Best viewed from across the street to appreciate its odd shape, the pastel structure is one of only two survivors of the 19th-century octagonal-house craze (the other is in Pacific Heights; *see p96*).

San Francisco Art Institute

800 Chestnut Street, between Leavenworth & Jones Streets (771 7020/www.sanfranciscoart.edu). Bus 30/cable car Powell-Hyde or Powell-Mason. **Open** *Diego Rivera Gallery* 10am-6pm Tue-Sat. **Admission** $6. **No credit cards**. **Map** p310 F2. This hip and prestigious art school offers the full spectrum of fine arts, including painting, film, photography, sculpture and new media. Its student shows are legendary. Most people visit to see Diego

Rivera's mural *The Making of a Fresco*, one of various works he completed in San Francisco in the 1930s. If you're worn out from climbing all those hills, have a rest in the pretty open-air courtyard, where plants and benches surround a fountain, or grab a cheap snack in the cafeteria.

Nob Hill

South of Russian Hill and overlooking the Tenderloin and Union Square, Nob Hill was named after the wealthy 'nabobs' who built their mansions in the area; it was described by Robert Louis Stevenson – who lived briefly on its lower flank – as 'the hill of palaces'. A short but incredibly steep jaunt up from Union Square, the summit stands 338 feet (103 metres) above the Bay. After a cable car started operating here in the 1870s, the once-barren hill began to attract wealthy residents, namely the 'Big Four' boom-era railroad tycoons: Charles

Barbary Lane

Armistead Maupin's *Tales of the City* column appeared in the *Chronicle* from 1976, but became internationally popular as novels in the '80s. The books offer a convincingly realistic snapshot of queer and straight life in San Francisco, but the apartment at their centre – Anna Madrigal's abode at 28 Barbary Lane – is a chimera. The 'narrow, wooded walkway' is supposed to be found off Leavenworth, between Union and Filbert, but the inquisitive find there only the pretty gardens of Havens Street.

Maupin has claimed the real inspiration behind Barbary Lane was a block away: the miraculously secluded **Macondray Lane**. One of San Francisco's 400 unmarked and overgrown public stairways, it has rickety wooden stairs and gives, through the idiosyncratic houses that line one side, tantalising views of the Bay. Its signpost is hard to spot (look for the name imprinted in the kerb), but you'll find it just north of Green Street, between Taylor and Jones.

If you want to explore more stairways (Adah Bakalinsky's *Stairway Walks in San Francisco* is invaluable), other Russian Hill favourites are Vallejo Street (between Jones and Mason) and Culebra Terrace (Chestnut, between Larkin and Polk).

Crocker, Leland Stanford, Mark Hopkins and Collis P Huntington. Their 'palaces' perished in the fire that swept through Nob Hill after the 1906 earthquake, and only the 1886 home belonging to James C Flood survived. Later remodelled by Willis Polk, the brownstone mansion is now the site of the private **Pacific-Union Club** (1000 California Street, at Mason Street). Next to it, at California and Taylor Streets, is the public but prissy **Huntington Park**, with its landscaped greenery and a fountain modelled on Rome's Tartarughe Fountain. Across the park, **Grace Cathedral** (*see below*) is another lovely landmark that was once a private home. Midnight Mass here, intoned by the celebrated boys' choir, is a marvellous Christmas tradition.

Surrounding the park and club are Nob Hill's elegant hotels. The **Fairmont Hotel** (950 Mason Street, at California Street, 772 5000) has a plush marble lobby and the fabulous **Tonga Room** (*see p153*) tiki bar. The quieter **Huntington Hotel** (*see p45*) is known as a royals' hideaway, but you don't have to stay there to use its luxurious Nob Hill Spa

(345 2888). Nearby, the **Top of the Mark** (*see p153*) bar, on the 19th floor of the Mark Hopkins Inter-Continental Hotel, offers fabulous views of the city. Moving down from the peak of the hill, the free **Cable Car Museum** (*see below*) on Mason Street displays antique cable cars and the mighty turbines that power the cables beneath the city's streets.

At the base of Nob Hill's western slopes, Polk Street (between Geary and Union) comprises a one-block-wide, mile-long neighbourhood known locally as **Polk Gulch**. Before the middle-class Castro came into its own, Polk was San Francisco's gay mecca: home to bold bars, adult bookshops and streetcorner encounters. In the mid 1970s, the area fell on hard times, as the exodus to the Castro left Polk Gulch with the unsavoury reputation as a last resort for runaway teenage boys resorting to selling sexual favours. While it has rebounded considerably and its ambience has mellowed – shops and restaurants crowd every block – the teenage boys have grown up into sad-eyed transvestites, and the area still seems to be searching for a new identity.

Grace Cathedral

1100 California Street, at Taylor Street (749 6300/www.gracecathedral.org). Bus 1, 27/cable car California. **Open** *Cathedral* 7.30am-6pm Mon-Fri, Sun; 8am-6pm Sat. *Tours* 1-3pm Mon-Fri; 11.30am-1.30pm Sat; 12.30-2pm Sun. **Map** p310 G3.
Begun in 1928, this Episcopalian house of worship was once a private mansion. It was later taken over by the Church and is, by US cathedral standards, an architectural extravaganza. Its façade is modelled on Paris's Notre Dame and it has a fine rose window, a magnificent organ, gilded bronze portals made from casts of the Doors of Paradise in Florence's Baptistery. Murals depict the founding of the UN and the burning of Grace's predecessor; an AIDS Interfaith Chapel has an altarpiece by Keith Haring.

Cable Car Museum

1201 Mason Street, at Washington Street (474 1887/www.cablecarmuseum.com). Bus 1, 12, 30, 45, 83/cable car Powell-Hyde or Powell-Mason. **Open** *Jan-Mar, Oct-Dec* 10am-5pm daily. *Apr-Sept* 10am-6pm daily. **Admission** free. **Map** p310 G3.
After the moo-ing foghorn, the sound most often associated with San Francisco is the clanging bells of the cable cars. The best way to study them is, of course, to ride one of the three lines that operate nowadays (*see p58* **You're on cable**); second best is to tour this museum, where you can view the cable winding machinery that actually powers the cars, as well as find out how the unusual vehicles work. You'll also learn about emergency procedures, bell-ringing competitions and the workmanship that goes into each car. Vintage cable cars, associated artefacts and dozens of old photos complete matters.

The Mission & the Castro

Hispanic, queer and quirky… a guaranteed taste of San Francisco's sassy neighbourhood life.

Looking for the beating heart of San Francisco? You'll find it right in the city's geographic centre, where the **Mission**, **Castro** and **Noe Valley** districts each boast a distinctive culture – Latino/hipster, queer and yuppie, respectively. From eclectic shops to vibrant nightlife to quaint Victorians, these neighbourhoods offer a taste of the thriving diversity that lends the city its charm.

The Mission

The city's oldest neighbourhood is still one of its most vital. Though only a block separates its two parallel corridors (Valencia and Mission Street), the difference between the two is striking. **Valencia** is chock-a-block with quirky boutiques and bars catering to urban hipsters, while **Mission Street** retains its longstanding working-class Hispanic flavour. Even the smells are different: the scent of seared meat and onions from the ubiquitous taquerias (*see p125* **Mr Big**) permeates the air along Mission Street, punctuated by the occasional whiff of urine in the dodgy alleys around 16th Street. Along Valencia, you're more likely to catch a whiff of scented candles

emanating from the trendy boutiques. But fascinating shops and local colour are plentiful along each corridor, and both are blessedly free of chain stores. (Navigators watch out: street numbers on Mission and Valencia Streets don't correspond to the number of blocks, unlike elsewhere in the city – *see p54*).

First settled by the Spanish in the 1770s and later by Irish, German, Italian and Asian immigrants, the Mission today is the centre of Latino culture in the city, thanks to a steady influx of families and workers from Mexico and Central America. Mission denizens also include well-heeled yuppies and many musicians and artists, though the invasion of *nouveaux riches* techies during the dot-com boom sent many artists scrambling for cheaper quarters. The arrival of a plethora of new venues – especially Luna Park (*see p133*) on Valencia Street and Foreign Cinema (*see p134*) and Beauty Bar (*see p153*) on Mission Street – did a great deal to cement the area's hipster credentials. Locals feared that an invasion of internet millionaires would change the area's face from brown to lily-white, gentrifying the place beyond recognition, but the exodus that followed the dot-com bust

The ever-vibrant **Mission**.

Walk 2 Sightseeing Mission

Meandering through the Mission on foot is by far the best way to experience its funky and flavourful soul. Begin at the landmark **Mission Dolores** (3321 16th Street, at Dolores; see p88); duck down Chula Lane, the tiny alley to the left of the adobe mission, to peek at the historic cemetery through an old wrought-iron fence. Then head north to **16th Street** and turn right along it to re-enter the modern world. Between Dolores and Guerrero, Creativity Explored (No.3245, 863 2108) is a nifty, non-profit gallery selling artwork by adults with developmental disabilities, and before Albion you'll find Café Macondo (No.3159, 431 7516), which prides itself on being 'best for your health, your pocket, and your politics'. Opposite, you'll find the excellent Adobe Books (No.3166, 824 8203). Keep on, passing the dilapidated red sign of the Roxie (No.3117; see p200), until you hit **Valencia Street**.

Turn right on to Valencia and head south. If you were here in the evening, you'd probably hear a roving mariachi band and the clink of Margarita glasses from Puerto Allegre (No.546, 255 8201), but during the day stick to the righthand pavement. You'll pass a number of excellent shops – orange-painted Therapy (No.541, 621 5902; No.545, 861 6213), Subterranean San Francisco (No.563, 431 9504) and Valencia Street Books (No.569, 552 7200) – but press on and cross 17th. Incongruously situated in the same building as a T-Mobile cellphone shop, you're now in the presence of **Good Vibrations** (No.603; see p185). Call in to see if its collection of antique vibrators is on display. Some date back to the 19th century, when a steam-powered model was patented for the admirable purpose of treating 'female disorders'; the collection does wander to the

other branches of the shop, but there will always be plenty of new models to keep you interested. **Clarion Alley**, right after Good Vibrations, is full of murals.

After another block, turn right off Valencia on to 18th. You'll head past the colourful **Women's Building** (No.3543; see p88) with its larger-than-life 'Maestrapeace' mural – an epic retelling of the history of women in the New World – and soon reach a tiny gourmet mecca: first there's **Tartine Bakery** (600 Guerrero Street, 487 2600) for wonderful pastries, then the Italian restaurant **Delfina** (No.3621; see p132) and, finally, a great selection of olives and other high-quality savouries at **Bi-Rite Market** (3639 18th Street; see p178). You could stop in at always-packed Dolores Park Café (501 Dolores Street, at 18th, 621 2936), but instead grab a cup to go and scoff your goodies in **Mission Dolores Park**. Then head back to Valencia and cross over the street.

You'll now be passing ADS Hats (No.758, 255 2787) and the mint green über-liberal **New College of California** (www.newcollege.edu), whose students loiter outside when they're not hard at work on their MFAs in Creative Inquiry. Between 19th and 20th there's a triptych of must-peeks. First are the taxidermist's curiosities of Paxton Gate (No.824; see p180). Next there's the chance of some celebrity-author stalking (the lovely Dave Eggers, of course) among the pirate supplies at 826 Valencia (see p196). Finally, you come to the small-press favourites and mainstream bestsellers at **Modern Times Bookstore** (No.888; see p166). If the book bug has really bitten, Modern Times is flanked to the north by Borderlands Books (No.866, 282 1901), a sci-fi specialist that's owned by a hairless cat

---

relieved some housing pressure, even though plenty of pricey live-work lofts – well out of the range of the average artist – are still being constructed. Still, the neighbourhood seems to have regained its equilibrium: increasingly upscale Valencia Street hasn't yet stopped the throbbing pulse of blue-collar Mission Street.

On Mission Street the cheque-cashing operations, bargain shops, taquerias and groceries selling sugar cane and prickly pears conduct brisk business, while Mexican pop music drifts out of open doors and windows.

The narrow, crowded pavements look as though they've been transported directly from Guadalajara. In autumn shops and art galleries are filled with traditional ghoulish items for **Día de los Muertos** (see p193). The barrio has its fair share of prostitutes, drug addicts and gangs (mostly deep in the inner Mission, east of Mission Street), and doorway drug-deals around scruffy 16th and Mission are enough to scare off the timid. Tourist buses limit their explorations to the fascinating **Mission Dolores** (see p88), but there's plenty else here

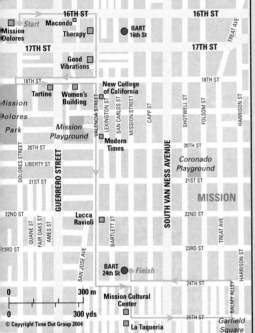

Sightseeing

the Marsh (No.1062; *see p247*), which lurks behind a distinctive swamp-green exterior. Just as you cross to 22nd, you'll see **Lucca Ravioli** (647 5581). If the name hasn't clued you in, the red, white and green awning will: this is the finest Italian deli in the area.

At 24th, turn left and head as far as **Mission Street**. As you probably noticed, what with all the discount stores, Latin American travel agencies and, above all, the taquerias, you're now in the neighbourhood's vibrant Hispanic barrio. Turn right on to Mission and head to 25th, passing the **Mission Cultural Center** (No.2868, 821 1155, www.missionculturalcenter.org) just before **La Taqueria** (No.2889, 285 7117). Here you simply must treat yourself to a burrito. Duly stuffed, push east along 25th Street. You'll be able to see lush green Bernal Heights, but there's little else apart from residential buildings for what feels like quarter of an hour. When you finally reach Garfield Square take the left up **Balmy Alley**, between Treat Avenue and Harrison Street. Suddenly, you're in among the famous and explosively colourful murals, each of them celebrating Latino heritage and encouraging community activism. Balmy Alley ends at 24th Street. Turn left there and walk west past the thriving restaurants, bakeries and shops back to Mission Street. The BART station there is the end of the walk.

Distance *about 2 miles (3.5km).* **Time** *40min.*

and run by its human slave, and to the south by Dog-Eared Books (No.900, 282 1901).

When enough browsing has been done, continue south up Valencia. It's worth picking up the pace a little here, but dawdlers can distract themselves with the local-made films shown at Artists' Television Access (No.992; *see p200*), the ultra-trendy clothes at Dema (No.1038; *see p170*) or some theatrics at

that's not be missed, not least **Ritmo Latino** (*see p184*), Latin music's answer to a Virgin Megastore, and the **Mission Cultural Center** (2868 Mission Street, 821 1155), which hosts a theatre and an art gallery showing out-of-the-mainstream visual artists.

Most famously Mission is home to a dazzling array of political and spiritual art, upholding the traditions of the Mexican muralists Diego Rivera, José Clemente Orozco and David Alfaro Siqueiros. There are more than 200 murals in this single district, many of which celebrate

the struggles and achievements of its Hispanic residents. The best-known mural street is **Balmy Alley** (which runs from 24th to 25th Streets, between Harrison Street and Treat Avenue), but you'll also find many murals near 24th Street, between Mission and Potrero. Perhaps the best resource for information about the city's murals is **Precita Eyes** (*see p88*).

On Valencia book-loving browsers can lose themselves for hours: **Dog Eared Books** (*see p168*) is only one of many bookshops in this literary neighbourhood. The **Women's**

Building (3543 18th Street, at Valencia, 431 1180/www.womensbuilding.org) houses a performance space and the headquarters of a dozen feminist non-profit groups. The pioneering, women-owned **Good Vibrations** (*see p185*) sex shop is a local favourite for women and men alike. Test the district's culinary reputation at **Truly Mediterranean** (*see p146*) – where you'll find truly fantastic falafel – or **Bombay Ice Creamery** (*see p178*). Numerous cafés populate both sides of Valencia between 16th and 24th Streets, each with its own unique ambience. A favourite destination for budget-conscious students and artists, the three-block stretch of 16th Street between Mission and Dolores Streets is packed full of colourful and inexpensive hangouts.

A short walk west to **Dolores Street** reveals the building which gave its name to the city, the 225-year-old Misión San Francisco de Asis, better known as Mission Dolores (*see below*). A couple of blocks south is **Mission Dolores Park**, worth visiting during daylight hours for great people- and dog-watching; on warm days, skimpily clad sunbathers line the upper end of the park (near Church and 20th), earning it the nickname 'Dolores Beach'.

At the neighbourhood's southern end **24th Street** offers numerous temptations – and plenty of Latino flavor. **El Nuevo Frutilandia** (*see p134*) serves Puerto Rican and Cuban delicacies, while the Mexican food is so good it draws in Financial District business types as well as local families (*see p125* **Mr Big**). If you just want a snack, the intersection of 24th and Alabama is a hub of *tipico* Mexican bakeries and quick-bite grills. And in a delicious universe of its own, the **St Francis Fountain Ice Cream Parlor** (2801 24th Street, at York, 826 4200) is a century-old, pink-and-chrome anachronism, complete with old-fashioned soda fountain. It's also reputedly the birthplace of the 49ers football team.

Mission Dolores

3321 16th Street, at Dolores Street (621 8203/ www.missiondolores.citysearch.com). BART 16th Street/Muni Metro J/bus 22. **Open** 8am-4pm daily. **Admission** $3; $1 concessions. **Credit** (groups only) AmEx, MC, V. **Map** p314 E6.
Founded by a tiny band of Spanish missionaries and soldiers in 1776 and completed in 1791, the historic mission is the oldest standing structure in the city, and bears the distinction of being San Francisco's Registered Landmark Number One. Built when the area was little more than a watery inlet, the mission takes its name from the swampy lagoon whose shores it was built upon (Laguna de los Dolores). Though the original

mission became an expansive outpost, housing over 4,000 monks and Indian converts, today only the tiny old church remains. The thick-walled adobe structure survived the 1906 earthquake unscathed, while the new church next door crumbled. Small wonder that the cool, dim interior looks and feels authentic – almost everything about it is unreconstructed and original, from the redwood logs holding up the roof to the ornate altars brought from Mexico centuries ago. (The modern-day church next door is a 20th-century basilica with no real architectural significance; it does, however, handle all the mission's religious services.) A small museum on the premises offers volunteer-led tours and access to a picturesque, flower-filled cemetery containing California's first governor and the city's first mayor, as well as Spanish settlers and the mass grave of 5,000 Costanoan Indians who died in their service. Fans of Hitchcock's *Vertigo* may recognise this as the very cemetery where an entranced Kim Novak leads Jimmy Stewart on a wild goose chase to the gravestone of the mysterious Carlotta Valdes (though you won't find Carlotta's stone, as it was a prop removed after filming).

Precita Eyes Mural Arts & Visitors Center

2981 24th Street, at Harrison Street (285 2287/ www.precitaeyes.org). BART 24th Street/bus 12, 27, 48. **Open** 10am-5pm Mon-Fri; 10am-4pm Sat, Sun. **Credit** MC, V. **Map** p314 G7.
If you want to know about San Francisco's fabulous and famous murals, this should be your first port of call. Established by Susan Cervantes in 1977, Precita Eyes is dedicated to preserving the Mission District's murals and specialises in guided tours; many of the murals visited were painted by Cervantes and her followers. Tours include Mission Mural Walks ($10), at 1.30pm on Saturdays and Sundays; BART Mural Walks ($7), at 1.30pm on Saturdays; BART Mural Tours ($5), at 11am on Saturdays; Bike Mural Tours ($10), at 11am on the second Sunday of every month; and Mexican Bus Mural Tours ($16), at 12.30pm on the third Sunday of every month.

Potrero Hill & Bernal Heights

On the outskirts of the Mission, the quiet **Potrero Hill** (to the east) and **Bernal Heights** (to the south) neighbourhoods are often sunny, even when the rest of the city is shrouded in fog. Both areas are a little off the beaten track and offer compact yet lively commercial districts. The neighbourhoods are home to a progressive mix of young families, dog-walking lesbians and hipsters who've fled the Mission.

Potrero locals live for the sourdough slices from **Goat Hill Pizza** (300 Connecticut Street, at 18th, 641 1440), and the **Bottom of the Hill** (*see p218*) lures regulars with a combination of great bands and an outdoor patio perfect for sunny afternoons. In the flatlands, where hilly Potrero bumps up against the Mission (also known as Multimedia Gulch), hipsters hang out at the **Slow Club** on Mariposa and the popular **Universal Café** on 19th (for both, *see p134*).

Bernal Hill boasts an eclectic mix of worthwhile hangouts on and around Cortland Avenue, including **Liberty Café** (No.410, at Bennington, 695 8777) for top-notch comfort food; **Zante's Indian Cuisine & Pizza** (3489 Mission Street, at Cortland, 821 3949) for their surprisingly excellent Indian pizza; and attitude-free lesbian bar **Wild Side West** (No.424, at Bennington, 647 3099),

which welcomes patrons of all genders and proclivities. Hike up the hill itself for a spectacular, 360° view of the city and bay.

The Castro

Bordered by Market, Church, 20th and Diamond Streets, festooned with rainbow flags, the **Castro** is an international gay mecca and one of the few places in the world where being gay is the norm. Straights are welcome, of course, and they get to experience the unusual sensation of, for once, being in the minority.

Along this stretch of trendy shops and see-and-be-seen cafés and bars (*see p227*), most of them gay-owned, a predominantly male populace enjoys a social and political influence that was hard-won, but is here to stay. A steadfastly working-class Irish-Catholic stronghold for nearly a century, the neighbourhood changed

A touch of glass

Founded by a lesbian couple in 1973, **Twin Peaks Bar** (401 Castro Street, at 17th, 864 9470) shattered taboos by becoming one of the first gay bars in the US, if not the very first, with large, pavement-facing windows. Prior to Twin Peaks, gay lifestyles were so utterly *verboten* that queers were forced to do their drinking, dating and socialising hidden in dark, windowless bars. Being gay was a felony (upgraded in the 1930s to a 'psychological disorder') in the United States for such a long time that there was every reason to try to protect your anonymity.

Twin Peaks' emergence was as timely as it was revolutionary. Its metamorphosis from a traditional pub to a gathering place for a (primarily male) gay clientele came just as the neighbourhood was undergoing its cataclysmic shift from working-class Irish-Catholic residents to out-and-proud queers. Twin Peaks' prime location on what was fast becoming the gayest corner of the gayest street in the country quickly attracted an ever-increasing crowd of upfront gay men who chatted and socialised unashamedly in the windows. And frequenting the bar was more than just a good time – it was a political act.

In a neighbourhood where youth and beauty are prized, the bar's predominantly grey-haired clientele has nowadays earned it the catty nickname 'the glass coffin'. Which hasn't daunted its many regulars, who are nothing if not survivors. The beautiful stained-glass lamps, interior balcony and carved

wooden bar create a dignified atmosphere, enhancing Twin Peaks' venerable reputation as a 'conversation bar'.

If you stop by, you won't see the original owners (they recently sold the business to some of their friendly, long-standing bartenders), but you will be seeing a living slice of gay history.

Sightseeing

rapidly in the 1970s as gay residents began moving in, buying businesses and battered Victorians and Edwardians at rock-bottom prices and renovating them, turning them into what is now some of the city's priciest – and prettiest – real estate. The neighbourhood was devastated, and politically galvanised, during the AIDS crisis of the 1980s and early 1990s. Today, with the availability of HIV drugs that can make the disease a long-term, manageable condition and with political clout that has put several mayors and numerous city supervisors into office, the locals seem more interested in shopping than storming City Hall.

During the week, the Castro is a relatively sleepy neighbourhood, a comfortable hub that lives up to its nickname of the 'Castro Village'. During the weekends (and of course, during June Pride; *see p189*), the streets explode with visitors and locals who come for the Castro's biggest commodity: the exuberantly queer party atmosphere.

Whatever the day, leather chaps and buffed biceps, long blond hair and divine drag are as comfortably at home here as Armani suits. A huge rainbow flag flies over **Harvey Milk Plaza** (the Muni stop at the corner of Market and Castro Streets). The plaza is named after the camera-shop owner and activist who in 1977 became California's first openly gay elected official, but was assassinated the following year (*see p15*). The dazzling art deco **Castro Theatre** (*see p230*) is the architectural flagship of the block, being the first building by Bay Area architect Timothy L Pflueger. In 1977 it became the 100th structure to be designated a US National Historic Landmark: a peek at the gold and murals inside will confirm why.

In the run-up to the Castro's uproarious Halloween (*see p192*) extravaganza, crowds fill **Cliff's Variety** (479 Castro Street, at 18th, 431 5365) to pick out costumes. During the rest of the year, Cliff's is an old-fashioned five-and-dime that functions as the local general/hardware store and toy shop. On the next block down Castro Street, **Skin Zone** (No.575, 626 7933) occupies Harvey Milk's former camera shop and campaign headquarters, considered by many to be as significant in the history of gay politics as New York's Stonewall bar; the martyred Milk (*see p15*) is now commemorated by a small plaque in the pavement and a modest mural. The other essential cultural landmark here is the Twin Peaks bar (*see p89* **A touch of glass**).

For a great view of the Castro from above, get lunch to go and wander up to **Corona Heights** (walk all the way up 16th Street to Flint Street, then take a right; the bare red rock of Corona looms overhead). Along with

Canine capers in the **Castro**.

beautiful vistas, you'll see plenty of Castro pooches and their human pets. If you've got tinies in tow, you can also check out the petting zoo at **Randall Museum** (*see p195*).

Noe Valley

Quaint **Noe Valley**, roughly bordered by 20th, Dolores, 30th and Douglass Streets, is a self-contained village cut off from the rest of the city by steep hills on every side. In the 1970s it was a fairly bohemian mix of straight, gay, working-class and white-collar residents. It became more family-oriented in the 1980s and 1990s, a place where well-paid young couples could retreat to raise a family away from the chaos of the rest of the city. The bustle of Mission Street feels a million miles away, though it's only ten blocks. **Twin Peaks** overlooks the area from the west and its flanks offer attractive views of the East Bay.

Noe Valley's high street, **24th Street**, is outfitted with all the amenities you might expect: gourmet groceries, romantic restaurants and boutiques where the owners welcome regulars by their first names. When hunger strikes there's a brunch at **Miss Millie's** (*see p146*) with your name on it, while a few blocks off the main drag, **Lovejoy's Antiques & Tea Room** (*see p146*) seems to think it's in the Lake District, complete with Victorian high teas. For all their bourgeois affectations, the Noe Valley crowd are very community-minded. When high rents nearly drove **Cover to Cover Booksellers** (1307 Castro Street, at at 24th, 282 8080) out of business, the neighbourhood rallied to support them with extra investment – now there are three independent bookstores here. All of which makes for pleasant strolling.

Haight, Western Addition & Hayes Valley

A notoriety of psychedelics, a diversity of cultures and a tourist centre coming out of the shadows.

The Haight's hippie heyday is long past, but there's still a relaxed anything-goes ethos round here that can make anyone feel at home. There's plenty of grit too, with the homeless problem in the **Haight** an ongoing political battle. The **Western Addition**, having faced good times and bad, remains one of the city's most interesting, least understood neighbourhoods. If this part of the city feels slightly separate from the rest, that's because people here are still intent on doing their own thing.

Haight-Ashbury

The ornate Victorians, many of them emblazoned with peace signs or painted funky colours, are a reminder of both the Haight's 19th-century resort-town beginnings and its more famous incarnation as the birthplace of free love. The district was born in the 1870s with the development of Golden Gate Park; at that time, it was mostly uninhabited except for dairy farms, but the Nob Hill elite soon began building weekend homes here. Spared by the 1906 earthquake, the neighbourhood continued to grow, with displaced citizens moving here and to the nearby Western Addition from other districts. In the 1950s, as part of the middle-class 'white flight' from inner city areas across the US, many residents fled for the suburbs, deserting the rambling Victorians. This set the stage for the Haight-Ashbury's most important era: student bohemians started moving in, *et voilà!* the hippie commune was born.

The flowering of the most famous youth culture movement in history was due to the confluence of huge anti-Vietnam War protests and 1967's Summer of Love, during which some 25,000 people gathered for the Human Be-In. Musicians and artists populated the old houses in the area: the Grateful Dead lived at 710 Ashbury Street and Jefferson Airplane at 2400 Fulton Street, while Janis Joplin and her band Big Brother & the Holding Company camped out at 124 Lyon Street, with Robert Crumb (*see p94* **SF heroes: Robert Crumb**) just down the street at No.301. As speed and heroin began

to replace LSD and marijuana as the drugs of choice, unsavoury characters like cult murderer Charles Manson (who lived at 636 Cole Street) descended on the area as gurus to the impressionable and the work of idealistic political groups like the Diggers and the San Francisco Mime Troupe (*see p247* **Mime's the word**) was buried beneath all the hangers-on.

Nearly 40 years later, teenage runaways still gravitate to the area's central axis **Haight Street** (*see p93* **Denizens of iniquity**). Shoe stores and edgy clothing boutiques line the main drag, although shops selling drug paraphernalia and Eastern esoterica still give the place a carnival atmosphere at weekends. Traces of the radical past linger at Bound Together Books (1369 Haight Street, at Masonic, 431 8355), run by an anarchist collective, and the Haight-Ashbury Free Clinic (*see p282*) and most people enjoy the peculiarly mellow coffee houses, but few can help but be disappointed to discover the fabled Haight-Ashbury is merely a corner at which Haight meets Ashbury Street.

Gorgeous Victorians in the **Western Addition**. *See p92*.

For a nostalgia trip, book the 'Flower Child' room at the Red Victorian (*see p49*), next door to worker-owned Red Vic Movie House (*see p200*). Amoeba Music (*see p182*), housed in a converted bowling alley, offers a huge variety of music and the Booksmith (*see p165*) holds frequent readings. The best place for a tipple is the Persian bar Aub Zam Zam (*see p156*).

At the western end of Haight Street, cross Stanyan Street and you'll enter **Golden Gate Park** (*see p107*). You can also walk a couple of blocks north and explore the park's grand entrance, the Panhandle.

The eastern half of Haight street, between Divisadero and Octavia Streets, is known as the **Lower Haight**. It's hipper, harsher and frankly more interesting than the Upper Haight. Browse the flea-market antique stores or take advantage of the higher-grade eateries (*see p136 and p146*). The area's main intersection is at Haight and Fillmore Streets, from which shops and cafés radiate in all directions. A good option for beer lovers is **Toronado**, while for Lower Haight nightlife try **Nickie's BBQ** or the **Noc Noc Bar** (for all, *see p156*).

Cole Valley

If Haight Street gets too intense, head south into stylish, small-town Cole Valley. Among the charming places on Cole Street are **Le Boulange de Cole** (No.1000, at Parnassus, 242 2442) and postage-stamp sized **Zazie** (No.941; *see p142* **Later than breakfast, sooner than Monday**). To walk off your full belly, wander south up Cole and then hike to the top of Tank Hill. The views are excellent.

The Western Addition

The Western Addition was not only the city's first suburb, it was its first multicultural neighbourhood. Mapped out in the 1860s to accommodate the post-Gold Rush population boom, the Western Addition was home to a thriving Jewish community from the 1890s and 1930s, with three synagogues, a Yiddish cultural centre and dozens of kosher butchers, bakers and restaurants in the area.

Recovering quickly from the 1906 earthquake and fire, the **Fillmore District** – the heart of the Western Addition – sprang to life as displaced residents, including the Japanese, began moving in. **Japantown** grew to cover more than 20 city blocks, but its residents were interned after the attack on Pearl Harbor and lost their homes and businesses. The thousands of black Southerners who had come west for work moved into the empty houses, and the character of the place changed again. Because

the Western Addition didn't observe racial covenant laws that prevented African-Americans from owning land elsewhere in the city, a vibrant neighbourhood took shape. Soon it was known as the 'Harlem of the West'.

Fillmore District

In the 1940s and 1950s Fillmore was a mecca for jazz and blues, but in the 1960s it was declared a slum by the San Francisco Redevelopment Agency and torn apart in the guise of urban renewal. The windy intersection of Fillmore and Eddy Streets is a legacy of the ill-conceived plan. Long an empty lot, it was to be the site of a Blue Note jazz club, a movie theatre, even a jazz museum – none of which has yet to come to fruition. Today there are some hopes that the 'Fillmore Jazz Preservation District' will finally begin to live up to its name (*see p214* **Stompin' in the Fillmore**).

The area has already hosted one musical revival. In the 1960s and 1970s Bill Graham's **Fillmore Auditorium** (at the corner of Geary; *see p218*) was its epicentre, booking such acts as the Grateful Dead, Jimi Hendrix and the Velvet Underground. Another rock 'n' roll icon, the now-defunct Winterland, was where the Sex Pistols gave their famous last performance. Look closely in the lobby at Post and Steiner and you'll find a small photo exhibit commemorating the spot. An eerier landmark is next door to the Fillmore. Now the Geary Station Post Office, this was the first home of the notorious Jim Jones and his People's Temple. In 1978 Jones and almost 1,000 disciples – the majority of them Fillmore residents – committed suicide or were murdered in Jonestown, Guyana.

Today the Western Addition is a mix of African-Americans, young hipsters, Russian senior citizens and other immigrants, with architecture that ranges from spectacular Victorians to bland high-rises and dismal housing projects. Even here there are signs of gentrification. In 2000 the Church of St John Coltrane was evicted after three decades of jazz services; designer boutique **Joe Pye** (351 Divisadero Street, at Oak, 355 1051) now occupies the site. (The church may find a new home at 930 Gough Street, at Turk Street; call 673 3572 and press 6 for details.) Still, the area remains mostly chain-free. Browse the smattering of antique and novelty stores on Divisadero, between Page and Fulton Streets, or join locals at the always-packed **Café Abir** (1300 Fulton Street; *see p146*). Keeping things real on the 'D' (as the drag is sometimes called) are African-American barbershops and braiding salons, emporiums selling tribal masks and incense, and African restaurants.

Denizens of iniquity

Haight-Ashbury may have been world news in the late '60s, but over the years the counter-culture has atrophied into several subtypes of putative outsider, all of whom are denizens of Haight Street. In Zona Rosa (No.1797, at Shrader Street, 668 7717) you'll find **Faux-Homeless Punk Kid** sporting ripped Dead Milkmen T-shirts and studded leathers. They're most likely listening to the Beatles on a concealed iPod, though, for they are the spawn of nice families in suburban East Bay. At the excellent Noc Noc (No.557; *see p156*) you'll encounter **Party Goth**. Paying respect to Robert Smith with pewter-coloured skin, inky-black hair and got-a-habit slenderness, their devotion to dark nihilism visibly wavers as they happily quaff Sierra Nevadas and smoke clove cigarettes, tackling such edgy subjects as 'George Bush is an assclown' and 'Yuppies go to hell'.

And why should the young 'uns have all the fun? Ben & Jerry's (corner of Haight and Ashbury Streets, 626 4143) is the natural habitat of **Alt-Lifestyle Dabbler**. More of a frequent browser than a Haight Street mainstay (usually coming in from Marin), he pledges allegiance to the organic lifestyle by ordering soy chai lattes at Starbucks and scorns the devastation wrought by SUVs while driving an oversize Suburu Outback. He drinks mass-marketed microbrews rather than 'too corporate' Budweiser, says 'yoga not Zoloft' but scores medicinal marijuana off his glaucomic friends, and loudly abhors mainstream cinema before rushing home to catch *Survivor*.

Finally, head to Planetweavers Treasure Store (No.1573, at Clayton Street, 864 4415, www.planetweavers.com) where you'll get to shop with **Middle-Aged Ponytail Man**. He is recognised not by the rat's tail hanging from his balding pate, but by his conversation: a litany of narcolepsy-inducing tales designed to convince you he was part of the original Haight scene. His uniform is pleated khaki shorts, jewellery from developing nations and an iridescent water bottle that could survive a fall from Yosemite's Half Dome but will never make it to the top of Mount Tam. Tread carefully. MAPM is a peace-loving animal, but could bore you to death. In an emergency, point to the nearest Latino, say 'Omigod, Carlos Santana!' and run like hell.

Alamo Square

Most visitors come here to see the famous **Postcard Row** of tidy pastel Victorians on the east side of Alamo Square Park, and the sweeping view of downtown behind them. The park is one of the loveliest in town, and there are many fine Victorians in the area; among them the ornate Italianate **Westerfield House**, at Fulton and Scott, dates to 1882.

SF heroes Robert Crumb

Sightseeing

From his early childhood in Philadelphia, when his older brother forced him to draw comics, Robert Crumb's twisted sensibility has bled into virtually everything he has put on paper.

In 1966, at the age of 23, Crumb moved to Haight-Ashbury. It was here that he first dropped acid – and the creations resulting from his experimentation were to make him the father of underground comics. LSD and the counter-culture that sprang up around its use removed virtually all boundaries for Crumb, liberating him financially, artistically and psychologically from the need to be accepted by the American mainstream (he once held a job drawing greetings cards in Cleveland, Ohio). He was able to indulge his lust for plush-bottomed women with impunity, while gaining notoriety for his wildly inventive and intensely surreal portrayals of American life. Heaping derision on 'normal' society became his ticket into a culture he alternately worshipped and mocked. Crumb's *Zap* comics introduced Mr Natural and Devil Girl, his object of perpetual desire, the hedonistic and oversexed Fritz the Cat, Whiteman and Flakey Foont. Such characters gave voice and, perhaps more importantly for those under the influence of hallucinogens, visual inspiration to the psychedelic sensibility of Haight-Ashbury throughout the 1960s and into the 1970s.

Early successes in San Francisco (including his now-emblematic *Keep on Truckin'* panels and the album sleeve for Big Brother & the Holding Company's *Cheap Thrills*), as well as a growing string of publications devoted to his work, made Crumb realise that he despised all the things for which he'd previously yearned. Over time, Crumb began to lambast even the hippies that first recognised his talents, but his work continued to evolve beyond acid-addled pseudo-pornography to become thoroughgoing social critique.

Now in self-imposed exile in France, Crumb is what he was before gaining notoriety: a misogynist, bespectacled geek, bitter misanthrope, rejected romantic and an acerbic satirist. Even what he hoped would be his ultimate revenge – becoming so famous and successful that it provoked jealousy in those who had belittled him – has failed to staunch his venom. Yet Crumb's prodigious influence in forging the hippie aesthetic can still be seen today in touches like the massive, disembodied female legs (complete with fishnet stockings and bright red pumps) that sprout from the front of the Piedmont Boutique costume shop on Haight Street. A true misfit, Crumb's skilled appropriation of the art of childhood – comics and cartoon books – as a tool for brutal social satire has become one of the closest things to an original artistic vision that American culture has produced over the last 40 years.

What a Crumb.

Japantown

Three long commercial blocks and a compound-like shopping centre is all that's left of what once may have been the country's largest Japantown. Devastated by the forced relocation of all Japanese-Americans during World War II, the community is now home to only a tiny percentage of the city's 12,000 Japanese-American citizens. Japantown provides support for the elderly, history lessons for its youth, and a banquet of aesthetic and pop cultural delights.

At the heart of it all is the **Japan Center** (*see p160*), a complex of shops, restaurants, an eight-screen movie theatre and a popular traditional bathhouse. Anchoring the centre is the **Peace Pagoda**, which becomes a hub of activity during the Cherry Blossom Festival (*see p188*) and the Nihonmachi Street Fair on the first weekend in August.

On Saturdays the Center is thronged with multi-generational family groups eating lunch, and youngsters feeding their obsession for all things Japanese. Browse the latest manga at the only branch outside Japan of **Kinokuniya Bookstore** (Kinokuniya Building, 1581 Webster Street, 567 7625) or pick your way through the numerous speciality shops selling teas, kimonos and Hello Kitty accessories.

For a change of scene, the block-long pedestrian-only **Buchanan Mall** (at Post Street) is an attractively authentic re-creation of a Japanese shopping district. To gain some cultural context, the **National Japanese American Historical Society** (684 Post Street, between Buchanan and Laguna, 921 5007, www.nikkeiheritage.org) and nearby **Japanese American Community Center** (1840 Sutter Street, at Webster, 567 5505, www.jcccnc.org) display archive photographs and host exhibitions on Japanese-American life. You can also relax in the **Kabuki Springs & Spa** (*see p182*) or drop in to **Sain Saine** (upper level of the Miyako Mall, adjacent to the Radisson Miyako, corner of Post and Laguna Streets, 292 3542) for some reflexology.

East of the Japan Center you'll also find the impressively modern **St Mary's Cathedral**.

Cathedral of St Mary of the Assumption

1111 Gough Street, at Geary Boulevard (567 2020/ www.stmarycathedralsf.org). Bus 2, 3, 4, 38.
Open 6.45am-4pm Mon-Fri; 6.45am-5.30pm Sat; 6.45am-4pm Sun. **Map** p310 F4.
Dominating the skyline for miles around, the exterior resembles the blades of a gigantic washing machine, but the inspiring interior has towering stained-glass windows and a massive pipe organ.

Hayes Valley

Typical San Francisco. Take an urban planning nightmare – let's say a freeway has been built that completely rips apart the fabric of a community – then just reverse it. Hayes Valley, a small neighbourhood just west of the Civic Center, was overshadowed by the Central Freeway. Then the 1989 quake all but destroyed it. Its removal completed the transformation of Hayes Valley from drug- and prostitution-riddled red-light district to possibly the hippest urban shopping area in San Francisco (*see p167* **Hayes Street chic**). Streets that once sat under a tangle of concrete overpasses now have sidewalk cafés, boutiques and art galleries – and even True Sake (*see p179*), the country's first specialist sake shop.

Though new shops and cafés open all the time, many have stayed the course, like **Powell's Place** (511 Hayes Street, at Octavia, 863 1404), a soul-food cafeteria and long-time neighbourhood fixture. It's also home to an active community association that fights to keep the chainstores out – it recently blocked plans to open a Starbucks – and has battled for years to close the Fell Street Exit ramp. The activists won in 2003, sounding the final death knell for the ill-fated Central Freeway. Plans for a tree-lined boulevard along Octavia Street are under way; it should be completed in 2005.

During the day Hayes Street is full of well-dressed couples shopping for modernist furniture and brunching on champagne and oysters at **Absinthe** (No.388; *see p136*), a *belle époque* French restaurant with tables spilling on to the pavement; pre- and post-symphony or opera, punters fill the tables at **Hayes Street Grill** (No.320, at Franklin, 863 5545, www.hayesstreetgrill.com), open since 1979. **Suppenküche** (525 Laguna; *see p136*) feels like an alpine lodge and makes the ideal restaurant/bar in which to end a Hayes Street jaunt. But a word of caution: be wary of walking west of Laguna Street at night – the area changes abruptly and can feel a bit dicey.

The internationally touted **Zuni Café** (1658 Market Street; *see p123*) anchors a mini-neighbourhood of its own along Market Street, just south of Hayes Valley. During the dot-com boom this was a shopping hub for antiques and upmarket interior accessories; it remains a good area to explore. Nearby, the city's oldest Harley-Davidson dealership is **Dudley Perkins Co** (66 Page Street, at Gough, 703 9494, www.dpchd.com). In operation since 1914, it's a veritable museum of gleaming hogs, vintage artefacts and rare photographs.

Sightseeing

Pacific Heights to the Golden Gate Bridge

High society, engineering brilliance and some simply stupendous views.

Crissy Field. See p98.

Pacific Heights and San Francisco's northern waterfront command some of the best views the city has to offer, but most people visit for one sight alone: the **Golden Gate Bridge**. A shame given that this area, which stretches from Bush Street to the Bay and from Van Ness Avenue to the Presidio, has much more to offer than that single engineering marvel. The **Pacific Heights** mansions overlook some of the most revered coastline in the United States, while the vast expanses of wooded trails and stunning cliffs in the **Presidio** run up against the well-scrubbed opulence of the **Marina**.

Pacific Heights

True to its name twice over, Pacific Heights (known to those from more ethnically diverse parts of the city as 'Specific Whites') is perched high over the water and its mansions are home to the cream of San Francisco's high society: billionaire socialites Gordon and Ann Getty have a house here; novelist Danielle Steel lives in the ornate **Spreckels Mansion**, which spans the entire block between Jackson, Gough,

Washington and Octavia Streets. (The address is 2080 Washington, but don't attempt a personal visit.) Thousands of lesser-known millionaires pass unnoticed, shopping for milk and caviar in their neighbourhood corner marts.

A Pacific Heights stroll is optimal for either trying to make rich friends or marvelling at sumptuous real estate (the average price of a home in Pacific Heights was $2,330,585 in 2002 and hasn't stopped rising). The stretch of **Broadway** between Divisadero Street and the Presidio affords some of the best architecture, although the blue-and-white **Octagon House** (*see p98*) on Gough Street, open for viewing a few days a month, is on the other side of the hill. The city's only Queen Anne-style Victorian that is open to the public, **Haas-Lilienthal House** (*see p97*), is also here, offering a rare chance to see the pristine insides of one of the city's grand residences. A rest stop at nearby **Lafayette Park** (Washington and Gough Streets) or **Alta Plaza Park** (Jackson and Steiner Streets) has the added benefit of views of nearby homes, the city and pedigreed dogs walking their pedigreed owners.

Upper Fillmore Street, between Bush and Jackson, is the region's central shopping hub, with plenty of smart shops and restaurants. **Vivande Porta Via** (2125 Fillmore Street, at California, 346 4430) made a name for itself as cookery queen Elizabeth David's favourite San Francisco lunch spot – quite a recommendation, since she had several thousand others to choose from. A few blocks west, you'll find pricey and elegant antique shops, ateliers and boutiques on **Sacramento Street,** between Presidio Avenue and Spruce Street, while nearby charity shops stock the cast-offs of the rich and famous. For the ultimate in canine decadence, **George** (*see p185*) on California Street proffers gourmet own-baked doggy confections and couture canine sweaters. It seems hardly conceivable now that poet Allen Ginsberg should have launched a literary renaissance in 1955 when he gave his

first public reading of *Howl* at the long-vanished Six Gallery (*see below* **Go! Go! Gone**). The site now occupied by a rug shop, the **Silkroute International Oriental** (3119 Fillmore Street, between Filbert and Pixley Streets, 563 4936).

Haas-Lilienthal House

2007 Franklin Street, between Washington & Jackson Streets (441 3000/www.sfheritage.org/ house.html). Bus 1, 12, 19, 27, 47, 49. **Open** noon-3pm Wed, Sat; 11am-4pm Sun. **Admission** $8. **Credit** AmEx, MC, V. **Map** p310 F3.
Built in 1886 by Bavarian William Haas, the house has elaborate wooden gables, a circular tower and 28 rooms, clearly marking it as being in the Queen Anne style. Fully restored and filled with period furniture, the house also contains photos documenting its history and that of the family that lived in it until 1972. It's maintained by San Francisco Architectural Heritage, which also organises walking tours.

Go! Go! Gone

The poster promised a 'remarkable collection of angels on one stage reading their poetry... No charge, small collection for wine, and postcards. Charming event.' The event was to be held on 7 October 1955 at the **Six Gallery,** a former auto repair shop at 3119 Fillmore Street that had been renovated to include a raised area of the floor for a stage. As the evening got under way Jack Kerouac dutifully took up the collection from an audience that included Neal Cassady and Lawrence Ferlinghetti, and toddled off to purchase a few gallon jugs. Suitably fortified, the assembled listeners settled down to hear Philip Lamantia, Michael McClure, Philip Whalen, Gary Snyder and an unknown 29-year-old named Allen Ginsberg, all introduced by the well-established pacifist poet Kenneth Rexroth.

Ginsberg had never read in public, but as he began to incant his as-yet unfinished long poem *Howl* at an increasingly infectious tempo, the crowd took up Kerouac's cries of 'Go! Go! Go!' in time to Ginsberg's delivery. When he had finished, the audience was transfixed and the elder statesman Rexroth was seen wiping tears from his eyes. Regardless of how the story is retold or mythologised, one thing is clear: those present had witnessed a seminal event in American letters. They had heard what the world at large would soon know as one of the most recognisable voices of American poetry, reading what would become his best-known work. For reasons no one is able to recall

there are recordings of every other reading that night, including Gary Snyder's 'A Berry Feast' that followed Ginsberg's performance, but there is no surviving recording of that night's *Howl*.

After the Six Gallery closed, the space was to become Silkroute International Oriental (*see above*), a store whose proprietors sell Asian rugs and curiosities, making a strange contrast with the store's counter-culture legacy. The portion of raised floor is, however, still visible. There Ginsberg first chanted: 'I saw the best minds of my generation destroyed by madness, starving hysterical naked,/ dragging themselves through the negro streets at dawn looking for an angry fix...'.

City Lights (*see p165*), the bookstore and press that in 1956 first published *Howl and Other Poems* in 1956, remains a vital presence in North Beach. Under Beat icon Lawrence Ferlinghetti, the shop still champions the cause of civil liberties, as it had to when defending its right to publish the poem following the seizure of copies of *Howl* by US Customs on grounds of obscenity. Ferlinghetti's impassioned words in defence of the book are as salient now as then: 'It is not the poet but what he observes which is revealed as obscene. The great obscene wastes of *Howl* are the sad wastes of the mechanised world, lost among atom bombs and insane nationalisms.' *Howl and Other Poems,* still published by City Lights in the original black-and-white Pocket Poets Series format, remains one of its bestsellers.

Octagon House

2645 Gough Street, at Union Street (441 7512). Bus 41, 45. **Open** *noon-3pm 2nd & 4th Thur, 2nd Sun of mth.* **Admission** *free.* **Map** *p310 E2.*

The 1861 Octagon House houses the small Museum of Colonial and Federal Decorative Arts, but is most notable as one of two surviving examples of eight-sided homes in San Francisco. Nationwide over 700 such houses were built in the belief that they improved their occupants' health by letting in more natural light. Originally owned (when nearby Cow Hollow still contained cows) by wealthy dairyman Charles Gough, Octagon House stands on the street to which he magnanimously gave his own name while on the city's naming commission – he also named an adjacent street 'Octavia' in honour of his sister.

Cow Hollow

From Pacific Heights it's a few blocks downhill towards the Bay to Cow Hollow. Once a dairy pasture, hence the name, the area is still serene, but its grazers are now of the well-heeled, two-legged kind. Centred on **Union Street**, between Broderick and Buchanan, you'll find chic bars and restaurants in carefully restored Victorians. Hiding in an alleyway is Carol Doda's **Champagne and Lace Lingerie Boutique** (1850 Union Street, between Octavia and Laguna, 776 6900), owned by the city's first topless dancer (*see p76* **SF heroes: Carol Doda**). Even more impressive than Carol's fabled 44 inches are the domes of the **Vedanta Temple** (2963 Webster Street, at Filbert Street, 922 2323) a short stroll away. Dating to 1905, the temple is dedicated to an ancient strain of Hinduism that holds all religions to be viable paths to spiritual awareness; accordingly, its six domes each represent a different architectural style, with elaborate Moorish arches, a Saracenic crescent, a Russian onion-style dome and Victorian gingerbread trim.

Marina & the waterfront

In a city justifiably famous for its gay scene, the pastel-painted Marina, between Fort Mason and the Presidio, is conspicuously straight. It's also one big pick-up joint. By night its bars fill with bare-bellied twentysomethings sipping cocktails and making eye contact, and for decades even the Safeway at 15 Marina Boulevard was a famous pulling spot. Built on soft rubble from the 1906 earthquake, the Marina shook harder than any other part of San Francisco in 1989's Loma Prieta quake. Buildings collapsed hither and thither, but the only reminders are renovated pavements and suspiciously new structures among the otherwise staid townhouses.

The main drag is **Chestnut Street**. The stretch between Fillmore and Divisadero Streets is a shrine to self-indulgence, with clothing boutiques and beauty salons seeming to occupy fully half the shopfronts. The **House of Magic** (No.2025, at Fillmore, 346 2218) lowers the tone with fright wigs, fake dog-doo and other unforgivable practical jokes, while the recently renovated **Presidio Cinema** (No.2340, at Scott, 922 1381) lends the place a little culture. Woodsy **Grove** (*see p147*) café is a good stopping point if you need more time to watch the preened denizens of the area 'fabu-lapping' – looking fabulous while walking laps up and down the street, sipping gourmet coffee.

The vast sloping lawns of the **Marina Green** (Marina Boulevard, between Scott and Webster Streets) are San Franciscans' favourite place to fly kites, jog or picnic, with dizzying views of the Golden Gate Bridge and the Bay. At the end of the yacht harbour jetty to the west of the Marina Green is the amazing **Wave Organ**, an underwater artwork whose pipes and benches, built from the remains of San Francisco's dismantled cemeteries, make music with the ebb and flow of the Bay currents.

At the eastern edge of the Marina waterfront, **Fort Mason** (*see p100*) started as a US Army command post in the 1850s. Today the reconditioned military buildings maintain a forbidding mien, but actually house some fine little museums and exhibition spaces. For the 1915 Panama-Pacific Exposition, a mile-long (1.6-kilometre) swath of temporary structures was erected all the way from here to Fort Point. When the fair was over the fantastical city-within-a-city was torn down to make way for the houses we see today. Yet a small part of the fantasyscape survived: the **Palace of Fine Arts** (*see p100*), set in a little park at the western edge of the Marina. The original plaster edifice was expensively converted to concrete just in time for the 1969 opening of the adjacent **Exploratorium** (*see p196*), one of the world's first hands-on science museums, still deservedly popular with children.

Further along is **Crissy Field**. Originally dunelands, it became a dump and staging ground for the Army, before being paved over and converted into a military airfield after World War II. Years of restoration work paid off in 2001, when a revamped Crissy Field opened to the public. Some of the original marshland and coastal dunes have been restored and the airfield is now an endless, beautiful lawn. It's the traditional place to watch the Fourth of July fireworks and the Fleet Week military airshow (for both, *see p188*). Under Golden Gate Bridge, the northernmost tip of the Presidio is **Fort Point** (556 1693), which is open to the public.

Mansions, hills...

...and beautiful bridges.

HILL

PREPARE TO STOP FOR VEHICLES EXITING DRIVEWAYS

Salty batteries

Though associated with the peace movement in recent times, San Francisco has been a military outpost since Spanish explorers first landed on its shores. Due to the tactical significance of the Bay as a major shipping port and base for military operations, fortifications lined every coastal point that could conceivably hold them. Ruins of US military fortifications can be seen throughout San Francisco, Marin County, on Angel Island and even on Alcatraz. Their careful placement ensured a number of guns could be brought to bear on any single target within the Bay; in the case of the massive 16-inch guns, they could hit targets over 25 miles (40 kilometres) out to sea. The guns are long gone – as are the US military activities that accompanied them – but the bunkers and batteries remain as silent testament to the ship spotters and artillery men, who were once the only souls authorised to view the spectacular landscape from its best vantage points.

Soldiers would often sleep through the frigid coastal nights alongside their guns amid shells and magazines of explosives, but the bunkers now play host to hikers taking in views of the coastline or of massive cargo ships slowly migrating through the Golden Gate. Batteries Godfrey and Crosby are good to visit, as both of them are easily accessible on foot.

Construction began on **Battery Godfrey** in 1892 and required 10,800 cubic yards (8,257 cubic metres) of concrete and 17,000 pounds (7,711 kilogrammes) of steel reinforcement – a large portion of which were recycled streetcar rails. In 1895 three massive 12-inch guns were installed, each firing 1,700-pound (485-kilogrammes) shells up to ten miles (16 kilometres). It was at that time the largest battery in the United States, and the first to use 12-inch guns. Built seven years later, the **Battery Crosby** held two six-inch guns with a range of eight miles (13 kilometres). Designed to defend the underwater minefields outside the Golden Gate, they could fire two rounds per minute. With their guns rendered obsolete by new military technology, the batteries were decommissioned in 1943 having never fired an angry shot.

Arm yourself with a bottle of sake and a blanket, and head south from Fort Point down the trail that parallels Lincoln Boulevard. You'll find Godfrey just past the intersection of Lincoln Boulevard, Ralston Avenue and Merchant Road, through the parking lot at Langdon Court and past an abandoned building; the dirt track to Battery Crosby is signposted further down the same trail. (If you reach Baker Beach, you've gone too far.) Whichever you choose, make sure you're still there for sunset.

Fort Mason

Marina Boulevard, at Buchanan Street (441 3400/ www.fortmason.org). Bus 10, 22, 28, 30, 47, 49. **Map** p310 E1.

This collection of ex-military buildings houses a bevy of cultural institutions. In Building C the African-American Historical and Cultural Society Museum (441 0640) is right across the hall from the Museo ItaloAmericano (673 2200, www.museoitaloamericano. org). Both museums have changing exhibitions on their respective ethnic themes. Shows at the Museum of Craft and Folk Art (775 0991, www.mocfa.org) in Building A range from bookbinding to handmade furniture. All the museums offer free admission on the first Wednesday of the month. Other outlets include the airy SFMOMA Artists' Gallery (Building A, 441 4777), which sells and rents out contemporary works by Northern Californians, while the Book Bay Bookstore (Building C, 771 1076) sells rejected stock from the public library, as well as LPs and art at rock-bottom prices. Fort Mason also houses the Magic Theatre (*see p245*) and other small performance spaces. Greens (Building A, 771 6222) is one of the city's favourite vegetarian restaurants, with high ceilings framing a wide view of the Marina and the Bay. A constant array of changing displays is on view at two waterside pavilions (actually reconstituted shipbuilding bays); concerts, gardening competitions and even the Spiral Dance, which is the local pagan community's major Halloween fête, are held here. Note that all the museums are closed on Mondays, only MoCFA is open on a Tuesday.

Palace of Fine Arts

Lyon Street, at Bay Street (567 6642/ www.palaceoffinearts.org). Bus 22, 28, 29, 30, 41, 43, 45. **Map** p309 D2.

Local architect Bernard Maybeck's pièce de résistance, the Palace is a neo-classical domed rotunda supported by a curved colonnade topped with friezes and statues of weeping women, and flanked by a pond alive with ducks, swans and lily pads. Initially meant to be only a temporary structure, it has been repeatedly saved by generations of San Franciscans. The Palace has served as everything from lighted tennis courts in 1934 to a motor pool for dignitaries assisting in the creation of the United Nations after World War II. As it fell into neglect and disrepair, it ignominiously served as a telephone book distribution centre and Fire Department headquarters. Demolished in 1964 – only the shell of the rotunda remained – it was reconstructed at ten times the original cost. You can see its magnificent dome from many parts of the city and it remains one of the most atmospheric spots in San Francisco.

Golden Gate Bridge

Few cities need bridges as much as San Francisco does. Without the Golden Gate Bridge connecting it to the northern half of the state and the Bay Bridge (see p64) connecting it to the rest of the country, San Francisco would be isolated at the tip of a mountainous peninsula. Yes, it thrived that way for almost a century, but the rise of the automobile meant that ferries and ocean liners were no longer sufficient. So bridges were built, and built with a bang. Within a few years the city's spans were the most famous in the US and now for the princely sum of $5 (the toll is charged only on southbound journeys) motorists can enjoy one of the greatest bridges in the world.

Luminous symbol of San Francisco and of the Golden State itself, the **Golden Gate Bridge** (linking the Toll Plaza near the Presidio to Marin County, 921 5858, www.goldengatebridge.org) may not be the longest in the world, but it is surely the most beautiful, certainly the most recognisable. Completed in 1937 after nearly five years under construction, the bridge's statistics alone are impressive: the towers are 746 feet (227 metres) high, the roadway 1.75 miles (nearly three kilometres) long, and enough cable was used in its construction to encircle the globe three times. Since its completion more than 1,000 people have committed suicide plunging 250 feet (76 metres) or more into the water below.

Raw statistics can't convey the sense of awe the grandeur of the bridge inspires, especially close up, and no trip to San Francisco is complete without walking across. Drive, walk or catch a bus to the Toll Plaza, and head out on foot along the pedestrian walkway. Once you feel it thrumming beneath your feet, you'll understand even more why people feel such a strong connection to the span. There's no need to hike all the way if the 3.5-mile (5.5-kilometre) round-trip is too much, just go to the midway point and return.

The person most responsible for making the bridge a reality was a pugnacious Chicago engineer named Joseph Strauss. He spent over a decade lobbying to promote the idea and circumventing innumerable financial and

legal hurdles. But it was a little-known freelance architect named Irwin F Morrow who actually designed it, with his brilliantly simple plan selected in preference to Strauss's hideous and complicated cantilever design. The result was the unforgettable, curvaceous swoop that we still marvel at today.

Reputedly five times stronger than it needs to be, the Golden Gate Bridge has survived earthquakes, hurricane-force winds and 65 years of abuse without the slightest defect or sign of damage. Built to flex under pressure, it can sway 21 feet (more than six metres) and sag 10 feet (3 metres) while withstanding winds of up to 100mph (161kph), and can support the weight of bumper-to-bumper traffic across all six lanes at the same time as shoulder-to-shoulder pedestrians covering the walkways. When the massive 1989 earthquake devastated large portions of the Marina (see p98), the Golden Gate Bridge survived unscathed, but the virtual certainty of another earthquake of a similar (if not greater) magnitude prompted officials to undertake a seismic retrofitting project at a scale commensurate with the vastness of the bridge itself. This entailed a vehicle toll hike from $3 to $5 to help pay for the project. Reinforcing the bridge will require an estimated total of 22.3 million pounds (10.1 million kilogrammes) of structural steel and 24,000 cubic yards (680 cubic metres) of concrete; the second of three works phases is due for completion in 2005.

The bridge's name has nothing to do with its colour. Rather, it follows the official title of the narrow strait it spans: the **Golden Gate**. And the strait itself was not named (as logic might suggest) after the city's historical association with the Gold Rush, but was thus named by Captain John Fremont in 1846, two years before gold was discovered in the California foothills. He borrowed the name from the Golden Horn, the geologically similar channel linking the Black Sea to the Mediterranean. The bridge's stroke-of-genius orange colour was also an accident of fate: San Franciscans were so delighted by the reddish tint of the bridge's primer paint that the builders decided to stick with it, rather than paint the whole bridge the traditional grey or silver. Many myths surround the repainting of the bridge. It is not continually repainted, nor is it repainted every seven years. It has, in fact, been repainted only once. That required 2,206 gallons (8,350 litres) of paint, equivalent to more than 17,000 pints of beer. Completed in 1995, the repainting replaced the former lead-based paint with primer and topcoat designed to withstand the corrosive salt and fog that continually bathe the bridge; it should now require only periodic touchups.

Sightseeing

The Presidio

Called 'the prettiest piece of real estate in America', the **Presidio** is unquestionably among the most valuable. Situated perfectly at the northern tip of the city, overlooking the Bay, the Pacific Ocean and the Golden Gate Bridge, it is a location fit for gods but for centuries endured the workaday drudgery of life as a military base. Then, in 1994, a miracle happened: after 220 years in the hands of soldiers, the US Army handed the Presidio over to the Park Service, claiming it could no longer afford the expensive upkeep. Technically a National Park (along the lines of Yosemite or Yellowstone), the Presidio is actually managed by a confusing welter of agencies, including the Golden Gate National Recreation Area, the National Park Service and the controversial Presidio Trust, whose mission is to make the Presidio self-sustaining by building resorts and business parks on the more than seven million square yards (around six million square metres) of property, while maintaining its historic character. One such deal has allowed for construction of a massive complex due to house George Lucas's Industrial Light & Magic and LucasArts operations. Set to open in 2005, annual rent will be around $5.8 million. With continuing protests from the conservationists, development battles are likely to continue for some time. So, much of the Presidio remains in a state of arrested decay, artful and picturesque.

The tip of the **San Francisco Peninsula** was first established as a military outpost in 1776, when a group led by Captain Juan Bautista de Anza planted the Spanish flag here to protect the newly discovered San Francisco Bay. Claimed as a garrison first for Spain (*presidio* means fortress in Spanish) and then for Mexico, the United States took it over with the rest of California in 1848. The base grew rapidly and the US military embarked on a massive landscaping project that converted hundreds of acres of sandy, windswept moors into a tree-lined garden. Now totally demilitarised, it includes some 11 miles (18 kilometres) of hiking trails, 14 miles (22.5 kilometres) of bicycle routes and three miles (five kilometres) of beaches. The gate from Pacific Heights on Presidio Avenue and Jackson Street leads into fairytale woods, often shrouded in mist for an extra dash of melancholy. You can pick up a map for free at the various visitor centres; without a map, you'll probably get lost – often a pleasant experience in itself. Below we detail some of the main points of interest.

The centre of the Presidio is the **Main Post**, a complex of old buildings arrayed along parallel streets on the site of the original Spanish fort. Here you'll find a visitor centre (Officer's Club, Building 50, between Moraga and Arguello Streets, 561 4323), two 17th-century Spanish cannons on Pershing Square, and rows of Victorian-era military homes along Funston Avenue. Building 102 is home to the small **Presidio Museum**, which contains two earthquake shacks, reconstructed and furnished as they were when provided as housing after the 1906 quake. In the **San Francisco National Cemetery** (Lincoln Boulevard, at Sheridan Avenue) lie the remains of several notables, including over 450 'Buffalo Soldiers', African-American servicemen. Known to many only as the subject of the eponymous Bob Marley song, they served not only at the Battle of San Juan Hill (the only battle namechecked by Marley) alongside future President Theodore Roosevelt, but also throughout the Civil War, the Indian Wars, the Spanish-American War and virtually every conflict up to and including the Korean War – after which the US armed services were officially integrated. Two of the Buffalo Soldiers interred in the cemetery received the Medal of Honor, the highest military decoration.

Along the Presidio's western edge, **Baker Beach** (*see below* **Beaches: City sands**) is a favourite getaway, while **Mountain Lake Park** (access from Lake Street and Funston Avenue, at the southern end of the Presidio) is a relaxing idyll. Golfers nationwide were ecstatic when the ultra-exclusive **Presidio Golf Course** (*see p238*), formerly a private, officers-only club favoured by presidents and generals, opened its manicured fairways to the public. But most San Franciscans just love to wander hiking trails and little-used roads that criss-cross the park, admiring the remarkable hillside vistas and beautifully restored officers' homes. All in all, some 500 structures from the former military base remain, ranging from Civil War mansions to simple barracks. There are also many decommissioned batteries (*see p100* **Salty batteries**) that invite exploration.

Fort Point

Marine Drive, beneath Golden Gate Bridge (556 1693/www.nps.gov/fopo). Bus 28, 29. **Open** 10am-5pm Fri-Sun. **Admission** free. **Map** p308 A1.
The spectacular brick-built Fort Point was built between 1853 and 1861 to protect the city from a sea attack that never came. Its 126 cannons remained idle, and the fort was closed in 1900. Today the four-storey, open-roofed building houses various military exhibitions; children love to scamper among the battlements and passageways. You can climb on to the roof for a fabulous view of the underbelly of the Golden Gate Bridge. Interestingly, the bridge was built over Fort Point, whose construction predates it by more than seven decades. The fort's pier is famous as the spot where Kim Novak's character pretends to attempt suicide in Hitchcock's *Vertigo*.

Beaches City sands

Unlike in Southern California, the majority of beaches in and around San Francisco aren't great for swimming (*see p241* **Beaches: Shark attack!**), but their exceptional beauty makes for joyous strolling, picnicking and simply lounging around sucking in the extraordinary views. Free spirits may be more interested in some other spots around the city (*see p106* **Beaches: Bare-faced cheeks**), but even in San Francisco 'clothing optional' isn't obligatory – so here is a selection of locations for the more modest (beach) bum.

Running for almost a mile along the craggy Presidio shoreline, **Baker Beach** (*pictured*) is a great place to start. It's accessible, has great views and offers easy access to the city's most popular 'clothing optional' beach – the north end of the same stretch. In 1905 the US Army decided to use Baker as the hiding place for a huge 95,000-pound (43,091-kilogramme) cannon. The naval invasion it was built to repel never came, but a replica of the original has been installed for the curious.

Hidden between Baker Beach and Lincoln Park in the exclusive Seacliff neighbourhood, you'll find the exquisitely sheltered James D Phelan Beach. Better known as **China Beach** (Seacliff Avenue, off 26th Avenue, bus 1, 18, 29), it takes its nickname from the settlement of Chinese fishermen who camped here in the 19th century. Many locals consider it the finest of all San Francisco's beaches – indeed Seacliff residents would prefer to keep it for themselves, though by law it remains open to the public. Pacific Heights nannies, rich kids and avoiders of the hoi polloi all favour China Beach. There's plenty of parking and a pleasant hike down to the sand, then a free sundeck, showers and changing rooms once you get there. Should you be there at sunset, with Marin Headlands opposite, the Golden Gate Bridge to your right and sea lions swimming in the ocean ahead of you, it will be your favourite too.

Extending from Cliff House (*see p105*) south past the city limits, **Ocean Beach** (Great Highway, between Balboa Street and Sloat Boulevard, Muni Metro N, L/bus 5, 18, 31, 38, 48, 71) is by far San Francisco's biggest beach: a three-mile (five-kilometre) sandy strip along the Pacific. Widening into dunes and plateaus at the end of the fog-bound Sunset District, Ocean Beach is a fine place for strolling, dog-walking and the odd illicit midnight ritual. But look, don't taste: tremendous waves come thundering ashore when the weather's up, and even on seemingly calm days the tides and currents can be lethal.

Richmond, Sunset & Golden Gate Park

Where lived-in means lovable.

The resplendent **Conservatory of Flowers**. *See p108.*

In a city that often seems to be just a series of inter-connected suburbs or villages, the **Richmond District** and **Sunset District** may be the most sub-urban of them all. That sense is only enhanced by the presence of **Golden Gate Park** – one of San Francisco's greatest attractions – sandwiched between them. Practically bedroom communities within the city, the primarily residential outermost districts in the west of the city remain largely unexplored by tourists and even many locals. Which is just fine with the residents, who tend to be a bit more unassuming, a bit less concerned with appearances and a bit more friendly than those in other neighbourhoods. If places like **Fisherman's Wharf** (*see p80*) and the **Marina** (*see p98*) represent the larger-than-life opera sets of San Francisco, residents of the Richmond and Sunset are the masters of that stagecraft. This happy mélange of active immigrant communities, students, families, working-class folk and, by the ocean, surfers also enjoys the city's very best coastal trails. Less crowded and touristy, less flashy if more foggy – for some, this is the real San Francisco.

Richmond

Bordering the northern edge of Golden Gate Park, from beyond Arguello Boulevard to the ocean and from Fulton to California Streets, the largely residential Richmond is a highly flavoured cultural mix, predominantly Russian, Chinese and Irish immigrants. Once a sandy waterfront wasteland, the region was developed for housing after construction of the Geary Boulevard tramway in 1906. Eastern European Jews formed a strong community after World War I, and their synagogues and delicatessens still a thriving presence here.

San Francisco University and the peculiar **Columbarium** (*see p107*) hover at the extreme easterly edge of the Richmond, but **Clement Street** is the district's primary commercial centre. Stretching from Second Avenue all the way to 34th, Clement Street is arguably a more authentic Chinatown than the more famous one downtown (*see p73*). Its wider streets and fewer tourists make browsing the no-nonsense emporia for Asian groceries, cheap kitchenware, shrine accoutrements and ginseng a pleasure; literary types have long been enamoured of **Green Apple Books** (*see p166*). Restaurants are also beautifully mixed: traditional Chinese cuisine next to an American diner, sushi opposite a pasta joint. Super-funky Q Restaurant (*see p140*) serves up American comfort food in a surreal setting, Chapeau! (*see p140*) offers a comfortable setting for Provençal food, and the takeout dumplings from **Good Luck Dim Sum** (No.736, at Eighth Avenue, 386 3388) are recommended by Chinese grandmothers for their authenticity and by everyone else for their flavour and price (you can get stuffed for under $5). Near Seventh Avenue, Wing Lee Bakery (No.503, 668 9481) and the cavernous Chinese market New May Wah (No.547, 668 2523) also make it worth your while to journey out here.

One block south of Clement is **Geary Boulevard**, the Richmond's main artery. Excellent own-made ice-cream can be found at Joe's (No.5351, between 17th and 18th Avenues, 751 1950), including such exotica as azuki bean and pumpkin. North towards **Ocean Beach** (*see p103* **Beaches: City sands**) and deeper into the avenues is Tommy (No.5929, at 23rd Avenue, 387 4747), a family-run Mexican restaurant renowned for its 250 pure agave tequilas – the largest selection outside Mexico – and the encyclopedic tequila knowledge of proprietor Julio Bermejo. The much-admired 'free wine while you wait' policy at Pacific Café (No.7000, at 34th Avenue, 387 7091) puts a premium on avoiding getting your table for its fresh-from-the-sea seafood.

Now you're at 34th Avenue, turn north back over Clement into Lincoln Park to find the **California Palace of the Legion of Honor** (*see p106*), built by architect George Applegarth to pay homage to the Palais de la Legion d'Honneur in Paris. A memorial to Californians who died in World War I, it stands on a promontory that now overlooks the Golden Gate Bridge (*see p101*). Just north of the Palace's car park is the haunting **Jewish Holocaust Memorial** by George Segal. The surrounding wooded and hilly park contains the 18-hole Lincoln Park Golf Course (*see p238*) and a number of well-maintained hiking trails,

shaded by twisted cypress, meander along the spectacular cliffs of **Land's End** (*see p106* **Beaches: Bare-faced cheeks**).

At the westerly end of the Richmond, **Sutro Heights Park** is a tiny idyll, virtually empty except for a few Russians walking their dogs or playing chess or and a statue of the goddess Diana that is often decorated with flowers by local pagans. In the nearby garden, you can enjoy a secluded picnic and marvel at the spectacular panoramic view of the Pacific. Just across the street below Sutro Park is modestly priced (and modestly appointed) **Louis** (902 Point Lobos Avenue, 387 6330), a classic American 'greasy spoon' – and a San Francisco institution since 1937. It serves up milkshakes and ham steaks at Formica counters and booths that all offer views of the ocean and the remains of Sutro Baths rivalling those of the Cliff House.

Perched on the very verge of the city is the somewhat touristy – and pricey – **Cliff House Bar and Restaurant** (*see p107*), the brainchild of silver baron Adolph Sutro. San Francisco's 24th mayor, Sutro owned most of the land on the western side of the city and his house once stood above Sutro Park. Below the Cliff House to the north are the ruins of **Sutro Baths**. Built by Sutro in 1896, these were once the world's biggest swimming baths. Fed by the Pacific, seven pools holding 1,375,578 gallons (6,253,500 litres) in total could be filled or emptied by the tides in one hour. Destroyed by fire in 1966, the pool ruins are strangely photogenic, famously used in a scene in the 1971 film *Harold and Maude*. A windswept three-mile (five-kilometre) coastal path winds all the way north from here to the Golden Gate Bridge. The pathside shrubbery is notorious as a rendezvous for lovers, so it can be scenic in more ways than one.

South of the Cliff House, on the edge of Golden Gate Park, is the **Beach Chalet** (*see below*). The main floor is now a visitor centre for the park, with a good restaurant upstairs that boasts beers brewed on the site.

Beach Chalet

1000 Great Highway, in Golden Gate Park (visitor centre 751 2766/restaurant 386 8439/ www.beachchalet.com). Bus 18. **Open** *Visitor centre* 9am-6pm daily. *Restaurant* 9am-10pm daily. **Credit** AmEx, MC, V.

A perfect spot for sunset cocktails, the historic Willis Polk-designed building is home to a quality restaurant and brewpub. The walls on the bottom floor are awash in WPA frescoes by Lucien Labaudt. They depict notable San Franciscans, among them sculptor Benny Bufano and Golden Gate Park's famous gardener, John McLaren. The views of the ocean from upstairs are stupendous.

California Palace of the Legion of Honor

Lincoln Park, at 34th Avenue & Clement Street (863 3330/www.thinker.org). Bus 1, 2, 18, 38. **Open** 9.30am-5pm Tue-Sun. **Admission** $8; $6 seniors; $5 12-17s; free under-12s; free every Tue. **Credit** AmEx, MC, V.

In a wooded spot overlooking the Pacific Ocean, the Palace of the Legion of Honor is San Francisco's most beautiful museum, its neo-classical façade and Beaux Arts interior virtually unchanged since it was completed in 1924. A cast of Rodin's Le Penseur still dominates the entrance, which has now been enhanced by a glass pyramid that acts as a skylight

Beaches Bare-faced cheeks

In a nation that still wrestles with its Puritan conscience, San Francisco strives to be an oasis of Continental sophistication – or at least a Dutch brand of tolerance. Evidence of this is the popularity of clothing optional beaches throughout the Bay Area. In fact, with the exception of China Beach (*see p103* **Beaches: City sands**), almost all beaches are 'clothing optional', given that local law enforcement has little interest in enforcing the laws prohibiting public nudity.

If you're after somewhere a bit secluded, it might require a brief hike to get there. Still, the spectacular scenery and relative privacy when you arrive make more out-of-the-way spots well worth the effort. Baker, Fort Funston and Land's End beaches are all great for starters, but the little extra effort and care it takes to explore the Golden Gate Bridge Beach will be more than rewarded.

At the southern terminus of Ocean Beach, windy **Fort Funston Beach** (right off Skyline Boulevard) is a good spot for suitless sunning during the week when crowds are minimal. The same wind currents that keep hang-gliders and kites wheeling overhead have created dunes that are perfect for preserving one's modesty. Which is just as well, because you need to be a little discreet here if you're planning to shed your clothes. Although there have been no complaints since 2000, nude sunbathing is still technically illegal. To get here, head south on the Great Highway beside Ocean Beach (*see p103* **Beaches: City sands**) and bear right on to Skyline Boulevard as the highway comes to an end. Pass the first stoplight and look for the entrance on the right.

Just near the Cliff House (*see p105*), the quarter-mile stretch of **Land's End Beach** offers small islands of sand in otherwise rocky terrain, ideal for catching rays *au naturel*. This beauty isn't the easiest to find. Follow Geary Boulevard until it turns into Point Lobos. After the intersection of 48th Avenue and Point Lobos, take your first right at Merrie, which is not a street, but a parking lot overlooking the ruins of the Sutro Baths (*see p105*). To find the beach, locate the trail head at the end of the parking lot. Approximately 120 paces from the trailhead, bear left at a large tangle of dead trees and vegetation and follow the narrow trail (which eventually widens) down towards the ocean. Like Golden Gate Bridge Beach (*see below*), trails can be steep and aren't well marked – be careful.

The area around the Golden Gate Bridge offers two fabulous options. The first and simplest is **Baker Beach**. The south end is reserved for the clothed, with more liberated folk hanging out in the bit to the north of the 'Hazardous Surf' sign. Easy access (a ten-minute downhill walk on well-maintained trails from Lincoln Boulevard), spectacular views, beautiful sand and an interesting cross-section of locals have helped to make this the most-visited urban nude beach in the US.

Caution is advised (as is a keen eye for the poison oak) if you opt for the second choice, but a clamber down to **Golden Gate Bridge Beach** allows the cooked and the raw to relax together almost directly below the bridge. There are three coves here, all surrounded by wildflowers and accessible by trails that the Golden Gate National Recreation Area (GGRNA) rangers warn are treacherous. They are steep and should not be attempted for a few days following rain. Following Lincoln Boulevard, keep an eye out for Langdon Court, a small street that turns into a little parking lot. Head around to the left of the building as you enter and park in the inner lot closest to the ocean. Step over the guard rails, following the narrow trail down, and turn right at the first opportunity. You can then follow a number of trails down to the beach. You can also sit out on the fabulous bunkers (*see p100* **Salty batteries**) should you wish.

If you want to visit any of these beaches using public transport, bus 29 goes to Baker and Golden Gate Bridge beaches, bus 3 to Land's End and bus 18 to Fort Funston.

A golden afternoon in **Golden Gate Park**.

for galleries containing more than 87,000 works of art, spanning 4,000 years but with the emphasis on European painting and decorative art (El Greco, Rembrandt, Monet). The personal passion of the museum's founder, Alma Spreckels, was Rodin and the collection of his sculpture on display is second only to that of the Musée Rodin in Paris. There is an expanded garden level that houses temporary exhibitions, the Achenbach Foundation for Graphic Arts and the Bowles Collection of porcelain. Bus 18 goes directly to the museum and visitors with a Muni ticket get $2 off admission.

Cliff House

1090 Point Lobos Avenue, at the Great Highway (386 3330/www.cliffhouse.com). Bus 18, 38.
Open *Bar* 11am-2am daily. *Restaurant* 9am-10.30pm Mon-Fri; 8.30am-10.30pm Sat, Sun. *Walkways* 24hrs daily. **Credit** AmEx, MC, V.

The first house was built on this spot in the 1860s. After a fire in 1894, a magnificent, eight-storey Victorian turreted palace replaced it. That also burned down, only a year after surviving the Great Quake of 1906. Today's nominally neo-classical architectural muddle was the final replacement. It's now rather touristy, but the superb views almost compensate for the crowds. Extensive restoration, due to be completed in summer 2004, has displaced the whimsical Musée Mécanique (*see p81*) but the camera obscura (*see below*), a 19th-century optical marvel, was saved after public outcry halted its demolition. The National Park Service maintains on the premises a visitor centre (556 8642) for the Golden Gate National Recreation Area.

Columbarium

1 Loraine Court, off Anza Street (752 7891). Bus 31, 33, 38. **Open** 10am-4pm Mon-Fri; 10am-2pm Sat, Sun. **Admission** free. **Map** p312 C5.

This round, domed neo-classical rotunda is honeycombed with hundreds of niches. Its cremation urns are lavishly and individualistically decorated, alternately dignified and flamboyantly whimsical. The niches house the remains of many of the city's first families, such as the Folgers (of coffee fame), Magnins and Kaisers. This is the only active funereal resting place in the city and the sole remnant of what was once a vast burial ground.

Holographic Museum & Camera Obscura

Cliff House, 1090 Point Lobos Avenue, at the Great Highway (386 3330/www.cliffhouse.com). Bus 18, 38. **Open** 11am-sunset daily. **Admission** $2. **No credit cards**.

Closed during the renovations at the Cliff House (*see above*), this museum is one of a kind. Several dozen holographs are displayed at eye level around the tiny chamber that houses the camera obscura, a Victorian creation that projects an image of the outside world (including a large stretch of Ocean Beach) on to a giant parabolic screen.

Golden Gate Park

Golden Gate Park is one of the largest manmade parks in the world and a testament to human dominion over nature, encompassing five million square yards (4,115,653 square

Walk 3 Free parking

Start at **McLaren Lodge** (John F Kennedy Drive, 831 2700). Once the residence of the famed gardener John McLaren, who dedicated more than 50 years of his life to the park, it's now the site of the park offices and visitor centre (open 8am-5pm Mon-Fri). Strike out south from the lodge down the tree-lined path running parallel to Stanyan Street, bearing right until you come to **Alvord Lake.** Keep right beside the lake and pass under Alvord Lake Bridge, which dates way back to 1809, heading on through Mothers' Meadow until you reach a fork. The left fork brings you to the **Children's Playground** and the wonderful Herschel-Spillman Carousel, built in 1912. North, past the Sharon Building is Sharon Meadow. You'll hear **Hippie Hill**, in the middle of the meadow, before you see it. Ever since 25,000 people gathered for the Human Be-In on 17 January 1967, hippies and alt-lifestylers have been visiting here – and the drums still sound today.

Follow the path north to the tennis courts and continue round their right-hand side. Cross John F Kennedy Drive after you emerge from the trees: the gleaming, white-domed **Conservatory of Flowers** should be in full view up to your left. Badly damaged in a storm in 1995, it reopened to considerable excitement in 2003 after an eight-year, $25-million restoration. It's the oldest glass-and-wood Victorian greenhouse in the Western Hemisphere, and home to more than 10,000 plants from all over the world.

Take the stairs down to JFK Drive and hear along Middle East Drive. On your left is the 36,300-square-yard (30,351-square-metre) **National AIDS Memorial Grove**. Inaugurated in 1991, it has the names of some of the city's nearly 20,000 dead engraved in stone amid redwoods, oaks and maples. (For a guided tour, call 750 8340.) Opposite, a path leads north to the beautiful **Lily Pond**. Follow it round the west side of the pond to the crossroads. On the right is a grove of ferns – some of them reaching 20 feet (6 metres) – that dates back to 1898. Head straight on, though, taking the footpath to your left that parallels JFK Drive. You'll soon wind up at another botanical delight: the **John McLaren Rhododendron Dell**, all agapanthus, raspberries and, of course, rhododendrons.

Amble south along the leafy walkways until you reach the looming **California Academy of Sciences** complex. It's closed until 2008, so press on west across the Music Concourse through the arch in the Temple of Music to find yourself at everyone's favourite: the **Japanese Tea Garden** (752 1171, open 9am-6pm daily). Built in 1893 for the Exposition, it still delights visitors with its nearly vertical bridges, bonzai trees, a huge bronze Buddha and an outdoor tearoom with kimono-clad servers. Admission is $3.50 with $1.25 concessions, although it's half price on the first Wednesday of each month. Another essential stopping-off point is just south of the Tea Garden. The **Strybing Arboretum &**

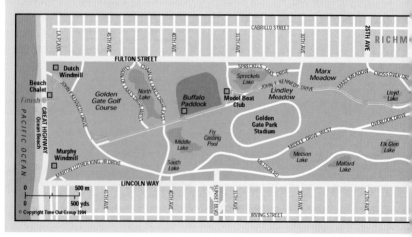

Botanical Gardens (661 1316) house some 7,000 species from diverse climates, all arranged by country and connected by a looped boardwalk path. There's a fragrant garden designed for the visually impaired and a particularly appealing moon-viewing garden. The John Muir Nature Trail, in the west of the gardens, focuses on local flora.

Return to Martin Luther King Jr Drive, then head west up the hill and take the concrete stairs to Stow Lake. Wandering along the broad path on the south side of the lake, you'll come to the **Rustic Bridge** – cross here if you fancy exploring Strawberry Hill island and its Chinese pavilion. A gift from the people of Taipei, it was shipping here in 6,000 pieces and reassembled in 1981. (The Pioneer Log Cabin is on the far side, if you fancy paying it a visit.) Head on round the lake to the **Boathouse** (open summer 10am-5pm Mon-Fri, 9am-5pm Sat, Sun; winter 9am-4pm daily), where paddleboats and canoes are available for rent.

From the Boathouse walk north. Pick up the path to the left of the restrooms that are situated across the parking lot and you'll come out opposite **Rainbow Falls** and the **Prayer Book Cross**, which commemorates Francis Drake's chaplain offering up prayers during their brief holiday in the Bay Area in 1579. Follow the little waterway west under Cross Over Drive Bridge and across Transverse Drive to Lloyd Lake and the **Portals of the Past** – an ornate archway

saved from a Nob Hill home that was destroyed in the 1906 earthquake. From there JFK Drive takes you through meadows that offer plenty of picnicking opportunities. After about half a mile, you'll come to **Spreckels Lake**. Rest on a bench here and watch the ducks and model sailing boats, before gearing up for the home stretch.

When you're ready, get back on to JFK (Model Boat Club on your right) and press ever west. Almost immediately, on your right, you'll be passing the large **Buffalo Paddock**, where a small herd of bison roams on a 'prairie'. Pass Chain of Lakes Drive West on your right and keep going for about five minutes. Just past the golf course (watch out for stray balls) you'll find a pleasant tree-lined pedestrian path that will take you round to the north, and soon to **Queen Wilhelmina's Tulip Gardens** and then the **Dutch Windmill**, gifts from the eponymous Dutch monarch in 1902.

Head south on another wooded path rather than getting straight on to the Great Highway. You'll soon be at journey's end: the **Beach Chalet** (*see p105*). Opened in 1925 as a restaurant and bathhouse, the building, designed by Willis Polk, houses a magnificent 1936 mural and offers staggering views of the Pacific across **Ocean Beach**. Sup on own-brewed ales and linger for a dramatic sunset. If you linger too long to walk back, never fear: bus 5 will take you back to civilisation.
Distance over 8 miles (13.5km).
Time 2.5hrs.

metres) of forests, meadows and landscaped gardens. The ambitious task of creating all this pastoral loveliness out of barren sand dunes began in 1870, both to meet the growing public demand for a city park and to solidify San Francisco's position as a new modern urban centre. While William Hammond Hall, a civil engineer, prepared the initial design for the park – and implemented some innovative sand reclamation techniques – the true 'father of Golden Gate Park' is certainly the eccentric Scottish-born John McLaren. He spent more than 50 years as park superintendent, planting more than a million trees.

The park's true public debut was in 1894, when more than 1.3 million people visited for the Midwinter International Exposition. Covering 968,000 square yards (nearly 810,000 square metres), the six-month fair filled more than 100 temporary buildings. As the park's fame spread, horticulturists from all over the world sent in seeds and cuttings. Today a rose garden, a Shakespeare garden, a rhododendron dell and a tulip garden are among hundreds of living delights whose colours dazzle on a sunny day and console on a foggy one. Among the soaring eucalyptus and pine trees, the city is so rarely in view it is easily forgotten.

With the **MH de Young Memorial Museum** having been torn down (it will be replaced by a new Herzog & de Meuron building in 2005), the **Japanese Tea Garden** and the **Music Concourse** are now the only Exposition structures still standing. The park's other museum – the **California Academy of Sciences** (*see p195*) – is also closed for renovations, but the park is still a wonderful day out. Join the throngs of locals biking, walking, jogging and in-line skating on a Sunday afternoon when **John F Kennedy Drive** (the park's main east–west artery) is closed to traffic and you'll soon understand why the park is known as San Francisco's collective backyard.

Sampling all the park's attractions would take days, but a great way to see it in one afternoon is to stroll all the way from the entrance of the park along the pedestrian footpaths beside JFK Drive to the ocean – it takes a few hours if you stop along the way (which you will want to), but the reward is the crashing waves of the Pacific (*see p108* **Walk 3: Free parking**). If you prefer wheels, bicycles and in-line skates can be rented for various locations (*see p234*).

If you're in the Haight-Ashbury (*see p91*), it's easy to access the park directly from the west end of Haight Street by crossing Stanyan Street. Otherwise come in via the **Panhandle**, a couple of blocks north. This was the grand entrance to the park, designed with paths wide enough to accommodate carriages. It brings you out next to the park headquarters in **McLaren Lodge**, where you can pick up information.

Sunset

South of Golden Gate Park, the large southern twin to the Richmond District usually belies its own name. The residential district is habitually swathed in fog from June to September, often in other months as well. If you do catch one of the rare fair days, however, the sunsets can be spectacular. **Irving Street**, between Fifth and Tenth Avenues, is the main shopping area. On Ninth Avenue, you can not only dine on San Francisco's best sushi at Ebisu (*see p140*), but also enjoy affordable Asian, American and Italian at Park Chow (*see p132* **On the cheap: White-collar taste, blue-collar budget**). But the Sunset's main attractions are Ocean Beach, the zoo and Fort Funston.

Ocean Beach (*see p103* **Beaches: City sands**) is great for a blustery wander and to watch surfers (who sometimes count Chris Isaak among their numbers) battling strong rip tides and chilly water. Take a warming break either over coffee at the Java Beach Cafe (*see p240*) or with a garlic whole-roasted crab at the Vietnamese restaurant Thanh Long (4101 Judah Street, at 46th Avenue, 665 1146).

In the south-west corner of the district, the **San Francisco Zoo** (*see p195*) has all the Sumatran tigers, gorillas, African warthogs, otters and penguins you could hope for, and a hands-on 'family farm'. It is also one of few zoos to house koalas (two of which were bear-napped by some teenage boys, who wanted to give them as gifts to their girlfriends – they were safely returned). Beyond the zoo is the Harding Municipal Park & Golf Course (*see p237*), cradled by the picturesque Lake Merced and encircled by lovely biking and jogging trails. North of the lake is Stern Grove, 305,000 square yards (255,000 square metres) of eucalyptus and redwood, which hosts the annual Stern Grove Festival (*see p191*).

Fort Funston Reservation is a large natural area, also in the south-west of the city. It is criss-crossed with hiking trails, dramatic promontories and jagged beaches, and is a favourite place for dog-walkers. (For more on the beaches, *see p103* and *p106*.) Many Sunset residents steal a few hours here to run, take a stroll or meditate. Other worthwhile jaunts in the area include the hike up **Mount Davidson**. At 927 feet (283 metres), this is the highest point in San Francisco. The summit provides great views – if you can ignore the enormous cross that sits at its apex.

The East Bay

A transcontinental terminus and the beginnings of a culinary obsession.

Visitors to San Francisco don't always think to visit the city's world-famous neighbours, but the best-known East Bay cities – **Oakland** and **Berkeley** (for tourist offices in both cities, *see p290*) – are only half an hour away by BART or car, and offer museums, a world-renowned university and miles of parkland, as well as being the birthplace of California cuisine. Hell, the temperatures in East Bay even run an average 10˚C higher than at the Golden Gate.

Oakland Museum of California

Sightseeing

Oakland

Named after its now-vanished oak forests, San Francisco's stepsister has had image problems since it made headlines in the 1960s as the headquarters of both radical Black Panthers and mobhanded Hell's Angels. The murder rate still runs high, but the once-notorious Panthers are now the subject of the two-and-a-half-hour **Black Panther Legacy Tour** (1-510 986 0660, www.blackpanthertours.com). Oakland's earliest fame, back in 1869, was as the western terminus of the 3,000-mile (4,800-kilometre) transcontinental railway. The slow bells of passing freight trains are still strangely evocative of Oakland's working heritage.

After the 1906 earthquake, thousands of displaced San Franciscans moved here. Today many residents commute to San Francisco across the Bay Bridge or by BART (the City Center/12th Street and 19th Street stations are best for downtown). There are also ferries (1-510 522 3300, www.eastbayferry.com).

On the waterfront, **Jack London Square** (at Broadway and Embarcadero) is named after the noted local author, who used to carouse at the **First & Last Chance Saloon** (*see p158*). The square also has a lovely Sunday morning farmers' market (10am-2pm).

Having undergone huge redevelopment, Oakland's downtown is much more inviting than of old. **Chinatown**, which covers the few blocks south of Broadway around Seventh, Eighth and Ninth Streets, is less tourist-focused than its San Francisco counterpart, but still packed with places to eat, snack and shop. Among the gems are **Sherry's Shop** (388 Ninth Street, at Franklin Street, 1-510 763 6321), stuffed with cheap oriental clothes and bags, and **KV Mart** (303 Tenth Street, at Alice Street, 1-510 893 1838), a veritable Hello Kitty shrine.

Your next stop should surely be **Oakland Museum of California** (*see p112*), a great place to learn about the state, but it's well worth negotiating the rather unpleasant road that separates it from **Lake Merritt**. There you'll find the largest collection of gondolas outside Venice. Rides start at $45 for a couple and reservations are required (1-510 663 6603, www.gondolaservizio.com). In the adjacent park, **Children's Fairyland** (*see p198*) is full of scenarios based on classic nursery rhymes. As musicians and artists were priced out of San Francisco, Oakland developed strong theatre, dance, ballet and classical music, and it now boasts one of the West Coast's best jazz venues: **Yoshi's at Jack London Square** (*see p213*). Timothy L Pflueger's beautiful **Parkway Theater** (*see p201*) is another treat. Oakland also has a dizzying array of national cuisines: Burmese, Ethiopian, Peruvian, African-American, Caribbean – many clustered in Chinatown and Rockridge.

East Oakland merits a visit for the **Oakland Zoo** (*see p198*). Situated in Knowland Park, the zoo has done much to shake off its poor reputation, creating large areas of naturalistic habitat for its 1,000-plus species of animal.

Walk 4 The ice-cream's academic

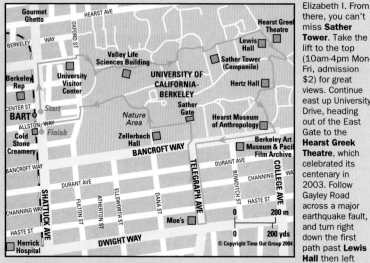

Elizabeth I. From there, you can't miss **Sather Tower**. Take the lift to the top (10am-4pm Mon-Fri, admission $2) for great views. Continue east up University Drive, heading out of the East Gate to the **Hearst Greek Theatre**, which celebrated its centenary in 2003. Follow Gayley Road across a major earthquake fault, and turn right down the first path past **Lewis Hall** then left

Jump off the BART at Downtown Berkeley and then walk the few blocks up Shattuck Avenue to University Avenue. Turn right, cross Oxford Street and enter the campus at University Drive. Pass the Valley Life Sciences Building until you come to **Bancroft Library**. This houses a plate that was supposedly left by Sir Francis Drake to claim California for Queen

over a bridge. Continue down the path as it swings to the right and take a sharp left. Have a peek at Hertz Hall and, if you're interested, visit the **PA Hearst Museum of Anthropology**. On Bancroft Way you can take a break with the students and locals at **Caffe Strada** (at College Avenue), but make sure you visit the ultra-modern **Berkeley Art Museum** (see

Oakland Museum of California

1000 Oak Street, at Tenth Street (1-510 238 2200/ www.museumca.org). **Open** 10am-5pm Wed-Sat; noon-5pm Sun. **Admission** $8; free under-5s. Free 2nd Sun of mth. **Credit** AmEx, MC, V.
The Oakland Museum's art collection includes sketches by early explorers and genre pictures from the Gold Rush, along with sculpture, landscapes and Bay Area figurative, pop and funk works. The Hall of California Ecology uses stuffed mammals, reptiles and birds to exemplify the state's extraordinary range of habitats, while the Cowell Hall of California History houses curiosities going back to the Spanish incursion. The collection of priceless Chinese artefacts also includes some stunning pieces.

Berkeley

Buoyed up on a river of coffee, Berkeley works hard to live up to its reputation as a hotbed of avant-garde arts, left politics and revolutionary food. The Downtown Berkeley BART station is

most convenient for all attractions, and hence the starting point for our suggested walk, *see p112* **Walk 4: The ice-cream's academic**. Near the BART Berkeley station, bustling coffee houses suggest the proximity of students. The campus of the **University of California** (known locally as just Cal) is indeed only a short distance east. Thirty years ago this was the birthplace of America's youth revolution: students protesting against campus rules and the Vietnam War radicalised and turned against mainstream society, with a nation of disgruntled youths following their lead. These days the sprawling campus, with its creeks and redwood groves, is calm, and studious undergraduates and Nobel laureates absent-mindedly stroll between the historic buildings. As well as **Sather Tower** (*see above*), you'll find museums dedicated to art, anthropology, palaeontology and other disciplines dotted about the property. Prime among these has

p113). This is also where you can visit the
Pacific Film Archive (*see p200*), with its
frequent showings of interesting (often
challenging) international films.

Now take a detour south into what
has been called 'Haight-Ashbury East'.
Telegraph Avenue is lined with street
traders and shops selling hip clothes,
wickedly cool music and tons of books.
Moe's (No.2476; *see p166*), which made
all too brief appearance in *The Graduate*,
and **Cody's** (No.2454; *see p165*) are the
best bookstores.

Head back up Telegraph and, from the
university entrance opposite, fight your
way through the students in **Sproul Plaza**,
site of student protests past and present.
Admire **Sather Gate** at the end of the strip
but don't go through. Instead turn left and
walk down to the lower courtyard with the
ultra-modern **Zellerbach Hall**. Turn right
at the end of the courtyard, crossing over
the south fork of Strawberry Creek at Bay
Tree Bridge. On your left is a **nature area**,
complete with some of the world's tallest
eucalyptus trees.

Head back west on to Shattuck. For
serious eats go north into the **Gourmet
Ghetto** (*see p113*). Otherwise, **Cold Stone
Creamery** (No.2204, at Allston Way, 1-510
849 4928) mixes anything you want into
your ice-cream – on a frozen granite stone.
Distance *2.5 miles (4km).* **Time** *45min.*

to be the **Berkeley Art Museum** (*see below*).
Drop in on the **Visitors' Center** (University
Hall, 2200 University Avenue, at Oxford Street,
1-510 642 5215, closed Sat & Sun) for maps
and information. The **Lawrence Hall of
Science** (*see p198*), above the campus on
Centennial Drive, is a fascinating science
museum with commanding views over
the entire Bay Area. Spiking southwards,
Telegraph Avenue is home to jewellery,
crafts and brilliant bookstores.

North-west of campus, the culinary hot zone
known as the **Gourmet Ghetto** runs along
Shattuck Avenue between Delaware and Rose.
The star of the show, **Chez Panisse** (No.1517,
between Cedar and Vine Streets; *see p137* **East
Bay dining**), is owned by Alice Waters, the
elfin leader of California's cuisine revolution
since the 1970s. Between Telegraph and 45th,
you'll find **Cheese Board Pizza** (No.1512,
1-510 549 3055), an employee-owned collective

that offers a single type of vegetarian pizza to
crowds that inevitably begin to form before
opening time each evening; **César** (No.115,
1-510 883 0222) for tapas, wine and whiskey;
and the **French Hotel Café** (No.1538, 1-510
548 9930) with its killer espressos. Talking
of which, some have hailed the coffee at the
original **Peet's** (2124 Vine Street, at Walnut
Street, 1-510 841 0564) the world's strongest
and best. Opened in 1966, this Peet's was also
where the founder of Starbucks got his training.
So now you know who to blame. After all that
coffee you'll probably need some chocolate:
Scharffen Berger (914 Heinz Avenue, at
Seventh Street, www.scharffenberger.com) is
an upmarket chocolatier. For a free tour of the
West Berkeley factory, call 1-510 981 4066.

Hardcore capitalists will love newly trendy
Fourth Street (between Hearst Avenue and
Virginia Street) near the waterfront, which
has exclusive and stylish shops by the dozen.
Traditionalists can sample the fish at century-
old **Spenger's** (No.1919, 1-510 845 7771) and
Brennan's (Fourth Street and University
Avenue, 1-510 841 0960), a cavernous, old-
fashioned Irish pub and cafeteria.

Berkeley's residential districts are also worth
exploring. South Berkeley rewards wanderers
with the **Judah L Magnes Museum** (2911
Russell Street, at Pine Street, 1-510 549 6950,
closed Fri & Sat), a large mansion bursting at
the seams with Jewish history and culture, and
the **Claremont Resort & Spa** (41 Tunnel
Road, at Claremont Avenue, 1-510 843 3000,
www.claremontresort.com), a decadent holiday
getaway. The latter is a sprawling hillside
palace, straddling the Berkeley-Oakland border.
It serves both as an architectural landmark and
as a famously indulgent splurge.

Many visit Berkeley just for its hills. Above
the city, the lovely and magnificently wild
Tilden Regional Park (1-510 525 2233) offers
hiking, nature trails and pony rides, a farm and
a steam train, while those who manage the trip
up to **Inspiration Point** or **Wildcat Peak**
are rewarded with 180° views.

Berkeley Art Museum

*2626 Bancroft Way, at Bowditch Street (1-510 642
0808/www.bampfa.berkeley.edu).* **Open** 11am-5pm
Wed, Fri-Sun; 11am-7pm Thur. **Admission** $8;
free under-12s. Free 1st Thur of mth.
Credit AmEx, DC, MC, V.
Opened in 1970, this dramatic exhibition space is
arranged in terraces so visitors can see the works
from various vantage points. The collection's
strength is 20th-century art, be it sculpture, painting,
photography or conceptual work, but there's also a
good collection of Asian pieces. Ten galleries and a
bookstore occupy the upper level, while a sculpture
garden and café share the lower floor.

Eat, Drink, Shop

Restaurants	**116**
Cafés	**141**
Bars	**148**
Shops & Services	**159**

Features

The best Restaurants	118
Small plates get big	121
Mr Big	125
On the cheap Blue-collar price,	
white-collar taste	132
East Bay dining	137
The best Cafés	141
Later than breakfast,	
sooner than Monday	142
Sake tsunami	150
Staffa outing	152
A cocktail and bull story	157
The best Shopping	159
On the cheap Thrift, fleas	
& second-hand	162
The best Bookshops	164
Hayes Street chic	167
No poseurs, please	170
Vinyl junkies	184

Restaurants

Food City, USA.

San Francisco is one of the world's greatest places to be hungry. Few cities count their food an attraction in the way that San Francisco does. With nearly 4,000 restaurants huddled into this tiny city, you'll be able to find every persuasion under the sun – and even a few from outside the culinary solar system.

The chief reason for such a proliferation of eating dens is the region's climate and topography. Likened to the great Mediterranean towns of Europe, the Bay Area's mild weather and rich soil make for great growing conditions for ingredients of all kinds. Similarly, excellent fish, fowl and meat are produced within an arm's reach of any chef lucky enough to cook in a San Francisco kitchen. This happy aspect combines with a huge population of foodies to create one of the best dining scenes in America.

Widespread appreciation of fine cuisine took root locally in the 1970s, when Alice Waters of Chez Panisse in Berkeley (*see p137* **East Bay dining**) gained global fame for her 'California cuisine' – the infusing of local seasonal ingredients and traditional recipes with cross-cultural influences. The scene enjoyed unprecedented growth during the halcyon days of the 1990s dot-com boom. Top-end restaurants with interesting food ideas popped up like mushrooms in a spring rain. Many of the restaurants were very good, more were very expensive. And like the dot-coms, several high-profile restaurants were ill-conceived and over-valued. The dot-com bust and economic downturn quickly separated the wheat from the chaff, and San Franciscans watched in wonder as restaurants closed or restructured.

Unfortunately, the bust took its toll on some good places as well. Customer flow slowed to a trickle and dining rooms struggled to remain open. There was, however, a positive aspect to the whole thing as the slowdown forced restaurateurs to focus on value. Comfort food became the official San Francisco food for a while, as loyal patrons soothed their souls over hearty fried chicken, roast beef and mashed potatoes. What's more, service was better than ever as establishments realised any customer was a great customer.

While comfort is still on the menu, California cuisine hasn't gone very far. It continues to be a source of inspiration for chefs whose ideas are increasingly inspired by regions far and wide.

Locals delight in their ability to dine on fare from all points of the globe, from Afghan to Asian-fusion and Vietnamese to vegetarian. With taquerias in the Mission, Italian bakeries in North Beach, an endless array of Thai, Chinese, Vietnamese and Korean restaurants in the Sunset, and in-and-out noodle shops in Japantown, it's possible to take a round-the-world gourmet trip during a single San Francisco weekend.

Our cuisine categories are by necessity quite broad. 'American', for example, includes both new-wave Californian and old-fashioned grills, while 'Asian' covers such options as Japanese, Chinese, Thai, Vietnamese, Korean and Asian-fusion. And one thing to remember: always tip. The exact amount is up to you, but 15 to 20 per cent is standard. A handy rule of thumb is to double the sales tax (currently 8.75 per cent).

Union Square

Union Square is best known for its huge retail establishments and many of its dining rooms are more like eating emporiums than restaurants, well regarded as much for their splashy decor and big-name chefs as for the cuisine they offer. It's fun to visit spots like **Farallon** (450 Post Street, between Powell and Mason Streets, 956 6969, www.farallonrestaurant.com) and **Postrio** (545 Post Street, between Taylor and Mason Streets, 776 7825, www.postrio.com) for their cachet, but the food doesn't always match the hype – and often comes with a hefty tab. If you want the experience without the hassle, visit for lunch or sidestep the reservations process by sitting at the bar where you can sample the menu without the full-service effect.

European

Fifth Floor

Hotel Palomar, 12 Fourth Street, at Market Street (348 1555/http://fifthfloor.citysearch.com). BART Powell/Muni Metro F, J, K, L, M, N/bus 5, 6, 7, 9, 21, 31, 66, 71/cable car Powell-Mason. **Open** 7-10am, 5.30-9.30pm Mon-Thur; 7-10am, 5.30-10.30pm Fri; 8-11am, 5.30-11pm Sat; 8-11am Sun. **Main courses** $30-$45. **Credit** AmEx, DC, Disc, MC, V. **Map** p311 G4.
The Fifth Floor feels like an exclusive club for the tragically hip. The room is fabulous: an idyllic blend of romance and chic, complete with zebra-print rug

Asia de Cuba. *See p119.*

beneath your feet as you stroll to your table. Chef Laurent Gras stepped in for the award-winning opening chef and actually took things up a notch. Gras brings three-Michelin-star weight to the restaurant and a culinary motto of 'Flavor, esthetic and perfection, in that order.' He delivers: this remains one of the best dining experiences in town.

Masa's

648 Bush Street, between Stockton & Powell Streets (989 7154/www.masas.citysearch.com). Bus 2, 3, 4, 76/cable car California. **Open** *5.30-9.30pm Tue-Sat.* **Main courses** *Set menus* $65 for 3 courses; $75 for 6 courses; $115 for 9 courses. **Credit** AmEx, DC, Disc, MC, V. **Map** p311 G3.

Masa's helped create fine dining in the city; it was the first notable restaurant to combine SF haute cuisine with the French dining aesthetic. Staving off the threat of irrelevance with a brilliant remodel and 're-introduction' to the community, Masa's also snared local legend Ron Siegel to run the kitchen. Arguably the best chef in town, his dishes are at once sumptuous and verging on scientific, showing influences that range from Jamaica to Japan. It's worth the splurge to go with the sommelier's wine pairings.

For waterfront dining
Butterfly Embarcadero (*see p120*), **A Sabella's** (*see p128*) and vegetarian **Greens** (*see p139*).

For old-fashioned class
Swan Oyster Depot (*see p131*), **Harris'** (*see p138*) and **Alfred's** (*see p126*).

For sushi lovers
Ebisu (*see p140*) and **Kabuto** (*see p140*) are the best, but neither **Ozumo** (*see p120*) nor **Sushi Groove** (*see p128*) will disappoint.

For a special occasion
Look no further than award-winning **Gary Danko** (*see p128*), romantic **Fifth Floor** (*see p116*) or hipper-than-thou **Asia de Cuba** (*see p119*).

For ethnic eats
Dim sum at **Yank Sing** (*see p123*), Thai at **Thep Phanom** (*see p136*), Vietnamese at **Slanted Door** (*see p123*) and **Helmand** (*see p128*) for the only Afghani cuisine in town.

For late-night dining
For sit-down eats, **Globe** (*see p120*) is open until 1am, but if you really need to eat, head to **El Farolito** (*see p134*) or **Taqueria Cancun** (*see p135*).

Scala's Bistro

Sir Francis Drake Hotel, 432 Powell Street, between Post & Sutter Streets (395 8555/www.scalasbistro. com). BART Powell/Muni Metro F, J, K, L, M, N/bus 2, 3, 4, 76/cable car Powell-Hyde or Powell-Mason. **Open** *Breakfast* 7-10.30am Mon-Fri; 8-10.30am Sat; Sun. *Lunch* 11.30am-4pm daily. *Bistro menu* 4-5.15pm daily. *Dinner* 5.15pm-midnight daily. **Main courses** $12-$21. **Credit** AmEx, DC, MC, V. **Map** p311 G3.

This bustling bistro is frequented by tourists staying in Union Square and locals attracted by the reasonably priced Mediterranean food. The fare is spot on, from the daily risotto to the fresh-made pasta. Salads feature the season's freshest produce, and the wine list is well chosen from nearby regions with the occasional surprise from beyond the borders. One of the most reliable restaurants in town.

Financial District

When it comes to cuisine, the domain of the towering skyscraper is mostly associated with the power lunch. To be sure there are some great places to lunch over a Martini and sign on the dotted line. But the Financial District contains standard-bearer eateries of all types and for several of them it's well worth leaving the briefcase behind. Recently, the **Ferry Building** (*see p65* **Foodie frenzy**) was reborn with the idea of celebrating San Francisco's cuisine culture.

American

500 Jackson

500 Jackson Street, between Montgomery Street & Columbus Avenue (772 1940/www.500 jackson.com). Bus 12, 15, 41, 83. **Open** 11.30am-10pm Mon-Wed; 11.30am-11pm Thur; 11.30am-midnight Fri; 5pm-midnight Sat; 5-10pm Sun. **Main courses** $9-$25. **Credit** AmEx, DC, Disc, MC, V. **Map** p311 H3.

Opening recently in one of San Francisco's great festive restaurant locations, 500 Jackson toned it down a bit with a seasonal, no-nonsense menu of American-styled seafood and a Craftsman-inspired interior that is a far cry from the fantastical decor of the previous tenant. The amazingly fresh shellfish at the raw bar is a main attraction, but great steak and chops complete the upscale surf-and-turf scenario. The bar is shaping up to be quite a scene.

Sam's Grill

374 Bush Street, between Montgomery & Kearny Streets (421 0594). Bus 15, 45, 76. **Open** 11am-9pm Mon-Fri. **Main courses** $15-$40. **Credit** AmEx, DC, Disc, MC, V. **Map** p311 H3.

Sam's has been keeping it simple and straightforward for around 130 years. The restaurant holds fast to its historic charm, with a friendly atmosphere and a dining room panelled in dark wood and dotted by bright white tablecloths. The American menu is largely driven by seafood, while house specialities include the wonderful Hangtown Fry. The sand dabs *à la* Sam are also a treat. Save room for dessert, as all are priced out of time at $2.50.

Asian

Harbor Village
4 Embarcadero Center, between Sacramento & Clay Streets (781 8833/www.harborvillage.net). BART Embarcadero/Muni Metro F, J, K, L, M, N/bus 1, 15, 41, 42/cable car California. **Open** 11am-2.30pm, 5.30-9.30pm Mon-Fri; 10.30am-2.30pm, 5.30-9.30pm Sat, Sun. **Main courses** $14-$25. *Dim sum* $3-$6. **Credit** AmEx, DC, Disc, MC, V. **Map** p311 H3.
This place built a strong reputation in Hong Kong before opening this spacious downtown location. It's not much to look at, but locals love the dim sum – many claim it's the best to be found in town. Come midday, the place is packed with patrons pointing out their favourite steamed dumplings to the smiling waitresses as they wheel delicacies by on a cart. The evening dinners aren't bad either, a gourmet take on Cantonese cuisine, heavy on seafood specialities.

European

Kokkari Estiatorio
200 Jackson Street, at Front Street (981 0983/ www.kokkari.com). BART Embarcadero/bus 1, 12, 42, 83. **Open** 11.30am-10pm Mon-Thur; 11.30am-11pm Fri; 5-11pm Sat. **Main courses** $18-$35. **Credit** AmEx, DC, MC, V. **Map** p311 H2.
Kokkari's authentic Hellenic cuisine – jealously traditional Greek food – though highly priced, is a treat to experience and a sizeable hit with locals. The *pikilia* (appetiser plate) is a good place to start, featuring three traditional Greek dips with fresh pitta bread. Mains like swordfish, lamb chops and moussaka are standouts, although we like everything here.

Plouf
40 Belden Place, between Bush, Pine, Kearny & Montgomery Streets (986 6491/www.plouf. citysearch.com). Bus 2, 3, 4, 15. **Open** 11.30am-3pm, 5.30-7pm Mon-Wed; 11am-midnight Thur-Sat. **Main courses** $10-$18. **Credit** AmEx, MC, V. **Map** p311 H3.
A wonderful slice of European alfresco dining beneath the French word for the sound a pebble makes when it's dropped into water, most dishes come from the sea and are prepared with French panache. The waitstaff seem to come from clothing catalogues: striped-shirt servers whisk buckets of speciality steamed mussels to tables so close together everyone is a neighbour. The fish is also excellent, with an especially fine fish and chips.

Seafood

Aqua
252 California Street, between Battery & Front Streets (956 9662/www.aqua-sf.com). BART Embarcadero/bus 1, 12, 41, 42/cable car California. **Open** Lunch 11.30am-2pm Mon-Fri. Dinner 5.30-9.30pm daily. **Main courses** $32-$52. **Credit** AmEx, DC, Disc, MC, V. **Map** p311 H3.
Founding chef Michael Mina's downtown restaurant is one of the most expensive in town and once typified power dining. Now, Mina himself has the power. He's fashioning a culinary empire, with restaurant offshoots in Las Vegas and San Jose. This sleek, handsomely appointed space is punctuated with enormous floral arrangements and good-looking servers. Dishes dazzle the eye and palate: seafood is richly sauced and surprisingly spiced, while the foie gras is to be written home about in postcards.

Tenderloin

Asian

Asia de Cuba
Clift Hotel, 495 Geary Street, at Taylor Street (929 2300/www.clifthotel.com). Bus 2, 3, 4, 27, 38, 76. **Open** 7am-1am daily. **Main courses** $15-$60. **Credit** AmEx, DC, MC, V. **Map** p310 G4.
The ultra-swanky Asia de Cuba has managed to cling to its hip clientele in spite of the economic downturn and its sky-high prices. A big part of the draw is the sleek Redwood Room (*see p151*) bar inside Ian Schrager's only San Francisco property, the Clift Hotel (*see p38*). The fun and interesting menu is good for groups and many dishes, including the excellent paella, are designed to be shared. Rich, sweet sauces characterise most items on the intensely flavoured Chino-Latino menu. Well suited to its richly flavoured clientele, most of whom never met a fashion trend they didn't like.

European

Cortez Restaurant & Bar
550 Geary Street, between Taylor & Jones Streets (292 6360/www.cortezrestaurant.com). Bus 27, 38. **Open** *Bar* 5.30pm-1am daily. *Restaurant* 5.30-10.30pm daily. **Main courses** $15-$25. **Credit** AmEx, DC, MC, V. **Map** p310 G4.
This is a surprising find, set off the lobby of a stylish new Adagio Hotel (*see p38*), which is itself nestled into a rather seamy stretch of Geary Street in the Tenderloin. The room is highly styled and energetic; one of the new in-spots, to be sure. Small plates is the theme here, but the influences range from the Far East to the American West. It's a good idea to order up a bunch of plates and graze your way through the maze of tasties – washed down with a few of the Cortez speciality cocktails.

Eat, Drink, Shop

Fleur de Lys

777 Sutter Street, between Jones & Taylor Streets (673 7779/www.fleurdelyssf.com). Bus 2, 3, 4, 27, 76. **Open** 6-9.30pm Mon-Thur; 5.30-10.30pm Fri, Sat. **Main courses** *Set menu* $65-$85. **Credit** AmEx, DC, MC, V. **Map** p310 G3.

The grand, tent-draped interior of Fleur de Lys is synonymous with fine dining and, over the years, chef Hubert Keller's cuisine hasn't missed a step. He has a vast culinary repertoire and his menu is lush, exorbitant even. But the quality of the French food and the splendid wine list help you forget you're spending a fortune, and the service is attentive without being overbearing. Splash out on the *prix fixe* five-course tasting menu (there's a version for vegetarians as well).

Vegetarian

Millennium

Savoy Hotel, 580 Geary Street, at Jones Street (345 3900/www.millenniumrestaurant.com). BART Powell/bus 27, 38. **Open** 5.30-9.30pm Mon-Thur, Sun; 5.30-10pm Fri, Sat. **Main courses** $12-$18. **Credit** MC, V. **Map** p310 F/G4.

The award-winning and ever-popular gourmet vegetarian restaurant pulled up stakes in the Civic Center area and headed for the Theatre District not long ago. Happily, it took with it its refreshing, surprisingly hearty and inventive meatless menu. The new dining room is sophisticated yet casual. The menu changes frequently, but rarely misses, and is accompanied by what may well be the first all-organic wine list in the United States.

Embarcadero

American

Boulevard

1 Mission Street, at Steuart Street (543 6084/ www.boulevardrestaurant.com). BART Embarcadero/ Muni Metro F, J, K, L, M, N/bus 1, 2, 6, 7, 9, 14, 21, 31, 66, 71. **Open** *Lunch* 11.30am-2pm Mon-Fri. *Dinner* 5.30-10pm Mon-Wed, Sun; 5.30-10.30pm Thur-Sat. **Main courses** $14-$35. **Credit** AmEx, DC, Disc, MC, V. **Map** p311 J3.

Since 1993 this handsome room has been one of San Francisco's most consistently reliable restaurants. Always packed, it attracts locals and visitors with its waterfront views and hearty food. Self-taught chef Nancy Oakes specialises in elaborate New American dishes: pork chops, steaks and risottos are always on offer. Wood-roasted dishes are another strength. Service is casual although the prices are not: try the bar at lunchtime as a cheaper option.

Globe Restaurant

290 Pacific Avenue, at Battery Street (391 4132). Bus 12, 42, 83. **Open** 11.30am-1am Mon-Fri; 6pm-1am Sat; 6-11.30pm Sun. **Main courses** $12-$26. **Credit** AmEx, MC, V. **Map** p311 H2.

As diners are often reminded, this is where local chefs eat when they're not working. Chef Joseph Manzare is a New Yorker and one-time protégé of LA's Wolfgang Puck, which explains both the Globe's late opening hours and its penchant for California cuisine. An exposed-brick dining room adds a SoHo touch, as standards such as wood-oven pizzas and grilled salmon with buttery pasta and watercress are transformed by the freshness of their ingredients. The Globe is best known for its innovative meat dishes: try the T-bone steak for two.

One Market

1 Market Street, at Steuart Street (777 5577/ www.onemarket.com). BART Embarcadero/Muni Metro F/bus 14. **Open** *Lunch* 11.30am-2pm Mon-Fri. *Dinner* 5.30-9pm Mon-Sat. **Main courses** $14-$36. **Credit** AmEx, DC, Disc, MC, V. **Map** p311 H3.

There may be no restaurant that shows off San Francisco better than this one. The gracious picture windows allow diners to gaze out towards the soaring clock tower of the Ferry Building as the vintage streetcars amble past. Inside, the sincere American fare has never been better, with chef Adrian Hoffman preparing an inventive mix of straightforward classics (Caesar salad) and European-inspired brilliance (braised and glazed Berkshire pork shoulder with green onion farro). Meat and fish dishes from the rotisserie grill are a speciality. For a dining experience you won't forget, come in a group and request the chef's table located inside the kitchen.

Asian

Butterfly Embarcadero

Pier 33, at Bay Street (864 8999/www.butterflysf. com). Muni Metro F/bus 12. **Open** *Lunch* 11am-3pm daily. *Dinner* 5.30-10pm Mon-Wed, Sun; 5.30-11.30pm Thur-Sat. **Main courses** $8-$38. **Credit** AmEx, Disc, MC, V. **Map** p311 H1.

The Mission-based hangout has branched out to this new waterfront location. Chef-owner Robert Lam's pan-Asian cuisine is quite good, but nearly incidental to the stylish surroundings – beautiful views of the Bay without and beautiful crowd within. Local art adorns the walls and music from DJs fills the air. Highlights on the innovative menu include braised ribs, pumpkin risotto and soy-glazed black cod. **Other location**: 1710 Mission Street, between Duboce & 14th Streets, Mission (864 5585).

Ozumo

161 Steuart Street, at Mission Street (882 1333/ www.ozumo.com). Muni Metro F/bus 1, 2, 6, 7, 9, 14, 21, 31, 66, 71. **Open** 11.30am-midnight Mon-Fri; 5.30pm-midnight Sat, Sun. **Main courses** $12-$38; sushi omakase from $50. **Credit** AmEx, DC, Disc, MC, V. **Map** p311 J3.

There aren't enough 'e's in sleek to describe this beautiful contemporary Japanese restaurant, where some 6,000sq ft (560sq m) of design panache swaddle an equally chic crowd. The front area holds a bar and lounge serving an exhaustive menu of sakes and

Small plates get big

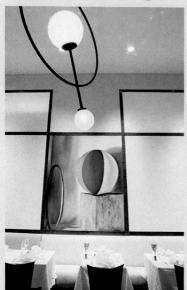

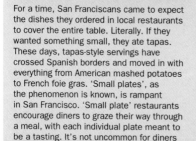

For a time, San Franciscans came to expect the dishes they ordered in local restaurants to cover the entire table. Literally. If they wanted something small, they ate tapas. These days, tapas-style servings have crossed Spanish borders and moved in with everything from American mashed potatoes to French foie gras. 'Small plates', as the phenomenon is known, is rampant in San Francisco. 'Small plate' restaurants encourage diners to graze their way through a meal, with each individual plate meant to be a tasting. It's not uncommon for diners to try six or seven different dishes in a single dinner. The appeal of such an approach is hardly mysterious, and the thanks should go to one man: **Pascal Rigo**.

Rigo hails from a small village in France, but his ever-expanding empire now includes a three-starred destination restaurant (La Table in Presidio Heights) and several of San Francisco's most popular casual dining spots. First apprenticed to a baker in France, Rigo moved in the late 1980s to Los Angeles, where he opened the wholesale bakery Bread Only. Soon he was selling bread to the top

70 restaurants and hotels in the city. He then moved to San Francisco where his new bakery business, Bay Bread, gave rise (sorry) to **Chez Nous** (average plate $10; see p139). It was Chez Nous that took the small plate concept beyond tapas. Rigo's Panissimo Group continued to expand, with new boulangeries as well as the restaurants **Galette** (plates $4-$15; see p146), **Le Petit Robert** (2300 Polk Street, at Green Street, Polk Gulch, 922 8100, average plate $12) and, his latest offering, **Cortez Restaurant & Bar** (pictured; average plate $12; see p119), right in the heart of the Theatre District. Each has a distinct style: Chez Nous is Mediterranean, Le Petit Robert is French and Cortez is globally inspired.

But Rigo has by no means cornered the small-plate market. Others interpreting the concept to high acclaim include **Andalu** (average plate $10; see p134), which draws inspiration from cuisines as different as Japanese and Swiss, and super-stylish **RNM** (average plate $12; see p135), where chef Justine Miner creates miniature versions of American comfort food – with the occasional Italian reference for good measure.

The Experience

161 Steuart Street, San Francisco, CA 94105 T 415.882.1333 F 415.882.1794 www.ozumo.com

Sushi Bar•Robata Grill•Sake Lounge•Open 7days a week

San Francisco
Contemporary Japanese Cuisine

Executive chef
Shotaro "Sho" Ka

rare teas. Amble past the robata grill – the robata menu's meat, fish and vegetables are the real attractions here – and you'll come to an enormous main dining room, with sushi bar and Bay Bridge views.

Slanted Door

100 Brannan, at Embarcadero (861 8032/ www.slanteddoor.com). Muni Metro N. **Open** *Lunch 11.30am-2.30pm daily. Dinner 5.30-10pm Mon-Thur, Sun; 5.30-10.30pm Fri, Sat.* **Main courses** $8-$27. **Credit** AmEx, MC, V. **Map** p311 J4.

Chef Charles Phan moved his wildly popular Vietnamese restaurant from the Mission to the less pedestrian-friendly Embarcadero while the original underwent remodelling. As we went to press, he was also planning a splashy new dining room at a high-profile corner of the new-look Ferry Building. If the shaking beef makes the move too, all will be well. Other popular dishes are spicy short ribs and shrimp-and-crab spring rolls. The original 540 Valencia Street location is slated to reopen in autumn 2004.

Yank Sing

Rincon Center, 101 Spear Street, at Mission Street (957 9300/www.yanksing.com). BART Embarcadero/ Muni Metro F, J, K, L, M, N/bus 1, 2, 6, 7, 9, 14, 21, 31, 66, 71. **Open** 11am-3pm Mon-Fri; 10am-4pm Sat, Sun. **Main courses** *Dim sum* $3-$8. **Credit** AmEx, DC, MC, V. **Map** p311 J3.

For many San Franciscans, Yank Sing is the de facto place for dim sum. Since closing its flagship location, the restaurant has lost a bit of lustre, but it still thrives here in a corner of the massive office complex. Non-English-speaking waitresses roll out an endless array of steaming dumplings, filled with everything from shrimp to pork to vegetables, and the on-the-go business crowd snap them up.

Civic Center

American

Indigo

687 McAllister Street, at Gough Street (673 9353/ www.indigorestaurant.com). Bus 5, 42, 47, 49. **Open** 5-11pm Tue-Sun. **Main courses** $15-$20. **Credit** AmEx, MC, V. **Map** p310 F4.

This cool restaurant has not only survived its non-descript location, but blossomed in it. The key is good food that is well priced, and an edgy, chic environment that defies trends and pretension. The lounge-like setting features a long, open kitchen from which emerges a never-ending mix of inventive New American dishes. To feel like you're entering the truly unknown, the Crimson Lounge downstairs is an ultra-swank candlelit hideaway.

Zuni Cafe

1658 Market Street, between Franklin & Gough Streets (552 2522). Muni Metro F, J, K, L, M, N/bus 6, 7, 66, 71. **Open** 11.30am-midnight Tue-Sat; 11am-11pm Sun. **Main courses** $10-$37. **Credit** AmEx, MC, V. **Map** p314 F5.

In its twenties but still full of life, Zuni marches to its own beat in a city of ever-newer rhythms. Chef Judy Rodgers is something of an icon, praised for Cal-Ital food that manages to be both memorable and transparently simple. The art-filled setting can be quite a scene before and after performances at the Davies (*see p210*), but the sourdough bread and oysters on an iced platter or the roast chicken and pizzettas from the wood-fired oven are enough of an attraction all by themselves.

European

Jardinière

300 Grove Street, at Franklin Street (861 5555/ www.jardiniere.com). Bus 21, 42, 47, 49. **Open** 5-10.30pm Mon-Wed, Sun; 5-11.30pm Thur-Sat. **Main courses** $25-$30. **Credit** AmEx, DC, Disc, MC, V. **Map** p314 F5.

When celebrity chef Traci des Jardins left her post at Rubicon in the late 1990s to set up her namesake eaterie, she single-handedly revived the city's flagging pre-opera and symphony dining scene. While some places in the area have caught up (and done so for less money), this whimsically shaped restaurant is still one of the best high-dollar special-occasion spots in the state. Des Jardins seeks tirelessly to find the best and most environmentally friendly local ingredients for her seasonal cuisine. Starters can be a meal in themselves, but mains like the wine-braised shortribs with horseradish potato purée are worth writing home about. The wine list features pages of sparkling wine selections.

Soluna

272 McAllister Street, at Larkin Street (621 2200/ www.solunasf.com). BART Civic Center/bus 5, 42, 47, 49. **Open** 7am-2.30pm Mon; 7am-9.30pm Tue-Fri; 5-9.30pm Sat. **Main courses** $8-$16. **Credit** AmEx, MC, V. **Map** p310 F4.

Soluna is a bit of an everyman: morning coffee shop, casual lunch spot at midday, tasty and affordable dinner option by evening. But for many the draw is after dinner, when DJs and the occasional live band turn the place into a hangout for a good-looking, dressed-down crowd. With its eye-popping views of the City Hall dome and proximity to the Asian Art Museum (*see p68*), this unassuming little spot has quickly built up a loyal daytime following as well, with a simple menu of earnest, well-priced fish and chicken dishes, plus a few tasty vegetarian choices.

SoMa

American

Acme Chop House

24 Willie Mays Plaza, corner of King & Third Streets (644 0240/www.acmechophouse.com). Muni Metro N/bus 15, 30, 42, 45, 76. **Open** 5.30-9pm Tue-Wed, Sun; 5.30-10pm Thur-Sat. **Main courses** $17-$36. **Credit** AmEx, DC, MC, V. **Map** p315 J5.

Traci des Jardins (of Jardinière fame; *see p123*) over-sees this handsome operation on the corner of SBC Park. It is her commitment to sustainable agriculture and fishing, and to organically raised meat, that sets this restaurant apart from most steak houses. The beef melts in the mouth, while the raw bar, with an assortment of oysters, mussels and fresh shrimp, is a fine way to start the meal. Lunch is served from 10.30am and 2pm when there's an afternoon ballgame on. It also opens from 4.30pm until after the finish of the night games.

Bacar

448 Brannan Street, between Third & Fourth Streets (904 4100/www.bacarsf.com). Bus 15, 30, 42, 45, 76. **Open** 5.30-11pm Mon-Wed, Sun; 5.30pm-midnight Thur-Sat. **Main courses** $16-$38. **Credit** AmEx, DC, MC, V. **Map** p315 H4/5.

One of the city's most talked-about restaurants when it opened in 2000, Bacar has felt the buzz subside somewhat, unlike the quality of the wine list: it's a cork-dork's Valhalla of 1,000 varietals, 100 of them available by the glass. The bottles loom over the guests in a glass-enclosed 'wine wall', the most eye-catching aspect of this remarkable three-level converted warehouse. Pair your wine with a wood-fired pizza, mesquite-grilled meat or reliable fish from the mix of approachable US and Mediterranean dishes.

Paragon

701 Second Street, at Townsend Street (537 9020/ www.paragonrestaurant.com). Muni Metro N/bus 15, 30, 42, 45, 76. **Open** 11.30am-2.30pm, 5.30-10pm Mon-Fri; 5.30-10pm Sat. **Main courses** $12-$19. **Credit** AmEx, DC, Disc, MC, V. **Map** p311 J4.

Paragon is a magnet for fans 'warming up' for the baseball. They eagerly press shoulder-to-shoulder at the huge bar, and the attractive dining room is similarly energy-charged. The classic American brasserie fare is rustic and reliable, but overpriced. Steaks and seafood come with hearty side orders like mashed potatoes and vegetable gratin. Paragon is part of an expanding empire these days: there are duplicates in three other cities.

The Public

1489 Folsom Street, at 11th Street (552 3065/ www.thepublicsf.com). Bus 9, 12, 42. **Open** 6-10pm Mon-Thur; 6pm-2am Fri, Sat. **Main courses** $13-$16. **Credit** MC, V. **Map** p314 G5.

Once upon a time the 11th Street corridor was a shopping mall for partiers. Now, with the Public, there are hints the stars may shine again. Skilfully blending nightclub energy with fine dining sophistication, the Public is built into a historic brick building that makes it feel as if it's been here longer. On the mezzanine is a stylish lounge with multiple bars. In the kitchen, American-Italian comfort is the theme. Highlights include eggplant napoleon with romesco sauce and ricotta and Niman Ranch flank steak with onion rings – straightforward, but executed with flair. Note: despite extended opening hours at weekends, the kitchen closes at 11pm.

Town Hall Restaurant

342 Howard Street, at Fremont Street (908 3900/ www.townhallsf.com). Bus 12, 30, 45, 76. **Open** 11.30am-2.30pm, 5.30-10pm Mon-Thur; 11.30am-2.30pm, 5.30-11pm Fri, Sat; 5.30-10pm Sun. **Main courses** $16-$25. **Credit** AmEx, MC, V. **Map** p311 H3.

Perhaps a hint of SoMa reawakening, certainly a little slice of New England, Town Hall is a collaboration between Postrio (*see p116*) chefs Mitchell and Steven Rosenthal and legendary front-of-house man Doug Washington. Together they've put together a great-looking restaurant in a historic brick building. The menu recalls classics from the American cookbook, with highlights including the Shrimp Etouffe (a rarity in these parts), the Town Hall cioppino (enough to feed Washington's army) and, at lunch, a true New York-style triple-decker sandwich.

21st Amendment

563 Second Street, between Bryant & Brannan Streets (369 0900/www.21st-amendment.com). Bus 15, 30, 42, 45, 76. **Open** 11.30am-9pm Mon, Tue; 11.30am-10pm Wed-Fri; noon-10pm Sat; 3-9pm Sun. **Main courses** $7-$17. **Credit** AmEx, Disc, MC, V. **Map** p311 J4.

Having a microbrewery this close to the ballpark is, of course, a brilliant idea. But to make it as good as this one is even better. A big, open, industrial space, with dining on two levels and a large social bar, it's always packed before games. Once you squeeze in, though, you'll happily quaff excellent own-made brews (the Amendment Pale Ale and Shot Tower Stout are recommended) and chow down on above-average pub grub, such as wood-fired pizzas.

Asian

For something with extra sizzle, dine with the 'gender illusionists' at **AsiaSF** (*see p233*).

Azie

826 Folsom Street, at Fourth Street (538 0918/ www.restaurantazie.com). Bus 12, 30, 45, 76. **Open** 5.30-10.30pm Mon-Wed, Sun; 5.30-11.30pm Thur, Fri; 5-11.30pm Sat. **Main courses** $15-$25. **Credit** AmEx, DC, Disc, MC, V. **Map** p311/315 H4.

With its soaring ceiling, flowing red drapery and swanky lighting fixtures (always dimmed), Azie is one of the most interesting-looking restaurants in town. After an ambitious but poorly received start, Azie has settled into serving French-inspired Asian dishes. Presentations are artful and wonderfully geometric, with small plates of, say, duck spring rolls combining with green bean and wild mushroom tempura for an interesting and ultimately satisfying meal. Quietly, Azie has become a true SoMa gem.

Loft 11

316 11th Street, at Folsom Street (701 8111/ www.loft11sf.com). Bus 9,12, 42. **Open** 6pm-midnight Tue-Sat. **Main courses** $8-$18. **Credit** AmEx, MC, V. **Map** p314 G5.

Part of the 11th Street revival, this bar/restaurant is a fun hangout for the casually hip. Yet if you pay attention, there's much from the kitchen to appreciate. Erik Hopfinger is adept at creating eclectic food 'ideas', here presenting such delicacies as lamb lollipops and sake-braised pork ribs. That the place has a nightclub vibe (opening until 2am on Fridays and Saturdays) shouldn't overshadow the food.

European

Le Charm

315 Fifth Street, at Folsom Street (546 6128/ www.lecharm.com). Bus 12, 27, 30, 45, 76. **Open** 11.30am-2.30pm, 5.30-9.30pm Mon-Thur; 11.30am-2.30pm, 5.30-10pm Fri; 5.30-10pm Sat; 5-8.30pm Sun. **Main courses** $7-$17. **Credit** AmEx, MC, V. **Map** p315 H4.
This rather nondescript little restaurant is as charming as its name suggests once you get inside. One of the few places in town where you can enjoy a true French bistro menu without parting with major cash, Le Charm has a three-course *prix fixe* ($25) that can include such mains as grilled tuna Provençal, chicken chasseur with pomme fondant and tarragon sauce, or grilled beef brochettes. Try the tarte tatin for dessert. The wine list is tiny, but well chosen.

Fringale

570 Fourth Street, between Bryant & Brannan Streets (543 0573). Bus 15, 30, 42, 45, 76. **Open** 11.30am-3pm, 5.30-10.30pm Mon-Fri; 5.30-10.30pm Sat. **Main courses** $8-$19. **Credit** AmEx, MC, V. **Map** p315 H4/5.
Literally translated, the name means 'the urge to eat', neatly describing a menu that reads classic French, but informed by chef Gerald Hirigoyen's Basque heritage. Frisée salads, beef carpaccio, lamb sweetbread fricassee… all with a rural air that cuts their elaborate richness. Book well in advance and come prepared to sit close to your fellow diners, but every noisy bite is worth the trouble.

LuLu

816 Folsom Street, between Fourth & Fifth Streets (495 5775/www.restaurantlulu.com). Bus 12, 27, 30, 45, 76. **Open** 11.30am-10.30pm Mon-Thur, Sun; 11.30am-11.30pm Fri, Sat. **Main courses** $7-$23. **Credit** AmEx, DC, MC, V. **Map** p311 H4.
Executive chef Jody Denton turns out consistently delicious, rustic, Italian-influenced cuisine, including specialities from the wood-fired oven, rotisserie and grill, with pizzas, pasta and shellfish coming on large platters that are meant to be shared. The industrial-looking space is usually filled to capacity, so be sure to book a table or take your chance at the bar. Conversation is difficult in the noisy and crowded room, but LuLu's wine bar next door offers a more intimate and quieter alternative if you primarily want to chat. Denton also owns stylish Azie (*see p124*) and a petite version of LuLu is open in the Ferry Building marketplace.

Thirsty Bear Brewing Company

661 Howard Street, between Second & Third Streets (974 0905/www.thirstybear.com). Bus 12, 14, 15, 30, 45, 76. **Open** 11.30am-10.30pm Mon-Thur; 11.30am-midnight Fri; noon-midnight Sat; 5-10pm Sun. **Main courses** $8-$17. **Credit** AmEx, DC, MC, V. **Map** p311 H4.
Gamers, barflies and diners all enjoy the Thirsty Bear, known for its pool tables and dartboards, microbrewed beers and a rotating selection of good Spanish tapas. The famous *kokotxas* (fish cheeks) and numerous paellas standout. Patrons are often corporate clones out for an after-work beer and quick meal, but don't let that put you off. Everybody feels at home here, and the beer is outstanding.

XYZ

W Hotel, 181 Third Street, at Howard Street (817 7836/www.xyz-sf.com). Bus 12, 14, 15, 30, 45, 76. **Open** *Breakfast* 6.30-10.30am Mon-Fri. *Brunch* 8am-2.30pm Sat, Sun. *Lunch* 11.30am-2.30pm Mon-Fri. *Dinner* 5.30-10.30pm Mon-Thur, Sun; 5.30-11pm Fri, Sat. **Main courses** $11-$36. **Credit** AmEx, DC, Disc, MC, V. **Map** p311 H4.
Adjacent to the lobby of the swanky W Hotel (*see p42*), XYZ holds fast to its austere decor and sophisticated clientele. Young chef Malachi Harland is only

Mr Big

In the window of a Mexican restaurant on New York's Upper West Side is a sign that boasts of 'San Francisco Mission-style Burritos'. They're that good? They're really that good.

Often imitated but seldom matched, the Mission burrito is as much of an attraction as the Golden Gate Bridge or a cable car ride. Indeed, some of them are bigger than cable cars. The big burrito is, in fact, more a Californian invention than Mexican, but its roots are strong in the authenticity of the ingredients. All over town everything from grilled steak (*carne asada*) and refried beans (*frijoles*) to shrimp (*camarones*) and black beans is wrapped into massive fresh-made tortillas.

The burrito is the best bet at most of the city's taquerias, typically simple and unassuming places, with basic Latin American decor, tiled floors and open-grill kitchens flanked by a counter and a cash register. They're located in all parts of town – one of the best is **Los Hermanos** (*see p139*) – but found in great numbers in the Mission District (*see p134*). And every San Franciscan has their favourite. Before long, you will too.

the most recent in a long line of talents in the kitchen, but he seems to have found his niche here and the flavourful menu is one of the longest running in the restaurant's short history (opened in 2000). Among his greatest hits are roasted sea scallops with ginger carrot sauce and maple leaf duck breast with caramelised red onions.

Chinatown

American

Alfred's Steak House

659 Merchant Street, between Kearny & Montgomery Streets (781 7058/www.alfredssteakhouse.com). Bus 1, 15, 41, 42. **Open** 5.30-9.30pm Mon, Sun; 11.30am-9.30pm Tue-Thur; 11.30am-9pm Fri; 5.30-9pm Sat. **Main courses** $7-$36. **Credit** AmEx, DC, Disc, MC, V. **Map** p311 H3.

After decades with its trademark sign above the Broadway tunnel, Alfred's moved to a new location near the Chinese Cultural Center. Loyal patrons eagerly followed, proving that this is still quite possibly the best steak house in town – it's certainly the best steak house experience in town. With giant Chicago rib-eyes, tender T-bones and a porterhouse that covers the dish, Alfred's feels like a bit of San Francisco gone by. The fish and pasta are excellent and the bar, which prepares a superlative Martini, stocks more than 100 single malts.

Asian

The best Chinese food in San Francisco is actually found in the Richmond District (*see p140*), but we've listed Chinatown's best below. There are also a few low-profile spots with good dim sum, potstickers or healthy soup: the Chinese crowd at **Dol Ho's** (808 Pacific Avenue, at Stockton Steet, 392 2828) speaks volumes about the food's authenticity, and **House of Nanking** (919 Kearny Street, at Jackson Street, 421 1429), although avoided by locals as too touristy, never disappoints with its food.

R&G Lounge

631 Kearny Street, at Clay Street (982 7877). Bus 1, 15, 41. **Open** 11am-9.30pm Mon-Thur, Sun; 11am-10pm Fri, Sat. **Main courses** $6-$28. **Credit** AmEx, DC, MC, V. **Map** p311 H3.

This blindingly bright restaurant features two levels of dining, neither much to look at, but each serving authentic Hong Kong-style food. The emphasis is on seafood, most of which comes direct from in-house tanks. People come from miles around for the deep-fried salt-and-pepper crab and barbecue pork.

Yuet Lee

1300 Stockton Street, at Broadway (982 6020). Bus 12, 15, 30, 39, 41, 45, 83. **Open** 11am-3am Mon, Wed-Sun. **Main courses** $5-$15. **No credit cards. Map** p311 G2.

Chefs and restaurant folk are often spotted at this tiny, bright-green Chinese eatery, probably because the seafood is excellent and the place stays open until 3am. Worth trying are the roasted squab with fresh coriander and lemon, sautéed clams with black bean sauce and 'eight precious noodle soup', made with eight kinds of meat. The lighting is glaringly unflattering and service matter of fact.

North Beach

American

Moose's

1652 Stockton Street, between Union & Filbert Streets (989 7800/www.mooses.com). Bus 15, 30, 39, 41, 45. **Open** 5.30-10pm Mon-Wed; 11.30am-11pm Fri, Sat; 10am-10pm Sun. **Main courses** $18-$33. **Credit** AmEx, DC, MC, V. **Map** p310/11 G2.

Long-time restaurateurs Ed and Mary Etta Moose create environments that are uniquely San Franciscan. A full bar, an open kitchen serving consistently good California cuisine and an extensive wine list are the draws here, as well as the excellent Sunday brunch. Regardless of changes to the menu, the storied Mooseburger keeps right on satisfying local celebs, high-profile business types and big-ego politicos. Despite the uneven service.

Washington Square Bar & Grill

1707 Powell Street, at Union Street (982 8123). Bus 15, 30, 41, 45/cable car Powell-Mason. **Open** *Brunch* 10.30am-3pm Sat, Sun. *Lunch* 11.30am-3pm Mon-Fri. *Dinner* 5.30-10pm Mon-Wed; 5.30-11pm Thur, Fri; 5-11pm Sat; 5-10pm Sun. **Main courses** $17-$24. **Credit** MC, V. **Map** p310 G2.

Like so many of San Francisco's citizens, this restaurant went through an identity crisis. For years known as the WashBag, it abruptly changed ownership and its name. To Cobalt. Many loyalists were shocked, but happily, after a couple of years, it has switched back to comfy old WashBag. Today it plays a familiar role as neighborhood watering hole and reliable American-Italian restaurant. The best dishes are the classics, like double cut pork chops and the sturdy WSB&G burger. Live music jazz lends the place an energetic tone.

Asian

House

1230 Grant Avenue, at Columbus Avenue & Vallejo Street (986 8612/www.thehse.com). Bus 15, 30, 41, 45. **Open** *Lunch* 11.30am-3pm Mon-Sat. *Dinner* 5.30-10pm Mon-Thur; 5.30-11pm Fri; 5-11pm Sat; 5-10pm Sun. **Main courses** *Lunch* $8-$14. *Dinner* $15-$21. **Credit** AmEx, DC, MC, V. **Map** p311 G2.

Welcome respite from all the Italian spots in the area, this no-frills (though often deafeningly loud) Chinese fusion dining room works wonders with fresh, seasonal produce and East-meets-West

Low on lighting but high on character, **Sodini's** is a neighbourhood Italian to cherish.

preparations. The Chinese chicken salad with sesame soy illustrates the menu: light and tangy and big enough to be a meal on its own. The menu changes frequently, resisting fickle trends while remaining decidedly sophisticated. Wines are rock-bottom priced.

European

Enrico's

504 Broadway, at Kearny Street (982 6223/ www.enricossidewalkcafe.com). Bus 12, 15, 30, 41, 83. **Open** 11.30am-11pm Mon-Thur, Sun; 11.30am-12.30am Fri, Sat. **Main courses** $9-$23. **Credit** AmEx, Disc, MC, V. **Map** p311 G2.

Enrico's is a quintessential North Beach hangout, where locals and tourists happily bump elbows. The outdoor patio has prime people-watching and live jazz most nights. Pizzas baked in wood-fired ovens are the top draws, but the kitchen also ably cranks out savoury pasta, meat and fish. A noisy, friendly environment with a long wooden bar where, oddly, the Cuban-inspired Mojito is the speciality drink.

Sodini's

510 Green Street, at Grant Avenue (291 0499). Bus 15, 30, 41, 45. **Open** 5-10pm Mon-Thur; 5-11pm Fri, Sat. **Main courses** $13-$20. **Credit** MC, V. **Map** p311 G2.

Off the beaten track (but no less popular because of it), this little place offers a bit of romance and a lot of good food. Small and dark, with red, flickering candle lanterns, Sodini's jams its patrons in together and servers squeeze past carrying some of the

best pizza in town. The rib-sticking lasagne and rich ravioli are also noteworthy, and the Chianti cheap and plentiful. Arrive early, sign the waiting list and drop over to a neighbouring bar while you wait for a table.

Tommaso's Ristorante Italiano

1042 Kearny Street, at Broadway (398 9696). Bus 12, 15, 30, 41, 45, 83. **Open** 5-10.30pm Tue-Sun. **Main courses** $8-$20. **Credit** AmEx, DC, Disc, MC, V. **Map** p311 G2.

Tommaso's has been a no-affectation, no-frills San Francisco dining institution since 1935. Known citywide for simply good Italian food, served family-style in a tiny, boisterous dining room, the wood-fired thin-crust pizzas and calzones are worthy of their high reputation. Surprisingly good house red wine is served in ceramic jugs. There are no reservations, so join the queue and keep your eyes peeled: you never know who might walk in.

US Restaurant

515 Columbus Avenue, at Green Street (397 5200/ www.originalusrestaurant.com). Bus 15, 30, 41, 45. **Open** 11am-9pm Tue-Thur, Sun; 11am-10pm Fri, Sat. **Main courses** $8-$14. **Credit** AmEx, DC, Disc, MC, V. **Map** p310/11 G2.

Rising from the ashes of a temporary closure in 1997, this is another of the few places to go for a true slice of historic North Beach. Named after the Unione Sportiva, an Italian sports club active when the restaurant originally opened in 1919, the US has a menu that features hearty northern Italian cuisine like *bollito* (boiled beef) and rib-eye steak. Portions are huge, the service downright familial.

Middle Eastern

The Helmand
*430 Broadway, between Kearny & Montgomery
Streets (362 0641). Bus 12, 15, 30, 41, 83.*
Open 5.30-10pm Mon-Thur, Sun; 5.30-11pm Fri,
Sat. **Main courses** $12-$17. **Credit** AmEx, MC, V.
Map p311 G/H2.
Still the city's only Afghan restaurant, the Helmand
is consistently on lists of recommended eateries. The
food is cheap and deliciously aromatic, with specialities of baked baby pumpkin and scallion and leek
ravioli. Influenced by the flavours of India, Asia and
the Middle East, marinades and fragrant spices give
each dish unique character. Highlights include the
spiced own-made yoghurts, tender rack of lamb and
koufta challow (meatballs in cinnamon tomato sauce).

Fisherman's Wharf

European

Gary Danko
*800 North Point Street, at Hyde Street (749 2060/
www.garydanko.com). Bus 19, 30, 42/cable car
Powell-Hyde.* **Open** 5.30-10pm daily. **Main courses**
Set menus $58, $68, $78. **Credit** AmEx, DC, Disc,
MC, V. **Map** p310 F1.
Critics lined up to hand out stars to Gary Danko
even before he opened his eponymous 75-seat restaurant. It turns out praise was in order. Danko has created a fabulous – and fabulously understated – spot
for fine dining. The best way to experience Danko's
dexterity and genius is via the tasting menus, which
change seasonally but might include chickpea-
crusted black grouper starter, beef medallion with
orzo risotto as a main, and a selection of farmhouse
artisan cheeses to finish. If you don't want to go all
in, a more casual adventure can be found at the bar.

Seafood

Alioto's
*8 Fisherman's Wharf, at Taylor & Jefferson Streets
(673 0183). Muni Metro F/bus 39, 42.* **Open** 11am-
11pm daily. **Main courses** $7-$24. **Credit** AmEx,
DC, Disc, MC, V. **Map** p310 F1.
Alioto's began as a sidewalk stand offering crab and
shrimp cocktails served in a paper cup. Now, more
than 70 years later, it is a hugely popular restaurant
owned by a prominent San Francisco family. It
offers an amazing view of the Bay, so hordes of
tourists fight their way in year-round, but the
kitchen still manages to turn out fine (if somewhat
overpriced) seafood, as well as fish-centred Sicilian
specialities. The wine list is outstanding.

A Sabella's
*Third floor, 2766 Taylor Street, at Jefferson Street
(771 6775/www.asabella.com). Muni Metro F/bus
39, 42.* **Open** 9.45pm daily. **Main courses** $13-$56.
Credit AmEx, DC, MC, V. **Map** p310 F/G1.

Fisherman's Wharf has its share of pirates, but
Sabella's remains one of those fighting for what's
right in the sea of culinary tricksters. Family-owned
for four generations, the restaurant takes great pride
in its food and service. The huge dining room, with
great Bay views, is comfortable for kids and adults.
Wait while impossibly fresh local Dungeness crab
and lobster are cooked for you, or try the cioppino
for a real taste of local cuisine. The pasta and steak
are certainly worthwhile, but it would be a shame to
pass up the seafood when it's done this well.

Blue Mermaid
*Argonaut Hotel, 471 Jefferson Street, at Hyde Street
(771 2222/www.bluemermaidsf.com). Cable car
Powell-Hyde/Muni 10, 19, 30.* **Open** Lunch 11.30-
5pm daily. *Dinner* 5-9pm Mon-Thur, Sun; 5-10pm Fri,
Sat. **Main courses** $12-$24. **Credit** AmEx, DC,
Disc, MC, V. **Map** p310 F1.
A welcome addition to the Fisherman's Wharf dining scene, this rustic-looking restaurant is set off the
lobby of the Argonaut Hotel (*see p44*) and was
designed to recall the history of the working wharf.
The menu is great for fogged-in days, with hearty
chowders spooned up from large cauldrons – specialities include New England clam, sweetcorn and
Dungeness crab varieties. A great spot for families.

Russian Hill, Nob Hill & Polk Gulch

American

Tablespoon
*2209 Polk Street, between Vallejo & Green Streets,
Russian Hill (268 0140). Bus 19, 41, 42, 45, 47, 49,
76.* **Open** 6pm-midnight Mon, Wed-Sat; 10am-10pm
Sun. **Main courses** $17-$20. **Credit** AmEx, MC, V.
Map p310 F2.
Two young guys with big vision took over an under-
managed spot and have turned it into a delightful
treat. The concept of offering well-above-par food at
neighbourhood prices seems obvious, but it's much
easier said than done. Here, John Jasso and Rob
Reischer do it with panache: four-star service at
casual prices. The food is inventive (too inventive at
times), but appeals to the home-cooking heart –
braised lamb shank is top-notch. The bar's hip too.

Asian

Sushi Groove
*1916 Hyde Street, between Union & Green Streets,
Russian Hill (440 1905). Bus 41, 45/cable car
Powell-Hyde.* **Open** 5.30-10pm Mon-Thur, Sun; 5.30-
10.30pm Fri, Sat. **Main courses** $13-$16; sushi $3-
$8. **Credit** AmEx, Disc, MC, V. **Map** p310 F2.
An inventive, highly charged sushi restaurant, with
rich, postmodern decor and drum 'n' bass mood
music to underscore the atmosphere. The original
rolls and salads attract a stylish clientele, who don't

Eat, Drink, Shop

Gary Danko.
See p128.

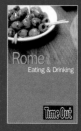

seem to mind elbow-to-elbow seating in a dining room the size of a postage stamp. Fresh crab, sea urchin and eel join favourites like mackerel, tuna and salmon; most of it is very good indeed. The impressive sake selection is itself worth the trip.

Cuban

Habana

2080 Van Ness Avenue, at Pacific Avenue, Polk Gulch (441 2822/www.habana1948.com). Bus, 1, 42, 47, 49. **Open** 5.30-10pm Mon-Fri; 5.30-11pm Sat, Sun. **Main courses** $18-$20. **Credit** AmEx, DC, Disc, MC, V. **Map** p310 F3.

Like an accelerated phoenix, this place is constantly reborn. Currently meant to evoke the spirit of Cuba in 1948, Habana's uncosy space is full of swaying banana palms and over two tons of wrought iron. Luckily, the lack of atmosphere is compensated for by some very nice modern interpretations of Cuban classics. Three seasonal ceviches start things off nicely, the main courses are highlighted by the delicious Ropa Nueva, a whimsical braised beef ragout served with cumin-marinated skirt steak with chimmichurri sauce, and don't miss the coconut flan. At the bar, the Mojito is king.

European

Acquerello

1722 Sacramento Street, between Van Ness Avenue & Polk Street, Polk Gulch (567 5432/www.acquerello. com). Bus 1, 42, 49, 76/cable car California. **Open** 5.30-10.30pm Tue-Sat. **Main courses** $29-$32. **Credit** AmEx, Disc, MC, V. **Map** p310 F3.

Blink and you might miss this unassuming restaurant, but it soon becomes a favourite. For ten years the dining room, with its big bold floral arrangements and exposed beams, has been regularly voted as among the city's most romantic. Yet chef and co-owner Suzette Gresham's contemporary Italian food remains the draw: the light salads and pastas are never wimpy, the wine list earns numerous awards.

The Dining Room

Ritz-Carlton Hotel, 600 Stockton Street, at California Street, Nob Hill (773 6198). Bus 1, 30, 45/cable car California. **Open** 6-9pm Tue-Thur; 5.30-9.30pm Fri, Sat. **Main courses** Set menus $62, $75, $81. **Credit** AmEx, DC, Disc, MC, V. **Map** p310 G3.

The place that puts the 'fine' in fine dining, the Ritz-Carlton's Dining Room is San Francisco's most honoured restaurant. It has a global reputation and eating here is nothing short of an event – the wait-staff-to-diner ratio is close to 1:1. Opulent without being over the top, the refined dining room is, if anything, a little too serious. More elegance is found in the modern French menu, all inventively imagined and artfully executed; also well known are its seasonal speciality menus, like the annual white-truffle festival, while the *prix fixe* menus (mostly) steer clear of lobster-and-caviar obviousness. Master

sommelier Stephane Lacroix will ably guide you through appropriate libations; and the bar has one of the country's longest lists of single-malt scotch.

La Folie

2316 Polk Street, between Union & Green Streets, Polk Gulch (776 5577/www.lafolie.com). Bus 19, 41, 42, 45, 47, 49, 76. **Open** 5.30-10.30pm Mon-Sat. **Main courses** Set menus $58, $72, $82. **Credit** AmEx, DC, Disc, MC, V. **Map** p310 F2.

Chef Roland Passot enjoys a passionate following at this delightful French-Californian eatery. Prices are steep, but the cooking is exquisite. Opt for the five-course discovery menu ($75), which allows you to sample such dishes as lobster and albacore salad, roti of quail and squab or a trio of rabbit (loin, rack and braised). The Provençal decor and attentive staff add to La Folie's charm – the recently opened Green Room is a nice option for intimate dining.

Zarzuela

2000 Hyde Street, at Union Street, Russian Hill (346 0800). Bus 41, 45/cable car Powell-Hyde. **Open** 5.30-10pm Tue-Thur; 5.30-10.30pm Fri, Sat. **Main courses** $9-$14. **Credit** MC, V. **Map** p310 F2.

Cosy Zarzuela serves up Spanish cuisine amid posters of bull fights and maps of Spain. The tapas are always a treat, but old standbys like grilled eggplant filled with goat's cheese, sautéed shrimps in garlic and olive oil, and fried potatoes with garlic and sherry vinegar never disappoint.

Seafood

Pesce

2227 Polk Street, between Green & Vallejo Streets, Polk Gulch (928 8025). Bus 19, 41, 42, 45, 47. **Open** 5-11pm Mon-Thur; 5pm-midnight Fri, Sat. **Main courses** $7-$15. **Credit** AmEx, MC, V. **Map** p310 F2.

This simple seafood restaurant and bar is wildly popular with locals, who love having a place nearby that proves fabulous seafood doesn't have to be fancy or expensive. Starters include excellent mussels, cod cakes and calamari, while mains tend to the Italian. Modest and comfortable, this is where you can feel happy making a mess with your cioppino.

Swan Oyster Depot

1517 Polk Street, between California & Sacramento Streets, Polk Gulch (673 1101). Bus 1, 19, 42, 47, 49, 76/cable car California. **Open** 8am-5.30pm Mon-Sat. **Main courses** $5-$15. **No credit cards.** **Map** p310 F3.

A San Francisco institution since 1912, the Depot is half fish market and half counter-service hole in the wall. The best time to visit is between November and June, when the local Dungeness crab is in season, but at any time the selections are straight-from-the-water fresh. Specialities include classic clam chowder, the smoked salmon plate and an obscenely large variety of oysters. You can buy shellfish to take away – a good option if the place is too crowded. The staff are boisterous and friendly. Don't miss this one.

On the cheap Blue-collar price,

In many cities there are two options: dine at a fancy restaurant for fancy money or have your fast food off Formica under the strip lights. Here, where people take their dining as seriously as their budgets, it's no surprise to find many places where you can eat like a gourmet without breaking the bank.

At **Barney's** (4138 24th Street, near Noe Street, 282 7770, main courses $5-$7) in Noe Valley the theme is hamburgers and the style gourmet. Grilled perfectly to taste, there are all manner of clever toppings, as well as 21 burger varieties, including chicken, turkey, tofu and grain versions. **Park Chow** (*pictured above*; 1240 Ninth Avenue, at

Lincoln Way, Sunset, 665 9912, main courses $7-$15; *see also p135* **Chow**) not only serves top-quality fare, but is also perfectly located for a bite after an exhausting day spent exploring Golden Gate Park. Its flatiron steak with fries is a favourite, as are the huge chicken salad, the noodles and the wood-fired pizzas. If the notion of 'fresh food for a hungry universe' appeals, **Pluto's** (*pictured right*; 3258 Scott Street, at Chestnut Street, Marina, 775 8867, main courses $4-$8) is where to go. It lacks the great atmosphere of Park Chow, but more than makes up for it in mouth-watering, health-conscious cuisine. Ordering is

Mission

You want burritos? Talk to **Mr Big** (*see p125*), then check our selection on p134-135.

American

Delfina

3621 18th Street, between Dolores & Guerrero Streets (552 4055). Muni Metro J/bus 33. **Open** 5.30-10pm Mon-Thur, Sun; 5.30-11pm Fri, Sat. **Main courses** $12-$19. **Credit** MC, V. **Map** p314 F6.
Chef Craig Stoll was all over the local press when his charming little restaurant opened a few years ago. Which may be why it's now a charming

big restaurant. In an era of fusion-food madness, Stoll keeps it simple but never ordinary. His fresh-made pasta, fish and braised meats burst with flavour – you actually want to order the chicken. The menu changes daily, reflecting Stoll's desire to stay on his toes. The staff don't always share his ambition.

Luna Park

694 Valencia Street, at 18th Street (553 8584/ www.lunaparksf.com). BART 16th Street/bus 14, 26, 33, 49. **Open** 11.30am-2.30pm, 5.30-10.30pm Mon-Thur; 11.30am-2.30pm, 5.30-11.30pm Fri; 11.30am-3pm, 5.30-11.30pm Sat; 11.30am-3pm, 5.30-10pm Sun. **Main courses** $9-$15. **Credit** AmEx, MC, V. **Map** p314 F6.

white-collar taste

cafeteria-style, but swift and friendly. Choose a big selection of pasta salads as a side and you can easily put together a tasty meal, while spending little more than spare change.

Given San Francisco's legendary fusion of cultures, it's surprisingly hard to get quality Middle Eastern fare cheaply. If you're in the Mission, though, you're in luck. The falafels at **Truly Mediterranean** (3109 16th Street, near Valencia Street, Mission, 252 7482, main courses $3.75-$6.95; *see also p146*) are always fresh and filled with wonderfully flavourful lamb, chicken or eggplant. There's the full complement of top-notch sides, including rich houmous and tangy baba ganoush, but a group of four can eat heartily for less than $30.

If you fancy a bit of class, head to **Blue** (*see p231*) in the Castro, a bistro-like diner whose inexpensive American fare is served by sassy waitstaff in blue shirts. The minimalist decor isn't echoed by the food, which comes in ample portions and with familiar American names. The meaty chilli is noteworthy, as is the chicken pot pie. Until you've had too much of both. Finally, inner Richmond contains quirky little **Q** (*see p140*), home to big salads and massive plates of crispy fried chicken and fluffy mashed potatoes – all at prices that leave the wallet as full as the belly. Its days as a barbecue specialist mean the short ribs are still top drawer, but the menu is now as adventurous and eclectic as the decor. The service? Four-star friendly. At least.

Eat, Drink, Shop

The concept is obvious: no-nonsense food at decent prices in an environment that makes people want to linger. Its diminutive size (just 50 seats) doesn't deter locals from queuing; the highly charged lounge bar catches the spillover. Once you get a table, expect swift, courteous service and an accessible selection of hearty dishes, including flatiron steak and french fries, the amazing tuna poke and earthy stomach-fillers like 'pot on fire' – slowly simmered beef brisket with carrots, turnips, leeks and potatoes in broth. The duo behind this operation now has LPs in other cities, as well as another popular spot nearby called Last Supper Club (1199 Valencia Street, at 23rd Street, 695 1199, www.lastsupperclubsf.com), serving Italian cuisine.

Pauline's Pizza

260 Valencia Street, between Duboce Avenue & 14th Street (552 2050). Bus 14, 26, 49. **Open** 5-10pm Tue-Sat. **Main courses** $12-$21. **Credit** MC, V. **Map** p314 F6.

Pauline's specialises in inventive, thin-crust pizzas made with top-quality produce. This is gourmet pie, with ingredients like roasted peppers, goat's cheese, smoked pork, edible flowers and exotic vegetables, plus several without tomato sauce. The pesto pizza is particularly renowned, and comes with basil and pesto baked into the crust. Complement your main course with an organic salad or own-made soup. The original headquarters of Levi Strauss is next door.

Slow Club

2501 Mariposa Street, at Hampshire Street
(241 9390/www.slowclub.com). Bus 9, 22, 27, 33,
53. **Open** 11.30am-2.30pm, 6.30-10pm Mon-Thur;
11.30am-2.30pm, 6.30-11pm Fri; 10am-2.30pm, 6.30-
11pm Sat; 10am-2.30pm Sun. **Main courses** $7-$17.
Credit MC, V. **Map** p315 G6.

This is a true local post, partly because of its remote
locale, but also because people love to hang out here.
Slow Club's laid-back atmosphere and understated
charm make it one of the coolest restaurant/bars
in town. The dinner menu changes nightly. Typical
mains include pan-roasted duck breast and
chipotle-glazed pork chops. There are no reservations, but waiting is tolerable in the cosy bar area.
Also a great spot for brunch.

Universal Café

2814 19th Street, between Bryant & Florida Streets
(821 4608). Bus 27. **Open** 5.30-10pm Tue-Thur;
5.30-11pm Fri; 9am-2.30pm, 5.30-11pm Sat; 9am-
2.30pm Sun. **Main courses** $7-$24. **Credit** AmEx,
DC, MC, V. **Map** p314 G7.

One of the first upmarket spots to open in this area,
near what became the centre of the gentrified
Mission, Universal Café has held its own with an
understated, industrial-look dining room and fresh,
interesting food. It's a great spot for a weekend
breakfast, when you can enjoy potato pancakes at
an outside table; lunch features focaccia sandwiches,
salads and tiny pizzas. Dinner brings higher prices,
but a decent menu too. Don't pass it by.

Asian

Firecracker

1007 Valencia Street, at 21st Street (642 3470).
BART 16th Street/bus 14, 26, 33, 49. **Open** 5.30-
10.30pm Mon-Thur; 5.30-11pm Fri, Sat. **Main courses**
$9-$15. **Credit** DC, Disc, MC, V. **Map** p314 F7.

Always reliable when fun is the order of the evening,
Firecracker lives up to its name with fire-red
walls and an often ear-splitting din. The place has
withstood the onslaught of Asian-inspired food
trends and carved a niche for itself with Chinese
standards. Spring rolls, dumplings and seafood
specialities are among the most popular orders. A
good choice before stepping out into the Mission
District night.

European

Andalu

3198 16th Street, at Guererro Street (621 2211/
www.andalusf.com). BART 16th Street/bus 14,
22, 33, 49, 53. **Open** 5.30-10.30pm Mon-Tue,
Sun; 5.30-11pm Wed-Thur; 5.30-11.30pm Fri, Sat.
Main courses *Plates* $5-$12. **Credit** AmEx, DC,
MC, V. **Map** p314 F6.

This big spacious room fills up with Mission hipsters who have figured out that you can have style
and good food too. The long bar at the back is great

when you're waiting for a table, but once you sit
down the focus shifts from the crowd to cuisine.
Small plates are given an inventive twist here, with
such surprises as glazed chicken yakitori skewers
and seared scallops with truffled leeks. Save room
for a fresh-made plate of donuts for dessert.

Foreign Cinema

2534 Mission Street, between 21st & 22nd Streets
(648 7600/www.foreigncinema.com). Bus 14, 49.
Open 6pm-2am Tue-Fri; 11pm-2am Sat, Sun.
Main courses $18-$27. **Credit** AmEx, MC, V.
Map p314 F7.

After surviving some unfortunate growing
pains, Foreign Cinema has emerged as one of the
Mission's best spots for dining; the opening of a
bar, Laszlo, contributed to the steady stream of
customers. The decor is dominated by the screen on
one side of the outdoor dining room. Classic films
are projected on to it each night, and there are speakers at each table for those who want to listen. But
the food remains the focus, a frequently updated
list of classically rooted Mediterranean favourites
and stellar oysters.

Ti Couz Creperie

3108 16th Street, between Valencia & Guerrero
Streets (252 7373). BART 16th Street/bus 14, 22,
26, 33, 49, 53. **Open** 11am-11pm Mon-Fri; 10am-
11pm Sat; 10am-10pm Sun. **Main courses** $2-$10.
Credit MC, V. **Map** p314 F6.

All walks of urban life can be found in this modest
crêperie. Savoury buckwheat galettes as well as
sweet crêpes are cooked captivatingly before your
eyes in classic Breton style, with more than 100
fillings on offer, from smoked salmon to lemon and
brown sugar. Ti Couz Two, next door, has seafood
and a full bar.

Latin American

El Farolito

2779 Mission Street, at 24th Street (824 7877).
BART 24th Street/bus 14, 26, 48, 49, 67.
Open 11am-1am Mon-Thur, Sun; 11am-3am Fri, Sat.
No credit cards. Map p314 F7.

El Farolito is wildly popular for its mouth-watering
burritos and fine quesadillas, enhanced by complimentary warm tortilla chips and fresh salsa.

El Nuevo Frutilandia

3077 24th Street, between Folsom & Treat Streets
(648 2958). BART 24th Street/bus 12, 48, 67.
Open 11.30am-3pm, 5-9pm Tue-Thur; 11.30am-3pm,
5-10pm Fri; noon-10pm Sat; noon-9pm Sun. **Main
courses** $6-$13. **Credit** MC, V. **Map** p314 G7.

Specialising in Cuban and Puerto Rican food, this
tiny, noisy eaterie near Balmy Alley dishes up appe-
tisers such as meat-filled plantain and yucca fritters,
as well as *higado a la Frutilandia*, a succulent
concoction of calf's liver cooked with green peppers
and onions in a spicy sauce. Vegetarian dishes
include yucca with garlic, black beans and rice.

El Toro Taqueria

598 Valencia Street, at 17th Street (431 3351). BART 16th Street/bus 14, 22, 26, 33, 53. **Open** 10am-10pm daily. **Credit** AmEx, MC, V. **Map** p314 F6.
Frequented on weekends by truly devoted fans of the *menudo*, an eye-opening traditional soup (don't ask about the ingredients) served with fresh tortillas. The burritos are massive. Set apart from the crowd by its insistence on fresh ingredients, El Toro also rejects conventional recipes in favour of those without lard.

La Taqueria

2889 Mission Street, at 25th Street (285 7117). BART 24th Street/bus 12, 14, 26, 27, 49, 67. **Open** 11am-9pm Mon-Sat; 11am-8pm Sun. **No credit cards. Map** p314 F7.
Regarded as the best in town, the made-to-order burritos are stuffed with fresh *carne asada* or *carnitas*. Try the refreshing *aguas frescas* fruit drinks.

Taqueria Cancun

2288 Mission Street, at 19th Street (252 9560). Bus 14, 33, 49. **Open** 10am-1am Mon-Thur, Sun; 10am-2am Fri, Sat. **No credit cards. Map** p314 F7.
This place is so popular it's got three locations to satisfy demand. Grilled chicken, spicy *carne asada* and a dangerously delicious *mojado* (with red and green sauces and sour cream) are among the many temptations stuffed into tortillas.
Other locations: 1003 Market Street, at Sixth Street, Tenderloin (864 6773); 3211 Mission Street, at Valencia Street, Outer Mission (550 1414).

Taqueria La Cumbre

515 Valencia Street, at 16th Street (863 8205). BART 16th Street/bus 14, 22, 26, 33, 53. **Open** 11am-10pm Mon-Sat; noon-9pm Sun. **No credit cards. Map** p314 F6.
La Cumbre has been in the neighbourhood forever, and is jealously defended by Valencia Street hipsters as offering the city's top burritos. The long queue leads to an assembly-line kitchen, where your burrito is created by committee to your specifications. The *carne asada* is the signature order: tender, flavourful and huge (around 3lb or 1.5kg). Oh yes.

Castro & Noe Valley

American

Chow

215 Church Street, at Market Street, Castro (552 2469). Muni Metro F, J, K, L, M/bus 22, 37. **Open** 11am-11pm Mon-Thur; 10am-midnight Fri; 10am-11pm Sat, Sun. **Main courses** $7-$14. **Credit** MC, V. **Map** p314 E6.
This is a simple, no-gimmick spot for good food. Its central Castro location ensures a vivacious clientele, but then who wouldn't be happy with food this good, at prices this low? Simple American fare like roast chicken and burgers shares the menu with more 'exotic' Asian bok choi noodles. Portions are huge. (For Chow's sister restaurant Park Chow, *see p132*.)

Firefly

4288 24th Street, at Douglass Street, Noe Valley (821 7652). Muni Metro N/Bus 37, 43. **Open** 5.30-9.30pm Mon-Thur; 5.30-10pm Fri, Sat; 5.30-9pm Sun. **Main courses** $14-$19. **Credit** AmEx, MC, V. **Map** p313 D7.
Fairly remote, but well worth seeking out, this neighbourhood spot is warm, cosy and utterly charming, white-topped tables aglow with soft lights and the room buzzing with good conversation. If the fried chicken is offered, get it – it's among the best-made in town. Otherwise, the eclectic menu might feature garlic and herb-crusted rack of lamb or rib-sticking chicken and dumplings.

Mecca

2029 Market Street, at Dolores & 14th Streets, Castro (621 7000/www.sfmecca.com). Muni Metro F, J, K, L, M/bus 37. **Open** 6-11pm Tue-Thur, Sun. 5.45pm-midnight Fri, Sat. **Main courses** $16-$27. **Credit** AmEx, DC, MC, V. **Map** p314 E6.
Big, bustling and unswervingly fashionable, this restaurant has become the de facto headquarters of Castro cuisine. The food has always struck a harmonious accord with the surroundings, but Stephen Barber has recently taken it to a higher level. His world-influenced menu features wonderfully flavourful spare ribs, a divine seared ahi and one of the best New York strip steaks in town. Back at the bar, the mood becomes ever looser as the evening progresses, cocktails flow and the DJ spins his platters.

Asian

Alice's

1599 Sanchez Street, at 29th Street, Noe Valley (282 8999/http://alicesrestaurant.citysearch.com). Muni Metro J/bus 24, 26. **Open** 11am-9.15pm Mon-Fri; 11am-10pm Sat; noon-9.15pm Sun. **Main courses** $7-$10. **Credit** MC, V.
It's worth trekking down to Noe Valley for Alice's spicy Hunan and Mandarin cooking. The clean, airy setting enhances such dishes as asparagus salmon in a black bean sauce or delicate orange beef; the spicy fried string beans will sear you in the best possible way. Reasonable prices and punctual (if slightly dull) service complete the experience.

Haight, Western Addition & Hayes Valley

American

RNM

598 Haight Street, at Steiner Stree, Lower Haight (551 7900/www.rnmrestaurant.com). Muni Metro N/bus 37, 43. **Open** 5.30-10pm Tue-Thur; 5.30-11pm Fri, Sat. **Main courses** *Plates* $12-$20. **Credit** MC, V. **Map** p313/14 E5.

A sleek little restaurant in this up-and-coming dining destination. RNM is like a slice of New York's SoHo transplanted for a laid-back Californian crowd. The high-style dining room (complete with massive chandelier) belies the food, which is almost entirely without pretension and mostly off-the-charts delicious. Don't miss garlic and rosemary roasted baby chicken or grilled Maine lobster on corn risotto.

Asian

Eos Restaurant

901 Cole Street, at Carl Street, Haight-Ashbury (566 3063/www.eossf.com). Muni Metro N/bus 37, 43. **Open** 5.30-10pm Mon-Wed, Sun; 5.30-11pm Thur-Sat. **Main courses** $6-$16. **Credit** AmEx, MC, V. **Map** p313 C6.

This comfortably spare, highly designed restaurant presents the best of East-West fusion, with classically trained chef/owner Arnold Eric Wong producing such dishes as tea-smoked Peking Duck and taramind chilli-glazed spare ribs, backed up by one of the Bay Area's best wine lists. The same menu is served in the wine bar next door (101 Carl Street).

Mifune

Japan Center, 1737 Post Street, between Webster & Buchanan Streets, Japantown (922 0337). Bus 2, 3, 4, 22, 38. **Open** 11am-9.30pm Mon-Thur, Sun; 11am-10pm Fri, Sat. **Main courses** $8-$12. **Credit** AmEx, DC, Disc, MC, V. **Map** p310 E4.

The lowly noodle is prepared in at least 30 different ways here. Orders come quickly, inexpensively and deliciously to your table. It's a good place to take kids, and great for vegetarians. Mifune's motto is: 'It's okay to slurp your noodles', so be noisy.

Sanppo

1702 Post Street, at Buchanan Street, Japantown (346 3486). Bus 2, 3, 4, 22, 38. **Open** 11.30am-midnight daily. **Main courses** $5-$9. **Credit** MC, V. **Map** p310 E4.

For nearly 25 years, this small, casual restaurant opposite the Japan Center has been turning out consistently good, rustic Japanese food – soups, tempura, fresh fish and East-West salads – all at just the right price. Charming service, charming place.

Seoul Garden

22 Peace Plaza, Geary Boulevard, at Laguna Street, Japantown (563 7664/www.seoulgardenbbq.com). Bus 2, 3, 4, 22, 38. **Open** 11am-midnight daily. **Main courses** $7-$25. **Credit** AmEx, MC, V. **Map** p310 E4.

Grill marinated beef at your table and try the myriad little dishes that typically make up Korean cuisine. A good place for times when all the Japanese restaurants hereabouts are too crowded for comfort.

Thep Phanom

400 Waller Street, at Fillmore Street, Lower Haight (431 2526). Bus 6, 7, 22, 66, 71. **Open** 5.30-10.30pm daily. **Main courses** $9-$16. **Credit** AmEx, DC, Disc, MC, V. **Map** p313/14 E5.

Possibly the best Thai restaurant in San Francisco. If you're smart, you'll make a reservation; if you're brilliant, you'll order the *tom ka gai* (coconut chicken soup) as a starter. The 'angel wings' – fried chicken wings stuffed with glass noodles – are a universally popular choice.

European

Absinthe

398 Hayes Street, at Gough Street, Hayes Valley (551 1590/www.absinthe.com). Bus 21, 42, 47, 49. **Open** 11.30am-2am Tue-Fri; 10.30am-2am Sat; 10.30am-10.30pm Sun. **Main courses** $9-$32. **Credit** AmEx, DC, Disc, MC, V. **Map** p314 F5.

In late 19th-century Europe, absinthe was outlawed as a poisonous libation. A century later, it has been reborn in San Francisco as a boisterous brasserie. The restaurant's grand feel is perhaps a little forced, but the French menu features great coq au vin and cassoulet. Try the veal sweetbreads or the seafood platter to start. You can't get absinthe here, but 'Death in the Afternoon' (Pernod and champagne) has a similar effect. Minus the blindness.

Suppenküche

601 Hayes Street, at Laguna Street, Western Addition (252 9289/www.suppenkuche.com). Bus 21. **Open** 5-10pm Mon-Sat; 10am-2.30pm, 5-10pm Sun. **Main courses** $7-$16. **Credit** AmEx, MC, V. **Map** p314 F5.

If you're craving the polar opposite of California cuisine, Suppenküche is a good choice. Its menu (including *spaetzle*, schnitzels and dense, dark breads) is authentically German and not for the faint of belly. There is, however, a nice selection of vegetarian offerings. An impressive array of flavoursome German beers are served in tall steins, and seating is on benches.

Pacific Heights to Golden Gate Bridge

American

Elite Café

2049 Fillmore Street, at California Street, Pacific Heights (346 8668). Bus 1, 3, 22. **Open** 5-11pm Mon-Sat; 10am-3pm, 5-10pm Sun. **Main courses** $17-$28. **Credit** AmEx, Disc, MC, V. **Map** p309 E3.

This handsome Fillmore Street stalwart has withstood every cuisine trend and restaurant fashion that the city could throw at it, and locals still queue for the Creole- and Cajun-inspired seafood, served by smiling, white-aproned staff. It offers authentic New Orleans gumbo and an unbeatable jambalaya, coming with a large leg of duck confit on top. There's a great Cajun brunch on Sunday mornings, complete with one of the best Bloody Marys in town.

East Bay dining

serving a *menu prix fixe* ($50 Mon, $65 Tue-Thur, $75 Fri, Sat) downstairs in the restaurant and a more casual, à la carte menu in the upstairs café. Ingredients are fresh, local, organic and of the very best quality – and the excellent wine list combines French and Californian options. Also in Berkeley is **Rivoli** (1539 Solano Avenue, between Neilson Street and Peralta Avenue, 1-510 526 2542, www.rivolirestaurant.com), a small, French-inspired restaurant run by talented chef Wendy Brucker. The menu changes every three weeks, but the portabello mushroom fritters (Brucker's signature dish), Caesar salad and a great hot fudge sundae are constants.

Chef Paul Bertoli, who earned his stripes at Chez Panisse, has brought Panisse's savvy reputation to **Oliveto** (*pictured*; 5655 College Avenue, at Shafter Avenue, 1-510 547 5356, www.oliveto.com) in Oakland. This fantastic traditional Northern Italian restaurant has a menu in which nearly every ingredient, down to the olive oil, is made from scratch. The speciality is house-cured, grilled and rotisseried meat. Also in Oakland, the **Bay Wolf** (3853 Piedmont Avenue, between 40th Street and MacArthur Boulevard, 1-510 655 6004, www.baywolf.com), opened by Michael Wild in 1975, serves a blend of California and Mediterranean food that uses impeccably fresh seasonal produce.

Further east is the charming little suburb of Walnut Creek, where a growing population of former San Franciscans is demanding restaurants that keep pace with their sophisticated tastebuds. Among those answering their call is **Lark Creek Inn** (1360 Locust Street, at Diablo Street, 1-925 256 1234, www.larkcreek.com), an outpost of chef Bradley Ogden and restaurateur Michael Dellar's growing empire. Lark Creek boasts a charming dining room with a bustling neighbourhood feel and a kitchen where American fare is prepared with considerable imagination. You'll find fish, fowl and grilled meats served here in huge portions, along with signature dishes, including a wonderful clam chowder, that can be found at all Lark Creek restaurants.

The argument can be made that the Bay Area's current high culinary standing can be traced to the East Bay. The area just across the Bay Bridge – which includes the cities of Oakland, Berkeley, Alameda, Walnut Creek, and many others – is no slouch when it comes to great food. In fact the East Bay's dining scene is at least as good as San Francisco's, albeit with fewer restaurants. There are certainly several dining options that make a quick jaunt over the bridge or BART trip a mighty temptation.

Berkeley is where it all began. The town, known for its liberal politics and freewheeling populace, is home to **Chez Panisse** (1517 Shattuck Avenue, between Cedar and Vine Streets, 1-510 548 5525, www.chezpanisse.com), where chef/owner Alice Waters created California cuisine way back in the 1970s. The modest wood-framed restaurant continues to reign supreme,

Eat, Drink, Shop

Elite Café.
See p136.

Harris'

*2100 Van Ness Avenue, at Pacific Avenue, Pacific
Heights (673 1888/www.harrisrestaurant.com).
Bus 12, 42, 47, 49, 83.* **Open** 5.30-9.30pm Mon-Fri;
5-10pm Sat; 5-9pm Sun. **Main courses** $17-$38.
Credit AmEx, DC, Disc, MC, V. **Map** p310 F3.
Unchanged for decades (save for a recent dust-off-
like refurbishment), Harris' offers the kind of classy
old-style dining your great-uncle would have loved.
Sink into your booth, start with a strong cocktail,
then proceed with a textbook Caesar salad (put
together at your table), a prime piece of steak and a
baked potato with all the trimmings and, of course,
a hefty dessert.

PlumpJack Cafe

*3127 Fillmore Street, between Greenwich &
Filbert Streets, Cow Hollow (563 4755/www.plump
jack.com). Bus 22, 28, 41, 43, 45, 76.* **Open**
11.30am-2pm, 5.30-10pm Mon-Fri; 5.30-10pm Sat.
Main courses $7-$28. **Credit** AmEx, DC, MC, V.
Map p309 E2.
Following the success of PlumpJack Wines down the
street, this high-profile restaurant is a blend of new
ideas and old money: dashing owner Gavin Newsom
is the city's mayor, his partner the son of magnate
Gordon Getty. PlumpJack Cafe is a special-occasion
eaterie that produces outstanding California cuisine,
with a penchant for interesting takes on seafood and
Mediterranean recipes – such as pan-roasted organic
wild Pacific steelhead with quinoa pilaf, grilled
Portobello mushroom, roast baby beets and red wine
sauce. An extensive, inexpensive wine list culls
the best from the wine shop.

Asian

Betelnut

*2030 Union Street, between Webster &
Buchanan Streets, Cow Hollow (929 8855/
www.betelnut.com). Bus 22, 41, 45.* **Open** 11.30am-
11pm Mon-Thur, Sun; 11am-midnight Fri, Sat.
Main courses $5-$18. **Credit** DC, Disc, MC, V.
Map p309 E2.
Despite being in a notoriously fickle neighbourhood,
this cool-looking restaurant has managed to retain
its popularity, probably due to its relatively exotic
South Pacific concept and consistent execution. Sidestep the can't-be-bothered attitude up front, squeeze
into the crowd of beautiful people at the bar and you
can peruse a menu made for grazing. The best bet
is to keep ordering small plates (tea-smoked duck,
braised short ribs, papaya salad) until your waist-
line or your credit card goes pop.

European

Baker Street Bistro

*2953 Baker Street, between Lombard & Greenwich
Streets, Cow Hollow (931 1475/www.bakerstbistro.
citysearch.com). Bus 28, 41, 43, 45, 76.* **Open** *Lunch*
11.30am-2.30pm Tue-Fri; 7.30am-2.30pm Sat, Sun.
Dinner 5.30-9.30pm Mon; 5.30-10.30pm Tue-Sat; 5-
9.30pm Sun. **Main courses** $5-$17. **Credit** AmEx,
MC, V. **Map** p309 D2.
On a lost stretch of Baker Street near the Palace of
Fine Arts, this gem oozes French charm. Wooden
floors, lots of sunlight and a temperate outdoor patio

attract a loyal clientele, but the place's good looks are complemented by great food and unbelievable prices. The three-course *prix fixe* is only \$14.50.

Chez Nous

1911 Fillmore Street, at Pine Street, Pacific Heights (441 8044). Bus 1, 3, 22. **Open** 11.30am-3pm, 5.30-10pm Mon-Thur, Sun; 11.30am-3pm, 5.30-11pm Fri, Sat. **Main courses** *Plates* \$4-\$13. **Credit** MC, V. **Map** p309 E3.

This small neighbourhood eaterie seems always to be crowded, sometimes frustratingly so. It's a recommendation, of sorts, for the delicious, small, tapas-like plates of Mediterranean food, typified by options such as Moroccan spiced duck confit and a luscious salad Niçoise. Breads are unbelievably fresh, from the owner's bakery around the corner. If a table takes too long to materialise, ask to sit at the bar.

Florio

1915 Fillmore Street, between Bush & Pine Streets, Pacific Heights (775 4300). Bus 1, 3, 22. **Open** 5.30-10.30pm Mon-Wed; 5.30-11pm Thur-Sat; 5.30-10pm Sun. **Main courses** \$14-\$28. **Credit** AmEx, MC, V. **Map** p309 E4.

A quintessential neighbourhood bistro, Florio is warm and welcoming, with just the right degree of refinement. Dark wood and white tablecloths set the tone for food influenced by French rural cooking. The steak frites and the roast chicken and fries (available to be shared by two) are the best choices, always soul-warming on a foggy evening. The lobster bisque is also rich and reliable.

Fresca

2114 Fillmore Street, at California Street, Pacific Heights (447 2668/www.frescaperuviancuisine.com). Bus 1, 3, 22. **Open** 11am-10pm Mon-Thur, Sun; 11am-11pm Fri, Sat. **Main courses** *Average lunch entrée* \$9. *Average dinner* \$18. **Credit** AmEx, DC, MC, V. **Map** p309 E3.

It bills itself as San Francisco's only ceviche bar, but there's so much more on offer. The tables are crammed together and the place can be very loud, but the Peruvian fare easily makes up for any discomfort. Try the tangy halibut ceviche or the *flambé pisco* prawns to start. For mains, try the sweet soy-roasted trout – though the grilled rib-eye steak with fries and plantains also bears close inspection.
Other locations: 24 West Portal Avenue, at Ulloa Street (759 8087).

Restaurant Isa

3324 Steiner Street, between Chestnut & Lombard Streets, Marina (567 9588). Bus 22, 28, 30, 43, 76. **Open** 5-10pm Tue-Thur, Sun; 5-10.30pm Fri, Sat. **Main courses** *Plates* \$5-\$16. **Credit** MC, V. **Map** p309 D2.

French meets Spanish at this Marina district discovery, with a tapas-like menu that includes such interesting fare as roast mussels with shallots and white wine or hanger steak with tarragon mustard and roast garlic potatoes. Charmingly cosy (the back patio is truly secluded), it is also free of the prevalent neighbourhood affectations.

Latin American

Los Hermanos

2026 Fillmore Street, at Fillmore Street, Marina (921 5790). Bus 22, 30. **Open** 11am-10pm Mon-Sat. **Main courses** \$5-\$8. **No credit cards**. **Map** p309 E2.

A misplaced bit of the Mission, this utterly nondescript spot serves some amazingly authentic Mexican food. The burritos are enormous and freshly made up before your eyes. The atmosphere is chaotic, with people three rows back shouting orders to the hardworking and friendly crew. Cash only.

Vegetarian

Greens

Building A, Fort Mason Center, Marina Boulevard, at Buchanan Street, Marina (771 6222). Bus 28. **Open** 5.30-9pm Mon-Sat; 10.30am-2pm Sun. **Main courses** \$8-\$19. **Credit** AmEx, Disc, MC, V. **Map** p309 E1.

With a great view of the Golden Gate Bridge and an award-winning, all-vegetarian menu, Greens keeps its reputation sterling, despite occasionally spacey service. Fresh produce and an extensive wine list complement mesquite-grilled vegetables and wood-fired pizzas topped with wild mushrooms. If you don't fancy queuing for a table, take advantage of the takeaway counter for sandwiches and soups.

Eat, Drink, Shop

Richmond

American

Q Restaurant

*225 Clement Street, at Third Avenue (752 2298).
Bus 1, 2, 33, 38.* **Open** *11.30am-3pm; 5-11pm Mon-Fri; 10am-11pm Sat; 10am-10pm Sun.* **Main courses**
$7-$14. **Credit** MC, V. **Map** p308/12 B4.
Squeezed into a tiny shopfront, this delightful restaurant serves up some of the tastiest comfort food in town. The name comes from earlier ambitions as a barbecue joint, but the kitchen expanded its repertoire to grilled steaks and seafood, pasta and some of the top fried chicken in the city. A good wine list and the funky decor round out this outstanding find.

Asian

Kabuto

*5121 Geary Boulevard, between 15th & 16th
Avenues (752 5652). Bus 2, 28, 38.* **Open** *Lunch*
11.30am-2pm. *Dinner* 5.30-10.30pm Tue-Sat;
5.30-10pm Sun. **Main courses** $9-$15; sushi $2.50-
$10. **Credit** MC, V. **Map** p312 A4.
Miles from Japantown, Kabuto's uninteresting exterior gives no hint of the excellent raw fish within. Another favourite with restaurateurs and chefs, this tiny sushi bar has few tables. So grab a seat at the sushi bar, where the chefs will give you a show – and a meal – you won't forget.

Khan Toke

*5937 Geary Boulevard, between 23rd & 24th
Avenues (668 6654). Bus 2, 29, 38.* **Open** *5-10.30pm
daily.* **Main courses** $8-$12. **Credit** AmEx, MC, V.
Slip off your shoes and choose a seat on the floor (well, a low chair with a padded back support) in one of the city's most attractive and overlooked Thai restaurants. Fiery, colourful curries and excellent noodles, plus a good selection of Sauvignon Blancs.

Mayflower

*6255 Geary Boulevard, at 27th Avenue (387 8338).
Bus 2, 29, 38.* **Open** *11am-2.30pm, 5-9.30pm Mon-Fri; 10am-2.30pm, 5-9.30pm Sat, Sun.* **Main courses**
$8-$10; dim sum $2-$6. **Credit** MC, V.
This large, noisy and family-oriented Cantonese restaurant is consistently good. Perhaps best known for mid-morning dim sum, the Mayflower's house speciality is seafood and its clay pot dishes and roast chicken or duck are all good. Mongolian beef is another perennial favourite. Arrive after 8pm if you want to avoid the hordes of families at dinnertime.

Ton Kiang

*5821 Geary Boulevard, between 22nd & 23rd
Avenues (387 8273/http://tonkiang.citysearch.com).
Bus 2, 29, 38.* **Open** *10.30am-10pm Mon-Thur;
10.30am-10.30pm Fri; 10am-10.30pm Sat; 9am-
10.30pm Sun.* **Main courses** $7-$24. **Credit** AmEx,
DC, MC, V.

Very popular for dim sum on weekend mornings, this large restaurant is also known for its traditional Chinese gypsy cuisine *hakka*. Among the authentic items is salt-baked chicken served with a ground garlic and ginger paste. Around Chinese New Year, it features a delicious seasonal menu.

European

Chapeau!

*1408 Clement Street, at 15th Avenue (750 9787/
http://bistrochapeau.citysearch.com). Bus 1, 2, 28, 38.*
Open 5-10pm Tue-Thur, Sun; 5-10.30pm Fri, Sat.
Main courses $16-$19. **Credit** AmEx, DC, Disc,
MC, V. **Map** p308/12 A4.
'Hat!', in case you're wondering, is more or less French for 'Wow!' – which is just about right. This place is a proper little charmer, with homely bistro decor and friendly staff. The Provençal fare is just as comforting, with excellent coq au vin, onion soup and duck à l'orange. There's a fine brunch on Sunday – an ideal time to explore the bubbly list.

Sunset

American

The **Beach Chalet** (*see p105*) is well worth a visit: the food is good, the location superlative.

PJ's Oyster Bed

*737 Irving Street, between Eighth & Ninth Avenues
(566 7775). Muni Metro N/bus 6, 43, 44, 66.* **Open**
Lunch 11.30am-2.30pm daily. *Dinner* 5-10pm Mon-
Thur, Sun; 5-11pm Fri, Sat. **Main courses** $12-$20.
Credit AmEx, DC, MC, V. **Map** p312 B6.
A noisy, friendly neighbourhood seafood restaurant, PJ's dishes out some of the freshest and most authentic Cajun food in San Francisco. The seafood is displayed on ice (the place used to be a fish market), oysters are shucked to order, portions are generous and the place is always packed. The jovial chef, sporting Mardi Gras beads, eventually slips out from the kitchen to jaw with his customers.

Asian

Ebisu

*1283 Ninth Avenue, between Irving Street & Lincoln
Way (566 1770/http://ebisu.citysearch.com). Muni
Metro N/bus 6, 43 44, 66.* **Open** 5-10pm Mon-Fri;
11.30am-11pm Sat, Sun. **Main courses** $7-$19; sushi
$3-$6. **Credit** AmEx, DC, MC, V. **Map** p312 B6.
Considered by many to serve the best sushi in town, Ebisu might as well be Japanese for 'long wait'. But put your name on the list and get a drink at the bar with light heart, because you're going to enjoy house specialities like the 'pink Cadillac' (salmon sushi roll), seafood salad, the '49er roll… And good as they all are, you can happily forgo sushi for Ebisu's traditional Japanese cooked food. Excellent, excellent.

Cafés

Join San Francisco's favourite cult: café culture.

Cafés in San Francisco are a way of life. No matter the day of the week, there always seem to be weekending throngs huddled around sidewalk tables or sitting windowside in front of giant cappuccinos at the city's numerous cafés. Does anybody work in this town?

The definition of the word 'café' is a hazy one here. It can mean anything from a place serving just coffee and pastries to somewhere you can have a full meal and a bottle of wine. Of course, you'll find as many Starbucks here as cars during rush hour, but don't bother with them. Head instead for the city's one-off establishments – each distinct neighbourhood has a coffee house on nearly every corner, at least one of which will reflect the area's unique character.

Downtown

Arabi

Rincon Center, 101 Spear Street, at Mission Street, Embarcadero (243 8575). BART Embarcadero/Muni Metro F, J, K, L, M, N/bus 2, 7, 9, 14. **Open** 7am-2.30pm Mon-Fri. **No credit cards. Map** p311 J3.
Rincon Center is alive with worker-bees buzzing down from the offices above to nosh at this marvellous little spot at the foot of the skyscraper. Serving such specialities as shawerma (pitta-bread sandwich with a meat filling) and tabouleh, as well as salads and small plates, you can take a culinary trip to the Middle East in 20 minutes.

Café Claude

7 Claude Lane, between Sutter & Bush Streets, Kearny Street & Grant Avenue, Union Square (392 3515/www.cafeclaude.com). BART Montgomery Street/Muni Metro F, J, K, L, M, N/bus 2, 3, 4, 15, 30, 45, 76. **Open** *Lunch* 11.30am-4pm Mon-Sat. *Dinner* 5.30-10pm Tue-Thur; 5.30pm-11pm Fri, Sat. *Bar* from 11am Mon-Sat. **Credit** AmEx, DC, Disc, MC, V. **Map** p311 H3.
The story is now almost a legend: owner Stephen Decker purchased Le Barbizon café in Paris and shipped it over one piece at a time. The result is a real slice of France, from the setting to service by slender model-like drones to its little alleyway locale. Signature dishes such as cassoulet and mousse au chocolat maintain the delightful illusion.

Cafe de la Presse

352 Grant Avenue, at Bush Street, Union Square (398 2680/www.cafedelapresse.com). Bus 2, 3, 4, 15, 30, 45, 76. **Open** 7am-10pm daily. **Credit** AmEx, DC, Disc, MC, V. **Map** p311 G3.

Near the Chinatown gateway, this is a cosmopolitan café. It stocks a variety of foreign newspapers and magazines, and serves a French bistro-type menu morning to night. Celebs filming in the city tend to find their way here, as do fashion-industry mavens patronising the Hotel Triton (*see p35*) next door.

Cafe de Stijl

1 Union Street, at Front Street, Embarcadero (291 0808). Muni Metro F/bus 42. **Open** 6.30am-5pm Mon-Fri; 8.30am-2.30pm Sat. **Credit** AmEx, Disc, MC, V. **Map** p311 H2.
Named after the early 20th-century Dutch art movement, de Stijl is a rarity: it offers easy parking, pavement seating and hearty food with a Middle Eastern flair. Try the chicken sandwich with tahini or a mixed platter complete with baba ganoush, tabouleh and kibbeh (ground lamb patty).

Cheesecake Factory

Eighth floor, Macy's, 251 Geary Street, at Stockton Street, Union Square (391 4444/ www.thecheesecakefactory.com). BART Powell Street/Muni Metro F, J, K, L, M, N/bus 2, 3, 4, 15, 30, 38, 45, 76/cable car Powell-Hyde or Powell-Mason. **Open** 11am-11pm Mon-Thur; 11am-12.30am Fri, Sat; 10am-11pm Sun. **Credit** AmEx, DC, Disc, MC, V. **Map** p311 G4.
Inside Macy's (*see p160*) fancy department store, Cheesecake Factory has a menu long enough to be considered a novel. Everything from cheeseburgers to cappuccino, turkey sandwiches to tiramisu is on offer, as well as more than 30 flavours of the eponymous dessert. At lunchtime be prepared to wait if you're after an outside seat.

The best Cafés

Blue Danube
To make a start on those books. *See p147.*

Cafe Abir
To kick back with the laid-back. *See p146.*

Imperial Tea Court
For the world's finest tea. *See p144.*

Mario's Bohemian Cigar Store
For that Italian espresso. *See p145.*

Zazie
For a boozy brunch. *See p143.*

Later than breakfast, sooner than Monday

If it is true that (as every American is told from the moment they gingerly tooth their first solids) 'breakfast is the most important meal of the day', then brunch is the most important meal of the week. Eaten so late in the morning it's usually afternoon, portions are larger – yes, larger – than normal to accommodate the amount of reading and talking you need to get through before the eating's over.

For the best places, you'll have to wait for a table. If you think queuing for breakfast is a weird waste of time, here's a thought experiment: how good would breakfast at your local caff have to be for you to line up every Sunday? So join the locals, because that's exactly how good this is going to be. **Dottie's True Blue Cafe** (*see p142*) near Union Square, **Ella's** (*see p146*) in Pacific Heights, **Kate's Kitchen** (*see p146*) in the Lower Haight, **Miss Millie's** (*see p146*) in Noe Valley and **Mama's on Washington Square** (*see p145*) don't mark the end of SF café society, but on a weekend they surely mark the beginning. You can also hob-nob with local big wigs at **Moose's** (*see p126*) and relax at **Slow Club** or **Universal Café** (for both, *see p134*).

When you need more than mere food, brunch with booze is a decadent pastime San Franciscans excel at. **Foreign Cinema** (*see p134*) has great cocktails to accompany a truly gourmet brunch: how about a champagne omelette with golden chanterelles, crème fraîche, fontina, crispy potatoes, or two poached eggs with grilled duck breast, warm salad greens, shiitakes and sherry? If that's too fancy, try the Bloody Mary bar at **Home** (2100 Market Street, at Church & 14th Streets, 503 0333, www.home-sf.com, brunch 11am-3pm Sun) in the Castro. The brunch is hearty and affordable, the surroundings comfortable, if a bit generic, but the kick is creating your own mix from the selection of tomato juices, spicy sauces and garnishes. Don't panic if you mess the first one up: they're relatively inexpensive, so order just one more until you no longer care. If that's too complicated, the **Elite Café** (*see p136*) will make you what is reputed to be the best Bloody Mary in town; if you're feeling sophisticated, the Champagne at **Chapeau!** (*see p140*) can't be beat.

To make the most of a sunny day, the sidewalk tables at **Perry's** (1944 Union Street, between Laguna & Buchanan Streets, Marina, 922 9022, www.perrysunionst.city search.com, brunch 9am-3pm Sat, Sun) are perfect for checking out the polished and perfumed classes as they take their laps along Union Street. Perry's offers a large brunch menu and probably the best selection of brunch drinks in town. But the Ramos Fizz is what you need to try: rarely made at all, here it's cocktail perfection. If you need serious help after the night before, you might prefer the New York steak and eggs and a

Dottie's True Blue Cafe

522 Jones Street, at O'Farrell Street, Union Square/ Tenderloin (885 2767). Bus 27, 38. **Open** 7.30am-3pm Mon-Thur. **Credit** Disc, MC, V. **Map** p310 G4. Arrive early to avoid the queue (you can't book) at this legendary brunch spot. Tiny and always busy, Dottie's is a quaint slice of Americana, complete with checked tablecloths and a Formica countertop. All the standards are here, including pancakes that cover the plate and eggs any way you want them. Most choices come with flour tortillas and home fries.

Kuleto's Cafe

Villa Florence Hotel, 221 Powell Street, at Geary Street, Union Square (397 7720/www.kuletos. citysearch.com). BART Powell Street/Muni Metro F, J, K, L, M, N/bus 5, 6, 7, 21, 30, 31, 38, 45, 66, 71/cable car Powell-Hyde or Powell-Mason. **Open** 7am-11pm Mon-Fri; 8am-11pm Sat, Sun. **Credit** AmEx, DC, Disc, MC, V. **Map** p311 G4.

Kuleto's Cafe is great for a refuel break from shopping around Union Square. This humble annexe of the popular Kuleto restaurant offers eye-opening coffee drinks, as well as fresh juices and own-made Italian pastries. For lunch, there is a good selection of heartier picks, such as pizza by the slice, panini, antipasti and rich desserts.

Saigon Sandwich Cafe

560 Larkin Street, between Turk & Eddy Streets, Civic Center (474 5698). Bus 5, 19, 31. **Open** 7am-4.30pm Mon-Sat; 7.30am-4.30pm Sun. **No credit cards. Map** p310 F4.

This lunch spot is popular with workers in the many nearby government buildings, who file in for huge sandwiches at rock-bottom prices. The bare-bones menu shows Vietnamese influences, such as roast pork with a sweet-and-sour sauce. The meatball sandwich is brilliant, and big enough for two.

Bull Shot: vodka, beef bouillon, dash of Tabasco, dash of Worcestershire, salt and pepper to taste. The thought of it alone cures all ills. Another alfresco joy is the large outdoor deck at **Pier 23** (Embarcadero, 362 5125, www.pier23cafe.com, brunch 10am-3pm Sat, Sun), perfect for a crab, shrimp and jack cheese omelette or fresh seafood. When

the weather's right, patrons get a bucket of Coronas on ice and stay put until the evening's live music begins.

Or you could combine two pleasures: just a block from SBC Park (*see p234*) in South Beach, you'll find **Primo Patio Cafe** (214 Townsend Street, between Third & Fourth Streets, 957 1129, www.primopatiocafe. com, open 8am-4pm Mon-Sat). With Jamaican, Cuban and Mexican dishes to spice up the breakfast and a partially covered outdoor patio with heat lamps to maintain the island vibe in cooler weather, you'll be set up for a Mango Mimosa, sangria or a Cuban Buli Buli (beer, lime juice, sugar and ice).

Of all good things, there is surely a best: for a boozy brunch, that best is Cole Valley's **Zazie** (941 Cole Street, between Carl Street & Parnassus Avenue, 564 5332, brunch 9am-3pm Sat, Sun; *pictured*). This French bistro serves a delicious brunch throughout the week, both indoors and in its cosy garden. Selections such as their eggs Monaco (poached eggs, tomatoes provençal and prosciutto on an English muffin slathered with hollandaise sauce) or thick, fluffy gingerbread pancakes are perfectly complemented by the selection of champagne cocktails. Their Mimosas are made with fresh-squeezed orange juice, and the Kir Royale's blackcurrant sweetness is perfect with the many items on the menu that include fresh fruit.

SoMa

There's also a decent café at **SFMOMA** (*see p56*), which is a good place for lunch after a morning in the galleries.

Brain Wash Cafe & Laundromat

1122 Folsom Street, at Seventh Street (861 3663/www.brainwash.com). Bus 12, 19, 27, 42. **Open** *7am-11pm daily.* **Credit** MC, V. **Map** p315 G5.
Brainwash is an extraordinary place: launderette, bar, café and performance space, all located in one quirky industrial structure. It offers a simple menu of soups, salads and burgers, and most nights of the week young hipsters can watch live bands play, hear spoken word artists and comedians, or get down to the DJs (all ages, no cover). And do their laundry, of course. It's a great pick-up spot.

The Butler & the Chef

155 South Park, at Third Street (896 2075). Bus 15, 30, 45, 76. **Open** *7.30am-5.30pm daily. Lunch 11.30am-3pm daily.* **Credit** MC, V. **Map** p315 H4.
This oh-so-Gallic pavement café always has a very tempting mound of toothsome sandwiches made with Boulangerie Bay Bread (*see p178*), ideal for munching in sunny South Park. Breakfast on *pain au chocolat* or sip a Pernod while chatting with Pierre, the amiable owner. The Butler & the Chef runs a warehouse of French antiques and collectibles (*see p164*), so everything here's for sale.

Caffe Centro

102 South Park, at Jack London Place, between Bryant & Brannan Streets (882 1500/ www.caffecentro.com). Bus 15, 30, 42, 45, 76. **Open** *7am-4.30pm Mon-Fri; 8am-2.30pm Sat.* **Credit** AmEx, MC, V. **Map** p315 H/J4.

Eat, Drink, Shop

Mario's Bohemian Cigar Store: perfection is in the waiting. *See p145.*

Now that the queues of earnest dot-commoners no longer snake out the door, the mix of friendly service, fresh soups, salads and sandwiches (much of it organic) once again attracts a quirky mix of local residents, creative types and other workers. Large windows open on to South Park, and the proximity of interesting shops (Jeremy's, *see p173*; William Stout, *see p166*) is an added attraction.

Town's End Restaurant & Bakery
2 Townsend Street, at Embarcadero (512 0749). Muni Metro N/bus 15, 42. **Open** *Breakfast 7.30-11am Tue-Fri. Lunch 11.30am-2.30pm Tue-Fri. Dinner 5pm-9pm Tue-Sat.* **Credit** AmEx, DC, MC, V. **Map** p311/15 J4.
This modern-looking place near the ballpark is one of the area's few breakfast spots. Most of the patrons live nearby or are picking up sandwiches for the game. Baked goods are the highlight, but weekend breakfasts have been picking up steam of late.

Chinatown

Imperial Tea Court
1411 Powell Street, at Broadway (1-800 567 6080/ 788 6080/www.imperialtea.com). Bus 15, 30, 39, 41, 45/cable car Powell-Mason. **Open** 11am-6.30pm Mon, Wed-Sun. **Credit** AmEx, MC, V. **Map** p310 J2.
There is no better place in the city for tea. This serene, wood-panelled tea house seemingly offers all the tea in China, served to the accompaniment of birds chirping in their cages. The endless assortment of rare and fine teas, brought to your table in ornate pots, includes 'fancy dragon well', 'silver needle' and 'snow water'. Teas are available to take away too – an expensive habit, but one you'll definitely want to acquire. **Other locations**: 27 Ferry Market Place, Ferry Building, Embarcadero (544 9830).

North Beach & Polk Gulch

Bob's Donut Shop
1621 Polk Street, at Sacramento Street, Polk Gulch (776 3141). Bus 1, 19, 42, 47, 49/cable car California. **Open** 24hrs daily. **No credit cards. Map** p310 F3.
It's not much to look at – and you certainly won't want to look too long at some of the characters who frequent the place – but this round-the-clock joint serves up possibly the best doughnut you'll find in town. The sugary wheels have been the salvation of many a Polk Street nightclubber; they make great pick-me-ups in the morning as well. The coffee here is good and strong.

La Boulange de Polk
2310 Polk Street, at Green Street, Polk Gulch (345 1107). Bus 19, 42, 47, 49. **Open** 7am-6.30pm Tue-Sun. **No credit cards. Map** p310 F2.
Few places in town so thoroughly evoke the feel of a Parisian boulangerie as this little place. Pavement tables are highly coveted, which is understandable: they're a great place to enjoy a fresh brioche, croissant or quiche while watching the locals amble by.

Caffe Puccini
411 Columbus Avenue, at Vallejo Street, North Beach (989 7033). Bus 12, 15, 30, 41. **Open** 6am-12.30am daily. **No credit cards. Map** p311 G2.
Be prepared to listen to opera at Graziano Lucchese's place. He's from the same town as the composer after whom he named this intimate North Beach café. The sandwiches, stuffed with prosciutto, mortadella and salami, are outstanding, while the antipasto plate is ample for two.

Caffe Trieste

*609 Vallejo Street, at Grant Avenue, North Beach
(982 2605/http://caffetrieste.citysearch.com). Bus
12, 15, 30, 41, 45, 83/cable car Powell-Mason.* **Open**
6.30am-11pm Mon-Thur, Sun; 6.30am-midnight Fri,
Sat. **No credit cards. Map** p311 G2.

One of the city's great cafés. A Beat-era landmark,
it was the espresso bar of choice for Kerouac and
Ginsberg. Near City Lights (*see p165*) bookshop,
its dark walls are plastered with photos of opera
singers and famous regulars. There are muffins,
pastries, sandwiches and wonderfully potent
lattes. Don't miss the opera sessions held here on
Saturday afternoons.

Mama's on Washington Square

*1701 Stockton Street, at Filbert Street, North Beach
(362 6421). Bus 15, 30, 39, 41, 45.* **Open** 8am-3pm
Tue-Sun. **No credit cards. Map** p310 G2.

The weekend wait is part of the fun at this comfy
North Beach fixture, with its mix of locals and
tourists milling about with newspapers and the
menu. Once seated, you'll be faced with such temptations as a giant made-to-order 'm'omelette' or the
Monte Cristo sandwich. Service is swift and homey.

Mario's Bohemian Cigar Store

*566 Columbus Avenue, at Union Street, North
Beach (362 0536). Bus 15, 30, 39, 41, 45/cable
car Powell-Mason.* **Open** 10.30am-11pm daily.
Credit MC, V. **Map** p310 G2.

Located on the edge of Washington Square Park,
Mario's offers a light menu of focaccia sandwiches
and salads, beer and coffee drinks. It's always
packed and lunch may be slow in coming, but there
is no more essential North Beach café. Despite its
name, you won't find a cigar in sight, nor will you
be allowed to smoke one. Instead sip a flavoured
Italian soda and watch the neighbourhood.
Other locations: 2209 Polk Street, between Vallejo
& Green Streets, Polk Gulch (776 8226).

Steps of Rome

*348 Columbus Avenue, between Green
& Vallejo Streets, North Beach (397 0435/
www.stepsofrome.com). Bus 12, 15, 30, 41, 45,
83/cable car Powell-Mason.* **Open** 8.30am-3am
daily. **No credit cards. Map** p311 G2.

Steps of Rome's huge windows are usually open,
providing excellent seats for people-watching. Open
until 3am, it's often filled with party-goers staving
off the next day's hangover or making a pit stop on
the way to an after-hours club in SoMa. Though it
can at times be quite loud, it is ideal for a caffeine
break and a quick dessert.

Zero Degrees

*490 Pacific Avenue, at Montgomery Street, North
Beach (788 9376). Bus 12, 15, 41.* **Open** 6.30am-
8pm Mon-Wed; 6.30am-11pm Thur; 6.30am-1am Fri;
noon-1am Sat. **Credit** AmEx, MC, V. **Map** p311 H2.

Probably the most stylish place in town for a cup
of coffee, this offshoot of the (now defunct) MC2
restaurant is mainly known as a dessert café.

You'll find soups and light sandwiches alongside
the fabulous own-made ice-cream and pastries,
plus an impressive range of tequilas and single
malts. The enormous flatscreen plasma TV
provides an ambient glow.

Fisherman's Wharf

Boudin Sourdough Bakery & Cafe

*2890 Taylor Street, at Jefferson Street (776 1849/
www.boudinbakery.com). Muni Metro F/bus 39,
42/cable car Powell-Mason.* **Open** 8am-6pm Mon-
Thur; 8am-7pm Fri-Sun. **Credit** AmEx, MC, V.
Map p310 G1.

Fact: sourdough bread was invented in San
Francisco. The Boudin family has been making it
here since 1849; it has numerous outlets in the Bay
Area, and even a few in Chicago. This bakery-cum-
café is a relaxing alternative to the many frenetic
crab and seafood stands of Fisherman's Wharf. Try
the sourdough pizzas, or clam chowder served in a
fresh-baked, hollowed-out, sourdough bowl.
Other locations: throughout the Bay Area.

Mission & Castro

For good cafés and restaurants in the Castro,
see p231. And don't miss out on the **Bombay
Ice Creamery** (*see p178*).

Atlas Cafe

*3049 20th Street, at Alabama Street, Mission
(648 1047/www.atlascafe.net). Bus 27.* **Open**
7am-10pm Mon-Fri; 8am-10pm Sat; 8am-8pm Sun.
No credit cards. Map p313 G7.

The comfy funk of this unassuming café represents
the Mission at its best. A daily list of grilled
sandwiches, including many vegetarian specialities,
along with fresh soups and salads is chalked on the
wall; order yours and grab a sunny seat on the patio
at the back (where dogs are allowed).

Cafe Commons

*3161 Mission Street, at Precita Avenue, Mission
(282 2928). BART 24th Street/bus 12, 14, 26, 27,
67.* **Open** 6am-5pm Mon-Fri; 8am-5pm Sat, Sun.
No credit cards.

Located in the limbo between the Mission and
Bernal Heights, this relaxed neighbourhood café is
worth finding for its own-made soups and
sandwiches. Grab something from the stack of
magazines and head for the sun-drenched deck.
There's live music on Saturdays, plus bluegrass on
Thursday night.

Chloe's Cafe

*1399 Church Street, at 26th Street, Noe Valley
(648 4116). Muni Metro J.* **Open** 8am-3pm Mon-
Fri; 8am-3.30pm Sat, Sun. **No credit cards.**

Long known only to Noe Valley residents, Chloe's
serves a great brunch at weekends and is always
packed. The tables outside are popular, but inside
there's still a friendly hubbub and the great food.

Lovejoy's Tea Room

1351 Church Street, at Clipper Street, Noe Valley (648 5895). Muni Metro J/bus 48. **Open** 11am-6pm Wed-Sun; 11am-7pm Fri. **Credit** MC, V.
Come to Lovejoy's for high tea that's served in a cosy room scattered with a mishmash of antique furniture. You can choose from six different teas, including the Queen's Tea ($18.95) and the Wee Tea ($8.25) for children.

Miss Millie's

4123 24th Street, between Diamond & Castro Streets, Noe Valley (285 5598). Bus 24, 35, 48. **Open** 6-10pm Wed-Fri; 9am-2pm, 6-10pm Sat; 9am-2pm Sun. **Credit** MC, V. **Map** p313/4 E7.
Like having brunch in your favourite aunt's house, this is quaint Noe Valley at its last-of-a-lost-era best. Renowned for its lemon ricotta pancakes and hearty brunch fare, Millie's offers great French toast, omelettes and classic American standards. Vegetarians will love the curried tofu scramble. Typically crowded, the best seats for brunch are at the outdoor patio tables.

Just For You Bakery & Cafe

732 22nd Street, at Third Street, Potrero Hill (647 3033). Bus 22. **Open** 7.30am-3pm Mon-Fri; 8am-3pm Sat, Sun. **No credit cards. Map** p314 J7.
Having recently left Potrero Hill for larger premises in Dogpatch, this stylish, lesbian-run eaterie is big on taste, serving the best grits and huevos rancheros in this up-and-coming area. If you're in before 8.30am, you can get a full eggs-and-toast breakfast for about $3. It also does a decent burger.

Haight, Western Addition & Hayes Valley

Cafe Abir

1300 Fulton Street, at Divisadero Street, Western Addition (567 7654). Bus 5, 24. **Open** 6am-12.30am daily. **No credit cards. Map** p313 D5.
Abir, in the Gen-X-meets-rasta climes of the Western Addition, has grown wildly since its modest opening. It now comprises a large café, organic grocery store, coffee roastery, international newsstand and bar. Choose from freshly made sandwiches, deli salads and mountains of bagels; complete your meal with a latte and a copy of the *Times* (London, New York or Los Angeles). With friendly staff and well-chosen house music, these days it's as much about nightlife as morning life.

Citizen Cake

399 Grove Street, at Gough Street, Hayes Valley (861 2228/www.citizencake.com). Bus 21, 42, 47, 49. **Open** 8am-10pm Tue-Fri; 10am-10pm Sat; 10am-5pm Sun. **Credit** AmEx, MC, V. **Map** p314 F5.
Only in San Francisco: a bakery with a high hipness quotient. This swanky eaterie sells some of the best-looking desserts you'll ever see to some great-looking people. Don't ignore the non-dessert offerings, either: the lunch/dinner menu is excellent. Though you might prefer just cake with cake afters.

Grind Cafe

783 Haight Street, at Scott Street, Lower Haight (864 0955). Bus 6, 7, 66, 71. **Open** 7am-8pm daily. **No credit cards. Map** p313 E5.
Casual but classic, the Grind is populated with hip and ratty denizens of the Lower Haight, who are likely to be spending the morning leafing through Sartre or sweating off a hangover. The café's open-air patio hosts smokers and dog lovers. Don't miss vegetable-packed omelettes and tall stacks of pancakes.

Kate's Kitchen

471 Haight Street, between Fillmore & Webster Streets, Haight (626 3984). Bus 6, 7, 22, 71. **Open** 9am-2.45pm Mon; 8am-2.45pm Tue-Fri; 8.30am-3.45pm Sat, Sun. **No credit cards. Map** p313/4 E5.
Unofficially brunch central for the denizens of the Lower Haight, who come here to read the Sunday papers as they nurse hangovers over a giant bowl of granola or a huge omelette. 'Hush puppies' are a signature dish. Don't worry: the queue moves fast.

Truly Mediterranean

3109 16th Street, at Valencia Street, Mission (252 7482). Bus 6, 7, 33, 43, 66, 71. **Open** 11am-midnight Mon-Sat; 11am-10pm Sun. **Credit** MC, V. **Map** p313 C6.
Truly Mediterranean has two city locations (the original is in the Mission; *see p132* **On the cheap: Blue-collar price, white-collar taste**), but the Haight version has beer on tap and much better people-watching. The menu's heavy on falafels, houmous and baba ganoush. Eat in or take away, this is some of the best-ever fast food.
Other locations: 627 Vallejo Street, at Columbus Avenue, North Beach (362 2636).

Pacific Heights to Golden Gate Bridge

Ella's

500 Presidio Avenue, at California Street, Pacific Heights (441 5669/www.ellassanfrancisco.com). Bus 1, 3, 4, 43. **Open** 7-11am, 11.30am-9pm Mon-Fri; 8.30am-2pm Sat, Sun. **Credit** AmEx, MC, V. **Map** p309 D3.
This comfy and stylish corner restaurant in Presidio Heights is famed for its weekend brunch. The wait can be long, but well worth it. The chicken hash with eggs and toast is a favourite, as is potato scramble with pea sprouts, mushrooms, roasted garlic and manchego cheese. The thick and delicate French toast is arguably the best in town.

Galette

2043 Fillmore Street, between Pine & California Streets, Pacific Heights (928 1300). Bus 1, 3, 22. **Open** 11am-10pm daily. **Credit** MC, V. **Map** p309 E3.

Close company and comfort food at **The Grove**.

A chic, unassuming getaway in the hustle and bustle of Fillmore Street. So authentically Gallic is Galette that most of the staff have French accents. Crêpes are the star attraction, made fresh to order and crisped to perfection, with a bowl of cider the perfect accompaniment. Grab one of the few outdoor seats for prime people-watching action.

The Grove

2250 Chestnut Street, at Avila Street, Marina
(474 4843). **Bus** *28, 30, 43, 76.* **Open** *7am-11pm*
daily. **Credit** AmEx, MC, V. **Map** p309 D2.
This corner café could pass for a frat house, but it's the Marina's most happening spot, albeit with more people talking on cellphones than to each other. As well as coffee, beer, wine and comfort food (chicken pot pie, lasagne), patrons can enjoy chess, checkers and backgammon. The Grove is so popular that a time limit is imposed during peak hours. The Fillmore Street location offers the same kind of woodsy interior and big cappuccinos, but for a less trend-conscious clientele.
Other locations: 2016 Fillmore Street,
at Pine Street, Pacific Heights (474 1419).

Richmond & Sunset

Blue Danube Coffee House

306 Clement Street, at Fourth Avenue, Richmond
(221 9041). **Bus** *2, 4, 38, 44.* **Open** *7am-9.30pm*
daily. **No credit cards. Map** p308/12 B4.

Still going strong after 25 years, the Danube was one of the city's first hipster coffee houses – an anomaly given its location in the decidedly unhip Richmond District. Most afternoons, bookish types sit in the large streetside windows perusing something from Green Apple Books & Music (*see p166*) and watching the sidewalk scene. A recently acquired beer and wine licence and extended night hours also make this a great bar alternative for low-key locals.

Java Beach Cafe

1396 La Playa Boulevard, at Judah Street, Sunset
(665 5282). **Muni Metro** *N/bus 18.* **Open** *5.30am-*
9.30pm Mon, Tue; 5.30am-10pm Wed, Fri; 5.30am-
9pm Thur; 6am-10pm Sat, Sun. **Credit** MC, V.
A hangout for surfers, cyclists and passers-by on their way to the oceanfront, Java Beach has a basic sandwich, soup and pastry menu. It's both funky and civilised, with all the wetsuits and the grand Pacific view making it feel like a café at LA's Hermosa Beach. Without the tans.

Tart to Tart

641 Irving Street, between Seventh & Eighth
Avenues, Inner Sunset (504 7068). **Muni** *N/bus*
6, 43, 44, 66. **Open** *6am-2am Mon-Sat; 6.30am-*
1am Sun. **Credit** MC, V. **Map** p312 B6.
There are surprisingly few late-night options in the Inner Sunset, one of the city's best unsung neighbourhoods. Standard fare ranges from freshly made cookies and cakes to above-average salads and sandwiches. Oh, and the tarts aren't bad either.

Bars

From premium sake to microbreweries, there's no drinking this city dry.

San Franciscans spend more than twice the national average on alcohol – 85 per cent more than even New Yorkers. Many have attempted to fix the reasons for this, but a single answer has proved elusive. Is it because they drink pricier wine thanks to their proximity to wine country? Do they consume more premium spirits due to their more discerning palates? Or do San Franciscans just like to binge? Whatever the final analysis, these hoochers benefit from a vast array of drinking holes that cater to any and all of their desires.

Restaurant culture has taken a hit since the boom days of the late 1990s, but bars continue to thrive, but an ample selection of old favourites and newcomers. Each neighbourhood has a different feel, but the highest density of bars continues to be found in the Mission.

On weekends parts of Mission and Valencia Streets teem with revellers. Finding a happy spot, however, requires proficient hunting skills due to the diaspora from the Marina who are seeking something edgier than the yuppie pick-up joints on Union or Chestnut Streets. If you do fancy picking up a yuppie, the Marina is still the place: vibe with the moneyed crowd, who pack out bars catering to well-heeled singles on the prowl (foreign strangers with intriguing accents can work wonders here).

In North Beach, prepare to be shaken, not stirred, and slowly strained into your seat. This is where locals mix with the Bridge and Tunnel crowd as they stroll from bar to bar past an array of strip joints on the main drag, Broadway Avenue. Yet there are a number of haunts away from the neon that deserve consideration. Their virtues are well-mixed cocktails accompanied by old-school Italian crooners or mellow trance on jukebox rotation.

Bars in the Haight are usually less crowded. It's here that wide selections of beer and an earthy ethic prevail. Nowhere more so than Lower Haight, which is free of glitz and glamour in the best way. Elsewhere, the Financial District and the Tenderloin empty out at night, but for a snifter after work or Union Square shopping there are many notable spots hidden down the narrow alleyways.

Given the San Franciscan taste for cultural hybrids – gallery-club-bar 111 Minna (see p205, p221) is a good example, Canvas Café Gallery (see p157) another – it's small wonder that some

clubby venues are great for drinking too: DJ bars we like to booze in are below, those where we show off our shuffle or goggle at the platter-meisters are in the nightlife chapter, see p219. For the best bars for the queer crowd, see p227.

BOOZE AND THE LAW

You have to be aged 21 or over to buy and consume alcohol (take ID even if you look older) and it can be sold only between 6am and 2am. Last orders vary between 1.15am and 1.30am and, technically, staff are obliged to confiscate unconsumed alcoholic drinks after 2am. They take it seriously, so it's best you do too.

Downtown & SoMa

Bix
56 Gold Street, between Montgomery & Sansome Streets, Financial District (433 6300/ www.bixrestaurant.com). Bus 12, 15, 41. **Open** 4.30am-10.30pm Mon-Thur; 11.30am-11pm Fri; 5.30-11pm Sat; 5.30-10pm Sun. **Credit** AmEx, DC, Disc, MC, V. **Map** p311 H2.
Named for owner Doug 'Bix' Beiderbeck (who is 'very vaguely related' to the '20s and '30s jazz cornet tootler Biederbecke), its secretive locale and supper-club menu evoke the opulence of the Jazz Age. Combining the glamour of Harlem's Cotton Club with the splendour of a cruiseliner's dining room, you expect to spy Rita Hayworth sipping a Martini in a booth.

Bubble Lounge
714 Montgomery Street, between Washington & Jackson Streets, Financial District (434 4204/ www.bubblelounge.com). Bus 15, 41, 83. **Open** 4.30pm-1am Mon; 4.30pm-2am Tue-Fri; 5.30pm-2am Sat. **Credit** AmEx, DC, MC, V. **Map** p311 H3.
After the stock market closes, stockbrokers and short-skirted execs tickle their noses with an incredible selection of sparkling wines and champagnes. These are paired with fine pâté, salads and caviar for a top-drawer taste of the Wall Street of the West.

Butter
354 11th Street, between Folsom & Harrison Streets, SoMa (863 5964/www.smoothasbutter.com). Bus 9, 12, 19, 27, 42. **Open** 5pm-2am Wed-Sat. **Credit** AmEx, DC, Disc, MC, V. **Map** p314 G5.
With the pun-on-Beck motto 'two turntables and a microwave', Butter combines a chill-room vibe (complete with DJ) with trailer-trash kitsch and food. While the hipsters may have moved on, their absence doesn't spoil the magic of a corn dog, Twinkie and Pabst Blue Ribbon repast.

Julip Cocktail Lounge. *See p150.*

Eat, Drink, Shop

C Bobby's Owl Tree

601 Post Street, at Taylor Street, Tenderloin (776 9344). Bus 2, 3, 4, 27, 38, 76/cable car Powell-Hyde or Powell-Mason. **Open** 5pm-2am daily. **No credit cards. Map** p310 G3/4.

Small and cosy, the Owl Tree is frozen in time somewhere around 1953. Every available perch features stuffed owls, carved owls, owl paintings… owls. Details from the tiny dog lounging in a doggy bed next to the bar to the self-serve bin of snack mix would make David Lynch feel right at home. Rumour has it that the owl theme is connected to the Bohemian Club, a secret society whose headquarters are located in the ivy-covered building across the street. Conspiracy buffs talk of smuggled video footage showing rituals performed in front of a giant stone owl. But we're just here for a drink.

Edinburgh Castle

950 Geary Street, between Larkin & Polk Streets, Tenderloin (885 4074/www.castlenews.com). Bus 2, 3, 4, 19, 38. **Open** 5pm-2am daily. **Credit** Disc, MC, V. **Map** p314 F4.

This Korean-owned, Scottish-operated pub is one certainly not to be missed, despite the dodgy neighbourhood it sits in. Upstairs you'll find a venue for local bands, DJ nights and original plays (the stage version of Irvine Welsh's *Trainspotting* made its world debut here), and the patrons are an unpretentious mix of expats, mods and hipsters. Fish and chips are hand-delivered in rolled-up newspaper from a shop just around the corner and a vast, excellent and affordable selection of single malt scotch is available for quaffing the night away.

Sake tsunami

Fine sake has never been widely available outside Japan and its rarer Korean counterpart, soju, is rarely even heard of outside its native country. But luckily for San Franciscans – and anyone wise enough to pay them a visit – the Bay Area is fast becoming a great place for sampling rice-based booze. San Francisco has the first sake-only store in the United States, **True Sake** (see p179), and one of the largest Japanese producers of sake has opened a sake brewery across the Bay in Berkeley: **Takara Sake USA** (708 Addison Street, between Third and Fourth Streets, 1-510 540 8250, www.takara sake.com). Offering free tastings of about a dozen different kinds of sake, as well as tours of the brewery, a trip to Takara is the surest way to learn about the drink. Unfiltered, unpasteurised, junmai, ginjo and organic sake can be sampled here.

For the less scholarly, a quick and inexpensive (no mean feat) introduction to drinking sake is the sampler flight at **Memphis Minnie's BBQ** (576 Haight Street, between Fillmore and Steiner Streets, 864 7675, www.memphisminnies.com) in Lower Haight. Order up a brisket sandwich with a side of sweet potatoes and get the sake sampler. More like fission than fusion cuisine, the two radically different tastes of down-home barbecue and sake somehow complement each other perfectly, perhaps because both require the best ingredients and expert timing. At $8 for three small glasses (one each of junmai, ginjo and daiginjo), you can't go wrong. For the full soju experience, **Rohan** (3809 Geary Boulevard, between Second and Third Avenues, 221

5095, www.rohanlounge.com) is the only place to go. One of the few soju bars in San Francisco, it also offers 'small plate' Asian fusion cuisine.

A relative newcomer to the scene, North Beach has a super-slick option: **Sake Lab** (498 Broadway, at Kearny Street, 837 0228, www.sakelab.com; *pictured*). It boasts more than 50 sakes and a menu that includes a chart of how sakes are classified. You can order sakes in various sizes, served in small cedar boxes for $4 to $7 apiece. Sampling a flight of such boxes will provide you with an entire evening of tasting. Alternatively, head into the bottle range for some of the finer and rarer varieties (if you're out with a group, buying by the bottle can help defray the costs of sake sampling). If your sake pleasure is incomplete without a few bits of raw fish, high-end **Ozumo** (see p120) and funky **Sushi Groove** (see p128) are great for sushi.

If these aren't in the neighbourhood, never fear: **Movida Lounge** (see p156), **Fly Bar** (762 Divisadero Street, between Fulton and Grove Streets, 931 4359) or **Midori Mushi** (465 Grove Street, between Gough and Octavia Streets, 503 1377) are all great quaff-spots.

So what caused this explosion in the number of places in San Francisco serving sake and soju? First of all, local drinkers are not only discerning but adventurous, welcoming new drinking experiences with open mouths. Second, thank the US Bureau of Alcohol, Tobacco and Firearms. San Francisco issues a 'limited liquor license' that allows restaurants and bars to serve beer and wine, and a much more limited number of 'full

Le Colonial

20 Cosmo Place, alley between Jones & Taylor Streets, Tenderloin (931 3600/ www.lecolonialsf.com). Bus 2, 3, 4, 27, 38, 76. **Open** 4.30-10pm Mon-Wed, Sun; 4.30-11pm Thur-Sat. **Credit** AmEx, DC, MC, V. **Map** p310 G4.

Designed to approximate Vietnam circa 1920 (when the country was still a French colony), this elegant hideaway has a capacious dining room to host the restaurant crowd, while the stylish upstairs lounge serves tropical cocktails, exotic teas and offers a lounge menu highlighting Vietnamese fusion cuisine. Le Colonial's comfortable couches invite cocktailing and more amid the lush environment of palm trees, rattan furniture and shuttered windows.

Julip Cocktail Lounge

839 Geary Street, between Hyde & Larkin Streets, Tenderloin (474 3216). Bus 19, 38. **Open** 5pm-2am Tue-Fri; 7pm-2am Sat. **No credit cards**. **Map** p314 F4.

Lurking behind the retro façade of Julip Cocktail Lounge, you'll find an exemplary DJ bar to remind you what DJ bars should all be like. Run by the owners of Dalva (see p153) in the Mission District, Julip draws cool kids to its handkerchief-sized dancefloor with fine DJs spinning funk, jazz and broken beat on Tuesdays, futuristic lounge on Wednesdays and finger-licking soul on Fridays. The bar's drinks selection, meanwhile, boosts your self-confidence to exactly the same degree as they undermine your dancefloor co-ordination.

liquor licenses' that permit the sale of beer, wine and spirits. Despite their alcohol content being on par with vodka and whisky, sake and soju are both classified as 'wine' by the ATF.

Confusing? Well, yes. But reason has never governed US law concerning the use and sale of controlled substances. Still, the happy result of all this befuddlement is that anywhere with a 'limited liquor license' can legally sell sake and soju. Which not only means enthusiastic consumers can try out premium labels without investing in a flight to Asia, but also has encouraged the development of inventive 'non-liquor' cocktails, the sake- and soju-based versions

prime among them. They're served throughout the city, but we recommend the Tokyo Manhattan (soju with a dash of plum sake) or Monkey Screw (unfiltered sake, soju, orange juice and triple sec) at low-key **Tsunami** (1306 Fulton Street, at Divisidero, Western Addition, 567 7664, http://tsunami-sf.com), as well as Rohan's great array of colourful soju cocktails, like the Asian Blonde (soju, fresh carrot and orange juice with a splash of lemon and lime, shaken and served) or the Happy Family (soju, koko creme, fresh pineapple and orange juice with a splash of grenadine on the rocks).

Kampai!

The Ramp

855 Terry Francois Street, at Mariposa & Third Streets, China Basin (621 2378). Bus 15, 22. **Open** 11am-8pm Mon-Fri; 11am-10pm Sat, Sun. **Credit** AmEx, MC, V. **Map** p315 J6.

The Bay laps right up to the edge of the Ramp, almost hidden among the waterfront warehouses and new construction throughout China Basin. This is a hideaway in which to have a drink and watch the ships rust on a sunny afternoon. Salsa and 'tropical' bands perform on summer weekends.

Red Room

Commodore International Hotel, 827 Sutter Street, between Jones & Leavenworth Streets, Tenderloin (346 7666). Bus 2, 3, 4, 27. **Open** 5pm-2am Mon-Sat, 7pm-2am Sun. **Credit** MC, V. **Map** p310 G3.

Enough to inspire a craving in any vampire, this slick bar inside the Commodore Hotel is entirely blood red: the walls, the tables, the semicircular bar, even one of the many speciality Martinis. It's wildly popular but tiny – an uncomfortable combo at the weekend. Come during the week when it's cosier.

Redwood Room

Clift Hotel, 495 Geary Street, at Taylor Street, Tenderloin (775 4700). Bus 2, 3, 4, 27, 38, 76. **Open** 5pm-2am Mon-Thur, Sun; 4pm-2am Fri, Sat. **Credit** AmEx, DC, Disc, MC, V. **Map** p310 G4.

No time was wasted in adding a bar to the Clift Hotel after the repeal of prohibition in 1933, and the magnificent result has been a fixture of high-end cocktailing ever since. Indeed, when hotelier Ian Schrager (former owner of New York's Studio 54) announced that he and designer Philippe Starck were renovating and modernising the Clift, there was a candlelight vigil to 'save' Redwood. Happily, despite the decor shifting from art deco to PoMo, the bar is neither tacky nor too flamboyant, and its towering walls are still panelled in lustrous redwood rumoured to have come from a single giant tree. A DJ spins four nights a week and the bar opens on to the Asia de Cuba (*see p119*) restaurant.

Tunnel Top

601 Bush Street, at Stockton Street, Union Square (986 8900). Bus 30, 45/cable car Powell-Hyde or Powell-Mason. **Open** 4pm-2am Mon-Sat. **No credit cards.** **Map** p311 G3.

The two-storey Tunnel Top perches above the Stockton Tunnel, between Chinatown and Union Square. On approach it looks like the dodgiest of dives. Inside, however, the decor is urban-decay cool. Films are projected against rust-coloured walls, while a DJ graces the balcony. Outside is the spot where Sam Spade surveys the scene of his partner's murder at the beginning of *The Maltese Falcon*.

W Hotel

181 Third Street, at Howard Street, SoMa (817 7836). Bus 12, 15, 30, 45, 76. **Open** 5pm-1.30am Tue-Fri; 7pm-1.30am Sat. **Credit** AmEx, DC, Disc, MC, V. **Map** p315 H4.

The two bars at this ultra-trendy SoMa hotel are both packed with the beautiful people. The first bar is a circular affair in the lobby, while the main bar, next to the XYZ (*see p125*) restaurant, lies behind a beaded curtain above. Some find the atmosphere a bit competitive, but the scene shifts nightly and the banquettes upstairs encourage an intimate vibe.

North Beach & around

Li Po

916 Grant Avenue, between Washington & Jackson Streets, Chinatown (982 0072). Bus 1, 12, 15, 30, 45. **Open** 2pm-2am daily. **No credit cards.** **Map** p311 G3.

A fun spot for a pick-me-up when you're done with the junk shops on Grant Avenue. Li Po is basically a dive, but the cave façade and giant, tattered Chinese lantern inside set it nicely apart from its neighbours. It'll take you back to a Barbary Coast-era San Francisco with no risk of being shanghaied by anything – except the potent cocktails.

Rosewood

732 Broadway, between Stockton & Powell Streets, North Beach (951 4886). Bus 12, 15, 30, 41/cable car Powell-Mason or Powell-Hyde. **Open** 5.30pm-2am Tue-Fri; 7pm-2am Sat. **Credit** MC, V. **Map** p310 G2.

This stylish bar, opened in early 2001, boasts rosewood panelling and is furnished with low, black leather benches – think retro-modern. Located on a neglected commercial strip at the edge of North Beach and Chinatown, and with no sign outside, it's not yet overrun. For now, it's one of the best places in the city to sip a cocktail, while DJs spin mellow tunes.

San Francisco Brewing Company

155 Columbus Avenue, at Pacific Avenue, North Beach (434 3344/www.sfbrewing.com). Bus 12, 15, 30, 41. **Open** 11.30-1am Mon-Fri; 11.30-1.30am Sat, Sun. **Credit** AmEx, MC, V. **Map** p311 G2.

Housed in a restored 1907 saloon, with a mahogany bar and belt-driven ceiling fans, this brew pub offers several own-made microbrews, pub grub and free

Staffa outing

You're draped over the bar in an appealingly louche location, really getting in touch with the charming barkeep. Suddenly you're asked if you fancy a shot. Forget about tequila, you could well be poured... a tiny glass of brown gloop. Welcome to Fernet.

Fernet Branca is a dark-brown bitter digestif. Made from a secret recipe of over 40 herbs created in 1845 by a young Milanese woman, Maria Scala, it's believed to hold powers as a restorative that are second to none – as bar and restaurant staff throughout San Francisco will attest. Whether used as a bracer to help maintain awareness through a late shift or as a 'staffa' (Italian for stirrup, a kind of 'one for the road') before heading home for the night, the tradition of consuming Fernet separates worker from civilian in San Francisco's boozing and eating world.

Still produced by Fratelli Branca (Maria Scala became Maria Branca once one of the Fratelli realised what he'd found) in Italy, Fernet contains aloe, chamomile, gentian, saffron, St John's wort, myrrh, rhubarb and cardamom, among other ingredients – and it's mighty bitter. Some, in fact, question the wisdom of offering it to newcomers. At first you're stunned by the pungent aroma, bold taste and sinus-searing finish, but then, as it settles into the bloodstream, many are won over by the undeniable exhilaration it provokes in mind and body. It may be a bit rough, but its consumption is an ongoing affirmation of fellowship among those who toil in common circumstance and a rite of passage for new initiates.

In other words, knock it back and smile sweetly. Your barkeeper loves you.

tours of the brewery. It was at this location, formerly the Andromeda Saloon, that Depression-era gangster 'Baby Face' Nelson was captured. Nowadays the scene is more staid, but it's hard to pass up the $1 brews from 4pm to 6pm and midnight to 1am.

Spec's

William Saroyan Place, off Columbus Avenue, at Broadway, North Beach (421 4112). Bus 12, 15, 30, 41. **Open** *4.30pm-2am Mon-Fri; 5pm-2am Sat, Sun.* **No credit cards. Map** p311 G2.

Spec's is the quintessential old-school San Francisco bar: one part North Beach bohemian, one part Wild West saloon, with a dash of weirdness for good measure. Tucked away in a false alley (you'll see what we mean), nearly every inch is covered with dusty detritus from around the world – this was once a sailor's haunt. If you're feeling a bit peckish, a basket of Saltines and a wedge of cheese hacked from a massive wheel of Gouda can be had for $2.

Tonga Room

Fairmont Hotel, 950 Mason Street, at California Street, Nob Hill (772 5278). Bus 1/cable car California, Powell-Hyde or Powell-Mason. **Open** *5pm-midnight Mon-Thur, Sun; 6pm-1am Fri, Sat.* **Credit** *AmEx, Disc, MC, V.* **Map** p310 G3.

This classic, long-lived Tiki bar has all-you-can-eat happy-hour dim sum, waitresses in sarongs and huge, exotic cocktails (Bora Bora Horror, anyone?). The real attraction, however, is the spectacle of house musicians performing off-key covers of cheesy pop songs while afloat on a raft on the Tonga's indoor 'lagoon', with patrons twirling on the ship's-deck dancefloor. There's even an indoor thunderstorm every 20 minutes, complete with rain.

Top of the Mark

Mark Hopkins Inter-Continental Hotel, 1 Nob Hill, between California & Mason Streets, Nob Hill (392 3434). Bus 1/cable car California, Powell-Hyde or Powell-Mason. **Open** *5pm-midnight Mon-Thur, Sun; 4pm-1am Fri, Sat.* **Admission** *$10 after 9pm Fri, Sat.* **Credit** *AmEx, DC, Disc, MC, V.* **Map** p310 G3.

Top of the Mark offers spectacular panoramic views of the city. It's worth a quick visit just to check the view and sip a Martini from the extensive '100 Martinis' menu, but arrive early in the evening to avoid the cover charge and dress code.

Tosca Café

242 Columbus Avenue, between Broadway & Pacific Avenue, North Beach (986 9651). Bus 12, 15, 30, 41. **Open** *5pm-2am Tue-Sun.* **No credit cards. Map** p311 G2.

SF nightspots seldom boast a high concentration of celebrities. Tosca is an exception. Its bada-bing Italian ambience and Hollywood-connected owner, Jeannette Etheridge, draw such stars as Bono, Francis Ford Coppola, Tom Waits and Sam Shepard. It's one of the city's oldest bars, with Formica-topped tables, deep-red vinyl booths, massive copper espresso machines and Caruso warbling from an ancient jukebox. If you're trying

to get your second wind, try a cappuccino. But beware: here it's the house speciality, a concoction of coffee, steamed milk and brandy, that really packs a punch.

Vesuvio

255 Columbus Avenue, between Broadway & Pacific Avenue, North Beach (362 3370/www.vesuvio.com). Bus 12, 15, 30, 41, 83. **Open** *6am-2am daily.* **No credit cards. Map** p311 G2.

A funky old saloon with a stained-glass façade, Vesuvio preserves the flavour of an earlier era. It's next to the famous City Lights (*see p165*) bookshop, across Jack Kerouac Alley (the writer was a regular here), and its walls are covered with Beat memorabilia. Sit on the narrow balcony and check out the scene downstairs and on the street.

Mission & Castro

The Argus Lounge

3187 Mission Street, between Cesar Chavez (Army) & Valencia Streets, Mission (824 1447). Bus 12, 14, 26, 27, 49, 67. **Open** *4pm-2am Mon-Sat; 5pm-12am Sun.* **No credit cards.**

Known by some as the Peacock because of the illuminated peacock feather out front (there's no other sign), the Argus is far enough down Mission Street to escape the gentrifying masses. A clean, simple hangout, it draws a happy crowd, including local indie-rock heroes. A superlative jukebox selection and a backroom pool table add to quirky touches such as a stuffed peacock and a working version of one of those 1950s exercise belts. Shake it, baby.

Beauty Bar San Francisco

2299 Mission Street, at 19th Street, Mission (285 0323/www.beautybar.com). Bus 14, 33, 49. **Open** *5pm-2am Mon-Fri; 7pm-2am Sat, Sun.* **Credit** *MC, V.* **Map** p314 F7.

This little cocktail bar, modelled after its sister bar in New York, is decorated with bric-a-brac salvaged from a Long Island hair salon. Instead of a couch, curl up on a Naugahyde salon chair, with hairdryer still attached. On Wednesday to Saturday evenings, buy a $10 cocktail and get a free manicure.

Dalva

3121 16th Street, between Guerrero & Valencia Streets, Mission (252 7740). BART 16th Street/ bus 14, 22, 26, 33, 49, 53. **Open** *4pm-2am daily.* **No credit cards. Map** p314 F6.

An unspoiled oasis of cool in the manic Mission bar scene, Dalva worships good music (these good people also run Julip, *see p150*). The jukebox, named Orpheus, carries a wonderfully diverse array of sounds, from Cuban music to Tiki kitsch. DJs spin drum 'n' bass, jazz, soul, funk, salsa and more.

Doc's Clock

2575 Mission Street, at 22nd Street, Mission (824 3627). Bus 14, 14L. **Open** *4pm-2am Mon-Fri; 6pm-2am Sat; Sun 8pm-2am.* **No credit cards. Map** p314 F7.

Eat, Drink, Shop

The neon sign alone warrants at least one quick drink at Doc's Clock. Though no longer a complete dive, the pours are generous and atmosphere is laid back, with the exception of heated games of shuffle-puck that take place on the full-size table in back.

Hotel Biron

45 Rose Street, alley between Market & Gough Streets,Mission (703 0403/www.hotelbiron.com). Muni Metro F, J, K, L, M/bus 6, 7, 66, 71. **Open** 5pm-2am Tue-Sun. **Credit** AmEx, MC, V. **Map** p314 F5.
Home to a wine bar and gallery, this hotel is named after the Rodin museum in Paris. Stylish yet unpretentious, the walls showcase the work of local artists. The impressive wine list boasts 80 wines by the bottle, with 35 or so by the glass, a selection of beers and a small menu of cheeses, caviar and olives. A great, low-key place for drinkers who like to talk.

Lucky 13

2140 Market Street, at Church Street, Castro (487 1313). Muni Metro F, J, K, L, M/bus 22, 37. **Open** 4pm-2am Mon-Thur; 2pm-2am Fri-Sun. **No credit cards. Map** p314 E6.
Dark, spacious and always busy, Lucky 13 has long been a favourite with those who crave the aura of a punk/biker bar without the risk. There's pinball, pool and foosball for diversion, but the main entertainments are people-watching and draining pints from one of the best German beer selections in the Bay Area. There are even Black Forest liqueurs.

Mecca

2029 Market Street, between Dolores & Church Streets, Upper Market (621 7000/ www.sfmecca.com). Muni Metro F, J, K, L, M, N/ bus 22. **Open** 5-11.30pm Tue-Thur; 5pm-1am Fri, Sat; 4-11pm Sun. **Credit** AmEx, Disc, DC, MC, V. **Map** p314 E/F6.
Armani's best customers hold holy congregation at Mecca. Inside frosted-glass doors, the urban warehouse look is melded successfully with baroque red velvet and chiffon drapery. The lounge area is an excellent place to get used to the finery. It's a favourite with svelte, immaculately dressed guppies, but draws a mixed crowd too. Soul and jazz singers perform on Mondays (8pm and 10pm, no cover).

Odeon Bar

3223 Mission Street, between Valencia & 29th Streets, Outer Mission (550 6994/ www.odeonbar.com). Bus 14, 26, 49, 67. **Open** 6pm-2am daily. **Credit** MC, V.
To confirm your stereotype of San Francisco as the land of lunatics, check out this dive. It was recently bought by Chicken John – locally notorious as the ringmaster of punk Circus Redickuless – who has turned the bar into a gathering spot for 'geeks, freaks, squids'. On most nights there's something strange going on. Possible events include the Mongoloid Lounge (a lounge night featuring a Devo cover band) and Porn-E-Okie (karaoke set to dirty movies). The Odeon is popular with the Burning Man (*see p188*) crowd.

Sadie's Flying Elephant

491 Potrero Avenue, at Mariposa Street, Mission (551 7988/www.flyingelephant.com). Bus 9, 33. **Open** 3pm-2am daily. **No credit cards. Map** p315 G6.
A dive bar with a heart of gold, Sadie's offers comfy couches, a superb jukebox, free popcorn and two pool tables. Most of the walls are large chalkboards – inspired patrons are encouraged to contribute their own graffiti, chalk murals, epitaphs, admonitions, hexes and/or pearls of wisdom. Philanthropic activities (monthly benefits and neighbourhood trash pick-up days) make Sadie's a worthy place to binge as well.

Treat Street Cocktails

3050 24th Street, at Treat Avenue, Mission (824 5954). BART 24th Street/bus 12, 48, 67. **Open** 5pm-2am daily. **No credit cards. Map** p314 G7.
Fans of cult TV hit *Northern Exposure* will appreciate this bar's style. Effects include deer heads, fish trophies and poor lighting, all quite an anomaly for a venue on the city's most Hispanic corner. Is that why the erudite-looking thirtysomethings come here?

Zeitgeist

199 Valencia Street, at Duboce Avenue, Mission (255 7505/http://zeitgeist.citysearch.com). Muni Metro F, J, K, L, M/bus 26. **Open** 9am-2am daily. **No credit cards. Map** p314 F5/6.
Zeitgeist, on the unofficial border between SoMa and the Mission, is one of the hippest and most chilled-out bars in town. It's popular with bikers (Hondas rather than Harleys), bike messengers and people from every walk of alternative life. On sunny early evenings, it's hard to sit, let alone move, at the dozens of benches and tables in the giant beer-garden-meets-junkyard back patio. The jukebox places special emphasis on underground punk.

Haight, Western Addition & Hayes Valley

An Bodhrán

668 Haight Street, between Pierce & Steiner Streets, Lower Haight (431 4724/www.anbodhran.com). Bus 6, 7, 22, 66, 71. **Open** 4pm-2am Mon-Fri, Sun; 6pm-2am Sat. **Credit** MC, V. **Map** p313 E5.
This dark, low-ceilinged Irish bar seems to fly beneath the radar of both the scenesters and the yuppies in the Lower Haight. It's a friendly place to raise a pint or have a game of darts. Trad Irish music sessions are held on Sunday afternoons.

Hayes & Vine

377 Hayes Street, between Franklin & Gough Streets, Hayes Valley (626 5301). Bus 21, 47, 49. **Open** 5pm-midnight Mon-Thur; 5pm-1am Fri, Sat; 3-10pm Sun. **Credit** MC, V. **Map** p314 F5.
This elegant wine bar caters to symphony-goers, shoppers and anyone up for good vino in comfortable surroundings. No stuffy wine snobs, either. Ask for suggestions from the list of 1,000 wines by the bottle, and more than 40 by the glass.

The/debonair **Tosca Café**.
See p153.

Hobson's Choice

1601 Haight Street, at Clayton Street, Haight-Ashbury (621 5859/www.hobsonschoice.com). Bus 6, 7, 33, 37, 43, 66, 71. **Open** 2pm-2am Mon-Fri; midnight-2am Sat; 8am-2am Sun. **Credit** Disc, MC, V. **Map** p313 C7.

Billing itself as a 'Victorian punch bar', bartenders ladle out tall glasses of tasty rum punch and offer huge bowls of the stuff for larger parties. The menu boasts more than 60 kinds of rum. Fresh, grilled kebabs delivered from neighbouring Asqew Grill feed the collegiate-cum-jam-band set that fills the bar almost every night of the week.

Mad Dog in the Fog

530 Haight Street, between Fillmore & Steiner Streets, Lower Haight (626 7279/ http://maddog.citysearch.com). Bus 6, 7, 22, 66, 71. **Open** 11.30am-2am Mon-Fri; 10am-2am Sat, Sun. **No credit cards. Map** p314 E5.

A congenial spot for anyone fancying a live broadcast of real football (aka soccer), the Mad Dog offers 20 beers on tap and another 30 in bottles. DJs wax their vinyl on Fridays and Sundays and bands play everything from punk to Scottish folk on Saturdays. Traditional English breakfasts (the 'Greedy Bastard' is $7) are served mid-morning, with pub grub available in the afternoon and evening.

Movida Lounge

200 Fillmore Street, at Waller Street, Lower Haight (934 8637). Bus 6, 7, 22, 66, 71. **Open** 4pm-midnight daily. **No credit cards. Map** p314 E5.

A great place to start the evening (it gets packed and horrid later on). Mural-sized re-creations of Picasso's *Don Quixote* series adorn Movida's exterior, while red lighting bathes the inside during the evening. Curl up on banquettes along the windows or mingle as a DJ provides the background music. Closing time can be as late as 2am, depending on the crowd.

Nickie's BBQ

460 Haight Street, between Fillmore & Webster Streets, Lower Haight (621 6508/www.nickies.com). Bus 6, 7, 22, 66, 71. **Open** 9pm-2am Mon-Sat. **No credit cards. Map** p314 E5.

No longer a barbecue joint, Nickie's now serves up a heapin' helping of spicy-sweet soul and deep funk. The down-home atmosphere makes this small, divey DJ bar a good groove, but at weekends it can get absurdly crowded with drunken louts and the ladies who tolerate them. Come on Thursday for hardcore soul or Tuesday for increasingly renowned DJ Cheb I Sabbah's Asian, African and Arabian dance party. Other nights you'll get house, reggae, funk or disco.

Noc Noc

557 Haight Street, between Fillmore & Steiner Streets, Lower Haight (861 5811). Bus 6, 7, 22, 66, 71. **Open** 5pm-2am daily. **Credit** MC, V. **Map** p314 E5.

An eternally hip institution. If Dr Seuss and Trent Reznor had gone into the bar business together, this is what they'd have come up with. The decor is described as 'post-apocalyptic industrial', and the

whole place has an oddly organic Gaudi feel. Always plunged in near darkness and with a mellow chill-room vibe, Noc Noc attracts a multi-ethnic lot.

Persian Aub Zam Zam

1633 Haight Street, between Clayton & Belvedere Streets, Haight-Ashbury (861 2545). Bus 6, 7, 33, 37, 43, 66, 71. **Open** 3.30pm-2am daily. **No credit cards. Map** p313 C6.

This tiny bar was a legend thanks to its notoriously cantankerous owner, Bruno Mooshei; he inherited the bar from his father and waged a one-man campaign to keep it exactly as it must have been circa World War II. This meant inexpensive drinks and proper bar etiquette – only ladies got cocktail napkins. It also meant you stood an excellent chance of getting tossed out if you ordered the 'wrong' drink (a Martini was the only choice), the bar was crowded or he just didn't like your looks (bland suburbanites were more likely to get the boot than bohemians). Bruno died in 2000, but long-time patrons bought the place and are devoted to keeping its *Casablanca* aura intact.

Place Pigalle

520 Hayes Street, between Laguna & Octavia Streets, Hayes Valley (552 2671/www.place-pigalle.com). Bus 21, 47, 49. **Open** 4pm-2am daily. **Credit** AmEx, MC, V. **Map** p314 F5.

While the decor says 'at-risk youth drop-in centre', the well-selected wine and beer menu says otherwise. Both conspire to keep the vibe laid-back. The crowd is eclectic: gay and straight, bohemian and yuppie, young and not-so-young. The back room (with pool table) doubles as an art gallery.

Toronado

547 Haight Street, between Fillmore & Steiner Streets, Lower Haight (863 2276/www.toronado.com). Bus 6, 7, 22, 66, 71. **Open** 11.30am-2am daily. **No credit cards. Map** p313/4 E5.

Toronado is a beer drinker's delight. A board posted on the wall shows the massive, ever-changing selection of draughts (slanted in favour of the Belgian), while the chalkboard behind the bar highlights bottled beer and non-alco options. Patrons are encouraged to bring in fresh sausages from Rosamunde Sausage Grill next door, so relax – everything's taken care of.

Pacific Heights to Golden Gate Bridge

G Bar

Laurel Inn, 444 Presidio Avenue, between Sacramento & California Streets, Presidio Heights (409 4227). Bus 1, 3, 4, 43. **Open** 5.30pm-2am daily. **Credit** AmEx, MC, V. **Map** p309 D4.

If you're saddened that San Francisco doesn't look like Los Angeles, head to G. The Laurel Inn was a non-descript motel until the folks behind the Commodore (home to the Red Room, *see p151*) and Phoenix (Bambuddha Lounge, *see p219*) got hold of it. It now has a neo-'50s look and a bachelor-pad atmosphere.

A cocktail and bull story

Sazerac, Ramoz Fizz, Rusty Nail, the Scofflaw, Knickerbocker, Greyhound. There was a time in America when, perhaps due to the scarcity of quality alcohol, mixing a cocktail was a creative and celebratory act. Major publishing houses printed cocktail manuals penned by the bartenders of upmarket hotel bars, speciality cocktail menus celebrated contemporary icons, international events and local heroes. The Gold Rush was to yield a number of recipes that are still favoured by the cocktailing classes, and the Bull Shot at Perry's (*see p142* **Later than breakfast, sooner than Monday**) proves that San Francisco remains unafraid of even the most brutal inventiveness of the cocktail chef. Yet it is to the classic, the most simply perfect cocktail that all others pay homage: the Martini.

According to one version of history, the Martini was invented in California. In 1849 a prospector who'd struck it rich was heading through Martinez, some 40 miles (64 kilometres) north-east of San Francisco, on his way back to town. Stepping into a bar, he ordered a bottle of champagne, which this 19th-century miners' bar in the sticks had

apparently neglected to stock. In lieu of of champagne, the bartender whipped up his 'Martinez Special'. Over time 'Martinez' evolved into 'Martini' – perhaps thanks to the use of Martini vermouth in certain versions of the Martinez Special.

Regardless of origins, mixologists at such places as **Blondie's Bar & No Grill** (540 Valencia Street, at 16th Street, Mission, 864 2419, www.blondiesbar.com) create elaborate Martinis that are served in a convenient pint size. Artworks like their Almond Mocha (Stoli Kafya, chocolate liqueur and Frangelico garnished with a chocolate kiss and served in a chocolate-rimmed glass – heaven) are poured to the top of a half-pint Martini glass. What about the other half pint you ask? The bartender leaves the remainder in the shaker next to the glass so that indulgers can refill at their leisure. A Martini at **Martuni's** (*see p228*) is nearly as massive. The relaxed and elegant environs invite serious cocktailing, but the rigidly straight-laced should note that the clientele, like the address, borders the Castro: that piano means showtunes, sister.

Liverpool Lil's

2942 Lyon Street, between Lombard & Greenwich Streets, Marina (921 6664). Bus 28, 41, 43, 45, 76. **Open** 11am-2am Mon-Fri; 10am-2am Sat, Sun. **Credit** MC, V. **Map** p309 D2.
The façade looks like it's made out of driftwood and the main decorative touch inside is a wall of old sports photos. There's a considerable pub menu and the crowd ranges from square old things to young hipsters. Caught in a '70s timewarp, this is the Marina's least pretentious bar. Easily.

Matrix

3138 Fillmore Street, between Filbert & Greenwich Streets, Marina (563 4180/www.plumpjack. com). Bus 22. **Open** 5.30pm-2am daily. **Credit** AmEx, MC, V. **Map** p309 E2.
Things have changed at the Matrix. At the original, you might have seen Hunter S Thompson in the bathroom sucking LSD off a stranger's sleeve (it's in *Fear and Loathing…*, sweetie), maybe catch a set from Jefferson Airplane or the Grateful Dead. Now the place belongs to SF mayor Gavin Newsom and his Plumpjack restaurant group. If you can choke down a cocktail between nostalgic sobs, be prepared for label-conscious fashionistas and financiers sipping selections from the extensive, and expensive, cocktail menu at this high-style pick-up joint.

Richmond, Sunset & the Golden Gate Park

Also try the **Beach Chalet** for cocktails or **Cliff House** for the view (for both, *see p105*).

Canvas Café Gallery

1200 Ninth Avenue, at Lincoln Way, Inner Sunset (504 0060/www.thecanvasgallery.com). Muni Metro N/bus 6, 16, 44, 66, 71. **Open** 6am-midnight Mon-Thur; 7am-2am Fri; 8am-2am Sat; 8am-midnight Sun. **Credit** AmEx, MC, V. **Map** p312 B6.
The Canvas combines beer and wine bar, and café, with art gallery and live performance space. The decor is Scandinavian modern, with plate-glass windows overlooking Golden Gate Park. From Wednesday to Saturday there's live music, usually folk, rock and jazz, plus the occasional DJ.

The Plough & Stars

116 Clement Street, at 2nd Avenue, Inner Richmond (751 1122). Bus 2, 31, 33, 38. **Open** 4pm-2am Mon-Fri; 2pm-2am Sat, Sun. **Credit** Disc, MC, V. **Map** p308 B4.
Located in the hear of the city's Irish community it doesn't get much more Irish than the Plough & Stars. Live traditional Irish music fills this hall-like space most nights (and has done for more than 25 years).

Eat, Drink, Shop

Trader Sam's

6150 Geary Boulevard, at 26th Avenue, Richmond (221 0773). Bus 29, 38. **Open** 10am-2am daily.
No credit cards.
A local fave since 1939, this unabashedly traditional Tiki bar serves the kind of cocktails that can only be described as dangerous. Planter's Punch, Mai Tais, Singapore Slings and the ever-popular Volcano & Goldfish Bowl – a guaranteed hangover under every cheesy umbrella. It's just a shame Trader's is so far from any nightlife hub.

East Bay

The places where East Bay folk congregate to raise a glass reflect a more proletarian sensibility than those in San Francisco, with points awarded for substance over style and absence of frills over large bills. Genuinely down-to-earth, the East Bay bar scene offers honest booze at an honest price, plus oddities like the **Alley** (*see below*) or the **First & Last Chance** (*see below*). Then there's the **Parkway Theater** (*see p201*): beer isn't traditionally served at US cinemas unless you sneak in a six-pack, but at the Parkway…

Albatross Pub

1822 San Pablo Avenue, between Delaware & Hearst Streets, Berkeley (1-510 843 2473/ www.albatrosspub.com). BART Berkeley, then AC Transit bus 51. **Open** 6pm-2am Mon, Tue, Sun; 4.30pm-2am Wed-Sat. **No credit cards.**
The Albatross has the pub concept locked down. The homey atmosphere allows its diverse crowd to take part in a range of activities. For the (relatively) active there is a huge variety of boardgames, four separate dart stalls, a poolroom and regular live music. For the supine? A nice fireplace, a large selection of beers, free popcorn, adjustable lamps at the tables for reading and a host of quiet corners.

The Alley

3325 Grand Avenue, between Elwood Avenue & Lake Park Avenue, Oakland (1-510 444 8505). BART 19th Street, then bus 12/AC Transit bus K, N, V. **Open** 4pm-2am Tue-Sat. **No credit cards.**
The Alley is designed to look like a shanty-town street, complete with knickers strung between building façades and jagged fences separating the booths. At the end of the bar is a piano surrounded by bar stools, each with a microphone. Anyone is free to take a seat and join the sing-along that takes place every Thursday through Saturday night. Participants are from all walks of life. Don't worry if you're not sure of the words – neither is the pianist.

Club Mallard

752 San Pablo Avenue, between Portland & Washington Avenues, Albany (1-510 524 8450/ www.clubmallard.com). BART El Cerrito Plaza, then 8 blocks south down San Pablo. **Open** 2pm-2am Mon-Fri; noon-2am Sat, Sun. **Credit** MC, V.

Though all are remnants of a time when the San Pablo Avenue was one of the most notorious streets in the region, the good-natured crowd you'll find at the half log-cabin, half Tiki-style Club Mallard are more congenial than the salty folk that frequent the Hotsy Totsy and the Ivy Room just along the street. The two pool tables on the main floor cost only 25 cents, with more tables upstairs for hire by the hour. The eclectic jukebox ranges from funk and reggae to campy lounge tunes, heightening the surreal atmosphere.

First & Last Chance Saloon

Jack London Square, at Webster Street, Oakland (1-510 839 6761/www.heinoldsfirstandlastchance.com). BART Oakland City Center, then bus 58, 72L, 301. **Open** noon-midnight Mon-Thur; noon-1am Fri, Sat; 11am-10pm Sun. **No credit cards.**
Listed on the National Register of Historic Places, this tiny building is made from wood salvaged from a whaling ship in 1883. As a schoolboy Jack London did his homework at the tables still used today and the bar itself is mentioned 17 times in his memoir *John Barleycorn*. The floor and bar are tilted at an extreme angle, and have been since the 1906 earthquake.

Hotsy Totsy

601 San Pablo Avenue, at Garfield Avenue, Albany (1-510 525 9964). BART El Cerrito Plaza, then 8 blocks south down San Pablo. **Open** 6am-2pm daily. **No credit cards.**
If you always wanted to re-enact scenes from Charles Bukowski's movie *Barfly*, then the Hotsy Totsy and the Ivy Room (just down the street at No.858) are the places to do it. Order a drink for all your friends or engage in impromptu back-alley bare-knuckle boxing. Maybe not, but stepping into this joint, you might as well be at a steelworker's bar outside Allentown, PA, or in a George Thorogood song. Don't expect nuthin' fancy.

Ruby Room

132 14th Street, between Madison Street & Lakeside Drive, Oakland (1-510 444 7224). BART 12th Street, then bus 13, 59, 82. **Open** 5pm-2am Mon-Fri; 8pm-2am Sat, Sun. **Credit** AmEx, MC, V.
Neither the fantastic jukebox nor the new-wave DJs seem able to entice people on to the tiny dancefloor, but everyone hums or sings along. The crowd is young, hip, tattooed and pierced, and happy to while away the hours in Ruby Room's dim, smoky, womb-like space, all red walls and black ceiling.

Spats

1974 Shattuck Avenue, between Berkeley Way & University Avenue, Berkeley (1-510 841 7225/ www.spats.citysearch.com). BART Berkeley. **Open** 4pm-1am Mon-Thur; 4pm-2am Fri, Sat. **Credit** AmEx, DC, MC, V. **Map** p315 L3.
Modelled on a gents' club, this is a plush bar full of lovely deep chairs. The giant novelty drinks are quite a production: the Borneo Fogcutter, for instance, comes trailing dry-ice smoke from its base.

Shops & Services

From hipster thrift demons to designer addicts, San Francisco is everyone's consumer fix.

Whether you're hung on haute couture or your style notes (and light wallet) dictate second-hand chic, you're likely to find exactly what you're looking for here. Burdened with neither the skeletal shop girls who rove LA's boutiques nor the rabid Upper East Side cashmere hounds who menace midtown Manhattan, San Francisco offers a refined and diverse shopping experience, all squeezed into a refreshingly bijou space by the ocean and the Bay.

In a city heavily determined by the unique personality of individual neighbourhoods, there is only one centralised shopping district: Union Square. But, with its overwhelming collage of chain stores and designer shops, this consumer hub is least likely to provide original finds. The rest – and best – of the retail opportunities line neighbourhood streets and hide down secluded alleyways. You'll find almost every district, from Noe Valley to Russian Hill, has a 'shopping street' replete with boutiques and speciality shops indicative of that area's particular flavour. Seek them out and you'll discover a plethora of disparate and unique retailers, the majority of which remain proudly disdainful of homogenised mall culture.

SHOPPING AREAS

The recently renovated and restored (to the tune of $25 million) **Union Square** in downtown San Francisco hosts monolithic retail stores (**Macy's, Niketown, Disney Store**), as well as designer boutiques (**Ferragamo, Marc Jacobs, Gucci**) and long-standing department stores whose sombre, historical architecture reflects the classic, if somewhat bland, inventory within (**Neiman Marcus, Gump's, Saks Fifth Avenue**). From Union Square, a short stroll up **Grant Avenue** takes you into another world. Not just a tourist magnet but a thriving community, the streets of **Chinatown** are thronged with locals who make their daily expeditions to overflowing vegetable markets, fish shops and herbal apothecaries. A haven for knick-knacks, porcelain, lanterns, embroidered jackets and other Chinoiserie, there are many hidden gems to be found here, such as the **Sam Bo Trading Co** (*see p164*).

Keep walking along Grant Avenue and you'll end up at **North Beach**. Upper Grant Avenue has evolved from a sleepy corner of North Beach to a bona fide mecca for those with a few dollars to drop on local couture, while Columbus Avenue hosts the legendary **City Lights** (*see p165*) bookstore.

The struggle over gentrification in the **Mission** seems to have ebbed a little; artists and original residents have begun to accept their digs are now home to upscale restaurants, yuppie DJ bars and fashionable boutiques and both sides of the cultural divide exist in a state of uneasily peaceful symbiosis. It's a sign of the best such boutiques,

The best Shopping

Amoeba Music
An imperative for music lovers, Amoeba has a dizzying selection *and* free gigs. *See p182.*

Anthropologie
This colossal girlie-cute emporium is perfect for everything from faux-fur wraps to willowy silk dresses with butterfly appliqués. *See p169.*

Crossroads Trading Company
New and used items that run the retail gamut from elegant Valentino coat to fly Adidas tracksuit. *See p175.*

Dema
Mod styles from local designers, including the owner's funkafied retro-chic threads. *See p170.*

George
Ideal for the stylish pet: smashing plaid doggie jackets, iridescent cat collars, gourmet petfood and charming people clothes. *See p185.*

Lombardi Sports
Those who do the hard yards and those who merely watch are equally welcome. *See p186.*

places like **Dema** (*see p170*), that they feel comfortably integrated into the ever-evolving district.

Far away from the Mission geographically and demographically, along the northern waterfront below **Pacific Heights**, young urban professionals happily exist in a parallel universe of spiky gelled hair, Coors Light binges and yoga classes. The main drags – **Union Street** and **Chestnut Street** – offer myriad retail opportunities and, if you look hard enough, a few gems like **Ambiance** (*see p170* **No poseurs, please**) and **Rin** (*see p172*). Running up off Union Street over the sizeable hill, **Fillmore Street** offers a stridently top-class selection of shops filled with clothing, beauty products and vintage threads. Continuing down Fillmore Street leads you to the **Japan Center**, a mall housing Japanese-language bookshops, sushi bars, noodle joints and purveyors of Japanese iron, bronze and incense for that touch of legitimacy in your newly installed meditation room.

Continuing south, you'll arrive at **Hayes Valley**, three blocks of Hayes Street running between **Laguna Street** and the **Civic Center**. Now liberated from the Fell Street Freeway Exit (torn down in early 2003), this area is brimming with shops that make up in hipster cachet what they lack in affordability (*see p167* **Hayes Street chic**). Those in the know stroll down **Gough Street** as far as Market to wander through the droves of antique stores, full of vintage deco and '50s furnishings, then cross Market Street to search the shops around tiny **Brady Street** for everything from imported ribbons to valuable Eames chairs.

Combining sightseeing with shopping is particularly easy on **Haight Street**. Its heyday more than three decades hence, Haight still pays over-the-top homage to the Summer of Love. Fortunately, it also maintains progressive clothing, shoe and record boutiques among the hokey head shops. The **Castro** (*see p85*) is lively too, with the young, hip and fit getting poured into club-worthy threads from stores such as **Rolo on Market** (*see p172*) and **Citizen Clothing** (*see p169*).

TAX & DUTY

Most shops accept travellers' cheques, but don't forget that local sales tax (currently 8.5 per cent) will be added to all purchases. You can avoid paying this if you live out of state and either arrange for the shop to ship your purchase or arrange shipment yourself by US mail or courier. If you are taking goods out of the country, remember that you'll be liable for duty and tax on goods worth more than a certain amount (£145 for the UK).

The sublimely cool **AB Fits**. *See p168.*

Department stores

You will find all of the following located in and around Union Square – and most have extended opening hours between Thanksgiving and Christmas.

Gump's

135 Post Street, between Grant Avenue & Kearny Street (1-800 766 7628/984 9439/www.gumps.com). BART Montgomery Street/Muni Metro F, J, K, L, M, N/bus 2, 3, 4, 15, 30, 38, 45, 76/cable car Powell-Hyde or Powell-Mason. **Open** 10am-6pm Mon-Sat; noon-5pm Sun. **Credit** AmEx, DC, Disc, MC, V. **Map** p311 H3.

Established in 1861, Gump's is the city's original emporium of good taste and the place where moneyed San Franciscans buy wedding presents, china and a variety of baubles – including oriental ware, jade, antiques and pearls, pearls, pearls.

Macy's

170 O'Farrell Street, between Powell & Stockton Streets (397 3333/www.macys.com). BART Powell Street/Muni Metro F, J, K, L, M, N/bus 2, 3, 4, 15, 30, 38, 45, 76/cable car Powell-Hyde or Powell-Mason. **Open** 10am-8pm Mon-Sat; 11am-7pm Sun. **Credit** AmEx, DC, Disc, MC, V. **Map** p311 G4.

This is the mother of all department stores, offering racks crammed with goods at all prices. Theory, DKNY, Ralph Lauren and INC lines are all available,

frequently discounted. Upstairs Cheesecake Factory (*see p141*) is perpetually packed, but the view is as huge as the slices of cheesecake.
Other locations: Stonestown Galleria, Winston Drive, at 19th Avenue, Park Merced (753 4000/www.macys.com).

Neiman Marcus
150 Stockton Street, at Geary Street (362 3900/1-877 634 6264/www.neimanmarcus.com). BART Powell Street/Muni Metro F, J, K, L, M, N/bus 2, 3, 4, 15, 30, 38, 45, 76/cable car Powell-Hyde or Powell-Mason. **Open** 10am-7pm Mon-Wed, Fri, Sat; 10am-8pm Thur; noon-6pm Sun. **Credit** AmEx, DC. **Map** p311 G3/4.
Now commonly referred to as 'Needless Markup', Neiman Marcus was revered by old San Francisco society back when labels said 'Exclusively for Neiman Marcus'. Today luxury of the mink-covered coat-hangar variety can still be yours, alongside new designer and diffusion labels (Prada to Blahnik).

Nordstrom
San Francisco Centre, 865 Market Street, at Fifth Street (243 8500/www.nordstrom.com). BART Powell Street/Muni Metro F, J, K, L, M, N/bus 5, 21, 27, 30, 31, 38, 45/cable car Powell-Hyde or Powell-Mason. **Open** 9.30am-9pm Mon-Sat; 10am-7pm Sun. **Credit** AmEx, DC, Disc, MC, V. **Map** p311 G4.
While its commitment to customer service may have flagged in recent years, Nordstrom still offers accessible luxury. As well as well-appointed departments for every type of fashion, there's live piano music and even, in the Men's Department, a lounge.
Other locations: Stonestown Galleria, 285 Winston Drive, at 19th Avenue, Park Merced (753 1344).

Saks Fifth Avenue
384 Post Street, at Powell Street (986 4300/www.saksfifthavenue.com). BART Powell Street/Muni Metro F, J, K, L, M, N/bus 2, 3, 4, 15, 30, 38, 45, 76/cable car Powell-Hyde or Powell-Mason. **Open** 10am-7pm Mon-Wed, Fri; 10am-8pm Thur; 11am-6pm Sun. **Credit** AmEx, DC, Disc, MC, V. **Map** p311 G3.
The San Francisco branch of this upmarket store is airier and less claustrophobic than most of its ilk. The second floor offers designers like Marc Jacobs, Ann Demeulemeester, Gucci and Moschino, but two floors up you'll find less pricey but just as trendy lines by Katayone, Miu Miu and Tocca. (At the menswear store, the more cutting-edge creations are to be found on the fifth floor.)
Other locations: (menswear) 220 Post Street, at Powell Street, Union Square (986 4300).

Shopping centres

Crocker Galleria
50 Post Street, between Montgomery & Kearny Streets, Union Square (393 1505/www.shopatgalleria.com). BART Montgomery Street/Muni Metro J, K, L, M, N/bus 2, 4, 5, 15, 30/cable car Powell-Hyde or Powell-Mason. **Open** 10am-6pm Mon-Fri; 11am-6pm Sat. **Map** p311 H3.

This open-ended arcade a couple of blocks off Union Square mixes individually owned shops and eateries with European and US designers' boutiques (Ralph Lauren, Versace).

Embarcadero Center
Sacramento Street, between Battery & Drumm Streets, Financial District (772 0700/www.embarcaderocenter.com). BART Embarcadero/Muni Metro F, J, K, L, M, N/bus 1, 2, 7, 9, 10, 14, 15, 21, 31, 41, 66, 71/cable car Van Ness-Embarcadero. **Open** 10am-7pm Mon-Fri; 10am-6pm Sat; noon-5pm Sun. **Map** p311 H3.
The shopping areas on the ground and first floors of these four downtown office towers represent most of the major chains: Banana Republic, Gap, Victoria's Secret, Pottery Barn, Nine West *et al*. There's also a well-stocked international newsstand and excellent multiscreen cinema featuring an eclectic range of independent films and documentaries.

Fisherman's Wharf
Jefferson Street, between Hyde & Powell Streets, Fisherman's Wharf (626 7070/www.fishermanswharf.org). Muni Metro F/bus 10, 15, 30, 39, 47/cable car Powell-Hyde or Powell-Mason/Golden Gate Ferry, Blue & Gold Ferry. **Open** times vary. **Map** p310 F1.
Fisherman's Wharf hawks tourist fare like 'Property of Alcatraz' T-shirts and crab-shaped ashtrays. It's worth a wander, if only for the striking bay views, cacophonous street bands and an Irish coffee at the Buena Vista (on North Point and Hyde Streets).

Ghirardelli Square
Beach Street, between Larkin & Polk Streets, Fisherman's Wharf (775 5500/www.ghirardellisq.com). Muni Metro F/bus 10, 15, 30, 39, 47/cable car Powell-Hyde or Powell-Mason/ferry Golden Gate Ferry, Blue & Gold Ferry. **Open** *Apr-May* 10am-7pm Mon-Thur; 10am-8pm Fri, Sat; 11am-6pm Sun. *June-Aug* 10am-9pm Mon-Sat; 10am-6pm Sun. *Sept-Mar* 11am-7pm Mon-Thur; 10am-8pm Fri, Sat; 11am-6pm Sun. **Map** p310 F1/2.
At this home of the Ghirardelli chocolate factory, you can watch the stuff being made and scoff it as you wander through the mostly souvenir-themed shops. Take a break at Fritz Frites or sip an elegant cocktail at Ana Mandara, local (anti-)hero Don Johnson's upscale Vietnamese restaurant.

Metreon
Fourth Street, at Mission Street, SoMa (369 6000/www.metreon.com). BART Powell Street or Montgomery Street/Muni Metro F, J, K, L, M, N/bus 9, 12, 14, 15, 30, 45/cable car Powell-Hyde or Powell-Mason. **Open** 10am-10pm daily. **Map** p311 H4.
While the idea of a technology-themed mini-emporium now seems very '90s, there's still something in the Metreon for technophiles, including Sony Style and a Microsoft shop. But the real draw is 15 cinemas, including a monolithic Sony IMAX screen. There's also an interactive exhibit, based on Maurice Sendak's *Where the Wild Things Are*, where kids can cavort with giant monsters.

On the cheap Thrift, fleas & second-hand

There can be little doubt that the reigning dress and decorating code in San Francisco is shabby chic, and there are myriad shops that cater to the desire for upscale cast-offs and carefully sourced vintage gear (for listings, *see p173*). But, really, why spend top dollar for that de rigueur plether jacket or oh-so-ironic school T-shirt at the vintage or resale shops? The truth is that you can outfit yourself, your home, your children, probably even your pet just as well, for a quarter of the price, at the city's staggering array of bargain outlets. And then there's the thrill of beating granny to the rummage thrown in as well.

The best place to start is in the Mission, which boasts the city's largest concentration of thrift stores. Visiting the **Goodwill Superstore** (1580 Mission Street, at Van Ness Avenue, 575 2240; *pictured*) doesn't guarantee you'll find a $4 Betsey Johnson skirt, but it's big enough to maximise the odds. (For the city's many other Goodwill stores, check www.sfgoodwill.org). It should come as no surprise either that, whenever he's in town, Latin rocker El Vez calls in on **Thrift Town** (2101 Mission Street, at 17th Street, 861 1132) for the outrageous pant suits. But hardcore thrifters will still demand the can't-be-beat prices and no-nonsense displays at the **Salvation Army** (1509 Valencia Street, at 26th Street, 643 8040). If bulk is the objective, you can pick up clothes by the pound: as we went to press, $8 would buy you exactly 1lb (400 grammes) of clothes at **Clothes Contact** (473 Valencia Street, at 16th Street, 621 3212).

For collectibles, make sure to visit the Bay Area's flea markets. The two best are on Alemany Boulevard and, across the Bay, at Alameda Point. **Alemany Flea Market** (100 Alemany Boulevard, between Putnam & Crescent Streets, 647 2043) takes place every Sunday. Nestled under the US 101 & I-280 intersection, just east of Bernal Heights, you can find everything from vintage Fiestaware to dusty ham radio manuals. It's well known as the cool person's flea, so there are more Gazelle-clad young 'uns sifting the sales bins than pack-rat wrinklies – arrive early (8am) for the bargains. If you have a car and an entire day to spare, head to **Alameda Point Antiques and Collectibles Faire** (www.antiquesbybay.com) on the first Saturday of the month. Held on a former naval base, this monster has over 800 vendors.

But if you're on holiday, it's probably best to combine sightseeing and bargain-seeking at one of the city's numerous weekend **sidewalk sales**. Check the comprehensive listing at www.craigslist.org and choose one in a neighbourhood you'd be visiting anyway. That way you enjoy the day out even if that Betsey Johnson skirt is still evading your clutches.

Pier 39

Beach Street & The Embarcadero, Fisherman's Wharf (705 5500/www.pier39.com). Muni Metro F/bus 10, 15, 39, 47/cable car Powell-Mason. **Open** *Jan-Feb* 10.30am-7pm Mon-Thur, Sun; 10am-9pm Fri, Sat. *Mar-mid May, mid Sept-Oct* 10am-8pm Mon-Thur, Sun; 10am-9pm Fri, Sat. *Mid May-mid Sept* 10am-9pm Mon-Thur, Sun; 10am-10pm Fri, Sat. *Nov-Dec* 10.30am-8pm Mon-Thur, Sun; 10.30am-9pm Fri, Sat. **Map** p310 G1.
A bustling tourist trap, all T-shirt shops and people flogging music boxes, plus the recently opened Hard Rock Café and a working carousel. Don't be put off, though: there are good views and, best of all, noisy and extremely smelly sea lions.

San Francisco Centre

865 Market Street, at Fifth Street, Union Square (512 6776/www.westfield.com/us/centres). BART Powell Street/Muni Metro F, J, K, L, M, N/bus 5, 21, 27, 30, 31, 38, 45/cable car Powell-Hyde or Powell-Mason. **Open** 9.30am-8pm Mon-Sat; 11am-6pm Sun. **Map** p311 G4.
Spiral elevators wind slowly up this vast vertical mall, enticing shoppers with mid-priced chain stores including J Crew, Abercrombie & Fitch, Wet Seal, BCBG and Club Monaco. Nordstrom resides on top like a society matron; you can take express elevators that whizz past the retail riff-raff and deposit you directly in its majestic shoe department.

Antiques & collectibles

In the serpentine streets (Kansas, Henry Adams, 16th and Brannan) that surround the **Design Center** on Potrero Hill, you'll find upmarket places that cater to interior designers and decorators. Several more are clustered in the **Jackson Square Historical District** (call 296 8150 for the Jackson Square Art & Antique Dealers Association), while the antique and novelty shops in **Hayes Valley** at Gough and Market Streets are a frequent haven for stylists and photographers. The now revitalised stretch of **Polk Street** on Russian Hill (between Pacific and Green Streets) is also now rich with shops for furniture and collectibles. For flea markets, *see p162* **On the cheap: Thrift, fleas & second-hand**.

Aria

1522 Grant Avenue, at Union Street, North Beach (433 0219). Bus 15, 30, 39, 41/cable car Powell-Mason. **Open** 11am-6pm Mon-Sat; noon-5pm Sun. **No credit cards. Map** p311 G2.
The ultimate curiosity shop, with everything coated in just the right amount of dust. Bill Haskell's treasure trove includes a little bit of everything from everywhere: German marionettes, Victorian mirrors, World War II photos and eerie 19th-century mannequins – all illuminated by original Nelson lamps.

Eat, Drink, Shop

The Butler & the Chef

1011 25th Street, at Third Street, Potrero Hill (642 6440/www.thebutlerandthechef.com). Bus 15. **Open** 10am-6pm Mon-Fri; 11am-5pm Sat. **Credit** MC, V.

This huge warehouse is full of French antique bar and kitchen furniture, from copper cauldrons to art deco tables. Fun to browse, less fun to buy: prices are steep.

Dishes Delmar

558 8882/www.dishesdelmar.com. **Open** by appointment.

Inside a Haight Victorian, Burt Tessler and his partner have assembled a pristine collection of mid-20th-century American dishware: Fiesta, Harlequin, Lu-Ray and the like. Visits are only by appointment, but it's often possible to stop by the same day.

Arts & crafts

In the Mission, **Studio 24**, part of **Galeria de la Raza** (*see p205*), embraces everything from kitsch to crafts, with Latin American folk art alongside works by contemporary artists.

The African Outlet

524 Octavia Street, between Hayes & Grove Streets, Hayes Valley (864 3576). Bus 21, 47, 49. **Open** 10.30am-7pm daily. **Credit** AmEx, MC, V. **Map** p314 F5.

Gathered by a Nigerian expat and his wife, this is a gorgeous jumble of authentic tribal artefacts and antiques – brilliantly coloured textiles, beads and jewellery, sculpture, fetishes, ceremonial masks. The proprietors delight in explaining their pieces.

Polonco

393 Hayes Street, at Gough Street, Hayes Valley (252 5753). Bus 21, 47, 49. **Open** 11am-6pm Tue-Sat; 1-6pm Sun. **Credit** AmEx, MC, V. **Map** p314 F5.

Even on grey days, this fine and folk art gallery exudes warmth and colour. New and emerging Mexican artistry shares space with a refined collection of antique and contemporary crafts: *retablos*, *santos* figures and handmade silver jewellery.

Sam Bo Trading Co

51 Ross Alley, off Washington Street, between Stockton Avenue & Grant Avenue, Chinatown (397 2998). Bus 12, 15, 30, 41, 45/cable car Powell-Hyde or Powell-Mason. **Open** 11am-5.30pm daily. **No credit cards. Map** p311 G3.

The best things in Chinatown are found down the sidestreets. This tiny shop of Buddhist and Taoist religious items is like a secret shrine. You'll find buddhas, ceremonial candles, incense and intriguing paper goods that are burnt in honour of ancestors or to ask a favour of the gods.

Tibet Shop

4100 19th Street, at Castro Street, Castro (982 0326/www.tibetshopsf.com). Muni Metro F, K, L, M/bus 24, 33, 35, 37. **Open** 10am-6pm Mon-Sat; noon-5pm Sun. **Credit** AmEx, Disc, MC, V. **Map** p313 E6.

Incense, singing bowls, carved skulls, prayer beads, lapis lazuli, turquoise, silver, coral necklaces and the clothing and crafts of Tibet come together in this shop, which is run by a disciple of the Dalai Lama.

Bookshops

San Francisco is crawling with wordsmiths, which means there are fantastic bookshops to supply them with reading matter. Many serious antiquarian booksellers are clustered at 49 Geary Street, near Union Square, but if you're looking for good used bookshops that keep a few rare editions tucked away, your best bet is the Mission. Whatever you do, don't miss out on the bibliophile paradise of Berkeley's **Telegraph Avenue**. There you'll find esoteric religious works at Shambala Booksellers (No.2482, 1-510 848 8443) and reasonably priced second-hand books at Shakespeare and Company (No.2499, 1-510 841 8916), plus Comics and Comix (No.2502, 1-510 845 4091) and Revolution Books (2425C Channing Way, 1-510 848 1196). Best of all, though, are Cody's and Moe's (for both, *see below*).

Abandoned Planet Bookstore

518 Valencia Street, between 16th & 17th Streets, Mission (861 4695). BART 16th Street/bus 12, 22, 26, 33, 49, 53. **Open** 2pm-9pm Mon-Fri; 11am-9pm Sat, Sun. **Credit** MC, V. **Map** p314 1Y.

Cultivating a homey feel with two in-store cats and a comfy couch on which to give your putative purchase a test-read, Abandoned Planet mostly sells used books, with all the Bukowski you can stomach and original paintings by Beat author Jack Micheline.

The best Bookshops

City Lights

A 'literary meeting place' since 1953, City Lights is still a great bookshop. See *p165*.

Cody's Books/Moe's

The best across the Bay. No self-respecting bibliophile should – or would – miss these two. See *p165* & *p166*.

Green Apple Books

For a gargantuan array of new and used books and CDs. See *p166*.

Modern Times Bookstore

Browse the sizable selection of socially and politically progressive books and magazines. See *p166*.

Modern Times Bookstore – a community thing. *See p166.*

Acorn Books

1436 Polk Street, at California Street, Polk Gulch (563 1736/www.acornbook.com). Bus 1, 19, 27, 47, 49, 76/cable car California. **Open** 10.30am-8pm Mon-Sat; noon-7pm Sun. **Credit** AmEx, Disc, MC, V. **Map** p310 F3.

A large selection of rare books in all genres – and a superlative collection of vintage sci-fi magazines.

The Booksmith

1644 Haight Street, between Clayton & Cole Streets, Haight-Ashbury (1-800 493 7323/863 8688/www.booksmith.com). Muni Metro N/bus 6, 7, 33, 37, 43, 66, 71. **Open** 10am-9pm Mon-Sat; 10am-6pm Sun. **Credit** AmEx, Disc, MC, V. **Map** p313 C6.

This is the Haight's best bookshop. It hosts many authors' readings and events, and stocks a decent selection of magazines both literary and obscure.

City Lights

261 Columbus Avenue, at Jack Kerouac Alley, between Broadway & Pacific Avenue, North Beach (362 8193/www.citylights.com). Bus 12, 15, 30, 41, 45. **Open** 10am-midnight daily. **Credit** AmEx, Disc, MC, V. **Map** p311 G2.

The legacy of Beat anti-authoritarianism lives on in this publishing company and bookshop, founded by poet Lawrence Ferlinghetti in 1953. Make sure to head upstairs to the Poetry Annex, where well-established Beat poets sit proximate to small-press works and the photocopied ravings of 'shroom-addled hippies. The European literature selection is also strong, and the occasional readings real events.

A Clean Well-Lighted Place for Books

Opera Plaza, 601 Van Ness Avenue, between Golden Gate Avenue & Turk Street, Civic Center (441 6670/ www.bookstore.com). Bus 5, 31, 42, 47, 49. **Open** 10am-11pm Mon-Sat; 10am-9pm Sun. **Credit** AmEx, MC, V. **Map** p314 F4.

This well-stocked, general interest bookshop hosts frequent and popular events (John Watters, They Might Be Giants and Hillary Clinton all stopped by in 2003).

Cody's Books

2454 Telegraph Avenue, at Haste Street, Berkeley (1-510 845 7852/www.codysbooks.com). BART Downtown Berkeley/bus 7, 40, 51. **Open** 10am-10pm daily. **Credit** AmEx, Disc, MC, V.

Fred and Pat Cody opened their store in 1956 on a loan and a prayer; it's now one of the most staunchly and successfully independent bookstores in the US. Their tradition of supporting writers who might not otherwise be heard continues under owner Andrew Ross, with regular readings (legendary in intellectual circles) by authors ranging from unknowns to Isabel Allende and Salman Rushdie. On non-reading days, bookworms huddle in the stacks perusing the latest greats to have missed out on the bestseller lists. **Other locations**: 1740 Fourth Street, between Virginia & Cedar Streets, Berkeley (1-510 559 9500).

A Different Light

489 Castro Street, at 18th Street, Castro (431 0891/ www.adlbooks.com). Muni Metro F, K, L, M/bus 24, 33, 35, 37. **Open** 10am-11pm daily. **Credit** AmEx, Disc, MC, V. **Map** p312 E6.

A Different Light has an extensive and impressive stock of books and magazines for and about the queer community.

Get Lost Travel Books, Maps & Gear

1825 Market Street, at Guerrero Street, Upper Market (437 0529/www.getlostbooks.com). Muni Metro F, K, L, M/bus 26. **Open** 10am-7pm Mon-Fri; 10am-6pm Sat; 11am-5pm Sun. **Credit** AmEx, DC, Disc, MC, V. **Map** p314 F5.

A compelling assortment of hands-on guides and literature, plus a variety of other things that might help you get on your way: maps, travel accessories and readings, for instance.

Green Apple Books & Music

506 Clement Street, at Sixth Avenue, Richmond (387 2272/www.greenapplebooks.com). Bus 1, 2, 4, 5, 31, 38, 44. **Open** 10am-10.30pm Mon-Thur, Sun; 10am-11.30pm Fri, Sat. **Credit** Disc, MC, V. **Map** p312 B4.
Green Apple is paradise regained for used-book lovers. This longstanding inner Richmond bookstore features a staggering selection of new and second-hand titles, all crammed together in glorious disarray (don't miss the fiction and music annexe a few doors down). On Sundays the shop is packed.

Kayo Books

814 Post Street, between Hyde & Leavenworth Streets, Tenderloin (749 0554/www.kayobooks.com). Bus 2, 3, 4, 27, 38/cable car Powell-Hyde or Powell-Mason. **Open** 11am-6pm Wed-Sun. **Credit** AmEx, Disc, MC, V. **Map** p314 F/G4.
For those who like their mysteries hard-boiled and their juveniles delinquent, this emporium of pulp delivers. Specialising in vintage paperbacks and dime-store novels from the '40s to the '70s, Kayo also stocks rare and out-of-print books, as well as delicious exploitation ephemera.

Limelight Film & Theater Bookstore

1803 Market Street, at Octavia Street, Hayes Valley (864 2265/www.limelightbooks.com). Muni Metro F, J, K, L, M, N/bus 6, 7, 26, 66, 71. **Open** noon-7pm daily. **Credit** AmEx, Disc, MC, V. **Map** p314 F5.
As you might gather from the name, this shop is dedicated to the thespian arts. Books, plays, books about plays, movie scripts and more plays line every shelf.

Marcus Book Stores

1712 Fillmore Street, between Post & Sutter Streets, Western Addition (346 4222). Bus 2, 3, 4, 22, 38. **Open** 10am-7pm Mon-Sat. **Credit** AmEx, MC, V. **Map** p310 E4.
Marcus specialises in books by African and African-American writers, and about both African and African-American culture. It puts on great reading series: the mighty Chaka Khan recently made an appearance here.
Other locations: 3900 Martin L King Jr Way, between 39th & 40th Streets, Oakland (1-510 652 2344).

Modern Times Bookstore

888 Valencia Street, between 19th & 20th Streets, Mission (282 9246/www.mtbs.com). BART 16th Street or 24th Street/bus 14, 26, 33, 49. **Open** 10am-9pm Mon-Sat; 11am-6pm Sun. **Credit** AmEx, MC, V. **Map** p314 F7.
Originally a source of left-wing political tracts, Modern Times is now more like a community centre, with political readings and forums taking place amid the new and used literature, non-fiction, alternative 'zines and scholarly journals.

Moe's

2476 Telegraph Avenue, at Dwight Way, Berkeley (1-510 849-2087). BART Downtown Berkeley/bus 7, 40, 51. **Open** 10am-11pm daily. **Credit** AmEx, Disc, MC, V.

A Berkeley literary landmark, Moe's has 100,000 volumes spread over four floors. It's the place to find a first edition of *Naked Lunch* or a 17th-century Bible. Collectors head to the fourth floor for the antiquarian, out-of-print and art books.

Rand McNally Map & Travel Store

595 Market Street, at Second Street, Financial District (777 3131/www.randmcnally.com). BART Montgomery Street/Metro Muni F, J, K, L, M, N/bus 2, 3, 4, 6, 7, 9, 21, 31, 66, 71. **Open** 9am-7pm Mon-Fri; 10am-6pm Sat; 11am-5pm Sun. **Credit** AmEx, Disc, MC, V. **Map** p311 H3.
If you're hitting the road, stop in here first. This is downtown San Francisco's source for domestic and international guidebooks, globes, folded and wall maps, and all kinds of essential travel accessories.

San Francisco Mystery Bookstore

4175 24th Street, between Castro & Diamond Streets, Noe Valley (282 7444/ www.sfmysterybooks.com). Muni Metro J/bus 24, 35, 48. **Open** 11am-6pm Mon-Thur, Sun; 11am-8pm Fri, Sat. **Credit** AmEx, MC, V. **Map** p313/4 E7.
Shelf after shelf of mystery and detective fiction (both in and out of print), with a large selection of everything Sherlock Holmes.

Smoke Signals

2223 Polk Street, between Vallejo & Green Streets, Polk Gulch (292 6025). Bus 12, 19, 30, 76/cable car Powell-Hyde. **Open** 8am-8pm Mon-Sat; 8am-6pm Sun. **Credit** AmEx, DC, Disc, MC, V. **Map** p310 F2.
Homesick expats can smooth the process of assimilation with the latest *Le Monde* or Italian *Vogue* from this international newsstand. It also has a comprehensive selection of national and local papers, design annuals and obscure literary journals.

Stacey's

581 Market Street, between First & Second Streets, Financial District (1-800 926 6511/421 4687/ www.staceys.com). BART Montgomery Street/Metro Muni F, J, K, L, M, N/bus 2, 3, 4, 6, 7, 9, 21, 31, 66, 71. **Open** 8.30am-7pm Mon-Fri; 11am-6.30pm Sat; 11am-5.30pm Sun. **Credit** AmEx, DC, Disc, MC, V. **Map** p315 H3.
The city's oldest and largest independent bookshop (established in 1923), Stacey's offers an impressive selection of autographed books, makes excellent staff recommendations, and maintains a healthy association with the Commonwealth Club (co-sponsoring lectures from the likes of Gore Vidal).

William Stout Architectural Books

804 Montgomery Street, between Jackson Street & Pacific Avenue, North Beach (391 6757/ www.stoutbooks.com). Bus 1, 10, 12, 15, 30, 41. **Open** 10am-6.30pm Tue-Fri; 10am-5.30pm Sat. **Credit** MC, V. **Map** p311 H2.
Architect and publisher William Stout's shop stocks every type of architectural tome, plus books on urban planning, landscaping, interior and industrial design, furniture, graphics, art and photography. Rare editions are everywhere you look.

Hayes Street chic

Mexican art. The gallery-shop hybrid also sells traditional cookbooks, intricate dolls and rare photography prints.

One block away on **Octavia Street**, get hoofed up in Miu Miu or Puma at **Gimme Shoes** (*see p176*) or cross the street for the schizophrenic collection of styles at **Azalea Boutique** (411 Hayes Street, 861 9888), where you can scoop up a blazing pink Birkin bag or Von Dutch jeans – minus the SoHo attitude. The **African Outlet** (*see p164*) on Octavia imports gorgeous textiles, carvings and jewellery, as well as incense and sarongs, while tops, bottoms and everything in-between find happiness at **Dark Garden** (*see p173*) on Linden Street.

From Octavia move on to Laguna Street, where you can hop aboard **Flight 001** (*see p176*). The interior here, which resembles the inside of a 747, is a haven of sleek, colourful luggage and upscale travel accessories. A different kind of fly describes the booty at **Dish** (541 Hayes Street, 252 5997), where finicky ladies peruse piles of Seven Jeans or take the tailored approach with items by Theory and Nanette Lapore. Next door, **Propeller** (555 Hayes Street, 701 7767; *pictured*)

Department stores are *so* depressing. All those precious shopping hours lost in the maze of confusing displays, hopelessly seeking advice from out-there salespeople. Thankfully, friendly San Francisco has a street where the concentration of boutiques and designer shops truly reflects the city's spirit of individualism. As you stroll the three-block stretch of **Hayes Street**, from Franklin to Laguna, it's hard to believe this was once the preserve of drug dealers, prostitutes and their clients. Now, more than a decade after the Loma Prieta quake felled the freeway overpass that cast the area in gloom, Hayes Valley has become a luscious little pocket of restaurants and high-end shops.

On the block between Franklin and Gough Streets, **Champ de Mars** (347 Hayes Street, 252 9434) is like a French flea market, offering everything from pooch portraits to antiques and collectibles, but perhaps most revered for its fine linens. Heading south, **Polonco** (*see p164*) is a shrine devoted to

hawks swanky mod furniture and urban lifestyle accessories: geometric pillows, whimsical stationery modelled after library due-date cards, and intriguing furniture by local designer Melanie Schnack. Opposite, **BUU** (506 Hayes Street, 626 1503) has everything a metrosexual needs, from sterling silver sake sets to Votivo candles.

Alabaster (*see p180*) sells furniture and more in a spry space, mingling vintage (mother-of-pearl caviar spoons) with fresh (lilac-scented bath salts), while **Alla Prima** (*see p173*) stocks underwear candy that make Victoria's Secret look like a regrettable one-night stand. There's also **BPM Music Factory** (*see p183*), brimming with 12-inch vinyl, rare live compilation CDs, and sage advice about turntable repairs.

Look up now: you're at the sign of the french fry, which means **Frjtz** (579 Hayes Street, 864 7654). Just the place for a pile of hot, crisp Belgian fries washed down with a cold beer.

Eat, Drink, Shop

Foreign-language bookshops

San Francisco is one of the most multicultural of US cities, which is good news for anyone after foreign-language books. On Valencia Street in the Mission, the following bookshops sell Spanish-language newspapers and *libros en Español*: **Dog Eared Books** (900 Valencia Street, at 20th Street, Mission, 282 1901); **La Casa del Libro** (973 Valencia Street, at 20th Street, Mission, 285 1399) and **Modern Times Bookstore** (*see p166*). The magnificent **Kinokuniya** (1581 Webster Street, between Post and Geary Streets, 567 7625) in Japantown is the city's largest Japanese-language bookshop. Italians can pick up the latest instalment of *Diabolik* at **Cavalli Italian Bookstore** in North Beach (1441 Stockton Street, at Columbus Avenue, North Beach, 421 4219). In the Tenderloin, the **European Book Company** (925 Larkin Street, between Geary and Post Streets, 474 0626) stocks publications in various languages; it also has a small branch at **Cafe de la Presse** (*see p141*).

Computers & electronics

San Francisco remains at the (diminished) helm of technological advancement, so a laptop or notebook computer can cost half the European price. Two warnings, though: first, whatever you buy, make sure that your item will work in the country in which you want to use it; second, many of the downtown stores that advertise cheap cameras and electronics are fly-by-night – if a deal seems too good to be true, it probably is. Most locals head to the **Good Guys** (1400 Van Ness Avenue, at Bush Street, 775 9323; 2675 Geary Boulevard, at Masonic, 202 0220) or **Circuit City** (1200 Van Ness Avenue, at Post Street, 441 1300). Both have low prices, and offer installation services and delivery.

Franklin Covey

350 California Street, at Sansome Street, Financial District (397 1776/www.franklincovey. com). BART Embarcadero/Muni Metro F, J, K, L, M, N/bus 2, 3, 4, 6, 7, 8, 9, 15, 21, 30, 31, 45, 66, 71/cable car California. **Open** 9am-7pm Mon-Fri. **Credit** AmEx, DC, Disc, MC, V. **Map** p311 H3.
All the latest PDAs, laptops and accessories (modems, cables, stylus writers), plus assorted cases for schlepping it all around.

International Electronics

1163 Mission Street, between Seventh & Eighth Streets, SoMa (1-800 962 4715/626 6382). BART Civic Center/Muni Metro F, J, K, L, M, N/bus 12, 14, 19, 26. **Open** 10am-6pm Mon-Sat. **Credit** AmEx, Disc, MC, V. **Map** p314 G5.

IE sells electronics that work in the UK: portable CD players, camcorders, DVD players, plus voltage converters and transformers ($50-$400) for computers.

MacAdam Computers

1062 Folsom Street, between Sixth & Seventh Streets, SoMa (863 6222). Bus 12, 14, 19, 27. **Open** 9am-6pm Mon-Fri; 10am-5pm Sat. **Credit** AmEx, Disc, MC, V. **Map** p315 G5.
MacAdam has been serving the Bay Area's Macintosh community since the time when Macs resembled petrified loaves of bread. These days you're more likely to be picking up a PowerMac G5 with a 20-inch flat monitor. MacAdam offer excellent technical support if your iPod is misbehaving.

Fashion

If it's the monoliths you're looking for (Banana Republicans get almost a full city block, Gap and Old Navy addicts similarly catered for), you'll find the flagships on U nion Square, with additional branches almost everywhere you go. Union Square is also the place for those familiar high-end labels – Chanel, Prada, Gucci, Armani, Hermes, Ralph Lauren and Versace – and sub-stellar chains like **Express, BCBG, Bebe, Guess, Club Monaco, Laundry Industry** and **French Connection**. Below we've listed the places San Franciscans love, the shops with a bit more nous or character or style. We've also given you the low-down on local shops with a particularly friendly face (*see p170* **No poseurs, please**).

AB Fits

1519 Grant Avenue, between Union & Filbert Streets, North Beach (982 5726/www.abfits.com). Bus 15, 39, 41. **Open** 11am-6.30pm Tue-Sat; noon-6pm Sun. **Credit** AmEx, MC, V. **Map** p311 G2.
Jean genies Howard Gee and Christopher Louie carry a barge-load of brands. Some are familiar (Earl, Dope, Levi's Red, Seven), others more rarefied (hand-loomed inky jeans with silver buttons by Japan's Hollywood Ranch Market) and a few plain fabulous (Blueline from Rome). You'll also find separates and accessories by designers like Fresh Hype here.

American Rag

1305 Van Ness Avenue, between Bush & Sutter Streets, Cathedral Hill (474 5214). Bus 2, 3, 4, 47, 49, 76/cable car California. **Open** 10am-9pm Mon-Sat; noon-8pm Sun. **Credit** AmEx, MC, V. **Map** p310 F3/4.
American Rag is the ideal place for the SF creative community to cultivate their laissez-faire look. Less daunting than a used-clothing shop and a cut above obvious institutions such as Diesel, you can sort through the racks of used and new threads here with the solid assurance that the poly-blend button-down you finally decide on will be the one and only.

Eat, Drink, Shop

Funky threads and friendly service at **Heather**. *See p171*.

Anthropologie

*880 Market Street, between Powell &
Stockton Streets, Union Square (434 2210/
www.anthropologie.com). BART Powell Street/
Metro Muni F, J, K, L, M, N/bus 2, 3, 4, 6, 7, 9,
14, 15, 21, 30, 31, 45, 66, 71/cable car Powell-
Hyde or Powell-Mason.* **Open** 10am-8pm Mon-Sat;
10am-7pm Sun. **Credit** AmEx, Disc, MC, V.
Map p311 G3/4.

Girlie, girlie and girlie. Indulge your desire for beaded cardigans, A-line skirts and fuzzy fur-lined jackets, as well as home furnishings, decadent scented
candles, too-cute pyjamas and coquettish lingerie.
Unlike its sister store Urban Outfitters (*see p172*),
Anthropologie traffics more in treacle than trend-
setting. And, more or often than not, it's all done
with considerable charm.
Other locations: 750 Hearst Avenue, between
Fourth & Sixth Streets, Berkeley (1-510 486 0705).

The Bar

*340 Presidio Avenue, between Sacramento & Clay
Streets, Presidio Heights (409 4901). Bus 1, 3, 4, 43.*
Open 10am-6pm Mon-Sat; noon-5pm Sun. **Credit**
AmEx, MC, V. **Map** p309 D3.

Snugly located in posh Laurel Heights, the Bar displays a healthy mix of trendy, tried-and-true and
old San Francisco society (think cashmere) pieces
on its distinguished rails.

Behind the Post Office

*1510 Haight Street, between Ashbury & Clayton
Streets, Haight-Ashbury (861 2507). Muni Metro
N/bus 6, 7, 33, 37, 43, 66, 71.* **Open** 11am-7pm
daily. **Credit** AmEx, Disc, MC, V. **Map** p313 D5/6.

This Haight Street boutique packs a lot of style into
a tiny space. You'll find vibrant T-shirts, edgy new
designers and a killer shoe collection, all at moderate
prices. The owners are committed to helping find you
the right fit – and as anyone who's ever struggled to
find the perfect pair of jeans knows, an expert opinion is worth its weight in denim.

Betsey Johnson

*2031 Fillmore Street, between California & Pine
Streets, Pacific Heights (567 2726/www.betsey
johnson.com). Bus 1, 3, 22.* **Open** 11am-7pm Mon-Sat;
noon-6pm Sun. **Credit** AmEx, MC, V. **Map** p309 E3.

When you need a fix of something fresh, girlish or
frankly vampy, Betsey is there for you. The slip
dresses, stretchy velvets, feathered boas and floaty
skirts are all at digestible prices, and the neo-
bordello sex 'n' roses decor is simply delicious.
Other locations: 160 Geary Street, between
Stockton Street & Grant Avenue, Union Square
(398 2516).

Citizen Clothing

*536 Castro Street, between 18th & 19th Streets,
Castro (558 9429/www.bodyclothing.com). Muni
Metro F, K, L, M/bus 24, 33, 35, 37.* **Open** 10am-
8pm Mon-Sat; 11am-7pm Sun. **Credit** AmEx, Disc,
MC, V. **Map** p313/4 E7.

Citizen's London-born proprietor outfits queer and
straight alike in his own brand of utilitarian chic:
streetwear, Calvin Klein suits and shoes, French
Connection, Swiss Army, Ike & Dean, Gucci and
Giraudon. Round the corner, Citizen's brother
establishment Body (4071 18th Street, 861 6111)
gets guys into the latest sportswear-chic.

No poseurs, please

It may be the mild weather. It may be the lack of an all-consuming status-based industry (we mean you, Hollywood). Whatever it is, the fact remains that a sense of civility pervades San Francisco. Locals' lack of pretension takes many visitors by surprise, but it is indeed possible to shop at lush boutiques in track pants without being treated like a common housefly. Those slick gits in head-to-toe Prada are going to make a sudden and immediate bad impression in this cultured city, where high fashion is never a set standard and 'trendy' can be found at Marc Jacobs or Thrift Town (*see p162* **On the cheap: Thrift, fleas and second-hand**) or, often, a combination of both. And there is a handful of small shops, often run by independent-minded locals, where the commitment to friendliness goes above and beyond the call of retail.

Workshop (*see p173*) exists in relative anonymity up in Cow Hollow. A delightful high-end boutique, it features comfortably stylish items from Aussie designer Easton Pearson, hand-crafted Emma Hope shoes, divine Henry Beguelin bags and, in the back, swimsuits. But the best thing about the place is that staff will give you an honest opinion here. Not too honest, either. While it might take a lot to coax you out of the dressing room for appraisal, at **Rabat** (4005 24th Street, at Noe Street, 282 7861) the huge variety of shoes, accessories and women's clothing ('sparkly-chic' decribes it) provides reams of material for you to work with – as well as staff accommodating enough to happily suggest ways to co-ordinate it all.

Then at **Ambiance** (1458 Haight Street, 552 5095) they just get it if you've put on ten pounds and need to look like you've lost 20. Located in a hectic block of Haight-Ashbury, with branches on Union Street and Noe Street, Ambiance is committed to finding the perfect ensemble for whatever occasion requires it: its vibrant collection of retro-style dresses and flirty skirts is even arranged by colour for your shopping convenience. Also uncommonly friendly is **Heather** (*see p171*), unlike bitchy elder sibling Heidi Says two blocks further up Fillmore Street. Its selection of fur-trim wool and cashmere sweaters, elaborate brocade wool coats and clever little cocktail dresses will ensure you're the hit of the party.

For friendship-inspired designs, however, head to independently owned boutique **Sunhee Moon** (142 Fillmore Street, at Waller Street, Lower Haight, 355 1800). Flourishing alongside less-affable dive bars and head shops, Sunhee Moon (*pictured*) has created clean-lined, '50s-influenced and personalised fashions – each style is named after a friend, such as the Eva button-front shirt or Lily satin-lined coats. Even further away from the world of pretension is **Huff** (808 Sutter Street, 614 9414), an Nob Hill/Tenderloin outpost where skate culture meets high-concept design. Initially focusing just on shoes, former pro skater Keith 'Huff' Hufnagel has expanded into a clothing outlet next door at No.816, cultivating a streamlined aesthetic that would make a Japanese minimalist smile in polite envy.

Dema

1038 Valencia Street, between 21st & 22nd Streets, Mission (206 0500). BART 24th Street/ bus 14, 26, 49. **Open** 11am-7pm Mon-Fri; noon-7pm Sat; noon-6pm Sun. **Credit** Disc, MC, V. **Map** p314 F7.

Got a yen for a denim bias-cut skirt? Dreaming of a '60s swing coat? Wanna be a mod but don't know how? Dema is your church, owner Dema Grim your guide to brash (but refined) clothes that let you do flair without the Elton John.

Diana Slavin

3 Claude Lane, between Sutter & Bush Streets, Union Square (677 9939/www.dianaslavin.com). BART Montgomery Street/Muni Metro F, J, K, L, M, N/bus 2, 3, 4, 15, 30, 38, 45, 76/cable car Powell-Hyde or Powell-Mason. **Open** 11am-6pm Tue-Fri; noon-5pm Sat. **Credit** AmEx, MC, V. **Map** p311 H3.

In this haberdashery for women, Diana Slavin designs and displays her trademark fashions: menswear-inspired clothing in rich, subtle colours and lush fabrics. Cutler & Gross sunglasses and Clergerie shoes complete the look.

Diesel

101 Post Street, at Kearny Street, Union Square (982 7077/www.diesel.com). BART Montgomery Street or Powell Street/Muni Metro F, J, K, L, M, N/bus 2, 3, 4, 15, 30, 38, 45, 76/cable car Powell-Hyde or Powell-Mason. **Open** 10am-8pm Mon-Fri; 10am-7pm Sat; noon-6pm Sun. **Credit** AmEx, DC, Disc, MC, V. **Map** p311 H3.

Three tragically hip floors of Italian street fashion, with a zillion styles of jeans, trendy-retro sneakers and edgy separates. Those feeling extra experimental should check out the StyleLab line upstairs, for the labels more edgy ensembles.

Eat, Drink, Shop

Store policy dictates that walk-ins get first dibs on the exclusives, so there's no irritating wait list.

At Grant Avenue's perpetually cool **AB Fits** (*see p168*), celebrity-endorsed SF designer Jeanine Payer creates silver rings, bracelets, pendants, earrings, cufflinks and necklaces, all adorned with clever scrawled inscriptions. Along with a rotating array of local designers' wares, AB Fits also imports the latest jeans

from across the world. Also on Grant, you'll find the charming **Ooma** (No.1422, 627 6963). The puzzling name stands for 'Objects Of My Affection' and it's clear that every item in the store is positively adored by owner Kate Logan. The sentiment seems retchingly saccharine until you see the clothes: smart, sexy and fun takes on halter tops, cocktail dresses or cropped pants, as well as bold jewellery, hats and handbags, largely by local designers.

Heather

2408 Fillmore Street, between Jackson & Washington Streets, Pacific Heights (409 4410). Bus 3, 12, 22, 24. **Open** 10.30am-6pm Mon-Sat; noon-5pm Sun. **Credit** AmEx, MC, V. **Map** p309 E3.

The friendliest shop on Fillmore Street has a fresh approach to dressing up or down, with soft separates from the likes of John Smedley, Ginka and Nuala (model Christy Turlington's casual collection, in partnership with Puma). There are tiny treasures – such as precious little cameo earrings – in the display case.

Levi's Jean Store

300 Post Street, at Stockton Street, Union Square (501 0100/www.levi.com). BART Powell Street/ Muni Metro F, J, K, L, M, N/bus 2, 3, 4, 15, 30, 38, 45, 76/cable car Powell-Hyde or Powell-Mason. **Open** 9am-9pm daily. **Credit** AmEx, DC, Disc, MC, V. **Map** p311 G3.

Levi's remain an American icon as indisputable as a glass of Coca-Cola. Visit this vast, bumpin' Union Square emporium and slip into a pair of classic 501s.

MAC

1543 Grant Avenue, at Union Street, North Beach (837 1604). Bus 15, 30, 39, 41, 45. **Open** 11am-6pm Mon-Sat; noon-5pm Sun. **Credit** AmEx, MC, V. **Map** p311 H3.

Any eclectic wardrobe will love the cosy, intimate MAC (Modern Appealing Clothing) for women, offering the likes of Yoshi Kondo's tweaked British designs (off-register argyle mohairs) and Anna Sui's dramatic embroidery. The downtown men's shop has laid-back streetwear, edgy sportswear by William Reid, John Bartlett and Paul Smith, and a nice collection of vintage *Playboy* magazines. **Other locations**: 5 Claude Lane, between Bush & Sutter Streets, Union Square (837 0615).

Kids love **Murik**. *See p173.*

Metier

*355 Sutter Street, between Stockton Street & Grant
Avenue, Union Square (989 5395). BART Powell
Street/Muni Metro F, J, K, L, M, N/bus 2, 3, 4, 15,
30, 38, 45, 76/cable car Powell-Hyde or Powell-
Mason.* **Open** 10am-6pm Mon-Sat. **Credit** AmEx,
MC, V. **Map** p311 G3.

Neo-bohos lap up Anna Molinari's sexy sweaters and
dresses, Rozae Nichols' gossamer separates and
Katayone's street-smart slacks. Not to mention the
fantastic contemporary and vintage jewellery.

Rin

*2111 Union Street, at Webster Street, Cow Hollow
(922 8040). Bus 22, 41, 45.* **Open** 11am-7pm
Mon-Sat; noon-6pm Sun. **Credit** AmEx, MC, V.
Map p310 E2.

Contemporary, fun, flirty… the rails at this subterranean boutique feature adorable Tocca dresses,
Blue Cult jeans and Ruth cocktail dresses.

Rolo on Market

*2351 Market Street, between Castro & 16th Streets,
Castro (431 4545/www.rolo.com).* **Open** 11am-8pm
Mon-Sat; 11am-7pm Sun. **Credit** AmEx, DC, Disc,
MC, V. **Map** p313/4 E7.

While the Rolo empire has lost its stranglehold on San
Francisco (two locations have closed recently), Rolo
on Market still peddles label-conscious and edgy
menswear (Helmut Lang, G-Star, Paul Smith), as well
as streetwear catering to hip working gals (Triple Five
Soul, Adidas). Head South of Market to the Howard
Street Garage for mark-downs, sale items and steals.
Other locations: 1301 Howard Street, at
Ninth Street, SoMa (861 4862/www.rolo.com).

Susan

*3685 Sacramento Street, between Locust & Spruce
Streets, Presidio Heights (922 3685). Bus 1, 3, 12,
22, 24.* **Open** 10.30am-6.30pm Mon-Fri; 10.30am-
6pm Sat. **Credit** AmEx, MC, V. **Map** p308 B3.

A splurgefest in the heart of Laurel Heights: Yohji,
Comme des Garçons, Dolce & Gabbana, Helmut Lang,
Marni, Margiela and Prada. Check out its sister shop,
the Grocery Store (3615 Sacramento, 928 3615) for its
collection of diffusion lines.

Urban Outfitters

*80 Powell Street, at Ellis Street, Union Square
(989 1515/www.urbanoutfitters.com). BART Powell
Street/Muni Metro F, J, K, L, M, N/bus 2, 3, 4, 15,
30, 38, 45, 76/cable car Powell-Hyde or Powell-
Mason.* **Open** 9.30am-9.30pm Mon-Sat; 10.30am-9pm
Sun. **Credit** AmEx, Disc, MC, V. **Map** p311 G4.

Brace yourself: there are seriously dope finds here,
at seriously affordable prices. Everything from sturdy Ben Sherman pants to adorable Free People cardigans, plus old-school T-shirts, funky jewellery and
tons of jeans, both new and recycled. Ideal for those
just out of college – and those who wish they were.
Other locations: 2590 Bancroft Way, at Bowditch
Street, Berkeley (1-510 486 1300).

Villains

*1672 Haight Street, between Clayton & Cole Streets,
Haight-Ashbury (626 5939). Muni Metro N/bus 6, 7,
33, 37, 43, 66, 71.* **Open** 11am-7pm daily. **Credit**
AmEx, DC, Disc, MC, V. **Map** p313 C6.

Cropped trousers, experimental fabrics and tiny
T-shirts that scream 'I party'. Next door you'll find
an excellent selection of covetable shoes.

Children

Kids Only

*1608 Haight Street, at Clayton Street, Haight-
Ashbury (552 5445). Muni Metro N/bus 6, 7, 33, 37,
43, 66, 71.* **Open** 10.30am-6.30pm Mon-Fri; 10am-
6pm Sat; 11am-5pm Sun. **Credit** AmEx, DC, Disc,
MC, V. **Map** p313 C/D5/6.

Black clothing for baby goths, leopard-print blan-
kets and hats, handmade grape and strawberry
caps, and tie-dyed duds for tiny Deadheads.

Laku

*1069 Valencia Street, between 21st & 22nd Streets,
Mission (695 1462). BART 24th Street/bus 14, 26,
49.* **Open** 11.30am-6.30pm Mon-Sat; noon-5pm Sun.
Credit AmEx, DC, Disc, MC, V. **Map** p314 F7.

Head to the fanciful Laku for beguiling Lilliputian
slippers wrought from velvet and shantung silk, and
topped with a confection of velvet roses.

Mudpie

*1694 Union Street, between Franklin & Gough
Streets, Cow Hollow (771 9262). Bus 41, 45.* **Open**
10am-6pm Mon-Sat; 11am-5pm Sun. **Credit** AmEx,
MC, V. **Map** p310 E2.

A charming shop for clothes and toys, unique accessories and pricey gifts for privileged tots.

Peek-a-Boutique

*1306 Castro Street, at 24th Street, Noe Valley (641
6192). Bus 24, 48.* **Open** 10.30am-6pm Mon-Sat;
noon-5pm Sun. **Credit** MC, V. **Map** p313 E7.

Previously worn children's clothing gets a new lease
of life at this second-hand shop, along with back-
packs, strollers, car seats and toys.

Murik

*73 Geary Street, at Grant Avenue, Union Square
(395 9200/www.murikwebstore.com). BART Powell
Street/Muni Metro F, J, K, L, M, N/bus 2, 3, 4, 15,
30, 38, 45, 76/cable car Powell-Hyde or Powell-
Mason.* **Open** 10am-6pm daily. **Map** p311 H3.

The affordable Belgian, Dutch and Danish minimalist togs at Murik are understated and adorable,
with simple folk motifs and subtle patterns.

Discount

As is always the case, all sizeable outlet
malls are well outside town. About an hour
north on Highway 101 are some of the best.
Petaluma Village Premium Outlets
(2200 Petaluma Boulevard North, 1-707 778
9300) has 60 shops including Donna Karan,
Gap Outlet, Nine West, and Bose. At
the **Napa Premium Outlets** (Highway 29
to First Street exit, 629 Factory Stores Drive,
1-707 226 9876), about 90 minutes from the
city, there's a Barneys New York outlet, as
well as J Crew, Timberland, BCBG, Kenneth
Cole and more. For a complete list of stores,
check www.premiumoutlets.com.

Jeremy's

*2 South Park, off Second Street, between Bryant &
Brannan Streets, South Beach (882 4929/
http://jeremys.com). Bus 10, 15.* **Open** 11am-6pm
Mon-Sat; 11am-5pm Sun. **Credit** AmEx, MC, V.
Map p315 J4.

A well-guarded local secret, Jeremy's sits on a sunny
corner of South Park, hawking designer wares at dis-
count-store prices. It's a label whore's dream come
true, especially when it comes to shoes: Jimmy Choo
pumps, Prada slides and Dolce & Gabbana boots
live here on the tables out front and, if you look carefully, in smaller cubby holes in the rear.

Other locations: 2967 College Avenue, at Ashby,
Berkeley (1-510 849 0701).

Loehmann's

*222 Sutter Street, between Grant Avenue & Kearny
Street, Union Square (982 3215/www.loehmanns.
com). BART Montgomery Street/Muni Metro F, J,
K, L, M, N/bus 2, 3, 4, 15, 30, 38, 45, 76/cable car
Powell-Hyde or Powell-Mason.* **Open** 9am-8pm
Mon-Fri; 9.30am-8pm Sat; 11am-6pm Sun.
Credit Disc, MC, V. **Map** p311 H3.

The communal dressing rooms at Loehmann's send
many shoppers running, but joining 60-year-old
women shimmying into spandex pedal pushers can
be oddly liberating. Cut-rate designer clothes
(DKNY, Versace, Moschino) hang from the rafters.

Lingerie

Alla Prima

*1420 Grant Avenue, at Green Street, North Beach
(397 4077). Bus 15, 30, 39, 41, 45.* **Open** 11am-
7pm Tue-Sat; noon-5pm Sun. **Credit** AmEx, Disc,
MC, V. **Map** p311 G2.

From slinky, ribbed chemises by local designers
Underwriters to high-concept panty-pushers La
Perla and Leigh Bontivoglio, Alla Prima stocks it all
in sizes ranging from gamine to well-rounded.

Other locations: 539 Hayes Street, between Octavia
& Laguna Streets, Hayes Valley (864 8180).

Dark Garden

*321 Linden Street, at Gough Street, Hayes Valley
(431 7684/www.darkgarden.net). Bus 21.* **Open**
noon-6pm Mon-Wed, Fri, Sat; noon-7pm Thur.
Credit AmEx, Disc, MC, V. **Map** p314 F5.

Autumn Carey-Adamme has a calling: corsets. The
off-the-rack models are seductive, but her métier is
bespoke creations. You select the style, fabric and
colour, and 12 individual measurements create a gar-
ment that laces you into delightful submission.

Workshop

*2254 Union Street, between Fillmore & Steiner
Streets, Cow Hollow (561 9551). Bus 22, 41, 45.*
Open 10am-6pm Mon-Sat. **Credit** AmEx, MC, V.
Map p309 E2/3.

Pass through the main shop here to Lingerie Cottage
out back. There brilliant concoctions by Laura
Urbinati and Capucine Puerari lie in quiet sophistication beside a year-round selection of swimsuits.

Vintage & second-hand

The most fertile hunting grounds for previously worn clothing are **Haight Street**, **Fillmore Street** and in the **Mission**. Listed here are the most likely spots if you've specific style ideas; if you're after the thrill of the chase, *see p162* **On the cheap: Thrift, fleas & second-hand**.

Aardvark's Odd Ark
1501 Haight Street, at Ashbury Street, Haight-Ashbury (621 x3141). Muni Metro N/bus 6, 7, 33, 37, 43, 66, 71. **Open** 11am-7pm daily. **Credit** AmEx, Disc, MC, V. **Map** p313 D5/6.
Pass happy hours hunting for diamonds in the rough at this packed-to-the-rafters shop.

Buffalo Exchange
1555 Haight Street, between Clayton & Ashbury Streets, Haight-Ashbury (431 7733/ www.buffaloexchange.com). Muni Metro N/bus 7, 33, 37, 43, 66, 71. **Open** 11am-7pm Mon-Thur, Sun; 11am-8pm Fri, Sat. **Credit** MC, V. **Map** p313 D6.
While the trade-in process at Buffalo can be tough on the ego (the look of contempt, for instance, while trying to hawk your stone-washed Gap reverse-cut jeans), the payoff is in the vast selection on sale.
Other locations: 1800 Polk Street, at Washington Street, Polk Gulch (346 5726); 2585 Telegraph Avenue, at Parker Street, Berkeley (1-510 644 9202).

Crossroads Trading Company
2231 Market Street, at Church Street, Castro (552 8740/www.crossroadstrading.com). Muni Metro F, K, L, M/bus 24, 35, 37. **Open** 11am-7pm Mon-Thur; 11am-8pm Fri, Sat; noon-7pm Sun. **Credit** MC, V. **Map** p313 E6.
The Market and Haight Streets branches of this favourite local trading shop house mostly '80s wear, while the Fillmore Street branch is better for jeans, dresses and classic vintage pieces.
Other locations: 1901 Fillmore Street, at Bush Street, Pacific Heights (775 8885); 1519 Haight Street, at Ashbury Street, Haight-Ashbury (355 0555); 555 Irving Street, at Seventh Avenue, Inner Sunset (681 0100); 2338 Shattuck Avenue, between Bancroft & Durant Streets, Berkeley (1-510 843 7600).

Departures from the Past
2028 Fillmore Street, between Pine & California Streets, Pacific Heights (885 3377). Bus 1, 3, 22. **Open** 11am-7pm Mon-Sat; noon-6pm Sun. **Credit** AmEx, MC, V. **Map** p309 E3.
The theme here is theatrical, with a focus on costumes and formal attire. Like most of the vintage haunts on Fillmore, the pickings here are much richer than at shops in less upmarket districts.

GoodByes
3483 Sacramento Street, between Laurel & Walnut Streets, Presidio Heights (674 0151). Bus 1, 4. **Open** 10am-6pm Mon-Wed, Fri, Sat; 10am-8pm Thur; 11am-5pm Sun. **Credit** Disc, MC, V. **Map** p313 C4.
Light years from the Haight/Mission scene in pristine Laurel Heights, GoodByes is where you might stumble across a barely worn Miu Miu sweater, last season's Prada coat or a little Chanel suit.
Other locations: (menswear) 3464 Sacramento Street, Presidio Heights (346 6388).

Schauplatz
791 Valencia Street, between 18th & 19th Streets, Mission (864 5665). BART 16th Street/bus 14, 33, 49. **Open** 1-6pm Mon, Wed-Sun. **Credit** DC, MC, V. **Map** p314 F6/7.
The offerings here are more self-consciously curated than at other Mission haunts (*schauplatz* is German for 'happening place'), which makes those Italian Riviera sunglasses, the intricately beaded Moroccan mules or that Swedish policeman's leather jacket (with special map pocket) easier to spot.

Ver Unica
437B Hayes Street, between Gough & Octavia Streets, Hayes Valley (431 0688/www.ver-unica.com). Bus 21. **Open** 11am-7pm Mon-Sat; noon-6pm Sun. **Credit** AmEx, DC, Disc, MC, V. **Map** p313 E6.
Vintage vultures graduate to Ver Unica when they get a few dollars and grow weary of pawing through crammed-together cast-offs; the unique retro finds here are a cut above the norm.

Wasteland
1660 Haight Street, between Clayton & Cole Streets, Haight-Ashbury (863 3150). Metro Muni N/bus 7, 33, 37, 43, 66, 71. **Open** 11am-7pm Mon-Fri; 11am-8pm Sat, Sun. **Credit** AmEx, MC, V. **Map** p313 C6.
Possibly the most popular used clothier in town, Wasteland sells second-hand clothing with history, including a rich supply of vintage costume jewellery, fancy gowns and worn-in leather jackets.

Fashion accessories

Handbags

Whether you're after a chic little clutch or a tote the size of a bowling ball, these selections should provide the goods. If not, try **Gimme Shoes** (*see p176*), **Susan** (*see p172*) or the **department stores** (*see p160*).

Coach
190 Post Street, at Grant Avenue, Union Square (392 1772/www.coach.com). BART Powell Street or Montgomery Street/Muni Metro F, J, K, L, M, N/bus 2, 3, 4, 15, 30, 38, 45, 76/cable car Powell-Mason or Powell-Hyde. **Open** 10am-7.30pm Mon-Sat; 11am-6pm Sun. **Credit** AmEx, DC, Disc, MC, V. **Map** p311 G/H3.
Forgive the logo-fabric parade in the window and browse this pristine designer outpost for high-quality leather or suede handbags and accessories. The returns policy here is incredible (they hand you a new bag if but a single stitch comes out).
Other locations: 1 Embarcadero Center, at Sacramento Street, Financial District (362 2518); San Francisco Centre, 865 Market Street, at Powell Street, Union Square (543 7152).

Kate Spade

227 Grant Avenue, between Post &
Sutter Streets, Union Square (216 0880/
www.katespade.com). BART Powell Street or
Montgomery Street/Muni Metro F, J, K, L, M, N/
bus 2, 3, 4, 15, 30, 38, 45, 76/cable car Powell-
Mason or Powell-Hyde. **Open** 11am-7pm Mon-Sat;
noon-5pm Sun. **Credit** AmEx, MC, V.
Map p311 G/H3.
Once a neatly stitched label on a simple black nylon
handbag, Kate Spade is now a full-blown lifestyle.
You can buy your luggage, shoes, fragrances,
jewellery – even drinking chocolate (at $25) – here.
And then, of course, there's the bags.

Jewellery

Metier (*see p172*) in Union Square also has
a delicious selection of contemporary and
vintage jewellery.

De Vera

29 Maiden Lane, between Grant Avenue
& Kearny Street, Union Square (788 0828/
www.deveraobjects.com). BART Montgomery Street
or Powell Street/Muni Metro F, J, K, L, M, N/bus 5, 6,
7, 9, 21, 27, 30, 31, 45, 66/cable car Powell-Hyde or
Powell-Mason. **Open** 10am-6pm Tue-Sat.
Credit AmEx, MC, V. **Map** p311 H3.
Federico De Vera's necklaces, bracelets, rings and
earrings – many a rarefied mix of old and new elements – catch the light and ignite desire. Intricate
beadwork unites precious gemstones, rosecut diamonds and Indian gold beads. Don't miss the stunning collection of objets d'art, ancient and modern,
at the nearby sister shop on Sutter.
Other locations: 580 Sutter Street, between
Powell & Mason Streets, Union Square (989 0988).

Gallery of Jewels

2115 Fillmore Street, between California &
Sacramento Streets, Pacific Heights (771 5099).
Bus 1, 2, 3, 4, 12, 24. **Open** 10.30am-6.30pm Mon-
Sat; 11am-6pm Sun. **Credit** AmEx, Disc, MC, V.
Map p309 E3.
Peruse local creations of silver and semi-precious
stones, as well as funky beads and antique bracelets.
Designs run the gamut from fresh and modern to
something your mum would find 'just adorable'.

Leather goods & luggage

Edward's Luggage

3 Embarcadero Center, between Davis &
Drumm Streets, Financial District (981 7047/
www.edwardsluggage.com). BART Embarcadero/
Muni Metro F, J, K, L, M, N/bus 2, 3, 4, 6, 7, 8,
9, 15, 21, 30, 31, 45, 66, 71/cable car California.
Open 10am-7pm Mon-Fri; 10am-6pm Sat; noon-
5pm Sun. **Credit** AmEx, Disc, MC, V.
Map p311 H3.
Edward's offers everything you need to hit the road,
including easy-rolling, ultra-sturdy Tumi luggage.
Other locations: throughout the Bay Area.

Flight 001

525 Hayes Street, at Octavia Street, Hayes Valley (487
1001). Bus 21. **Open** 11am-8pm Mon-Sat; noon-6pm
Sun. **Credit** AmEx, Disc, DC, MC, V. **Map** p314 F5.
This streamlined store applies cutting-edge modern
design to all things travel, including Japanese metal
suitcases and fabulous travel accessories.

Johnson Leather Corporation

1833 Polk Street, between Jackson &
Washington Streets, Polk Gulch (775 7392/
www.johnsonleather.com). Bus 1, 12, 19, 27, 47, 49,
76. **Open** 10.30am-6.30pm Mon-Sat; noon-5pm Sun.
Credit AmEx, DC, Disc, MC, V. **Map** p310 F3.
A favourite with local motorcyclists, Johnson's is
both a factory and a shop, which means good buys
on lambskin unisex jackets and alterations done
while you wait. You'll also find custom-made jackets
at laughably low prices.

Kenneth Cole

166 Grant Avenue, between Post & Geary Streets,
Union Square (981 2653/www.kennethcole.com).
BART Powell or Montgomery Streets/Muni Metro
F, J, K, L, M, N/bus 2, 3, 4, 15, 30, 38, 45, 76/cable
car Powell-Hyde or Powell-Mason. **Open** 9.30am-8pm
Mon-Sat; 11am-6pm Sat. **Credit** AmEx, MC, V.
Map p311 G/H3.
The socially conscious national shoe tsar flogs more
than footwear. There's also a tasty selection of men's
and women's leather outerwear, sportswear, brief-
cases, wallets and purses at decent prices.
Other locations: 865 Market Street, at Grant
Avenue, Union Square (227 4536); 2078 Union Street,
between Webster & Buchanan Streets, Cow Hollow
(346 2161).

Lava 9

542 Hayes Street, between Laguna & Octavia
Streets, Hayes Valley (552 6468). Bus 21. **Open**
noon-7pm Mon-Sat; noon-5pm Sun. **Credit** AmEx,
MC, V. **Map** p314 F5.
Buy off the rack, or have owner Heidi Werner take
your measurements, spread out some skins and get
that customised jacket you finally convinced yourself you're cool enough to wear.

Shoes

Fetish

344 Presidio Avenue, between Clay & Sacramento
Streets, Presidio Heights (409 7429). Bus 1, 3, 6, 43.
Open 10am-6pm Mon-Sat; noon-5pm Sun. **Credit**
AmEx, MC, V. **Map** p309 D3.
Ultra-femme, delicate and dangerous heels by Jimmy
Choo, Patrick Cox, Emma Hope and others.

Gimme Shoes

50 Grant Avenue, between O'Farrell & Geary
Streets, Union Square (434 9242). BART Powell
Street or Montgomery Street/Muni Metro F, J, K,
L, M, N/bus 5, 6, 7, 9, 21, 27, 30, 31, 45, 66.
Open 11am-7pm Mon-Sat; noon-6pm Sun.
Credit AmEx, Disc, MC, V. **Map** p311 H4.

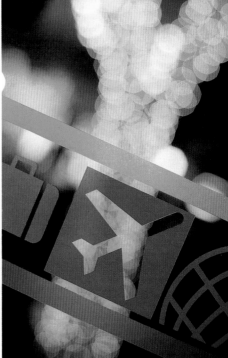

Flight 001 prepares you for take-off. *See p176.*

Shoe-mad locals flock here each season. Richer fare includes Demeulemeester, Miu Miu, Kelian, Costume National and Martine Sitbon, while Momo and Clone are among many moderately priced, forward-looking lines. There's an impressive cache of trainers and casual shoes too, ranging from Adidas to Prada.

Other locations: 416 Hayes Street, at Gough Street, Hayes Valley (864 0691); 2358 Fillmore Street, at Washington Street, Pacific Heights (441 3040).

Shoe Biz

1446 Haight Street, between Ashbury Street & Masonic Avenue, Haight-Ashbury (864 0990/ www.shoebizsf.com). Metro Muni J/bus 6, 7, 33, 66, 71. **Open** 11am-7pm Mon-Sat; 11am-6pm Sun. **Credit** AmEx, DC, Disc, MC, V. **Map** p313 D5.
Towering, pointy, chunky, clunky – the emphasis here is on the fun and the fashionable. For trainers (Pumas galore), Shoe Biz II is but a block away.
Other locations: Shoe Biz II, 1553 Haight Street, between Ashbury & Clayton Streets, Haight-Ashbury (861 3933); Super Shoe Biz, 1420 Haight Street, between Masonic Avenue & Ashbury Street, Haight-Ashbury (861 0313).

Subterranean Shoe Room

877 Valencia Street, at 20th Street, Mission (401 9504/http://subshoeroom.com). BART 16th Street or 24th Street/bus 14, 26, 33, 49. **Open** noon-7pm daily. **Credit** AmEx, DC, Disc, MC, V. **Map** p314 F7.
This place is full of hard-to-find gems such as Redwing, Frye Boots, Blundstone from Australia, molto-trendy Italian lines Holler and Fornarina, and vintage cowboy boots, along with trainers by Puma and Fly London.

Shoe repair

Anthony's Shoe Service

30 Geary Street, between Grant Avenue & Kearny Street, Union Square (781 1338). BART Montgomery Street/Muni Metro F, J, K, L, M, N/ bus 2, 3, 4, 15, 30, 38, 45, 76/cable car Powell-Hyde or Powell-Mason. **Open** 8am-5.30pm Mon-Fri; 9am-5pm Sat. **Credit** AmEx, DC, Disc, MC, V. **Map** p315 G/H3.
A well-known cobbler, Anthony's Shoe Service will undertake any kind of shoe repair. Handy for downtown – if a tad pricey.

They're thinking what you're thinking: **Gimme Shoes**. *See p176.*

For details of Berkeley's world-famous 'Gourmet ghetto', *see p113.*

Bi-Rite Market

3639 18th Street, at Dolores Street, Mission (241 9773). Muni Metro J/bus 22, 33. **Open** 9am-9pm Mon-Fri; 9am-8pm Sat, Sun. **Credit** AmEx, MC, V. **Map** p314 F6.

First opened in 1940 and now restored to its original pre-war lustre, this speciality grocery store sells house-smoked salmon, own-made sausages, cakes, salads, Middle Eastern dips and pasta sauces. It also has an olive bar and more than 100 cheeses.

Bombay Ice Creamery

522 Valencia Street, between 16th & 17th Streets, Mission (431 1103). BART 16th Street/bus 14, 26, 33, 49. **Open** 11am-9pm Tue-Sun. **Credit** AmEx, Disc, MC, V. **Map** p314 F6.

Don't deny yourself this pleasure. Chai, rose, saffron-pistachio and cardamom are among the ice-cream flavours on offer and the menu on hand to help you decipher Indian names for ingredients.

Boulangerie Bay Bread

2325 Pine Street, at Fillmore Street, Pacific Heights (440 0356). Bus 1, 2, 3, 4, 22. **Open** 8am-6pm Tue-Sat; 8am-4pm Sun. **No credit cards. Map** p309 E3.

The crusty breads here are all baked from organic flour in Pavailler ovens imported from France; the tarts and eclairs meltingly sweet, without being cloying. You'll also find delicious fresh sandwiches and a delightful rustic salad.

Other locations: 2310 Polk Street, at Green Street, Polk Gulch (345 1107).

Ferry Plaza Farmer's Market

Ferry Building, on Embarcadero at Market Street. MUNI Metro F. **Open** 10am-2pm Tue; noon-dusk Thur; 8am-2pm Sat; 9am-3pm Sun. **Credit** MC, V. **Map** p311 H2/3.

After ten years of transient existence, this Saturday market is now a sightseeing attraction in its own right (*see p65* **Foodie frenzy**). Foodies flock to find all-organic fruit and veggies, local goat's cheeses, fresh bread and pasta, and gourmet sausages in the open-air market. The new shops inside the building – including Recchiuti Chocolate, which is beyond decadent – are open daily.

Liguria Bakery
1700 Stockton Street, at Filbert Street, North Beach (421 3786). Bus 15, 30, 39, 41, 45/cable car Powell-Mason. **Open** 8am-5pm Mon-Fri; 7am-5pm Sat; 8am-noon Sun. **No credit cards.** **Map** p310/311 G3.
In 1911 three brothers from Genoa had the foresight to set up this tiny North Beach focacceria, which sells their famous flatbreads from morning until whenever they sell out.

Molinari Delicatessen
373 Columbus Avenue, at Vallejo Street, North Beach (421 2337). Bus 12, 15, 30, 39, 41, 45. **Open** 8am-6pm Mon-Fri; 7.30am-5.30pm Sat. **Credit** MC, V. **Map** p311 G2.
Molinari's own-made gnocchi, meatballs and killer sandwiches (particularly the Joe's Special: mozzarella, just-sliced prosciutto and pesto) are so good that they make even huge the crowds and the chaotic deli-style ordering system tolerable.

Whole Foods
1765 California Street, at Franklin Street, Pacific Heights (674 0500/www.wholefoodsmarket.com). Bus 1, 42, 47, 49, 76. **Open** 8am-10pm daily. **Credit** AmEx, Disc, MC, V. **Map** p310 F3.
San Franciscans call this place 'Whole Paycheck' – the challenge here is to leave with anything left in your wallet. The bakery, gourmet deli and outstanding cheese, fish, sushi and meat counters are all tempting, with mostly organic produce and lots of vegetarian options. In 2003 a new, even larger branch opened in SoMa.
Other locations: 399 Fourth Street, at Harrison Street, SoMa (618 0066); 3000 Telegraph Avenue, at Ashby Avenue, Berkeley (1-510 649 1333).

Food delivery
You don't even have to leave your room to eat well in this city: **Waiters on Wheels** (452 6600, www.waitersonwheels.com) delivers meals from many of the better dining establishments, albeit with a 90-minute wait, and many of the smaller restaurants offer delivery of a minimum food order. Ask at the local restaurants near your hotel.

Tea & coffee
The **Imperial Tea Court** (*see p144*) sells (and serves) an exemplary range of teas.

Graffeo Coffee Roasting Company
735 Columbus Avenue, at Filbert Street, North Beach (1-800 222 6250/986 2429). Bus 15, 30, 39, 41, 45/ cable car Powell-Mason. **Open** 9am-6pm Mon-Fri; 9am-5pm Sat. **Credit** MC, V. **Map** p310 G2.
This San Francisco institution is stocked with fresh coffees from around the world. Even better, staff roast the beans right here on the premises.

Ten Ren Tea Company of San Francisco
949 Grant Avenue, between Washington & Jackson Streets, Chinatown (362 0656). Bus 1, 9, 15, 30, 41, 45. **Open** 9am-9pm daily. **Credit** AmEx, Disc, MC, V. **Map** p311 G3.
Ten Ren stocks around 40 different types of Chinese tea, ranging from the ordinary cuppa to more expensive infusions for special occasions. You can taste before you buy.

Alcoholic drinks
For the **Wine Country**, *see p256*.

Amphora Wine Merchant
384 Hayes Street, between Franklin & Gough Streets, Hayes Valley (863 1104/www.amphorawine.com). Bus 16, 21, 47, 49. **Open** 11am-8pm Mon-Sat; 12-6pm Sun. **Credit** AmEx, MC, V. **Map** p314 F5.
If their grand selection of limited-production wine baffles you, ask owners Neil Mechanic and John Ogden for advice – their viticultural prowess seems to know no bounds. The tastings should also assist in preparing you to drop, let's say, $120 on a '99 Ridge Montebello.

Jug Shop
1567 Pacific Avenue, at Polk Street, Polk Gulch (885 2922). Bus 12, 19, 27, 42, 47, 49, 76. **Open** 9am-9pm Mon-Sat; 9.30am-7pm Sun. **Credit** AmEx, DC, MC, V. **Map** p310 F3.
Knowledgeable staff here will help you select vintages from around the world. Look for in-store wine tastings and weekly specials, with an emphasis on California and Pacific Northwest vintages. Especially good if you're buying in bulk.

Napa Valley Winery Exchange
415 Taylor Street, between Geary & O'Farrell Streets, Tenderloin (771 2887/www.napavalleywineryex.com). Bus 27, 38. **Open** 10am-7pm Mon-Sat; 10am-5pm Sun. **Credit** AmEx, DC, Disc, MC, V. **Map** p310 G4.
Specialising in California wines, including unusual and hard-to-find varieties, this shop has 500 wine brands in stock and will ship anywhere in the world.

True Sake
560 Hayes Street, between Laguna & Octavia Streets, Hayes Valley (355 9555/http://truesake.com). Bus 21. **Open** noon-6pm Tue-Fri, Sun; noon-7pm Fri. **Credit** AmEx, DC, MC, V. **Map** p314 F5.
The first shop in the US dedicated entirely to sake. Owner Beau Timken shepherds customers through his stock, ready to give a primer on sake basics, offer tasting notes on any of the beautiful and elegant bottles in the shop, and to suggest food pairings.

The Wine Club
953 Harrison Street, between Fifth & Sixth Streets, SoMa (1-800 966 7835/www.thewineclub.com). Bus 12, 27, 47. **Open** 9am-7pm Mon-Sat; 11am-6pm Sun. **Credit** AmEx, MC, V. **Map** p311 H5.

Some of the best wine bargains around are found in this warehouse of a shop, with prices on very drinkable varieties starting at $5 and going as high as you like. The enthusiastic staff will guide you through the 1,200 options. Tastings are held each month.

Gifts

If the recipient is going to be a furry friend, **George** (*see p185*) is a good bet.

Alabaster

597 Hayes Street, at Laguna Street, Hayes Valley (558 0482/www.alabastersf.com). Bus 21. **Open** 11am-6pm Tue-Sat; noon-5pm Sun. **Credit** AmEx, Disc, MC, V. **Map** p314 F5.
A homage to all things pale (alabaster lamps that glow from within, French ivory boxes, Burmese buddhas) sparked by objects of colour, from vintage globes to vivid, framed African butterflies.

Dandelion

55 Potrero Avenue, at 15th Street, Mission (436 9500/www.tampopo.com). Bus 9, 33. **Open** 10am-6pm Tue-Sat. **Credit** AmEx, MC, V. **Map** p315 G6.
Brave the seedy underbelly of the Mission/Potrero underpass to find this enchanting gift shop, which carries exquisite gifts both familiar (porcelain carafes) and obscure (snail windchimes). Prices are startlingly reasonable.

Nest

2300 Fillmore Street, at Clay Street, Pacific Heights (292 6199). Bus 1, 3, 12, 22, 24. **Open** 10.30am-6.30pm Mon-Sat; noon-6pm Sun. **Credit** AmEx, MC, V. **Map** p309 E3.
Like the flea market of your dreams, Nest sells gauzy Chinese lanterns, tin jack-in-the-boxes, woodcut prints, adorable kids' clothes and unusual ceramics. **Other locations**: 2340 Polk Street, between Union & Green Streets, Polk Gulch (292 6198).

Paxton Gate

824 Valencia Street, at 20th Street, Mission (824 1872/www.paxton-gate.com). Bus 14, 26, 33, 49. **Open** 11am-7pm Mon-Thur, Sun; noon-8pm Fri; 11am-8pm Sat. **Credit** AmEx, MC, V. **Map** p314 F7.
Dedicated to 'treasures and oddities inspired by the garden', Paxton Gate has everything from bulbs and flower-arranging tools to hand-painted glass eyes used for taxidermy and silver necklaces cast from the bones of rats and pelicans. Bizarre and unique.

Sakura Flowers & Gifts

1371A Ninth Avenue, between Irving & Judah Streets, Inner Sunset (731 6060/ www.sakuraflowers.com). Muni N/bus 44, 71. **Open** 9am-7pm Mon-Fri; 10am-6pm Sat. **Credit** MC, V. **Map** p312 B6.
In her long-standing florists, Elena creates remarkably abstract seasonal bouquets, all painstakingly custom designed. Orders for Sakura's delivery service are taken in English, German or Russian.

SFMOMA MuseumStore

SFMOMA, 151 Third Street, between Mission & Howard Streets, SoMa (357 4035/www.sfmoma.org). BART Powell or Montgomery/Muni Metro F, J, K, L, M, N/bus 9, 15, 30, 45, 76. **Open** 10am-6.30pm Mon-Wed, Fri-Sun; 10.30am-9.30pm Thur. **Credit** AmEx, MC, V. **Map** p311 H4.
A lot of people never make it past the gift shop to the galleries. You'll find art and photography books, monographs and catalogues, a vast selection of cards, posters, videos, jewellery and children's toys. **Other locations**: San Francisco International Airport (1-650 553 8040).

Swallow Tail

2217 Polk Street, between Vallejo & Green Streets, Polk Gulch (567 1555/www.swallowtailhome.com). Bus 19, 41, 45, 47, 49, 76. **Open** noon-6pm daily. **Credit** AmEx, MC, V. **Map** p310 F2.
Owners Sheri Sheridan and Kari Lobdell's expertise spans the art world and the realm of theatre design, resulting in a vast, beyond-eclectic array of collectibles, antiques, and mid-century and modern objets d'art.

Health & beauty

Complementary & alternative medicine

Scarlet Sage Herb Co

1173 Valencia Street, between 22nd & 23rd Streets, Mission (821 0997/www.scarletsageherb.com). BART 24th Street/bus 14, 26, 48, 49. **Open** 11am-6.30pm daily. **Credit** AmEx, Disc, MC, V. **Map** p314 F7.
The owners of this herbal apothecary stock more than 300 organic herbs, essential oils, tinctures and plant essences, with a section dedicated specifically to homoeopathic remedies. It also offers a variety of teas, sweet-smelling soaps and plenty of books.

Vinh Khang Herbs & Ginsengs

512 Clement Street, between Sixth & Seventh Avenues, Richmond (752 8336). Bus 1, 2, 4, 44. **Open** 9.30am-7pm Mon, Wed-Sun. **No credit cards. Map** p308 B4.
Thanks to the city's large Asian population, Chinese herbalism has thrived in San Francisco. Inspect the splendid array of roots and remedies, while herbal specialists create a customised concoction for you.

Cosmetics & skincare

Kiehl's

2360 Fillmore Street, between Washington & Clay Streets, Pacific Heights (359 9260). Bus 1, 3, 12, 22, 24. **Open** 11am-7pm Mon-Sat; noon-5pm Sun. **Credit** AmEx, MC, V. **Map** p309 E3.
The first Kiehl's botanical apothecary opened in New York's East Village in 1851; 150 years later, the second opened in Pacific Heights. Gentle and justifiably beloved, these products (especially the lip balm) are a fave with models and Hollywood types.

MAC Cosmetics

*1833 Union Street, between Laguna & Octavia
Streets, Cow Hollow (771 6113/www.maccosmetics.
com). Bus 41, 45.* **Open** 11am-7pm Mon-Sat;
10am-7pm Sun. **Credit** AmEx, Disc, MC, V.
Map p310 E2.
Favoured by party girls and drag queens from LA
to New York (although the company itself is based
in, gulp, Canada) MAC has gritty downtown palettes
as well as sparkly pink pastels for those early
Britney moments. Ask for a free makeover.

Sephora

*33 Powell Street, at Market Street, Union Square
(392 1545/www.sephora.com). BART Powell
Street/Muni Metro F, J, K, L, M, N/bus 5, 6, 7, 9,
21, 27, 30, 31, 45, 66/cable car Powell-Hyde or
Powell-Mason.* **Open** 10am-9pm Mon-Sat; 11am-7pm
Sun. **Credit** AmEx, Disc, MC, V. **Map** p315 H4.
Recently moved from its flagship Stockton Street
location, Sephora's cosier digs still accommodate its
interactive floor plan: you can touch, smell and try
on most of the premier perfumes and make-up
brands without suffering the hard-sell. Try the
Sephora brand make-up, high quality and a cut
above in terms of value for money.
Other locations: 2083 Union Street, at Webster
Street, Cow Hollow (614 2704).

Hair salons

Backstage Salon

*2134 Polk Street, at Vallejo Street, Russian Hill
(775 1440). Bus 19, 47, 49.* **Open** 11am-7pm
Tue-Sat. **Credit** MC, V. **Map** p310 F2.
This full-service hair salon/gallery showcases local
art while coaxing Russian Hill yuppies out of their
cookie-cutter bobs and George Clooney caesar cuts.
International stylists offer intense colour treatments
and innovative haircuts at affordable prices.

De Kroon Salon & Spa

*303 Sutter Street, at Grant Avenue, Financial
District (398 6464). BART Montgomery Street or
Powell Street/bus 2, 3, 4, 30, 45, 48.* **Open** 10am-
7pm daily. **Credit** AmEx, MC, V. **Map** p311 H3.
Perched two storeys up in an airy, window-encased
space, De Kroon is where you get pampered any
which way but cheap. Hair, nails, massage and
facials ensure those self-esteem boosts so necessary
when fatigue, ex-lovers or problem skin descend.

Elevation Salon & Café

*451 Bush Street, between Kearny Street & Grant
Avenue, Union Square (392 2969). BART Powell
Street/Muni Metro F, J, K, L, M, N/bus 5, 6, 7, 9,
21, 27, 30, 31, 45, 66.* **Open** 9am-6pm Mon, Tue;
9am-8pm Wed; 9.30am-7pm Thur; 9am-6pm Fri, Sat.
Credit MC, V. **Map** p311 G/H3.
Newly elected San Francisco mayor Gavin Newsom
is a client (although those who saw his hair during
the mayoral debates may call this a dubious distinction). Political follicles aside, some of the best
colour in the city is done here.

De Kroon Salon & Spa.

Vidal Sassoon

359 Sutter Street, between Stockton Street & Grant Avenue, Union Square (397 5105/ www.vssassoon.com). BART Powell Street/Muni Metro F, J, K, L, M, N/bus 5, 6, 7, 9, 21, 27, 30, 31, 45, 66/cable car Powell-Hyde or Powell-Mason. **Open** 9am-5.15pm Mon-Wed, Fri; 9am-6pm Thur; 8.30am-5.30pm Sat. **Credit** AmEx, MC, V. **Map** p311 G3.

Visit when price is immaterial and a precision cut is your goal. Remember that breezy Farrah Fawcett blow-dry? This was the chain that made it. If they don't look good, you don't look good. Or something.

Zip Zap

245 Fillmore Street, at Haight Street, Lower Haight (621 1671). Bus 6, 7, 22, 66, 71. **Open** 11am-7pm daily. **Credit** MC, V. **Map** p313 E5.

Drop into this trendy shop in the Lower Haight and improve your look for about $35.

Pharmacies

Walgreens Drugstore

3201 Divisadero Street, at Lombard Street, Marina (931 6417/www.walgreens.com). Bus 28, 30, 43, 76. **Open** 24hrs daily. **Credit** AmEx, Disc, MC, V. **Map** p309 D2.

Prescriptions and general drugstore purchases are available at this pharmacy around the clock.

Other 24hr locations: 498 Castro Street, at 18th Street, Castro (861 6276); 25 Point Lobos Avenue, at 43rd Avenue, Richmond (387 0706).

Spas, saunas & bathhouses

International Orange

2044 Fillmore Street, between Pine & California Streets, Fillmore (563 5000/www.international orange.com). Bus 1, 22. **Open** 11am-9pm Mon-Fri; 9am-7pm Sat, Sun. **Credit** AmEx, Disc, MC, V. **Map** p309 D3.

Leave life's clutter at the door and receive refined treatments from the serious – almost clinical – massage and facial professionals at International Orange. Try the 'extra sensual' Swedish massage, with fragrant body balms, which is designed to Zen the tension out of tight, aching muscles.

Kabuki Springs & Spa

Japan Center, 1750 Geary Boulevard, at Fillmore Street, Western Addition (922 6000/www.kabuki springs.com). Bus 22, 38. **Open** 10am-10pm daily. **Admission** *Day pass* $15. *Evening pass* $18. **Credit** AmEx, MC, V. **Map** p310 E4.

This traditional Japanese bathhouse has deep ceramic communal tubs, a steam room, saunas, a cold plunge pool and a restful tatami room. Shiatsu, Swedish and deep-tissue massages, body scrubs and a host of other soothing services are available by appointment. Women-only days are Wednesday, Friday and Sunday; men-only days are Monday, Thursday and Saturday.

Osento

955 Valencia Street, at 21st Street, Mission (282 6333/www.osento.com). BART 24th Street/ bus 14, 26, 49. **Open** 1pm-1am daily (last admission midnight). **Admission** $10-$20. **No credit cards**. **Map** p314 F7.

A women-only bathhouse. Walk into the peaceful surroundings, leave your clothes in a locker and relax in the whirlpool. After a cold plunge, you can choose between wet and dry saunas. An outdoor deck offers the chance to enjoy the weather on a sunny day. Massages available by appointment.

Tattoos & body piercing

Body Manipulations

3234 16th Street, between Guerrero & Dolores Streets, Mission (621 0408/www.bodym.com). BART 16th Street/Muni Metro J/bus 22, 26, 53. **Open** noon-7pm daily. **Credit** AmEx, Disc, MC, V. **Map** p314 F6.

Custom body-piercing, scarring, branding and just about anything else – except tattooing.

Lyle Tuttle Tattooing

841 Columbus Avenue, at Lombard Street, North Beach (775 4991). Bus 15, 30/cable car Powell-Mason. **Open** noon-9pm daily. **No credit cards**. **Map** p310 G2.

Tuttle was one of the world's most respected tattoo artists and his parlour is still an essential stopoff for the cognoscenti. Though he has himself retired, the talented Tanja Nicklish is usually available for those who want to add a little plumage to their skin – she specialises in designs in bright colours. The associated tattoo museum is, sadly, no more.

Launderettes

Don't miss **Brainwash** (*see p143*), SoMa's still popular café/bar/launderette.

Star Wash

392 Dolores Street, at 17th Street, Mission (431 2443). Muni Metro J/bus 22, 33. **Open** 7am-9pm daily. **No credit cards**. **Map** p314 F6.

A hip gathering place for cinephiles, Star Wash shows old and new movies as you sort through your socks. The images of Fred, Ginger, Bogey and Bacall on the walls seem to be surveying your scanties.

Music

CDs, tapes & records

See also p184 **Vinyl junkies**.

Amoeba Music

1855 Haight Street, between Shrader & Stanyan Streets, Haight-Ashbury (831 1200/ www.amoebamusic.com). Muni Metro N/bus 7, 33, 71. **Open** 10.30am-10pm Mon-Sat; 11am-9pm Sun. **Credit** Disc, MC, V. **Map** p313 C6.

Be free: gigging at **Amoeba Music**. *See p182.*

There's no denying the powerful presence of Amoeba, whose 25,000sq ft/23,225sq m (it used to be a bowling alley) premises are packed with every imaginable type of recorded music, both new and used. DJs and musicians love this place, not least because of the free gigs, some with surprisingly big-name bands.
Other locations: 2455 Telegraph Avenue, at Haste Street, Berkeley (1-510 549 1125).

BPM Music Factory
573 Hayes Street, at Laguna Street, Hayes Valley (487 8680). Bus 21. **Open** 11am-8pm Mon-Sat; 11am-7pm Sun. **Credit** AmEx, MC, V. **Map** p314 E/F5.
Local DJs gather at BPM Music Factory to gossip and buy their carefully chosen 12-inches to add to their already expansive personal collections. The rest of us go to eaves-shop.

Grooves Vinyl Attractions
1797 Market Street, between Guerrero & Valencia Streets, SoMa (436 9933). Muni Metro F, J, K, L, M/bus 6, 7, 26, 71. **Open** 11am-7pm daily. **Credit** AmEx, Disc, MC, V. **Map** p314 F5.
Dive into the dollar bin for '70s crooners and vintage vinyl. This place is also excellent for out-of-print soundtracks.

Jack's Record Cellar
254 Scott Street, at Page Street, Lower Haight (431 3047). Bus 6, 7, 24, 71. **Open** noon-7pm Wed-Sat. **Credit** MC, V. **Map** p313 E5.
Think *High Fidelity* in the Lower Haight, with hard-to-find jazz, R&B, pop and country, mostly on vinyl.

Jazz Quarter
1267 20th Avenue, at Irving Street, Sunset (661 2331). Muni Metro N/bus 29, 71. **Open** 1-6pm Tue-Sat. **No credit cards. Map** p312 A6.
Cool cats come here to score Mingus, Miles, Chet and Charlie, Parker and Coltrane, that is.

Livity
505 Divisadero Street, at Fell Street, Western Addition (922 2442). Bus 21, 24. **Open** 11am-9pm daily. **Credit** AmEx, Disc, MC, V. **Map** p313 D/E5.
For those who see beyond reggae's pass-the-bong reputation, this is the place. There's a juice bar and Jamaican food for extra atmosphere.

Medium Rare Records
2310 Market Street, at 16th Street, Castro (255 7273/www.modsystem.com/mediumrare). Muni Metro F, K, L, M/bus 24, 33, 35, 37. **Open** 11am-9pm Mon-Thur; 11am-9pm Fri, Sat; noon-7.30pm Sun. **Credit** AmEx, MC, V. **Map** p313/4 E6.
Owner Arnold Conrad has lovingly assembled a collection that meanders widely across decades and genres. This is a tiny shop that definitely packs a lot of sonic punch.

Rasputin Music
69 Powell Street, between Eddy & Ellis Streets, Downtown (1-800 350 8700/www.rasputinmusic.com). Muni F, J, K, L, M, N/bus 2, 5, 7, 9, 14, 21, 66, 71. **Open** 11am-8pm Mon-Thur; 11am-9pm Fri, Sat; noon-7pm Sun. **Credit** AmEx, Disc, MC, V. **Map** p310 G4.
Hosting a staggering collection of new and used CDs, tapes (remember those?) and LPs, as well as DVDs and VHS, Rasputin remains the Bay Area's

Vinyl junkies

Through the '90s, the Lower Haight's vinyl craze exploded with San Francisco's burgeoning house and trance scenes. With dance music rapidly mutating, record-buying and -collecting took on a whole new face, with DJs – the professionals, not just the hobbyists – largely replacing the area's typical Mojo-scouring clientele. These days vinyl shops could likely survive on the city's contingent of techno, house, drum 'n' bass and hip-hop jocks alone.

Those wax purists who haven't succumbed to CD players or fancy software simulations pop up in the strangest places. Some eschew the regular club outlets in favour of setting up shop in their apartments, blasting tunes out of the window to the neighbours' annoyance. When they're in a buying mood, though, they're likely to be found in the Lower Haight. Electronic dance music shops come and go as quickly as the Haight's fashion fads, but you can rest assured this stretch of real estate will always have a few purveyors of the funkiest 180-gram. It's only a hop, a skip and a jump between **Tweekin Records** (593 Haight Street, at Steiner Street, 626 6995, www.tweakin.com) and **Future Primitive Sound** (597 Haight Street, also at Steiner, 551 2328, www.futureprimitivesound.com). These aren't for the casual shopper, though: staff stand around staring at whatever slab's on the platter rather than trying to sell you any records and the racks aren't exactly what you'd call user-friendly.

The neighbourhood's more rarefied **Groove Merchant** (687 Haight Street, at Pierce Street, 252 5766) may not have the largest or cheapest selection, but its bins of hard-to-find jazz, funk, soul and other dusty 12-inch delights offer even the most discerning collector a feast for the ears. (Our word isn't enough? Well, listen up to the Beastie Boys in 'Professor Booty'.)

Of more interest to chin-stroking minimal soundscape aficionados than clubby rump shakers is **Open Mind Music** (342 Divisadero Street, at Oak Street, 621 2244, www.open mindmusic.com), just a few blocks north of Haight Street. Whether it's fresh Deutsch schaffel, innovations from Detroit or glitchy house from local favourites Kit Clayton and Kid606, Open Mind has the Bay's best selection for experimental dance vinyl, all just begging to have its wrapping split at the pressure-free listening stations.

With 45rpm discs gaining renewed popularity, soul and funk classics are never too far away from the city's DJ sets. Often the best place to find the tiny gems is a mess known as **Rooky Ricardo's** (448 Haight Street, at Fillmore Street, 864 7526), another staple of the Lower Haight. That the owner and his friends play cards in the shop's only open floor space should lead one to suspect that this is where to get 7-inchs for a special occasion. Racks and racks are covered with old R&B and dance 45s sold at bargain-basement prices. The closet in the front of the place holds the special stuff, haphazardly stacked in cardboard boxes for your mining pleasure. You may have to dig your way out when you're finished, but you'll emerge with a Stax or Motown treasure.

largest independent record store. Helpful computer-aides guide you through the maze of obscurities and familiarities from local punk to Czech art-rock. **Other locations:** 2401 Telegraph Avenue, at Channing Way, Berkeley (1-800 350 8700).

Ritmo Latino

2401 Mission Street, at 20th Street, Mission (824 8556). Bus 14, 26, 33, 49. **Open** 10am-9.30pm daily. **Credit** MC, V. **Map** p314 F7.
Inside, indulge your Latin fantasies. Outside, there's handprints of stars like Celia Cruz and Ricky Martin.

Tower Records

2525 Jones Street, at Columbus Avenue, North Beach (885 0500/www.towerrecords.com). Bus 10, 30, 47/ cable car Powell-Mason. **Open** 10am-11pm Mon-Thur, Sun; 10am-midnight Fri, Sat. **Credit** AmEx, Disc, MC, V. **Map** p310 F2.

Reviled on principle by music snobs, Tower Records is actually a smaller, friendlier kind of corporate entity (at least at its North Beach location). The Classical Annex (2568 Jones Street, 441 4880) provides an oasis of calm and a comprehensive selection. In-store musician appearances are frequent.
Other locations: 2280 Market Street, between Noe & 16th Streets, Castro (621 0588); 660 Third Street, at Brannan Street, SoMa (957 9660); Stonestown Galleria, Winston Drive, at 19th Avenue, Park Merced (681 2001).

Instruments & sheet music

Byron Hoyt

333 Hayes Street, at Franklin Street, Hayes Valley (431 8055). Bus 21. **Open** noon-6pm Mon-Sat. **Credit** AmEx, Disc, MC, V. **Map** p314 F5.

At this venerable sheet music and instrument shop, you'll find a stunning view, helpful, solicitous and knowledgeable staff, along with copies of every possible score from Bach to Irving Berlin.

Clarion Music

816 Sacramento Street, at Waverly Place, Chinatown (391 1317/www.clarionmusic.com). Bus 1, 30, 45/cable car California. **Open** 11am-6pm Mon-Fri; 9am-5pm Sat. **Credit** AmEx, Disc, MC, V. **Map** p311 G3.

This is world music central: didgeridoos, sitars, Tibetan singing bowls, African drums, Native American flutes, Chinese stringed instruments and other non-Western noisemakers are all stocked here. Concerts, usually on Fridays, feature everything from Latin and blues to the more obscure varieties of world music.

Haight-Ashbury Music Center

1540 Haight Street, at Ashbury Street, Haight-Ashbury (863 7327/www.haight-ashbury-music.com). Muni Metro N/bus 6, 7, 33, 37, 43, 66, 71. **Open** 11am-7pm Mon-Fri; 10am-6pm Sat; noon-6pm Sun. **Credit** AmEx, DC, Disc, MC, V. **Map** p313 D5/6.

A stopoff point for local musicians and rockers in town for a gig, this shop sells new and second-hand instruments, microphones, mixers, amps and sheet music, along with hundreds of guitars. It's also the proud sponsor of Haight Street's Carnivale, a sprawling mass of reggae, hip hop, calypso and salsa.

Opticians

City Optix

2154 Chestnut Street, between Pierce & Steiner Streets, Marina (921 1188/www.cityoptix.com). Bus 22, 28, 30, 43, 76. **Open** 10am-6pm Mon-Wed, Fri, Sat; 10am-8pm Thur; noon-5pm Sun. **Credit** AmEx, MC, V. **Map** p309 D2.

The most comprehensive collection of great frames in most price ranges, sold by friendly staff. Look for Matsuda, Oliver Peoples, LA Eyeworks and more. **Other locations**: 1685 Haight Street, between Belvedere & Cole Streets, Haight-Ashbury (626 1188).

Invision Optometry

1907 Fillmore Street, between Pine & Bush Streets, Pacific Heights (563 9003). Bus 1, 2, 3, 4. **Open** 10am-6pm Mon-Sat; noon-4pm Sun. **Credit** AmEx, MC, V. **Map** p309 E4.

Four eyes are definitely better than two, as you will quickly learn while browsing through this spacious shop, which is filled with more than 600 frame styles.

Pets

George

2411 California Street, at Fillmore Street, Pacific Heights (441 0564/www.georgesf.com). Bus 1, 3, 22. **Open** 11am-6pm Mon-Fri; 10am-6pm Sat; noon-6pm Sun. **Credit** AmEx, MC, V. **Map** p309 E3.

Pampered pets (and their pamperers) will love this fabulous pet boutique founded by a pair of fox-terrier owners from Texas, which sells eye-catching accessories for pets to wear, eat, play with and sleep on. Treats, organic catnip, natty jackets and patterned ceramic bowls complement an enticing array of people clothes, such as a bright, stripy Dogpatch ski hat or a 'Best in Show' bracelet. **Other locations**: 44 Fourth Street, at Hearst Avenue, Berkeley (1-510 644 1033).

Photography

Adolph Gasser

181 Second Street, between Mission & Howard Streets, SoMa (495 3852/www.gassers.com). BART Montgomery Street/Metro Muni F, J, K, L, M, N/ bus 2, 3, 4, 6, 7, 9, 12, 15, 21, 31, 71, 76. **Open** 9am-6pm Mon-Fri; 10am-5pm Sat. **Credit** AmEx, Disc, MC, V. **Map** p311 H4.

This justly famous photographic shop has the largest inventory of photo and video equipment in Northern California. It stocks SLR cameras by Canon and Nikon (far cheaper than in the UK), all sorts of lenses, point-and-shoot cameras, and an expanding selection of digital cameras and scanners.

Discount Camera

33 Kearny Street, between Post & Market Streets, Union Square (392 1103/www.discountcamera.com). BART Montgomery Street/Metro Muni F, J, K, L, M, N/bus 2, 3, 4, 6, 7, 9, 14, 15, 21, 30, 31, 45, 71/cable car Powell-Hyde or Powell-Mason. **Open** 8.30am-6.30pm Mon-Sat; 9.30am-6pm Sun. **Credit** AmEx, Disc, MC, V. **Map** p311 H3.

Concierges at downtown hotels steer guests here to help them avoid the unscrupulous tourist traps by the Powell Street turnaround. Discount Camera carries all major brands and has an on-site photo lab.

Photoworks

2077A Market Street, at Church Street, Castro (626 6800/www.photoworkssf.com). Muni Metro F, J, K, L, M/bus 22, 33, 35, 37. **Open** 9am-8pm Mon-Fri; 10am-8pm Sat; 10am-6pm Sun. **Credit** AmEx, Disc, MC, V. **Map** p314 E6.

On the fringes of the Castro, this is the favourite photo processor for amateurs and pros alike. It is staffed by photographers and they take unusual care with your film. Turnaround is two to three days.

Sex shops

Good Vibrations

603 Valencia Street, at 17th Street, Mission (522 5460/www.goodvibes.com). BART 24th Street/bus 14, 26, 48, 49. **Open** 11am-7pm Mon-Wed, Sun; 11am-8pm Thur-Sat. **Credit** AmEx, Disc, MC, V. **Map** p314 F6.

Some call it the Blockbuster Video of vibrators. The staff here pride themselves on providing a clean, safe environment for buying sex toys of every imaginable kind. Shop without shame for the popular Hitachi 'Magic Wand', the 'I Rub My Duckie' or the infamous 'Rabbit', as seen (and used) on *Sex and the City*. Although run by and catering mainly to women, everyone is welcome to shop and browse their large stock.

Other locations: 1620 Polk Street, at Sacramento Street, Polk Gulch (345 0400); 2504 San Pablo Avenue, at Dwight Way, Berkeley (1-510 841 8987).

Stormy Leather

1158 Howard Street, at Seventh Street, SoMa (626 1672/www.stormyleather.com). Bus 12, 14, 19, 26. **Open** noon-7pm daily. **Credit** AmEx, Disc, MC, V. **Map** p314 G5.

More titillating than Good Vibrations because of its less clinical atmosphere, Stormy Leather will provide that rubber nurse or French maid outfit, or leather and latex bustiers. Friendly female staff.

Other locations: 582C Castro Street, at 19th Street, Castro (671 1295).

Smoking

Ashbury Tobacco Center

1524 Haight Street, at Ashbury Street, Haight-Ashbury (552 5556). Bus 6, 7, 33, 43, 71. **Open** 10am-9.30pm daily. **Credit** AmEx, DC, Disc, MC, V. **Map** p313 D5/6.

The full array of psychedelic sundries are available here, at one of Haight's better head shops. In addition to the hookahs and honeybear bongs, there's a vast offering of tobacco products.

Grant's Tobacconists

562 Market Street, between Sansome & Montgomery Streets, Financial District (981 1000). BART Montgomery Street/Muni Metro F, J, K, L, M, N/bus 1, 2, 3, 4, 15, 76. **Open** 9am-5.30pm Mon-Fri; 10am-5.30pm Sat. **Credit** AmEx, Disc, MC, V. **Map** p311 H3.

Grant's offers pipes, cigars, humidors, tobacco, sundry posh accessories and a walk-in humidor reputed to be stocked with 100,000 cigars. Smokin'.

Sport

For other shops selling and renting skis, snowboards, in-line skates and other sports equipment, *see p234*.

Lombardi Sports

1600 Jackson Street, at Polk Street, Russian Hill (771 0600/www.lombardisports.com). Bus 12, 19, 27, 47, 49, 76. **Open** 10am-7pm Mon-Wed; 10am-8pm Thur, Fri; 10am-6pm Sat; 11am-6pm Sun. **Credit** AmEx, Disc, MC, V. **Map** p310 F3.

A mecca for the serious eco-challengers, Lombardi Sports also attracts those whose idea of camping is four cases of beer and a cosy SUV. An affable institution full of equipment, accessories, footwear and clothing for almost any sport you can imagine – with assistance from staff who look like they've come straight out of a Mountain Dew commercial.

See Jane Run Sports

3870 24th Street, at Sanchez Street, Noe Valley (401 8338/www.seejanerunsports.com). Muni Metro J/bus 48. **Open** 11am-7pm Mon-Fri; 10am-6pm Sat; 11am-5pm Sun. **Credit** AmEx, Disc, MC, V. **Map** p313/4 E7.

This shops stocks a well-compiled selection of gear for women who run, cycle, swim, hike or do yoga, and staff who are more than happy to spend time matching you to the right shoes for the right sport – which every keen athlete knows is essential.

Sports Basement

1301 Sixth Street, at Channel Street, SoMa (437 0111/www.sportsbasement.com). Bus 10, 15. **Open** 10am-6pm Mon-Wed, Fri; 10am-8pm Thur; 10am-6pm Sat, Sun. **Credit** AmEx, MC, V. **Map** p315 H5.

This huge SoMa warehouse – the new Presidio branch manages to be even larger – gathers end-of-line goods from top-tier brands such as North Face, Teva, Speedo, Pearl Izumi and Cannondale, and offers them at savings of 30-60%. The shop can be tricky to find, so staff advise that you call ahead for directions.

Other locations: 610 Mason Street, opposite Crissy Field, Presidio (437 0100).

Toys

Ambassador Toys

1981 Union Street, at Buchanan Street, Marina (345 8697). Bus 45. **Open** 10am-6pm daily. **Credit** AmEx, Disc, MC, V. **Map** p310 E3.

This straightforward store has a charming and lovingly displayed selection of toys, dolls, books, games and plushy animals. Blessedly free of the chaos of larger emporiums, it specialises in international toys. Opening hours change with the seasons, so it's a good idea phone ahead.

Chinatown Kite Shop

717 Grant Avenue, at Sacramento Street, Chinatown (989 5182). Bus 1, 15, 30, 45/ cable car California. **Open** 10am-9pm daily. **Credit** AmEx, Disc, MC, V. **Map** p311 G3.

A breezy city like San Francisco is a kite-flyer's dream, and this shop its fruition, stocked with hundreds of different kites in every imaginable shape and colour. The perfect place to get kitted out before you head out to Marina Green.

Sanrio

San Francisco Centre, 865 Market Street at Fifth Street, Tenderloin (495 3056/ www.sanrio.com). BART Powell Street/Muni Metro F, J, K, L, M, N/bus 5, 6, 7, 9, 21, 27, 30, 31, 45, 66/cable car Powell-Market. **Open** 10am-8pm Mon-Sat; 11am-6pm Sun. **Credit** AmEx, Disc, MC, V. **Map** p311 G4.

From the creative folks behind Hello Kitty, Sanrio is the place to find Japanese candy, pencil boxes, irresistible toys and charmingly dated cartoon stuff, including '70s-style *Peanuts* merchandise.

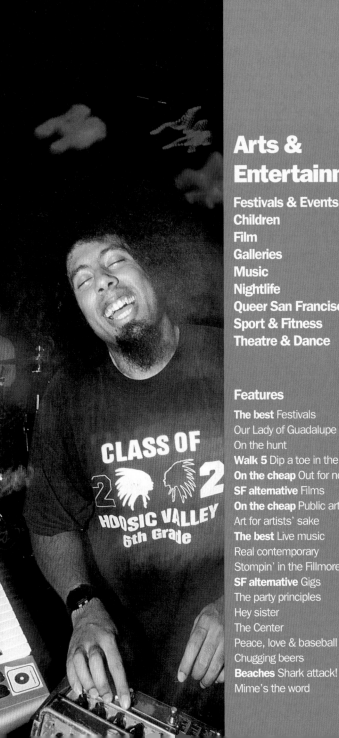

Arts & Entertainment

Festivals & Events	**188**
Children	**195**
Film	**199**
Galleries	**204**
Music	**209**
Nightlife	**219**
Queer San Francisco	**224**
Sport & Fitness	**234**
Theatre & Dance	**244**

Features

The best Festivals	189
Our Lady of Guadalupe	190
On the hunt	193
Walk 5 Dip a toe in the Marina	197
On the cheap Out for nowt	198
SF alternative Films	202
On the cheap Public art	207
Art for artists' sake	208
The best Live music	209
Real contemporary	210
Stompin' in the Fillmore	214
SF alternative Gigs	216
The party principles	223
Hey sister	226
The Center	232
Peace, love & baseball	235
Chugging beers	236
Beaches Shark attack!	241
Mime's the word	247

Festivals & Events

Raucous revelry or chilling in the park? San Francisco is a festival mega-mix.

Christmas lights, Union Square. *See p194.*

The number and variety of public events held in this city are a source of pride for its citizens. Temperate spring and summer are punctuated by neighbourhood fairs, parades and park entertainments, while autumn and winter see events move indoors to performance spaces and studios. No matter the season, public celebrations are great for mingling with the locals, as the city often caters to residents first and visitors second – a commitment returned in kind by the multitudes of inhabitants who attend the same events year after year. Be prepared for crowds and take public transport: parking in San Francisco is notoriously difficult.

The dates listed below are as accurate as possible, but always check before you make plans. For the most up-to-date information, consult the San Francisco Visitor Information Center (*see p290*) or local papers, including the free alternative press. For a list of annual public holidays, *see p291*.

Spring

St Patrick's Day Parade

Second & Market Streets (675 9885). BART Montgomery Street/Muni Metro F, J, K, L, M, N S/bus 5, 15, 21, 31, 38, 66, 71. **Date** Sun before 17 Mar. **Map** p311 H3.

San Francisco has a sizeable Irish population, so this parade is one of the city's biggest. Festivities begin at noon, with the parade heading from Second and Market to the Civic Center, before dispersing into a host of pubs and celebrating into the night.

St Stupid's Day Parade

Usually Justin Herman Plaza, Embarcadero (www.saintstupid.com). BART Embarcadero/Muni Metro J, K, L, M, N/bus 1, 2, 7, 9, 12, 14, 21, 41, 42, 66, 71. **Date** 1 Apr. **Map** p311 H3.

For more than 20 years, Bishop Joey of the First Church of the Last Laugh has led the St Stupid's Day Parade, which gathers at noon to snake through San Francisco's Financial District before coming to a halt on the steps of the Pacific Stock Exchange. There sermons are given and everyone removes a sock for the 'Pacific Sock Exchange'. Indeed many go home entirely sockless, as the event usually degenerates into a sock fight. The starting point varies, so check the website or local papers for the latest information.

Cherry Blossom Festival

Japan Center, Geary Boulevard, between Fillmore & Laguna Streets, Japantown (922 6776/www.sf-osaka.org/Pages/events.html). Bus 2, 3, 4, 22, 38. **Date** Apr. **Map** p309/10 E4.

For two consecutive weekends in April, the Cherry Blossom Festival transforms the ordinarily sleepy Japantown into a celebratory whirlwind. The festivities pay tribute to the delights of Japanese cuisine, as well as to traditional arts and crafts, and there are dance and martial arts demonstrations.

San Francisco International Film Festival

931 3456/www.sfiff.org. **Date** mid Apr-early May.

The SFIFF may not be the largest film festival, but over its annual fortnight it screens enough films to make a good stab at being the world's most eclectic. It is strong on independent documentaries and films from developing countries that are rarely shown at other US festivals. Tickets sell out quickly, so book in advance. *See also p203.*

Cinco de Mayo

Civic Center Plaza, between McAllister, Grove, Franklin & Hyde Streets, Civic Center (256 3005). BART Civic Center/Muni Metro F, J, K, L, M, N/bus

---

Arts & Entertainment

5, 19, 21, 42, 47, 49. **Date** wknd before 5 May.
Map p314 F4.
A raucous weekend of parades, fireworks and music
during which San Francisco's Latino residents and
their friends celebrate General Ignacio Zaragoza's
defeat of the French army at Puebla in 1862. It's one
of the best parties of the year.

AIDS Candlelight Memorial March & Vigil
*Castro & Market Streets, Castro (331 1500/www.
aidscandlelightvigil.org). Muni Metro F, K, L, M/bus
24, 33, 35, 37.* **Date** 3rd Sun in May. **Map** p313 E6.
This annual candlelit vigil begins at 8pm with a
solemn procession from the Castro along Market
Street, ending on the steps of the Main Library.
There crowds gather for speeches, an award
ceremony, celebrations and remembrances.

Examiner Bay to Breakers Foot Race
*Howard & Spear Streets, SoMa (359 2800/www.
baytobreakers.com). BART Embarcadero/Muni
Metro F, J, K, L, M, N, S/bus 1, 12, 14, 41.* **Date**
3rd Sun in May. **Map** p311 J3.
The *San Francisco Examiner* and other corporate
sponsors encourage 70,000 athletes, weekend
warriors, jog-walkers, joggers-for-a-day and fleet-
footed zanies to run to Ocean Beach from SoMa. The
course is about 12km (7.46 miles), a perfect length
for most to make it without much training. The race
is famous for its costumes, party atmosphere and
nudity – there are always a few running free and
bouncy – as well as a school of runners dressed as
salmon who attempt to run the course 'upstream'.
On the subject of futility, don't attempt to cross the
city from north to south on the morning of the race.

Carnaval
*Harrison Street, between 16th & 22nd Streets (920
0125/www.carnavalsf.com). BART 16th or 24th
Streets/bus 12, 14, 22, 27, 33, 48, 49, 53.*
Admission $5. **No credit cards**. **Date** Memorial
Day wknd. **Map** p314 G6/7.
As of 2003, Carnaval has returned to its natural home
in the Mission. The dazzling parade of skimpily
costumed samba dancers starts at Mission and 24th
Streets, arriving in due course at the festival on
Harrison, where there's fine food and more music.

Summer

Haight Street Fair
*Haight Street, between Masonic Avenue & Stanyan
Street, Haight-Ashbury (666 9952/www.haightstreet
fair.org). Muni Metro N/bus 6, 7, 33, 43, 66, 71.*
Date early June. **Map** p313 C6/D5.
The Haight Street Fair boasts more than 200 booths
of greasy food, hippie crafts and all sorts of drug
paraphernalia, plus live music stages and plenty of
folks tripped out of their gourds. The Haight Street
Fair attracts a younger, earthier crowd than its well-
heeled rival, the North Beach Festival (*see below*).

North Beach Festival
*Grant Avenue, Green Street, Stockton Street &
Washington Square, North Beach (989 2220/
www.sfnorthbeach.com). Bus 15, 30, 39, 41, 45/cable
car Powell-Mason.* **Date** June. **Map** p310/11 G2.
San Francisco's oldest street shindig, the North
Beach festival is heavy on art and crafts, including
a contest for the best chalk street 'painting'. Initially
smaller than the city's other fairs, in recent years the
North Beach
Festival's popularity has exploded in recent years.
There's live music and top-quality Italian food.

San Francisco LGBT Pride Celebration Parade
*Market Street, between Embarcadero & Eighth
Street, Downtown (864 3733/www.sfpride.org).
BART Embarcadero, Montgomery Street, Powell
Street or Civic Center/Muni Metro F, J, K, L, M, N/
bus 5, 6, 7, 9, 21, 31, 66, 71.* **Date** Sun in late June.
Map p311 J3.
A San Francisco rite of passage, the Lesbian, Gay,
Bisexual and Transgender Pride Parade and the
celebrations that follow are every bit as wonderful
and outlandish as you'd expect. Local politicians
cruising for votes share the route with drag queens,
leather daddies, Harley-revving dykes, parents
pushing strollers and gay marching bands. It's the
wildest, friendliest parade you'll ever witness.
Arrive at least an hour early for a kerbside seat, then
join the masses for a celebration at the Civic Center.

Summer Solstice
Date 21 June.
On this longest day of the year, pagans and their
sympathisers meet on the city's hills and beaches to
drum, dance and celebrate. At sunset, pound along
with a drum circle in Justin Herman Plaza at the
Embarcadero or join bonfires on Baker Beach.

The best Festivals

Chinese New Year
The biggest outside Asia. *See p194.*

Folsom Street Festival
Eye-bogglingly filthy fun. *See p192.*

Hardly Strictly Bluegrass Festival
The newest, bluest free festival. *See p192.*

San Francisco International Film Festival
For a great range of films, SFIFF can't be
beat. *See p188.*

San Francisco LGBT Pride Celebration Parade
Simply unforgettable. *See above.*

Arts & Entertainment

Our Lady of Guadalupe

In a city that prides itself on its liberalism, the 5am mass celebrated each 12 December in honour of Our Lady of Guadalupe is surprising. It marks an apparition of the Virgin Mary in 1531 to a Nahuatl peasant in Mexico called Juan Diego. The Spanish authorities were, it is said, rather sceptical until Juan opened his cloak and roses fell out, though the flowering season was long over. From this proof some trace the further 'miracle' of the conversion over two decades of nine million Mexicans to Christianity. The annual ceremonies in San Francisco involve hymn-playing mariachis and costumed Aztec dancers outside St Mary's Cathedal (*see p77*), while the petals of 300 roses are dropped from the dome of Mission Dolores (*see p88*) basilica. Given that Our Lady of Guadalupe was in 1999 appointed protector of innocent children, 'especially those... in danger of not being born', by Pope John Paul II, such acts of reverence in this of all cities could also be seen as some sort of miracle.

Fourth of July Waterfront Festival

Between Aquatic Park & Pier 39, Fisherman's Wharf (San Francisco Visitor Information Center 777 7120). Muni Metro F/bus 10, 15, 19, 30, 39, 42, 47/cable car Powell-Hyde, Powell-Mason. **Date** 4 July. **Map** p310 F/G1.

Spend the day on the waterfront, where you'll find live entertainment and food stalls, but make sure you stay for the spectacular firework display.

Fillmore Street Jazz Festival

Fillmore Street, between Jackson & Eddy Streets, Western Addition (1-800 731 0003). Bus 1, 2, 3, 4, 12, 22, 31, 38. **Date** early July. **Map** p309/10 E3/4.

Politicians and locals are struggling to breathe life back into Fillmore Street by capitalising on its jazz legacy (*see p214* **Stompin' in the Fillmore**). This steadily growing festival is one promising result. Alongside live music stages you'll find crafts and handiwork, mixed up with booths selling fine art.

San Francisco Chronicle Marathon

Embarcadero & Mission Street, Embarcadero (284 9653/www.chroniclemarathon.com). BART Embarcadero/Muni Metro F, J, K, L, M, N, S/bus 1, 12, 14, 41. **Date** 1st Sun in Aug. **Map** p311 J3.

It may not be as well known as the London or New York versions, but the San Francisco marathon has grown larger every year since its inception in 1999. The course starts at the Embarcadero and heads round the entire city, through the Mission, the Haight, Fisherman's Wharf and the Marina.

Books by the Bay

Yerba Buena Gardens, Mission Street, between Third & Fourth Streets, SoMa (561 7686/www. booksbythebay.com). BART Powell or Montgomery Streets/Muni Metro F, J, K, L, M, N/bus 9, 12, 15, 30, 45, 76. **Date** July. **Map** p311 H4.

San Francisco's reputation as a literary city is especially well deserved during this weekend of open-air events. You can browse booksellers' booths, attend author signings and participate in book panel discussions. A plethora of children's activities makes this a great stop for literary folk with kids.

Stern Grove Festival

Stern Grove, 19th Avenue, between Sloat Boulevard & Wawona Street, Sunset (252 6252/www.stern grove.org). Muni Metro K, M/bus 23, 28. **Date** early June-late Aug.

A local favourite, this free concert series includes jazz, classical and world music. The amphitheatre, set in a grove of eucalyptus trees, is idyllic – for as long as the fog holds off. Go early to claim your patch of grass, and bring snacks, a picnic blanket and an extra sweater.

Gilroy Garlic Festival

Gilroy, south of San Jose on US 101 (1-408 842 1625/www.gilroygarlicfestival.com). **Date** last wknd in July.

For 25 years this food and wine fest has featured the 'stinking rose' of Gilroy: the celebrated garlic clove, made into every edible concoction you can imagine, from ice-cream to jelly. There are more than 100 craft booths and three stages of entertainers, including puppeteers, magicians and musicians. Garlic-lovers should be aware that Gilroy is at least a two-hour drive from San Francisco.

Mime Troupe in the Park

Mission Dolores Park, 18th & Dolores Streets, Mission, then various parks (285 1717/www.sfmt. org). Muni Metro J/bus 33. **Date** early July-early Sept. **Map** p314 E7.

Only in San Francisco does the local mime troupe perform leftist, political musicals about the evils of genetic engineering and dot-com gentrification. Only in San Francisco does the local mime troupe not do mime. *See also p247* **Mime's the word**.

Comedy Day

Sharon Meadow, between Kezar & John F Kennedy Drives, Golden Gate Park (www.comedyday.com). Muni Metro N/bus 5, 7, 21, 33, 66, 71. **Date** early Sept. **Map** p312 C6.

Lie back on a blanket in the park, drink, scoff and laugh at local and national stand-up comedians. There are often cameos by famous figures from San Francisco's days as a comedy launchpad – Robin Williams or Rob Schneider, for instance.

A La Carte, A La Park

Sharon Meadow, Kezar & John F Kennedy Drives, Golden Gate Park (458 1988/advance tickets 478 2277/www.eventswestca.com/alchome.html). Muni Metro N/bus 5, 7, 21, 33, 66, 71. **Tickets** $12 ($10 in advance); $10 ($8 in advance) seniors; free under-12s. *Tastings* $1-$5. **No credit cards. Date** late Aug/early Sept. **Map** p312 C6.

Sample culinary creations from the Bay Area's best restaurants during this popular Labor Day event. More than 40 eateries are represented, as well as dozens of wineries and local microbreweries.

Autumn

Burning Man

Black Rock Desert, Nevada (863 5263/www.burning man.com). **Rates** $150-$200. **Date** Labor Day wknd.

Every year more than 25,000 people gather in the desert around a 50-foot-tall (15-metre) wooden man, laced with neon and packed with fireworks. For a week a temporary city appears, complete with radio stations, newspapers, huge works of art and crazy performances, then the man is burned and partici- pants cart off every vestige of their campsites. If you want to attend, click on the Survival Guide to find out what you're up against. Bay Area-based Burning Man events happen all through the year.

Ghirardelli Square Chocolate Festival

Ghirardelli Square, between North Point, Beach, Larkin & Polk Streets, Fisherman's Wharf (775 5500/www.ghirardellisq.com). Muni Metro F/bus 10, 19, 30, 47/cable car Powell-Hyde. **Date** early Sept. **Map** p310 F1.

A chocolate lover's dream come true. Sample a variety of luscious treats, including chocolate- covered strawberries, brownies, chocolate cheese- cake and more. The self-indulgence comes guilt-free too: the proceeds go to a local charity.

San Francisco Fringe Festival

931 1033/www.sffringe.org. **Tickets** free-$8. **No credit cards. Date** early Sept.

This dramatic, non-juried, non-censored theatre marathon features around 260 performances by some 50 local, national and international theatre companies, covering a broad spectrum from comedy to classic theatre or performance art.

San Francisco Shakespeare Festival

Golden Gate Park (422 2222/www.sfshakes.org). Muni Metro N/bus 5, 7, 21, 28, 29, 44, 71. **Date** Sept. **Map** p312 B6.

It seems the Bard knows no chronological or geographical limit. There are no fewer than five Bay Area theatre companies that produce Shakespeare plays during the summer, but the Shakespeare Festival is closest to home, being performed free on outdoor stages in Golden Gate Park throughout September. Shows begin at 1.30pm, but locals usually arrive at noon with their picnics.

San Francisco Blues Festival

Great Meadow, Fort Mason Center, Marina Boulevard, at Laguna Street, Marina (979 5588/ www.sfblues.com). Bus 22, 28, 30, 43, 49. **Tickets** $25-$65. **Credit** (in advance only) AmEx, DC, Disc, MC, V. **Date** 3rd or 4th wknd in Sept. **Map** p310 E2.

The oldest blues festival in the US, this weekend- long shindig blurs into one eternal afternoon. Hear set after set of plangent chords from some of the best blues musicians in the world. Shades, a blanket and a cooler full of refreshments are all essential, though

Arts & Entertainment

you can pick up food and drinks on-site if picnics aren't your vibe. Tickets are also available from Ticketmaster (421 8497, www.ticketmaster.com).

Folsom Street Fair
Folsom Street, between Seventh & 12th Streets, SoMa (861 3247/www.folsomstreetfair.org). Bus 9, 12, 14, 19, 27, 47. **Date** last Sun in Sept. **Map** p314/15 G5.
The Queen Mother of all leather street fairs: 'twenty years of fun, frolic and fetish', and still as enjoyably kinky as ever. The Folsom Street Fair is a visitors' gawkfest, with eyes on stalks almost as much the uniform as bottomless leather trousers. Be prepared for whips, chains and public fellatio. Parental advisory for children; grans and grandads welcome.

ArtSpan Open Studios
861 9838/www.artspan.org. **Date** Oct.
Get a behind-the-scenes peak at San Francisco's creative visionaries throughout October. More than 900 artists' studios are open to the public, with a different neighbourhood getting to show off its paintings, sculpture, ceramics, glass and jewellery every weekend. A free map and the *Directory of San Francisco Artists* are available from bookshops; a map is also published in the *Chronicle* in September.

Hardly Strictly Bluegrass Festival
Speedway Meadow, Golden Gate Park (no phone/ www.strictlybluegrass.com). Bus 5, 28, 29, 71. **Date** 1st wknd in Oct. **Map** p312 B6.
In 2003 country superstars Willie Nelson and Emmy Lou Harris, as well as the excellent Gillian Welch, graced San Francisco's newest festival. Established by Warren Hellman in 2001, the festival takes place over three fabulous days of pickin' and singin'. Although the organisers have added 'Hardly' to the original name to reflect the festival's broadening remit, the festival still focuses on bluegrass and, amazingly, it's still free. God bless you, Warren.

San Francisco International Art Exposition
Fort Mason Center, Marina Boulevard, at Laguna Street, Marina (391 2000/www.sfiae.com). Bus 22, 28, 30, 43, 49. **Tickets** $12; $10 concessions; free under-10s. **Credit** AmEx, MC, V. **Date** mid Jan. **Map** p310 E1.
This highbrow event includes work from some 100 art galleries that represent more than 2,000 artists from 12 countries. Prices are considerably higher than those at the ArtSpan Open Studios (*see p192*).

Castro Street Fair
Market & Castro Streets, from 16th to 19th Streets, Castro (841 1824/www.castrostreetfair.org). Muni Metro F, K, L, M/bus 24, 33, 35, 37. **Date** early Oct. **Map** p313 E6/7.
Presenting the softer side of gay life here, this one-day fair – started in 1974 by Harvey Milk – features food, crafts and community activists' stalls, along with plenty of rainbow merchandise.

Reggae in the Park
Sharon Meadow, between Kezar & John F Kennedy Drives, Golden Gate Park (458 1988). Muni Metro N/bus 5, 7, 21, 33, 66, 71. **Tickets** $25 ($20 in advance); $35 2-day pass; $10 6-12s; $17.50 6-12s 2-day pass; free under-5s. **Credit** (in advance only) AmEx, Disc, MC, V. **Date** early Oct. **Map** p312 C6.
You'll hear it from blocks away and smell the smoke long before you get there: RITP is quickly becoming one of the city's best-attended music festivals, mainly because it always seems to take place during the best autumn weather. A two-day event, it attracts artists and fans from all over the world.

Fleet Week
Fisherman's Wharf & Piers 30-32, Embarcadero (705 5500/www.fleetweek.com/sf). Muni Metro F/bus 15, 39, 42. **Date** Oct. **Map** p310 F1.
For more than two decades the US Navy's Blue Angels have torn up the skies over San Francisco (and under the Golden Gate Bridge) on Columbus Day weekend – although whether they'd visit in 2004 was a matter of dispute as we went to press. Still, the fleet will sail into harbour as usual on the Saturday morning (the best view is from the Golden Gate Bridge) and free ship tours should be on offer during this celebration of the entrance of the Navy's Great White Fleet into the Bay in 1908.

San Francisco Jazz Festival
788 7353/www.sfjazz.org. **Tickets** $5-$65. **Credit** AmEx, MC, V. **Date** 3rd & 4th wks in Oct.
Despite being in competition with the better-known Monterey festival, the SFJF still manages to attract some of the biggest names in jazz – witness Herbie Hancock's opening night in 2003. More than 30 swinging and singing festival events take place in venues around San Francisco and Oakland.

Exotic Erotic Ball
Cow Palace, 2600 Geneva Avenue, at Santos Street, Daly City (1-888 396 8426/www.exoticeroticball. com). Bus 9, 9AX. **Tickets** $50-$125. **Credit** MC, V. **Date** late Oct.
It's obnoxious, it's exploitative, it's 25 years old and it's the bridge-and-tunnel crowd's annual excuse to pull on the latex and fishnets and party with other sex kittens at the world's largest indoor masquerade ball. Strippers, sideshows and a costume competition are among the tamer perks.

Halloween San Francisco
Market Street from 15th to Castro Streets, Castro Street from Market to 19th Streets, Castro (www.halloweensf.com). **Date** 31 Oct. **Map** p313 E6.
All attempts by city leaders to divert Halloween revellers from the traditional fray in the Castro to the staid Civic Center have been a monumental flop, though the alcohol ban imposed in 2003 looks likely to stick. Head for the Castro, nip through the SFPD cordon, and find a land where crazy costumes, dressy drag queens and half-naked pagans are the exhilarating norm. If you're going to stare, return the favour and wear something outlandish.

On the hunt

Sometimes numbers are important. Each year nearly 1,600 people indulge their inner Sam Spade in the streets of Chinatown. Amid the dancing dragons and firecrackers, these crazed sleuths are taking part in San Francisco's **Annual Chinese New Year Treasure Hunt** (www.sftreasurehunts.com).

The Treasure Hunt begins at Justin Herman Plaza on the Embarcadero at 4.30pm and ends at the same place at 9pm. Beginners', Regular and Masters' Hunts ensure anyone can participate, and ticket prices are the same for all three ($30-$35 per person in advance or $40 per person on the day) with proceeds donated to the city's largest provider of housing and support services to homeless families. Don't just assume tickets will be available though: the Beginners' event often sells out months in advance.

If you're on your own or haven't got enough people to make up one of the four- to nine-person teams, turn up anyway and the staff will put you together with an appropriate group of hunters. 'Appropriate' is a key concept here, since some teams take the whole thing very seriously, with members dressed in matching shirts and forbidden to deviate from the Hunt, while others chase down a few simple clues then get distracted by some dim sum restaurant and never quite rejoin the Hunt. Whether or not your team completes the Hunt, head back to Justin Herman Plaza to hear the clues explained. The winners get a key-shaped cake, a bottle of champagne and, most importantly, gloating rights for the rest of the year.

Comfortable shoes and a flashlight come in handy, and many teams use a map and street index of the city. Some even carry phone books, almanacs and dictionaries. While it's acceptable to consult any publicly available resource – one team phoned a librarian in Hawaii because the local libraries were shut – calling a brainy friend is strictly forbidden, and team members must always remain within sight and earshot of one another. Plus, even if you're not local, you stand a chance: deep knowledge of San Francisco is less important than a good handle on current affairs, pop culture and puzzle-solving. Plus a healthy sense of when to spy on your rivals and a hearty appetite for dim sum.

Día de los Muertos
24th & Bryant Streets, Mission (826 8009). Bus 27, 33, 48. **Date** 2 Nov. **Map** p315 G7.
Hundreds of marchers gather at the intersection of 24th and Bryant to celebrate the Mexican Day of the Dead. After a traditional blessing, the music starts and the procession begins: Aztec dancers, hippie musicians, women in antique wedding dresses clutching bouquets of dead flowers and sleepy children in papier-mâché skeleton masks. Ending up in Garfield Square, people leave candles at a huge community altar. A focal celebration for the

Halloween.
See p192.

Hispanic community here, wear dark, sombre clothes (the dressier the better) if you want to attend. If you want to look like a local, paint your face a ghoulish white and bring a noisemaker.

Holiday Lighting Festivities

Union Square, between Geary, Powell, Post & Stockton Streets, Downtown; Ghirardelli Square, 900 North Point Street, at Polk Street, Fisherman's Wharf (705 5500). Muni Metro F/bus 10, 19, 30, 47/cable car Powell-Hyde. **Date** late Nov. **Map** p311 G3/4; p310 F1/2.

The holiday season kicks off with food, ice skating and a variety of lighting ceremonies. The most important is in Union Square, where a 67ft (20m) living white fir tree, decorated with 2,000 lights, 400 ornaments and 500 bows, is lit up each year. A 22ft (7m) wooden menorah is also lit as part of the Jewish Chanukah celebrations. A slightly smaller tree is lit each year in Ghirardelli Square.

Run to the Far Side

Music Concourse, Ninth Avenue & John F Kennedy Drive, Golden Gate Park (759 2690/www.cal academy.org). Muni Metro N/bus 16, 21, 44, 71. **Date** wknd after Thanksgiving. **Map** p312 B5.

Dress as your favourite Gary Larson character for this annual footrace. A fundraiser for the California Academy of Sciences, participants can walk or run 5km (3 miles) or run 10km (6 miles) through Golden Gate Park. The entrance fee is $20-$30.

Winter

The Nutcracker

War Memorial Opera House, 301 Van Ness Avenue, at Grove Street, Civic Center (865 2000/

www.sfballet.org). BART Civic Center/Muni Metro F, J, K, L, M, N/bus 6, 7, 21, 42, 47, 49, 66, 71. **Tickets** $12-$130. **Credit** AmEx, MC, V. **Date** Dec. **Map** p314 F5.

San Francisco Ballet (*see p248*), America's oldest ballet company, presents Tchaikovsky's beloved classic every holiday season. The company puts on dozens of performances, so you have no excuse not to see it, but be quick: performances always sell out.

New Year's Eve

Date 31 Dec.

San Franciscans traditionally throng to Union Square to see the New Year in, but in recent years the city fathers have been discouraging such street celebrations. Check local papers or call the Visitor Center (*see p290*) before heading into town. Other traditional festivities include a cavalcade of bands performing in tents along the Embarcadero.

Martin Luther King Jr Birthday Celebration

Yerba Buena Gardens, Mission Street, between Third & Fourth Streets, SoMa (771 630/http://glide.org). BART Powell or Montgomery Streets/Muni Metro F, J, K, L, M, N/bus 9, 12, 15, 30, 45, 76. **Date** Mon after 15 Jan. **Map** p311 H4.

The whole United States takes the day off to honour Dr King's birthday. The route of the parade in San Francisco varies, but it always finishes with a rally in Yerba Buena Gardens.

Tet Festival

Civic Center & Tenderloin (885 2743). BART Civic Center. **Date** Jan-Feb.

San Francisco has a sizeable population of Vietnamese-Americans who, with Cambodian, Latino- and African-American families, transform the centre of the city into a multicultural carnival.

San Francisco Tribal, Folk & Textile Arts Show

Fort Mason Center, Marina Boulevard, at Laguna Street, Marina (1-310 455 2886). Bus 22, 28, 30, 43, 49. **Admission** $12; free under-16s. **No credit cards.** **Date** early Feb. **Map** p310 E1.

More than 100 folk and ethnic art dealers converge to sell pottery, baskets, textiles and jewellery.

Chinese New Year

Market Street, at Second Street (982 3071/www. chineseparade.com). BART Montgomery Street/Muni Metro F, J, K, L, M, N/bus 5, 6, 7, 9, 21, 31, 66, 71. **Date** Feb. **Map** p311 H3.

San Francisco's Chinese New Year is the biggest event of its kind outside Asia, and quite simply the best parade in the city. With beauty pageants, drumming, martial arts, mountains of food, endless fireworks and a huge procession of dancing dragons, acrobats and stilt-walkers, the party turns the city jubilant and upside-down. It's also the occasion of the hugely popular Annual Treasure Hunt (*see p193* **On the hunt**). If you're in town on the right day, make sure you don't miss it.

Children

Don't expect to keep the kids quiet, there's far too much to shout about.

The City by the Bay is very child-friendly. There's the sea and the sea lions, Golden Gate Park and outdoor activities galore, as well as a plethora of museums and discovery centres. As well as permanent attractions, look out for special events and workshops listed under 'Children's events' in the Sunday pink section of the *San Francisco Chronicle* (www.sfgate.com) or 'Kids' Stuff' in *SF Weekly* (www.sfweekly.com). And don't neglect to head out beyond the city bounds. Hire a car and a whole new range of activities open up. For East Bay attractions, *see p196. See also p111, p250.*

When you're ready for an adults-only evening (and the more than $50 it's going to cost you) try **Bay Area Childcare Agency** (115 Lawton Street, at Seventh Avenue, Sunset, 309 5662). It's been a reliable option for more than 50 years.

The **Zeum** carousel. *See p196.*

Aquariums & zoos

For **Oakland Zoo** and the **Marine Mammal Center**, *see p198*; for the world-class **Monterey Bay Aquarium**, *see p271*.

Aquarium of the Bay
Pier 39, Embarcadero, at Beach Street, Fisherman's Wharf (1-888 732 3483/ www.aquariumofthebay.com). Muni Metro F/ bus 10, 15, 39, 47. **Open** *Summer* 9am-8pm daily. *Winter* 10am-6pm Mon-Fri; 10am-7pm Sat, Sun. **Admission** $12.95; $6.50 3-11s; $2 off with coupon from website. **Credit** MC, V. **Map** p310 G1.
Renovated in 2001, this aquatic attraction gives you a diver's-eye view of the Bay through clear plastic underwater tunnels. Home to 23,000 creatures, it's an amazing place to spy on crabs and sharks, touch live bat rays and watch the slow, gentle combat of octopuses. You can combine a visit with a pricey Bay cruise (every 45mins daily, $23, $15 3-11s).

Randall Museum
199 Museum Street, off Roosevelt Way, Buena Vista (554 9600/www.randallmuseum.org). Bus 24, 37. **Open** 10am-5pm Tue-Sat. **Admission** free. **Map** p313 D/E6.
A small, friendly museum in Corona Heights Park with a petting zoo (lambs, racoons, hawks and creepy crawlies), a kid-friendly earthquake display, and drop-in arts and crafts classes most Saturdays.

San Francisco Zoo
Sloat Boulevard, at 45th Avenue, Sunset (753 7080/www.sfzoo.org). Muni Metro L/bus 18, 23. **Open** *Main zoo* 10am-5pm daily. *Children's zoo*

mid June-Labor Day 10.30am-4.30pm daily. Labor Day-mid June 11am-4pm daily. **Admission** $10; $7 12-17s, concessions; $4 3-11s. **Credit** AmEx, MC, V.
One of few zoos to have koalas, SF Zoo contains a total of more than 1,000 species of mammals and birds. Kids love Lemur Forest, Gorilla World and Wolf Woods, and the petting and egg-gathering at the Family Farm. Recent zoo babies include twin lion cubs, baby penguins and a pair of fishing cats.

California Academy of Sciences
875 Howard Street, between Fourth & Fifth Streets, SoMa (750 7145/www.calacademy.org). BART Powell or Montgomery/Muni Metro F, J, K, L, M, N/bus 9, 15, 30, 45, 76. **Open** 10am-5pm daily. **Admission** $7; $4.50 12-17s, students, seniors; $2 4-11s; free under-4s. Free 1st Wed of mth. **Map** p311/15 H4.
The Academy, along with its impressive Steinhart Aquarium, has shut its Golden Gate Park location for total renovation. Its temporary premises will be in operation until 2008, when the new academy opens in the park. This temporary venue is smaller than the original site, but it stocks an impressive 5,000 live animals, from ants to penguins, fish and frogs.

Circus

San Francisco is right on the cutting edge of 'new circus', taking the traditional three-ring circus and adding elements of dance, theatre and comedy. In the Haight-Ashbury you'll find the **Circus Center** (755 Frederick Street, at Arguello Boulevard, 759 8123, www.circus center.org), which offers courses in Chinese acrobatics, clowning and on the flying trapeze, as well as performances. Most classes last several weeks; call for details. Also in the

Arts & Entertainment

Haight, **Acrosports** (639 Frederick Street, at Willard Street, 665 2276, www.acrosports.com) offers all sorts of gymnastics, tumbling and circus classes for children as young as two. It's home to the **Acrosports Performance Troupe** (242 1414), a kids-only outfit that performs throughout California.

Libraries & museums

San Francisco's gorgeous **Main Library** (see p68) boasts half a floor just for children, with a storytelling room, a creative centre for crafts and performances, and a teenagers' drop-in section. Many local libraries also offer **story hours** – multilingual branches in the Mission (300 Bartlett Street, between Mission and Valencia Streets, 355 2800) and Chinatown (1135 Powell Street, near Jackson Street, 355 2888) are especially recommended.

Museums of equal interest to kids and grown-ups include the **Cable Car Museum** (see p84), **National Maritime Museum** (see p81) and **Musée Mécanique** (see p81).

826 Valencia

826 Valencia Street, between 19th & 20th Streets, Mission (642 5905/www.826valencia.org). BART 16th Street/bus 14, 26, 49. **Open** *Drop-in tutoring 3-6pm Mon-Thur, Sun. Pirate store noon-7pm Tue-Sun.* **Admission** free. **Map** p314 F7.
Literary lion Dave Eggers opened this non-profit kids' writing centre in 2002. In addition to tutoring young authors and hosting events and classes, 826 is the Bay Area's only independent pirate supply store. There's even a fish auditorium in which a handful of guests can sit to watch Karl the Fish.

Exploratorium

3601 Lyon Street, at Marina Boulevard, Marina (563 7337/www.exploratorium.edu). Bus 22, 28, 30, 41, 43, 45, 76. **Open** 10am-5pm Tue-Sun. **Admission** $12; $9.50 13-17s, concessions; $8 4-12s; free under-4s. Free 1st Wed of mth. **Credit** AmEx, MC, V. **Map** p309 C2.
This museum is designed to be touched. There are more than 700 hands-on experiments based around perception, weather, botany, mechanics, health and the physics of sound and light. A favourite attraction is the Tactile Dome, a geodesic hemisphere of total blackness in which you fumble around trying to identify different objects; you must book in advance (561 0362), but the $15 admission is truly worth it. The Exploratorium is also parent of the Wave Organ (see p197 **Walk 5: Dip a toe in the Marina**).

Zeum

221 Fourth Street, at Howard Street, SoMa (777 2800/www.zeum.org). BART Powell or Montgomery/Muni Metro F, J, K, L, M, N/bus 9, 15, 30, 45, 76. **Open** 11am-5pm Wed-Sun. **Admission** $7; $6 concessions; $5 4-18s. **Credit** AmEx, MC, V. **Map** p311/15 H4.

The city's newest art and technology centre is aimed at 8-18s, which means the kids love it and parents get a headache. Exhibits are interactive: kids direct their own video productions, create sculptures or experiment with computer-aided animation design. Nearby is a bowling alley (with gutter bumpers, so that no one strikes out), a garden, a labyrinth, ice skating and a lovely carousel.

Outdoors

San Francisco is blessed with wonderful parks (see p198 **On the cheap: Out for nowt**), but for a wilder walk try **Ocean Beach** (see p103 **Beaches: City sands**). Warm up with a hot chocolate in the **Cliff House** and watch sea lions on Seal Rocks below, then visit the **Camera Obscura** (for both, see p107). You'll also find sea lions at nearby Point Lobos.

Child-friendly attractions near **Fisherman's Wharf** (see p80) include the historic ships at Hyde Street Pier and, at Pier 45, the relocated Musée Mécanique (see p81), the submarine USS Pampanito (see p81) and the Jeremiah O'Brien (see below). It is also the departure point for trips to **Alcatraz Island** (see p80) and **Angel Island** (see p81). Organised outings include the **Fire Engine Tour** (see p54).

Jeremiah O'Brien Liberty Ship

Pier 45, Embarcadero, at Taylor Street, Fisherman's Wharf (544 0100/www.ssjeremiahobrien.com). Muni Metro F/bus 10, 15, 39, 47/cable car Powell-Hyde. **Open** 9am-5pm daily. **Admission** $7; $5 concessions; $4 6-14s; free under-6s. **No credit cards**. **Map** p310 F1.
Kids can explore the faithfully restored ship's engine room and officers' bunk rooms, and operate the foghorn. The ship occasionally leaves the dock for cruises or events, so call ahead to be sure it's there.

East Bay & beyond

Bay Area Discovery Museum

557 McReynolds Road, East Fort Baker, Sausalito (339 3900/www.baykidsmuseum.org). **Open** 9am-4pm Tue-Fri; 10am-5pm Sat, Sun. **Admission** $7; free under-1s. Free 2nd Sat of mth after 1pm. **No credit cards**.
These army barracks have been imaginatively transformed into a place for kids aged up to ten. The newly remodelled facilities are nestled beneath the north tower of the Golden Gate Bridge and feature a theatre and expanded Tot Spot, with an outdoor play area due to open in summer 2004. The main hall has rotating interactive exhibits, and the museum hosts events like storytelling and the singing Miss Kitty. There's also an art room and pleasant café.

Chabot Space & Science Museum

10000 Skyline Boulevard, Joaquin Miller Park, Oakland (1-510 336 7300/www.chabotspace.org).

Walk 5 Dip a toe in the Marina

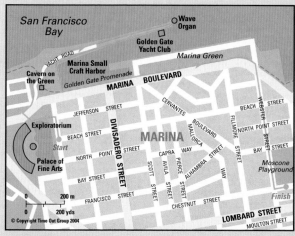

San Francisco Bay

Wave Organ

Golden Gate Yacht Club

Marina Green

Marina Small Craft Harbor

YACHT ROAD

Cavern on the Green

Golden Gate Promenade

MARINA BOULEVARD

CERVANTES

JEFFERSON STREET

DIVISADERO STREET

BEACH STREET

WEBSTER STREET

NORTH POINT STREET

FILLMORE STREET

BAY STREET

BOULEVARD

MALLORCA

Exploratorium

BEACH STREET

MARINA

Start

NORTH POINT STREET

CAPRA WAY

ALHAMBRA STREET

WAY

Moscone Playground

Palace of Fine Arts

BAY STREET

SCOTT STREET

AVILA STREET

PIERCE STREET

0   200 m

FRANCISCO STREET

CHESTNUT STREET

Finish

0   200 yds

LOMBARD STREET

© Copyright Time Out Group 2004

MOULTON STREET

The Marina's bars, bistros and shops are full of urban preppies in designer duds (dashing young mayor Gavin Newsom, who lives next door in Pacific Heights, is the area's darling) but there are great activities here for the kids.

Start on Beach Street, at the intersection with Baker Street. You're at the **Palace of Fine Arts** (*see p100*). The colonnade of this grand Beaux Arts rotunda is adorned with sculpted male torsos and melancholy female figures, but the lagoon facing the Palace will be of more interest to the offspring. There are ducks and elegant swans, though the kids often prefer to feed the scavenging pigeons.

Wander around the lagoon, towards the **Exploratorium** (*see p196*), San Francisco's quirky science museum. Here hungry brains can learn all about static electricity, Tesla coils and sound waves. With all the brouhaha about the red planet, Mars will be a big topic at the museum in the near future.

After leaving the museum, cross Marina Boulevard towards the Bay – be cautious, traffic headed east from the Golden Gate Bridge can be fast and furious. Keep walking straight ahead past **Crissy Field** – which quite often hosts events for kids (561 4778 for up to date information) – and along to the small boat harbour. You'll pass the **Cavern on the Green** – a play on the famous Tavern on the Green in New York's Central Park – which has great snacks and extremely friendly service.

Keep going to the end of the boat harbour, and turn right through a parking lot. Pause to enjoy the spectacular views of the Golden Gate Bridge, Alcatraz Island and Marin County, then (with the Marina Yacht Harbor and the Golden Gate Yacht Club on your right) keep walking to the end of the jetty. The sunken **Wave Organ** is here. Built by artist Peter Richards in 1985 out of granite and marble from a demolished cemetery, this is a 'wave-activated acoustic sculpture'. Sit down on one of the stone benches and listen to the ocean as it sings you a siren song. The waves rush in under the organ, pushing air up through its tubes and resulting in a symphony of eerie tones and sighs.

Once you've had enough of communing with the depths, retrace your steps, but turn left once you reach Marina Boulevard. Walk beside the boat harbour to Marina Green. On any dry and windy day, here you'll be able to see kites of every stripe and trick. If you want to join in, head beforehand to the **Chinatown Kite Shop** (717 Grant Avenue, at Sacramento Street, 989 5182, www.chinatownkite.com) for one of their impressively elaborate butterfly, moth and dragon kites.

If the kids are still ready to go, go, go, turn right on to Webster Street and head over to the **George R Moscone Center** playground at the corner of Chestnut. It was named after the assassinated 1970s city mayor (*see p15*), whose killer Dan White used the infamous 'Twinkie defense' at his trial – claiming he was driven mad by eating too many Twinkie bars. The playground has an Adventure Ship and enough swings to prevent arguments between the kids. Very important if they've been on the Twinkies. **Distance** over 2 miles (3.5km). **Time** 40min.

Arts & Entertainment

On the cheap Out for nowt

For San Francisco's most entertaining free ride, jump in one of the five glass elevators that cling to the outside of the **Westin St Francis Hotel** (335 Powell Street, at Sutter Street, 397 7000). They whoosh you from ground to 32nd floor in less than 30 seconds, at a speed of 1,000 feet (305 metres) per minute. The lift used to run twice as fast, but it was deemed too scary so the engineers slowed it down a notch. The four brass and glass lifts at the **Hyatt Regency San Francisco** (*see p38*) are only half as quick, but they do offer breathtaking views of the hotel's 17-storey atrium. Pick the right one and you'll go the extra three storeys up to the 20th-floor restaurant.

On a beautiful autumn day, nothing beats San Francisco's public parks. **Golden Gate Park** (*see p107*) offers far too many activities to exploit in a single visit, but don't overlook the huge children's playground in Sharon Meadow in the south-east corner of the park. There's a carousel, a tree house, swings and summer Punch and Judy

shows. At Stow Lake you can hire rowing boats and pedalos, while the herd of buffalo in the west of the park, by the golf course, is another big favourite.

Handily for the adults, SoMa's **Yerba Buena Park** (701 Mission Street, between Third and Fourth Streets) is only a few blocks from the hustle and bustle of Market Street and at the centre of the city's biggest concentration of museums, including Zeum (*see p196*). It's also a delightful, calming urban oasis. Kids love ducking under the *Revelations* fountain on the south side of the park.

For that 'only in San Francisco' feeling, visit Pier 39 (*see p80*) where you can see and hear – and smell – the **sea lions** who have taken up residence. There are plenty of street performers too. And while the **cable cars** may be too much for very young children, they don't have to miss out: tiny Cow Hollow Playground (hidden at the end of Miley Street, a half-block alley between Greenwich and Filbert Streets) has a tot-sized replica cable car.

Open 10am-5pm Wed-Thur; 10am-10pm Fri, Sat; noon-5pm Sun. **Admission** $11 (incl admission, plantetarium show & parking); $8 children. *Mega-Dome Theatre* $6; $5 children. *Planetarium* $6; $5 children. **Credit** MC, V.

High in the Oakland Hills, this is the next best thing to space travel. Gaze at the night sky through one of two giant telescopes or experience a total solar eclipse. Kids love waving their hands through the cauldron of billowing fog that makes up 'Planetary Landscapes: Sculpting the Solar System'.

Children's Fairyland

699 Bellevue Avenue, at Lake Merritt, Oakland (1-510 452 2259/www.fairyland.org). BART 19th Street, then short walk down 20th Street. **Open** times vary, call for details. **Admission** $6. **Credit** MC, V.

Legend has it that Walt Disney was so taken with this whimsical theme park when he visited it in 1950 that he decided to build his own. The place recently got a facelift, but retains its unique charm. Kids can follow Alice down the rabbit hole, ride a tiny Ferris wheel and catch daily puppet shows. The pirate ship is open again and there are crooked toddler-sized houses to climb through.

Lawrence Hall of Science

Centennial Drive, near Grizzly Park Boulevard, Berkeley (1-510 642 5132/www.lhs.berkeley.edu). BART Berkeley, then AC Transit 8, 65. **Open** 10am-

5pm daily. **Admission** $7; $5 5-18s, concessions; $3 3-4s; free under-3s. **Credit** Disc, MC, V.

Perched on the hills facing the Bay (a great spot for daytime views and evening star-gazing), this science museum has computers to explore the inside of your brain, a Young Explorers Area and a huge DNA model to scramble over. Don't miss the telescope and the wind-driven organ pipes at the back.

Marine Mammal Center

1065 Fort Cronkhite, Sausalito (289 7325/www. tmmc.org). **Open** 10am-4pm daily. **Admission** free. **Credit** AmEx, Disc, MC, V.

See seals, sea lions, sea otters and even turtles up close at this non-profit centre, which rescues sick or stranded animals, nurtures them back to health and then releases them back into the Pacific. Spring is pupping season, so that's when you'll see the most animals. There's a gift shop (289 7373) at Pier 39.

Oakland Zoo

9777 Golf Links Road, off I-580, Oakland (1-510 632 9525/www.oaklandzoo.org). AC Transit 56, 98. **Open** 10am-4pm daily. **Admission** $8.50; $5 2-14s, concessions; free under-2s. **Credit** AmEx, Disc, MC, V.

There are more than 1,000 species here, most of which are not caged. Kids can visit Bititi, the baby giraffe, and ride the miniature train, a replica Civil War-era locomotive. The old children's zoo is now closed, but will reopen in spring 2005, complete with alligator, bat and lemur discovery areas.

Film

From blockbuster to small-scale independent, film – watching, making and talking about it – is this city's vocation.

Local lore has it that there are more cinema screens and bars per capita in San Francisco than anywhere else in the United States. Fact or fiction (the San Franciscans themselves are too busy drinking and watching films to actually count) this pretty much sums up film culture here. Film is woven into the fabric of the city, from the unique locations for classic films like *Vertigo* or contemporary ones like *The Hulk*, to the multifarious film festivals to the odd places where films are shown (*see p202* **SF alternative: Films**). The city is a breeding ground for film buffs, cinema junkies and amateur critics. Whether you're chatting to a grizzled barfly or an amiable software engineer, you'll be able to enjoy some movie-talk – and to get the flaws in your analysis pointed out to you.

From the city that invented electronic television transmission (Philo T Farnsworth created the current method in 1927, *see p64*), from the region that George Lucas and Francis Ford Coppola call home, you'd expect nothing less than groundbreaking cinema. Most recently the Bay Area has been spearheading the digital film revolution. Lucas's Industrial Light & Magic (ILM) dominates the live-action digital FX industry, Pixar Studios (creators of *Toy Story* and *Finding Nemo*) leads the digital animation field and the creators of *The Matrix* trilogy developed their 'bullet-time' effect using gigantic stages in the recently redeveloped Alameda naval base.

Perhaps as important as the technical innovations has been SF's role in fostering independent filmmakers and auteurs in so-called 'under-represented' communities. The emergence of a Gay and Lesbian film aesthetic and the Asian-American film movement owes much to the Bay Area. Equally important is the area's role as a hotbed of documentary filmmaking: locals have won prizes for such work at Sundance (Terry Zwigoff for *Crumb*) and Academy Awards (Robert Epstein for *The Times of Harvey Milk*, Allie Light and Irving Saraf's *In the Shadow of the Stars*).

Then there are the cinema houses. The beautifully restored **Castro Theatre** (*see p231*) is the exemplar. When the Wurlitzer organ descends into the pit, with the audience cheering as the organist bangs out the last rousing chords to 'San Francisco', and the curtains part to reveal a beautifully restored print of a classic film, you know this is why God created movie houses – and why that surround-sound home cinema will never replace a living and breathing motion picture house.

TICKETS AND INFORMATION

You can usually purchase tickets direct from cinema box offices immediately before a film showing. Most cinemas also run bargain-price matinées: contact the venue direct to check details. Most local newspapers have listings (the *Chronicle, Examiner, SF Weekly* and *Bay Guardian* all have up-to-date information and reviews), but showtimes, locations and tickets are also often available from Moviefone (777 3456, www.moviefone.com); there's a $1 surcharge per ticket. You can also reserve or buy tickets at www.movietickets.com.

Cinemas

Mainstream

San Franciscans used to have more than a dozen grand movie palaces to choose from; now there are only a precious few. Among them are the colossal **United Artists Coronet** (3575 Geary Boulevard, at Arguello Street, 752 4400) in the Richmond District, the **United Artists Metro** (2055 Union Street, at Webster Street, 931 1685) in Cow Hollow and the gorgeous **Castro Theatre** (*see p231*). As elsewhere, the decline of San Francisco's movie palaces was hastened by the coming to power of massive and relentlessly upbeat modern multiplexes: the gleaming escalators and long hallways of **AMC Kabuki 8** (1881 Post Street, at Fillmore Street, 931 9800) in Japantown, the 14-screen **AMC 1000** (1000 Van Ness Avenue, at O'Farrell Street, 922 4262) on the western edge of the Tenderloin, and the 15-screen **Sony Metreon** (Fourth Street, at Mission Street, 369 6200) in SoMa have all the gentle ambience of an airport waiting room. To their credit, the screens are state-of-the-art, the seats high-backed and comfortable, and the sound systems excellent. Kabuki 8 is also the main venue for the **International Film Festival** (*see p203*).

Arts & Entertainment

Other good movie houses within easy reach of the town centre include the Marina's funky **Presidio** (2340 Chestnut Street, at Scott Street, 922 1318) and the **Embarcadero Cinema** (Building 1, Embarcadero Center, Battery Street, between Sacramento and Clay Streets, Financial District), one of four quality movie houses that make up the Landmark Theaters chain (for details of the others, consult www.landmarktheater.com). The Embarcadero even serves popcorn with real butter.

Tickets at all of the cinemas mentioned above cost around $10 and AmEx, MasterCard and Visa cards are accepted.

Repertory

San Francisco's repertory theatres are often an excellent combination of independent ownership and unique buildings: look no further than the **Castro Theatre** (see p231), **Roxie** and **Red Vic** if you want to tick both boxes. A repertory-film scene also thrives across the Bay (see below). The **San Francisco Cinematheque** (see below) is renowned for putting on avant-garde screenings at a variety of venues.

Red Vic

1727 Haight Street, at Cole Street, Haight-Ashbury (668 3994/www.redvicmoviehouse.com). Metro Muni N/bus 7, 33, 37 43, 77. **Tickets** $6.50; $4.50 concessions. **No credit cards. Map** p313 C6.
Old sofas, popcorn in wooden bowls with butter and brewer's yeast, and a choice of films ranging from revivals to the best current movies. You're in your best friend's living room, right? Wrong. This is the worker-owned and -operated Red Vic. Hell, even your ticket money is supporting a good cause.

Roxie & Little Roxie

3117 16th Street, between Valencia & Guererra Streets, Mission (863 1087/www.roxie.com). BART 16th Street/bus 14, 22, 33, 49, 53. **Tickets** $8; $5 concessions. **No credit cards. Map** p314 F6.
World premières of cutting-edge documentaries (Nick Broomfield's *Biggie and Tupac*, say), classic noirs and '60s horror only gesture towards the range of films the Roxie puts on. Better still, an alternative screening space has recently opened up next door. Called, appropriately enough, Little Roxie, it has a state-of-the-art sound system and both film and video projection systems. And it programmes stuff that's even too weird for daddy Roxie.

Experimental

With the opening of the **Little Roxie** (see above) and the **Jewish Community Center** getting a fresh lick of paint, times are good for experimental cinema. Longer established venues include the 278-seat cinema in **SFMOMA** (see p56) and the 96-seat media

screening room in the **Yerba Buena Center for the Arts** (see p247), both of which put on contemporary and experimental work, often themed with current exhibitions. But the **SF Cinematheque** remains the major driving force for innovative film in the city.

Artists' Television Access

992 Valencia Street, at 21st Street, Mission (824 3890/www.atasite.org). BART 24th Street/ bus 14, 26, 48, 49. **Open** 10am-10pm Mon; 3-10pm Thur-Fri; 6-10pm Sat. **Tickets** from $5. **No credit cards. Map** p314 F7.
Experimental and unusual programming, including open screenings, usually from Thursday to Sunday.

Jewish Community Center

3200 California Street, at Presidio Avenue, Laurel Heights (292 1233/www.jccsf.org). Bus 1, 3, 4, 43. **Tickets** from $8. **Credit** AmEx, MC, V. **Map** p311 C4.
This newly remodelled 450-seat theatre will host cutting-edge international Jewish-themed films and videos, as well as the Jewish Film Festival (see p203).

San Francisco Cinematheque

522 1990/www.sfcinematheque.org. **Tickets** $7. **No credit cards.**
The people putting on stuff you can't see anywhere else, be it documentary, feature film, animation or whatever. At the centre of avant-garde film in the Bay Area, the Cinematheque offers programmes twice weekly from late September until July. Venues vary, but include the Yerba Buena Center (see p247) and San Francisco Art Institute (see p203).

East Bay

The East Bay has an embarrassment of cinematic riches. As well as Berkeley's **Fine Arts Cinema** and **Pacific Film Archive**, there are the **Paramount** and **Parkway** in Oakland, the first East Asian megaplex in the US – **Naz8** – and a wealth of film festivals like **Black Filmworks Festival** (see p201).

Naz8 Cinema

39160 Paseo Padre Parkway, in Fremont (information 1-510 797 2000/797 1000/ www.naz8.com). BART Fremont. **Tickets** $8; $5 concessions. **Credit** AmEx, DC, Disc, MC, V.
This Bollywood bonanza was the brainchild of Shiraz Jivani. It's just a short freeway or BART ride from San Francisco (it's directly opposite the BART station) and mainly features first-run movies from India and Pakistan. You can even gorge yourself on samosas or a pistachio kulfi while catching the flick.

Pacific Film Archive

2575 Bancroft Way, at Bowditch Street, Berkeley (1-510 642 1124/www.bampfa. berkeley.edu). BART Berkeley, then AC Transit bus 7, 8, 42, 51, 65. **Tickets** $8; $5 concessions. **Credit** AmEx, Disc, MC, V.

The opulent **Castro Theatre**. See p199.

The PFA, just off the university campus, has a collection of more than 7,000 titles (including Soviet, US avant-garde and Japanese cinema). It screens some 650 of them annually to a dissecting audience.

Paramount Theatre
2025 Broadway, between 20th & 21st Streets, Oakland (1-510 465 6400/www.paramounttheatre. com). BART 19th Street. **Tickets** $6. **Credit** AmEx, Disc, MC, V.

An art deco masterpiece outside and in, the Paramount shows old classics on a Friday night. Like the Castro, it's a National Historic Landmark; also like the Castro it was designed by Pflueger.

Parkway Theater
1834 Park Boulevard, at E 18th Street, Oakland (1-510 814 2400/www.picturepubpizza.com). BART Lake Merritt, then AC Transit bus 14. **Tickets** $3-$6. **No credit cards**.

Two separate screens (one has comfy chairs, the other regulation seats), a dinner menu and a friendly atmosphere are just some of the reasons to hit the Parkway. You can even buy beer. Along with mainstream movies, the cinema hosts the Thrillville (www.thrillville.net) cult movie cabaret, with obscure delights like Chilean horror flicks and Elvis Presley tributes.

Foreign language

As if to prove its Europhile tendencies, the city offers screenings of European films in their original languages: try **Alliance Française** (1345 Bush Street, 775 7755, www.afsf.com) in Polk Gulch, the **Goethe Institut** (530 Bush Street, 263 8760, www.goethe.de/uk/saf/enindex.htm) near Union Square and the **Istituto**

Italiano di Cultura (425 Washington Street, 788 7142, www.sfiic.org) in the Financial District. You'll also want to check out the South American offerings at **Festival ¡Cine Latino!** (*see below*).

Festivals

The Bay Area's love affair with film is amply demonstrated by the range and sheer number of film festivals that take place here, many drawing international stars along with the hardcore and off-beat independents. Local movie-makers feature prominently and the quality varies from extremely high to, erm, challenging. As well as the major fests listed, there are numerous tiny festivals that come and go, plus a number of touring festivals – notably, the New York-based **RESFEST** (1-212 217 1154, www.resfest.com), an international celebration of digital video experiments.

Black Filmworks Festival of Film & Video
1-510 465 0804. **Venues** *Paramount Theatre, Parkway Theater, Laney College, Oakland Museum, all in Oakland.* **Date** late Sept-early Oct.

This ten-day competitive fest features films by, for and about Africans and African-Americans. It has included tributes to US director Spike Lee and the late Marlon Riggs, whose *Tongues Untied* explored the experiences of African-American gay men.

Festival ¡Cine Latino!
553 8135/www.cineaccion.com. **Venues** principally Victoria Theatre, Mission; phone for details. **Date** mid Sept.

Arts & Entertainment

For over a decade Cine Acción has presented this formidable showcase of Latin American cinema, screening the best of recent works from Central and South American filmmakers. With interest in Latin films blossoming, this is a rare opportunity to see the challenging and obscure alongside major works.

Film Arts Festival of Independent Cinema
552 8760/www.filmarts.org. **Venues** Castro Theatre, Castro; Zeum, SoMa; Fine Arts Cinema, Berkeley; and others, phone for details. **Date** early Nov.

SF alternative Films

Sick of the multiplexes? Bored of spending evenings trapped in the darkened theatre? If you're after somewhere fresh to catch a movie, this film-crazed city has the solution. For starters there's the movie restaurant **Foreign Cinema** (*see p134*). If you then spill the soup on your trousers, you can get them cleaned while-u-watch at **Star Wash** (*see p182*) launderette. There's even film for when you're working out. **Gorilla Sports Club** (2330 Polk Street, between Green and Union Streets, Russian Hill, 292 5444, www.gorillasports.com; *pictured*) opened inside the Alhambra Theater, once a shining art deco movie house. Then some visionary at Gorilla Sports realised that they could combine pain and pleasure: a state-of-the-art sports club, with the latest cardio machines, free weights and a dedicated Pilates studio, plus feature films projected on a big screen in the main exercise area.

Of course, life in San Francisco isn't all about eating too much and working it off again. There's nightlife for you too. Every Monday night the funky Red Devil Lounge

(1695 Clay Street, at Polk Street, Polk Gulch, 921 1695, 648 7600) plays host to a short-film minifest known as **ViV and a Movie** (www.vivandamovie.com, admission $10). ViV, the local alt-rock band behind the evening, open the night with a set at 7pm. Then the audience is treated to several short films and videos, before ViV wind up proceedings with another set. More mysterious is the **Werepad** (2430 Third Street, between 20th and 22nd Streets, Potrero Hill, information 824 7334, www.werepad.com, admission $8), tucked away in an industrial area at the base of Potrero Hill. If you didn't know what you were looking for, you'd never find the place, but the innocuous wooden door leads into a cosy, padded bar, rigged up with '50s and '60s accoutrements (think Tiki plus lava lamps) and a DJ booth. On a Friday and Saturday night, the hosts – dressed, like many of their patrons, in period costume – unleash delights from their huge cache of exploitation flicks and B-movies. Big-screen trash projected from low-tech 16mm prints? Celluloid wonderland.

The essential festival for a real snapshot of Northern Californian independents. All programming for the six-day fest is drawn from Bay Area filmmakers, featuring documentary, experimental and traditional narrative pieces in formats that range from Super-8 shorts to high-end DV.

Jewish Film Festival

621 0556/www.sfjff.org. **Venues** Castro Theatre, Castro; Wheeler Auditorium, Berkeley; Fox Theatre, Redwood City; Jewish Community Center, Laurel Heights. **Date** late July-early Aug.

Now the world's largest Jewish film fest, the SFJFF spends two weeks presenting contemporary (and some archival) films celebrating Jewish culture.

MadCat Women's International Film Festival

436 9523/www.madcatfilmfestival.org. **Venues** vary; phone for details. **Date** Sept.

The radical, alternative women's film festival, MadCat happens over three weeks. It's tiny, but squeezes in pioneering films that range from earnest feminist polemics to raunchy sexploitation.

Mill Valley Film Festival & Videofest

383 5256/www.finc.org. **Venues** Cine Arts Sequoia, Mill Valley; Rafael Film Center, San Rafael. **Date** early Oct.

One of the state's best-known and most influential film events, with local celebs practically able to walk from their home to a film première. Dozens of new American films and international indies are screened over the ten days. There's also a six-day Videofest, special events and various children's programmes.

San Francisco International Asian American Film Festival

863 0814/www.naatanet.org/festival. **Venues** Kabuki 8 Cinema, Japantown; Pacific Film Archive, Berkeley. **Date** mid Mar.

One of the longest running (over 20 years) and most prestigious Asian-American filmmaking showcases in the US, this fest provides a meeting ground for ethnic communities of all types (Filipino-Americans, Pakistani-Americans, Cambodian-Americans…), bringing in films from across the globe, premièring important local talent and showcasing work by the new generation of Asian-American makers, including Justin Lim and Gene Cajyon.

San Francisco International Film Festival

931 3456/www.sfiff.org. **Venues** Kabuki 8, Japantown; Castro Theatre, PFA; and others. **Date** mid Apr-early May.

Produced by the San Francisco Film Society, this nearly 50-year-old festival is North America's longest-running and considered one of its best. Over a few weeks, more than 200 films and videos are screened, and it's sure to find a clunker in the bunch. Glitterati attend (Wim Wenders, Clint Eastwood and Wayne Wang have all showed up in recent years) and more than 80,000 tickets sell like hot starlets.

San Francisco International Lesbian & Gay Film Festival

703 8650/www.frameline.org. **Venues** Castro Theatre, Castro; Victoria Theatre & Roxie, Mission; and others. **Date** late June.

This two-week festival is a crucial part of the month-long Gay Pride celebration, as well as the world's oldest and largest event of its kind – it has been running for 28 years. It is both a potent political statement and an unbridled celebration, comprising mainstream queer features alongside independent shorts, experimental works and documentaries. Programmes are available a month in advance from bookshops and cafés or in the San Francisco *Bay Guardian*.

San Francisco Silent Film Festival

777 4908/www.silentfilm.org. **Venue** Castro Theatre, Castro. **Date** early July.

This two-day festival focuses exclusively on lost silent-era masterpieces. Most performances are accompanied by the Castro's wonderful organist, but one film at least is always accompanied by more unusual orchestration – an Indian duo, Mexican folk music or perhaps an avant-garde orchestral group.

Spike & Mike's Festival of Animation

1-800 457 7453/www.spikeandmike.com. **Venues** Victoria Theatre, Mission; Castro Theatre, Castro; Palace of Fine Arts, Presidio; and East Bay cinemas. **Date** late Apr-early May; Oct-Dec.

Part of Bay Area film culture for years, Spike & Mike's showcases the very best animated shorts. Mainstream animators (among them Oscar-winners Nick Park and Pixar's John Lasseter) have shown early works at the festival, but it's the 'Sick and Twisted' segment that really raises the bar: rude, raucous and cutting edge. (It gave *Beavis and Butthead* their debut. Enough said.)

Schools & classes

San Francisco State University, **UC Berkeley**, the **San Francisco Art Institute** and **City College** (for all, *see p288*) have thriving film study or filmmaking programmes, each encouraging and developing new and established film and video artists. In addition, two San Francisco institutions – both the **Film Arts Foundation** (145 Ninth Street, Suite 101, at Mission Street, 552 8760, www.filmarts.org) and the **Bay Area Video Coalition** (861 3282, www.bavc.org) – provide services and continuing education and networking for filmmakers and videographers in the area. For Bay Area film casting and production details, contact the **San Francisco Film Commission** (554 6244, www.ci.sf.ca.us/film).

Arts & Entertainment

Galleries

San Francisco's art scene celebrates the brave, the political and the new.

SoMarts Gallery.
See p205.

Art-world heavy hitters like New York and Los Angeles may look down on San Francisco, but the city boasts a rich and provocative scene. Given the small size of the city, San Francisco's galleries pack a mighty punch, with radical politics, breathtaking locations and an edgy sensibility fusing into an exhilarating whole. The city authorities do their bit to help, championing home-grown artists through a host of non-profit, community-oriented spaces and running one of the country's most progressive public arts programmes. Works by emerging local and international artists are to be found all over the city (*see p207* **On the cheap: Public art**).

Ever since the dot-coms went belly up, local arts have found more stable ground. Rents are no longer outrageous, which means galleries and artists are no longer being pushed out to the edges of the city. Most commercial galleries are clustered within a few blocks of **Union Square** – some stacked within single buildings like a club sandwich – although cutting-edge work is primarily found in **SoMa** and the **Mission** areas. One of the best ways to sample the full range of local artists' work is during the **ArtSpan Open Studios** weekends that run throughout

October (they're based in SoMarts Gallery, *see p205*; for details, *see p192*). Otherwise **First Thursdays** run throughout the year, with many galleries scheduling openings or opening late on the first Thursday of each month, plying visitors with wine and cheese. In July new work by emerging artists can be viewed on the **Introductions and Summer Art Walk**, presented by the San Francisco Art Dealers Association (278 9818, www.sfada. com), a non-profit organisation comprising 35 Bay Area galleries.

The city's three major art schools are worth a visit too: the **San Francisco Art Institute** in North Beach; the **Academy of Art College**, with campuses in SoMa and on Nob Hill; and the **California College of the Arts** (CCA), formerly known as the California College of Arts and Crafts, with campuses on Potrero Hill and in Oakland – each offering student and faculty shows as well as independently curated exhibitions. CCA's **Wattis Institute for Contemporary Arts** consistently exhibits the best contemporary artists, including Wolfgang Tillmans, Steve McQueen and Paul McCarthy. **San Francisco State University** (out by Lake Merced) has also opened a new gallery. For contact details, *see p288*.

INFORMATION

Pick up a copy of either the bi-monthly *San Francisco Bay Area Gallery Guide* or the monthly *Art Now Gallery Guide – West Coast*, available in galleries all over town. Both are handy for addresses and details of individual shows or special events. *San Francisco Arts Monthly* (www.sfarts.org) has a more complete calendar of monthly exhibitions, as well as music, dance and theatre listings. Copies can be found in bookshops, hotels and museums. Admission is free to all galleries listed below.

Non-profit galleries

Don't miss the fabulous gallery at the **Intersection for the Arts** (*see p246*) – this gallery/performance space is at the centre of the burgeoning arts community centred around Mission and 16th Streets.

Galeria de la Raza/Studio 24

2857 24th Street, at Bryant Street, Mission (826 8009/www.galeriadelaraza.org). BART 24th Street/bus 9, 27, 33, 48. **Open** noon-6pm Wed-Sat. **Credit** MC, V. **Map** p314 G7.

Since 1970 this tiny shopfront gallery has celebrated contemporary Mexican-American culture with bi-monthly exhibits and the ongoing (Re)generation project. The diversity of talent on display is superb, as is its archive of protest and political art.

The Lab

2948 16th Street, between Mission Street & S Van Ness Avenue, Mission (864 8855/www.thelab.org). BART 16th Street/bus 14, 22, 26, 33, 49. **Open** 1-6pm Wed, Fri, Sat; 1-7pm Thur. **No credit cards**. **Map** p314 F6.

A ground-floor space on a slightly seedy corner, the Lab favours political, subversive and controversial punk photography, painting and multimedia works. It holds art auctions several times a year, and can always be counted on for edgy pieces at decent prices. Of particular interest are the CAMP collective's murals in the stairwells and mezzanine level corridors, depicting various moments in San Francisco's riotous history.

The Luggage Store

1007 Market Street, near Sixth Street, Tenderloin (255 5971/www.luggagestoregallery.org). BART Powell Street/Muni Metro F, J, K, L, M, N/bus 6, 7, 9, 71. **Open** noon-5pm Wed-Sat. **Credit** MC, V. **Map** p310/14 G4.

Luggage is one of the city's original grassroots galleries. In addition to shows of modern and minimalist works by local artists maintaining the gallery's links with the *arte povera* tradition, Luggage develops public murals and street festivals. There are open-mic readings (Tues, 8pm) and a satellite space at 509 Ellis Street offers art classes, street photography workshops and internships for neighbourhood youth. After hours, murals by graphic artists Barry McGee

and Margaret Kilgallen are visible on the roll-down security doors next to the gallery entrance (*see p207* **On the cheap: Public art**). The Tenderloin location can be a little dodgy.

New Langton Arts

1246 Folsom Street, between Eighth & Ninth Streets, SoMa (626 5416/www.newlangtonarts.org). Bus 12, 19, 27. **Open** noon-5pm Tue-Sat. **Credit** MC, V. **Map** p314 G5.

At the forefront of the alternative arts scene, this diminutive gallery, located in a first-floor loft behind an unprepossessing black façade, is best known for installations and performance pieces. It shares its space with artist-run San Francisco Camerawork.

San Francisco Art Commission Gallery

Veterans' Memorial Building, 401 Van Ness Avenue, at McAllister Street, Civic Center (554 6080/www.sfacgallery.org). Muni Metro F, J, K, L, M, N/ bus 5, 21, 42, 47, 49. **Open** by appointment only Tue; 11am-5.30pm Wed-Sat. **No credit cards**. **Map** p314 F4.

This tidy space draws from local and national artists, and exhibits all kinds of media in many contexts. It also maintains Grove Street Windows (155 Grove Street, between Van Ness & Polk Streets), two blocks from the gallery, where you can watch video projections, soundworks and other site-specific installations through shopfront windows. City Site, a third exhibition programme in a vacant lot next door, is temporarily inactive – which doesn't stop guerrilla artists leaving occasional 'plop art' there.

SoMarts Gallery

934 Brannan Street, between Eighth & Ninth Streets, SoMa (552 2131/www.somarts.org). Bus 19, 27, 42. **Open** noon-4pm Tue-Sat. **No credit cards**. **Map** p314 G5.

Tucked under the freeway near the city's popular design and flower marts, this gallery is easy to miss. But it's one of the city's greatest and longest-lived alternative art spaces: a cavern-like series of rooms in an ancient warehouse. Besides being headquarters for ArtSpan, which runs the ever-popular Open Studios (*see p192*), SoMarts hosts its own group and solo shows, as well as live music. It's also home for Kearny Street Workshop (503 0520), the oldest Asian-American arts organisation in the country.

Southern Exposure

401 Alabama Street, at 17th Street, Mission (863 2141/www.soex.org). Bus 12, 22, 27, 33, 53. **Open** 11am-5pm Tue-Sat. **Credit** MC, V. **Map** p314 G6.

Much like Intersection for the Arts (*see p246*), Southern Exposure has made its reputation as the place for emerging artists to show – and to be discovered shortly thereafter. But where Intersection is small and focused, SoEx is large and inclusive. SoEx's group shows and parties are legendary, and its juried art shows have drawn nationally respected curators. The city's best non-profit gallery.

Arts & Entertainment

Commercial galleries

Bomani Gallery

296 8677. Muni Metro N/bus 6, 37, 43, 66.
Open by appointment only.
Located in a Victorian house in the Haight-Ashbury, the Bomani (owned by the wife of actor Danny Glover) was one of many galleries forced out of downtown by sky-rocketing rents. Visiting takes an effort (you must call to make an appointment before you're given the address) but it's the only gallery in the city to represent African-American masters alongside emerging artists from the Third World.

Catharine Clark Gallery

49 Geary Street, between Kearny Street & Grant Avenue, Union Square (399 1439/ www.cclarkgallery.com). BART Montgomery/Muni Metro F, J, K, L, M, N/bus 15, 30, 38, 45. **Open** 10.30am-5.30pm Tue-Fri; 11am-5.30pm Sat; 5.30-7.30pm 1st Thur of mth. **Credit** AmEx, MC, V. **Map** p311 H3.
Director Catharine Clark has a keen eye for modern art with legs – many of the works by her sculptors, painters and mixed-media artists walk straight into regional museums. The gallery's three rooms display art ranging from kinetic sculptures to figurative paintings. It's located in the Geary Street 'art mall', along with the Stephen Wirtz (*see below*), Fraenkel (*see p208*) and Robert Koch (*see p208*) galleries.

City Art

828 Valencia Street, at 19th Street, Mission (970 9900/www.cityartgallery.org). Bus 14, 26, 33, 49. **Open** noon-9pm Wed-Sun.
Credit AmEx, MC, V. **Map** p314 F7.
A no-frills, quirky, collective enterprise that's commercial in intent, but has the panache of a non-profit space. Filled floor to ceiling with art by co-op members, who also staff the gallery during the month-long exhibitions, prices are affordable ($100-$500) and there are gems among the odd and sometimes downright awful works – a large part of the gallery's charm.

Crown Point Press

20 Hawthorne Street, between Howard & Folsom Streets, SoMa (974 6273/www.crownpoint.com). BART Montgomery/Muni Metro F, J, K, L, M, N/bus 9, 12, 14, 15, 30, 45, 76. **Open** 10am-6pm Tue-Sat.
Credit MC, V. **Map** p315 H4.
Opened as a print workshop in 1962, the Press invites noted artists (Ed Ruscha and Nathan Oliveira, say – although the gallery's known for selling work by the late Richard Diebenkorn and John Cage) to create editions of prints, exhibited in a large, airy space. The Press also has a summer workshop and sells exquisite artist-made books from the shop Califia (284 0310).

Dolby Chadwick

210 Post Street, Suite 205, at Grant Avenue, Union Square (956 3560/www.dolbychadwickgallery.com). BART Montgomery/Muni Metro F, J, K, L, M, N/ bus 15, 30, 38, 45. **Open** 10am-6pm Tue-Fri; 11am-5pm Sat. **Credit** AmEx, MC, V. **Map** p311 3H.

Don't be intimidated by the creaky ride up in the old lift: it takes you directly into the gallery, which couldn't be friendlier. Tall windows frame a view as compelling as the clean-lined still lifes on the walls. There are paintings, drawings and monotypes by emerging and mid-career artists, many priced at under $1,000. It can be a funky place to hang out too.

Hackett-Freedman Gallery

250 Sutter Street, Suite 400, between Kearny Street & Grant Avenue, Union Square (362 7152/ www.realart.com). BART Montgomery/Muni Metro F, J, K, L, M, N/bus 15, 30, 38, 45. **Open** 10.30am-5.30pm Tue-Fri; 11am-5pm Sat. **No credit cards**.
Map p311 3H.
One of the city's 'art towers' – a building filled with galleries. Hackett-Freedman has a comprehensive stable of artists from the major West Coast schools: Bay Area figurative and realist, California colourist and expressionist works are all represented. With detailed colour catalogues for most shows, it's a one-stop visual art tour of California.

Modernism

685 Market Street, between Third & New Montgomery Streets, Financial District (541 0461/www.artnet.com/modernism.html). BART Montgomery/Muni Metro F, J, K, L, M, N/bus 5, 6, 7, 9, 15, 30, 38, 45, 71. **Open** 10am-5.30pm Tue-Sat. **Credit** AmEx, MC, V. **Map** p311 H3.
This place grapples with the age-old conundrum of how to show fine art that attracts high prices but still maintain hospitable atmosphere. And loses. If you're not rich and conservatively dressed (DKNY rather than Prada), you probably won't feel comfortable here. Which is a great shame, as the art is amazing.

111 Minna Street Gallery

111 Minna Street, at Second Street, SoMa (974 1719/www.111minnagallery.com). BART Montgomery/Muni Metro F, J, K, L, K, M, N/bus 9, 12, 14, 15, 30, 45, 76. **Open** noon-5pm Mon-Fri.
Bar 5pm-late Tue-Sat. **Credit** AmEx, MC, V.
Map p315 H4.
This innovative space is not only a contemporary painting and sculpture gallery, it's also a danceclub (*see p221*). This attempt to make connections between all media seems to be working: locals voted it the city's best gallery in a *Bay Guardian* poll. After an exhibition, stay on for happy hour (Wed, Fri 5-10pm). If you're already inside, you're lucky, because the queue on those nights stretches around the block.

Stephen Wirtz Gallery

49 Geary Street, between Kearny Street & Grant Avenue, Union Square (433 6879/www.wirtzgallery. com). BART Montgomery/Muni Metro F, J, K, L, M, N/bus 15, 30, 38, 45. **Open** 10.30am-5.30pm Tue-Fri; 10.30am-5.30pm Sat; 10.30am-7.30pm 1st Thur of mth. **No credit cards**. **Map** p311 H3.
All is hushed except for the click of expensive heels on polished wooden floors. There's a sophistication and restraint to the work, as well as the atmosphere. The contemporary, conceptual paintings and

On the cheap Public art

Where's the best place to see art in San Francisco? The answer is all around you. The city's well-established public artworks programme – funded by the **San Francisco Arts Commission** (www.sfgov.org/sfac/pubart) and occasionally local and corporate donors – has been around since 1969 and is heralded as one of the best in the US. Now works crop up in the most unexpected places, making the whole city feel like a gallery.

For a glimpse of leading local artists' work, head to **SoMa**. Artist Ricardo Gouveia (popularly known as Rigo) made a huge splash in the '90s with his faux street signs: check out *Innercity-Home* (*pictured*) at Sixth and Folsom and *One Tree* on the corner of Tenth and Bryant Streets. Closer to SFMOMA is Dustin Shuler's famous *Spider Pelt*. The shell of a red 1971 Fiat Spider, flattened against the wall of the Moscone Parking Garage at 255 Third Street, it looks like a beetle pinned in a collector's case. On the corner of Sixth and Howard, you'll find one of the city's most provocative public works: Brian Goggin's massive *Defenestration*. With furniture and home appliances dangling from the exposed sides of an empty building, this is art that's impossible to miss.

More great public art exists along **Market Street**. Celebrated local artist Barry McGee became a household name with his

melancholy, graffiti-inspired murals. One of the most popular is best viewed at night at New Step Fashion (No.1009): it's on its roll-down security door. As is the late Margaret Kilgallen's infamous tree mural, although this time the door belongs to the Luggage Store (*see p205*) gallery. Rigo's most political work is in Civic Center Plaza: his street sign *Truth* sits directly opposite City Hall.

Also in the Civic Center (outside the Davies Symphony Hall, *see p210*) is Henry Moore's strikingly sensual *Reclining Figure in Four Pieces*, just one of many pieces in the city by established international artists. In **Lincoln Park** (along El Camino del Mar) you'll find George Segal's potent and emotive *Holocaust Memorial*, while the **Embarcadero** boasts Claes Oldenburg and Coosje Van Bruggen's huge *Cupid's Span*, which frames the Bay Bridge and the waterfront beyond it. Nearby, at 199 Fremont Street, the artist Paul Kos joined poet Robert Hass to create a beautiful, restful and intellectually charged sculpture garden.

Not even the **airport** is spared the city's love of public art. Inside the new international terminal there's a literal maze of works by leading contemporary artists, among them Ann Preston, Vito Acconci, Lewis deSoto and Ned Kahn. The perfect welcome to San Francisco.

Arts & Entertainment

sculpture here prompt discussion, and launch young artists to major shows. This is where you come to watch the present unfold.

Gallery Paule Anglim

14 Geary Street, at Market Street, Union Square (433 2710/www.gellerypauleanglim.com). BART Montgomery/Metro Muni F, J, K, L, M, N/bus 9, 38. **Open** 10am-5.30pm Tue-Fri; 10am-5pm Sat. **No credit cards. Map** p311 H3.

The unimpressive exterior of this gallery gives no indication of its light-filled, airy interior, designed to accommodate two shows at once, one major and one minor; expect artists ranging from Bay Area legends David Ireland and Barry McGee to international superstars like Louise Bourgeois and Philip Guston.

Linc Real Art

1632-C Market Street, at Rose Street, between Franklin & Gough Streets, Hayes/Castro (503 1981/www. lincart.com). Muni Metro F/bus 6, 7, 9, 26, 66, 71. **Open** noon-6pm Wed-Sun. **Credit** AmEx, MC, V. **Map** p314 F5.

Intimate and warm, this new gallery has quickly made a name for itself, showcasing playful works by young and emerging artists. It hosts events and art classes, and is also one of the few places where you'll find inexpensive, rare art books.

Steel Gallery

3524 Sacramento Street, between Laurel & Locust Streets, Presidio Heights (885 1655/ www.steelgalleryinc.com). Bus 1, 3, 4. **Open** 10am-6pm Tue-Sat. **Credit** MC, V. **Map** p309 C4.

The queen of the romance novel, Danielle Steel, opened her own gallery in 2003. An avid collector, she mainly exhibits her own favourite artists: Wendy Robushi, Sofia Harrison and so on. The gallery's mission statement ('to assemble a collection of bright, exciting, well thought out pieces… that bring… joy, happiness, and are fun to live with') may set your teeth on edge, but the shows are often impressive.

Photography galleries

San Francisco Camerawork (863 1001, www.sfcamerawork.org) exhibitions are shown at New Langton Arts (*see p205*).

Fraenkel Gallery

49 Geary Street, between Kearny Street & Grant Avenue, Union Square (981 2661/ www.fraenkelgallery.com). BART Montgomery/Muni Metro F, J, K, L, M, N/bus 15, 30, 38, 45. **Open** 10.30am-5.30pm Tue-Fri; 10.30am-7.30pm 1st Thur of mth; 11am-5pm Sat. **Credit** MC, V. **Map** p311 H3.

Well known for showing major 20th-century photographers, the curators here use photography as a nexus of interchange between media, showing sculpture or film alongside the works on paper.

Robert Koch Gallery

49 Geary Street, 5th floor, between Kearny Street & Grant Avenue, Union Square (421 0122/ www.kochgallery.com). BART Montgomery/Muni Metro F, J, K, L, M, N/bus 15, 30, 38, 45. **Open** 10.30am-5.30pm Tue-Sat; 10.30am-5.30pm 1st Thur of mth. **Credit** MC, V. **Map** p311 H3.

This reliable, established gallery favours works with an environmental edge, alongside more experimental pieces and a good selection of 19th-century artists.

Shapiro Gallery

760 Market Street, Suite 248, at Grant Avenue, Union Square (398 6655/www.shapirogallery.net). BART Powell/Muni Metro F, J, K, L, M, N/bus 15, 30, 38, 45. **Open** 11am-5.30pm Tue-Fri; 11am-5pm Sat; 10.30am-7.30pm 1st Thur of mth. **Credit** MC, V. **Map** p311 H3.

This refined gallery deals primarily in 20th-century black-and-whites, along with vintage pieces. Shapiro is in an art mall, just near tribal art dealer Gallery de Roche (989 0300, www.galleryderoche.com) and the quirky Quotidian Gallery (788 0445, www.quotidian-gallery.com), which represents emerging local artists.

Art for artists' sake

Each year, in the grey parking lot of **SoMarts Gallery** (*see p205*), the city's art lovers gather to camp out on the concrete for a night. This is no collective work of performance art: they're here to bag first place in the queue for the **Big Deal** charity art fair, a unique opportunity to snap up work by top names from the San Francisco (and national and international) art world for a paltry $110 apiece. Plus tax.

It's staged by **Visual Aid** (777 8242, www.visualaid.org), a non-profit organisation founded in 1989 by a group of San Francisco artists, collectors and art dealers to support and promote Bay Area artists with life-threatening illnesses. Initially a response to the HIV/AIDS epidemic, it's now helped more than 250 such artists to continue work.

A decade old, the Big Deal is more like a party than an auction. Keeping your place in the queue is a serious matter, though. Some 600 works are sold on a first-come, first-served basis and it's your queue ticket that gives you priority when buying. When the doors open there's an hour's viewing time, then prospective buyers are called, one by one, to the sales desk. Then, if you're still feeling flush, there's a 'silent' auction – those who enter remain anonymous – of 12 major works, sold to the highest bidder.

Music

Tuned in and turned on, San Francisco's vibrant and hybrid music scene keeps right on growing.

San Francisco's famous liberalism extends to the city's freestyle musical tastes. Genres, scenes and even media seem to cross-pollinate and hyperlink faster and faster with each passing year. In the world of popular (for want of a better term) music, an active underground of young musicians and show organisers continues to flourish. While the high-tech boom and subsequent bust left its mark on the city and its music – reducing the number of rehearsal spaces available to struggling musicians and darkening many venues – some of those who came for the dot-com gold rush stayed on after the pink slip parties and now pour their energies into the arts and culture. Others washed up here after art school – recently, many seem to have ties with the Rhode Island School of Design – and work in sound as well as visual media. The results have been a surge in wild DIY house parties and homegrown music festivals (the Mission Creek Music Festival, Budget Rock Showcase and Bay Pop among them), with local bands eschewing the stage in favour of in-your-face, ground-level pranksterism (*see p216* **SF alternative: Gigs**).

San Francisco's classical music and opera scene is no less eclectic and forward thinking. The city has major symphony and professional opera companies, but also numerous smaller avant-garde outfits performing everything from early music to multimedia contemporary compositions. Venues are similarly varied: you'll be able to catch a recital or peformance in everything from the grand Opera House to one of the many churches and theatres.

Musicians may complain that Bay Area residents just don't go out to hear music as much as they used to – perhaps a result of higher rents and escalating real-estate prices forcing the more culturally active locals out of the city and leaving an older, more affluent and less curious population in SF proper. But whatever the truth of the matter, the current situation in San Francisco gives music lovers a great deal of hope. Only New York and Los Angeles attract more bands, few cities can boast visits by so many famous classical musicians and, perhaps most importantly, good public transport and the relatively small size of the city make it simple to get to pretty

much any event you fancy. You can hear great live music somewhere different every night of the week. Several times over.

If you're after ballet or modern dance, *see chapter* **Theatre & Dance**; if you fancy a jig yourself, *see chapter* **Nightlife**.

INFORMATION
The best overall sources of information are the *San Francisco Bay Guardian* (www.sfbg.com) and *SF Weekly* (www.sfweekly.com), both of which have extensive listings of live music. You can also try www.sfgate.com, website of the *San Francisco Chronicle*, or www.sfstation.com for background listings of events and venues.

TICKETS AND ADMISSION
Where possible, buy tickets from the box office of the venue itself (most of which accept credit cards). That way you avoid paying the surcharge levied by Ticketmaster (421 8497, www.ticketmaster.com). Ticket prices usually range from free to $25.

The best Live music

Bottom of the Hill
The top for rock. See p218.

Fillmore Auditorium
Historic shrine to the San Francisco sound. See p218.

Great American Music Hall
A gorgeous Barbary Coast-era bordello: dramatic mirrors and great stage views. See p216.

Hemlock Tavern
Unpretentious style and sounds from the edge – and a fabulous jukebox. See p216.

War Memorial Opera House
Catch the SF Opera here: sublime singing in a beautiful venue. See p211.

Yoshi's at Jack London Square
The best jazz on the Bay. Go see. See p213.

Arts & Entertainment

LATE-NIGHT TRANSPORT

The Muni Owl Service operates on the Muni Metro L and N lines and on the 5, 14, 22, 24, 38, 90, 91 and 108 bus lines from 1am until 5am. All other lines stop at 12.30am. BART runs roughly until midnight, although it's always best to check the time of the last train. For a list of taxi companies, *see p277*.

Classical & Opera

The **San Francisco Symphony** (864 6000, www.sfsymphony.org) is the oldest performing arts group in the city. Formed shortly after the 1906 earthquake and fire to boost public morale, it performed its first concert in 1911. Today, under the direction of Michael Tilson Thomas, the Symphony is internationally recognised for its innovative work. The **San Francisco Opera** (864 3330, www.sfopera.com), inaugurated in 1923, is renowned for its world premières of major operas. Both groups perform in the Civic Center neighbourhood. Meanwhile, **SF Performances** (398 6449, www.performances.org), directed by founder Ruth Felt, puts on a programme of over 200 performances annually – most of them at the Herbst Theatre (*see p244*) and the Yerba Buena Performing Arts Theater (*see p211*) – featuring a blend of chamber music, vocal and instrumental recitals and jazz. Another big name is the **Philharmonia Baroque** (252 1288, www.philharmonia.org), which enjoys nationwide fame and performs with medieval European instruments.

Of the more diminutive groups, the 16-member, conductorless **New Century Chamber Orchestra** (357 1111, www.ncco. org) brings an immediacy to the classics that is hard to find in larger ensembles – it regularly plays at the Herbst Theatre. Also watch out for the **Pocket Opera** (972 8930, www.pocket opera.org), a professional group that presents operatic works in English in intimate settings,

with an emphasis on accessibility. The company performs most often at the Florence Gould Theater in the Palace of the Legion of Honor (*see p106*).

The widely respected **Kronos Quartet** (731 3533, www.kronosquartet.org), founded in 1973, is dedicated to experimentation, focusing exclusively on new music, most of which is specially composed for the group. Also well reputed and now in its 26th season, Grammy Award-winning **Chanticleer** (252 8589, www.chanticleer.org) bills itself as an orchestra of voices. This all-male, 12-member a cappella group performs an eclectic variety of vocal music. Its traditional Christmas programme is superb: four concerts every December, two at St Ignatius (650 Parker Avenue, at Fulton Street) and two elsewhere in the Bay Area. Both Kronos and Chanticleer are often away touring the world, so make a point of seeing them if they're playing on home soil.

The gentler side of classical music is represented by **Lamplighters Musical Theater** (227 4797, www.lamplighters.org). One of the oldest theatre companies in San Francisco, Lamplighters is best known for its award-winning productions of Gilbert and Sullivan operettas, but has cemented a considerable following with contemporary musical comedies from Sondheim to Lerner and Loewe. The company's annual gala, usually staged in the autumn or winter, is a G&S-style satire on local issues. The company performs at the Yerba Buena Theater, the Herbst Theatre and at the Dean Lesher Regional Center for the Arts (1-925 943 7469) in Walnut Creek.

Downtown & SoMa

Louise M Davies Symphony Hall

201 Van Ness Avenue, at Hayes Street, Civic Center (864 6000/www.sfsymphony.org). BART Civic Center/Muni Metro F, J, K, L, M, N/bus 21, 42, 47, 49. **Tickets** $15-$88. **Credit** MC, V. **Map** p314 F5.

Real contemporary

Had enough of Beethoven and Bach? Then check out the 33-year-old **San Francisco Contemporary Music Players** (252 6235, www.sfcmp.org) for a jolt of pure musical energy. The SFCMP continue to push the boundaries of new music, commissioning new works from both young and established composers. The chamber group has built its much-deserved good reputation supporting the work of John

Adams and John Cage, experimenting with mixed media, collaborating with **Chanticleer** (*see above*) and other local groups, and generally infusing a major dose of creativity into San Francisco's classical music scene. Though the ensemble tours widely, each year it presents a series at Yerba Buena Performing Arts Theater (*see p211*). From music students to hip octogenarians, Bay Area music lovers attend in numbers.

Simply known as 'the Davies', this striking multi-tiered, curved glass edifice is home to the San Francisco Symphony. Opened in 1980 and later renovated, the hall is famous for nearly flawless acoustics and clear sightlines. It's said there isn't a bad seat in the house – even in the 'rush' section behind the orchestra; these are the least expensive seats ($15-$20) and go on sale a couple of hours before certain performances, first-come first-served.

War Memorial Opera House

301 Van Ness Avenue, at Grove Street, Civic Center (864 3330/www.sfopera.com). BART Civic Center/ Muni Metro F, J, K, L, M, N/bus 21, 42, 47, 49. **Tickets** $25-$165. **Credit** AmEx, MC, V. **Map** p314 F5.

This grand Beaux Arts building, designed by Arthur Brown Jr (also the architect of nearby City Hall), was built in 1932 as a memorial to the soldiers who fought in World War I. The 3,176-seat auditorium is modelled on European opera houses, with a vaulted ceiling, a huge silver art deco chandelier and a marble foyer. In 1997 an $84.5-million revamp not only restored the elegant building, but installed up-to-date electronics and stage gear. The San Francisco Opera (*see p210*) is the main draw (its season runs from early September to January, with a June summer season), but the San Francisco Ballet (*see p248*) is also outstanding.

Yerba Buena Performing Arts Theater

701 Mission Street, at Third Street, SoMa (978 2787/www.yerbabuenaarts.com). **Ticket** prices vary according to event; call for details. **Credit** AmEx, DC, MC, V. **Map** p311 H4.

Part of the innovative ten-year-old Yerba Buena Center for the Arts, this 757-seat auditorium plays host to some of the most exciting contemporary music and dance companies in the country, including Kronos Quartet and the San Francisco Contemporary Music Players (*see p210* **Real contemporary**). Designed by modernist architect James Stewart Polshek, the exterior of the cube-shaped theatre is covered in aluminium panels that catch the ever-changing San Francisco light.

East Bay & beyond

Just across the Bay Bridge, Zellerbach Hall is used by the **Berkeley Symphony Orchestra** (1-510 841 2800, www.berkeleysymphony.org), which attracts a roster of distinguished stars under its music director Kent Nagano. It's the venue for concerts, recitals and solo shows organised by Cal Performances (*see p248*) as well, and the **Berkeley Opera** (1-510 841 1903, www.berkeleyopera.org) puts on three productions a year there.

Other East Bay venues worth investigating include the First Congregational Church in Berkeley (1-510 848 3696, www.fccb.org) and

The **Yerba Buena Performing Arts Theater**.

the Paramount Theatre (*see p201*) in Oakland, where the **Oakland East Bay Symphony** (1-510 444 0801, www.oebs.org) and **Oakland Symphony Chorus** (1-510 207 4093, www.oakland-sym-chorus.org) perform.

The popular **Chamber Music Sundaes** series (1-415 584 5946, www.chambermusic sundaes.com), held at St John's Presbyterian Church (2727 College Avenue, between First & Garber Streets) in Berkeley at 3pm, takes place on Sunday afternoons. The season runs from October to May and employs the prodigious skills of San Francisco Symphony members and other local musicians.

Some of the most diverse programming in Northern California is at the **Robert and Margrit Mondavi Center for the Performing Arts** (University of California at Davis, One Shields Avenue, 1-530 754 5000, www.mondaviarts.org), a 90-minute drive from San Francisco. Since its much-heralded opening in 2002, this large performing arts complex has attracted Bay Area music lovers with performances by such as Paco de Lucia and the Ballet Folklórico de México.

Church venues

Recitals and concerts are performed in many of San Francisco's churches – they're often free too. They include the **Old First Presbyterian Church** (1751 Sacramento Street, between Polk Street & Van Ness Avenue, 776 5552, www.oldfirst.org) on the edge of Pacific Heights, where Chanticleer often performs; the **First Unitarian Universalist Church** (1187 Franklin Street, at Geary Street, 776 4580, www.uusf.org), near the Civic Center; and **Grace Cathedral** (749 6300, www.grace cathedral.org; *see also p84*) on Nob Hill. **St Patrick's** (756 Mission Street, 777 3211), a beautifully restored Catholic church just across the street from Yerba Buena Gardens, hosts noontime concerts every Wednesday. A great venue for organ recitals or performances by the San Francisco Bach Choir is **St Mary's Cathedral** (*see p95*).

Jazz & blues

San Francisco's roots as a hotspot for music, dancing and good times reach back as far as the rip-roaring Barbary Coast days, and continue through the city's heyday as the epicentre of Beat culture and West Coast jazz. (*See also p214* **Stompin' in the Fillmore**.) Despite reports of an ailing scene, the Bay Area continues to turn out vital jazz musicians. A single high-school programme, the Berkeley High Jazz Ensemble, has been responsible for some of today's brightest stars, including Joshua Redman, Benny Green, Jessica Jones and David Murray.

Downtown & SoMa

Biscuits & Blues

401 Mason Street, at Geary Street, Union Square (292 2583/www.biscuitandblue.citysearch.com). Bus 2, 3, 4, 38, 76/cable car Powell-Hyde or Powell-Mason. **Open** 5pm-1am daily. **Admission** varies. **Credit** AmEx, MC, V. **Map** p310 G4.

This subterranean nightclub/restaurant is, like any good blues joint, a pretty basic affair. It attracts mainly middle-aged tourists and suburbanites and can get fairly stuffy when crowded, but it's one of the few places in San Francisco where you can regularly see blues legends and national up-and-comers. It's also refreshing to see a genuinely excited crowd, unlike the jaded scenesters at so many cooler clubs. Biscuits and Blues serves up American food with a Southern accent and the portions are truly enormous; dinner is 5-7.30pm, with the kitchen closing soon after 10pm. Book if you want to be sure of getting in.

North Beach & around

The Saloon

1232 Grant Avenue, at Vallejo Street & Columbus Avenue (989 7666). Bus 15, 30, 41, 45. **Open** noon-2am daily. **Admission** free-$5. **No credit cards.** **Map** p311 G2.

A beer hall that scandalised the neighbourhood when it was built in 1861, the Saloon has survived earthquakes and shifting musical tastes to remain a no-nonsense, rough-edged joint with a busy calendar of blues and blues-rock. Psychedelic-era rockers you might see include former members of Jefferson Airplane and Country Joe & the Fish. It's now the oldest continuously operating bar in San Francisco.

Mission & Castro

The salsa party at **El Rio** (*see p218*) is a must.

Bruno's

2389 Mission Street, at 20th Street, Mission (648 7701/www.brunoslive.com). Bus 14, 26, 49. **Open** 6pm-2am Tue-Sun. **Admission** varies. **Credit** MC, V. **Map** p314 F7.

For such an attractive and popular place, Bruno's can't hold on to an owner for long: it's been bought and sold four times since 1994. First opened in the late 1930s, it retains an old supper-club feel, but with a sleek modern edge. There's a smart dining room, long bar and seating area, with the music happening in a narrow lounge. Bruno's was gaining a reputation for experimental jazz when the club was sold again in mid 2001; since then, owner and chef Chris Pastena has put the emphasis on affordable, appetising Italian-American comfort food, while the appealingly retro, streamlined live room does soul-, funk- and hip-hop-tinged jazz, as well as sporadic evenings of singer/songwriter music or live drum 'n' bass.

Elbo Room

647 Valencia Street, between 17th & 18th Streets, Mission (552 7788/www.elbo.com). BART 16th Street/bus 26, 33. **Open** 5pm-2am daily. **Admission** $5-$20. **No credit cards.** **Map** p314 F6.

Although the Elbo has been commandeered by yuppies, it continues to be a place to hear good music, usually performed in the open-raftered space upstairs. You're likely to hear jazz (usually with a funk edge), pure funk, soul or Latin jazz, but hip hop and random whacked-out experimentalists also appear. Sunday nights you'll catch the legendary Dub Mission DJ.

Haight, Western Addition & Hayes Valley

Boom Boom Room

1601 Fillmore Street, at Geary Boulevard, Fillmore (673 8000/www.boomboomblues.com). Bus 2, 3, 4, 22, 38. **Open** 4pm-2am daily. **Admission** $5-$12. **No credit cards.** **Map** p309/10 E4.

Yoshi's at Jack London Square – home of the finest jazz on the West Coast.

Located opposite the Fillmore (*see p218*), the Boom Boom Room stands on the site of what was once Jack's Bar, a blues dive and SF fixture for more than 50 years. It's been remade as a classy version of a trad blues joint. Until his death in 2001, blues legend John Lee Hooker held court at his personal booth up front. The club attracts solid blues acts with an occasional rock-star surprise, but the crowd can be obnoxious.

Rasselas Jazz

1534 Fillmore Street, at Geary Boulevard, Fillmore (346 8696/www.rasselasjazzclub.com). Bus 1, 22, 24, 38. **Open** 5pm-midnight daily. **Credit** AmEx, MC, V. **Map** p309/10 E4.

The Rasselas, like the Fillmore Historic Jazz District it's meant to anchor, is starting to live up to its potential. On the weekend the live combos usually get the crowd of African-American revellers and white yuppies on their feet. The decor – two-storey ceilings, bachelor-pad furniture and a crackling fireplace behind the band – is suggestive of a '60s Playboy Mansion. The music tends to be unadventurous jazz and needs more imagination; some hip-hop nights are hosted in the back room. The food is Ethiopian.

East Bay

Yoshi's at Jack London Square

510 Embarcadero West, at Jack London Square, Oakland (1-510 238 9200/www.yoshis.com). BART Oakland City Center, then bus 58, 72L, 301. **Open** 11.30am-2pm, 5.30pm-11.30pm Mon-Sat; noon-2pm, 5-10pm Sun. **Admission** $10-$30. **Credit** AmEx, DC, Disc, MC, V.

Yoshi's is the kind of refined setting that makes for a splendid occasion. Its separate dining room does good business on the strength of its Japanese food, but you should come here for the music: two sets a night, at 8pm and 10pm Monday to Saturday and at 2pm and 8pm on a Sunday. This is without doubt the premier Bay Area jazz house, and probably the best on the entire West Coast. Book in advance.

Rock, pop & hip hop

Some say the music scene here hit its high point (literally and figuratively) with the advent in the '60s of the so-called 'San Francisco sound'. Psychedelic rock royalty such as the Grateful Dead, Jefferson Airplane and Big Brother & the Holding Company governed the stage during the Summer of Love, an idyllic period that was brought to a symbolic end when the Rolling Stones moved their infamous free concert from Golden Gate Park up north to the Altamont Speedway with notorious results. Since then the Bay Area has been especially noted for innovative fusions of genres – funk-metal, acid jazz, laptop-thrash, pop-punk – and has produced a frightening array of headliners, among them Green Day, Carlos Santana, Black Rebel Motorcycle Club, the Dead Kennedys, the Donnas, Me'Shell Ndege'cello and Chris Isaak.

The Bay Area has also been a potent source for all kinds of hip hop, from gangsta rap to backpacker styles and Funkadelic-whimsy.

Arts & Entertainment

Stompin' in the Fillmore

The jazz heritage of the Fillmore District can be traced back to World War II and the arrival of African-Americans from the South, drawn by wartime work opportunities and the area's small but established black population. Filling vacancies left by interned Japanese-Americans, African-Americans turned the Fillmore into a community so vibrant it became known as 'the Harlem of the West', with shops, restaurants, newspapers, churches, theatres and nightclubs catering to a prosperous population eager for a good time after a hard week in the shipyards.

Black jazz artists such as Billie Holiday, Ella Fitzgerald and Louis Armstrong found gigs at Jack's Tavern, Club Alabam, the New Orleans Swing Club, the Blue Mirror and in the lounge of the Booker T Washington Hotel. Bop City, at 1690 Post Street, was perhaps the best-loved of them all. Named after a place in New

Important figures include resurgent old-schoolers like E-40 and Too $hort, fiery polemicists such as Paris and Michael Franti, and underground experimentalists like DJ Shadow and Blackalicious. The late, Daly City-based Invisibl Skratch Piklz, arguably the greatest practitioners of turntablism, have produced celebrated alumni, including DJ Q-Bert and Beastie Boys collaborator Mix Master Mike. In recent years, Oakland has emerged as a hotbed of hip hop/electronic experimentation informed by indie rock aesthetics: Anticon fills halls with grating, off-beat samples and oblique, anti-bling rhymes, while on his Tigerbeat6 label laptop lout Kid606 fosters such wide-ranging local performers as underground MC Gold Chains, jazzed-out panic-rockers Total Shutdown and emo-rapper Cex.

Downtown & SoMa

Avalon Ballroom

1268 Sutter Street, at Van Ness Avenue, Tenderloin (847 4043/tickets 421 8497/ www.morningspringrain.com). Bus 19, 38, 42, 47, 49. **Open** 1hr before showtime. **Credit** AmEx, DC, MC, V. **Map** p310 F4.

Avalon Ballroom only seems new. In truth it's been all the way to the movies and back. Built in 1911 in full Beaux Arts splendour, the one-time Puckett Academy of Dance became a bastion of the San Francisco sound in the '60s, with the work of Family Dog promoter Chet Helms. It was the site of Janis Joplin's first public appearance, and hippies flocked to shows by the likes of Moby Grape, Country Joe & the Fish and Bo Diddley. Converted into a cinema in the '70s, Avalon Ballroom found a new lease of

York, Bop City was no more than a stage in the back room of Jimbo's Waffle Shop, but the likes of Duke Ellington, John Coltrane, Miles Davis, Art Tatum, Dizzy Gillespie, Count Basie and Dinah Washington all sat in at sizzling all-night jam sessions there. It surprised no one at the time: celebrities like Joe Louis, Marilyn Monroe and Sammy Davis Jr would all visit the Fillmore clubs, as did a 16-year-old alto sax player named Clint Eastwood. It was here, too, that Etta James was discovered by Johnny Otis; she was 14 and singing with the all-girl Creolettes.

Once the shipyards closed, racial discrimination grew in step with the rising unemployment. The Fillmore became famous simply as a low-income ghetto. Residents battled the SF Redevelopment Agency over plans to drive the Geary Street thoroughfare through the area and construct the Japantown Center shopping mall, but to no avail. Many black residents sold up and moved away, businesses buckled and the area never quite regained its former lustre. Rappers San Quinn, Rappin' 4-Tay and Andre Nickatina have since come out of the district, but the paucity of venues (the Lower Haight's **Nickie's BBQ**, see p156, is one of the few still holding out) for young African-Americans the bitter '70s slogan rings horribly true: 'urban renewal equals Negro removal'.

Today the SF Redevelopment Agency is trying to correct its mistakes. Plans have been afoot for years to create a Fillmore Jazz Preservation District along Fillmore Street, between Golden Gate Avenue and Post Street. Anticipated anchors, such as Blue Note and House of Blues fell through, but in 2003 hopes for the jazz district were revived when a new promotions office began a Saturday farmers' market and regular film and music events. Momentum continued to build with the announcement that **Yoshi's** (see p213) will be the centrepiece of a $60-million development at Fillmore and Eddy Streets (a Fillmore Jazz Museum is also talked about – the precursors to it a poignant black-and-white photo exhibit and a 'walk of fame' with names of famous Fillmore-ites engraved in the sidewalk). Scheduled to open in 2007, the new Yoshi's will join **Rasselas Jazz** (see p213), which has already moved into the redevelopment zone from California Street. Indeed, the most exciting sign of a Fillmore revival is to be found in Rasselas at the weekend: the venue seems to be finally finding its beat with a raucous, racially diverse and footloose crowd.

Elsewhere, jazz and blues are in the air. There are free jazz performances on Fridays in summer, the **Fillmore Auditorium** (see p218) is hosting occasional big-ticket jazz concerts by artists like Soulive, and musicians of the calibre of Buddy Miles, the Meters, Van Morrison, Olu Dara and Elvis Costello have all dropped in for aftershow jams at the **Boom Boom Room** (pictured left; see p212). Best of all, early July each year sees the **Fillmore Street Jazz Festival** (see p190), a chance for the city's musos to really blow.

life as a live music venue. Steve Shirley (who grew up with the moniker Morning Spring Rain on the Hog Farm, Northern California's holdout hippie commune) took over and began putting on shows featuring such acts as Spearhead, Rob Halford, AFI and Buju Banton.

Bill Graham Civic Auditorium

99 Grove Street, between Polk & Larkin Streets, Civic Center (974 4060/www.billgrahamcivic.com). BART Civic Center/Muni Metro F, J, K, L, M, N/ bus 9, 19, 21, 26. **Open** *Box office* 1hr before shows. **Admission** varies. **Credit** MC, V. **Map** p314 F5.

In this 5,000-seat auditorium, on 26 September 1923, the San Francisco Opera (see p210) was born; by the '60s, it had become home to the NBA's San Francisco Warriors. Renamed after the city's famous rock impresario, it has now settled into hosting a variety of events, from not-quite-arena rock shows to conferences. Cavernous and with poor acoustics, it's nonetheless centrally located and hosts well-regarded acts, among them Beck and the Strokes.

Eagle Tavern

398 12th Street, at Harrison Street, SoMa (626 0880/www.sfeagle.com). Bus 9, 12, 27, 42. **Open** noon-2am daily. **No credit cards.** **Map** p314 G5.

Fly into venerable gay bar the Eagle for all-male leather action, some random mud-wrestling, all manner of goings-on in the beergarden and a chance to cosy up to your favourite gay – and straight – local indie rockers and punkheads Pansy Division, Panty Raid and Erase Errata. The tavern welcomes them onstage as well, poked in between meetings of International Gay & Lesbian Football and Leather Daddies organisations.

SF alternative Gigs

Care for a walk on the wild side of the local music scene? The Bay Area offers a slew of secret shows featuring local bands or bigger acts in performances that are often unpublicised due to difficulties with permits or conflicting larger club dates elsewhere. Gillian Welch and Cat Power have both played last-minute or unannounced dates at **Hemlock Tavern** (see below), while the Greenhornes and Soledad Brothers did the same at **Thee Parkside** (see p218). There are casual gigs at many of the city's music stores too. **Amoeba** (see p182), **Mod Lang** (2136 University Avenue, at Shattuck Avenue, Berkeley, 1-510 486 1880) and **Robotspeak** (589.5 Haight Street, at Steiner Street, 554 1977) all host free gigs to promote record sales, and if you're lucky, you'll catch some surprisingly big names.

So far, so much like any other city. But, blame it on the hippies or blame it on a DIY punker-prankster heritage, the Bay Area has a great line in unconventional venues: warehouses, label offices, live-work studios, parks and beaches. Something as staid as Flag Day suddenly spurs groups like the Coachwhips and Double Duchess to take their show on the road, with musical pit-stops at the Civic Center, Ocean Beach, Twin Peaks and 16th Street BART station. Rock Out SF puts a similar idea to a more focused end: one

day a year, organisers encourage musicians throughout the city to play on street corners or rooftops or in the parks – an action originally organised in 2000 as a protest against the closure of Downtown Rehearsal Studios.

For performances at less than above-board venues, websites are the first point of reference. **The List** (www.foopee.com/punk/the-list), a local concert guide, is well worth keeping an eye on. Also be alert on the street, in clubs and at music shops for posters and fliers, and pay attention to your favourite artists' websites or email lists for last-minute announcements.

Of course, it's in the nature of secret and unofficial gigs to be a little tricky to track down. But some unorthodox venues have become increasingly frequent hosts of excellent gigs. There certainly aren't going to be any complaints from the neighbours at Warm Water Cove – there simply are no neighbours to complain. **Toxic Beach**, as Warm Water Cove has been lovingly dubbed by the locals, is right on the water's edge in a small park at the end of 24th Street, at the intersection with Third Street. There, punk, rock, electronic and noise bands take the opportunity to get as loud and messy as they can, with underground aficionados biking to free summer shows on this rocky remnant of post-industrial landfill. (Those with less time or energy can take the

Great American Music Hall

859 O'Farrell Street, between Polk & Larkin Streets, Tenderloin (885 0750/www.musichallsf.com). Bus 19, 38, 42, 47, 49. **Open** *Box office 10.30am-6pm Mon-Fri; until 9pm on show nights; 1hr before show Sat, Sun.* **Admission** $8-$22. **Credit** MC, V. **Map** p310 F4.

Among the city's smaller venues, the Great American Music Hall is the grande dame. Originally a bordello, the hall was also owned by fan dancer Sally Rand – it has preserved its beauty admirably over the years. The lavish decor includes huge mirrors, rococo woodwork and gold-leaf trim. Now helmed by the owners of Slim's (see below), it presents a cutting-edge bill of highly regarded local and touring musicians, especially of the indie-rock variety. Be sure to snag a coveted seat in the upper balcony.

Hemlock Tavern

1131 Polk Street, at Post Street, Tenderloin (923 0923/www.hemlocktavern.com). Bus 19, 38, 42, 47, 49. **Open** *4pm-around 2am daily.* **No credit cards.** **Map** p310 F4.

Edgy, unpretentious and intelligent musical programming make this venue a must for eclectic listeners. The intimate live room – separate from the rest of the bar and well soundproofed – is easily filled with hipsters when the bill includes hot, emerging artists (Wolf Eyes, Dynasty, Deerhoof – who knows next year?). Outside, an intriguing mix of young tastemakers, college-age art snobs and wandering yuppies play pool, hang in the open-air smoking room or cluster around the stand-alone bar.

Slim's

333 11th Street, between Folsom & Harrison Streets, SoMa (255 0333/www.slims-sf.com). Bus 9, 12, 27, 42. **Open** *Box office 10.30am-6pm Mon-Fri.* **Admission** free-$25. **Credit** MC, V. **Map** p314 G5.

One of San Francisco's most important venues, offering two or more bands four or five nights a week. Holding about 550, Slim's isn't the most comfortable place to listen to music: most patrons have to stand and sightlines are compromised by floor-to-ceiling pillars. It gets pretty steamy on a busy night too. Mainly rock acts and post-punk singer/songwriters.

No.15 bus.) If the bands begin to pall, there are scenic views of the Port of Oakland, flowers peeping through the broken concrete and seabirds hovering overhead. Perfect with cheap beer and chips – that's crisps for all

Anglos. (Toxic Beach organisers have also put on shows at Potrero Del Sol Park's bandstand, at 25th Street and Potrero Avenue.)

If you're in Oakland, **40th Street Warehouse** (379 40th Street, between Opal & Shaffer, 1-510 625 1504) is known for great punk and underground rock gigs with thematic art shows, harking back to the era when anarchist co-ops proliferated in the Bay Area. It's a gallery, performance space and living quarters for artists and musicians, and local and touring bands like Schaffer the Darklord and Dance Disaster Movement have played here beside the crammed kitchen.

But the best named of these venues has to be **Recombinant Labs Compound** (1070 Van Dyke Street, off Griffith Street, 863 3068 ext 811, 971 4276, www.asphodel.com). Owner Naut Humon says shows are ramping up rapidly at the Compound, which otherwise functions as the headquarters for Asphodel, a respected experimental music label. About 150 people can partake in the surround sound and visuals of performers like electro-acoustic minimalist Francisco Lopez, German dub-meister Tiki Man, and Norwegian click-popster Sir Dupermann.

One important caveat: don't just roll up to any of these venues. Performances depend entirely on the organiser's whim and can be few and far between. Which is a large part of the appeal.

StudioZ.tv

314 11th Street, at Folsom Street, SoMa (252 7666/ www.studioZ.tv). Bus 9, 12, 27, 42. **Open** varies, usually 7-10pm. **Credit** MC, V. **Map** p314 G5.
The venue for a hodge-podge of events, the curiously named StudioZ.tv hosts everything from the regular Club Dread reggae night and live South Asian fusion jams to political fundraisers and hip-hop poetry slams. Graced with exposed red-brick walls, high ceilings and hardwood floors, the huge main room, several mezzanines and full bars here provide the ideal blank slate for party organisers.

Warfield Theater

982 Market Street, at Mason Street, Union Square (775 7722/www.thefillmore.com/warfield.asp). BART Powell/Muni Metro F, J, K, L, M, N/bus 7, 27, 31, 66, 71. **Open** *Box office* 10am-4pm Sun; 7.30-10.30pm on show nights. **Admission** $25-$35. **Credit** AmEx, MC, V. **Map** p310 G4.
The Warfield is an ornate 1922 theatre that has been converted into a 2,100-seat venue for popular music, especially rock. Major national and international

acts play here, sometimes as the last step before vaulting to arena-sized venues. It's well designed so that even the back balcony seats have a good view of the stage.

North Beach & around

Bimbo's 365 Club

25 Columbus Avenue, at Chestnut Street, North Beach (474 0365/www.bimbos365club.com). Bus 30/ cable car Powell-Mason. **Open** *Box office* 10am-4pm Mon-Fri. **Admission** $15-$25. **Credit** MC, V. **Map** p310 G2.
Bimbo's began its glamorous life in 1931, as a Market Street speakeasy, but took up residence in North Beach in 1951. It's still owned by the descendants of one of its original owners, Agostino 'Bimbo' Giuntoli, who have lovingly preserved it like a jewel from a more elegant time. Rita Hayworth once worked the boards as a dancer, but these days you're more likely to see Prefuse 73 or Kid Koala spinning vinyl, and rockers like the Strokes. It's a regular stop

on the touring circuit of world-class musicians, with shows four or five nights a week. A mermaid theme runs throughout; on some nights you can spot 'Dolfina' the naked fish-woman.

Mission & Castro

If the **Elbo Room** (*see p212*) has a vocation, it's the funkier end of jazz, but its hip hop and experimental gigs are worth checking out too.

Bottom of the Hill

1233 17th Street, at Missouri Street, Potrero Hill (box office 621 4455/tickets 1-866 468 3399/www. bottomofthehill.com). Bus 22, 53. **Open** 3pm-2am Mon-Thur; 2pm-2am Fri; 8pm-2am Sat; 4pm-2am Sun. **Admission** $5-$12. **Credit** MC, V. **Map** p315 H6.
This little club, wedged among warehouses at the bottom of Potrero Hill, has long been a favourite with the indie-rock crowd. Underground bands that play here this year may well become cult sensations or even major stars the next. It features a mix of local and touring acts most nights, as well as occasional name acts hankering to play an intimate show or big stars from abroad trying to get a toehold in the US. The decor is classic dive, with quirky touches.

Café Du Nord

2170 Market Street, between Church & Sanchez Streets, Castro (861 5016/www.cafedunord.com). Muni Metro F, J, L, N, M/bus 22, 37. **Open** 6pm-around 2am Mon-Wed, Sat, Sun; 5pm-around 2am Thur, Fri. *Dinner* 6.30-11pm daily. **Admission** varies. **Credit** AmEx, MC, V. **Map** p314 E6.
There are several SF nightspots with the feel of a Prohibition-era speakeasy, but none captures that spirit quite so well as the always-popular Café Du Nord. Perhaps that's because it really was one during its nearly 100-year existence. A subterranean place, the front room has red velvet walls and a 40ft (12m) mahogany bar bustling with scenesters.

Make-Out Room

3225 22nd Street, between Mission & Valencia Streets, Mission (647 2888/www.makeoutroom.com). BART 24th Street/bus 14, 26, 49. **Open** 6pm-2am daily. **Admission** free-$6. **No credit cards**. **Map** p314 F7.
One of the best places to see a good band, but one of the worst for encountering yuppies. The key is to go only when there's live music, when you're likely to see a laid-back, alternative and young crowd. The decor lives up to the name: there's a bearskin rug on one wall and a stag's head on another, with a rainbow of bras strung from the antlers.

El Rio

3158 Mission Street, at Cesar Chavez Street, Mission (282 3325/www.elriosf.com). Bus 12, 14, 26, 49, 67. **Open** 3pm-midnight Mon; 3pm-2am Tue-Sun. **Admission** free-$10. **No credit cards**.
You owe it to yourself to take part in this San Francisco tradition – 25 years and counting. Head to El Rio early on a Sunday afternoon between March and November and make your way to the back garden. There you'll find the city's most diverse and lively salsa party. There's an outdoor barbecue, dancing lessons, decent Margaritas and a friendly crowd of straights and queers. Other nights you might encounter experimental rock, DJs (including a Middle Eastern dance night on Thursdays) or, in the summer, outdoor films.

Thee Parkside

1600 17th Street, at Wisconsin Street, Potrero Hill (503 0393/www.theeparkside.com). Bus 22, 53. **Open** 11am-2am daily. **Credit** AmEx, MC, V. **Map** p315 H6.
San Francisco's latest rock 'n' roll roadhouse started life as a lunch spot for dot-com cube farmers. That plan fell by the wayside when the pink slips began to flutter. No matter, Thee Parkside has found new life as a rowdy joint specialising in roots, punk, country and, especially, garage rock. Things quickly get sweaty and loud in the main room, where the so-called stage abuts the door. In the Tiki patio out back, hard rockers and Pabst drinkers heat up with a bit of ping-pong. Ryan Adams and the Hives have been known to drop in before their shows elsewhere.

Haight, Western Addition & Hayes Valley

Fillmore Auditorium

1805 Geary Boulevard, at Fillmore Street, Fillmore (24hr hotline 346 6000/www.thefillmore.com). Bus 22, 38. **Open** *Box office* 10am-4pm Sun; 7.30-10pm on show nights. **Admission** $15-$30. **Credit** AmEx, MC, V. **Map** p309/10 E4.
The Fillmore began life in 1912 as a dance hall, but is better known as the place where the late Bill Graham launched his rock-promotion empire in the '60s with the likes of the Grateful Dead and Jefferson Airplane. It remains a favourite venue for all kinds of big-name musicians and their fans. With a capacity of 1,200, it's relatively intimate and quite relaxed.

Other neighbourhoods

Pound SF

Pier 96, 100 Cargo Way, near 3rd Street, Hunter's Point (826 5009/www.poundsf.com). Bus 15. **Open** shows usually begin between 7pm & 9pm. **Admission** varies. **No credit cards**.
Pound SF is hidden in the furthest reaches of one the city's sketchiest neighbourhoods (although it's only a quick cab ride from downtown), on a pier with a view of giant cranes and San Francisco Bay. It's your basic squat black box (with portions of it made from shipping containers), but the management has invested in decent lights and sound. When it opened in 2001, it booked mainly hard rock, punk and metal bands. Since then it has branched out into indie pop and funk. Shows are all ages, and plans are afoot to build a neighbouring outdoor stage.

Nightlife

Through even the darkest nights, pleasure is a San Franciscan artform.

San Francisco's nightlife has weathered a tide of troubles of late, with clubs closing and hitherto popular DJ nights biting the dust. The city is still suffering the lingering effects of the dot-com economic hangover. During the 1990s boom, lines would snake round the block at favoured nightclubs, but even then life for DJs (as for musicians and artists) was touch and go – the high-tech explosion brought in audiences and lucrative work for some, even as the skyrocketing rents ousted the less-commercially minded creators. On top of this, a change in zoning laws, dating all the way back to 1988, had turned previously industrial areas into residential ones. In increasing numbers, the inevitable noise complaints forced long-established clubs to turn down or get shut down. These changes had their most potent effects on the once-heaving South of Market corridor: 11th Street is but a shadow of its former clubbing self. Especially hard hit were bottom-rung clubs, where fledgling acts once honed their craft and built their audience.

San Francisco being San Francisco, the city wasn't about to let all this happen quietly. In reaction, and in the grand Bay Area tradition of activism, some musicians and scene boosters rallied to save the scene. Groups such as the Popular Noise Foundation, the San Francisco Late Night Coalition and Save Local Music emerged, and in 2003, after various police crackdowns on clubs, the city created a seven-member Entertainment Commission to regulate and promote nightlife. The power to issue entertainment-related permits went from the San Francisco Police Department (which was still applying laws instituted more than 80 years ago) to the new Commission.

Further challenges have come in the form of national legislation, especially the Illicit Drug Anti-Proliferation (or RAVE) Act. Yet Bay Area nightlife remains resilient. San Franciscans live to get down, and they'll go where fashion and music takes them. Glammed-up clubhoppers in heels and glitter can be found stepping over shattered crack pipes in the gritty, hustler-strewn Tenderloin, and among the hard-luck residential hotels of Sixth Street, suburban club kids get down and dirty with hard-bodied gay men to trash-electro. DJ-bar culture is also thriving, with places like **Julip Cocktail Lounge** (*see p150*), **Dalva** (*see p153*) and

Nickie's BBQ (*see p156*) no mere warm-up, pre-club venues. As a result, San Francisco still has more nightlife options than most visitors could ever hope to experience in a single trip.

This is San Francisco, sweetie, so for more clubs, *see chapter* **Queer San Francisco**. Clubs like **Cherry Bar** and **Stud** run excellent queer nights… excellent nights, period.

INFORMATION

SF Weekly (www.sfweekly.com) and the *San Francisco Bay Guardian* (www.sfbg.com) have extensive listings of clubs and special events, but for the latest info call the venerable **Be-At Line** (626 4087; call after 2pm), which lists daily details of where to be and when. **SF Raves** (www.sfraves.org, not to be confused with www.sfraves.com) has an exhaustive list of dance events, including underground parties. Alternatively, visit Amoeba Music (*see p182*), Tweekin Records (*see p184* **Vinyl junkies**) and BPM Music (*see p183* for fliers and free CD-sized dance-culture magazines with detailed listings.

ADMISSION

Admission prices depend on the night, but usually vary from nothing to $25. Many clubs stay open well past last orders, but by law they can't serve alcohol between 2am and 6am, nor to anyone under the age of 21. Some clubs are strictly 21 and over; if you're under 21, check the club's policy before you go.

LATE-NIGHT TRANSPORT

The Muni Owl Service operates on the Muni Metro L and N lines and on the 5, 14, 22, 38, 90, 91 and 108 bus lines from 1am until 5am. All other lines stop at 12.30am. BART runs roughly until midnight, although it's always best to check the time of the last train to your destination. For taxi companies, *see p277*.

Around Union Square

Bambuddha Lounge

Phoenix Hotel, 601 Eddy Street, at Larkin Street, Tenderloin (885 5088/www.bambuddhalounge.com). Bus 19, 31. **Open** 5pm-2am Tue-Sat. **Credit** AmEx, MC, V. **Map** p310 F4.

This bar/restaurant/nightclub is part of the Phoenix Hotel (*see p41*), a favourite of slumming rock stars. Once known as the Backflip, Bambuddha's general motif is New Age pan-Asian and the decor sleek

Six. *See p221.*

and minimal, with gentle lighting and plenty of conversational nooks, as well as a glittering bar and a roaring fireplace. A bamboo glade leads to another bar, with discreet DJ booth. The cabana-style pool is perfect for those 'lychee-tinis' and 'guavapolitans'.

Harry Denton's Starlight Room

Sir Francis Drake Hotel, 450 Powell Street, between Post & Sutter Streets, Union Square (395 8595/www.harrydenton.com). Bus 2, 3, 4, 30, 45, 76/cable car Powell-Hyde or Powell-Mason. **Open** 6pm-2am daily. **Credit** AmEx, MC, V. **Map** p311 G3.

Harry Denton's venues are a love 'em or leave 'em affair. Set aside the stunning 21st-floor view over Union Square, multiple mirrors and floral carpets, and you're left with a room of dressed-up social and financial climbers dancing to 'Mustang Sally' or lurking in booths. Harry Denton's Rouge (1500 Broadway, at Polk Street, 346 7683) offers the delights of Vegas-style showgirls jiggling on the bar and mingling among starry-eyed punters.

Ruby Skye

420 Mason Street, between Geary & Post Streets, Union Square (693 0777/www.rubyskye.com). Bus 2, 3, 4, 38, 76/cable car Powell-Hyde or Powell-Mason. **Open** 7pm-3am Wed-Sat. **Admission** varies. **Credit** AmEx, Disc, MC, V. **Map** p310 G3/4.

Ruby Skye is an attractive place, with a huge dancefloor. Converted from an elegant 1890s theatre, the designers retained plenty of ornate Victorian touches while installing a thoroughly modern sound and light system. But the whole scene feels like it's been imported from LA – one of the few clubs here where young women proudly parade their breast implants.

SoMa

Arrow

10 Sixth Street, at Market Street (255 7920). BART Powell/Muni Metro F, J, K, L, M, N/bus 14, 26. **Open** 9pm-2am daily. **Admission** varies. **Credit** AmEx, MC, V. **Map** p310/14 G4.

The street outside is as grungy as they come, but the vibe inside this funky dive is cool as art school. Complete with a tiny but pristine cave-like dance area, as well as a three-headed neon Hydra over the bar, the trendiest kids and enthusiastic dancers get into rock DJs, pop-locking new-wave funk sets and Trouble – a session that brings out the frustrated DJ in local music writers and musicians.

DNA Lounge

375 11th Street, at Harrison Street (626 1409/ www.dnalounge.com). Bus 9, 12, 27, 42. **Open** 8 or 9pm-2 or 4am Tue-Sat. **Admission** $5-$20. **No credit cards**. **Map** p314 G5.

The DNA is a long-time fixture of the local music scene but, like the scene itself, had trouble staying alive a few years ago as owner Jamie Zawinski (one of the creators of Netscape) ran the gauntlet of permit and remodelling issues. It reopened in mid 2001 with a full schedule of DJ nights and has

flourished ever since. The dancefloor below the stage is flanked by stairs to a mezzanine level, where corner booths encourage drinking and necking.

Mezzanine

444 Jessie Street, at Sixth Street (820 9669/ www.mezzaninesf.com). BART Powell/Muni Metro F, J, K, L, M, N/bus 14, 26. **Open** 10pm-2am Thur, Fri; 10pm-7am Sat; 7pm-10pm 1st Tue of mth; 7pm-midnight 1st Wed of mth. **Admission** varies. **No credit cards**. **Map** p310/14 G4.

This massive club and art gallery can take 900 dancers, with two long bars bordering the ample dancefloor. San Fran-London DJ Jamie Sanchez's tribal house on Saturdays (10pm-7am) brings out the crowds, while respected techno artists such as Richie Hawtin make this venue their sole stop in SF.

111 Minna

111 Minna Street, at Second Street (974 1719/ www.111annex.com). BART Montgomery/Muni Metro F, J, K, L, M, N/bus 9, 12, 14, 15, 30, 45, 76. **Open** 7pm-2am Mon-Sat. **Admission** $3-$10. **Credit** AmEx, MC, V. **Map** p311 H3/4.

This concrete box down an alley just south of Market Street is an art gallery (*see p206*) by day, but a truly happening dance club by night. It draws an unusual hybrid – serious rave yuppies – but is popular with all kinds of dance-music freaks owing to music ranging from garage to Afrobeat to South Asian. Check out long-running Qoöl, a techno party from 5pm to 10pm on Wednesdays.

Paradise Lounge

1501 Folsom Street, at 11th Street (621 1911/www. paradiseloungesf.com). Bus 9, 12, 47. **Open** 9pm-2am Thur-Sat. **Admission** $5-$12; free before 10pm. **Credit** MC, V. **Map** p314 G5.

Once the premier showcase for local bands, the Paradise recently had a major makeover, jettisoning its three stages and being transformed into a two-storey dance club. At nights like Dirrty, they mash up smut rock, new wave, no wave and hip hop.

Six

60 Sixth Street, between Market & Mission Streets (863 1221/www.clubsix1.com). BART Powell/Muni Metro F, J, K, L, M, N/bus 14, 26. **Open** 10pm-2am Wed-Sat. **Admission** $5-$12. **No credit cards**. **Map** p310/14 G4.

Six sits on one of the scariest blocks in the city – although south of Market Street, it's considered part of the Tenderloin – so it's best to go in a group and avoid looking rich or touristy. Inside you'll find a high-ceilinged chill room/bar, with a low-ceilinged dancefloor below. Created by the guy responsible for Liquid (*see p222*), the club offers house, dub, breaks and whatever else may be filling dancefloors at the moment. And an upstairs art gallery.

Sno-Drift

1830 Third Street, at 16th Street (431 4766/ www.sno-drift.com). Bus 15. **Open** 10pm-4am Mon, Wed-Sun. **Admission** $5-$20. **Credit** AmEx, MC, V. **Map** p315 J6.

This place is a beauty. Located on a barren commercial strip near SBC Park, it's easy to spot: foreign movies are beamed on to the windows. Inside, the cocktail lounge has the feel of a swinging-'60s ski lodge, with circular fireplace, deer statue and a long, curved bar behind which sit cocktail glasses chilling atop mountains of crushed ice. Sno-Drift is fairly small, so come early or during the week if you don't like crowds – and its days of operation shift constantly so make sure you call in advance.

Sublounge
628 20th Street, at Third Street (552 3603/ www.sublounge.com). Bus 15, 22. **Open** 6pm-2am Mon-Sat. **Admission** $5-$10. **Map** p315 J7.
The city's outstanding new dance club, according to both the *Bay Guardian* and *SF Weekly*, is lodged inauspiciously between a taqueria and factory warehouses on a dusty sidestreet. But club kids from all over the city have been strapping in to the deep-cool decor and taking off in relaxed but playful mood: genuine aeroplane seats are scattered beneath space-ace bachelor-pad light fixtures. Deep house, hip hop, indie pop and funky beats provide the in-flight entertainment. Things will really hot up when the new Muni Metro line arrives and construction of the nearby college campus is complete.

Ten 15 Folsom
1015 Folsom Street, between Sixth & Seventh Streets (431 7444/recorded information 431 1200/ www.1015.com). Bus 12, 27, 42. **Open** 9.30pm-7am Thur, Fri; 10pm-7am Sat; 10pm-5.30am Sun. **Admission** free-$20. **No credit cards**. **Map** p315 G5.
San Francisco's meat-and-potatoes dance club, this is always a safe bet for dancing, before, during and after hours. The three rooms each have their own vibe, so you move through space and time without changing venues. You'll find the same suburban crowd of sad pick-up artists and bimbos as in any big club, but they don't overwhelm the place.

330 Ritch
330 Ritch Street, between Brannan & Townsend Streets (541 9574). Bus 15, 30, 42, 45, 76. **Open** 5pm-2am Wed-Fri; 10pm-2am Sat, Sun. **Admission** varies. **Credit** AmEx, MC, V. **Map** p315 H/J4/5.
The young crowd seems right at home in this spacious yet intimate spot, which is hidden down an alley. Sounds include hip hop and classic soul, but Thursdays belong to long-running Popscene, a Britpop night (spot the scooters out front). If you've got a British accent, you'll make friends easily.

North Beach

Blind Tiger
787 Broadway, at Powell Street (788 4020/ www.blindtigersf.com). Bus 12, 83/cable car Powell-Mason. **Open** 8pm-2am Thur-Sat. **No credit cards**. **Map** p310 G2.

DJs spin hip hop, house and breaks to an enormously varied crowd. The space is attractive, though the dancefloor is small and near the toilets, but the real draw is location: a quiet stretch of Broadway at the edge of North Beach. If nothing's happening, nip into the ultra-cool Rosewood (*see p152*).

Mission & Castro

Amnesia
853 Valencia Street, between 19th & 20th Streets, Mission (970 0012). Bus 14, 26, 49. **Open** 6pm-2am daily. **Admission** free-$10. **No credit cards**. **Map** p314 F7.
Amnesia is still resisting the party-hearty armies that take over most of this stretch of the Mission at weekends. Instead, it draws a diverse, friendly, multi-ethnic crowd, and the DJ spins suitably eclectic sounds.

Liquid
2925 16th Street, between South Van Ness Avenue & Mission Street (431 8889). BART 16th Street/bus 14, 22, 26, 53. **Open** 9pm-2am Mon-Sat. **Admission** free-$5. **Credit** MC, V. **Map** p314 F6.
A favourite spot for fans of DJ culture, Liquid is a narrow bar with a small dancefloor. It can get uncomfortably crowded during the weekend, but it's a different club every night. On Fridays DJs spin house, leftfield, funk and disco rarities.

Metronome Ballroom
1830 17th Street, at De Haro Street, Potrero Hill (252 9000/www.metronomeballroom.com). Bus 19, 22. **Open** 7.30pm-midnight Fri, Sat; 5-11pm Sun. **Admission** free-$15. **Credit** AmEx, MC, V. **Map** p315 H6.
If you love to dance, but clubbing isn't your thing, then the spacious, airy Metronome Ballroom is the place for you. It offers a friendly place for civilised tush-shaking, as well as lessons in tango, swing, cha cha, salsa and many other styles.

Haight, Western Addition & Hayes Valley

Milk DJ Bar & Lounge
1840 Haight Street, at Stanyan Street, Haight-Ashbury (387 6455/www.milksf.com). Bus 6, 7, 33, 66, 71. **Open** varies; contact venue. **Admission** free-$10. **No credit cards**. **Map** p313 C6.
Milk replaces Galaxy, which stepped in for the Boomerang, a starting point/last resort for local bands trying to gain an audience. Its disappearance left the Haight, home of the 'San Francisco sound', almost devoid of live rock. Still, Milk is a cool place to catch some vibrant local hip hop, with smooth modern decor and a decent-sized dancefloor. DJ Shadow has been known to drop in, and True Skool and Future Primitive Sound are worthy proponents of the art of hip hop.

The party principles

Much has changed since then. Economic tides have ebbed and flowed, coming almost full circle to the pre-boom climate of London's Summer of Love and its undeniable influence on clubbing in the City by the Bay. While punters locally and abroad fretted over the infamous **RAVE Act**'s possible effect on the average enthusiast's ability to get ripped to the tits and dance all night, make no mistake about it: drugs and dancing remain integral to SF club culture.

The heady days of scoring pure MDMA in the sweaty bathroom of **Ten 15 Folsom** (*see p222*) may be over, but all that has really done is to force E-tards to take care of their drug issues before getting in line. A routine scan of any of the classic old-school haunts will still turn up a healthy slathering of dilated pupils and demented gazes in the wee hours, much as it did ten years ago.

There's no doubt that casual chemical consumers have to be a tad smarter about their proclivities than back in '94 though. The legacy of the RAVE Act has been security routines only slightly less intrusive than those undergone to get on the bloody plane here – and the death of conspicuous drug consumption inside clubs. Don't try to sneak in the odd spliff or pill: door guards are as likely to arrange for you to spend a fun night out with the San Francisco Police Department as see you on your way. And valid ID is a must: attempts to penetrate even the less swanky clubs without one (or, worse, with a fake) are simply futile.

Nevertheless, with a little forward-planning, skill, brains and some local mates to score the ill-gotten booty, you can still enjoy a night staring at the lights stoned out of your gourd, listening to the signature soulful San Francisco house sound – a unique and blissful experience to be found elsewhere on this continent (hell, this planet) rarely, if ever.

It's been around 15 years since San Francisco's drug culture started taking its first steps from Grateful Dead hippie heaven to DJ-culture community. Not that the menu changed much. With the exception of an increase in MDMA ingestion – already considerable here compared to the rest of the country, courtesy of the city's iconoclastic queers – the same copious quantities of pot, cocaine, LSD and mushrooms were smoked, snorted and gobbled whether the soundtrack was Phish or Mark Farina.

Arts & Entertainment

1751 Social Club

1751 Fulton Street, between Masonic & Central Avenues, Western Addition (441 1751). Bus 5, 43. **Open** 5pm-2am daily. **Admission** $3-$5. **Credit** AmEx, Disc, MC, V. **Map** p313 D5.

An odd club in an odd (residential) location, 1751 Social was once a jazz house and supper club called Storyville. Remodelled as a more trad dance club, it's more likely to be playing pop, soul and dance music these days. The venue's DJs are starting to get into the Boogie Down swing of things on Wednesdays.

The Top

424 Haight Street, between Fillmore & Webster Streets, Lower Haight (864 7386). Bus 6, 7, 22, 66, 71. **Open** 7pm-2am daily. **Admission** $5. **Credit** MC, V. **Map** p314 E5.

Just down the street from Nickie's BBQ (*see p156*), on a somewhat sketchy stretch of Lower Haight, the Top is little more than a converted dive with a smallish dancefloor. But set the Top's looks aside and watch with your ears: it has a deservedly good reputation as a centre of turntable culture.

Queer San Francisco

Every day is gay in San Francisco.

Stepping out on **Castro**, the queer heart of San Francisco.

Arts & Entertainment

What makes San Francisco one of the world's most gay-friendly cities? Some say the wild gold miners of the mid 1800s stamped the region with an indelible 'anything goes' *joie de vivre*. Others say the city's development into a raucous port town, with the freewheeling sailors and dens of iniquity that go along with it, cemented permissive attitudes. Then there's the long-standing influence of queer cultural icons like the late Allen Ginsberg, which fed into the Free Love movement in the late 1960s and inspired generations of young people to reject their parents' conservative social mores and instead flock to 'Baghdad by the Bay'. Whatever the exact mix of influences was, San Francisco is now home to a thriving, politically influential gay community. They're here, they're queer and everybody's used to it.

At the heart of it all is the **Castro**. Once a quiet, working-class enclave populated by Irish, German and Scandinavian immigrants, by the early 1970s the neighbourhood had hit hard times, a victim of the nationwide 'white flight'

that sent many city dwellers scuttling to the suburbs. The Castro's first gay bar, the Missouri Mule, arrived in the mid 1960s (its Market Street location, still a gay bar, is now the **Detour**; *see p228*) and by 1972 gay men had begun moving to the Castro in droves, opening shops and returning shabby homes to their former glory. The Castro quickly became ground zero for gay civil rights activism and, after the devastation wrought by AIDS in the '80s, HIV-related activism. But nowadays the neighbourhood is less politicised and more mainstream, boasting one of the city's busiest commercial districts.

Of course, not all San Francisco's queers live in the Castro: some choose not to live in what local literary luminary Armistead Maupin dubbed 'the gay ghetto', others can't afford the pricey rents and mortgages there. Indeed, you'll find a refreshing diversity of queers from all walks of life throughout the city. From yuppie lesbian moms in Bernal Heights to avant-garde artists in SoMa to slick City Hall lobbyists downtown, queers are just about everywhere.

The city's biggest queer celebration is, hands-down, the month-long **Pride** (*see p189*) celebration in June. The festivities culminate in an action-packed weekend that includes the rowdy, popular Dyke March (women only, though men heartily cheer from the sidelines) and a massive Pride Parade down Market Street. For more information, call 864 3733 or check www.sfpride.org. Leather lovers of all persuasions flock to the **Folsom Street Fair** (*see p192*) in September; the **Dore Up Your Alley Fair** (861 3247, www.folsom streetfair.com/alley) in July is smaller, and known locally as the more 'authentic' queer S&M festival. The Castro's other big party is **Halloween** (*see p192*). It gained renown as a block party with impromptu drag performances, but recent Halloweens have drawn panic-inducing crowds (large numbers of whom don't even bother to dress up), gang violence and even some queer-bashing. If you do plan to attend, either show your respect by putting some thought into your costume or earn a deserved tongue-lashing from the drag divas patrolling the entryways. Recent anti-alcohol rules have made the Castro Halloween party more peaceful, if a little less raucous.

For an in-depth look at San Francisco's gay life past and present explore **The Center's** Reading Room (*see p232* **The Center**), the **James C Hormel Gay & Lesbian Center** at the Main Library (*see p68*) or join a walking tour: the vivacious docent Trevor Hailey hosts the popular **Cruisin' the Castro** outing (*see p54*). The **International Museum of Gay and Lesbian History** (657 Mission Street, Suite 300, between Third and Fourth Streets, 777 5455, www.glbthistory.org, admission $4, $2 concessions) has gallery exhibitions and extensive archives. It's open Tuesday to Saturday from 1pm to 5pm.

NEIGHBOURHOODS

The Castro remains the most visible mecca of queer culture in San Francisco, though some women visitors are surprised to be so outnumbered by men. Women do patronise Castro bars, cafés and restaurants, but the predominance of gay male cruising and fashion has prompted local dykes to put their marks on other districts: the **Mission**, **Bernal Heights** and **Hayes Valley** are all popular with lesbians. A perennial favourite is **Osento** (*see p182*), a women-only spa where you can soak in a hot tub or eucalyptus-scented sauna, then lie on the outside deck beneath the stars.

Gay male life in San Francisco also extends beyond the Castro. **Polk Street** is poorer, rougher and draggier. **SoMa** has bars, trendy restaurants, sex clubs and dance venues packed with hot, muscled men. And queer parents of all genders have taken refuge in cosy, family-friendly, out-of-the-way neighbourhoods like **Bernal Heights** and **Noe Valley**.

INFORMATION

The best sources for up-to-date information on new clubs, shows, films, events and gay news are the free newspapers, notably the *Bay Times* and the *Bay Area Reporter (BAR)*, found in cafés or street-corner boxes. The Center (*see p232* **The Center**) has numerous fliers and listings for queer events. The **Women's Building** (*see p87*) houses various non-profit organisations; you'll find newspapers, bulletin board postings and information here too. Local queer-about-town Larry-bob Roberts regularly updates his website listings – click 'event listings' at www.holytitclamps.com. The free *Bay Guardian* and *SF Weekly* are also worth a look.

Where to stay

Most San Francisco hoteliers either openly welcome same-gender couples or are utterly indifferent to their guests' sexuality: for a complete listing, *see p31*. But here are Castro's best, plus a couple of favourites.

The Castro

Beck's Motor Lodge

2222 Market Street, CA 94114, at 15th Street (621 8212/fax 421 0435). Muni Metro F, J, K, L, M/bus 22, 37. **Rates** single $89-$104; double $93-$109. **Credit** AmEx, Disc, MC, V. **Map** p314 E6. The quintessential American motel: tacky carpets, garish soft furnishings, glasses sealed in plastic. Relatively cheap rates, a sun deck and its prime Castro location keep the Lodge popular. **Hotel services** *Air conditioning (some rooms). Business services. Concierge. Parking (free). Safe. Sun deck.* **Room services** *Dataport. Refrigerator. TV: cable.*

Inn on Castro

321 Castro Street, CA 94114, at Market Street (861 0321/www.innoncastro2.com). Muni Metro F, K, L, M/bus 24, 33, 35, 37. **Rates** single $85-$165; double $100-185; suite $185. **Credit** AmEx, Disc, MC, V. **Map** p313 E6. Twenty years old, this beautifully restored Edwardian is still going strong. Its eight rooms and four apartments are decorated in a contemporary meets traditional style, with original modern art. Elaborate flower arrangements throughout the Inn are a highlight, along with the hotel's famous breakfast, featuring delicious own-made muffins and fresh fruit. **Hotel services** *Business centre. Concierge. Parking ($15).* **Room services** *Complimentary brandy. Dataport. TV: cable.*

Arts & Entertainment

Hey sister

According to legend, the history ('sistory' might be more fitting) of the Sisters of Perpetual Indulgence can be traced to a convent in Iowa where, in 1976, a group of local theatre buffs who claimed that they were preparing to stage a production of *The Sound of Music* borrowed habits from some unsuspecting nuns. Years later, those very habits appeared in San Francisco: four men in nun drag marched across the cruisy gay hotspot, Land's End Beach (*see p106* **Beaches: Bare-faced cheeks**), delighting naked sun worshippers. It was Easter weekend 1979.

The Sisters of Perpetual Indulgence – an antidote to the 'Castro Clone' aesthetic of tight jeans, flannel shirts and moustaches – offered such a sassy theology of liberated love, raunchy humour and unbounded individualism that the Order quickly grew. Each Sister cultivated her own unique and outrageous persona, adopting monikers such as Sister Lily White Superior Posterior, Sister Edith Myflesh, Sister Constance Craving and Sister Vicious Power Hungry Bitch. Their unique approach to performance – they were renowned for their pom-pom routines – and activism coincided with the onset of AIDS in

Nancy's Bed

In Twin Peaks, near the Castro; phone for exact address (239 5692). **Rates** single $35; double $65. **No credit cards. Map** p313.

Those seeking respite from San Francisco's numerous cookie-cutter hotels should head here. Nancy and her partner share their home, with women travellers, who can rent the guest room. Patrons have access to the kitchen and (beware, allergy-sufferers) the hosts' cats. **Room services** *TV: VCR.*

The Parker Guest House

520 Church Street, CA 94114, at 18th Street (1-888 520 7275/621 3222/fax 621 4139/ www.parkerguesthouse.com). Muni Metro J/bus 22, 33. **Rates** $119-$199. **Credit** AmEx, Disc, MC, V. **Map** p314 E6.

This beautifully renovated 1909 Edwardian mini-mansion expanded into the next door property in 2002, but Bill, Bob and the eponymous Parker,

their adorable pug, ensure the place remains as relaxed and welcoming as ever. There are now 21 rooms (two with shared baths, all with terrycloth robes), a gorgeous garden, a steam room, a communal lounge and an airy breakfast room and balcony for morning coffee. Muni Metro runs outside until 11.30pm, but only the lightest sleepers need be concerned.

Hotel services *Breakfast room: complimentary breakfast & afternoon wine. Concierge. Fax. Internet. Parking ($15).* **Room services** *Dataport. TV: cable. Voicemail.*

24 Henry Guesthouse & Village House

24 Henry Street, CA 94114, between Sanchez & Noe Streets (1-800 900 5686/864 5686/fax 864 0406/www.24henry.com). Muni Metro F, J, K, L, M, N/bus 22, 24, 37. **Rates** single $65-$109; double $89-$119. **Credit** AmEx, MC, V. **Map** p313/14 E6.

the early '80s, and they were among the first groups to create a sex-positive safer sex pamphlet for gay men.

The Sisters' spin on religion did not escape the notice of conservatives, who denounced their antics as a sacrilegious affront. But the good ladies welcomed controversy: during Pope John Paul II's visit to San Francisco in 1987, the Sisters' protests, objecting to the Pope's stand on homosexuality and contraception, landed them on the official Papal List of Heretics. Then in 1999 the Sisters drew fire from a Catholic archbishop, who objected to their request to and permission from the city to close Castro Street on Easter Sunday for their 20th anniversary party and fundraiser.

The Sisters' presence is now de rigueur at all major queer events. Over 25 years of glitter and rabble-rousing have made them a beloved institution. They're also a money-raising force to be reckoned with, collecting around $90,000 each year.

You're likely to catch the Sisters *en masse* at their Easter Sunday anniversary (often in Dolores Park), as a contingent in the Pride Parade or working as door divas and hostesses at the Folsom Street Fair and Dore Alley Fair, as well as in the Castro for Pink Saturday, organising Children's Halloween and, in December, at their Saturnalia Grants Giveaway. Check out their website (www.thesisters.org) for a calendar of appearances.

These two refurbished late 1800s Victorian houses-turned-hotels cater to queer vacationers. Everyone is welcome, though – just as long as they don't smoke in their rooms. Both hotels are conveniently located a mere pigeon's spit away from Castro Street (you'll find the Village House at 4080 18th Street), each has a parlour and five bedrooms, with shared or private bath.
Hotel services *Breakfast room: complimentary breakfast.* **Room services** *Dataport. Voicemail.*

The Willows Inn

710 14th Street, CA 94114, between Sanchez & Church Streets (431 4770/fax 431 5295/ www.willowsf.com). Muni Metro F, J, K, L, M, N/bus 22, 24, 37. **Rates** *single $99-$119; double $109-$139.* **Credit** AmEx, DC, Disc, MC, V. **Map** p314 E4.
Located close to the wild heart of the Castro, this converted 1903 Edwardian home has 12 comfy rooms decked out in bentwood willow and antique

furnishings. Baths are shared here, but all rooms do have sinks. Guests are served complimentary breakfast and cocktails daily.
Hotel services *Complimentary evening drinks. Concierge. Fax. Parking (limited, $15).* **Room services** *Dataport/Wi-fi. Minibar. Turndown (late arrivals). TV: VCR/cable. Voicemail.*

Other neighbourhoods

Alamo Square Inn

719 Scott Street, CA 94117, at Fulton Street, Western Addition (922 2055/fax 931 1304/ www.alamoinn.com). Bus 5, 21, 22, 24. **Rates** single $95-$210; suite $165-$210. **Credit** AmEx, MC, V. **Map** p313 E5.
Located on pretty Alamo Square, directly opposite the famous row of Victorians known as the 'Painted Ladies', this is one of the most charming guesthouses in the city. An old-fashioned bed and breakfast, it's housed in two beautiful specimens – an 1895 Queen Anne and an unusual 1896 Tudor Revival. It's also right on Alamo Square Park, and just a block away from lively Divisadero Street, with its cafés and shops.
Hotel services *Breakfast room: complimentary breakfast & afternoon tea/wine. Business centre. Parking (free).*

Hayes Valley Inn

417 Gough Street, CA 94102, at Hayes Street, Hayes Valley (431 9131/www.hayesvalleyinn.com). Bus 21, 47, 49. **Rates** single $58-$88; double $79-$99. **Credit** AmEx, DC, MC, V. **Map** p314 F5.
With the collapse of the freeway that once (literally and figuratively) overshadowed this area (*see p95*), Hayes Valley is becoming super chic. This pleasant 28-room pension sits on the edge of the trendy 'hood, not far from the newly refurbished City Hall. There's a friendly bar downstairs, pets are welcome and rooms have their own sink; baths are shared. Parking is available nearby for $10 a day.
Hotel services *Breakfast room: complimentary breakfast. Business centre. Concierge.* **Room services** *Dataport. TV: cable.*

Bars

The Castro

Badlands

4121 18th Street, at Castro Street (626 9320). Muni Metro F, K, L, M/bus 24, 33, 35, 37. **Open** 2pm-2am daily. **No credit cards. Map** p313 E6/7.
The ever-popular Badlands is one of the hottest hangouts in the heart of the Castro. Pop in to check out its slick interior. During the weekend rush, boys bust a move on the 'fishbowl' dancefloor.

Bar on Castro

456 Castro Street, between 18th & Market Streets (626 7220). Muni Metro F, K, L, M/bus 24, 33, 35, 37. **Open** 5pm-2am Mon-Fri; noon-2am Sat, Sun. **No credit cards. Map** p313 E6.

Arts & Entertainment

Call 'em young and cute or call 'em 'twinkies', the boys who come to party at Bar on Castro have some attitude – and they're fun to watch. After-work crowds congregate too for the weekday happy hour (4-8pm Mon-Thur). Happy hours, that is.

Castro Country Club

4058 18th Street, at Castro Street (552 6102/ www.castrocountryclub.org). Muni Metro F, K, L, M/bus 24, 33, 35, 37. **Open** noon-11pm Mon-Thur; noon-1am Sat; 10am-11pm Sun. **No credit cards. Map** p313 E6/7.
Part coffee house, part hangout, the Country Club is a good alternative to the many surrounding bars and home to clean and sober queers and their friends. Located in a renovated Victorian, the club has a parlour, a room for boardgames and a sunny back patio. The front steps are the prime spot for cruising.

Detour

2348 Market Street, at Noe Street (861 6053). Muni Metro F, K, L, M/bus 24, 37. **Open** 2pm-2am daily. **No credit cards. Map** p313/14 E6.
If you haven't found Mr Right, this is the place to pick up Mr Right Now. A newly spruced-up interior (the memorable chain-link fence remains) and progressive music make this spot a hit with twenty- and thirtysomething guys intent on ferocious cruising.

Daddy's

440 Castro Street, at 18th Street (621 8732). Muni Metro F, K, L, M/bus 24, 33, 35. **Open** 9am-2am everyday. **No credit cards. Map** p313 E6/7.
This is the Castro's premier leather and denim bar, and really packs them in when leather events such as the Folsom Street Fair (*see p192*) are under way. Friendly locals enjoy the daily drink specials, and it's popular year-round as a gathering place for leather daddies and their boys.

Harvey's

500 Castro Street, at 18th Street (431 4278). Muni Metro F, K, L, M/bus 24, 33, 35, 37. **Open** 11am-2am Mon-Fri; 9am-2am Sat, Sun. **Credit** AmEx, DC, MC, V. **Map** p313 E6/7.
This friendly neighbourhood bar and restaurant used to be called the Elephant Walk, and was the site of an infamous brawl between queers and cops during the White Night riot of 1979 (*see p16*). Now named after slain San Francisco supervisor Harvey Milk, memorabilia and photos line the walls. Monday is popular for the bar's trivia quiz night.

Martuni's

4 Valencia Street, at Market Street (241 0205). Muni F, K, L, M/bus 6, 7, 26, 66, 71. **Open** 4pm-2am daily. **Credit** MC, V. **Map** p314 F5.
Martuni's is classy in an '80s sort of a way: namely, glass, chrome and lots of them. The location's perfect, though (on the outskirts of the Castro, Hayes Valley and Mission districts) and the atmosphere warm and welcoming. Friendly staff serve up great drinks and a jazz pianist, and occasional tipsy torch song at the open mic, soothe the weary of heart.

The Midnight Sun

4067 18th Street, between Castro & Noe Streets (861 4186). Muni Metro F, K, L, M/bus 24, 33, 35, 37. **Open** 2pm-2am Mon-Fri; noon-2am Sat, Sun. **No credit cards. Map** p313/14 E6/7.
Guys who want to prove they *can* multi-task will like it here. Cruise for hours while pretending to watch music vids and comedy skits showing on the bar's walls. The two-for-one cocktail hour (2-7pm weekdays) is generous; weekends are a boy fest.

The Mix

4086 18th Street, between Castro & Noe Streets (431 8616). Muni Metro F, K, L, M/bus 24, 33, 35. **Open** noon to 2am Mon-Fri; 8am-2am Sat, Sun. **No credit cards. Map** p313/14 E6/7.
Formerly known as Uncle Bert's Place, this friendly sports bar draws queer jocks and the folks who love them. Avid fans gather to root for the Giants or the '49ers, and on sunny weekends the grill on the back patio is a gem for tasty burgers and hot dogs.

Moby Dick's

4049 18th Street, at Hartford Street (no phone). Muni Metro F, K, L, M/bus 24, 33, 35, 37. **Open** 2pm-2am Mon-Fri; noon-2am Sat, Sun. **No credit cards. Map** p313/14 E6/7.
A cross between a neighbourhood pub and a gay bar, some locals consider this the friendliest spot in the Castro. Popular with pool players (although there's only one table) and pinball addicts (four machines at the back), those with other interests will find the big windows and prime Castro location make street cruising easy as well.

Orbit Room

1900 Market Street, at Laguna Street (252 9525). Muni Metro F, K, L, M/bus 6, 7, 66, 71. **Open** 2pm-2am daily. **No credit cards. Map** p314 F5.
This high-ceilinged art deco retreat is a coffee house by day and a cocktail bar by night. Its location on the edge of the Castro attracts a mellow crowd of straights and queers, with tasty cocktails making it a relaxing place to flutter away a gentle evening.

Whiskey Lounge

4063 18th Street, at Hartford Street (255 2733). Metro Muni F, K, L, M/bus 24, 33, 35. **Open** 5pm-midnight Mon-Sat; 10am-midnight Sun. **Credit** AmEx, MC, V. **Map** p313/14 E6/7.
The Whiskey Lounge sits above the Red Grill restaurant (which serves tasty Asian-influenced comfort food) in a renovated Victorian and is a throwback to more elegant times. Soft lighting, plush leather seats and a classy ambience makes this the perfect spot for romantic murmurings or dignified cruising.

The Mission

Although not strictly a gay bar, **El Rio** (*see p212*) hosts one-of-a-kind salsa parties and numerous queer-friendly events. Check its website (www.elriosf.com) for listings.

The Stud gets pie-eyed. *See p230.*

Esta Noche

3079 16th Street, at Mission Street (861 5757).
BART 16th Street/bus 14, 22, 26, 33, 49, 53.
Open 1pm-2am daily; closed Wed at 3am.
No credit cards. Map p314 F6.

In business more than 20 years, this unique
Latino drag club hosts a spectacular lip-synching
drag show (11.30pm Mon-Thur); go-go dancers
strut their stuff on Fridays (hourly, 10.30pm-
12.30am); and there are two drag shows on
Saturdays (7pm and 11.30pm) and three on Sundays
(7pm, 10.30pm and midnight). At weekends divas
spill on to 16th Street to smoke, and flaunt a little
tough-girl glamour.

Lexington Club

3464 19th Street, at Lexington Street (863 2052).
BART 16th Street or 24th Street/bus 14, 26, 33,
49. **Open** 3pm-2am daily. **No credit cards.**
Map p314 F7.

One of the city's most popular grrrl bars, the
Lexington is funky and mellow. Blood-red walls and
church pews give it a naughty atmosphere. Grab a
bar stool to flirt with the cute dyke bartender or settle at a corner table to suck face with your sweetie.

SoMa

Hole in the Wall

289 Eighth Street, between Howard & Folsom
Streets (431 4695). Bus 12, 19. **Open** noon-2am
daily. **No credit cards. Map** p314 G5.

One of the most popular hangouts for Gen-X queers
who have turned their backs on the Castro's clone
scene. Compare tattoos with hot boys in torn clothes.

Loading Dock

1525 Mission Street, between 11th Street & South
Van Ness Avenue (864 1525/www.loadingdocksf.com).
Muni Metro F, J, K, L, M, N/bus 9, 14, 26, 57.
Open 8pm-2am Thur-Sat; 6pm-2am Sun.
No credit cards. Map p314 F5.

This S&M bar prides itself on its strictly enforced
dress code (leather, latex, Levi's with boots, uniforms). Dabblers and drag queens need not apply.

Lone Star Saloon

1354 Harrison Street, between Ninth & Tenth
Streets (863 9999). Bus 12, 19, 27, 47. **Open**
noon-2am Mon-Fri; 9am-2am Sat, Sun. **No credit**
cards. Map p314 G5.

As the name suggests, country music is the prevalent sound (albeit interspersed with other styles) at
this biker bar that is an important centre for San
Francisco's leather scene. Bear heaven.

Powerhouse

1347 Folsom Street, between Ninth & Tenth
Streets (552 8689). Bus 12, 19, 27, 47.
Open 4pm-2am Mon-Sat; 2pm-2am Sun.
No credit cards. Map p314 G5.

Hard and hot, this is one of the most popular (male)
gay bars in the city. Underwear night, leather night,
blackout night, uniform and boot night. You get the
idea. Sexy customers complement sexy bartenders.

Other neighbourhoods

Aunt Charlie's Lounge

133 Turk Street, at Taylor Street, Tenderloin (441
2922/www.auntcharlieslounge.com).
Open noon-12am Mon-Thur; noon-2am Fri; 10am-
2am Sat, Sun. **No credit cards. Map** p310 G4.

Drag revues, sports nights, stiff drinks and a long-
standing location in the Tenderloin make this a popular spot. The slightly older crowd could probably
teach the Castro boys a thing or two.

Marlena's

488 Hayes Street, at Octavia Street, Hayes Valley
(864 6672). Bus 21, 47, 49. **Open** 3pm-2am Mon-Fri;
noon-2am Sat, Sun. **No credit cards. Map** p314 F5.

An eclectic crowd (including drag queens on the
weekends) shows up for the great Martinis at this
Hayes Street treasure. The building is a former
speakeasy, and it shows in the bar's cosy ambience.

The Lion Pub

2062 Divisadero Street, at Sacramento Street,
Pacific Heights (567 6565). Bus 1, 24. **Open**
4pm-2am daily. **No credit cards. Map** p309 D3.

Arts & Entertainment

The Lion Pub is not just the only gay bar in chi-chi Pacific Heights, but also the oldest continuously operating gay bar in the city. Its location on the first floor of a renovated Victorian makes it easy to miss, but queers with an eye for moneyed honeys and Martha Stewart-style decor should check it out.

Wild Side West

424 Cortland Avenue, at Wool Street, Bernal Heights (647 3099). Muni Metro J/bus 24. **Open** 1pm-2am daily. **No credit cards.**
This place has been around forever (though it used to be in North Beach) and has gathered some myths: it's said Janis Joplin picked up girls at the Wild Side's wooden bar. The walls are a shifting art installation, the pool table is cherry red, the patio sunny and the clientele mixed – it might be the city's longest-standing lesbian bar, but it's totally het friendly. There's a fabulous jukebox too: Joplin, Patsy Cline and, of course, Lou Reed's *Walk on the Wild Side*.

Dance clubs

The dance scene changes with dizzying rapidity, but the places listed are likely to be around for some time. It's always smart to check club-scene magazines *Odyssey* and *Gloss* to be sure a particular night is still happening. In the Mission, Rebel Girl spins for dykes and their friends at **26 Mix** (3024 Mission Street, at 26th Street, 826 7378, www.26mix.com) every first and third Thursday; glossy **Mezzanine** (*see p221*) is a big hit with the boys.

Most clubs are 21 and over, so bring photo ID. Even if you think you don't need it.

The Castro

The Café

2367 Market Street, at Castro Street (861 3846). Muni Metro F, K, L, M/bus 24, 33, 35, 37. **Open** 3pm-2am daily. **Admission** varies. **No credit cards. Map** p313 E6.
The Café is the Castro's most popular dance club. It helps that it's often free, but the two bars, dancefloor, patio and pool table add to the allure – it also contains the hottest young things (male and female) in town. Expect to queue on Friday and Saturday and wear something lightweight and revealing: temperatures soar as the night gets going.

SoMa

Cherry Bar & Lounge

917 Folsom Street, at Fifth Street (974 1585/www. thecherrybar.com). Bus 12, 27. **Open** times vary. **Admission** varies. **No credit cards. Map** p315 H4.
There are surprisingly few women's clubs in San Francisco, and Cherry (owned by the woman who founded the Dinah Shore Weekend, a renowned lesbian golf frolic) lives up to its reputation for the

city's slickest and sleekest nights for gals. Gorgeous babes descend for Girl Spot on Saturdays, Deep (every second Friday) and hip-hop junket Nasty (third Fridays). Third Sundays are 'for bears and their friends' and there are some straight nights, so it pays to check in advance.

The Endup

401 Sixth Street, at Harrison Street (357 0827/ www.theendup.com). Bus 12, 27, 47. **Open** 10pm-4.30am Thur; 10pm-6am Fri; 6am-noon, 10pm-4am Sat; 6am-8pm Sun. **Admission** $6-$12. **No credit cards. Map** p315 H5.
Saturday night has turned into Sunday morning and you're still going strong? Then the party continues here, with the T-Dance starting at 6am. Fag Friday is also a regular. This club just is gay San Francisco – it's been going since 1973.

The Stud

399 Ninth Street, at Harrison Street (252 7883/ www.studsf.com). Bus 19, 27, 47. **Open** 5pm-3am daily. **Admission** free-$15. **No credit cards. Map** p314 G5.
Buried in SoMa (take a cab both ways), this San Francisco institution boasts the most varied crowd in the city. Trannyshack (Tuesdays, 10pm-3am, $6) is a gender-bender's delight, hosted by SF's rowdiest drag diva, Heklina; the midnight show is a must. Every Friday is the Cheap Trick electro-funk party, Thursdays is for butch dancers, while Planet Big (second and fourth Sundays) is for chubby chasers.

Bernal Hill/South City

Space 550

550 Barneveld Avenue, at Apparel Way, Bernal Heights (550 8286/www.space550.com). Bus 23, 24. **Open** 10pm-4am daily. **Admission** varies. **No credit cards.**
This warehouse club has been around for ages, but recent renovations have spiffed it up enough to draw increasing crowds on the weekends – having three sizeable dancefloors doesn't hurt either. Club Papi (Saturdays) attracts sexy Latino queers and those who love them, while monthly blowout Metropolis draws dedicated partiers and enthusiastic go-go boys. Call or check the website for up-to-date info.

Entertainment

Check local alternative weeklies for information on specific upcoming performances. For full listings of other venues, *see p200, p210 & p244.*

The Castro

Castro Theatre

429 Castro Street, at Market Street (621 6120/ www.thecastrotheatre.com). Muni Metro F, K, L, M/bus 24, 33, 35, 37. **Tickets** $8; $5 concessions. **No credit cards. Map** p314 X1.

This is one of the city's finest rep houses: painted murals line the art deco walls and the ceilings shimmer with gold. Before each screening the audience is entertained by a battery of favourites played on the Mighty Wurlitzer. But the theatre really comes into its own for screenings of gay and camp classics. Until you've seen *Mommie Dearest, Valley of the Dolls* or *All About Eve* in a queer-packed theatre, with everyone joining in for the killer lines, you haven't seen audience participation. The *Sound of Music* sing-along is an institution.

Comedy Showcase

LGBT Community Center, 1800 Market Street, at Octavia Street (541 5610/www.qcomedy.com). Muni Metro F, J, K, L, M, N/bus 6, 7, 9, 10, 14, 21, 26, 47, 49, 66, 71. **Open** 7.30pm, shows begin 8pm. **Admission** $8-$15. **Map** p314 F5.

What's so funny about queers? This is the place to find out. Picking up from where much-loved Josie's Cabaret left off, QComedy at the Center (*see p232* **The Center**) features queer stand-up every other Monday. Local stars Marga Gomez and Scott Kennedy have made recent appearances.

The Mission

Brava! For Women in the Arts

Theatre Center, 2781 24th Street, between York & Hampshire Streets (641 7657/www.brava.org). BART 24th Street/bus 9, 27, 33, 48. **Tickets** free-$50. **Credit** MC, V. **Map** p315 G7.

Housed in a former vaudeville theatre, Brava specialises in new work by women of colour and lesbians. Founded in 1986, the group has put on more than 1,000 performances for some 150,000 people.

In Bed with Fairy Butch

Club Galia, 2565 Mission Street, at 22nd Street (339 8000/www.fairybutch.com). BART 24th Street/bus 15, 49. **Tickets** $15-$20. **Open** 8pm-2am; show begins at 9.30pm. **No credit cards**. **Map** p314 F7.

On the first and third Saturdays of each month, the charming and talented Fairy Butch (aka Karlyn Lotney) hosts a camp, erotic cabaret for dykes, trannies and their pals. Femme and butch strippers make this a fave with local women. After the show, the DJ spins retro tunes (disco and '80s) and hip hop.

Theatre Rhinoceros

2926 16th Street, between Mission Street & South Van Ness Avenue (861 5079/www.therhino.org). BART 16th Street/bus 14, 22, 33, 49, 53. **Tickets** $15-$30. **Credit** MC, V. **Map** p314 F6.

Founded in 1977, the Rhinoceros claims to be the world's longest-running professional queer theatre; long enough, certainly, to help the development of important work like the one-act plays by Harvey Fierstein that were to become the stage and movie hit *Torch Song Trilogy*. With a main stage and a smaller studio space for newer work, the theatre continues to support a huge range of work.

Restaurants & cafés

San Francisco doesn't have queer restaurants per se: gay, lesbian and transgendered diners are welcome everywhere (*see p116*). But you're most likely to see same-sex sweeties snuggling over food in the Castro and Mission, Bernal Heights or SoMa – we've listed a few favourites.

The Castro

2223 Restaurant & Bar

2223 Market Street, between Noe & Sanchez Streets (431 0692). Muni Metro F, K, L, M/bus 24, 35, 37. **Open** 5.30-9.30pm Mon-Thur; 5.30-11pm Fri; 11am-2pm, 5.30-11pm Sat; 10.30am-2pm, 5.30-9.30pm Sun. **Main courses** $15-$24; *brunch* $6.50-$10.50. **Credit** AmEx, DC, MC, V. **Map** p313/p314 E6.

By far the most upscale restaurant in the Castro, 2223 is a popular place for queers celebrating everything from birthdays and anniversaries to hot dates. The excellent cuisine has Mediterranean, Mexican and Caribbean influences and the efficient waitrons serve exotic mixed drinks. Be warned: the din on crowded nights isn't conducive to romantic conversations. The popular weekend brunch is a little calmer, but equally delicious.

Bagdad Café

2295 Market Street, at Noe Street (621 4434). Muni Metro F, K, L, M/bus 24, 35, 37. **Open** 24hrs daily. **Main courses** $7-$12. **No credit cards**. **Map** p313/14 E6.

The Bagdad owes its popularity to its central location and to the fact that it's one of the very few 24-hour restaurants in the Castro. Lots of window tables make it an excellent place to scope out cute guys and gals, and generous portions make up for the so-so food.

Blue

2337 Market Street, at 16th Street (863 2583). Muni Metro F, K, L, M/bus 24, 35, 37. **Open** 11.30am-11pm Mon-Thur; 11.30am-11.30pm Fri; 10am-11pm Sat; 10am-10pm Sun. **Main courses** $6.50-$18. **Credit** AmEx, MC, V. **Map** p313/14 E6.

Down-home cooking in a hip diner atmosphere. Slide into a smooth black booth, stare at the beautiful people passing by, and nosh on a gourmet macaroni cheese, own-made meatloaf or pork chops. Skip the dinky sidewalk tables, though: it's a busy street, so you don't want to eat on it.

Catch

2362 Market Street, at Castro Street (431 5000). Muni Metro F, K, L, M/bus 24, 33, 35, 37. **Open** 11.30am-3pm, 5.30-10pm Mon-Thur; 11.30am-3pm, 5.30-11pm Fri; 11am-3.30pm, 5.30-11pm Sat; 11am-3.30pm, 5.30-10pm Sun. **Main courses** $10-$20. **Credit** AmEx, DC, MC, V. **Map** p313 E6.

Catch is the Castro's newest restaurant, serving up seafood and traditional American chow in a swanky setting. The enclosed, heated patio out front is

The Center

Many have called the corner of Castro and 18th Streets the centre of queer San Francisco, but, since its much-anticipated opening in spring 2002, the Charles M Holmes Campus at The Center (known, for obvious reasons, simply as 'The Center') has been the vital nexus for the LGBT community.

Despite San Francisco's reputation as a gay hub, for years queers had no community centre of their own. Fundraising came first: the building bears the name of its largest single donor, the wealthy founder of the upscale gay porn empire Falcon Studios, but city government donated $6 million and 1,000 individuals pledged $1,000 each. Once the land was purchased, however, there was a battle with architectural conservationists fighting to save the lot's dilapidated Queen Anne-era Fallon Building from demolition. The architectural tussle ended in a compromise: merge the old and the new. Integrating the historic building and the new structure added $1.5 million and months of construction time to the project but, after more than nine years and $14 million, the Center was built.

Located at the intersection of the Castro, Haight and Mission neighbourhoods, the Center hosts dozens of events and welcomes over 2,000 visitors weekly. Its airy, colourful foyer holds an extensive information and advice service: there's a vast array of gay publications and events listings, free internet access, or help with everything from gay-friendly health services to roommate referrals.

The Center has children's services to support 'gayby boom' parents and their kids, while young queers find a safe haven in the welcoming youth space. There is a café, the Rainbow Room performance space and an art gallery, while in the evenings, dances are often held on the fourth-floor roof deck. Queer history is celebrated too: don't miss the Reading Room on the ground floor.

While you're here, make sure you visit the Psychiatric Survivors Memorial Skylight on the third floor of the beautifully renovated Fallon Building. Dedicated to transgender people who suffered under narrow-minded psychiatric care, it's a telling reminder of how times have changed: nowadays politicos ranging from the city supervisor to a Democratic presidential candidate are queuing up here for a photo-op.

The Center

1800 Market Street, at Octavia Street (865 5520/www.sfcenter.org). Metro Muni F, J, K, L, M, N/bus 6, 7, 9, 10, 14, 21, 26, 47, 49, 66, 71. **Open** noon-10pm Mon-Fri; 9am-10pm Sat. **Map** p314 F5.

perfect for watching the world go by, and there's live piano music. The bar fills up fast with yuppie locals on dates (or looking to snag a date), so make a reservation if you want to dine during the weekend rush.

Chow

215 Church Street, between Market & 16th Streets (552 2469). Muni F, J, K, L, M/bus 22, 37. **Open** 11am-11pm Mon-Thur; 11am-midnight Fri; 10am-midnight Sat; 10am-11pm Sun. **Main courses** $7-$15. **Credit** MC, V. **Map** p314 E6.

Chow is a noisy, friendly place with a menu that ranges from basic pasta dishes to heartier grilled fish and roast meat platters. Be sure to arrive early

if you want to secure a table for dinner, especially on weekends, otherwise you could find yourself with an hour-long wait.

Firewood Café

4248 18th Street, between Collingwood & Diamond Streets (252 0999). Muni Metro F, K, L, M/ bus 24, 33, 35. **Open** 11am-10.30pm Mon-Thur; 11am-11pm Fri, Sat; 11am-10pm Sun. **Main courses** $6.50-$13.50. **Credit** MC, V. **Map** p313 E7.

This hip, high-ceilinged bistro has a queue most nights – but don't let that put you off. Instead, make the most of your wait by perusing the large overhead menu, ordering before you get your table and thereby getting your food shortly after you sit down. House speciality is succulent roast chicken, but the pizzas and pasta are also consistently commendable.

La Mediterranee

288 Noe Street, between Market & 16th Streets (431 7210). Metro Muni F, K, L, M/bus 24, 33, 35. **Main courses** $8-$13. **Open** 11am-10pm Mon-Fri; 11am-11pm Sat, Sun. **Credit** AmEx, MC, V. **Map** p313/14 E6.

A long-standing local favourite, La Mediterranee serves up terrific houmous, baba ganoush and filo specials, all at reasonable prices. The warm, cosy interior makes the place feel like a genuine Mediterranean getaway, and the indecisive can plump for vegetarian or meat sample plates.

Samovar

498 Sanchez Street, at 18th Street (626 4700/www. samovartea.com). Metro Muni F, J, K, L, M/bus 24, 33, 35. **Open** 9am-10pm daily. **Main courses** $5.95-$8.95. **Credit** AmEx, MC, V. **Map** p313/14 E6.

As the Castro's only tearoom, this tranquil oasis has quickly become a hit with locals seeking a quiet Zen-like refuge. There are over 100 teas to try, as well as Asian-inspired small plates that are perfect affordable, healthy nosh. Don't miss high tea (weekdays, 3-6pm) or the tea brunch (weekends, 9am-3pm).

Other neighbourhoods

Asia SF

201 Ninth Street, at Howard Street, SoMa (255 2742/www.asiasf.com). Bus 14, 19, 26. **Open** *Restaurant* 6-10pm Mon-Wed; 5-10pm Thur-Sun. *Club* 7pm-3am Fri, Sat. **Main courses** $10-$20. **Credit** AmEx, DC, Disc, MC, V. **Map** p314 G5.

We'll start by answering the inevitable question: they're not. Not drag queens, that is. Nor are they women, so tread carefully if you're feeling flirty. Those sexy creatures who bring food to your table and dance seductively atop the long red bar are 'gender illusionists' and undoubtedly the stars of the show. But despite the visual and aural competition, the kitchen produces an inventive and tasty menu of Cal-Asian cuisine. A restaurant, nightclub and lounge all in one, the crowd here is a compelling mix of local party-goers and wide-eyed businessmen away from the family for a few days. Tables have a time limit of an hour and 45 minutes; reservations recommended.

Cup A Joe

1901 Hayes Street, at Ashbury Street, Haight (221 3378). Bus 5, 21, 43. **Open** 6am-8pm daily. **No credit cards. Map** p313 D6.

If your hotel room isn't wired, stop in here to check your email. Half a dozen iMacs are available for customer use (first 15mins free with purchase; $2 for every 15mins after that). And there's good coffee, alongside bagels, pastries and sandwiches. **Other locations**: 608 Geary Street, at Jones Street, Tenderloin (440 3437); 896 Sutter Street, at Leavenworth Street, Tenderloin (563 7745).

Da Flora

701 Columbus Avenue, at Filbert Street, North Beach (981 4664). Bus 15, 30, 39/cable car Powell-Mason. **Open** 5.30-9.30pm Tue-Sat. **Main courses** $16-$20. **Credit** MC, V. **Map** p310 G2.

This delightful osteria is a first for SF: a lesbian- and gay-friendly Italian restaurant in North Beach. The place is tiny, with kitsch decor and excellent food.

Mabel's Just for You Cafe

732 22nd Street, at Tennessee Street, Potrero Hill (647 3033/www.justforyoucafe.com). Bus 15, 48. **Open** 7am-2.30pm Mon-Fri; 8am-3pm Sat, Sun. **Main courses** $3-$9.95. **No credit cards. Map** p315 J7.

The popularity of the original Potrero Hill dyke-run café prompted the owners to move to bigger quarters ten blocks away. Since early 2002 they've been ensconced in the Dogpatch district, close to the Bay. House speciality is a Cajun-style breakfast, with superb grits and fluffy pancakes. Worth the trek.

Working out & health

All workout spaces are queer-friendly. The pick of the Castro is below, otherwise *see p238*.

Castro Yoga

4530 18th Street, at Douglass Street (552 9644/ www.castroyoga.com). Muni Metro F, K, L, M/bus 24, 35, 37. **Open** *Classes* from 7am Mon-Fri; from 9am Sat, Sun. **Rates** $15 per drop-in. **Map** p313 D7.

Locals love this small but clean Iyengar yoga studio. Classes are offered all day at different levels of difficulty (check the website for current details).

Gold's Gym Castro

2301 Market Street, at Noe Street (626 4488). Muni Metro F, K, L, M/bus 24, 35, 37. **Open** 5am-midnight Mon-Thur; 5am-11pm Fri; 5am-8pm Sat; 7am-8pm Sun. **Admission** $15 per day; $40 per week. **Credit** AmEx, Disc, MC, V. **Map** p313/14 E6.

Friendly staff and a booming sound system make this well-equipped gym a popular hangout.

Magnet

4122 18th Street, at Collingwood Street (581 1600/ www.magnetsf.org). Muni Metro F, K, L, M/bus 24, 35. **Open** 3-9pm Wed-Fri; 12-6pm Sat. **Map** p313 E7.

In response to rising HIV and STD rates among the city's queer men, community health groups launched an effort to put a new spin on gay men's health. Magnet is the result. This welcoming space looks more like an upscale café than a health clinic, with comfortable hangout areas and internet access. There's free, anonymous HIV and STD testing and counselling, community events, readings and workshops.

Muscle System

2275 Market Street, between Sanchez & Noe Streets (863 4700). Muni Metro F, K, L, M/bus 24, 35, 37. **Open** 5am-midnight Mon-Fri; 7am-10pm Sat; 8am-8pm Sun. **Admission** $8 per day; $27 per wk. **Credit** MC, V. **Map** p313/14 E6.

The ultimate Castro sweat palace. Men only.

Arts & Entertainment

Sport & Fitness

The watching is fun, but the taking part is a way of life.

San Franciscans may be a cultured bunch, but they still find time away from the opera to pull on a jersey and throw back scads of beer (or a supremely petulant Chardonnay) and cheer on their favourite team. The **49ers** (*see p236*) and the **Giants** (*see p236*) are the belles of the city ball, but the successes of their Oakland counterparts (the **Raiders**, *see p236*, and **Athletics**, *see below*) make for outstanding cross-bridge rivalry. The Bay Area is broad church too. San Jose, just down the peninsula, has professional ice hockey (the **Sharks**; *see p237*) and soccer (the **Earthquakes**; *see p237*) to add to Oakland's **Golden State Warriors** (*see p236*), a pro basketball team who maintain a noble tradition of futility.

This is also a city that gets fired up about joining in. It's not unusual to hear of lunch reservations at La Folie being exchanged for an afternoon's biking in the **Marin Headlands** (*see p237*) or an assault on **Mount Diablo**, shimmering tantalisingly across the Bay. The Bay itself offers many activities: sailing, surfing and windsurfing among them. For runners, there's **Bay to Breakers** (*see p189*) and superb paths at the **Marina** and round **Lake Merced**. If you're into aerobics or cross-training, there's a health club on nearly every corner, while new bike paths and glorious car-free Sundays in **Golden Gate Park** (*see p107*) keep wheel-freaks glowing. Even skiers and snowboarders can take off to the mountains (*see p242*). If it's all too much, there are plenty of **yoga** (*see p243*) classes available to help you achieve inner balance.

INFORMATION

The 'Sporting Green' section of the *San Francisco Chronicle* has a calendar of local events and broadcasts; every Thursday this includes the 'Outdoors' mini-section, which is full of listings and information on open-air activities. The *Chronicle* also hosts a superb webpage (www.sfgate.com/sports), as does KRON 4 (441 4444/www.kron.com). KNBR (680AM/1050AM/www.knbr.com) is a great source for up-to-the-minute news, as well as the endless sports chatter. There are also some outstanding specialist publications like *Sporting News*, *Sports Illustrated* and *Baseball Digest*. Useful for information on participatory sports

is *CitySports* (www.citysportsmag.com), a regional mag available in gyms and sports shops. For special events, also try the Visitor Information Center (*see p290*) on Market Street.

TICKETS, BROKERS AND SCALPERS

The best place to buy tickets is always at the box office of the team you want to see. There you can usually avoid the 'convenience' charges levied by brokers – between 5 and 50 per cent of the ticket price. Sometimes, though, the only place to get a ticket is through the big brokers (the 49ers, for example, only sell tickets this way). If so, Tickets.com (1-415 478 2277, www.tickets.com) and Ticketmaster (421 8497, www.ticketmaster.com) are good options, as they both work directly with the major teams. Other brokers include Premier Tickets (1-800 376 6876, www.premiertickets.com), Entertainment Ticketfinder (1-800 523 1515, www.ticketfinder.com) and Mr.Ticket (1-800 424 7328, www.mrtix.com). Scams abound, especially with scalpers, so be on your guard.

Spectator sports

Auto Racing

Infineon Raceway

Intersection of Highways 37 & 121, Sonoma (1-800 870 7223/www.searspoint.com). Golden Gate Bridge north to US 101, north to Highway 37, then east 10 miles to Highway 121. **Open** *Box office* 8am-5pm Mon-Fri & race days. **Tickets** $10-$60. **Credit** Disc, MC, V.

An hour away from the city, this is home to everything from NASCAR to monster-truck rallies, a surprisingly fun slice of Americana.

Baseball

Spend a summer afternoon at the ballpark and you'll see why baseball is adoringly called the 'national pastime'. Both the **San Francisco Giants** and **Oakland Athletics** are easily accessible. The Athletics' stadium is only a short train ride away, but the neophyte may well prefer to walk to the Giants' magnificent SBC Park (formerly Pacific Bell Park). Located in China Basin, the stadium has wonderful views of the glittering ocean. The baseball season runs from April to October.

Peace, love & baseball

and somehow keeping legendary batter Barry Bonds (*pictured*) hitting homers for the team (he won an unparalleled fifth Most Valuable Player award in 2003) – the Giants have yet to secure that elusive first World Series.

The roots of Bay Area baseball pre-date the Giants and A's, with a strong minor league tradition that goes back to the turn of the century. The San Francisco Seals and Oakland Oaks were hugely popular, not least because the nearest Major League team was 2,000 miles (3,219 kilometres) away in St Louis, and so the rivalry between San Francisco and Oakland was already in place long before the two Big League franchises began duking it out.

Even so, this city has an indomitable will to love everyone, and there are those who find it impossible to hate someone simply for backing the wrong side. In

The **Giants** arrived in San Francisco in 1958. Ten years later the **Athletics** moved west to Oakland (for both, *see p234*). But it's the latter that have the four World Series titles, not least one over the Giants from 1989. Their cross-bay rivalry became literally earth-shaking during this so-called 'Bay Bridge' World Series, with the massive Loma Prieta earthquake striking the city during one of the games. Despite winning the NL Western Division several times over the last decade –

other words, some San Franciscans genuinely root for both the Giants and the A's, a notion entirely foreign to the old baseball cities of the Midwest and East Coast, where loyalty to one specific team only is as natural and essential as breathing. The signpost for this patchouli-scented philanthropy? The A's/Giants split-panel cap, where the front is divided down the middle, giving equal time to both teams on one fence-riding noggin.

Oakland Athletics

Network Associates Coliseum, 7000 Coliseum Way, Nimitz Freeway, at Hegenberger Road, Oakland (1-510 568 5600/www.oaklandathletics.com). BART Coliseum. **Open** *Box office* 9am-6pm Mon-Fri; 10am-4pm Sat; 2hrs before game. **Tickets** $8-$34. **Credit** AmEx, Disc, MC, V.

San Francisco Giants

SBC Park, 24 Willie Mays Plaza, at Third & King Streets, South Beach (972 2000/www.sfgiants.com). Muni N/bus 10, 15, 30, 45, 47. **Open** *Box office* 8.30am-5.30pm Mon-Fri; 2hrs before game Sat, Sun. **Tickets** $12-$75. **Credit** Disc, MC, V. **Map** p315 J5.

Basketball

There's plenty of roundball here. The **Warriors** play in Oakland from November to May, while the thrilling college season runs from December through to the 'March Madness' national tournament. Both Stanford (1-800 782 6367, www.gostanford.com) and the University of California at Berkeley (1-800 462 3277, www.calbears.com) put out competitive teams.

Chugging beers

The 'Teal Terror' of the **San Jose Sharks** (*see p237*) may be more bark than bite, but they offer one attraction neither baseball nor football can match: when you get the CalTrain to the HP Pavilion, getting there really is half the fun.

CalTrain is ageing and rather slow (although the 'Baby Bullet', due in spring 2004, is expected to cut journey times in half), but it's cheap, comfortable and has one famous quality – you can drink on it. That's right, grab a six-pack, some seats with your friends and let someone else do the driving. The conductor will punch your tickets, but doesn't blink an eye when you pull out that extra large can of fizzy lager.

By the time your hour is up and you've arrived in San Jose, you're more than ready for sirens and the organ and the screaming. Just don't forget, as the zambonis start clearing the ice, you've got to catch that last train back – negotiated cab fares come in at around $100.

CalTrain Depot

4th Street & King Street, China Basin (1-800 660 4287/www.caltrain.com). Muni N/bus 10, 15, 30, 45, 47, 76, 91owl. **Tickets** $11 return. **Credit** Disc, MC, V. **Map** p315 H5.

If you think you've got game, there are pick-up contests across the city – the hoops at James Lick Middle School (Clipper and Castro Streets, Noe Valley) are the best if you're really serious.

Golden State Warriors

The Arena in Oakland (just behind the Network Associates Coliseum), 7000 Coliseum Way, Oakland (1-510 986 2200/www.warriors.com). BART Coliseum. **Open** *Box office* 10am-6pm Mon-Fri; 10am-4pm Sat. **Tickets** $10-$270. **Credit** AmEx, MC, V.

Football

The National Football League's **49ers** and **Raiders** were born with only the Bay to keep them apart and their supporters remain fanatically – almost religiously – opposed. Tickets are expensive and hard to come by, but sit in the 'Black Hole' in Oakland and you'll be terrified or enamoured. Most likely terrified. The annual college highlight is November's 'Big Game' between Stanford and Cal.

Oakland Raiders

Network Associates Coliseum, 7000 Coliseum Way, Nimitz Freeway, at Hegenberger Road, Oakland (toll-free 1-510 569 2121/www.raiders.com). BART Coliseum. **Open** *Box office* 10am-6pm Mon-Fri; 10am-4pm Sat; 2hrs before game Sun. **Tickets** $47-$91. **Credit** AmEx, Disc, MC, V.

San Francisco 49ers

3Com Park, Giants Drive, at Gilman Avenue, Bayview (656 4900/www.sf49ers.com). Ballpark Express Muni 9X from Sutter & Sansome Streets, 47X on Van Ness Avenue, or Muni 28X from Funston & California Streets. **Tickets** $58; single game tickets through Ticketmaster only (with $9 surcharge). **Credit** AmEx, Disc, DC, MC, V.

Horseracing

Bay Meadows Racecourse

2600 S Delaware Street, at Palm Avenue, San Mateo (1-650 574 7223/www.baymeadows.com). CalTrain to Bay Meadows. **Open** *Race days* Apr-June, Aug-Nov. *Box office* 9.30am-7pm Wed-Sat. **Tickets** $3-$15. **Credit** AmEx, Disc, MC, V.

Golden Gate Fields

1100 Eastshore Highway, Albany (1-510 559 7300/www.ggfields.com). BART North Berkeley, then AC Transit shuttle bus. **Open** *Race days* Nov-Apr Wed-Sun. *Box office* 9.30am-7pm Mon-Fri; 9am-5pm Sat. **Tickets** $3-$15. **Credit** MC, V.

Ice hockey

The National Hockey League's **San Jose Sharks** brought ice hockey to the Bay Area over ten years ago. They're still going strong, packing out the 'Shark Tank' with rabid fans.

(Side margin:) **Arts & Entertainment**

Games are immensely entertaining, especially after the beer train (*see p236* **Chugging beers**). The season runs from October to May.

San Jose Sharks

HP Pavilion, 525 West Santa Clara Street, at Autumn Street, San Jose (1-408 287 9200/www.sj-sharks.com). CalTrain to San Jose Diridon Station. **Open** *Box office* 9.30am-5.30pm Mon-Fri; from 3hrs before game Sat, Sun. **Tickets** $19-$112. **Credit** AmEx, MC, V.

Soccer

For a real football fix, look no further than the San Jose Earthquakes. They even boast a World Cup striker: American Landon Donovan.

San Jose Earthquakes

Spartan Stadium, Seventh Street, between Alma & Humboldt Streets, San Jose; box office 3550 Stevens Creek Boulevard, between San Tomas & Cypress Streets, San Jose (1-408 985 4625/www.sj earthquakes.com). CalTrain to San Jose. **Tickets** $12-$45. **Open** *Box office* 9am-5pm Mon-Fri; 2hrs before game Sat, Sun. **Credit** AmEx, MC, V.

Active sports/fitness

There can be few cities in the world as committed to active pastimes as San Francisco, so you shouldn't have any difficulty getting involved while you're here. If you're hiring expensive equipment, photo ID or a credit card is usually required for the deposit.

Bowling

Presidio Bowling Center

Building 93, at Montgomery Street & Moraga Avenue, Presidio (561 2695). Bus 29. **Open** 9am-12am Mon-Thur, Sun; 9am-2am Fri, Sat. **Rates** $2.50-$5/game. *Shoe rental* $3. **Credit** MC, V. **Map** p308 B2.

Yerba Buena Bowling Center

750 Folsom Street, between Third & Fourth Streets, SoMa (777 3727/www.skatebowl.com). Bus 12, 15, 30, 45, 76. **Open** 10am-10pm Mon-Thur, Sun; 10am-midnight Fri, Sat. **Rates** $3.50-$5/game. *Shoe rental* $3. **Credit** MC, V. **Map** p311 H4.

Cycling

There is no better way to get quickly around San Francisco than on a bicycle. Squeezed in by the peninsula, the city doesn't sprawl like most others and, mercifully, the precipitous hills go two ways. Bicycle lanes criss-cross in every direction (*see p279*), but be wary of the traffic – SUVs, Hummers and other such monstrosities are notorious for disregarding anything smaller than they are, namely everything. With windswept views of the sea, the aroma of

eucalyptus trees and the glorious Golden Gate Park, biking in the city is uniquely memorable.

Across the Bay, the endless biking trails in **Marin Headlands** (*see p251*) offer unmatched sights and pulmonary exertions: the mountain bike was born on the paths of **Bolinas Ridge** in Marin County and **Railroad Grade** along Mount Tamalpais. For information, call the Golden Gate National Recreation Area Visitor Center (331 1540) or the Pantoll Ranger Station (388 2070). Route maps, which include the street gradients, are available in most bike shops and some bookshops, where Roy Hosler's *Bay Area Bike Rides* ($14.95; www.chroniclebooks.com) can also be found.

Bicycles can be taken free of charge on BART, except during peak commuter hours (7-9am and 4-6pm weekdays). The Ferries will also take you and your beloved mountain bike across the rough Bay waters.

Golden Gate Park Skate & Bike

3038 Fulton Street, between Sixth & Seventh Avenues, Richmond (668 1117). Bus 5, 21, 31, 33. **Open** 10am-6pm Mon-Fri; 9am-7pm Sun. **Rates** *Bikes* $5/hr or $25/day. *Skates* $4/hr or $12/day. **Credit** MC, V. **Map** p312 B5.
This friendly shop rents out bikes, rollerskates and in-line skates and offers skateboarding lessons. Rates include a helmet and knee and elbow pads.

Solano Avenue Cyclery

1554 Solano Avenue, Albany (1-510 524 1094/ www.solanoavenuecyclery.com). BART El Cerrito Plaza, then AC Transit bus 43/AC Transit bus G. **Open** 11am-7pm Mon-Fri; 10am-6pm Sat; noon-5pm Sun. **Rates** $25/day. **Credit** Disc, MC, V.
Near Berkeley, this is a great place to launch into the East Bay trails – ask about the Nimitz Bike Path.

Surrey Bikes & Blades

50 Stow Lake Drive, at John F Kennedy & Cross Over Drives, Golden Gate Park (668 6699). Bus 5, 28, 29. **Open** 10am-5pm Mon-Fri; 9am-5pm Sat, Sun. **Rates** $8/hr or $25/day. **Credit** MC, V. **Map** p312 A6.

Golf

Golden Gate Park Course

John F Kennedy Drive, at 47th Avenue, Golden Gate Park (751 8987/www.goldengateparkgolf.com). Bus 5, 18, 31, 38. **Open** dawn-dusk daily. **Rates** $13 Mon-Fri; $18 Sat, Sun, holidays. **No credit cards.**
Just above Ocean Beach, a par-27 nine-hole course.

Harding Municipal Park & Golf Course

Harding Road & Skyline Boulevard, Lake Merced (750 4653). Metro Muni L/bus 18, 29. **Open** dawn-dusk daily. **Rates** *Non-residents* $76 Mon-Fri; $88 Sat, Sun. *Residents* $35 Mon-Fri; $45 Sat, Sun. **No credit cards.**

The second nine of this par-72 18-hole course is the par-32 Jack Fleming Golf Course, designed to provide golfers with a championship-quality course at a less difficult level.

Lincoln Park Golf Course

300 34th Avenue, at Clement Street, Lincoln Park (221 9911). Bus 1, 2, 18, 38. **Open** dawn-dusk daily. **Rates** $31 Mon-Thur; $35 Fri-Sun. **No credit cards.**

One of the most photographed courses in the US, because of a fabulous view of the Golden Gate Bridge from the 17th. Prices drop as the light fades.

Mission Bay Golf Center

1200 Sixth Street, at Channel Street, China Basin (431 7888). Bus 15. **Open** 11.30am-10pm Mon; 7am-10pm Tue-Sun. **Rates** $8 for a basket of balls. **Credit** MC, V. **Map** p315 H5.

Mission Bay Golf Centre offers a 300yd (274m), two-tiered driving range, as well as a restaurant and discount golf shop. And a 360° panorama of downtown, the freeway, East Bay and the south San Francisco hills.

Presidio Golf Course

300 Finley Road, at Arguello Gate, Presidio (561 4653/www.presidiogolf.com). Bus 28. **Open** dawn-dusk daily. **Rates** $52-$93. **Credit** AmEx, MC, V. **Map** p308 B/C3.

Built in 1885, former presidents Roosevelt and Eisenhower both played this 18-hole course when it was military only; it opened to the public in 1995.

Gyms

San Franciscans love their corner gyms every bit as much as their corner cafés and bars. Each neighbourhood seems to have at least one, some have many – a few of the best are listed here.

Embarcadero YMCA

169 Steuart Street, at Mission Street, Financial District (957 9622/www.ymcasf.org). BART Embarcadero/Muni F, J, K, L, M, N/bus 2, 6, 7, 9, 14, 21, 31, 32, 66, 71. **Open** 5.30am-9.45pm Mon-Fri; 8am-7.45pm Sat; 9am-5.45pm Sun. **Rates** *Day pass* $15. **Credit** MC, V. **Map** p311 J3.

San Francisco may have many YMCAs, but this is the only one that can boast a waterfront view. A day pass covers aerobics, free weights, Cybex and Nautilus machines, racquetball and basketball courts, and the 25m pool.

Koret Health & Recreation Center

University of San Francisco, 2130 Fulton Street, at Stanyan Street, Richmond (422 6821/www.usfca.edu/koret). Bus 5, 31. **Open** 6am-2pm Mon-Thur; 6am-10pm Fri, 8am-8pm Sat, Sun. **Day pass** $15. **Credit** MC, V. **Map** p313 C5.

Koret has an Olympic-sized pool, a gym and six racquetball courts. (For the latter you'll have to bring your own equipment.)

24 Hour Fitness Center

1200 Van Ness Avenue, at Post Street, Cathedral Hill (776 2200/www.24hourfitness.com). Bus 2, 3, 4, 19, 38, 47, 49, 76. **Open** 24hrs daily. **Rates** *Day pass* $15. **Credit** AmEx, Disc, MC, V. **Map** p310 F4.

Most classes are early morning, lunchtime and early evening. For other branches, call 1-800 249 6756.

Hiking

The beautiful hills of San Francisco make for hours of rewarding walking, but less than half an hour beyond the city are trails with astounding views and fragrant paths. Just across the Golden Gate Bridge, the short and easily hiked **Morning Sun Trail** climbs from a parking lot at Spencer Avenue (exit off US 101 north). It has lovely views east towards the city over the Bay and Angel Island and west to the thundering Pacific. You can also take Golden Gate Transit bus 10 to Mill Valley for the day-long **Dipsea Trail** to Stinson Beach. The **Bootjack Trail** to the summit of Mount Tamalpais is also popular. Call the Pantoll Ranger Station (388 2070) for trail information. **Bay Area Sierra Club** (1-510 848 0800, www.sanfranciscobay.sierraclub.org) in Berkeley has a wealth of hiking knowledge.

Horse-riding

If you want equestrian action, horses and tours are offered at the **Sea Horse & Friendly Acres Ranch** (1-650 726 9903) near Half Moon Bay or at the **Chanslor Guest Ranch & Stables** (1-707 875 3333, www.chanslor.com) next to Bodega Bay.

In-line skating

Sunday skating in Golden Gate Park is hard to beat: the beach at one end, plenty of sunny meadows along the way and no motor vehicles. For wide smiles (without wide polyester collars) join the mix of in-line skating, disco and break dancing near **Sixth Avenue** on JFK Drive. Skates are also for rent at Golden Gate Park Skate & Bike (*see p237*).

Skates on Haight

1818 Haight Street, at Stanyan Street, Haight-Ashbury (752 8375/www.skates.com). Bus 7, 33, 37, 66, 71. **Open** 8am-6pm Mon-Fri; 11am-6pm Sat, Sun. **Rates** $6/hr; $24/day. **Credit** AmEx, MC, V. **Map** p313 C6.

At least partly responsible for launching the world-wide skateboarding craze back in the 1970s, Skates on Haight rents and sells in-line skates, roller skates and snowboards. Cool place to visit.

Other location: 1219 Polk Street, at Sutter Street, Tenderloin (447 1800).

Crissy Field – running nirvana.
See p240.

Paragliding

Paragliding is the one without a boat. You'll be able to fly after less than a day's instruction, and you can do anything a hang-glider can do except turn upside-down. The equipment weighs only about 10lbs (4.5kg).

Glidell Paragliding

1-925 963 7802/www.glidell.com. **Open** Sat, Sun (by appointment). **Rates** *Tandem flight* $150. *Training packages* from $1,600. **Credit** MC, V.
Since 1990 this outfit has offered programmes for all levels from fledglings to fighter pilots. There are flying sites throughout the Bay Area.

Pool & billiards

There are pool tables in many bars but, for real enthusiasts, here are some of the specialists.

The Great Entertainer

975 Bryant Street, between Seventh & Eighth Streets, SoMa (861 8833/http://tge.com). Bus 19, 27, 42. **Open** 11am-2am daily. **Rates** $5-$15/hr. **Credit** AmEx, MC, V. **Map** p315 G5.
This is San Francisco's largest game room, with 40 billiard tables, shuffleboard, snooker, table tennis, darts, table football and a video arcade.

Rock climbing

Devoted Bay Area climbers travel to **Lake Tahoe** (*see p263*) and **Mount Shasta**, but **Yosemite** (*see p265*) is the California climbing mecca, with lessons available year-round. While you're still in the city, you can always warm up at **Mission Cliffs**.

Mission Cliffs

2295 Harrison Street, at 19th Street, Mission (550 0515/www.mission-cliffs.com). Bus 12, 27. **Open** 6.30am-10pm Mon-Fri; 10am-6pm Sat, Sun. **Rates** $10-$20/day. **Credit** AmEx, Disc, MC, V. **Map** p314 G7.
This 14,000sq ft (4,300sq m) of urban wilderness and polished jungle gym runs beginner's lessons from noon until 7.30pm on weekdays.

Running

Crissy Field, a former airstrip, is a gorgeous destination for runners. Each step of the route from Fort Mason past Marina Green along the Golden Gate Promenade is a postcard, leading all the way to historic Fort Point beneath the golden bridge herself. The **Embarcadero** offers another lovely path beneath the city's other beautiful bridge. If neither of those are convenient, **Golden Gate Park** is a third beautiful option, with the track at Kezar Stadium on the eastern edge of the park providing a perfect spot for sprints.

For something more sociable, the **San Francisco Dolphin South End Runners**, founded in 1966, have group runs at 9.30am every Sunday, for which non-members pay $5. Call 978 0837 or check www.dserunners.com for more details. Annual foot races in the city include **Bay to Breakers** (*see p189*), a 12-kilometre (7.2-mile) run from downtown to Ocean Beach each May, and the **San Francisco Marathon**, which is held in July.

Sailing, kayaking & rowing

There are numerous boating, sailing and kayaking outfits in the Bay Area and along the Pacific coastline, all of which offer equipment, lessons and trips. Rowing opportunities range from single sculls to whale boat racing; for details call **Open Water Rowing** (332 1091, www.owrc.com) in Sausalito or **South End Rowing Club** (776 7372, www.south-end.org) in San Francisco. For the romantic dabbler, pedalos and rowing boats are available for rent at **Stow Lake** in Golden Gate Park.

Cal Adventures

UC Aquatic Center, 100 University Avenue, at Shorebird Park, Berkeley Marina (1-510 642 4000/www.oksi.org). BART Berkeley, then AC Transit bus 9. **Open** noon-sunset Wed-Fri; 7.30am-sunset Sat, Sun. **Rate** *Kayaks* $12/hr. *Sailboats* $15/hr. **Credit** Disc, MC, V.
Cal Adventures rents out 15ft (4.6m) Coronados on the South Sailing Basin. Those without proper certification must be accompanied by an instructor, which costs an additional $60.

California Canoe & Kayak

409 Water Street, at Franklin Street, Jack London Square, Oakland (1-510 893 7833/www.cal kayak.com). **Rate** *Kayaks* $15/hr. *Canoes* $25/hr. **Credit** MC, V.
One of the Bay Area's best locations for hiring and buying kayaks and seagoing gear. Lessons and day trips navigate the nearby Oakland Estuary.

Sailing Education Adventures

Fort Mason Center, Laguna & Buchanan Streets, Marina (775 8779/www.sailsea.org). Bus 22, 28. **Open** 2.30-5.30pm Mon, Wed, Fri. **Credit** MC, V. **Map** p309/10 E1.
This Marina-based charity offers instruction for all levels of sailing skill and a summer camp for children. Only SEA members can rent boats.

Sea Trek

Schoonmaker Point Marina, at Libertyship Way, Sausalito (332 4465/www.seatrekkayak.com). Blue & Gold Fleet ferry from Pier 41, Fisherman's Wharf, or Golden Gate ferry from Ferry Building, Embarcadero/bus Golden Gate Transit 10. **Open** 9am-4pm Mon-Fri; 8.30am-4pm Sat, Sun. **Rate** *Kayak* $15/hr. *Tour* $65/hr. **Credit** AmEx, Disc, MC, V.

Sea Trek hosts summer camps for kids, books expeditions to Alaska and Baja, and supports waterway conservation. Beginner's classes in kayaking, guided tours and moonlight paddles are available; kayak rental is only to experienced kayakers.

Spinnaker Sailing

Pier 40, South Beach Harbor, Embarcadero, at Townsend Street, South Beach (543 7333/www. spinnaker-sailing.com). Muni N/bus 10. **Open** 8.30am-5.30pm daily. **Rates** *Boat rental* $140-$735/day. **Credit** AmEx, MC, V. **Map** p311/15 J4.
Professional instruction, boats from 22ft to 80ft (7-24m) and a great location near SBC Park.

Scuba diving

San Francisco doesn't cater for divers, but a trip south to **Monterey Bay** (*see p269*) will put the smile back on their faces.

Bamboo Reef Scuba Diving

584 Fourth Street, at Brannan Street, SoMa (362 6694/www.bambooreef.com). Bus 15, 30, 45, 76. **Open** 10am-7pm Mon-Fri; 9am-5.30pm Sat.
Rates *Scuba rental* $75/day. **Credit** AmEx, Disc, MC, V. **Map** p315 H5.
Bamboo Reef organises Monterey Bay trips, sells all the gear and offers rentals, repairs and training.
Other locations: 614 Lighthouse Avenue, Monterey (1-831 372 1685); 5702 Commerce Boulevard, Rohnert Park, Sonoma (1-707 586 0272).

Cal Dive & Travel

1750 Sixth Street, between Cedar & Virginia Streets, Berkeley (1-510 524 3248/www.caldive.net). BART North Berkeley, then AC Transit bus 19.

Open noon-6pm Tue-Fri; 10am-2pm Sat.
Rates *Scuba rental* $45/day. **Credit** AmEx, Disc, MC, V.
Arranges trips to Monterey Bay. Novices are welcome, but you can't hire masks, fins, boots, gloves or snorkels here.

Skateboarding

The police have done a pretty thorough job of eliminating skate rats from former favourite sites like Justin Herman Plaza and Pier 7 on the Embarcadero, though you'll be able to sniff out a Safeway parking lot or two and any number of downtown concrete ramps. If you're posing or want to learn, invest in helmet, gloves, knee and elbow pads at the places listed below. Dusting up on the slang won't hurt either.

DLX

1831 Market Street, at Guerrero Street, Mission (626 5588/www.dlxsf.com). Muni F, J, K, L, M, N/bus 26. **Open** 11am-7pm Mon-Thur; 10am-8pm Fri, Sat; 11am-6pm Sun. **Credit** AmEx, MC, V. **Map** p314 F5.
DLX (née Deluxe) is the mother of all skateboarding shops. It has a comprehensive range of clothes, boards, accessories and stickers.

FTC Skateboarding

1632 Haight Street, between Belvedere & Clayton Streets, Haight-Ashbury (626 0663/www.ftcskate. com). Bus 7, 33, 37, 43, 66, 71. **Open** 11am-7pm daily. **Credit** AmEx, Disc, MC, V. **Map** p313 C6.
FTC is the best of many small shops dedicated to baiting your riskier self. No rentals.

Beaches Shark attack!

f you're expecting Bay Area beaches to live up to *Baywatch* fantasies, you're in for a shock. The waves may be big but they're cold, the sands are often rocky and offshore waters are home to a sizeable contingent of sharks. Not just any old sharks. We're talking Great Whites.

But don't bin the swimsuit yet. Locals feel happy living with their finned neighbours – in fact, some surfers are alarmingly blasé about them – and, once you know a few facts, you might feel the same. First, a shark's natural prey is seals. They don't want to eat humans. Second, the Great Whites tend to hang out in particular places (Marin County's south-facing coast, the mouth of Tomales Bay, off Stinson Beach, Año Nuevo, Salmon Creek) and at certain times (August is when they spawn in Tomales Bay; October and November is

when they migrate past the Farallon Islands). Third, they don't want any trouble. So don't swim solo, take off anything glittery and stay away from fins – you should be fine. When a shark is sighted, lifeguards clear everyone out of the water.

So you can relax. Well, no. Riptides are a real danger. Formed by breaking waves pulling strongly away from the shore, they're commonplace at most Bay Area beaches. You should stay away from any water that looks especially foamy, as this is a sign that two currents are battling each other. If you do get caught in a rip, don't waste strength swimming against it towards the shore. Just tread water until someone rescues you, or swim parallel to the beach until you're out of the rip – then you can swim safely ashore.

Perfect your positions at the **Sivananda Yoga Vedanta Center**. *See p243.*

Skiing & snowboarding

Though the slopes could be hit and run in a day trip, most humans prefer at least a weekend for skiing in the Sierras. For leading resorts around **Lake Tahoe**, *see p263*. During the season (November to April) most ski shops have calendars of events and ads for package deals. Check www.goski.com for listings of all the major California resorts.

FTC Ski & Sports

1360 Bush Street, between Larkin & Polk Streets, Nob Hill (673 8363). Bus 2, 3, 4. **Open** 10am-7pm Mon-Fri; 10am-5pm Sat, Sun. **Rates** *Ski/snowboard rental* from $35/wknd. **Credit** AmEx, MC, V. **Map** p310 F3.
A great selection of skis, snowboards and all the accoutrements, as well as deals on used equipment.

SFO Snowboarding

618 Shrader Street, at Haight Street, Haight-Ashbury (386 1666/www.sfosnow.com). Bus 7, 33, 37, 43, 66, 71. **Open** 10am-7pm Mon-Fri; 10am-7pm Sat; 11am-6pm Sun. **Map** p313 C6.
Boards, boots, bindings and more for rent, plus an array of cold-weather clothes for sale.

Sullivan's Ski World

5323 Geary Boulevard, at 17th Street, Richmond (751 3515). Bus 38. **Open** 10am-6.30pm Mon-Fri; 10am-6pm Sat; 10am-5pm Sun. **Credit** AmEx, Disc, MC, V. **Map** p312 A5.
For more than 50 years Sullivan's has been selling everything you need for a ski trip to Tahoe. There is a four-day minimum on rentals: the snowboard package costs $60; the ski package $50.

Surfing

Here's the facts: the waves around San Francisco are dangerous – not a good place to learn (*see p241* **Beaches: Shark attack!**). An hour north of San Francisco on Highway 1, Stinson Beach (*see p254* **Beaches: All points north**) has gentler waves and fewer surfers, while the real pros head to Mavericks in Santa Cruz (*see p268* **Beaches: Shore thing**). But whether you're a pro headed to Ocean Beach and beyond or a newbie boogie-boarding the black sand beaches of Marin County, **Wise Surfboards** is the first choice for gear.

Wise Surfboards

800 Great Highway, at Cabrillo Street, Ocean Beach (750 9473). Bus 5, 18, 31, 38. **Open** 9am-6pm daily. **Credit** AmEx, MC, V.
Right on Ocean Beach, this shop sells boards, wet-suits and accessories, and hosts a 24hr surf info line (273 1618), which is updated at 9am, noon and 3pm.

Swimming

The ocean is usually too chilly and turbulent for a proper swim (*see p241* **Beaches: Shark attack!**), but there are plenty of swimming pools in San Francisco, including ones at the **Embarcadero YMCA** and the **Koret Center** (for both, *see p238*). The most central pools can be found at **Hamilton Recreation Center** (Geary Boulevard and Steiner Street, 292 2001) and the **North Beach Pool** (Lombard and Mason Streets, 274 0200). Adult admission is $3.

For your nearest municipal pool, check the White Pages under 'City Government Offices: Recreation and Parks'. For the best **beaches** in the city, *see p103* **City sands** and *p106* **Bare-faced cheeks**; for those further afield, *see p254* **All points north** and *p268* **Shore thing**.

Tennis

Indoor tennis in San Francisco is almost exclusively a members-only affair, but there are plenty of outdoor courts. **Golden Gate Park** has several (near the Stanyan Street entrance, 753 7001) and there are busy courts at **Dolores Park** (*see p88*). Both locations are free and open from sunrise to sunset. For a complete list of tennis facilities, see the 'Neighbourhood Parks' section of SBC Yellow Pages.

Volleyball

Although more popular in warmer Southern California, you can get your sets and spikes here too. The **Northern California Volleyball Association** (550 7582) organises leagues and there are pick-up games at the north end of **Marina Green** on weekend mornings. For details, check www.volleyball.org/bay_area.

Whale watching

Whale watching happens during the migration season (Nov-Dec and late Mar/early Apr), and occurs primarily just north and south of San Francisco. On occasion, however, it can be as easy as taking a pair of binoculars to the shore and having a look. Mendocino and Monterey are popular viewing spots, but we recommend the tip of **Point Reyes** (*see p255*), only an hour's drive north of the city. You might see glorious humpback and blue whales, as well as sea lions and other wildlife.

Oceanic Society Expeditions

Fort Mason Center, Laguna & Beach Streets, Marina (474 3385/www.oceanic-society.org). Bus 22, 28, 42, 47, 49. **Open** 9am-5pm Mon-Fri. **Rates** *Voyages* $61-$63. **Credit** AmEx, MC, V. **Map** p309/p310 E1.
This is a cut above most tourist trips as the staff are experts in natural history and marine life. On weekends (June-Nov), a full-day trip heads 26 miles (42km) west to the Farallon Islands, home of the largest seabird rookery in the continental US. Along the way, whales and orcas can be seen. From December to May there are gray whale cruises as well.

Windsurfing

San Francisco is a popular windsurfing centre with 32 launch sites. These include **Candlestick** and **Coyote Points**, as well

as **Crissy Field**, which is the site of several international competitions, including the World Cup.

City Front Boardsports

2936 Lyon Street, at Greenwich Street, Cow Hollow (929 7873/www.boardsports.com). Bus 28, 41, 43, 45. **Open** 11am-7pm Mon-Fri; 10am-6pm Sat, Sun. **Credit** AmEx, Disc, MC, V. **Map** p309 D2.
With locations in Berkeley and Marin, City Front is the place to go if you're a seasoned windsurfer with your own wetsuit and harness. Complete sailing rigs cost around $50.
Other locations: Berkeley Boardsports, 1601 University Avenue, at California Street, Berkeley (1-510 843 9283); Boardsports Marin, 113 Third Street, nr East Francisco Boulevard, San Rafael (288 9283).

Yoga

For many San Franciscans, daily yoga is as necessary as coffee during and drinks after work. Countless yoga schools offer a variety of styles for students of all levels; the Yoga Society (285 5537) is good for general info.

Bikram's Yoga College of India

2nd Floor, 910 Columbus Avenue, at Lombard Street, North Beach (346 5400). Bus 15, 30, 39/ cable car Powell-Mason. **Open** *Classes* 9am, 4.30pm, 6.30pm Mon-Fri; 9am, 4.30pm Sat, Sun. **Rates** $10/class. **Credit** MC, V. **Map** p310 G2.
Here one learns the 'hot yoga' techniques of Bikram Choudhury, who brought his style to the US in 1971. Bring a towel: the yoga is done in a sweltering room.

Mindful Body

2876 California Street, between Divisadero & Broderick Streets, Pacific Heights (931 2639/ www.themindfulbody.com). Bus 1, 24. **Open** 7am-9pm Mon-Fri; 8am-7.30pm Sat, Sun. **Rates** $13/class. **Credit** MC, V. **Map** p309 D3/4.
The popular Astanga class builds endurance, strength and flexibility.

Sivananda Yoga Vedanta Center

1200 Arguello Boulevard, at Lincoln Way, Inner Sunset (681 2731/www.sivananda.org). Metro Muni N/bus 66, 71. **Open** call for class schedule. **Rates** $14/class. **Credit** MC, V. **Map** p312 C6.
Part of a global network of yoga centres, offering courses, classes and workshops.

Yoga Tree

780 Stanyan Street, at Waller Street, Haight-Ashbury (387 4707/www.yogatreesf.com). Metro Muni N/bus 7, 33, 37, 43, 66, 71. **Open** 7am-9pm Mon-Fri; 9am-8pm Sat, Sun. **Rates** $12/class. **Credit** AmEx, MC, V. **Map** p313 C6.
There are numerous classes and styles here. **Other locations**: 1234 Valencia Street, at 23rd Street, Mission (647 9707); 519 Hayes Street, at Octavia Street, Hayes Valley (626 9707); 97 Collingwood Street, at 18th Street, Upper Market (701 9642).

Arts & Entertainment

Theatre & Dance

From blockbuster to avant-garde, San Francisco makes a song and dance of it.

With all the views, hiking trails and quaint alleys in San Francisco, why would anyone head indoors? Because you can see some of the best theatre and dance in the country performed here. From modern dance to Broadway tours, the Bay Area's performing arts scene rivals those of much bigger cities, appealing to and capturing the Bay Area's diversity.

Things have come a long way in the 150 years since the city's first recorded theatrical event in an old schoolhouse in front of an entirely male audience. The main theatres pack a powerful entertainment punch, but don't overlook the little guys – small in size, perhaps, but big on talent. From renovated church theatres to cosy basement venues, good theatre crops up in the most unexpected places.

In terms of dance, the **San Francisco Ballet** (*see p248*) is exemplary, but classical ballet is just the beginning. The city boasts an exciting modern dance scene, with extraordinary ethnic dance companies bringing forms from China, India, the Middle East… even Germany. If you're here in June, be sure to check out the **Ethnic Dance Festival** (www.ethnicdancefestival.org). If opera's more your style, *see p210*.

INFORMATION

For up-to-date information, the *San Francisco Chronicle*'s Sunday 'Datebook' section – look for the attention-grabbing pink pages – has extensive listings and is accessible online at www.sfgate.com. Free weeklies like the *Bay Guardian* and *SF Weekly* also run reviews and listings. For online listings, check out www.sanfranciscocitysearch.com, www.artsmonthlysf.org, www.bayinsider.com and www.laughingsquid.org. For Broadway shows, visit www.bestofbroadway-sf.com.

TICKETS

Ticket prices range from $5 for an experimental show to more than $80 for a Broadway-style extravaganza. Theatre box offices are usually cheapest for tickets (there's often a fee for telephone bookings), but there are also several good brokers: **TIX Bay Area** (433 7827), in Union Square, sells half-price tickets on the day of the show (cash only), as well as full-price tickets in advance (credit cards accepted); **Tickets.com** (776 1999, www.tickets.com) sells tickets by phone and email, as well as from outlets all over the city, with a hefty surcharge

of $2-$6 per ticket. Also try the **St Francis Theater Ticket Service** (362 3500), **Mr Ticket** (292 7328, 1-800 424 7328, 1-888 722 5737, www.mrticket.com) or **City Box Office** (392 4400, www.cityboxoffice.com). Some venues also sell tickets through **Ticketmaster** (512 7770, www.ticketmaster.com). A number of theatres run 'pay-what-you-can Thursdays' (or Tuesdays at the Magic, *see p245*).

Mainstream theatres

Curran Theater

445 Geary Street, between Mason & Taylor Streets, Tenderloin (551 2000). BART Powell/Muni Metro F, J, K, L, M, N/bus 27, 38/cable car Powell-Hyde or Powell-Mason. **Tickets** $20-$68. **Credit** AmEx, MC, V. **Map** p310 G4.

There's a fantasy castle feel to the Curran, with its enormous chandelier, carved-wood lobby and two-storey murals. Opened in 1922, the theatre seats about 1,600. It usually hosts non-musical Broadway-type shows, but in 2003 Peter Coyote and Robin Williams in *The Exonerated* (based on interviews with death-row inmates) were the talk of the theatre community.

Golden Gate Theater

1 Taylor Street, at Golden Gate Avenue, Tenderloin (551 2000). BART Powell Street or Civic Center/Muni Metro F, J, K, L, M, N/bus 5, 6, 7, 9, 21, 26, 31, 66, 71. **Tickets** $40-$81. **Credit** AmEx, MC, V. **Map** p310/314 G4.

Formerly a movie theatre and a vaudeville house, the 2,300-seater Golden Gate now often hosts travelling musicals for a longer-than-average run – *Mamma Mia*, for example, made a local stop here for the 'Best of the Broadway' series in spring 2004.

Herbst Theatre

Veterans' Memorial Building, 401 Van Ness Avenue, between Grove & McAllister Streets, Civic Center (621 6600/box office 392 4400). BART Civic Center/Muni Metro F, J, K, L, M, N/bus 5, 21, 47, 49. **Tickets** $30. **Credit** MC, V. **Map** p314 F4.

The Herbst, just across from City Hall, seats just over 900. It plays host to smaller touring shows, comedy and cabaret, but the eight Beaux Arts murals (painted for the 1915 Panama-Pacific Exposition) and glorious blue-and-gold ceiling often steal the show.

Orpheum

1192 Market Street, at Hyde Street, Civic Center (551 2000). BART Civic Center/Muni Metro F, J, K, L, M, N/bus 5, 6, 7, 9, 19, 21, 66, 71. **Tickets** $26-$160. **Credit** AmEx, MC, V. **Map** p314 F4.

A shining star – the **American Conservatory Theater**.

Like the Golden Gate (*see p244*), the 2,200-seat Orpheum was first a vaudeville house and later a movie palace, as the Moorish design and spacious lobby attest. Here *Hair* was first performed more than three decades ago, but more recently it was the venue for Julie Taymor's smash hit *The Lion King*.

Regional theatres

American Conservatory Theater (ACT)

Geary Theater, 415 Geary Street, between Mason & Taylor Streets, Tenderloin (834 3200/box office 749 2228/www.act-sfbay.org). BART Powell/Muni Metro F, J, K, L, M, N/bus 27, 38/cable car Powell-Hyde or Powell-Mason. **Tickets** $11-$70. **Credit** AmEx, MC, V. **Map** p310 G4.

In the late 1960s the ACT brought regional theatre to San Francisco. It still presents new works by new and established writers, such as Tom Stoppard and David Mamet, as well as classics. Despite the expensive tickets, the ACT draws good audiences, whether local theatre buffs catching a show before it goes Broadway or kids packed in for the annual presentation of *A Christmas Carol*. The glamorous downtown location is often blessed with street singers performing a cappella outside.

Magic Theatre

Building D, Fort Mason Center, Marina Boulevard at Buchanan Street, Marina (441 8822/www.magictheatre.org). Bus 22, 28, 30, 43, 49. **Tickets** $10-$53. **Credit** AmEx, Disc, MC, V. **Map** p309/10 E1.

The Magic Theatre represents a happy medium between brand new, mainstream plays and more experimental work. It has introduced San Francisco to shows that have gone on to considerable success,

most notably *Stones in His Pockets*, which became a hit in New York and London (1998-9 season), and by showing several of Sam Shepard's works helped bring him – and the theatre itself – to international attention. The Magic's two spaces each seat 150, and the theatre offers 'Rush Ticket Discounts' and 'Pay-what-you-can Tuesdays'.

Fringe theatres & companies

For queer theatre and cabaret, *see p230*.

Asian American Theater Company

543 5738/www.asianamericantheater.org. **Tickets** $10-25. **Credit** AmEx, MC, V.

Begun in 1973 from an initiative by the American Conservatory Theater, the AATC focuses on plays by and about Americans of Asian and Pacific Island descent. It also provides youth workshops and helps directors, writers and actors to develop new work.

Audium

1616 Bush Street, at Franklin Street, Pacific Heights (771 1616/www.audium.org). Bus 2, 3, 4, 42, 47, 49, 76. **Tickets** $12. **No credit cards.** **Map** p310 F3.

Behind its bland streetside façade, Audium is home to multi-dimensional audio sculptures – chirps and burps that ping-pong around the room; atonal synth passages that transmogrify into oppressive industrial static; an invisible marching band. The tiny theatre has 169 speakers, which are orchestrated by composer/sound manipulator Stan Shaff into producing a wealth of intriguing shapes and textures. Along with Shaff's post-performance pontifications, this is all surprisingly great entertainment. Shows are at 8.30pm every Friday and Saturday (box office opens 8pm).

San Francisco Ballet. *See p248.*

Arts & Entertainment

Beach Blanket Babylon

*Club Fugazi, 678 Green Street (or Beach Blanket
Babylon Boulevard), between Columbus Avenue
& Powell Street, North Beach (421 4222/www.
beachblanketbabylon.com). Bus 15, 30, 41, 45.*
Tickets $25-$62. **Credit** MC, V. **Map** p310 G2.
Beach Blanket Babylon enters its 30th year in 2004,
and it's been quite a ride. Featuring a changing array
of characters drawn from US popular culture, local
legend and the politics of the day, this musical revue
is the longest running in theatrical history. It's as
camp as it is clever, relying on formulaic visual gags,
especially the huge, elaborate headgear (a hat
bearing models of Big Ben *and* Buckingham Palace
greeted Queen Elizabeth II). Some may dismiss
Beach Blanket as sophomoric, but none can deny it's
a San Francisco institution. Evening performances
are for over-21s only.

EXITheater

*156 Eddy Street, between Mason & Taylor Streets,
Tenderloin (931 1094/festival information 673
3847/www.sffringe.org). BART Powell/Muni
Metro F, J, K, L, M, N/bus 27, 31.* **Tickets**
$10-$20. **No credit cards. Map** p310 G4.
This is the central complex – or 'theaterplex' as the
EXIT folks like to call it – for San Francisco's Fringe
Festival (*see p188*). The three-theatre group offers

a lively assortment of eclectic and provocative
shows, ranging from new one-acts to work by well-
known authors. Be warned: seating at the 277
Taylor Street location (between Eddy and Ellis
Streets) is cramped and there's no café. The main
location has the added attraction of Lily, the sweet
and sleepy pooch who guards the door.

Intersection for the Arts

*446 Valencia Street, between 15th & 16th
Streets, Mission (626 2787/box office 626 3311/
www.theintersection.org). BART 16th Street/bus
14, 22, 26, 33, 49.* **Tickets** $5-$15. **Credit** MC, V.
Map p314 F6.
The oldest alternative space in the city, Intersection
is a powerhouse, combining the talents of resident
theatre group Campo Santo with visiting playwrights such as Denis Johnson and John Steppling.
The small theatre isn't the most comfortable – there
are only folding chairs – but performances are
intense. There's a great art gallery upstairs.

Lorraine Hansberry Theatre

*620 Sutter Street, between Mason &
Taylor Streets, Nob Hill (474 8800/www.
lorrainehansberrytheatre.com). BART Powell/
bus 2, 3, 4, 76/cable car Powell-Hyde or Powell-
Mason.* **Tickets** $25-$32. **Credit** AmEx, Disc,
MC, V. **Map** p310 G3.

The Lorraine Hansberry Theatre is the best-known African-American theatre group in the Bay Area, producing plays either by black playwrights (August Wilson, Toni Morrison, Alice Walker, for example) or dealing with issues affecting the black community. The group stages a four- or five-play season in its 300-seat theatre each year. It usually includes a must-see musical Christmas offering, such as Langston Hughes's *Black Nativity*.

The Marsh

1062 Valencia Street, at 22nd Street, Mission (826 5750/www.themarsh.org). BART 24th Street/bus 14, 26, 49. **Tickets** $12-$22. **Credit** MC, V. **Map** p314 F7.

The Marsh works hard to present new works, priding itself on allowing performers to take risks. While performances here often move on to larger venues in the Bay Area or across the country (Josh Kornbluth's monologues were launched here), you should proceed with caution if you're looking for a sure thing. On the other hand, you wouldn't want to miss the Karen Carpenter Christmas.

New Conservatory Theatre

25 Van Ness Avenue, between Fell & Oak Streets, Hayes Valley (861 8972/www.nctcsf.org). Muni Metro F, J, K, L, M, N/bus 6, 7, 47, 49, 66, 71. **Tickets** $10-$35. **Credit** AmEx, Disc, MC, V. **Map** p314 F5.

The resident company at this well-designed performing arts complex is best known for its annual Pride Season, featuring works by and about the gay community, along with a series of musicals. The three theatres range from 50 to 132 seats, and there's a video studio, art gallery and classroom.

Project Artaud Theater

450 Florida Street, between 17th & Mariposa Streets, Mission (626 4370/www.artaud.org). BART 16th Street/bus 22, 27, 33, 53. **Tickets** $18-$25. **Credit** MC, V. **Map** p314 G6.

What was once dance-specialist Theater Artaud, now encompasses a range of performing and visual arts. The 70 individual spaces within this former warehouse are occupied not only by artists, but also by theatres including the Traveling Jewish Theatre (www.atjt.com) and Theater of Yugen/Noh Space (www.theatreofyugen.org). Plays range from the traditional to ethnic shows and performance art.

Word for Word

Various venues (437 6775/http://wordforword. zspace.org). **Tickets** $27. **Credit** MC, V.

It was only a matter of time before someone in this literary city decided to 'bring literature to its feet' by staging short stories verbatim as theatrical scripts. A decade old now, its well worth a visit: Tobias Wolff and Michael Chabon have both had works performed here. Wednesdays are 'pay-what-you-can'.

Yerba Buena Center for the Arts

701 Mission Street, at Third Street, SoMa (978 2787/www.yerbabuenaarts.org). BART Powell or Montgomery Streets/Muni Metro F, J, K, L, M, N/bus 9, 12, 15, 30, 45, 76. **Tickets** $5-$100. **Credit** AmEx, MC, V. **Map** p311 H4.

This angled, blue-tiled box is one of the city's most striking performance spaces. It boasts a wide variety of events, ranging from the Afro Solo Festival (*see p188*) to holiday season must-see *The Velveteen Rabbit*. The theatre entrance is at the intersection of Third and Howard Streets.

Mime's the word

If the words 'mime' and 'troupe' bring to mind silent, white-faced folk in leotards climbing out of imaginary boxes, then the **San Francisco Mime Troupe** (285 1717, www.sfmt.org) will give you pause. Founded in 1959 by RG Davis, this is a Mime Troupe that says a lot. Its July 2003 show, *Veronique of the Mounties*, said a lot about the US of A hunting down its next international victim: in this case, Canada. Previous shows have taken on the evils of live-work lofts, GM foods... you get the idea.

The Troupe's approach is refreshingly hands-on. The set for *Veronique* was still being assembled as audience members gathered in Dolores Park and the show was delayed because the actors were waiting for their costumes to be delivered. No matter the laid-back West Coast thing the Troupe has going on with the logistics, they're a pretty committed bunch of people. The Troupe cut its political teeth on such issues as the Vietnam War in the late '60s and it was the first US theatre to play in revolutionary Cuba and Sandinista Nicaragua. Often arrested and banned on obscenity charges, they had famed promoter Bill Graham put on some of his first Fillmore (*see p218*) shows to raise their bail money.

The Troupe's shows may be low budget but they're high energy. Stop by to catch a production (they play parks across the city) and you'll see local families feasting on home-made picnics – their kids having a boogie to tunes on catchy subjects like gentrification – alongside elderly couples and Mission hipsters kicking back with friends. As long as there's bad politician ass to be kicked, rest assured that the Mime Troupe will be there applying the boot.

East Bay theatres & companies

Aurora Theatre Company

2081 Addison Street, Berkeley (1-510 843 4822/www.auroratheatre.org). BART Berkeley/ AC Transit bus F. **Tickets** $28-$40. **Credit** AmEx, MC, V.

In 2001 Aurora moved from the Berkeley City Club to a custom-designed 150-seat theatre in the downtown Arts District, where the company now produces top-notch performances in five-play seasons, running the gamut from Shakespeare to Neil LaBute.

Berkeley Repertory Theater

2025 Addison Street, between Shattuck Avenue & Milvia Street, Berkeley (1-510 845 4700/ www.berkeleyrep.org). BART Berkeley/AC Transit bus F. **Tickets** $39-$55. **Credit** AmEx, Disc, MC, V.

The most acclaimed repertory theatre in the city, probably in the whole of California, Berkeley Rep expanded into a two-theatre complex a few years ago and now boasts a 400-seat thrust-stage auditorium and a newer 600-seat proscenium space. A season usually comprises a classic drama and several new works, as well as better-known plays by contemporary writers. The spaces are small; tickets can be difficult to find.

Shotgun Players

Julia Morgan Theatre, 2640 College Avenue, at Derby (1-510 704 8210/www.shotgunplayers.org). BART Rockridge/AC transit bus 51. **Tickets** free/donation. **Credit** MC, V.

They started out performing in the basement of a pizza parlour, but the Shotgun Players will soon be setting up their own downtown theatre (the kinks were being ironed out as we went to press). Under the direction of Patrick Dooley, the company takes risks that almost always pay off, whether performing Greek tragedies or *Under Milk Wood*.

Dance

The leading dance group in the Bay Area is the **San Francisco Ballet** (*see below*), but **LINES Ballet** (863 3040, www.linesballet.org) is also first-class. Performing primarily new works throughout the country, you can often catch LINES locally at Yerba Buena Center (*see p247*); its home season has been going since 1982.

There is a strong tradition of ethnic dance in San Francisco too. Performances by **TRANSIT** (621 6063, www.transitdance.com), a multi-ethnic company formed in 1995, borrow from German Expressionist dance, while the **Lily Cai Chinese Dance Company** (474 4829, www. ccpsf.org) has been blending ancient forms with modern dance since 1988. **Chitresh Das Dance Company** (449 1601, www.kathak.org) focuses on Kathak, a classical dance from India, and

Fat Chance Belly Dance (431 4322, www.fcbd.com) performs an 'American Tribal' style of traditional Middle Eastern dancing.

Cal Performances

Zellerbach Hall, UC Berkeley campus, Berkeley (1-510 642 9988/www.calperfs.berkeley.edu). BART Berkeley/AC Transit bus F. **Tickets** $18-$250. **Credit** AmEx, Disc, MC, V.

As an adjunct of UC Berkeley, Cal Performances offers a smattering of everything: dance, music and drama. It presents nationally regarded dance companies, such as Alvin Ailey and the Mark Morris Dance Group, plays by Brecht and performances by the likes of the American Ballet Theatre.

Joe Goode Performance Group (JGPG)

Various venues (561 6565/www.joegoode.org).

The JGPG has pushed modern dance to new heights, pursuing with gusto its founder's mission: to explore contemporary issues ranging from gender to AIDS. Keeping a toe in the community as well, the company teaches workshops to groups including at-risk youth and battered women. Despite worldwide tours, it has an annual season in SF.

ODC Performance Gallery

3153 17th Street, between South Van Ness Avenue & Shotwell Street, Mission (863 9834/ www.odcdance.org). BART 16th Street/bus 12, 14, 22, 33, 49, 53. **Tickets** $10-$40. **Credit** AmEx, MC, V. **Map** p314 F6.

Founded in 1971, ODC clambered on a yellow bus and headed for San Francisco in 1976. Since then the group has focused on creating innovative works of modern dance, but also has its own school and gallery. As we go to press, ODC is planning to complete a major expansion across the street by 2005.

San Francisco Ballet

War Memorial Opera House, 301 Van Ness Avenue, between Grove & McAllister Streets, Civic Center (863 2000/www.sfballet.org). BART Civic Center/Muni Metro F, J, K, L, M, N/bus 5, 21, 47, 49. **Tickets** $12-$130. **Credit** AmEx, MC, Visa. **Map** p314 F5.

Founded in 1933, this is the longest-running professional ballet company in the US. It presented the first full-length US production of *Coppélia*, followed in 1940 by the country's first complete *Swan Lake* and the first full-length *Nutcracker* in 1944. Based in the War Memorial Opera House (*see p211*), its annual season (February to May) is typically an even blend of traditional pieces and new works.

Smuin Ballets

Various venues (495 2234/www.smuinballets.com).

How many ballets can claim a film appearance, let alone in *Return of the Jedi*? Probably just this one. Founded in 1994 by Michael Smuin, former director of the SF Ballet (*see above*), this innovative group wowed the crowds with *Dancin' with Gershwin* in 2001 and *To the Beatles Revisited* in 2002.

Trips Out of Town

Introduction	250
Heading North	251
Wine Country	256
Heading East	263
Heading South	267

Features

The best Day trips	250
Beaches All points north	254
Stop wining	258
Grape expectations	260
Beaches Shore thing	268

Introduction

Enjoy nature at its wildest, and a host of alfresco activities.

If you're planning to explore the countryside around San Francisco, you're faced with an enormous number of choices. On even a short visit to the greater Bay Area, most people leave at least a bit of their heart behind, and for good reason. The region holds an embarrassment of travel riches, including empty beaches, windswept islands, craggy mountains, vast parks, gourmet restaurants and picturesque wineries. With so many options, often the biggest problem is finding a way to fit it all in. Whether you head north or south along the Pacific coast or strike inland to the east, each area has its own identity and array of offerings.

Close to San Francisco are the sleepy fishing villages, wildlife refuges and magnificent redwoods of **Marin County** (*see p251*), or **Wine Country** (*see p256*) with its vineyards and spas. Further afield lie the celebrated golf courses of the **Monterey peninsula** (*see p270*), the exhilarating ski slopes and watersports of **Lake Tahoe** (*see p263*) or the soaring peaks of **Yosemite** (*see p265*).

For more information, or to plan your trip in advance, contact the tourist information centres listed in this chapter; they're generally very well organised, have good websites and will send out a visitor pack on request. All phone numbers are listed as if dialled from San Francisco. For a map of the Bay Area and surrounding coast, *see p304*.

TRANSPORT

Most destinations listed in this chapter are in easy reach of the city and can be covered as a day trip or overnight stay, but many are ill-served by public transport. Try the BART rail service, which connects San Francisco with the East Bay, or Golden Gate Transit, which has a regular schedule of bus services to and from many Marin County destinations. It also has less frequent services to Sonoma County. You can also use Greyhound buses, Amtrak (although the nearest train station is in Oakland), a charter tour or one of the ferries that run frequently to the North Bay. But, if your budget permits it, rent a car; it's simply the best way to explore the area. For more information on public transport providers and car rental, *see p275*.

The best Day trips

Fancy a splash in the Pacific or some fabulous nature-watching? Do you want to soak in a spa, hike up a mountain or tour a vineyard? You're in luck – all these cravings, and plenty more, can be satisfied within a couple of hours' travel from San Francisco. The following are our recommendations for when you need time out of the city.

Feeling energetic
Drive to **Stinson Beach** (*see p254*) and hike until you drop, then revive yourself with a plunge in the chilly Pacific.

Feeling lazy
Just drive. Head south down **Highway 1** (*see p267*), through glorious Big Sur, and revel in the extraordinary views.

Feeling romantic
Tootle slowly through **Napa Valley** (*see p260*) or **Sonoma Valley** (*see p256*), then stop at a spa (*see p258* **Stop wining**) for an indulgent couple treatment.

Feeling urban overload
Hop on a ferry across the Bay for a leisurely lunch in **Sausalito** (*see p252*) or **Larkspur** (*see p253*), or get close to nature among the redwoods in **Muir Woods** (*see p254*).

Heading North

Land with plenty.

The Golden Gate Bridge, as seen from the **Marin Headlands**.

The Golden Gate Bridge serves as the border between the bustling city of San Francisco and its languid, wealthy, somewhat self-satisfied northern neighbour **Marin County**. The county extends up from Sausalito to Bodega and inland to Novato, with protected parkland and preserves sprawling across much of the county, rendering it immune to overpopulation. **Angel Island**, easily accessible by ferry from the city, is wonderful as a day trip or somewhere to spend a bit of time camping out in the wild.

The county has its towns too: **Tiburon**, with its bottom-up boat restaurants and singletons with pierced belly buttons; the dour fishermen and patchouli-scented trust-fund babies of Bolinas; and Corte Madera… any shopping you want, as long as it's expensive.

The main highway, **US 101**, progresses directly north through the heart of the county, dwindling from eight lanes in **Mill Valley** to a piddly four by the time it hits **Sonoma County**. Rather than battling the SUVs and BMWs on 101, take the scenic route: **Highway 1** (also called the Pacific Coast or Shoreline Highway) passing countless lesser-known North Bay gems as it weaves along, hugging

the coastline. Most Marin County destinations are within an hour's drive of San Francisco and therefore ideal for day trips, but there are plenty of other ways to see the sights: seaplane (*see p54*) or motorbike for the adventurous; ferry or tour bus for folks who just want to relax and take in the scenery.

Sausalito, Tiburon, Mill Valley & Larkspur

Stop at **Vista Point**, the first exit north of the Golden Gate Bridge, for a spectacular view of San Francisco (assuming, of course, there's no fog). Snuggled in Fort Baker at the northern foot of the bridge is the **Bay Area Discovery Museum** (*see p198*), an indoor/outdoor interactive museum geared toward youngsters. Just north, the **Marin Headlands** – part of the 364,926,320-square-yard (305,124,880-square-metre) Golden Gate National Recreation Area – offer nearly endless opportunities for outdoor activity, as well as breathtaking views of the city to the east and the wide-open Pacific Ocean to the west. Here also is the **Marine Mammal Center** (289 7325, www.tmmc.org), a sanctuary for sick or injured seals and sea lions.

Marin Civic Center. *See p253.*

The southernmost Marin County town, **Sausalito**, may not be as quaint as its reputation suggests, but it is undeniably picturesque, with a maze of tiny streets stretching from the shoreline all the way up to US 101. The best way to get to Sausalito (and the cheapest mode of sightseeing on water) is by ferry. It takes about half an hour to cross the Bay from San Francisco's Pier 41 or the Ferry Building (*see p276*), with unsurpassed views of the San Francisco waterfront, the Golden Gate Bridge and Alcatraz from the top deck. The boat docks in downtown Sausalito, all manicured gardens and pretty bungalows. Originally a fishing village, Sausalito is currently populated by well-heeled artist-types, yacht owners and successful businessmen and women. They, together with a constant flow of tourists, support the many T-shirt shops, waterfront restaurants and galleries.

Along North Bridgeway, opposite Spring Street, is the turn-off for Sausalito's only real visitor attraction: the **SF Bay Model Visitor Center** (2100 Bridgeway, at Olive Street, 332 3870, www.spn.usace.army.mil/bmvc, closed

Mon in summer & Sun in winter). A 7,260-square-yard (6,070-square-metre) 3-D hydraulic model of San Francisco Bay and beyond, it was built by the US Army Corps of Engineers as an actual engineering tool. From May through to October you can book passage from Sausalito on the **Hawaiian Chieftain** (331 3214, www.hawaiianchieftain.com), a replica late 18th-century sailing ship. Brunch, sunset and adventure cruises are on offer and on adventure cruises you help sail the ship, which is fun but exhausting.

Across Richardson Bay from Sausalito, and also accessible by ferry from San Francisco, is tiny downtown **Tiburon**. Again there are no real sights, though it's always tempting to enjoy a lingering brunch or lunch at one of the harbour-view restaurants on Main Street (also known as **Ark Row**, in honour of Tiburon's original, houseboat-dwelling denizens). If you're driving, park your car in one of the parking lots on Tiburon Boulevard and walk to the main drag. If you're biking, follow the bike path into the centre of town.

Tiburon's major attraction is, in fact, the Angel Island ferry (435 2131; $8 return, plus $1 supplement for bicycles), which runs hourly in summer from 10am to 4pm on weekdays and 10am to 5pm on weekends, in winter it sails weekends only (10am, 11am, 1pm and 3pm). The latest schedule information is at www.angelislandferry.com. Now a state park, **Angel Island** is not only the Bay's largest island, but also a delightfully wild place with an intriguing history. It was from 1910 the site of a US government immigration station, which became notorious as 'the Ellis Island of the West'. Boatloads of Chinese immigrants were detained for weeks and even months here while officials decided their fate; many of them were eventually sent home without ever touching the mainland. During World War II, the island housed German and Japanese POWs and, in the '50s and '60s, a Nike missile base. **Ayala Cove**, where the ferry docks, has a visitors' centre (information 435 1915, www.parks.ca.gov). It also marks the beginning of the five-mile (eight-kilometre) Perimeter Trail, which will take you past immigration quarantine buildings, picturesque Civil War barracks and the other military remnants that hide among the trees. You'll also find **Quarry Beach** – a sheltered, sandy sunbathing strip popular with kayakers. For those who can't deal with the walk, there's a tram tour round the island. The top of **Mount Livermore** (781 feet/238 metres) affords a lovely panoramic view of the Bay. The island has nine campsites and can be visited between 8am and sunset; for details of tours and bike or kayak rental, consult www.angelisland.com.

Marin lacks a real centre. San Rafael, Marin City, Corte Madera and Fairfield are sizeable towns, but they're not very interesting, unless you're shopping for a BMW or hot tub. Do, however, make the short detour to see the grand **Marin Civic Center** (Avenue of the Flags, North San Pedro Road exit on US 101, San Rafael, 499 6400, www.marincenter.org), designed by Frank Lloyd Wright and nicknamed 'Big Pink', and head to **Mill Valley**, at the bottom of Mount Tamalpais, for a taste of local yuppie culture. Home to charming boutiques, antique shops and restaurants, it also hosts the **Mill Valley Film Festival** (*see p203*).

Larkspur is also charming, but less visited (even though it's also on a ferry route). As well as a first-rate pub, the **Marin Brewing Company** (1809 Larkspur Landing Circle, 461 4677, www.marinbrewing.com), it has an old-fashioned downtown on the far side of the freeway from the ferry landing.

Nearby is the notorious **San Quentin Prison**, which out-of-towners often mistake for a holiday resort. The prison museum is only open by appointment (455 5000) and costs $2.

Where to eat

Bridgeway, Sausalito's main drag, offers several viable dining options. **Guernica** (No.2009, 332 1512, closed lunch, main courses $14-$21) has been serving unpretentious French-Basque cuisine and fantastic paella for more than 25 years. The early-bird specials and set meals at **Christophe** are a bargain (No.1919, 332 9244, closed Mon, lunch Tue-Fri, main courses $15-$25). **Horizons** (No.558, 331 3232, main courses $16-$28), a popular seafood restaurant, is housed in the lower two levels of a former yacht club.

In Tiburon most people come to **Guaymas** (5 Main Street, 435 6300, main courses $10-$25) to eat lunch, drink Margaritas and take in the view. Excellent for weekend brunch, **Sam's Anchor Cafe** (27 Main Street, 435 4527, www.samscafe.com, main courses $10-$25) invites you to accompany some hard liquor on to the waterfront deck to watch the boats go by: its colourful history spans back to Prohibition-era whiskey-running.

Larkspur's lovely and highly regarded **Lark Creek Inn** (234 Magnolia Avenue, 924 7766, www.larkcreek.com, main courses $20-$35) is a charming Victorian house with giant sloping skylights, located in a grove of redwoods. Its organic salads and vegetables come straight from the farmers' market and the butterscotch pudding is own-made. **Left Bank** (507 Magnolia Avenue, 927 3331, www.leftbank.com, main courses $12-$19) feels like a Parisian bistro, but caters to Bay Area dining sensibilities.

In Mill Valley visit the **Buckeye Roadhouse** (15 Shoreline Highway, 331 2600, www.buckeye roadhouse.com, main courses $13-$30), which offers all-American food in a setting reminiscent of a ski lodge. **La Ginestra** (127 Throckmorton Avenue, 388 0224, closed Mon, main courses $12-$20) is an old-time favourite; recommended dishes served here include linguine with clams, garlic and white wine, and the own-made cheese and spinach ravioli.

Getting there

By car

Take US 101 across the Golden Gate Bridge. For Sausalito (8 miles/13km from San Francisco), take the Alexander Avenue or Spencer Avenue exit. For Mill Valley (10 miles/16km) and Larkspur, take the East Blithedale exit; you can also reach Larkspur by the Paradise Drive or Lucky Drive exits. For Tiburon, turn off at the same point as for Mill Valley, but to the right, on to Highway 131.

By bus

Golden Gate Transit buses link San Francisco to Marin County. For Sausalito, take bus 22, 107 or 143; for Tiburon, bus 8 or 15; for Mill Valley, you need bus 4 or 10; and for Larkspur, take bus 97. Buses start from the Transbay Terminal at Mission and First Streets, but there are other pick-up points in the city. (See schedules at www.goldengate.org.)

By ferry

Golden Gate Transit ferries run daily from the Ferry Building on the Embarcadero to Sausalito and Larkspur; the Blue & Gold Fleet sails to Tiburon from the Ferry Building and to Sausalito and Angel Island from Pier 41, Fisherman's Wharf.

Resources

Tourist information

Mill Valley Chamber of Commerce *85 Throckmorton Avenue, Mill Valley (388 9700/www. millvalley.org)*. **Open** 10am-noon, 1.30-4pm Mon-Fri.
Sausalito Chamber of Commerce & Visitor Center *10 Liberty Ship Way, Bay 2, Ste 250 Sausalito (331 7262/www.sausalito.org)*. **Open** 9am-5pm Mon-Fri.

Mount Tamalpais & Muir Woods

Mount Tamalpais State Park covers some 30,491,999 square yards (25,495,195 square metres) on the mountain's western and southern slopes. Visible from as far away as Sonoma, Mount Tamalpais itself soars to nearly 2,600 feet (800 metres), its dramatic rise so steep it seems far taller. Beautiful at any time of day,

Trips Out of Town

Beaches All points north

To the north of San Francisco, Marin County has long proved irresistible for San Francisco's sybarites. Join them for an uplifting natural high among the several isolated coves north of the Marin Headlands. During the week or on brisk days the stretch of Highway 1 leading to **Stinson Beach** offers one of the most picturesque and exhilarating drives in the United States. When you arrive, it's the closest that the Bay Area comes to the Californian surfin' and sunnin' beach life of legend. (Would-be wave riders can rent open-top kayaks at Off the Beach Boats, 868 9445.) Further north, there is a different kind of heaven: **Point Reyes National Seashore** (*see p255*)

is miles and miles of surf-pounded shoreline, enhanced by deep valleys and lush forests of staggering beauty.

Brits may wish to knot a deferential hankie to the valiant not-yet-quite-Sir Francis Drake. The *Golden Hind* put in somewhere near **Drake's Beach** for six weeks in 1579, and Drake named the place 'Nova Albion' only for those pesky Puritans to steal the name and anglicise it for those dullards on the East Coast. But bypass this windswept bit of history and keep on Highway 1 as far as **Tomales Bay** (*pictured*), where tiny beaches offer mild tides and water that local swimmers swear is really not that cold. Here you'll find your heart's desire. Or, at the very least, the beach of that name.

the area is magnificent at sunset. The roads that snake over Mount Tam, though steep, are great for bicycling; indeed, the mountain bike was invented here.

Nearby **Muir Woods National Monument** (388 2595, www.visitmuirwoods.com, open 8am-sunset daily, admission $3) contains majestic groves of towering coastal redwoods, many between 500 and 1,000 years old. You'll find several miles of trails here, one of which (the one mile-/1.6-kilometre long Main Trail Loop) is accessible to the disabled. Redwood Creek is lined with madrone and big-leaf maple trees, wildflowers (even in winter), ferns and wild berry

bushes. Deer, chipmunks and a variety of birds live peacefully among the redwoods, while the creek is a migratory route for steelhead trout and silver salmon. The visitor centre at the entrance to Muir Woods has a gift shop, café and toilets, and offers walks led by park rangers. To avoid crowds, visit on weekday mornings and late afternoons. While in the area, take a spin on the **Panoramic Highway**, a beautiful two-lane spur with lots of hairpin bends that leads through sun-dappled forests to **Stinson Beach** (*see above*).

Just over three miles (4.8 kilometres) north of Stinson Beach is the **Bolinas Lagoon Preserve** (4900 Highway One, 868 9244, www.egret.org). It's one of the two wildlife sanctuaries run by **Audubon Canyon Ranch** (open weekends mid Mar-mid July), whose headquarters are a 19th-century white-frame house. In an old milking barn you'll find a natural history bookshop. The nearby **Alice Kent Trail** leads to an observation point for viewing egrets and great blue herons.

Where to stay & eat

The delightful, Elizabethan-style **Pelican Inn** (10 Pacific Way, at Highway 1, 383 6000, www.pelicaninn.com, rates from $201, closed dinner Mon, main courses $16-$26) could have been transplanted straight from England. Rooms are quaint, with canopied beds, balconies and private bathrooms, and though the food's not fantastic, you can get a nice table by the fire if you're staying for dinner.

Getting there

By car

Take US 101 across the Golden Gate Bridge, then turn on to Highway 1. Muir Woods is 15 miles (24km) from San Francisco.

By bus

There is no direct public transport to Muir Woods. Golden Gate Transit bus 63 goes from Marin City to Stinson Beach and local trailheads from mid Mar-mid Dec, and to Audubon Canyon Ranch from Mar to July.

Resources

Tourist information

Mount Tamalpais State Park (*388 2070*). **Open** 8am-5.30pm daily.
Muir Woods Visitor Center (*388 2595/ www.visitmuirwoods.com*). **Open** 9am-4.30pm daily.

Point Reyes National Seashore

Near Olema, north of Stinson Beach along Highway 1, is **Bear Valley Visitor Center** (*see below*). This is the entry point for the most famous parcel of land in these parts: the **Point Reyes National Seashore**, a vast wilderness, with beaches and ranchland from which one can still see San Francisco. This protected peninsula is an unforgettable wildlife refuge with sea mammals and waterfowl, miles of unspoilt beaches, waterfalls and campsites. From the visitor centre, head west towards the coast for **Drake's Beach** (*see p254* **Beaches: All points north**). Alternatively, go north via Inverness to the **Point Reyes Lighthouse**,

located at the tip of a peninsula; the perfect spot for whale-watching (*see p243*). Several trails start here, including the popular **Chimney Rock**.

Inverness is small and picturesque, with many homes still owned by the families that built them. It's also a good option for restaurants and places to bed down. Natural historians and those with more energy than is good for them should head along Highway 1 to **Tomales Bay** (*see p254* **Beaches: All points north**). **Blue Waters Kayaking** (12938 Sir Francis Drake Boulevard, Inverness, 669 2600, www.bwkayak.com) offers half- or full-day paddle trips, full-moon tours and overnighters by appointment, as well as basic kayak hire. Prices start at $30 for rental, and the company provides all the gear.

Where to eat

Vladimir's Czech Restaurant in Inverness (12785 Sir Francis Drake Boulevard, 669 1021, closed lunch, all Mon & Tue, main courses around $24) is one of a kind. Try the roast duckling, wiener schnitzel and delicious apple strudel. Also on Sir Francis Drake Boulevard, **Johnson's Oyster Company** (No.17171, 669 1149) hasn't changed after almost 50 years in business: same location, same family, same buildings, even the same Japanese method of farming oysters in clusters. **Manka's Inverness Lodge** (30 Callender Way, 669 1034, www.mankas.com, closed lunch and Jan, rates $185-$515, prix fixe menu $58-$88), built as a hunting and fishing lodge, has eight rooms, one suite, two cabins and a dramatic 1911 boat-house built over the water, with intimate quarters above. Owner/chef Margaret Grade's fresh seasonal cuisine and fire-roasted game make this the best food choice in Inverness.

Resources

Tourist information

Bear Valley Visitor Center (*464 5100/www.nps. gov/pore*). **Open** 9am-5pm Mon-Fri; 8am-5pm Sat, Sun.
Kenneth C Patrick Visitor Center (*669 1250/ www.nps.gov/pore*). **Open** 10am-5pm daily.
Lighthouse Visitor Center Point (*669 1534/ www.nps.gov/pore*). **Open** 10am-4.30pm Mon, Thur-Sun, weather permitting.

Getting there

By car

Take US 101 across the Golden Gate Bridge, then Highway 1. Point Reyes is 32 miles (51km) from SF.

By bus

There is no direct public transport to Point Reyes.

Trips Out of Town

Wine Country

Close to San Francisco, but in a world of its own.

Few visitors to San Francisco can resist making a visit to Napa and Sonoma Counties. Just an hour away from the city by car, the world-renowned wine regions are one of the most popular visitor attractions in the Western Region. The area is as perfect for a romantic weekend retreat as for a quick getaway for wine-tasting and touring among the lush rolling hills and tangled vineyards. It's always great to be here, but do try to avoid going during the height of summer when temperatures soar and tourists arrive in droves. The harvest season in October is also very busy. Off-season discounts are available in lush, colourful autumn and floral spring, when the area is more peaceful and far less inundated by traffic.

The region is essentially separated into the Napa and Sonoma Valleys, divided by a low-lying mountain range. Of the two, **Napa** is the largest and most famous, and subsequently the most popular. Napa's main thoroughfare, Highway 29, can during peak hours feel like a 20-mile-long (32-kilometre) parking lot. **Sonoma** is much smaller and slower, retaining much of its bucolic charm. If the traffic is slow in Sonoma, it's probably behind a farmer on his tractor. Most settlers in the area originally came from France, Italy or Germany, bringing with them their family traditions, foodstuffs and wine-making methods. They were drawn to the area by its similarity to their temperate European homelands. Indeed, that similarity gave rise to the world-class wines that ultimately made California's Wine Country famous. Most wineries are open daily and charge a nominal amount (a few are free) for tastings of several different wines and often a tour. For a guide to the labels and grapes, *see* *p260* **Grape expectations**. Several San Francisco operators run tours to the area: for more information, visit the San Francisco Visitor Information Center (*see p291*), a local tourist office or www.winecountryguide.com.

Sonoma Valley

The Sonoma Valley runs about 23 miles (37 kilometres) north from San Pablo Bay; Highway 12 goes through the centre of the valley. Besides the wine itself, one of the principal attractions of a Sonoma wine tour is the valley itself. The pristine rural surroundings offer glimpses of the region's pre-developed past, with working farms and rustic barns dotting the countryside. The **Sonoma County Wineries Association** (1-800 939 7666/1-707 586 3795) organises winery tours and daily tastings. It's located near US 101 in Rohnert Park.

The town of **Sonoma** was founded in 1823 as the Mission San Francisco Solano, the last and northernmost of the Franciscan missions. It developed around a Mexican-style plaza. For 25 days in 1846, during the riotous Bear Flag Revolt, it was the capital of the independent Republic of California. A monument to the revolt stands in the Plaza, which is now flanked by adobe and false-fronted buildings in an Old West style. Restaurants, bookshops, a cinema and places to grab picnic supplies – including a cheese shop, a bakery and a wine-tasting room – make the Plaza one of the top attractions in the valley. On Tuesdays in summer the Plaza hosts an excellent farmers' market.

It's worth picking up a leaflet on walking tours of the downtown area from the visitor bureau. Local landmarks include the whitewashed adobe **Sonoma Mission** (1-707 938 9560, www.iktome.com/svvb/mission.html) on the edge of the Plaza, which served as a Mexican outpost in the 17th century. Now restored, it houses a variety of relics. **Sonoma State Historic Park** (1-707 938 9559/939 9420) includes the mission building and town hall, as well as the Toscano Hotel and the Sonoma barracks, where troops under Mexican General Mariano G Vallejo were once stationed. About a mile south of the Plaza, **Sonoma Train Town** (20264 Broadway, at Highway 12, 1-707 938 3912, www.traintown.com) is a good stop for families. Take a 20-minute ride on a miniature steam train past scale models of buildings, a petting zoo and waterfalls.

The history of Sonoma is intertwined with that of the Californian wine industry, which first began here. A Hungarian count, Agoston Haraszthy, planted the first European grapevines in Sonoma in the 1850s at **Buena Vista Historical Winery** (18000 Old Winery Road, 1-800 926 1266, www.buenavista winery.com). It's open from 10am to 5pm daily. Of the nearly 40 wineries in the Sonoma Valley, several are near Sonoma's Plaza. One that also makes a great picnic choice is **Bartholomew Park Winery** (1000 Vineyard Lane, 1-707 935

One-time capital of the Republic of California, **Sonoma** is now in the heart of wine country.

9511, www.bartholomewparkwinery.com, tastings $3), which has a museum and a relief map dedicated to the appellation. The picnic grounds nestle beautifully atop a small overlook. Or you can head to the **Wine Exchange of Sonoma** (452 First Street East, 1-800 938 1794/www.wineexsonoma.com), which offers up to 18 Californian and European wines as well as a half-dozen beers for daily tasting.

North of Sonoma are the small settlements of Glen Ellen and Kenwood. Jack London – the famed adventurer, farmer and one of the most prolific authors of his day – made his home in Glen Ellen. In **Jack London Historic State Park** (2400 London Ranch Road, 1-707 938 5216, www.parks.sonoma.net/JLPark.html) are the charred remains of **Wolf House**, the once-magnificent four-storey house built of volcanic rock in which London lived. The park is a nice place to stroll in the shade among oak and madrone trees. Near the entrance to the park, the **Sonoma Cattle Company** (1-707 996 8566) leads horseback tours of the area.

To many people, Kenwood is synonymous with the **Kenwood Winery** (9592 Sonoma Highway, 1-707 833 5891, www.kenwood vineyards.com). This friendly, classic Sonoma winery is known for wine made from grapes grown on Jack London's former ranch. The original barn, now the tasting room and shop, dates from the pre-Prohibition days of the early 20th century. Tastings are free.

Further south is the Carneros region, straddling southern Sonoma and Napa. It is the area's only true appellation. Wineries here take advantage of the cooler climate to produce excellent Pinot Noirs and sparkling wines. The **Gloria Ferrer Champagne Caves** (23555 Highway 121, 1-707 996 7256, www.gloriaferrer.com) are worth a visit to witness the intricacies of the centuries-old process of making sparkling wine. They're open from 10.30am to 5.30pm daily; tastings cost $4-$7. The area is also home to the quaint **Schug Winery** (602 Bonneau Road, 1-800 966 9365, www.schugwinery.com), a family-run winery whose Pinot Noirs and Chardonnays have won awards. Near the southern entrance to the Valley is the **Viansa Winery and Italian Marketplace** (25200 Arnold Road, on Highway 121, Sonoma, 1-800 995 4740, 1-707 935 4700, www.viansa.com). A scion of one of the state's oldest wine families, Sam Sebastiani and his wife Vicki have built a Tuscan-style winery on a knoll facing the Sonoma Valley. Their tasting room (open 9.30am-5.30pm daily) also sells Italian foods, and trellis-topped picnic tables outside look out over the lower valley.

Where to eat

The **General's Daughter** (400 West Spain Street, 1-707 938 4004, main courses $9-$24, closed 1st 2wks Jan) is based in a beautifully restored Victorian building, and is an excellent place for brunch. The **Girl & the Fig** (110 West Spain Street, 1-707 938 3634, www.thegirlandthefig.com, main courses $11-$22) was an institution in Glen

Stop wining

It's called Wine Country for a reason. But among the rolling hills and ever-changing foliage of Napa and Sonoma Valleys there's a lot going on that isn't to do with wine. Fitness fans and self-pamperers, amateur photographers, thrill-seekers, even art critics find plenty to occupy them when they've had enough of the grape.

Nearly as famous as the vineyards of Wine Country are its many spas. They are largely concentrated in Calistoga, where there is a spa on almost every corner. Calistoga's speciality is mud baths that use volcanic ash from neighbouring St Helena Mountain, superheated with water from the underground hot springs. Bang in the centre of town, **Dr Wilkinson's Hot Springs** (1507 Lincoln Avenue, 1-707 942 4102/6257, www.drwilkinson.com) is sweet, old-fashioned and great value. For $99 you get a mud bath, mineral bath, steam, blanket wrap and a half-hour massage (a two-person package, including overnight lodgings as well as all the treatments, costs only $259). Also on Lincoln Avenue is the sumptuous **Indian Springs Spa** (No.1712, 1-707 942 4913, www.indianspringscalistoga.com), with pretty white cottages surrounded by lawns and contemplative fountains, and an enormous mineral-water swimming pool, while just half an hour's drive north of Calistoga you'll find **Harbin Hot Springs** (18424 Harbin Springs Road, Middletown, 1-800 622 2477, 1-707 987 2477, www.harbin.org), a hippie retreat offering yoga and meditation workshops alongside its spa treatments. Many people's favourite Bay Area spa resort is the **Sonoma Mission Inn & Spa** (100 Boyes Boulevard, 1-800 862 4945, www.sonomamissioninn.com) in Sonoma Valley. It seems to get brought bang up to date every year, staying at the leading edge of luxury; a romantic Couples Wine

and Roses Kur will set you back $418. For all, be sure to make an appointment, especially at weekends.

If you don't want to wallow in the mud, you could be floating across the skies. In these parts, colourful hot-air balloons are as common as clouds, and though the rides demand several rolls of film and mastery of any vestigial vertigo, they are well worth it. Many companies offer balloon flights, among them **Above the Wine Country Ballooning** (1-888 238 6359, 1-707 829 9850, www.balloontours.com), **Bonaventura Balloon Company** (1-800 359 6272, www.bonaventuraballoons.com) and **Balloon Aviation** (1-800 367 6272, www.nvaloft.com).

The remote waters of Lake Berryessa provide fishing and boating, while the surrounding countryside is wonderful for cycling, hiking and horse-riding. You can also take cycle tours around the wineries; these are arranged by companies like **Napa Valley Bike Tours** (1-800 707 2453, www.napavalleybiketours.com) and **Getaway Adventures** (1-800 499 2453, www.getaway adventures.com). Lazybones can let the **Napa Valley Wine Train** (1-800 427 4124, 1-707 253 2111, www.winetrain.com) do all the work. It runs lunch and dinner trips ($40-$140) up and down the valley every day. Cheesy, perhaps, but you don't have to fight the summer traffic and the food, paired with local wines, is really quite good.

Though it is mainly wine-oriented, **COPIA** (*see p260*) hosts brilliant exhibitions and runs programmes that explore other culinary innovations or investigate American approaches to food and drink in general. Several of the wineries themselves offer alternative activities. Art aficionados will delight in the **Di Rosa Preserve** (*pictured right*, 5200 Carneros Highway, Napa, 1-707 226

Ellen before it brought its delightful French-style country menu to this corner of Sonoma Plaza. The restaurant in Glen Ellen is now known as the **Fig Café** (13690 Arnold Drive, 1-707 938 2130) and offers lighter casual fare. Also near the Plaza is **Deuce** (691 Broadway, 1-707 933 3823, www.dine-at-deuce.com, main courses $14-$22), a bustling home-style dining room popular with locals for its fresh seasonal fare. For something meatier try **Saddles Steakhouse** (29 East MacArthur Street, 1-707 933 3191, main courses

$10-$30), which grills up some of the best steaks in either valley. For a spicy change of pace, try **Maya** (1-707 935 3500, www.maya restaurant.com, main courses $12-$20, closed lunch Mon & Sun), a casual spot on the square serving great Mexican fare and as many kinds of tequila as there are wines in the area. If you're in the mood for a picnic, pick up cheese and crackers at the **Sonoma Cheese Factory** (2 Spain Street, 1-707 996 1931, www.sonomajack.com), also located on the Plaza.

5991, www.dirosapreserve.org, admission $12), at the southern end of Napa Valley, as it houses one of the country's largest regional art collections. Built into a century-old stone winery, the Preserve's collection includes nearly 2,000 works of art, ranging from the beautiful to the bizarre. Then, at the northern end of the valley, there's the **Sharpsteen Museum** (1311 Washington Street, Calistoga, 1-707 942 5911, www.sharpsteen-museum.org) with its wonderful dioramas depicting 19th-century Calistoga life, as well as archive photos and other artefacts.

For geology buffs the little **Old Faithful geyser**, on Tubbs Lane, is a must. Water comes from an underground river, heating to around 350˚F (177˚C) before spewing high into the air four times an hour. Another quirk of nature is the **Petrified Forest**, a few miles

west on Petrified Forest Road. Here you can see fallen trees, some of them 150 feet (nearly 50 metres) long, fossilised by volcanic ash nearly three million years ago. North on Highway 29, **Robert Louis Stevenson State Park** (1-707 942 4575) is named after the writer who honeymooned here in 1880; the **Robert Louis Stevenson Museum** (1490 Library Lane, 1-707 963 3757) in St Helena provides more substantive memorabilia.

Finally, nature lovers should head to Calistoga's **Safari West Wildlife Preserve and Tent Camp** (1-707 579 2551). The 400 mainly African bird and mammal species who call this vast sanctuary home get to watch jeep-loads of strange humans on daily guided tours. Adults pay $58 for the privilege, children $28 and under-threes go free. A small enough price to pay for making a lemur laugh.

Where to stay

Two good options on Sonoma Plaza are the **Sonoma Hotel** (1-707 996 2996, rates $95-$245) and the luxurious **El Dorado Inn** (1-707 996 3030, rates $135-$190). Just a few blocks south is the **Lodge at Sonoma** (1325 Broadway Avenue, 1-707 935 6600) with comfy, cottage-style rooms ($199-$279) and the latest in spa amenities. If you're looking for peace and quiet, the **Gaige House Inn** (13540 Arnold

Drive, 1-707 935 0237) in Glen Ellen is worth the extra drive – and cash (rooms cost $275-$525): sit outside by the pool, where the creek gurgles, the sun shines and time seems to stop. Up-valley in Healdsburg is the sumptuous **Hotel Healdsburg** (25 Matheson Street, 1-707 431 2800, www.hotelhealdsburg.com, rates $245-$795), the area's only full-service resort and spa, and home to Charlie Palmer's award-winning **Dry Creek Kitchen** (317 Healdsburg Avenue, 1-707 431 0330, main courses $15-$25).

Trips Out of Town

Tourist information

Sonoma Valley Visitors Bureau
453 First Street East, Sonoma (1-707 996 1090/
www.sonomavalley.com). **Open** 9am-5pm daily.

Napa Valley

The 25-mile-long (40-kilometre) Napa Valley,
running almost parallel to the Sonoma Valley
on the east side of the Mayacamas Mountains,
forms the backbone of the Napa wine industry.
Napa was originally populated by the Nappa
Indian tribe; then Europeans settled, with
Charles Krug introducing grapes into the valley
in 1861. Highway 29 (also called the St Helena
Highway) runs up the centre of the valley and is
usually crowded with traffic because the largest
wineries are found on it. Boutique wineries are
mostly to be found on the **Silverado Trail**
(parallel to Highway 29 to the east) or on one
of the lanes that criss-cross the valley or lead
up one of the many hillsides.

Napa itself, at the bottom end of the valley,
has traditionally had little to offer the traveller
other than outlet stores. But that has changed,
especially in the historic downtown area
where a restoration of the Gold Rush-era
Opera House (1000 Main Street, 1-707 226
7372, www.napavalleyoperahouse.org) has been
indicative of renewed civic pride. The highly
publicised opening of **COPIA: The American
Center for Wine, Food & the Arts** (500
First Street, 1-707 259 1600, www.copia.org)
has also helped refocus attention on the city of
Napa. COPIA is a massive $50-million facility
dedicated to exploring food and wine and its
influence on American culture. Spearheaded by
Robert Mondavi, it offers everything from
art shows and cooking demonstrations to live
music. **Julia's Kitchen** (1-707 265 5700, closed
dinner Mon & Wed, all day Tue), COPIA's main
restaurant, is worth a visit for lunch or dinner.

Wine-tasting is the main attraction in Napa
Valley, with dining running a close second:
some of the Bay Area's best restaurants are
in this area. For a complete list of wineries, pick
up a map at any of the vineyards, but **Robert
Mondavi Winery** (7801 St Helena Highway,
1-888 766 6328, 1-707 259 9463, www.robert
mondaviwinery.com) in Oakville is a good bet
for first-time tasters. It's open from 9am to 5pm
daily, tastings cost $4-$8 and there are special
tours for $35-$95. Also worth investigation are
the historic German mansion of the **Beringer
Vineyards** (2000 Main Street, 1-707 963 7115,
www.beringer.com, $5-$65 for tasting/tours)
in St Helena and, in Yountville, **Domaine
Chandon** (1 California Drive, 1-707 944 2280,
www.dchandon.com). The latter an excellent
tour (Nov-Apr 11am-5pm, May-Oct 10am-6pm,
$5), introducing visitors to its stellar Californian
interpretation of *méthode champenoise*.

For a winery with a difference, visit film
director Francis Ford Coppola's **Niebaum-
Coppola Winery** (1991 St Helena Way,
1-800 782 4266, 1-707 968 1161, www.niebaum-
coppola.com) in Rutherford, where you can see
memorabilia from Coppola's movies, including
a vintage Tucker automobile and an Oscar
statuette from one of the *Godfather* films. Other
notable wineries in the area include **PlumpJack**
(620 Oakville Crossroad, 1-707 945 1220,
www.plumpjack.com, tastings $5-$7), which has
terrific Cabernets; **Cakebread Cellars** (8300 St
Helena Highway, 1-800 588 0298, www.cake

Grape expectations

Not all Californian wines are widely available
outside the state, so here's a guide to which
label does what. Huge volume of fruit and
flavour is the hallmark of today's Californian
wines; common varieties include crisp
Chardonnays, big Cabernet Sauvignons,
soft Merlots, Sauvignon Blancs, Pinot Noirs,
Rieslings and the versatile Zinfandel.

Sonoma labels

Cline (Zinfandel); Shug (Pinot Noir);
Dry Creek (Chardonnay); Field Stone
(Cabernet, Petite Syrah); Foppiano (Petite
Syrah, Zinfandel); Geyser Peak (Chardonnay);
Gundlach Bundschu (Merlot, Pinot Noir,
Chardonnay, Cabernet, Zinfandel); Lambert

Bridge (Fumé Blanc, Pinot Noir, Zinfandel);
Matanzas Creek (Chardonnay); Pezzi King
(Pinot Noir, Zinfandel, Cabernet); Roche
(Chardonnay, Pinot Noir).

Napa labels

Carneros Creek (Pinot Noir); Bouchon
(Pinot, Chardonnay); Chimney Rock
(Chardonnay, Cabernet); Clos Pegase
(Cabernet, Chardonnay, Merlot, Petite Syrah
port); Cuvaison (Cabernet, Chardonnay);
Joseph Phelps (Chardonnay); Opus One
(Cabernet); Pine Ridge (Chardonnay,
Cabernet, Merlot); Robert Sinskey (Pinot
Noir); Silver Oak (Cabernet); Stag's Leap
(Cabernet, Chardonnay, Sauvignon Blanc).

The classy **Carneros Inn**, a new vintage in the Napa Valley. *See p262.*

breadcellars.com) a great Chardonnay and
Cabernet house with an interesting tour (by
appointment); and the **Cliff Lede Vineyards**
(1473 Yountville Cross Road, 1-707 944 8642,
www.cliffledevineyards.com, tastings $5, tour
$10), which offers guided tours of its sparkling
wine caves and whose grounds feature a lovely
new mountainside inn. In addition to producing
award-winning wines, the **Hess Collection**
(4411 Redwood Road, 1-877 707 4377, www.hess
collection.com, tastings $3) has a museum-
quality selection of contemporary art, including
sculptures by Frank Stella and Robert
Rauschenberg. People with a palate for port
won't want to miss **Prager Winery & Port
Works** (1281 Lewelling Lane, St Helena, 1-800
969 7878, 1-707 963 7678, www.pragerport.com),
which explains how it's all made.

At the northern end of Napa Valley is
Calistoga, home of the hot springs and bottled
water. Calistoga has a distinct Western feel,
with saloons, wooden sidewalks, and a wide
main street, Lincoln Avenue, often festooned
with banners promoting beer tastings, mustard
festivals or other celebrations of the California
good life. Calistoga is famous for its spas; don't
leave without spending a few hours soaking in
a mud bath (*see p258* **Stop wining**).

Several wineries are located in and around
Calistoga. You can take the tram to **Sterling
Vineyards** (1111 Dunaweal Lane, 1-800
726 6136, 1-707 942 3345, www.sterling

vineyards.com). Famous for its Cabernet
Sauvignon as well as its white wines, this
hilltop winery has commanding views of the
countryside and an excellent self-guided tour
($10). **Château Montelena** (1429 Tubbs Lane,
1-707 942 5105, www.montelena.com, tastings
$10, tour $25) is an 1882 house overlooking
a Chinese garden complete with a lake, tea
houses, bridges and even the hull of a junk. The
winery produced the first bottle of California
white to win against the French, when its '73
beat all-comers in a 1976 competition and put
Napa on the wine-making map. **Clos Pegase**
(1060 Dunaweal Lane, 1-707 942 4981,
www.clospegase.com, tastings $5-$7.50) is a
large winery in a stunning structure designed
by postmodern architect Michael Graves. The
grounds contain a bewitching sculpture garden.

One of the best tours in the area is at
sparkling wine specialist **Schramsberg**
(1400 Schramsberg Road, 1-707 942 2414,
www.schramsberg.com). The tour ($20, by
appointment only) takes visitors through
a maze of caves dug at the turn of the 20th
century by Chinese labourers.

Where to eat

Known the world over, the **French Laundry**
(6640 Washington Street, 1-707 944 2380,
www.frenchlaundry.com, closed lunch Mon-
Thur) in Yountville prepares what may be

the best meal you'll ever eat for an average of around $70 a head. Make your dinner reservation at least three months in advance).

In central Napa, try **Cole's Chop House** (1122 Main Street, 1-707 224 6328, main courses $16-$42, closed lunch & 1st wk Jan), which takes its steaks and chops very seriously. Downtown Napa is home to **Tuscany** (1005 First Street, 1-707 258 1000, main courses $15-$50), a great choice for rustic Italian fare at reasonable prices. Also in Napa, **Mustards Grill** (7399 St Helena Highway, 1-707 944 2424, main courses $15-$20) is a popular upmarket diner. St Helena has a number of excellent restaurants, including newcomer **Market** (1347 Main Street, 1-707 963 3799, main courses $7-$20), established by San Francisco restaurateurs who brought together city-style service and affordable country-style American cooking. Another local favourite is **Pinot Blanc** (641 Main Street, 1-707 963 6191, main courses $16-$26, closed Mon), while for a quick bite **Taylor's Refresher** (933 Main Street, 1-707 963 3486, main courses $5-$8) can't be beat – locals have been driving up to get burgers and thick milkshakes for a generation.

For a picnic, pick up some gourmet delicacies from the West Coast installation of New York deli **Dean & Deluca** (607 South St Helena Highway, 1-707 967 9980). Both **Cantinetta Tra Vigne** (1050 Charter Oak Avenue, St Helena, 1-707 963 8888) and the **Oakville Grocery** (7856 St Helena Highway, Oakville, 1-707 944 8802) pack a picnic hamper if you phone the day before, and **Bale Grist Mill State Historic Park** (Highway 29, between St Helena and Calistoga) is a good place to eat it.

In Calistoga, the **Wappo Bar & Bistro** (1226 Washington Street, 1-707 942 4712, main courses $12-$23, closed Tue) is a long-time favourite that serves a surprising array of cuisines– from Asian to Italian – all of them very well. **Brannan's Grill** (1374 Lincoln Avenue, 1-707 942 2233, main courses $16-$28) captures the charm of the Old West with its decor and the hearts of diners with its magnificently prepared American classics. For snacks, the quintessentially Californian **Calistoga Natural** (1426 Lincoln Avenue, at Washington, 1-707 942 5822) healthfood store and café serves fabulous sandwiches, smoothies and vegetable and fruit juices.

Where to stay

For information on places to stay in Napa, contact **Napa Valley Reservations Unlimited** (1-800 251 6272, 1-707 252 1985, www.napavalleyreservations.com) – bear in mind that rooms are often booked up and most options are expensive.

A deluxe option is the **Vintage Inn** (6541 Washington Street, 1-800 351 1133, 1-707 944 1112, www.vintageinn.com, rates $210-$510) in Yountville. Similarly, the **Napa River Inn** (500 Main Street, 1-877 251 8500, 1-707 251 8500, www.napariverinn.com, rates $159-$500) has deluxe accommodation in the heart of downtown Napa. Even more expensive is the **Auberge du Soleil** (180 Rutherford Hill Road, 1-800 348 5406, rates $425-$3,500) on a hilltop in Rutherford, which is worth booking for very special occasions. St Helena's **Harvest Inn** (1 Main Street, 1-800 950 8466, 1-707 963 9463, www.harvestinn.com) offers Tudor-style cottages, all named after knights or romantic figures, set in pretty gardens and overlooking a vineyard. Rates range from $255 to $645. A welcome newcomer to the region is the luxurious and sleekly designed **Carneros Inn** (4048 Sonoma Highway, 1-707 299 4900, www.thecarnerosinn.com, rates $300-$1,200). Sandwiched between the towns of Napa and Sonoma, the Inn features 86 cosy cottages (including ten suites), all with wood-burning fireplaces, flat-panel TVs and ethernet hookups. The bathrooms are like mini spas. Check out the French-inspired cuisine at their Hilltop Dining Room; the Boon Fly Café is due to open in 2004.

In Calistoga, try the historic **Mount View Hotel** (1457 Lincoln Avenue, 1-707 942 6877, www.mountviewhotel.com, rates $125-$250) on the main street; it also has a first-class spa. The **Pink Mansion** (1415 Foothill Boulevard, at Main Street, 1-800 238 7465, 1-707 942 0558, www.pinkmansion.com, rates $165-$345) is an elegant restored building with in-house wine tastings, while the **Mountain Home Ranch** (3400 Mountain Home Ranch Road, 1-707 942 6616, www.mtnhomeranch.com, rates $55-$139) is a secluded resort with swimming pools, tennis and volleyball, fishing and hiking.

Tourist information

Calistoga Chamber of Commerce & Visitors Center *1458 Lincoln Avenue no.9, Calistoga (1-707 942 6333/www.calistogafun.com).* **Open** 10am-5pm Mon-Fri; 10am-4pm Sat; 11am-3pm Sun.
Napa Valley Conference & Visitor Center *1310 Napa Town Center, Napa (1-707 226 7459/ www.napavalley.com).* **Open** 9am-5pm daily.

Getting there

By car

Wine Country is about an hour by car from SF (44 miles/71km) over the Golden Gate along US 101. Turn east at Ignacio to Highway 37 and take Highway 121 north. From here, Highway 12 takes you along Sonoma Valley; Highway 29 along Napa Valley.

Heading East

Welcome to the Great Outdoors.

Everybody needs a break from city life, even life in a city as beautiful as San Francisco. The great thing is, for just the cost of renting a car, you really can get away from it all. Just a few hours out of the city you'll discover breathtaking scenery and a dazzling array of outdoor activities. **Yosemite** boasts some of the finest climbing terrain in the United States, along with stunning mountains, waterfalls and forests, while **Lake Tahoe** has winter sports, wonderful summer hiking and, for the cerebrally active, year-round gambling.

Lake Tahoe

At the eastern border of California, beautiful Lake Tahoe draws millions of visitors each year. No one knows how deep the lake actually is: locals simply call it 'Big Blue'. Flanked by snow-capped peaks, it has become California's primary playground for skiing, waterskiing, fishing and hiking. The California–Nevada border runs right through the middle of Tahoe, which means there are opportunities to gamble as well, at the casinos lining the main drag of aptly named **Stateline**, just over the border.

The north end of Lake Tahoe is a three-and-a-half hour drive from San Francisco. (It takes longer if there's heavy snow on I-80, in which case drive slowly and make sure you have snow chains.) The other route, via US 50, leads to the south shore, where hotels are usually packed with skiers and gamblers. From March to early November it's easy to drive the 72-mile (116-kilometre) perimeter of the lake, much of which is served by public transport. Alternatively, the **Tahoe Rim Trail** (call 1-775 298 0012 for info) provides extensive trails for those who prefer to explore on foot, bike or horse. On the California side you'll find such attractions as the **Sugar Pine Point State Park** (1-530 525 7982), near Meeks Bay, and further south the **Emerald Bay State Park** (1-530 541 3030), which overlooks the bay of the same name.

There are plenty of beaches around the lake: **Sand Harbour**, **Zephyr Cove** and **Camp Richardson** are all on the water. Only during August and September is the water, fed by snow melt, warm enough for swimming – and then barely so. A better idea is to book a scenic cruise on the **Tahoe Queen Paddlewheeler** (1-530 541 3364, www.laketahoecruises.com) or one of

Lose yourself in fathomless **Lake Tahoe** – the 'Big Blue'.

several other tour boats out of South Lake Tahoe. **Truckee**, an Old West town about 12 miles (19 kilometres) north of the lake, is worth a visit for its wooden sidewalks and wood-framed shopfronts. Designed to look like the backdrop for a John Wayne film, the effect is spoiled a little by the tourists and modern bars and restaurants. **Donner Memorial State Park**, a few miles west of Truckee off Highway 80, is named after the Donner family. This doomed group of pioneers suffered misfortune after misfortune as they attempted to cross the pass in the viciously cold winter of 1842, with starvation driving some of them to cannibalism. The visitor centre has a short movie detailing the grisly tale. The park's campsites were closed in August 2003 for renovations to the waterworks; they are scheduled to re-open in 2004.

For a bird's-eye view of the area, take a trip with **Mountain High Balloons** (1-888 462 2683) from Truckee or **Lake Tahoe Hot Air Balloons** (1-530 544 1221, www.laketahoe balloons.com) from South Lake Tahoe or in the slightly cheaper sightseeing gondolas operated by **Heavenly Valley** (1-775 586 7000, www.skiheavenly.com).

Skiing

The ski season varies each year, but usually starts around December and lasts until late April. Two of the most popular ski areas in the West are **Squaw Valley** (1-530 583 6985, www.squaw.com), site of the 1960 Winter Olympics, and **Alpine Meadows** (1-800 441 4423, 1-530 583 4232, snow conditions recorded message 1-530 581 8374, www.skialpine.com). Alpine is more family-oriented and has better snowboarding, while Squaw is glitzier, with more exciting runs.

Other ski areas include **Boreal** (1-530 426 3666, www.borealski.com), whose lower prices attract snowboarders; **Northstar** (1-530 562 1010, www.skinorthstar.com) at Tahoe, which has excellent beginners' slopes; and **Sugar Bowl** (1-530 426 9000, www.sugarbowl.com), where there's a creaky old gondola that takes you to the base lodge. Ski rental is available at the resorts, but if you're driving, it's probably cheaper to rent your gear in San Francisco – it also means you avoid the queues. Lift passes tend to be expensive, but most resorts offer half-day passes for the afternoon and sometimes mid-week special offers.

If you're not confident about your ability or haven't been on the slopes for a while, invest in a lesson – they include the cost of a lift pass for the day so it can work out to be a pretty good deal. If you're driving and are not tied to a particular schedule, avoid going on Friday afternoons: San Franciscans tend to leave work early to get a head start to the slopes. Likewise, Sunday evenings can be a nightmare if you're trying to get back into the city. You can even get some skiing in as a day trip. It means leaving San Francisco around 6am to arrive at the slopes by 9.30am, when the lifts open – you'll be among the first to experience the day's fresh powder snow as well. You can head back when the lifts close at 4pm.

Where to eat

Gourmet dining is rare in Tahoe, but you will find loads of unpretentious, family-owned restaurants that are easygoing and have friendly service – they're also cheap compared to the city. The bigger restaurant chains are in the hotel casinos, along with Vegas-style 'all-you-can-eat' buffets, quite an experience if you haven't tried one before.

South Lake Tahoe's **Cantina Bar & Grill** (765 Emerald Bay Road, 1-530 544 1233, www.cantinatahoe.com, closed breakfast, main courses $8-$14) is iconic. Hit its happy hour (3-6pm Mon-Fri) for delicious Margaritas and traditional Mexican fare. Also in South Lake Tahoe, **Evans American Gourmet Café** (536 Emerald Bay Road, 1-530 542 1990, www.evanstahoe.com, main courses $19-$30) serves up good Californian cuisine. Locals have voted it the best for fine dining.

In Truckee, you'll find the **Cottonwood Restaurant** (Highway 267 & Old Brockway Road, 1-530 587 5711, www.cottonwood restaurant.com, closed breakfast and lunch, main courses $9-$29). From outside it may seem rustic and worn down, but inside it serves up an eclectic range of eats accompanied by an adventurous wine list and (on Saturdays) live jazz. The elegant setting of **Le Petit Pier** (7238 North Lake Boulevard, Tahoe Vista, 1-530 546 4464, www.lepetitpier.com, closed breakfast, lunch & Tue, main courses $20-$40) makes it one of the most romantic restaurants in the area. The award-winning wine list and food (including herb-roasted rack of lamb with truffle sauce) mean reservations are recommended.

Where to stay

South of Lake Tahoe, **Kirkwood Ski & Summer Resort** (1501 Kirkwood Meadows Drive, off Highway 88, 1-800 967 7500, www.kirkwood.com, rates $125-$699) is a family-oriented resort. Guests stay in slopeside lodges or condos; the lodge itself has a spa, gym and massage room. Nearby, **Historic Camp Richardson Resort** (1900 Jameson Beach Road, South Lake Tahoe, 1-800 544 1801,

Yosemite Falls in spectacular **Yosemite National Park**.

www.camprich.com, rates $70-$270) has lakefront cabins with incredible views. Each cabin has a wood stove or fireplace and a basic kitchen, but if you don't feel like cooking, the camp's **Beacon Bar & Grill** (1-530 541 0630, main courses $18-$25) will do the work for you. In Truckee, the historic **Truckee Hotel** (10007 Bridge Street, 1-800 659 6921, www.truckeehotel.com, rates $45-$135) has 37 immaculate rooms decked out with antiques and clawfoot tubs. A good online resource is **Lake Tahoe Vacation Guide** (www.tahoevacationguide.com), full of information on where to stay in the region.

If you want to live large but don't have enough time to get to Las Vegas, **Caesars Tahoe** (55 Highway 50, 1-888 829 7630, www.caesarstahoe.com, rates $89-$200) on the south shore is the next best thing. As well as a spa and pool – and all the gambling, of course – the casino puts on sell-out shows by the likes of James Brown, Jewel and Macy Gray.

Resources

Tourist information
Donner Memorial State Park Visitors' Centre
12593 Donner Pass Road, Truckee (1-530 582 7892/ www.parks.ca.gov). Open June-Aug 10am-4pm daily. *Sept-May* 10am-5pm daily.
North Lake Tahoe Chamber of Commerce *380 North Lake Boulevard, Tahoe City (1-530 581 6900).* **Open** *Summer* 9am-5pm Mon-Fri; 9am-4pm Sat, Sun. *Winter* 8am-4pm Mon-Fri; 9am-4pm Sat, Sun.
South Lake Tahoe Chamber of Commerce *3066 Lake Tahoe Boulevard, South Lake Tahoe (1-530 541 5255/www.tahoeinfo.com).* **Open** 9am-5pm Mon-Sat.
Truckee Chamber of Commerce *10065 Donner Pass Road, Truckee (1-530 587 2757/ www.truckee.com).* **Open** 8.30am-5.30pm daily.

Getting there

By car
A car is your best means of transport for exploring Lake Tahoe, especially if you're skiing. It takes 3.5hrs from San Francisco, traffic and weather permitting. To reach the north shore, follow I-80 east over the Bay Bridge all the way to Truckee; then take Highway 89 to Tahoe City. To reach the south shore, take I-80 as far as Sacramento and then turn off on to US 50 east to South Tahoe.

By air
Reno-Tahoe International Airport, 58 miles (93km) north-east of the lake, is served by several airlines. United (1-800 241 6522, www.united.com) has 6 flights a day; booking 14 days in advance, a return fare from San Fran is around $150. The Tahoe Casino Express (1-800 446 6128, www.tahoecasinoexpress.com) offers a regular daily shuttle bus and limo service to South Lake Tahoe from the airport for around $36 return.

By bus
Greyhound buses (1-800-229-9424, www.greyhound. com) stop in Truckee and Reno and take about 6hrs. Buses to Truckee run 3-4 times a day and cost about $85 return; Reno buses cost about $63 and run all day.

By train
Amtrak (1-800 872 7245, www.amtrak.com) leaves once a day from Emeryville (take the free bus from several locations in San Francisco) at 8.40am. It arrives in Truckee at just after 3pm and Reno at 4pm (it costs around $50 one way).

Yosemite

The most enchanting, intoxicating, stunning, breathtaking... many adjectives can be applied to **Yosemite National Park**, all of them superlatives. The park covers some 1,200 square miles (3,108 square kilometres) of forest, alpine meadows, sheer granite cliffs, lush waterfalls and undisturbed wildlife. Park elevations range from 2,000 feet (609 metres) to over 13,000 feet (3,960 metres). Highway 120 runs east–west the entire length of the park, climbing to 9,945 feet (3,031 metres) at **Tioga Pass**, the highest automobile pass in California.

Admission to the park costs $20 per car. Most people head for seven-mile-long (11-kilometre) **Yosemite Valley**, where most of the park services and places to stay are located. It's touristy, but the views are spectacular. For **non-valley sites**, head for Crane Flat and Tuolumne Meadows (via Highway 120), Glacier Point (near Badger Pass) and the Hetch Hetchy Reservoir (north of Big Oak Flat). If you can, avoid visiting Yosemite in high summer: the bad traffic becomes almost unbearable, so make use of the free shuttle buses. Visit instead in the spring, when the wildflowers are in bloom, or in winter, when the untamed, snowcapped peaks (many of them famously snapped by photographer Ansel Adams) are awesome in their majesty. Much of the park is inaccessible during the winter months, so plan carefully.

Yosemite is all about views: as you drive into the valley, **El Capitan** is the first dramatic sight, a sheer rock wall 3,000 feet (914 metres) high. Look out for tiny, ant-like figures slowly crawling up its grey granite face – it's one of the most popular climbing spots in the US. You'll get a bird's-eye view from Glacier Point and a spectacular view of the Sierras from Tunnel View. There are hiking trails throughout the park. **Mist Trail** is the most popular: it's three miles (five kilometres) to Vernal Falls and back, or a seven-mile (11-kilometre) round trip to Nevada Falls. Standing beneath the pounding water of Yosemite Falls is heart-stopping, with an ambitious hike to the top of **Yosemite Point** (a round trip of just under seven miles/11 kilometres). The hike to **Glacier Point** is just as challenging, but you can cheat by driving there instead. Then there's the hike to **Half Dome** (16-mile/26-kilometre round trip), which is strictly for the hardcore, as you have to cling to cables anchored into a sheer rockface for the last half mile (nearly a kilometre). Allow 10 to 12 hours. Minimum.

Backpacking is the best way to avoid the crowds and get the most out of the park. However, the park has a visitors quota, so make sure you plan ahead. The **Yosemite Mountaineering School** (1-209 372 8344, www.yosemitemountaineering.com) offers excellent classes for first-time climbers (from $120 per person per day), as well as five-day climbs. Alternatively, you can hire rafts to float down the valley's winding **Merced River** or bikes to explore the area on two wheels. The

bulk of the park's accommodation and eating places, plus camping supplies, grocery stores and gift shops, are in the valley.

Some safety advice. First, stay out of the water: a lot of fatalities each year are caused by people taking nose dives over the falls. Second, take a decent map, compass and some sensible shoes. Third, heed the warnings about bears and lock food and cosmetics in bear-safe boxes.

Where to stay

Accommodation in the valley ranges from camp sites to the spectacular 1927 Ahwahnee Hotel. Camp sites can be booked months in advance; early booking is advised. To find out more or reserve a place, call **Yosemite Reservations** on 1-559 252 4848, or check www.yosemitepark. com. Another option, 25 miles (40 kilometres) from the valley, is the popular **Yosemite Bug Lodge & Hostel** (6979 Route 140, Midpines, 1-209 966 6666, www.yosemitebug.com, rates $14-$16 dormitory, $40-$125 private room, $17-$50 tent cabin or campsite).

Resources

Tourist information

General info is available from the National Park Service on 1-209 372 0200 and at www.nps.gov/ yose. The Yosemite Association (1-209 379 2646, www. yosemite.org) is a non-profit organisation that sells Yosemite-related books and interpretative materials. Other useful websites include www.yosemite.com.

Getting there

By car

There are three routes to Yosemite: Highway 41 from the south, Highway 140 from the west (the best entrance), and Highway 120 from the north-west. Highway 120 (the Tioga Road) is the only road across the park, and it closes in winter (usually Nov to May) due to snow. Allow 4hrs from San Francisco.

By bus

There is no direct public bus to Yosemite from San Francisco. However, several companies run private trips, including Gray Line Tours (558 9400, one-day tour from $110). Greyhound runs buses to Merced ($56 round trip, 4hrs). From Merced, Via Adventures (1-888 727 5287) runs buses to and from Yosemite daily ($10 one way, 2.5hrs). Green Tortoise (1-800 867 8647, www.greentortoise.com) runs 2- and 3-day camping tours to Yosemite. Prices start at $180, including most of your meals (which you'll help prepare) and a bed (sweet luxury!) on the bus.

By train

Each morning, Amtrak trains 712 and 714 from Oakland to Merced ($25-$35 one way, 3hrs) connect with a Via Adventures bus to Yosemite.

Heading South

Wind your way down dramatic coastal drives to peaceful beaches and the slick Silicon Valley.

In the eyes of most of the world, the San Francisco peninsula is merely an afterthought to the city itself, yet certain parts have acquired a reputation of their own: **Monterey** with its sea otters, **Santa Cruz** with its sun-splashed boardwalk, **Carmel** with its golf courses and famous former mayor. For a while it was even conceivable that **Silicon Valley** could become the local giant, with San Jose and neighbouring communities Los Altos and Palo Alto, buoyed by the dot-com frenzy, growing at a frenetic pace. But even Sandhill Road, once the Silicon Valley home of notoriously high-spending venture capitalists, has pretty much emptied out. While high-tech giants like Intel and Oracle remain robustly profitable, the South Bay is settling back into something closer to the suburban anonymity it once knew.

On the Pacific side, the pace of life remains steady and almost completely separate from the chaos on the Bay: farmers tend the artichoke and strawberry fields, surfers brave the chilly coastal waters and **Half Moon Bay** slumbers under a blanket of fog. San Francisco is a world away – but tourists don't seem to realise it.

Don't make the same mistake. Whether you're driving the picturesque I-280, gridlocked Highway 101 or the stunningly beautiful coastal curves of **Highway 1**, give yourself plenty of time to see the sights and explore the peninsula's towns. They deserve more than an afterthought.

Half Moon Bay & Silicon Valley

Half Moon Bay is a small, easygoing seaside town with a rural feel, just off Highway 1. It's perhaps most famous for growing Halloween pumpkins and Christmas trees. Quaint Main Street is filled with bookshops, health food stores, florists and antiques shops. Worth a visit too is the **San Gregorio General Store** (1-650 726 0565, www.sangregoriostore.com), eight miles (13 kilometres) south of Half Moon Bay on Highway 84. Serving the local farming community since 1889, it's a hybrid bar, music hall and general community gathering place.

Continuing south, a string of fine beaches stretches down the coast from Half Moon Bay. Probably the best is **San Gregorio State**

Beach, a strip of white sand distinguished by sedimentary cliffs and its proximity to a nudist beach further north. The **Sea Horse & Friendly Acres Ranch** (at Half Moon Bay and Highway 1, 1-650 726 9903), offering beach rides for all levels of experience. Another 15 miles (25 kilometres) down the coast are the historic buildings and rolling farmland of quaint **Pescadero**. Locals tend the artichoke fields and strawberry patches.

Silicon Valley, south of San Francisco and inland, is often dismissed as suburban sprawl, but there are surprisingly pretty, upscale villages. The downtown areas of Los Altos, Los Gatos and Saratoga are all worth a stroll, while **Palo Alto**, the site of Stanford University, should be visited for the on-campus **Rodin Sculpture Garden** (1-650 723 4177). But the concrete jungle of **San Jose** has the biggest draw. As well as the interactive **Children's Discovery Museum** (180 Woz Way and Auzerais Street, 1-408 298 5437, www.cdm.org, closed Mon & Sat, admission $7) and nearby **Monopoly in the Park** (Guadalupe River Park, West Fernando Street, 1-408 995 6487, www.sjbeautiful.org) – one of San Jose's newest attractions and the closest normal people will get to buying Silicon Valley property – don't miss the full-scale replica tombs of the **Rosicrucian Egyptian Museum** (1342 Naglee Avenue, 1-408 947 3636, www.egyptianmuseum.org, admission $9). There are six real mummies and a collection of more than 4,000 genuine ancient artefacts.

Where to eat

In Half Moon Bay, cosy **Pasta Moon** (315 Main Street, 1-650 726 5125, www.pastamoon.com, main courses $14-$18) serves elegant dishes of own-made pasta with produce fresh each day from nearby farms. Alternatively, there's pasta and local fish at **San Benito House** (356 Main Street, 1-650 726 3425, closed lunch, all Mon-Wed, main courses $15-$19), a gleaming old-fashioned saloon with brass chandeliers.

In Pescadero, enjoy a beer at **Duarte's Tavern** (202 Stage Road, 1-650 879 0464, www.duartestavern.com, main courses $14-$26), the town's most celebrated saloon since 1894. The crab sandwiches are legendary and the cream of artichoke soup is excellent.

Beaches Shore thing

Given the expense accounts, it's no surprise to find quality restaurants across Silicon Valley. Menlo Park has the **Wild Hare** (1029 El Camino Real, 1-650 327 4273, closed lunch, main courses $7.95-$31.95), known for – of course – game, while Palo Alto offers new American cuisine at **Zibibbo** (430 Kipling Street, 1-650 328 6722, www.restaurantzibibbo.com, main courses $13.25-$47.95) and an outpost of **Spago** (265 Lytton Avenue, 1-650 833 1000, main courses $21-$36). In San Jose, **AP Stumps** (163 W Santa Clara Street, 1-408 292 9928, www.ap stumps.com, closed lunch Sun, main courses $10-$30) is a venerable gem, and for high-priced but elegant French fare try **La Foret** (21747 Bertram Road, San Jose, 1-408 997 3458, closed lunch, all Mon, main courses $17.75-$26.75).

Where to stay

There's no shortage of places to stay in and around Half Moon Bay. The grandest is probably the 261-room **Ritz-Carlton** (1 Miramontes Point Road, 1-800 241-3333, 1-650 712 7000, www.ritzcarlton.com, rates $295-

$875), situated on scenic bluffs overlooking the rugged coastline. Opened in May 2001, it resembles a 19th-century seaside lodge and has two golf courses and a spa. More affordable are the 12 rooms at **San Benito House** (*see above*; rates $80-$176): nine are en suite, but some rooms are rather small. For more options, check the Chamber of Commerce's website (*see p269*).

About 25 miles (40 kilometres) south from Half Moon Bay, **Costanoa Coastal Lodge & Camp** (2001 Rossi Road at Highway 1, 1-650 879 1100, www.costanoa.com) is not your typical campground – it's more of a rustic resort. Accommodation comes in a 40-room lodge ($155-$235), individual wooden cabins ($115-$175) and canvas cabins ($65-$130), but you can also pitch a tent for a nominal fee. Activities include bicycle rentals, horse-riding and yoga, and the café even sells pre-marinated grub for the barbecue.

Getting there

By car

Half Moon Bay is 30 miles (48km) south of San Francisco on Highway 1 – about a 45min drive.

Snaking down the awesome coastline south of San Francisco, Highway 1 is the road to beach paradise. Escape the crowds by avoiding weekend afternoons, and in summer set out early to nab your spot on one of the many stretches of pristine sand.

San Pedro Point, 15 miles (24km) outside San Francisco, is a favourite with surf dudes; those who prefer their surf with turf can head to the nearby town of Pacifica for lunch, enjoying the views across **Rockaway Beach**. Reaching as far as Santa Cruz, the San Mateo County beaches are gems too, particularly **Gray Whale Cove** (clothing optional) and the great tidal pools of **James V Fitzgerald Marine Reserve**.

Mavericks Beach purportedly has the largest waves in North America. Plenty of mad-dog surfers believe it, and they're a compelling spectacle – especially during the annual Mavericks Surf Contest. This secret event depends on the weather conditions being exactly right; dates are given to surfers just two days in advance.

San Gregorio and **Año Nuevo** make it well worth extending your trip south. In season – December to March – elephant seals come here to mate.

Pescadero is 18 miles (30km) further south, and signposted off Highway 1. San Jose is 50 miles (85km) south of San Francisco on US 101.

By train & bus

From San Francisco, either take a BART train to Daly City (15min journey), pick up SamTrans bus 110 to Linda Mar and transfer to bus 294 for Half Moon Bay, or take CalTrain to Hillsdale and transfer to bus 294 there. Daly City to Half Moon Bay takes about 30mins; one-way fare is $2.50. SamTrans bus 15 runs between Half Moon Bay and Pescadero.

CalTrain travels every half hour from either of the San Francisco stations to **San Jose**, making several stops along the way. The fare is usually $6 one way.

Resources

Tourist information

Half Moon Bay Coastside Chamber of Commerce *1st floor, 520 Kelly Avenue, Half Moon Bay (1-650 726 8380/www.hmbchamber.com).* **Open** 9am-5pm Mon-Fri.

San Jose Convention & Visitor Bureau *150 West San Carlos Street, in the McEnery Convention Center (1-888 726 5673/www.sanjose.org).* **Open** 8am-5pm Mon-Fri.

Santa Cruz

Originally established as a mission at the end of the 18th century, **Santa Cruz** is a quirky and quintessentially Californian beach town well known for being easygoing and politically progressive. Home to the University of California at Santa Cruz (which has a clothing-optional campus and, until a few years back, wouldn't give its students grades), the city has a substantial population of young and lively folk, in addition to a permanent population of long-time residents. All are fiercely protective of the city's liberal heritage.

The small **Surfing Museum** (Mark Abbott Memorial Lighthouse, West Cliff Drive, 1-831 420 6289, www.santacruzmuseums.org/surfin.html, closed Mon & Tue in summer, Mon-Wed in winter) contains vintage boards and various other pieces of Santa Cruz's surfer heritage. **Steamer Lane**, one of the best surfing spots in California, is right outside the lighthouse.

Bang on the beach, the **Santa Cruz Beach Boardwalk** amusement park (400 Beach Street, 1-831 423 5590, www.beach boardwalk.com) is as tacky as it is nostalgic, hailing back to the city's 19th-century heyday as a beach resort. Among the rides are the Giant Dipper, a classic wooden rollercoaster, which has been declared a National Historic Landmark (as has the nearby 1911 carousel). The Boardwalk's **Cocoanut Grove Ballroom** (1-831 423 2053) is another remnant, but live music at weekends and during holidays brings it back to life.

All that remains today of the Misión la Exaltación de la Santa Cruz – the 12th of the 21 Californian Franciscan missions – is the Neary-Rodriguez Adobe, commonly known as the **Mission Adobe** (1-831 425 5849, closed Mon-Wed in winter). Located on the grounds of **Santa Cruz Mission State Historic Park**, it was originally used to house the mission's American Indian population. Just down the street is a replica, **Mission Plaza** (1-831 426-5686, closed Mon), built in the 1930s. The **Santa Cruz Museum of Natural History** (1305 East Cliff Drive, Tyrone Park, 1-831 420 6115, www.santacruzmuseums.org, closed Mon) contains vast information on the Ohlone people who originally populated the area. A few miles north, in the woods off Highway 17, is the kitsch roadside nonsense of **Mystery Spot** (465 Mystery Spot Road, 1-831 423 8897, www.mysteryspot.com, admission $5). Discovered in 1939, this 150-foot (46-metre) patch of ground supposedly confounds the laws of physics and gravity. Judge for yourself.

Fans of towering redwoods should head north to **Big Basin Redwoods State Park** (1-831 338 8860, www.bigbasin.org) and **Henry Cowell Redwoods State Park** (1-831 335 4598). You can also see the ruins of a Chinese labour camp, as well as the epicentre of the Loma Prieta earthquake, just south of Santa Cruz in the **Forest of Nisene Marks** (1-831 763 7063).

There are also approximately 50 **wineries** in the area, most of them open to the public for tastings and tours but lacking the offputting crowds of Napa. Notable among them are **Bonny Doon** (2 Pine Flat Road, Santa Cruz, 1-831 425 3625, www.bonnydoonvineyard.com), **David Bruce Winery** (21439 Bear Creek Road, Los Gatos, 1-800 397 9972, 1-408 354 4214, www.davidbrucewinery.com), the award-winning **Storrs Winery** (303 Potrero Street, Santa Cruz, 1-831 458 5030, closed Tue & Wed) and **Bargetto Winery** (3535 North Main Street, 1-831 475 2258, www.bargetto.com), widely known for its fruit wines.

Where to eat

High above Santa Cruz Yacht Harbor, the **Crow's Nest** (2218 East Cliff Drive, 1-831 476 4560, main courses $13-$19) offers magnificent views of Monterey Bay and great seafood. In town, try **Gabriella Café** (910 Cedar Street, 1-831 457 1677), a sweet little courtyard Italian, or **Cole's Barbecue** (770 26th Avenue, 1-831 476 4424), a weather-beaten rib shack.

Where to stay

Most of the hotels in Santa Cruz itself are substandard motels and cheap chains, but there are a few charming spots. The aptly named **Babbling Brook Inn** (1025 Laurel Street, 1-800 866 1131/1-831 427 2437, www.babbling brookinn.com, rates $179-$235) is surrounded by an acre of gardens with redwoods and, yes, a little warbling waterway. Built in 1909 on the site of a 2,000-year-old Native American fishing village, its 13 rooms are named after artists and poets (Cézanne, Tennyson and the like). Set overlooking the sea, the **Pleasure Point Inn** (2-3665 East Cliff Drive, 1-877 557 2567, 1-831 469 6161, www.pleasurepointinn.com, rates $187-$265) is a departure from traditional B&Bs, it's modern, upscale and well appointed, with four bedrooms and a large rooftop deck that features an eight-person jacuzzi. The **Adobe on Green Street** (103 Green Street, 1-888 878 2789, 1-831 469 9866, www.adobeongreen.com,

rates $140-$195) is an adobe B&B, with four mission-style rooms, antique furniture and Native American-influenced art, while **Darling House** (314 West Cliff Drive, 1-831 458 1958, www.darlinghouse.com, rates $85-$260) is an early 20th-century historic building a block away from the ocean.

Getting there

By car
Santa Cruz is 74 miles (119km) south of San Francisco on Highway 1 – about a 2hr drive.

By bus
Leaving San Francisco for Santa Cruz about four times a day, the Greyhound takes just under 3hrs and costs $11.

By train & bus
Take the CalTrain for San Jose (*see p276*). From San Jose station, ten daily Amtrak shuttle buses (journey time 45mins, $6 one way) go to Santa Cruz.

Resources

Tourist information
Santa Cruz County Conference & Visitors Bureau *1211 Ocean Street, near Washburn Avenue, Santa Cruz (1-800 833 3494/1-831 425 1234/www.scccvc.org/index.html)*. **Open** 9am-5pm Mon-Fri; 10am-4pm Sun.

Monterey peninsula

Jutting into the Pacific south of fun-loving Santa Cruz and north of the dramatic Big Sur coastline, Monterey peninsula has proved irresistible to writers and artists for decades, not least because of the stunning scenery all along the shore. Musicians and their fans are drawn here from all corners by the **Monterey Jazz Festival** (1-831 373 3366, www.monterey jazzfestival.org) in September and **Monterey Bay Blues Festival** (1-831 394 2652, www.montereyblues.com) at the end of June. There's also the shopping, family entertainment and spectacular golf courses.

The three major towns on the peninsula are Carmel, where Clint Eastwood famously served his stint as mayor, Monterey and Pacific Grove. **Carmel** is a love-it-or-hate-it place. Once a secluded seaside village favoured by the likes of Robert Louis Stevenson and Ansel Adams, it is now an over-trafficked town, full of hoity-toity shops (especially along Ocean Avenue) and faux-historic buildings. Much of it looks like a film set. The beach is a quasi-tropical crescent of white sand, but the water's as cold and prone to riptides as anywhere else along the coast. There are

For decades artists have been attracted to the magical light around **Monterey**.

a few must-see destinations though.
Carmel Mission (3080 Rio Road, 1-831
624 1271), the second of the Californian
missions, boasts three museums and
beautiful gardens. Its founder, Father Junípero
Serra, is buried inside the baroque church.
Mission Trail Park across the street is
popular with hikers and bikers, while just
below the Carmel Highlands, off Highway 1,
is one of the most beloved parks in California.
It's easy to spend the entire day exploring the
crannies, beaches and awesome promontories of
Point Lobos State Reserve (1-831 624 4909,
http://pt-lobos.parks.state.ca.us).

Capital of Alta California under successive
Spanish, Mexican and American governments,
Monterey itself is a big tourist centre, though
not entirely to its credit, especially downtown.
Popular sights include **Colton Hall Museum**
(Monterey City Hall, Pacific Street, 1-831 646
5640, www.monterey.org/museum), where
California's first constitution was written
in 1849, and the **Monterey State Historic
Park** (1-831 649 7118), and make certain

to brave the crowds for the world-class
Monterey Bay Aquarium (886 Cannery
Row, 1-831 648 4888, www.mbayaq.org).
Its spectacular, labyrinthine displays of
undersea forests, marine life, tide pools
and jellyfish are a real treat. If you can,
catch one of the sea otter feedings it will
make your day. The aquarium is open
9.30am-6pm daily (from 10am in winter);
admission is $17.95 for adults, $15.95 students
and seniors, and $8.95 for three- to 12-year-
olds. The aquarium is on **Cannery Row**,
made famous by native son John Steinbeck.
The canning factories were abandoned
in the 1940s when the commercial sardine
population was fished out, and now tacky
shops and mediocre restaurants occupy
the old warehouses.

Escape the tourist traffic to **Jacks Peak
Regional Park** (1-831 866 4899), located
just ten miles (16 kilometres) to the south of
town or make the most of the region's growing
reputation for wine, especially its Chardonnay.
Bargetto Winery (*see p270*) has a **Winery**

Trips Out of Town

Tasting Room (700 Cannery Row, 1-831 373 4053) and oenophiles can check out A Taste of Monterey (1-831 646 5446) in the same building.

Just a couple of miles west of Monterey is the smaller and much prettier town of Pacific Grove, founded in 1875 as a camping retreat for the Methodist Church. If you're in the area in winter, watch out for the annual migration of thousands of Monarch butterflies; the Pacific Grove Museum of Natural History (at Forest and Central Avenues, 1-831 648 5716, www.pgmuseum.org, closed Mon) has extensive information on the lovely creatures. You'll find the coast's oldest continuously operating lighthouse nearby too: tiny Point Pinos Light Station (Lighthouse Avenue, between Sunset Drive and Asilomar Avenue, 1-831 648 5716, closed mornings, all Tue and Wed).

Seventeen-Mile Drive, from Pacific Grove through Pebble Beach, takes you by some of the most famous and challenging golf courses in the country – although strategically placed toll booths force you to pay for the privilege of passing through. Save your pennies and walk the coastal path from Pacific Grove instead: the views are just as good and it's free.

Where to eat

There are plenty of places to eat, but many are tourist traps: bland food, high prices. The exceptions are expensive, but memorable. In Pacific Grove, the Old Bath House Restaurant (620 Ocean View Boulevard, 1-831 375 5195, www.oldbathhouse.com, closed lunch, main courses $23-$45) serves decent French/continental tucker, especially game and fresh seafood, and every table has a view of the ocean. Book ahead. Of all the restaurants on Monterey's Cannery Row, the Sardine Factory (701 Wave Street, 1-831 373 3775, www.sardinefactory.com, closed lunch, main courses $20-$59) is the best. The decor is a little ornate and staff can be over-attentive, but the seafood platter is especially good.

Where to stay

Most accommodation on the Monterey peninsula falls somewhere between pricey and extravagant. Some places are worth it, others overrated and overrun by tourists. If you're looking to splash out, Bernardus Lodge in Carmel Valley (415 Carmel Valley Road, 1-888 648 9463, 1-831 658 3400, www.bernardus.com) is an intimate retreat

with 57 luxurious rooms and suites ($375-$1,750), a full-service spa, swimming pool and a winery. Each room has a stone fireplace, a built-in wine grotto and a two-person tub. In the centre of Carmel, the 34-room Wayside Inn (Mission and Seventh Streets, 1-800 443 7443, 1-831 624 3871, www.ibts-wayside inn.com, rates $125-$395) is a small, old-fashioned hotel whose formal façade belies the atmosphere within: exposed rafters, overstuffed couches and a small library bar. For more Carmel options, contact the Carmel Area Reservation Services (see below). To get away from it all in Pacific Grove, try Andril Fireplace Cottages (569 Asilomar Boulevard, 1-831-375 0994, www.andrilcottages.com, rates $115-$485). As cosy and rustic as the name suggests, these bungalows have wood-burning fireplaces, as well as full-size modern kitchens, TVs and VCRs, and are walking distance from the ocean. Simple king bed units cost $74-$90.

Resources

Tourist information

Carmel California Visitor & Information Center *San Carlos Street, between Fifth & Sixth Streets (1-800 550 4333/1-831 624 2522/ www.carmelcalifornia.org).* Open 9am-5pm Mon-Fri. In summer and on Saturdays, you can also get maps and information from a small kiosk at Carmel Plaza.
Carmel Area Reservation Services *(1-888 434 3891/1-831 659 7061/www.carmel-california.com).* Open 8am-6pm Mon-Fri.
Monterey Visitors Center *(150 Olivier Street, 1-888 221 1010/1-831 649 1770/www.monterey info.org).* Open 9am-5pm daily.
Pacific Grove Information Center *Central & Forest Avenues (1-800 656 6650/1-831 373 3304/ www.pacificgrove.org).* Open 9.30am-5pm Mon-Fri; 10am-3pm Sat.

Getting there

By car

Carmel is 115 miles (200km) from San Francisco if you take US 101 to CA-17 to Highway 1, and a bit further if you take Highway 1 all the way. Plan on a 2-3hr drive. It's 5 miles (8km) to Monterey from Carmel, and 6 miles (10km) to Pacific Grove.

By bus

Greyhound buses run four times daily from San Francisco to Monterey. The 4-5hr trip costs $17.50. There is no direct bus service from San Francisco to Carmel or Pacific Grove, but Monterey-Salinas Transit (www.mst.org) goes from Monterey to the other two. For Carmel, take bus 4 or 5; for Pacific Grove, bus 1 or 2. Both journeys take about 40mins and cost $1.75.

Directory

Getting Around   **274**
Resources A-Z   **280**
Further Reference   **292**
Index   **294**
Advertisers' Index   **300**

Features

Passports & visas   275
Travel advice   281
Wi-Fi… why not?   285
Average monthly climate   290
Sun, wind & fog   291

Directory

Getting Around

San Francisco Airport (SFO)

SFO (1-650 821 8211, www.fly sfo.com) lies 14 miles (22.5km) south of the city, near US 101. The brand-new International terminal – the largest in the US – opened in December 2000. Gleaming, airy, spacious and well-served with shops and eating places, it's a pleasure to spend a few hours here. Artworks and exhibition cases dot the terminal, and there's a charming Aviation Museum. A new BART train station opened in SFO's international terminal in 2003, so it's now possible to get into downtown San Francisco in 30 minutes. Given that it allows you to avoid any traffic snafus, it's really the best option, and costs only $4.95. If there are problems with BART or you arrive at an odd hour, there are the following options:

By bus

SamTrans KX and 292 run every 30mins between the airport's lower level and the Transbay Terminal at First and Mission Streets. Bus 292 runs from 5.46am to 1.37am, costs $1.25, has no luggage restrictions and takes 32mins. Bus KX runs from 5.53am to 11.12pm, costs $3.50 and takes 30mins, but you can take only one small carry-on bag.

By passenger van or shuttle

Passenger vans (shuttles) are a definite step up from bussing it. It's a door-to-door service, costing $10-$20 per person (tickets can be bought from the driver). Ask about coupons or discounted rates for two or more travellers. Most passenger vans leave every 10-15mins from the upper level

of the terminal at specially marked kerbs – follow the red 'passenger vans' signs outside the baggage claim area. Vans run throughout the night, but are few and far between in the small hours; if you arrive late you may be faced with a long wait or an expensive taxi ride. For your return journey to the airport, book the shuttle at least 24hr in advance.

Companies include **Lorrie's Airport Service** (334 9000), **SuperShuttle** (558 8500), **Bay Shuttle** (564 3400), **American Airporter Shuttle** (202 0733, 1-800 282 7758) and **Quake City Airport Shuttle** (255 4899).

By taxi or limousine

The most expensive way of getting into town may be your only option in the wee hours. Expect to pay about $37 plus tip, and be sure to haggle for a flat rate. Taxis are found outside the baggage claim area in a zone marked with yellow columns.

For limousine service, use the toll-free white courtesy phones located in the terminal or phone **Associated Limousine** (1-800 258 2660).

Mineta San Jose International Airport (SJC)

Though it's 50 miles (80km) south of SF, San Jose Airport (1-408 277 4759, www.sjc.org) is the destination of choice for many Silicon Valley travellers. It's tiny and efficient, but more than an hour's journey from SF. CalTrain is the best way to get to the city from the SJC, though weekend service is suspended until at least spring 2004. Check www.caltrain.com or 1-510 817 1717 for details.

To get to the city from SJC, take Santa Clara Transit bus 10 to Santa Clara CalTrain station (every 20-30mins from 5.27am to 11.58pm; $1.50), then board the CalTrain for San Francisco (from 4.41am to 10.30pm, taking about 90mins

and costing $5.50). Purchase and validate tickets in the station before departure; those without valid tickets can be fined up to $250. Get off at the Fourth & Townsend terminus (not recommended if you're travelling alone at night).

Don't even think of taking a taxi or limo to San Francisco from San Jose. Unless you're a wealthy multimedia tycoon.

Oakland International Airport (OAK)

Many travellers opt to fly into tiny Oakland Airport (1-510 563 3300, www.oaklandairport. com). To get to San Francisco using public transport, catch the Air-BART shuttle from the airport terminal to the Coliseum/Oakland BART station ($2 – you'll need exact change for the perpetually malfunctioning machines; try the change machine inside the terminal before going to the shuttle stop). They run every 15mins (6.05am-11.50pm Mon-Sat, 8am-11.45pm Sun) from the central island outside terminals 1 and 2, and the journey takes about 15mins. Then catch the next Daly City or Millbrae BART to San Francisco ($3.15; about 25mins to downtown); schedule info is on 989 2278. Please note that this is not a safe option for passengers alone at night.

Other options are the **Super Shuttle** (1-800 258 3826) or a very expensive taxi/limo ride.

Major airlines

This is not an exhaustive list; for additional airlines, it's best to consult the Yellow Pages.

American Airlines
1-800 433 7300/www.aa.com
British Airways
1-800 247 9297/www.british-airways.com
Continental Airlines
1-800 523 3273/www.continental.com
Delta Airlines
1-800 221 1212/www.delta.com
Jet Blue
1-800 538 2583/www.jetblue.com
Northwest Airlines
domestic 1-800 225 2525/
international 1-800 447 4747/
www.nwa.com
Southwest Airlines
1-800 435 9792/www.iflyswa.com
United Airlines
1-800 241 6522/www.ual.com
USAir
1-800 428 4322/www.usairways.com
Virgin Atlantic
1-800 862 8621/www.virgin.com

Public transport

Unlike many US cities, San Francisco has a comprehensive and efficient public transport network. Buses, streetcars and cable cars are all run by the San Francisco Municipal Railway or Muni (673 6864, hearing-impaired 923 6373, www.sfmuni.com). The best way to find your way around the network is to buy a Muni Street & Transit map (you can get one online, at bookshops/drugstores or from the Visitor Information Center, *see p290*).

If you plan to use Muni often, purchase a one-day ($9), three-day ($15) or seven-day ($20) **Passport**, which is valid on all Muni vehicles. Passes are available at the Visitor Information Center, the Muni ticket booth/police kiosk at Powell and Market, the Muni ticket booth at Hyde and Beach, the Bay Area TIX booth in Union Square and Muni headquarters (949 Presidio Avenue, at Geary Boulevard, Western Addition). The **CityPass** gives you free travel on Muni as well as free admission to several museums. If you're staying for a while, the **FastPass** ($45) is valid from the first to the last day of the current month.

Buses

Muni's orange and white buses are the number one mode of public transport. Relatively cheap, they can get you to within a block or two of almost anywhere you want to go. Muni customer satisfaction rates have gone up in recent years, which may mean that the fume-spewing, off-schedule buses of former years have been consigned to the past.

Fares are $1.25 for adults (aged 18-64 years), 35¢ for seniors, disabled and kids; under-fives travel free. Exact change is required. Place your change or bills in the automatic toll-taker and take your proof-of-payment ticket; it doubles as a free transfer, valid for two changes within 90mins.

Bus stops are marked by a large white rectangle painted on a street with a red kerb; a yellow marking on a telephone or lamp post; a glass-walled bus shelter; and/or a brown and orange sign listing buses that serve that route.

Route numbers are posted on the front and (so you know which one you've just missed) rear of the bus. Buses operate 5am-1am Mon-Fri, 6am-1am Sat and 8am-1am Sun. On busy lines they run every 5-10mins during peak hours. Between midnight and 5am a skeleton crew operates the Owl Service – nine lines on which buses run every 30mins.

Outside San Francisco

AC Transit
817 1717/www.actransit.org
Service transbay and to Alameda and Contra Costa Counties. Buses A to Z go across the Bay Bridge to Berkeley and Oakland.

Passports & visas

All travellers entering the United States under the Visa Waiver Program must present a machine-readable passport (MRP), which has been the standard issue (burgundy) passport in the UK since 1988. However, at some point in the future, all visitors to the US will be required to present a passport with a biometric identifier (a microchip encoded with information such as fingerprints). The deadline for this requirement was, at the time of writing, under review. At a congressional hearing on 21 April 2004, the State Department lobbied for a two-year postponement of the original deadline, which stated that any passport issued after 26 October 2004 would require a biometric identifier. Call your nearest US Embassy and check http://unitedstatesvisas.gov or www.travel.state.gov/vwp.html for a final decision.

Meanwhile, all Visa Waiver Program travellers should expect to have their fingerprints scanned and have a digital photo taken when they arrive. This extra measure is supposed to add just 15 seconds to the arrival process, but queue times have increased. Also, children can no longer travel on their parents' passports.

Those travellers applying for a visa after 26 October 2004 will need to submit biometric data for an identifier, which will be added to their visa. Plenty of time should be allowed for visa applications (a process that can easily take anything from two to three months).

Golden Gate Transit
923 2000/www.goldengate.org.
Marin and Sonoma Counties from
Sausalito to Santa Rosa.
Greyhound Bus Line
1-800 231 2222/www.greyhound.com.
Long-distance buses across the US.
SamTrans
1-800 660 4287/www.samtrans.com.
San Mateo County with a service to
downtown San Francisco.

Muni Metro streetcars

The Muni Metro streetcar –
or tram – is used surprisingly
rarely by tourists. Five lines
(J, K, L, M and N) run under
Market Street in the downtown
area and above ground in the
outer neighbourhoods; the
recently revived F line runs
restored vintage streetcars
along Market Street and north
along the Embarcadero as
far as Fisherman's Wharf.
Along Market, Muni makes
the same stops as BART, but
past the Civic Center routes
branch towards the Mission,
Castro and Sunset. The 3rd
Street Light Rail extension
should take Muni down to the
Bayshore CalTrain station in
Visitacion Valley by 2005.
Fares and passes are the same
as for Muni buses, and lines
run 5am-midnight every day.

Cable cars

San Francisco's cable cars
are the most enjoyable ride
in town. There are 44 cars,
27 of them in use at peak
times, which travel at 9.5mph
(15kmh) on three lines:
California (along California
Street from the Financial
District to Van Ness Avenue),
Powell-Mason and Powell-
Hyde (both from Market Street
in downtown to Fisherman's
Wharf). Powell-Hyde has the
most thrills and most tourists.
    Lines operate from 6.30am
to midnight daily. If you don't
have a Muni pass or CityPass,
buy a $3 one-way ticket from
the conductor (under-fives go
free). No transfers are accepted

on cable cars. The stops are
marked by pole-mounted
brown signs with a cable car
symbol, and routes are marked
on Muni bus maps. Hold on
tight: you'll get thrown about
as the car lurches down the
precipitous hills. *See also p58*
You're on cable.

BART

Looking more like a ride
at Disneyland than a form
of public transport, BART
(Bay Area Rapid Transit –
989 2278, www.bart.gov) is
a $5-billion network of five
high-speed rail lines serving
San Francisco, Daly City,
Colma and East Bay. It's
modern and efficient, run by
computers at the Lake Merritt
station in Oakland with almost
everything – announcements,
trains, ticket dispensers, exit
and entry gates – automated.
    Passengers feed money
into a machine that dispenses
a reusable ticket encoded with
the amount entered. When you
reach your destination, the cost
of the ride is deducted from the
ticket as you pass through the
exit gate. Make sure you save
your ticket: any remaining
value can be used next trip.
    BART is of minor use for
getting around the city – it
only has six stops within San
Francisco, four along Market
Street and two on Mission –
but it's excellent for an
inexpensive tour of the Bay
Area because much of the rail
is elevated above the streets.
It's also the best way to get to
Berkeley and Oakland. Special
excursion-ride tickets allow
passengers to ride all lines for
up to three hours, as long as
they enter and exit from the
same station. Peak hours
travel (7-9am, 4-6pm Mon-Fri)
isn't recommended.
    BART stations close at
around midnight and open
at 4am on weekdays, 6am on
Saturday and 8am on Sunday.
Fares range from $1.25 to $7.45.

BART ticket dispensers take
cash, coins and now credit
cards (useful, as the machines
are notoriously picky about
which bills they'll accept –
sometimes rolling your dollar
up into a ball, smoothing it
out, then re-inserting it works).
A translink or 'smart card' is
to be introduced in 2005 that
will allows passengers to use a
single ticket for all major Bay
Area major transit systems.
    BART stations are clearly
marked with blue and white
'ba' signs at the escalators.

CalTrain

The CalTrain commuter line
(1-800 660 4287, www.caltrain.
com) connects San Francisco
with San Jose and ultimately
Gilroy, passing through
Burlingame, Redwood City,
Palo Alto, Mountain View,
Sunnyvale and several other
peninsula cities. Famously
punctual, it runs from 5am to
midnight. However, weekend
service is suspended until at
least spring 2004.
    One-way adult fares range
from $1.75 to $6.75 ($5.50 from
SF to San Jose, for instance);
senior, disabled and child
discounts are available, as is a
ten-ride ticket on some trains.
    You must purchase and
validate your Caltrain ticket
in the station; passengers
without valid tickets can
be fined up to $250.

Ferries

The completion of the Golden
Gate Bridge in 1937 marked
the end of ferries between San
Francisco and Marin – until
1970, when services resumed
to take a load off commuter
traffic. Used mainly by suits
during peak hours, the ferries
double as an inexpensive
excursion across the Bay
to Sausalito, Tiburon or
Larkspur. There are also
ferries to Alcatraz and Angel
Island in San Francisco Bay.

Blue & Gold Fleet

recorded information
773 1188/tickets 705 5555/
www.blueandgoldfleet.com.
Runs to Sausalito, Alcatraz and
Angel Island from Pier 41 at
Fisherman's Wharf. Its commuter
services to Alameda, Oakland (both
$5.25 one way), Tiburon ($7.25) and
Vallejo ($7.50) leave from the Ferry
Building on the Embarcadero.

Golden Gate Transit Ferry Service

923 2000/www.goldengate.org.
From the Ferry Building to Sausalito
and Larkspur (each $5.60 one way).

Taxis

As it's so small, getting around
San Francisco in a taxi is fairly
cheap. Fares average $10-$15,
with a base fee of $2.85 and
$2.25 for each additional mile.
But the trick is finding a cab.
On a weekday afternoon
downtown you'll easily flag
one from a street corner. But
in outlying areas, at mealtimes,
during holidays, in the rain,
if the commute is heavy that
day… forget about it. There
simply aren't enough taxis
because of a quirky local
law that limits the number
of cab licences, or medallions.
In a city with 25 per cent fewer
parking spaces than cars in
business districts, cabs would
seem to be a great solution, but
repeated efforts to deregulate
the medallion monopoly have
been thwarted by the cabbies.

If you're downtown, head
for the big hotels, where most
have a queue of cabs nearby.
If you're shopping or out to
dinner, ask the business to
call one for you. If you're in an
outlying area, phone early to
request one and ask how long
you'll have to wait.

Taxi companies

City Wide Dispatch 920 0700
Luxor 282 4141/www.luxorcab.com
National 648 4444
Veteran's 552 1300
Yellow 626 2345/
www.yellowcabsf.com

Limousine companies

MDM Limousine 775 6024
Pure Luxury 485 1764

Driving

It's not sensible to rent a car to
explore San Francisco. There's
no street parking and private
parking garages charge up to
$15/hr. The steep hills fry your
nerves and then your clutch,
and you're more than likely to
get a parking ticket – the city's
favourite source of revenue.
The only reason for renting a
car is to have wheels to explore
the Bay Area and beyond.

If you must drive in the
city, you should know the
following. Unless otherwise
posted, the speed limit within
the city is 25mph and everyone
must wear seatbelts. Cable
cars always have the right of
way and should be given a
wide berth. When parking in
residential neighbourhoods,
don't block driveways even
slightly, as you'll get fined and
towed away. When parking on
hills, set the hand brake and
'kerb' the front wheels (turn
them towards the kerb if
facing downhill, away from the
kerb facing uphill) or you'll get
a ticket. You must always park
in the direction of the traffic.

Parking spaces in San
Francisco are as rare as they
are tightly regulated: always
read the information on the
meter and/or all the signs on
your side of the block. One
missed warning could lead
to a towed car, in which case
you'll have to take a taxi to
the municipal garage, pay
$171 plus your parking ticket
and more in storage fees.

Don't park at white kerbs,
as these are passenger drop-
off zones; blue are reserved
for drivers or passengers
with disabilities; yellow are
for loading and unloading
commercial vehicles; and red
lie in front of bus stops or fire
hydrants. Green kerbs signify
parking for ten minutes only,
while some yellow and white
kerbs are only patrolled during
business hours. Infringement
could net you a $350 ticket.

Most parking meters accept
quarters only, and car parks
(public garages) are generally
your best bet in the downtown
area for long-term parking. If
you should venture across the
Golden Gate or Bay Bridges,
make sure you have enough
cash to pay the toll ($5 for the
Golden Gate Bridge and $2 for
the Bay Bridge), which is
levied on the return trip.

CalTrans Highway Information Service

511/www.dot.ca.gov/hq/roadinfo.
Open 24hrs daily.
This automated service gives
information on the latest highway
conditions but can only be accessed
by touchtone phone. Or there's the
recorded message on 1-916 445 1534.

Breakdown services

AAA Emergency Road Service

1-800 222 4357/www.aaa.com.
Open 24hrs daily.
AAA members (including members
of affiliated clubs, such as the British
AA) receive free towing and roadside
service. *See also p279.*

Golden Gate Towing Company

826 8866.
If you don't have a motorclub card,
phone this outfit for roadside service.
It will also recommend repair shops.

Fuel stations

Chevron

*2399 Market Street, between Castro
& Noe Streets, Castro (621 2570).*
Open 24 hrs daily. **Map** p313/4 E6.

Downtown Union

*390 First Street, between Folsom &
Harrison Streets, SoMa (957 1754).*
Open 24hrs daily. **Map** p311 J4.

76 19th

*1401 19th Avenue, at Judah Street,
Sunset District (681 3860).* **Open**
24hrs daily. **Map** p312 A6.

Parking

There are low-cost garages,
but prices shoot up for long-
term parking. Inquire about
discounted (or 'validated')
rates and times.

Directory

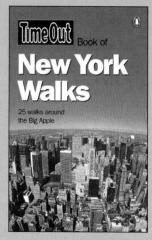
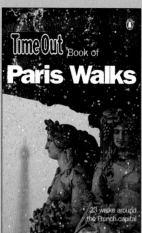

If you're parking during the day, look out for the few large city lots where you can plug a parking meter by the hour (keep your quarters handy).

Below we've listed some useful parking garages, all of which stay open late.

Embarcadero Center Parking

Between Battery, Drumm, Clay & Sacramento Streets, Financial District (772 0670). **Open** 6am-midnight. **Map** p311 H3.
Between certain hours, having your ticket validated at an Embarcadero establishment will decrease the rate.

Fifth & Mission Yerba Buena Gardens Garage

833 Mission Street, between Fourth & Fifth Streets, SoMa (982 8522). **Open** 24hrs daily. **Map** p311 G/H4.

Japan Center Garage

1610 Geary Boulevard, between Webster & Laguna Streets, Western Addition (567 4573). **Open** 6.30am-2.30am Mon-Thur, Sun; 24hrs Fri, Sat. **Map** p310 E4.

Lombard Garage

2055 Lombard Street, between Webster & Fillmore Streets, Marina (440 1984). **Open** 7am-midnight Mon, Sun; 7am-1am Tue, Wed; 7am-2.30am Thur; 7am-3am Fri, Sat. **Map** p309 E2.

New Mission Bartlett Garage

3255 21st Street, between Bartlett & Valencia Streets, Mission (821 6715). **Open** 6am-midnight daily. **Map** p314 F7.

St Mary's Garage

651 California Street, at Kearny Street, Chinatown (956 8106). **Open** 24hrs daily. **Map** p311 H3.

Union Square Garage

333 Post Street (enter on Geary Street), between Stockton & Powell Streets, Union Square (397 0631). **Open** 24hrs daily. **Map** p311 G3/4.

Vallejo Street Garage

766 Vallejo Street, between Stockton & Powell Streets, North Beach (989 4490). **Open** 24hrs daily. **Map** p310 G2.

Vehicle hire

A credit card and a driver's licence are required if you're renting a car. There are dozens of rental companies in the city and at SFO, and it definitely pays to shop around (national companies often have the best deals and service). Before you rent a car, make sure your own motor insurance or credit card company covers you, or you'll need to pay a surcharge. Car insurance is mandatory. Most companies stipulate age limits.

National rental companies

Alamo 1-800 462 5266/
www.alamo.com
Avis 1-800 831 2847/www.avis.com
Budget 1-800 527 0700/
www.drivebudget.com
Dollar 1-800 800 4000/
www.dollar.com
Enterprise 1-800 325 8007/
www.enterprise.com
Hertz 1-800 654 3131/www.hertz.com
Rent-A-Wreck 282 6293
Thrifty 1-800 367 2277/
www.thrifty.com

Local rental companies

A-One 771 3977
City Rent-A-Car 861 1312/
www.cityrentacar.com
Payless Car Rental 292 1000/
www.800-payless.com

Motorbike rental

Easy riders should head for **Dubbelju Motorcycle Rentals** (271 Clara Street, between Fifth and Sixth Streets, SoMa, 495 2774), which can set you up with the Harley or BMW of your choice (from $99 a day). You'll need a valid driver's licence and credit card deposit.

American Automobile Association (AAA)

150 Van Ness Avenue, CA 94102, between Fell & Hayes Streets, Civic Center (565 2012/touring info 565 2711/emergency service 1-800 222 4357). **Open** 8.30am-5.30pm Mon-Fri. **Map** p310 F5.
The fabulous Triple A provides excellent – and free – maps, guides, specific travel routes (TripTiks) and towing services to members of the AAA or an affiliated organisation (such as the British AA or RAC).

Cycling

Bike routes & rental

San Francisco is cycling city. A grid of major cycle routes across the city is marked by oval-shaped bike-and-bridge markers. North–south routes use odd numbers; east–west routes even; full-colour signs indicate primary crosstown routes; neighbourhood routes appear in green and white. The Yellow Pages has a map of the routes, but you can also call the Bicycle Information Line on 585 2453 for details.

There's also two scenic cycle routes: one from Golden Gate Park south to Lake Merced, the other heading north from the southern end of Golden Gate Bridge into Marin County.

You can take bicycles on BART free of charge (except 6.30am-9am, 3.30pm-6.30pm Mon-Fri, when they are banned). Bike racks on the front of certain Muni buses take up to two bikes. On CalTrain, cyclists can bring their bikes on cars that display yellow bike symbols. You can also stow bikes in lockers at CalTrain stations.

Walking

Exploring on foot is one of the most enjoyable and certainly the most complete ways to see the city. Not until you've hiked the twisting trails in the Presidio, slurped *gelato* while strolling Washington Square park or window-shopped wistfully in the Mission have you truly begun to experience the pleasure of San Francisco. In a city with more than its share of road rage, pedestrians nevertheless walk unimpeded, often arriving sooner than their petrol-consuming counterparts.

To avoid the steepest hills, be sure to get a copy of the *San Francisco Bike Map & Walking Guide*, which helpfully indicates the gradients of the city's streets. The Sunday edition of the *San Francisco Chronicle* includes the 'Datebook', which lists more than 20 walking tour companies. *See also p54.*

Directory

Resources A-Z

Age restrictions

In California you have to be 16 years old to drive, 18 to smoke and have sex (not necessarily at the same time) and 21 to drink. Drinking laws are strict; a major error is having an 'open container' in your car or any public area that isn't zoned for alcohol consumption. Cops will give you a ticket on the spot for walking down the street with a beer in your hand, or even having an empty beer can on your car's back seat. You don't want to know what happens if you're busted for drunk driving, so don't do it.

Business

There are few cities in the US that can match San Francisco's simultaneous qualifications as a world-class holiday and business destination. From MacWorld conferences to the UN's 50th Anniversary gala, conventions annually draw 1.4 million participants to the city. From a 1999 survey, San Francisco Convention & Visitor Bureau officials concluded that 1.2 million of the 17.3 million yearly visitors are on a combined business/pleasure trip.

The Bay Area is home to several of the country's biggest companies. Besides banking (the Pacific Stock Exchange, a Federal Reserve Bank and the California State Banking Department are all based in the city, as are Wells Fargo Bank and Charles Schwab & Co), resident industries include telecommunications, bio-medical technology, law, shipping and manufacturing. Another big business here is, of course, high technology. Silicon Valley, the stretch of the Bay Area from Redwood City to San Jose, is where the earliest personal computers

were developed more than 30 years ago. Despite the slump, Apple Computers, Sun Microsystems, Hewlett-Packard, Intel and Advanced Micro Devices are all still there.

Convention centres

Moscone Convention Center

747 Howard Street, between Third & Fourth Streets, SoMa (974 4000/ www.moscone.com). BART Powell or Montgomery/Muni MetroF, J, K, L, M, N/bus 12, 14, 15, 30, 45, 76. **Map** p311 H4.
San Francisco's exhibition and meeting facility is situated on two blocks bounded by Mission, Folsom, Third and Fourth Streets. Moscone is within walking distance of nearly 20,000 hotel rooms, although room reservations still need to be made as early as possible. The busiest times for conventions are usually the months of May and September, and mid January when the city hosts the MacWorld Expo.

Courier services

Local messenger & delivery services

Local companies include **Quicksilver Messenger Service** (431 2500), famous for its daring bikers; **Aero Special Delivery** (730 2603/ www.aerodelivery.com), which specialises in statewide message and parcel delivery; and **California Overnight** (1-877 334 500/www.cal over.com). The US Post Office (1-800 222 1811/www.usps.com) can make overnight deliveries to most US cities and will deliver express parcels on a Sunday to some neighbourhoods. Check the Yellow Pages for other couriers.

International couriers
DHL
1-800 225 5345/www.dhl.com.
Open 24hrs daily. **Credit** AmEx, Disc, MC, V.
Federal Express
24hr 1-800 238 5355/www.federal express.com. **Open** 9am-8pm Mon-Fri; 10am-5pm Sat. **Credit** AmEx, DC, MC, V.
UPS
24hr 1-800 742 5877/www.ups.com.
Open 9am-6pm Mon-Fri; 10am-4pm Sat. **Credit** (air deliveries only) AmEx, MC, V.

Message services

American Voice Mail
1-800 347 2861/www.american voicemail.com. **Open** 5am-7pm Mon-Fri; 6.30am-4pm Sat. **Credit** (after 1st payment only) MC, V.
Confidential voicemail service for unlimited messages, 24hrs a day.

Mail Boxes Etc
268 Bush Street, between Montgomery & Sansome Streets, Financial District (765 1515/www. mbe.com). Bus 28, 30, 43, 76.
Open 7.45am-5.45pm Mon-Fri.
Credit AmEx, DC, Disc, MC, V.
Map p309 D2.
Passport photos, mailbox rental, mail forwarding, packing shipping, copy and facsimile services.

Office services

Copy Central
705 Market Street, at Third Street, Financial District (882 7377/www. copycentral.com). BART Montgomery/ Muni Metro F, J, K, L, M, N/bus 5, 6, 7, 9, 15, 21, 31, 66, 71. **Open** 7.30am-10pm Mon-Thur; 7.30am-7pm Fri; 10am-6pm Sat; noon-6pm Sun. **Credit** AmEx, Disc, DC, MC, V. **Map** p311 H4.
Photocopying, printing, binding, faxing and overnight mail delivery; many branches have DTP centres.
Staff are friendly and helpful.
Other locations throughout the Bay Area.

Kinko's
369 Pine Street, at Montgomery Street, Financial District (834 1053/ www.kinkos.com). BART Montgomery/ Muni Metro F, J, K, L, M, N/bus 10, 15/cable car California. **Open** 7am-11pm Mon-Fri; 10am-6pm Sat, Sun.
Credit AmEx, DC, Disc, MC, V.
Map p311 H3.
Use of on-site computers, online facilities, printing, photocopying, fax and overnight mail delivery or collection. Be prepared to queue.
Other locations throughout the Bay Area, phone 1-800 254 6567.

Office Depot
33 Third Street, at Market, Financial District (777 1728/www.officedepot. com). BART Montgomery/Muni Metro F, J, K, L, M, N/bus 5, 6, 7, 9, 15, 21, 31, 66, 71. **Open** 8am-7pm Mon-Fri; 10am-6pm Sat. **Credit** AmEx, Disc, MC, V. **Map** p311 H4.
Photocopying, printing, DTP, custom stamps, engraved signs, faxes and every office product on the planet.

Directory

Useful organisations

The San Francisco Main Library (*see p68*) offers access to annual reports from most major US and Bay Area corporations; Standard & Poor's evaluations of publicly owned companies; the Dunn and Bradstreet Business Database; Securities and Exchange Commission data on US businesses; US Census information; environmental compliance records; and medical news/statistics. You don't need a library card for in-house print research or to read back-dated newspapers and magazines. The research desk staff are absolutely terrific and information professionals – journalists, in particular – often seek their help. Phone 557 4400.

Law Library

401 Van Ness Avenue, at McAllister Street, Civic Center (554 6821/www. ci.sf.ca.us/sfll). BART Civic Center/ bus 5, 19, 47, 49. **Open** 8.30am-5pm Mon-Fri. **Map** p310 F4.
Open to the public for research, but only San Francisco-based lawyers can borrow books and materials.

Mechanics' Institute Library

57 Post Street, between Montgomery & Kearny Streets, Financial District (393 0101/www.milibrary.org). BART Montgomery/Muni Metro F, J, K, L, M, N/bus 2, 3, 4, 7, 9, 21, 31, 38, 66, 71, 76. **Open** 9am-9pm Mon-Thur; 9am-6pm Fri; 10am-5pm Sat; 1-5pm Sun. **Admission** *Non-members* $5/day; $10/wk. **Map** p311 H3.
This private organisation offers many of the same data sources as the Main Library, especially CD-Rom search tools, but in only a fraction of the space. Its true source of fame, however, lies in its chess room (421 2258/www.chessclub.org; open 11am-10.50pm daily), which has long been considered one of the best places in town for a quiet game.

Consulates

For a complete list, consult the Yellow Pages, or phone directory assistance (411).

Australia 536 1970
Britain 617 1300/
www.britainusa.com
Canada 834 3180
EU Delegation (based in Washington, DC) 1-202 862 9500/
www.eurunion.org
Republic of Ireland 392 4214
New Zealand 399 1255

Consumer

Better Business Bureau

243 9999/www.bbbgoldengate.org. **Open** 24hrs daily.
Provides information on the reliability of a company or service and a list of companies with good business records. The bureau also has referral listings for anything from accountants to zipper repair services, plumbers to auto repair, and is the place to call to file a complaint about a company.

California Attorney General's Office Public Inquiry Unit

1-800 952 5225/http://caag.state.ca. us/consumers. **Open** 24hrs daily.
Reviews consumer complaints. Call to make a complaint about consumer law enforcement or any other agency.

Disabled

San Francisco is a highly accommodating city for most disabled travellers, despite its challenging topography. In fact, California is the national leader in providing the disabled with ready access to facilities and attractions. General privileges include unlimited free parking in designated (blue) areas and free parking at most metered spaces (display your blue and white 'parking placard' for both), plus special prices and arrangements for train, bus, air and sightseeing travel.

All public buildings within the city are required by law to be accessible to wheelchairs and have disabled-accessible toilets; most city buses can 'kneel' to make access easier and have handgrips and spaces designed for wheelchair users; most city street corners have ramped kerbs and most restaurants and hotels are designed (or redesigned) to accommodate wheelchairs.

What a building is supposed to have and what it really has can be different, so wheelchair-bound travellers should also contact the Independent Living Resource Center (543 6222/ www.ilrcsf.org).

Braille Institute of San Francisco

1-800 272 4553. **Open** 9am-4pm Mon-Fri.
Volunteers can connect anyone who has sight difficulties with services for the blind throughout the US.

California Relay Service

TTD to voice 1-800 735 2929/voice to TTD 1-800 735 2922.
Relays telephone calls between TTD and voice callers. The service is available 24hrs daily.

Travel advice

For up-to-date information on travel to a specific country – including the latest news on safety and security, health issues, local laws and customs – contact your home country government's department of foreign affairs. Most have websites packed with useful advice for would-be travellers.

Australia
www.dfat.gov.au/travel

Canada
www.voyage.gc.ca

New Zealand
www.mft.govt.nz/travel

Republic of Ireland
www.irlgov.ie/iveagh

UK
www.fco.gov.uk/travel

USA
http://www.state.gov/travel

Directory

Crisis Line for the Handicapped

1-800 426 4263. **Open** 24hrs daily.
Phoneline/referral service with advice on topics from transport to stress.

Electricity

US electricity voltage is 110-120V 60-cycle AC. Except for dual-voltage, flat-pin plug shavers, all European appliances need an adaptor, available at airport shops, some pharmacies, electronics stores (such as Radio Shack) and department stores.

Emergencies

Ambulance, fire brigade or police *Dial 911 (toll-free from any phone booth).*
Pacific, Gas and Electric Company (PG&E) *Emergency service 1-800 743 5000/information hotline 1-800 743 5002.* **Open** 24hrs daily.
Poison Control Center *1-800 523 2222/1-800 876 4766/1-800 222 1222.* **Open** 24hrs daily.
Water Department City & County of San Francisco *Emergency service 550 4911.*
Open 24hrs daily.

Health & medical

For complementary and alternative medicine, *see p180.* For opticians, *see p185.* For 24hr pharmacies, *see p182.*

Accident & emergency

In the United States you will have to pay for any emergency treatment you require. Contact the emergency number on your travel insurance before seeking treatment and they'll direct you to a hospital that deals directly with your insurance company at home. There are 24hr emergency rooms at:

California Pacific Medical Center

Castro Street, at Duboce Avenue, Lower Haight (600 6000). Muni Metro N/bus 24, 37. **Map** p313 E6.

St Francis Memorial Hospital

900 Hyde Street, between Bush & Pine Streets, Nob Hill (353 6300). Bus 2, 3, 4, 19, 27, 76/cable car California. **Map** p310 F3.

San Francisco General Hospital

1001 Potrero Avenue, between 22nd & 23rd Streets, Potrero Hill (206 8111). Bus 9, 27, 33, 48. **Map** p315 G/H7.

UCSF Medical Center

505 Parnassus Avenue, between Third & Hillway Avenues, Sunset (476 1000). Muni Metro N/bus 6, 43, 66. **Map** p312 B/C6.

Clinics

Haight-Ashbury Free Clinic

558 Clayton Street, at Haight Street, Haight-Ashbury (487 5632/www. hafci.org/medical). Muni Bus 6, 7, 33, 37, 43, 66, 71. **Open** 1-9pm Mon; 9am-9pm Tue-Thur; 1-5pm Fri; 24hr answerphone. **Map** p313 C/D6.
Free primary health care is provided to the uninsured. Speciality clinics include podiatry, chiropractics, paediatry and HIV testing. You will need to make an appointment.

Lyon-Martin Women's Health Services

1748 Market Street, between Octavia & Gough Streets, Upper Market (565 7667). Muni Metro F, J, K, L, M, N/bus 6, 7, 66, 71. **Open** 8.30am-5pm Mon, Thur; 11am-7pm Wed; 8.30am-5pm Tue, Fri. **Credit** MC, V. **Map** p314 F5.
Named after two of the founders of the modern lesbian movement in the US, the Lyon-Martin clinic offers affordable health care for women in a lesbian-friendly environment. Phone to make an appointment.

St Anthony Free Medical Clinic

121 Golden Gate Avenue, at Jones Street, Tenderloin (241 2600/www. stanthonysf.org). BART Civic Center/ Muni Metro J, K, L, M, N/bus 5, 6, 7, 9, 19, 21, 31, 66, 71. **Open** Drop-in clinic 8am-noon, 1-4.30pm Mon-Fri. **Map** p310/314 G4.
Free medical services for those with or without insurance. Arrive early.

Contraception & abortion

Planned Parenthood Clinics

815 Eddy Street, between Van Ness Avenue & Franklin Street, Tenderloin (1-800 967 7526). Bus 31, 47, 49. **Open** 9am-5pm Mon, Thur; 7.30am-5pm Tue, Fri; 11am-7pm Wed; 8am-2pm Sat. **Credit** MC, V. **Map** p310/314 F4.
In addition to contraception services and the morning-after pill, Planned Parenthood provides low-cost general health-care services, HIV testing and gynaecological exams.

Dentists

1-800 Dentist

1-800 336 8478. **Open** 24hrs daily. Referrals, based on geographic location and the services desired.

University of the Pacific School of Dentistry

2155 Webster Street, at Sacramento Street, Pacific Heights (929 6400). Bus 1, 3, 22. **Open** 8.30am-5pm Mon-Fri. *Late appointments* 5.30pm-8.30pm Mon, Thur. **Map** p309/10 E3.
Supervised dentists-in-training provide a low-cost service. Be warned, though: you'll spend little money for a long time in the chair.

HIV & AIDS

AIDS-HIV Nightline

434 2437. **Open** 5pm-5am daily. Crisis hotline offering emotional support. English only.

California AIDS Foundation Hotline

1-800 367 2437/863 2437. **Open** 9am-5pm Mon, Wed-Fri; 9am-9pm Tue.
Offers up-to-date information on the HIV virus, as well as advice on safe sex. Multilingual.

Helplines

Alcoholics Anonymous *674 1821.* **Open** 24hrs daily.
Drug Crisis Information *362 3400/hearing-impaired 781 2224.* **Open** 24hrs daily.
Phone this service to find out about the effects of a particular drug or overdose remedy, and how to get into a treatment programme. They'll also talk you through a bad trip.

Directory

Narcotics Anonymous
621 8600. **Open** 24hrs daily.

SF General Hospital
206 8125. **Open** 24hrs daily.
For anyone suffering a psychiatric breakdown or trying to find someone taken by the police or paramedics for acting out of control.

SF Rape Treatment Center
206 3222. **Open** 8am-5pm Mon-Fri.
Call here within 72hr of a sex crime for counselling and to be guided through medical/legal procedures.

Suicide Prevention
781 0500. **Open** 24hrs daily.

Talk Line Family Support
441 5437. **Open** 24hrs daily.
Counselling for children suffering abuse or parents involved in child abuse; follow-up services provided.

Victims of Crime Resource Center
1-800 842 8467. **Open** 8am-6pm Mon-Fri; 24hr answerphone Sat, Sun.

Women Against Rape Crisis Hotline
647 7273. **Open** 24hrs daily.
Counselling, support and legal services for victims and their partners.

ID

Even if you look 30, you'll need photo ID (preferably driver's licence with photo or passport) to get into the city's bars or clubs or to buy alcohol in a restaurant or shop.

Immigration & customs

Regulations apply to all visitors to the US, which means you may have to wait (maybe an hour or more) when you arrive at Immigration. During the flight you will have been issued two forms – an immigration form and a customs declaration form – to present to an official on the ground. You'll have to explain the nature of your visit and can expect close questioning if you're planning a long visit but don't have a return ticket or much money. Work permits are hard to get hold of, and you're not allowed to work without one (*see p291*). From 2004 there will be some new rules concerning passports (*see p275* **Passports & visas**).

US Customs allow visitors to bring in $100 worth of gifts ($400 for returning Americans) before paying duty. One carton of 200 cigarettes (or 100 cigars) and one litre of liquor (spirits) is allowed. No plants, fruit, meat or fresh produce are allowed in. For detailed information, contact your nearest US embassy or consulate. If you have any questions about US immigration policies, call the Northern California Coalition for Immigrant Rights (543 6767/ www.nccir.org).

Insurance

It's advisable to take out comprehensive insurance cover before arriving: it's almost impossible to arrange in the US. Make sure you have adequate health cover, since medical expenses can be high. For a list of hospitals and emergency rooms, *see p282.*

Internet

As you might expect, it is relatively easy to get online in San Francisco (wireless hotspots have made things even easier, *see p285* **Wi-Fi... why not?**). Most hotels have dataports in the rooms; the most expensive offer highspeed net access and laptops. Many hotels provide at least one computer for guests' use, where you can receive and send web-based email. If you already have an account with a global Internet Service Provider (ISP), such as AOL or CompuServe, all you need to do is change the dial-up access number (though you may have to pay a surcharge on top of your current plan). Otherwise set up a temporary account with a local provider. Outside your hotel, the best places to go online are office services centres (*see p280*) or the Main Library (*see p68*), which has express terminals on the first floor, available for free for 15

minutes on a first-come, first-served basis. For the best of SF-related websites, *see p293.*

AOL 1-800 392 5180, www.aol.com
CompuServe 1-800 848 8990
www.compuserve.com
Earthlink 1-800 327 8454
www.earthlink.net

Left luggage

Leaving luggage has got trickier since 9/11. No airports have lockers, but larger hotels may allow you to leave bags with them. Or use this agency.

Airport Travel Agency
1-650 877 0421.
Open 7am-11pm daily.
In SFO's international terminal, ATA stores everything from luggage to bicycles, priced by size and time.

Legal help

Lawyer Referral Service
989 1616. **Open** 8.30am-5.30pm Mon-Fri.
Legal interviewers refer callers to experienced attorneys and mediators for all legal problems, including criminal, business and immigration.

Libraries

For San Francisco Main Library, *see p68.* For legal and business libraries, *see p281.*

Lost property

Property Control
850 Bryant Street, between Sixth & Seventh Streets, SoMa (553 1377).
Bus 12, 27, 42. **Open** 8am-4.30pm Mon-Fri. **Map** p311 H5.
Make a police report – then hope.

Airports
For items lost during flight, contact the specific airline. If you leave a bag at the airport, it could well get blown up – but try one of these numbers.

San Francisco International Airport
1-650 821 7014. **Open** 8am-8pm Mon-Fri.

Oakland International Airport
1-510 563 3982. **Open** 8am-8pm daily (after hours, try 1-510 563 3300).

San Jose International Airport
1-408 277 5419. **Open** 7am-6pm Mon-Fri.

Directory

Public transport

The Muni lost-and-found office is on 923 6168. For BART, phone 1-510 464 7090; for AC Transit 1-510 891 4706; Golden Gate Transit 257 4476; and SamTrans 1-800 660 4287.

Taxis

Phone the relevant firm (*see p277*).

(*see p277*)

Media

The media exists in San Francisco not only to report what's going on, but to confirm the inhabitants' collective belief that they're living in the most trend-setting quadrant of the globe. The city supports only one major newspaper, the *San Francisco Chronicle*, as well as a faltering tabloid, the *Examiner*. Livelier are the alternative weekly tabloids, the *San Francisco Bay Guardian* and *SF Weekly*. The best media, though, is based out of town. The *San Jose Mercury News* remains the best read, and Oakland's KTVU (channel 2) gets the best news ratings.

Newspapers

Local papers are listed below. For broader national and international coverage try the regional edition of the *New York Times* ($1) or national edition of the *Los Angeles Times* ($1). *The Wall Street Journal* ($1) has an excellent news brief and some of the best feature writing in the country – though its op-ed page is dominated by famously reactionary conservatives. The vapid *USA Today* (50¢) makes good fishwrap; it's distributed free in many hotels.

San Francisco Chronicle

www.sfgate.com
Complaining about 'the Chron' ('the Comical', as locals call it) has become a San Francisco cliché. The region's largest circulation paper (50¢), it is the only real choice for local news since the Hearst Corporation bought it for $660 million in 2000 and closed down its only rival, the *Examiner*. The *Examiner* re-emerged in 2000 as a tabloid, but it's hardly the *Chron*'s

rival. After the buy-out, the paper doubled its staff, beefed up its local and international coverage, and was given a more mature look. Apart from good columnists who make it an entertaining Sunday read, the *Chron* still lacks the punch and vigour of a big-city newspaper. The Sunday 'Datebook' – what locals call the 'pink' (after the pink paper on which it's printed) – is a tabloid entertainment and arts supplement, complete with listings and reviews. It remains the most compelling reason to pick up the *Chron*.

San Francisco Examiner

www.examiner.com
This free tabloid is sometimes good for a laugh or a sensational story.

San Jose Mercury News

www.mercurynews.com
If you're thirsting for news outside San Francisco, this paper (25¢) offers the Bay Area's best overall news reporting, business and sport; its business coverage of Silicon Valley and internet commerce is first-rate.

San Francisco Bay Guardian

www.sfbg.com
One of a pair of free weekly arts tabloids (the other is *SF Weekly*) that battle for supremacy in San Francisco, this is a thick, lively rag that mixes an unapologetically progressive stance with a full range of arts listings. Exhaustive and opinionated, it's definitely the better of the two weeklies. It eagerly annoys the conservative local establishment by exposing cronyism, graft, fraud and double standards. Available free from newspaper boxes and in cafés and coffee-shops.

SF Weekly

www.sfweekly.com
Light on politics and in-depth, issue-oriented pieces, the *Weekly* is still an invaluable resource for keeping up with the arts and music scene. Highlights include Seattle-based syndicated columnist Dan Savage's brutally frank sex advice column, 'Savage Love', and a personal ads section so steamy it would make an exhibitionist blush. Available in the same places that carry the *Guardian*.

San Francisco Bay Times

A free fortnightly tabloid directed at the gay and lesbian community. It features listings, commentary, classified advertisements and personals. It can be found in coffee-shops and bookstores in the Castro.

BAR (Bay Area Reporter)

Similar to the *Bay Times*, free weekly *BAR* features listings and news that affects the gay community. Copies can be found in most of the same places as the *Times*.

Street Sheet

Written by the homeless and sold by them for $1. No need to look for it, it will come looking for you.

Magazines

San Francisco Magazine is an increasingly lively glossy monthly, covering everything from local politics and policy issues to the Bay Area's ravenous restaurant scene. Literary periodical *Zyzzyva* is produced three times a year, offering short stories, poetry, creative non-fiction and original art. Francis Ford Coppola's quarterly *Zoetrope: All-Story Magazine* moved to San Francisco from New York in 2000. It publishes short fiction and one-act plays. The quarterly *Juxtapoz* preaches to the alternative arts crowd. Most recently, 2003 saw the launch of *The Believer*, a literary and culture monthly associated with McSweeney's and alternalit crowdpleaser Dave Eggers.

There are several business publications, a few devoted to the tattered internet economy, still being published here, among them *Business 2.0* and the seminal *Wired*. Computer magazines such as *PCWorld* and *MacWorld* continue to thrive, proving the resilience of Bay Area geekdom.

Television

The Bay Area has affiliates of all three major networks: ABC (local station is KGO, found on channel 7), NBC (KNTV, channel 11) and CBS (KPIX, channel 5). KRON (channel 4) is now completely devoted to Bay Area news and syndicated sitcoms. Long-lasting independent

KTVU (channel 2) is now part of the Fox TV network. An alternative to the relentless advertising of commercial stations, PBS, the Public Broadcasting Service, has stations in San Francisco (KQED, on channel 9), in San Jose (KTEH, channel 54) and in San Mateo (KCSM, channel 60). Receiving a meagre subsidy from the federal government, these survive on viewers' donations.

Radio

San Francisco's constantly changing radio profile reflects a number of ongoing difficulties: attracting enough listeners in a competitive market and outsmarting weather and geography, which combine to undermine reliable radio signals. But Bay Area radio is still spectacular.

The weaker, non-commercial stations lie to the left of the FM dial; the powerhouses with the loudest ads cluster on the right. AM is mostly reserved for talk, news and sports

broadcasts, with a few foreign-language, oldie and Christian stations peppering the mix.

News & talk

For the latest news, KGO (810 AM), KQED (88.5 FM) and its competitor, KALW (91.7 FM), remain your best bets. Beyond that, Berkeley-based KPFA (94.1 FM) is also determined to give KQED a run for its money, and KCBS (740 AM), the local CBS affiliate, has likewise proved itself a station devoted to quality news (and priceless traffic reports, every 10mins). KSFO (740 AM), meanwhile, boasts reactionary talk radio shows in the morning and broadcasts the Oakland A's baseball games in the afternoon. KNBR (680 AM) is the voice of the SF Giants' baseball games and, later, the place to tune in for well-informed sporting debate.

Classical & jazz

KDFC (102.1 FM) advertises itself as a 'radio concert hall'; however, it remains a bit on the stuffy side, and interrupts its conservative classical repertoire to run hyperactive ads for cars, wine and singles clubs. Following the demise of KJAZ in the mid 1990s, San Francisco and the region have been hurting for a good jazz station. The adventurous KCSM (91.1 FM), a public radio station broadcast from a college in San Mateo, has taken up much of the slack, though its signal is relatively

weak. Local KKSF (103.7 FM) bills itself as a 'soft jazz' station, but all too often sounds more like muzak than anything worth an extended listening – never tune in while operating heavy machinery.

Dance, hip hop & soul

Rarely can one find more energy than on KMEL (106 FM), the Bay Area's foremost station for pop and hip hop. KYLD (94.9 FM) is something of a contender and definitely gets party-goers in the mood on weekend nights. For something different, tune in to tiny KPOO (89.5 FM), where innovative hip hop and hardcore rap alternate with cool blues shows on weekend nights. A Tuesday afternoon slot is dedicated to music by John Coltrane.

Rock & pop

The hot station for alt-rockers is KLLC (97.3 FM). 'Alice', as it calls itself, seems to have stolen listeners from the weakening KITS ('Live 105', 105 FM), which seems to focus too often on bands that made it big in the 1980s – U2 and Depeche Mode meet Nirvana and Alanis Morissette. KFOG (104.5 FM) manages to retain a loyal following with its above-average mix of classic rock, new material and live concerts, much of it local. Those in search of more eclectic listening tune in to college and independent stations such as KALX (90.7 FM), KUSF (90.3 FM), KFJC (89.7 FM) or KPOO (89.5 FM).

Wi-Fi… why not?

Turn on, tune in and drop out was a mantra of the 1960s counterculture in the Bay Area, but these days the mantra's changed to turn up, boot up and tune in. San Francisco boasts the largest number of Internet Wi-Fi 'hot spots' (as wireless access points are known) in the world; so while Paris may be the City of Lights, San Francisco remains – notwithstanding dotcom disasters – the City of Bytes. As wireless technology has become more widely deployed, many merchants, cafés, bars, restaurants and hotels have realised the value of offering free wireless connections to their patrons.

So you're in the city, with your laptop or PDA, and you want high-speed wireless Internet for free… how do you connect? Bay Area groups dedicated to providing free high-speed Internet access to all offer a number of Wi-Fi resources. Check out BAWUG, the Bay Area Wireless Users Group

(www.bawug.org), to find resources and contacts for local free wireless access advocates and a map of local free wireless hot spots (www.cheesebikini.com/wifi-cafes). There's also a searchable directory of hot spots across the United States (www.wi-fi hotspotlist.com/browse/us): to generate a list of hot spots for San Francisco or other towns in the Bay Area, simply click on 'California' in the 'Find a hot spot' menu, then in the next menu locate the nearest town or city. Click on individual listings for further details about that particular location and the type of service provided.

If you insist on paying for service, provider T-Mobile (www.t-mobile.com/hotspot) offers subscription rates that can be arranged monthly, daily or pay-as-you-go, as well as access through much of San Francisco International Airport and at every McDonalds, Starbucks and Borders location in the city.

Directory

On all these channels, you'll find diversity and innovative sounds, including acid jazz, Irish music, kids' shows, African and Latin music and the latest remixes. The best aural blend in the region, these indie stations represent the diverse, non-commercial musical bouillabaisse for which the Bay Area is known.

Money

The US dollar ($) equals 100 cents (¢). Coins range from copper pennies (1¢) to silver nickels (5¢), dimes (10¢) and quarters (25¢). Half-dollar and dollar coins do exist, but are rarely used. Bills are all the same size and colour and come in $1, $5, $10, $20, $50 and $100 denominations, though the $100 bill is not universally accepted. In an attempt to outwit forgers, there are new paper money designs (except the $1 bill); old bills remain legal tender.

ATMs/cashpoints

Most ATMs accept Visa, MasterCard and American Express, as well as other cards, but almost all of them charge a usage fee. If you don't remember your PIN number or have de-magnetised your card, most banks will dispense cash to cardholders. Wells Fargo is omnipresent in the city and offers cash advances at all of its branches. Phone these numbers for ATM locations:

Cirrus 1-800 424 7787
Plus System 1-800 843 7587
Wells Fargo 1-800 869 3557

Banks & bureaux de change

Most banks are open from 9am to 6pm Monday to Friday and on Saturday from 9am to 3pm. Photo ID is required to cash travellers' cheques. Many banks don't exchange foreign currency, so arrive with some US dollars. If you arrive in San Francisco after 6pm, change money at the airport or, if you

have US dollar travellers' cheques, buy something and get change. If you want to cash travellers' cheques at a shop, ask first – some require a minimum purchase. You can also obtain cash with a credit card from certain banks, but be prepared to pay interest rates that vary daily. Most banks and shops accept US dollar travellers' cheques.

American Express Travel Services

455 Market Street, at First Street, Financial District (536 2600/www. americanexpress.com/travel). BART Montgomery or Embarcadero/Muni Metro F, J, K, L, M, N/bus 2, 5, 6, 7, 9, 21, 31, 38, 66, 71. **Open** 9am-5.30pm Mon-Fri; 10am-2pm Sat. **Map** p311 H3.
American Express will change money and travellers' cheques, and offers (for AmEx cardholders only) a poste restante service.

Thomas Cook

75 Geary Street, between Grant Avenue & Kearny Street, Union Square (1-800 287 7362/www.us. thomascook.com). Muni Metro F, J, K, L, M, N/bus 2, 3, 4, 9, 15, 30, 45, 76. **Open** 9am-5pm Mon-Fri; 10am-4pm Sat. **Map** p311 H3.
A complete foreign exchange service, including money transfer by wire.
Other locations 2301 Shattuck Avenue, at Bancroft Way, Berkeley (1-510 849 8520). Closed Sat.

Western Union

1-800 325 6000/www.westernunion. com. **Open** 24hrs daily.
The old standby for bailing cash-challenged travellers out of trouble. Get advice on how to get money wired to you and where to pick it up out of a dozen city locations. You can also wire money to anyone outside the state over the phone, using your MasterCard or Visa. Expect to pay a whopping 10% or more commission when sending money. Western Union also takes telegrams over the phone and charges them to your credit card.

Credit cards

You are strongly advised to bring at least one major credit card on your trip. They are accepted (often required) at nearly all hotels, car rental agencies and airlines, as well as most restaurants, shops and petrol stations. The five major

credit cards most accepted in the US are American Express, Diners Club, Discover, MasterCard and Visa.

Lost/stolen cards

American Express 1-800 992 3404
Diners Club 1-800 234 6377
Discover 1-800 347 2683
MasterCard 1-800 826 2181
Visa 1-800 336 8472

Lost/stolen travellers' cheques

American Express 1-800 221 7282
Visa 1-800 227 6811

Police stations

Central Station

766 Vallejo Street, between Stockton & Powell Streets, North Beach (315 2400). Bus 12, 15, 41, 45/cable car Powell-Mason. **Map** p310 G2.

Southern Station

850 Bryant Street, between Sixth & Seventh Streets, SoMa (553 1373). Bus 19, 27, 42. **Map** p315 H5.

Postal services

Post offices mostly open from 9am to 5.30pm Monday to Friday, 9am to 2pm Saturday. All close on Sundays. (Phone 1-800 275 8777 for information on your nearest branch hours and mailing facilities.) Stamps can be bought at any post office and also at some hotel receptions, vending machines and ATMs. Stamps for postcards within the US cost 23¢; for Europe, Australia and New Zealand 70¢. To send a telegram, contact Western Union (*see above*). For couriers and shippers, *see p280*.

Poste Restante (General Delivery)

Main Post Office, 101 Hyde Street, at Golden Gate Avenue, Civic Center (1-800 275 8777). BART Civic Center/Muni Metro F, J, K, L, M, N/bus 5, 19. **Open** 10am-2pm Mon-Sat. **Map** p314 G4.
If you need to receive mail in SF and you're not sure where you'll be staying, have the envelope addressed with your name, c/o General Delivery, San Francisco, CA 94102, USA. Mail is only kept for ten days from receipt, and you must present some photo ID to retrieve it.

Queer

For fuller listings, *see p224*.

Helplines

For HIV/AIDS helplines, *see p282*.

Community United Against Violence

333 4357/www.cuav.org.
Open 24hrs daily.
A counselling group assisting gay, lesbian, bisexual and transgender victims of acts of domestic violence or hate crimes.

New Leaf

626 7000/www.newleafservices.org.
Open 9am-9pm Mon-Fri; 9am-8pm Sat; 9am-1pm Sun.
A counselling service for gay men, transgenders, lesbians and bisexuals, that deals with issues ranging from substance abuse to HIV.

Parents, Families & Friends of Lesbians and Gays (P-FLAG)

921 8850. **Open** 24hr answerphone.
A helpline offering support for families and friends of gay and lesbian teens and adults.

Other groups

Gay & Lesbian Medical Association

255 4547/www.glma.org.
Open 10am-2pm Mon-Fri.
Around 2,000 gay, lesbian and bisexual physicians and medical students make up this organisation, which publishes guides, holds forums, advocates rights of gay/lesbian doctors and offers medical referrals.

Religion

SF is teeming with temples, whether Baptist or Buddhist, Jewish or Jehovah's Witness, Nazarene, New Age or Satanic. For more, see the Yellow Pages.

Calvary Presbyterian

2515 Fillmore Street, at Jackson Street, Pacific Heights (346 3832). Bus 3, 12, 24. **Map** p309 E3.

Glide Memorial

330 Ellis Street, at Taylor Street, Tenderloin (771 6300/www.glide. org). BART Powell/Muni Metro F, J, K, L, M, N/bus 27, 31, 38. **Map** p310 G4.

Grace Cathedral

1100 California Street, at Taylor Street, Nob Hill (749 6300/www. gracecathedral.org). Bus 1, 15, 27/ cable car California. **Map** p310 G3.

Old St Mary's Cathedral

660 California Street, at Grant Avenue, Chinatown (288 3800). Bus 1, 15, 30, 45/cable car California. **Map** p311 G/H3.

St Boniface Catholic Church

133 Golden Gate Avenue, at Leavenworth Street, Tenderloin (863 7515). BART Civic Center/ bus 5, 19, 31. **Map** p310/14 G4.

St Mary's Cathedral

1111 Gough Street, at Geary Boulevard, Western Addition (567 2020). Bus 2, 3, 4, 37, 38, 49. **Map** p310 F4.

St Paul's Lutheran Church

930 Gough Street, between Turk & Eddy Streets, Western Addition (673 8088). Bus 31, 47, 49. **Map** p310 F4.

Temple Emanu-el

2 Lake Street, at Arguello Boulevard, Presidio Heights (751 2535). Bus 1, 4, 33, 44. **Map** p308 B/C4.

Zen Center

300 Page Street, at Laguna Street, Lower Haight (863 3136/www.sfzc. org). Bus 6, 7, 66, 71. **Map** p314 F5.

Safety & security

Crime is a reality in all big cities, but San Franciscans generally feel secure in their town. There is really just one basic rule of thumb you need to follow – use your common sense. If a neighbourhood doesn't feel safe to you, it probably isn't. Only a few areas warrant caution during daylight hours and are of particular concern at night. These include the Tenderloin (north and east of Civic Center); SoMa (near the Mission/Sixth Street corner); Mission Street between 13th and 22nd Streets; and the Hunter's Point neighbourhood near 3Com Park. Golden Gate Park should be avoided at

night. Many tourist areas are sprinkled with homeless people (notably the Union Square area), who beg for change but are, for the most part, harmless.

If you are unlucky enough to be mugged, your best bet is to give your attackers whatever they want, then call the police from the nearest pay phone by dialling 911. (Don't forget to get the reference number on the claim report for insurance purposes and to get travellers' cheque refunds.) If you are the victim of a sexual assault and wish to make a report, call the police. They will escort you to the hospital for treatment. For helplines that serve victims of rape or other crimes, *see p282*.

Smoking

Smokers may rank as the only group of people who are not particularly welcome in San Francisco. The city is party to some of the stiffest anti-smoking laws in the US (and possibly in the world). Smoking is banned in all public places, including banks, public buildings, sporting arenas, theatres, offices, the lobbies of buildings, shops, restaurants, bars, and any and every form of public transport.

There are many small hotels and B&Bs that don't allow you to light up anywhere inside (and, boy, do they get cross if you do). On the other hand, a select few bars cheerfully ignore the law.

Study

California's higher education system is a hierarchy that starts with publicly funded community colleges and city colleges at the lower end of the scale, followed by California State Universities, which cater primarily to undergraduates and do not grant doctorates, and then, at the top of the pile, the University of California system, which includes formal, research-oriented universities with rigorous entry demands (increasingly so as funding cuts started to bite in early 2004). There are also many private – and expensive – universities. These include Stanford and the University of San Francisco.

In general, universities in the United States are much more flexible about part-time studying than their European counterparts. Stipulations for non-English-speaking students might include passing the TOEFL (Test of English as a Foreign Language), and most students have to give proof of financial support.

The colleges

Academy of Art College

79 New Montgomery Street, CA 94105, between Mission & Market Streets, SoMa (274 2200/www. academyart.edu). BART Montgomery/ Muni Metro F, J, K, L, M, N/bus 2, 3, 4, 5, 9, 14, 30, 66, 76. **Map** *p311 H3.*
Foreign students flock to this visual arts college, which has satellite campuses all over the city. The Academy of Art offers practical graduate and postgrad courses in fine arts, history and graphic design.

California College of the Arts

1111 Eighth Street, CA 94107, between Mission & Minna Streets, SoMa (1-800 447 1278/www.cca. edu). BART Civic Center/Muni Metro F, J, K, L, M, N/bus 14, 19, 26. **Map** *p311 H6.*
With several campuses in San Francisco and Oakland, CCA specialises in architecture as well as fine arts and design.

City College of San Francisco

50 Phelan Avenue, CA 94112, at Ocean Avenue, Balboa Park (main switchboard 239 3000/international students 239 3837/www.ccsf.cc.ca.us). Muni Metro J, K/bus 15, 29, 36, 43, 49, 54.
The largest community college in the United States, City teaches more than 80 subjects on its eight campuses and 150 satellite sites. The most affordable place to study in San Francisco, it's a good choice for a foreign language or computer class over the summer.

Mills College

5000 MacArthur Boulevard, Oakland, CA 94613 (undergraduate admission 1-800 876 4557/graduate admission 1-510 430 3309/www. mills.edu). BART Coliseum, then AC Transit bus 57 to main entrance at Richards Gate/AC Transit bus N to Richards Gate.
A beautifully set, prestigious liberal women's college in Oakland, founded in 1852. Mills offers excellent MFA courses in art and creative writing. Graduate programmes include men.

San Francisco Art Institute

800 Chestnut Street, CA 94133, between Jones & Leavenworth Streets, North Beach (1-800 345 7324/771 7020/www.sanfrancisco art.edu). Bus 30/cable car Powell-Hyde or Powell-Mason. **Map** *p310 F2.*
This hip and prestigious art school offers the whole spectrum of fine arts, including painting, film, photography, sculpture and new genres. Expensive but well respected, SFAI has a good reputation for its one-to-one apprenticeships and puts on legendary student shows.

San Francisco Conservatory of Music

1201 Ortega Street, CA 94122, at 19th Avenue, Sunset District (564 8086/www.sfcm.edu). Bus 28. **Map** *p312 A7.*
Full- and part-time students study music at this small, independent conservatory, known for its excellent faculty and high standards.

San Francisco State University

1600 Holloway Avenue, CA 94132, at 19th Avenue, Stonestown (admissions 338 1111/www.sfsu.edu). Muni Metro M/bus 17, 18, 26, 28, 29.
Like all publicly funded California schools, SFSU is trying desperately to do more with fewer resources The largest school in the city, it has 27,000 students and is good for creative writing, business, ethnic studies and engineering. But be patient: undergrad classes are always full and many potential students are turned away at the beginning of each semester. As a result, it can take five or six years to complete a degree.

Stanford University

Stanford, CA 94305 (undergraduate admissions 1-650 723 2091/ graduate admissions 1-650 723 4291/www.stanford.edu). CalTrain to Palo Alto, then free Marguerite shuttle to campus.
A late 19th-century campus near Palo Alto, this private college is out of many students' league, with

tuition, room and board costing about $28,500 a year. Highly competitive in academic terms, Stanford is known for its business, law and medicine curricula.

UC Berkeley

Office of Undergraduate Admissions, 110 Sproul Hall, UC Berkeley, CA 94720 (1-510 642 6000/www. berkeley.edu). BART Berkeley.
The oldest in the nine-campus University of California system, Berkeley (called 'Cal' by locals) attracts some 30,000 students, including 9,000 postgrads. Famous globally for its history of radical student protest, Berkeley has highly reputed law and engineering schools and runs a controversial nuclear research lab in the East Bay suburb of Livermore. Admission standards have become increasingly rigid with the state's severe budget crisis. *See also p112.*

University of California, San Francisco

400 Parnassus Avenue, CA 94143, at Fourth Avenue, Parnassus Heights (476 9000/www.ucsf.edu). Muni Metro N/bus 6, 43, 66. **Map** *p312 B/C6.*
A top-notch health and sciences university with schools of medicine, dentistry, pharmacy and nursing. UCSF also operates one of the best and least expensive clinics in the city. Admission to the school is rigorous, but it's not impossible.

University of San Francisco

2130 Fulton Street, CA 94117, at Masonic Avenue, Richmond District (422 5555/www.usfca.edu). Bus 5, 31, 43. **Map** *p313 C5.*
One of the 28 Jesuit universities and colleges spread across the United States, USF has reputable business, law and communication arts courses. It has around 8,000 students, with international students making up 10% of the student body.

Visas & ID cards

To study in the Bay Area (or anywhere else in the United States) exchange students apply for a J-1 visa, while full-time students enrolled in a degree programme must apply for an F-1 visa. Both are valid for the duration of the course and for a limited period thereafter.

Foreign students need an International Student Identity Card (ISIC) as proof of student status. This can be bought from your local travel agent or student travel office. In San Francisco, an ISIC costs $22 at either of the two STA Travel offices (530 Bush Street, between Grant Avenue and Stockton Street, 421 3473; 36 Geary Street, between Kearny Street and Grant Avenue, 391 8407). You'll need proof you're a student, ID and a passport-size photo.

Tax

Sales tax of 8.5 per cent is added on to the label price in shops within city limits, and 8.25 per cent in surrounding cities. Hotels charge a 14 per cent room tax and the same percentage on hotel parking.

Telephones

Dialling & codes

The phone system is reliable and, for local calls, cheap. Long-distance, particularly overseas, calls are best paid for with a rechargeable, pre-paid phonecard ($6-$35) available from vending machines and many shops. You can use your MasterCard with AT&T (1-800 225 5288), MCI (1-800 532 8045) or Sprint (1-800 877 4646).

Direct dial calls

If you are dialling outside your area code, dial 1 + area code + phone number; on pay phones an operator or recording will tell you how much money to add. All phone numbers in this guide are given as if dialled from San Francisco, hence Berkeley numbers have the 1-510 prefix, Marin County numbers have no prefix.

Collect calls

For collect or when using a phone card, dial 0 + area code + phone number and listen for the operator/recorded instructions. If you're completely befuddled, dial 0 and plead your case with the operator.

Area codes

San Francisco & Marin County 415
Oakland & Berkeley 510
The peninsula cities 650
San Jose 408
Napa, Sonoma & Mendocino Counties 707

International calls

Dial 011 followed by the country code. If you need operator assistance with international calls, dial 00.

Australia 61
Germany 49
Japan 81
New Zealand 64
UK 44

Public phones

Public pay phones only accept nickels, dimes and quarters, but check for a dialling tone before you start feeding in your change. Local calls usually cost 35¢, though some companies operate pay phones that charge exorbitant prices. The price also rises steeply as the distance between callers increases (an operator or recorded message will tell you how much to add).

Operator services

Operator assistance 0
Emergency (police, ambulance and fire) 911
Local and **long-distance directory enquiries** 411
Toll-free numbers generally start with 1-800, 1-888 or 1-877, while pricey pay-per-call lines (usually phone-sex numbers) start with 1-900; don't confuse them.

Telephone directories

Directories are divided into Yellow Pages (classified) and White Pages (business and residential), and are available at most public phones and in hotels. They contain a wealth of travel info, including area codes, event calendars, park facilities, post office addresses and city zip codes. If you can't find one in the phone booth you're using, dial 411 (for directory assistance) and ask for your listing by name.

Mobile phones

Whereas in Europe mobile (cellular) phones work on the GSM network at either 900 or 1800mHz, the US does not have a standard mobile phone network that covers the whole country – which means that visitors from other parts of the US will have to check with their service provider that they can use their phone in San Francisco. However, the Bay Area does offer access to the GSM network at 1900mHz: European visitors with **tri-band phones** should contact their service provider a few days before they leave to set up international roaming. (If you are taking your mobile to San Francisco, don't forget to pack your charger and any adaptor you might need.)

Check the price of calls before you go; rates will be hefty (they're normally charged as if you were phoning from your home country) and you'll probably be charged for receiving as well as making calls. It might be cheaper to rent or buy a mobile phone while you're in town – try the dealer below, or check the Yellow Pages. Or you can just get a pre-paid SIM card when you arrive.

AllCell Rentals

1-877 724 2355/www.allcellrentals. com. **Open** 24hrs daily. **Credit** AmEx, DC, Disc, MC, V.
Rentals of mobile, GSM and satellite phones and pagers. You pay for the airtime ($1.95 per minute including domestic long-distance). There also may be a delivery fee.

Time & dates

San Francisco is on **Pacific Standard Time**, which is three hours behind Eastern Standard Time (New York) and eight hours behind Greenwich Mean Time (UK). Daylight Savings Time (which is almost concurrent with British Summer Time) runs from the first Sunday

Directory

in April, when the clocks are rolled ahead one hour, to the last Sunday in October. Going from the west to east coast, Pacific Time is one hour behind Mountain Time and two hours behind Central Time, three hours behind Eastern Time.

US **dates** are written in the order month, day, year: 2.5.98 is the fifth of February, not the second of May.

Tipping

Unlike in Europe, tipping is a way of life in the US: many locals in service industries rely on gratuities as part of their income, so you should tip accordingly. In general, tip bellhops and baggage handlers $1-$2 a bag; cab drivers, waiters and waitresses, hairdressers and food delivery people 15-20 per cent of the total tab; valets $2-$3; and counter staff 25¢ to 10 per cent of the order, depending on its size. In restaurants you should tip at least 15-20 per cent of the total bill; most will add this to the bill automatically for a table of six or more.

If you get good service, leave a good tip; if you get bad service, leave little and tip the management with words.

Toilets/restrooms

Restrooms can be found in prime tourist areas such as Fisherman's Wharf and Golden Gate Park, as well as in shopping malls. If you're caught short, don't hesitate to enter a restaurant or a bar and ask to use its facilities.

In keeping with its cosmopolitan standing, San Francisco has installed 20 of the French-designed, self-cleaning JC Decaux lavatories throughout the high-traffic areas of the city. Keep an eye out for these forest-green commodes (they're usually plastered with high-profile advertising). Admission is 25¢ for 20min; after that, you may be fined for indecent exposure, because the door pings open automatically. Be aware that some people use the toilets for purposes other than those for which they were designed.

Tourist information

One of the attractions of San Francisco is that there are many wonderful places to visit beyond the city itself. For full listings of the best of these options, *see p250*.

San Francisco Visitor Information Center

Lower level of Hallidie Plaza, corner of Market & Powell Streets (391 2000/www.sfvisitor.org). BART Powell/Muni Metro J, K, L, M, N/ bus 6, 7, 8, 9, 21, 26, 27, 31, 66, 71. **Open** 9am-5pm Mon-Fri; 9am-3pm Sat, Sun. **Map** p311 G4.
Located in downtown, this is the visitor centre for the efficient and helpful San Francisco Convention & Visitor Bureau. You won't find any parking, but you will find tons of free maps, brochures, coupons and advice. The number above gives access to a 24hr recorded message listing daily events and activities; you can also use it to request free information about hotels, restaurants and shopping. Or send a postcard with your address to PO Box 429097, San Francisco, CA 94102, USA.

Berkeley Convention & Visitors Bureau

2015 Center Street, Berkeley, CA 94704, at Milvia Street (1-800 847 4823/1-510 549 7040/www.visit berkeley.com). BART Berkeley. **Open** 9am-5pm Mon-Fri.
A block from the downtown Berkeley BART station. Will post a visitors' guide on request.

Oakland Convention & Visitors Bureau

463 11th Street, Oakland, CA 94609, between Broadway & Washington Streets (1-510 839 9000/www.oaklandcvb.com). BART 12th Street/City Center. **Open** 8.30am-5pm Mon-Fri.
Located in opposite the City Hall in downtown Oakland. Phone them if you would like to be sent a visitors' guide to Oakland.

Average monthly climate

	High temp	Low temp	Rainfall
Jan	56°F (13°C)	46°F (8°C)	4.5in (11.4cm)
Feb	60°F (15°C)	48°F (9°C)	2.8in (7.1cm)
Mar	61°F (16°C)	49°F (9°C)	2.6in (6.6cm)
Apr	63°F (17°C)	50°F (10°C)	1.5in (3.8cm)
May	64°F (17°C)	51°F (10°C)	0.4in (1cm)
June	66°F (19°C)	53°F (11°C)	0.2in (0.5cm)
July	66°F (19°C)	54°F (12°C)	0.1in (0.25cm)
Aug	66°F (19°C)	54°F (12°C)	0.1in (0.25cm)
Sept	70°F (21°C)	56°F (13°C)	0.2in (0.5cm)
Oct	69°F (20°C)	55°F (13°C)	1.1in (2.8cm)
Nov	64°F (18°C)	51°F (10°C)	2.5in (6.4cm)
Dec	57°F (14°C)	47°F (8°C)	3.5in (8.9cm)

Directory

Sun, wind & fog

San Francisco's bewildering weather is determined by an epic, unending battle between fog and terrain. The city's western third is comparatively flat, so there's little to prevent the fog from covering Richmond, Sunset and the Golden Gate Park. But the fog is often too heavy to climb over the city's hills into the centre, so areas east of Twin Peaks, Mount Davidson and Mount Sutro – the Mission, the Castro, Noe Valley and Potrero Hill – are often warm and sunny when the rest of town is grey and chilly. On any given day the sun is most likely to break through between noon and 4pm, though it is often a brief victory.

It's worth noting that, surprisingly, summer here isn't the warmest season (September and October are the hottest months; *see p290* **Average monthly climate**). Whenever you visit, dress in layers so that, as you pass from one neighbourhood (and microclimate) to the next, you can add or remove bits.

Here's a quick guide to the typical summer weather patterns in different neighbourhoods:
● **Sunny** The Mission, Potrero Hill, the Castro, Noe Valley, North Beach
● **Windy** Fisherman's Wharf, Financial District, Twin Peaks, Hunter's Point
● **Foggy** Richmond, Golden Gate Park, Sunset, Western Addition

Visas

Under the **Visa Waiver Scheme**, citizens of the UK, Japan and most West European countries (exceptions include Ireland, Portugal and Greece) do not need a visa for stays in the United States of less than 90 days (for business or pleasure). Visitors are required to have a passport that is valid for the full 90-day period and a return or open standby ticket. Canadians and Mexicans do not need visas but must have legal proof of their citizenship. All other travellers must have visas. From the end of October 2004, however, these arrangements look set to change (*see p275* **Passports & visas**).

Visa application forms and complete information can be obtained from the nearest US embassy or consulate. It's wise to send in your application at least three weeks before you plan to travel. If you require a visa more urgently you should apply via the travel agent who is booking your ticket.

For further information on visa requirements in the UK, phone the US Embassy Visa Recorded Information Line (0891 200 290).

Other contacts include: Visa Information Line: 09068 200 290 (24hr) 60p/min; Operator Assisted Visa Information: 09055 444 546 (8am-8pm Mon-Fri; 10am-4pm Sat; $1.30/min).

When to go

Climate

San Francisco may be in California, but its climate, like its politics, is all its own. When planning a trip, don't anticipate the normal seasons, climatically, at least. Spring and autumn are relatively predictable, with warm days and cool nights. During the summer, however, days are usually chilly and foggy, with just two or three hot days to momentarily lift the city's collective spirit. Conversely – or is it perversely? – the nights are usually mild. In midwinter, what seems like months of constant rain will suddenly break for a week of brilliant sunshine. Tourists shivering in T-shirts are a never-ending source of amusement for the always well-layered locals. For information on how the weather varies in different neighbourhoods of San Francisco, *see p291* **Sun, wind & fog**.

Public holidays

New Year's Day (1 Jan); **Martin Luther King Jr Day** (3rd Mon in Jan); **President's Day** (3rd Mon in Feb); **Memorial Day** (last Mon in May); **Independence Day** (4 July); **Labor Day** (1st Mon in Sept); **Columbus Day** (2nd Mon in Oct); **Veterans' Day** (11 Nov); **Thanksgiving Day** (4th Thur in Nov); **Christmas Day** (25 Dec).

Work permits

It's difficult for foreigners to find work in the United States. For you to work legally, a US company must sponsor your application for an **H-1 visa**, which enables you to work in the country for up to five years. For the H-1 visa to be approved, your prospective employer must attempt to convince the Immigration Department that there is no American citizen qualified to do the job as well as you.

Students have a much easier time. Your student union should have plenty of information on US working holidays. For more information on studying over the summer, get in touch with the **Council on International Education Exchange (CIEE)**, Work Exchanges Dept, 205 East 42nd Street, New York, NY10017, USA (www.ciee.org).

Further Reference

Fiction & poetry

Dave Eggers
A Heartbreaking Work of Staggering Genius (2000)
Beautiful memoir of bringing up a younger brother, wrapped in fun postmodern flim-flam.

Jim Fadiman
The Other Side of Haight
Details the early psychedelic experiments in the Haight-Ashbury neighbourhood.

Allen Ginsberg
Howl and Other Poems
Grab your chance to read the rant that caused all the fuss way back in the 1950s.

Dashiell Hammett
The Maltese Falcon
One of the greatest detective writers and one of the world's best detective novels, set in a dark and dangerous San Fran.

Jack Kerouac
On the Road; Desolation Angels; The Dharma Bums
Famous for a reason: bittersweet tales of drugs and sex in San Francisco and around the world, from the best Beat of them all.

Jack London *Tales of the Fish Patrol; John Barleycorn*
Early works, set in London's native city.

Armistead Maupin
Tales of the City (6 volumes)
Witty soap opera following the lives and loves of a group of San Francisco friends.

Frank Norris *McTeague*
Cult classic of the 1890s: working-class life and loss set in unromanticised Barbary Coast days.

John Steinbeck
The Grapes of Wrath
Grim tales of California in the Great Depression by the master of American fiction.

Amy Tan
The Joy Luck Club
Moving story of the lives and loves of two generations of Chinese-American women living in San Francisco.

Alfredo Vea
Gods Go Begging
A San Francisco murder trial has ties to the Vietnam War.

William T Vollmann
Whores for Gloria
The boozy story of a middle-aged alcoholic whose fall into decrepitude occurs in the underbelly of the Tenderloin.

Tom Wolfe
The Electric Kool-Aid Acid Test; The Pump House Gang
Alternative lifestyles in trippy, hippy, 1960s California.

Non-fiction

Walton Bean *California: An Interpretive History.*
Anecdotal account of California's shady past.

Po Bronson
The Nudist on the Late Shift
Unblinking treatise on the Silicon Valley scene.

Herb Caen
Baghdad by the Bay
Local gossip and lightly poetic insight from the much-missed *Chronicle* columnist.

Carolyn Cassady *Off the Road: My Years with Cassady, Kerouac and Ginsberg*
Not enlightened feminism, but an interesting alternative examination of the Beats.

Joan Didion
Slouching Towards Bethlehem; The White Album
Brilliant essays examining California in the past couple of decades by one of America's most respected authors.

Timothy W Drescher *San Francisco Bay Area Murals*
A well-resourced book with plenty of maps and 140 photos.

Lawrence Ferlinghetti & Nancy J Peters
Literary San Francisco
The city's literary pedigree.

Robert Greenfield
Dark Star: An Oral Biography of Jerry Garcia
The life and (high) times of the Grateful Dead's late frontman.

Malcolm Margolin
The Ohlone Way
How the Bay Area's original inhabitants lived, researched from oral histories.

John Miller (ed)
San Francisco Stories: Great Writers on the City
Contributions by Herb Caen, Anne Lamott, Amy Tan, Ishmael Reed and many others.

Ray Mungo
San Francisco Confidential
A gossipy look behind the city's closed doors.

John Plunkett & Barbara Traub (eds) *Burning Man*
Photo-heavy manual to the the annual insanity that is the Burning Man Festival.

Richard Schwartz
Berkeley 1900
An in-depth account of the early origins of complex and controversial Berkeley.

Joel Selvin *San Francisco: The Magical History*
Tour of the sights and sounds of the city's pop music history by the *Chronicle*'s music critic.

Randy Shilts
And the Band Played On
Still the most important account of the AIDS epidemic in San Francisco.

John Snyder *San Francisco Secrets: Fascinating Facts About the City by the Bay*
Amusing collection of city trivia, complete with facts and figures galore.

Sally Socolich *Bargain Hunting in the Bay Area*
A must for shopaholics. A truly useful guide that is regularly updated.

Gertrude Stein
The Making of Americans
Autobiographical work that includes an account of her early childhood in Oakland.

Robert Louis Stevenson
An Inland Voyage; The Silverado Squatters
Autobiographical narratives describing the journey from Europe to western America.

Directory

Film

Bullitt (1968)
This Steve McQueen film with the all-time greatest San Francisco car chase.

Chan Is Missing (1982)
Two cab drivers search for a man who stole their life savings; it gives an authentic, insider's look at Chinatown.

Crumb (1994)
Award-winning film about the comic book master and misanthrope Robert Crumb.

Dark Passage (1947)
This classic thriller starts in Marin County, where Bogart escapes from San Quentin Prison, and ends up in Lauren Bacall's SF apartment.

The Graduate (1967)
Hoffman at his best; with shots of Berkeley, as well as a a cool wrong-direction shot on the Bay Bridge.

Harold and Maude (1971)
Bay Area scenery abounds in this bittersweet cult classic about an unbalanced boy who falls in love with an elderly woman.

Jimi Plays Berkeley (1970)
Stirring footage of the town during its radical days, plus Hendrix at his very best.

The Maltese Falcon (1941)
Hammett's classic made into a glorious thriller, full of great street scenes.

Mrs Doubtfire (1993)
Relentlessly hammy Robin Williams as a divorcee posing as a nanny to be near his kids.

Pacific Heights (1990)
Pity the poor landlord: Michael Keaton preys on doting yuppie parents-to-be.

San Francisco (1936)
Ignore the first 90 minutes of moralising and sit back to enjoy the Great Quake.

The Sweetest Thing (2002)
Gross-out movie meets chick flick. With Cameron Diaz.

The Times of Harvey Milk (1984)
Oscar-winning documentary about the first 'out' gay politician in the United States.

Vertigo (1958)
A veteran cop becomes obsessed with a mysterious blonde. Die-cast classic.

The Voyage Home: Star Trek IV (1986)
The gang come to SF to to save some whales. Best of the series.

The Wedding Planner (2000)
Clunky update of the classic screwball comedy, but J-Lo's immaculately cast.

Music

Big Brother and the Holding Company *Cheap Thrills* (1968)
Classic Janis Joplin, included 'Ball and Chain' and 'Piece of My Heart'.

Black Rebel Motorcycle Club *Take Them On, On Your Own* (2003)
They smoke, they wear leather jackets, they rock.

Chris Isaak *Heart Shaped World* (1989)
What a 'Wicked Game' to be so good-looking, with a voice like that – and an SF boy too.

Creedence Clearwater Revival *Willie and the Poor Boys* (1969)
Classic southern rock with a San Francisco touch.

The Dead Kennedys *Fresh Fruit for Rotting Vegetables* (1980)
Excellent, angry SF punk, featuring the classic song, 'California Uber Alles'.

Digital Underground *Sex Packets* (1990)
Rap concept album. You're gonna laugh it up.

The Disposable Heroes of Hiphopricy *Hiphopricy is the Greatest Luxury* (1992)
Rap with a political conscience.

DJ Mark Farina *Mushroom Jazz Vol 4* (2003)
Latest from the DJ most likely to get the saucer-eyed folks jumping around.

Erase Errata *At Crystal Palace* (2003)
Angular, uplifting rock from the queens of the underground.

The Grateful Dead *Dick's Picks Vol 4* (1996)
Jerry Garcia and the boys in their 1970 prime at the Fillmore East.

Jefferson Airplane *Surrealistic Pillow* (1967)
Folk, blues and psychedelia. Grace Slick helps define the SF sound.

Joshua Redman *Wish* (1993)
Quality jazz from the Bay Area tenor saxophonist.

Primus *Pork Soda* (1993)
Wryly intelligent punk-funk in the Zappa tradition.

Rancid *And Out Come the Wolves* (1994)
If you don't like this solid, California ska, you just don't know how to have fun.

Sly and the Family Stone *Stand!* (1969)
Funk-rock masters – if you haven't heard this, you haven't heard the '60s.

Websites

http://sfbay.yahoo.com
An excellent online source, including restaurants, classifieds, traffic reports and an events calendar for the city and the Bay Area.

www.citysearch7.com
Exhaustive, daily-updated guide to SF and the Bay Area.

www.craigslist.org
How San Franciscans hook up. Hilarious and enlightening.

www.kpix.com/live
City Camera site with cameras perched atop the Fairmont Hotel and in the Presidio for breathtaking views.

www.mistersf.com
Delicious collection of local oddballs, notorious history and contemporary culture.

www.sfbayconcerts.com
Tells who's playing where at which Bay Area music venues.

www.sfstation.com
Upcoming events, clubs, parties, film and restaurant reviews and more.

www.transitinfo.org
Very useful for all forms of Bay Area public transport.

Directory

Index

Note Page numbers in **bold** indicate section(s) giving key information on a topic; *italics* indicate photographs.

a

abortion 282
Academy of Art College 204, **288**
accident & emergency services 282
accommodation **31-52**
best, the 33
by price
budget 37, 41, 42, 44, 47-49, 50, 51-52
deluxe 33-34, 37-38, 41-42, 44-47, 49-50
mid-range 34-37, 38-41, 42-44, 45, 47, 49, 50-51
chain hotels 34
hostels 52
hotels allowing dogs 19
queer 225-227
Acid Tests 15
Adams, Ansel 270
Aerosports 196
African-American Historical and Cultural Society Museum 100
African-Americans in San Francisco 92
age restrictions 280
AIDS 16, 90, 282
AIDS Candlelight Memorial March & Vigil 189
airlines 274-275
airports 274
getting to and from 274
Aitken, Robert 71
A La Carte, A La Park 191
Alameda Point Antiques and Collectibles Faire 163
Alamo Square 93
Alcatraz 6, 13, 23, 55, **80**, 196
alcoholic drinks shops 179
Alemany Flea Market 163
Alice Kent Trail 255
Allende, Isabelle 29
Alpine Meadows 264
Alta Plaza Park 96
Altamont Speedway concert, Rolling Stones 15
alternative medicine 180
Alvord Lake 108
American Conservatory Theater (ACT) 245, 245
And the Band Played On 16, 29
Angel Island 6, 80, **81**, 196, 251, **253**
Annual Chinese New Year Treasure Hunt **193**, *193*
antiques shops 163
Anza, Juan Bautista de 7
Applegarth, George 105
Aquarium of the Bay 195
Aquatic Park 80
Arbuckle, Fatty 48, 57
architecture **21-25**
Argonauts, the 9
Arneson, Robert 63
Arquitectonica 25
art
public 207
walk 204
see also galleries *and* museums; galleries in San Francisco
Artists' Television Access 87, 200
arts & entertainment 18, **187-248**
queer 230-231

art shops 164
ArtSpan Open Studios **192**, 204, 205
Asawa, Ruth 80
Asian Art Museum 23, 24, 25, 55, 56, **68**
Athletics *see* Oakland Athletics
ATMs 286
Audubon Canyon Ranch 255
Aulenti, Gae 24, 69
auto racing 234
Avalon Ballroom 28, **214-215**
Ayala Cove 252

b

Bahia de San Francisco 7
Baker Beach 102, **103**, 106
Bakewell, John 69
ballooning 258, 264
Balmy Alley 87
Bancroft Library 112
Bank of America 61
Bank of California 10
Bank of Canton 74
banks 286
'Barbary Coast' 10
Barbary Coast Trail 55
Barbary Lane 84
bargain-hunting 162-163
Bargetto Winery 270
bars **148-158**
DJ 148
queer 227-230
BART 20, **276**
Bartholomew Park Winery 256
Bartlett, Lieutenant Washington A 9
baseball 20, **234-236**
basketball 236
bathhouses 182
batteries 55, **100**, 106
Battery Crosby 100
Battery Godfrey 100
Bautista, Captain Juan 102
Bay Area Childcare Agency 195
Bay Area Discovery Museum **196**, 251
Bay Area Video Coalition 203
Bay Bridge 13, 20, 23, 63, **64**
Bay to Breakers Foot Race 189
Beach Blanket Babylon 246
beaches 242-243
city 103
naturist 106
north of San Francisco 254
south of San Francisco 268
Bear Flag Revolt 7, 256
Bear Valley Visitor Center 255
Beat Generation, the 14, **26-28**, 77, 97
Beat tour 28
Believer, The 29
Beringer Vineyards 260
Berkeley 112-113
walk 112
Berkeley Art Museum 112, **113**
Berkeley Opera 211
Berkeley Symphony Orchestra 211
Berkeley, University of California 15, **203**
Visitors' Center 113
Bernal Heights 88-89
Bernal Hill, queer clubs 230
Bierce, Ambrose 26, 28
Big Basin Redwoods State Park 270
Big Brother and the Holding Company 15, 94
'Big Four' businessmen **10**, 22, 83

Big Deal charity arts fair 208
Bill Graham Civic Auditorium 23, 68, **215**
billiards 240
Bird Man of Alcatraz **82**
Bi-Rite Market 86
Black Cat Café 62
Black Filmworks Festivals of Film & Video 201
Black Mask stories 27
Black Panther movement 15
Bloody Thursday 13
Bluegrass Festival, Hardly Strictly 192
Blues Festival 191
blues music 212-213
Bohemian Club 26, 28
Bolinas 29
Bolinas Lagoon Preserve 254
Bolinas Ridge 237
'Bonanza Kings, the' 10
Bonds, Barry 20, **235**, *235*
Bonny Doon 270
books
further reading 292
shops 164
the best 164
Books by the Bay 190
Boom Boom Room **212-213**, *214*, 215
Bootjack Trail 238
Boreal 264
Botta, Mario 24, 72
Bottom of the Hill 209, **218**
Bowan, James 26
bowling 237
Brady Street 160
Brangwyn, Frank 23
breakdown services 277
Bridges, Harry 13
Broadway 79, 96
Bronson, Po 28
Brown, Arthur 23, 68, 69, 80
Brown, Willie 19, 21
Bruce, Lenny 78
Brudden, Coosje Van 207
brunch 142-143
Buchanan Mall 95
Buena Vista Historical Winery 256
Bufano, Benny 105
Buffalo Paddock 109
'buffalo soldiers' 102
bureaux de change 286
Burnham, Daniel 23
Burning Man 191
bus 275
to & from the airport 274
tours 54
business services 280-281

c

Cable Car Museum 59, **84**, 196
cable cars 55, 57, 84, **58-59**, **276**
Cabrillo, Juan Rodriguez 7
Caen, Herb 78
cafés **141-147**
queer 231-233
Cakebread Cellars 260
Cal *see* Berkeley, University of California
Califia, Queen 7, **11**
California Academy of Sciences 18, **25**, 108, **110**, 195
California College of the Arts 204, **288**
California Culinary Academy 67

California Historical Society 71
California, origin of name 11
California Pacific Bank 61
California Palace of the Legion of Honor 105, **106**
California Star 74
Calistoga 258
Call of the Wild, The 27
CalTrain 236, **276**
Cameron, Donaldina 74
Cameron House 74
Camp Richardson 263
Canin, Ethan 28
Cannery Row 271
Cannery, The 24, **80**
Capitan, El 266
Capone, Al 82
'Car-Strangled Spanner' 20
Carmel 267, **270-272**
Carmel Mission 271
Carnaval 189
Carnelian Room 61
Carquinez Bridge 20
cars & car hire 277-279
Carson, Kit 7
Cartoon Art Museum 71
cashpoints 286
Cassady, Neal 14, 27, 28, 83, 97
Castro, the **85-90**, 224, *224*
arts & entertainment 230-231
bars 148, **153-154**, 227-228
cafés 145-146, 231-233
clubs 222, 230
jazz & blues 212
literary scene 28
restaurants 135, 231-233
rock, pop & hip hop 218
shopping 160
where to stay 49, 225-227
Castro Street Fair 192
Castro Theatre 56, 199, *201*, **230-231**
Cathedral of St Mary of the Assumption *see* St Mary's Cathedral
cathedrals *see* churches & other religious buildings
Celebrated Jumping Frog of Calaveras County, The 26
Center, The 225, **232**
Central Pacific Railroad 10
Cermeno, Sebastian Rodriguez 7
Chabon, Michael 29
Chabot Space & Science Museum 196-198
Chamber Music Sundaes 211
Chanticleer 210
Château Montelena 261
Cherry Blossom Festival 95, **188**
Chestnut Street **98**, 160
children **195-198**
clothes 173
sightseeing 195-198
Children's Discovery Museum, San Jose 267
Children's Fairyland 111, **198**
Chileans in San Francisco 9
Chimney Rock 255
Chin, Justin 29
China Beach 103, 106
Chinatown **73-77**
cafés 144
restaurants 126
shopping 159
where to stay 42
Chinatown (Oakland) 111
Chinatown Gate 74
Chinatown Post Office 74
Chinatown Tour 55
Chinese American National Museum & Learning Center 77

Chinese American Telephone
 Exchange 74
Chinese Culture Center 74, **77**
Chinese in San Francisco 6, 9, 10,
 12, 73-77
Chinese New Year 194
Chinese Six Companies Building
 74
Choy, Curtis 13
Church of John Coltrane 92
Church of St Peter & St Paul 78
churches & other religious
 buildings
 Church of St Peter & St Paul 78
 First Unitarian Universalist
  Church 212
 Glide Memorial United
  Methodist Church 67, **68**,
  287
 Grace Cathedral **84**, 212, 287
 Kong Chow Temple 74
 music in 212
 Old First Presbyterian Church
  212
 Old St Mary's Cathedral 74,
  77, 287
 St Boniface Catholic Church 67,
  68, 287
 St Mary's Cathedral 23, **95**,
  190, 190, 212, 287
 St Patrick's **71**, 212
 Tien Hau Temple 77
 Vedanta Temple 22, **98**
Cinco de Mayo 188-189
cinemas 199-201
circus 195-196
Circus Centre 195
'City Beautiful' project 23
City College of San Francisco
 203, **288**
City Hall 12, 14, 23, 68, **69**, 69
City Lights Booksellers &
 Publishers 28, 78, 97, 159,
 164, **165**
City of Angels 70
Civic Center 23, 56, **68**, 160
 restaurants 123
 where to stay 41
Civic Center Plaza 68
Civil War 10
Claremont Resort & Spa 113
Clarion Alley 86
classical music 210-212
Cleaver, Eldridge 15
Clemens, Samuel *see* Twain, Mark
Clement Street 105
Cliff House 22, 105, **107**
Cliff Lede Vineyards 261
climate 290-291
climbing **240**, 266
clinics 282
Clos Pegase 261
clothes
 second-hand 162-163
 shops 168-175
clubs *see* nightlife
cocktails 157
Cody's Books 113, 164, **165**
Coit, Lillie Hitchcock 80
Coit Tower 23, 55, 77, 79, **80**
Cole Valley 92
Colton Hall Museum 271
Columbarium 22, 105, **107**
Columbus Avenue **77**, 78
Columbus Tower 77
Comedy Day 191
complementary medicine 180
computer shops 168
Comstock, Henry 10
'Comstock Lode, the' 10
Condor Club **76**, 79
consulates 281
consumer information 281
contraception 282
convention centres 280
Coolbrith, Ina 28
COPIA: The American Center
 for Wine, Food & the Arts
 258, **260**

Coppola, Francis Ford 29, 77, 78,
 79, 199, 260
Corona Heights 90
Cortés, Hernán 7, 11
cosmetics & skincare shops 180
Costanoans, the 6
Country Joe and the Fish 15
courier servies 280
Cow Hollow 98
 where to stay 51
crafts shops 164
Craigslist 20, **62**
credit cards 286
Crissy Field 96, **98**, 197, *239*, 240
Crocker, Charles 10, 22, 84
Crocker Galleria 57, **161**
Crocker Mansion 22
Cruisin' the Castro (tour) 55
Crumb, Robert 91, **94**
Cupid's Span 207
Curran Theater 244
customs allowances 283
cycling **237**, 258, 279

d

Dain Curse, The 27
dance **244-248**
Dashiell Hammett Tour 55
dates, US style for 289
Daughters of Bilitis 15
David Bruce Winery 270
'Davies, the' *see* Louise M Davies
 Symphony Hall
Day of the Dead, the *see* Dia de
 los Muertos
day trips, the best 250
de Young Memorial Museum, MH
 18, 24, **110**
Defenestration 207
Democratic Party 19
dentists 282
department stores 160
Design Center 163
Design Museum 24
Desolation Angels 27
Dewey, Admiral 57
Dharma Bums, The 27
Di Rosa Preserve 258
Dia de los Muertos 86, **193-4**
Diller, Elizabeth 24
DiMaggio, Joe 68, 79
Dipsea Trail 238
directory **274-293**
disabled information 281
discount clothes 173
diving, scuba 241
Dr Wilkinson's Hot Springs 258
Doda, Carol 76, 79, 98
Dog Soldiers 28
Dogpatch 17
dogs 18-19
Domaine Chandon 260
Donner Memorial State Park 264
Dore Up Your Alley Fair 225
Downtown **56-72**
 bars 149-152
 cafés 141-142
 classical music & opera
  210-211
 jazz & blues 212
 rock, pop & hip hop 213-217
Drake, Sir Francis 7, 112
Drake's Bay 7
Drake's Beach **254**, 255
drinking 148
driving *see* cars & car hire
drug culture 223
Dubuffet, Jean 63
Ducks, the 9
Dutch Windmill 109
Dyke March 225

e

earthquake of 1906, the **11-12**,
 23, 61, 98
earthquake of 1989, the **16**, 63,
 95, 98

Earthquakes, the *see* San Jose
 Earthquakes
East Bay **111-113**
 bars 158
 Berkeley 111-113
 children 196-198
 cinemas 200-201
 classical music & opera 211
 jazz & blues 213
 Oakland 111-112
 restaurants 137
Eastlake, Charles 22
Eggers, Dave 29, 86
826 Valencia 196
Electric Kool-Aid Acid Test 28
electricity 282
electronics shops 168
Embarcadero, the 56, **63**, 207, 240
Embarcadero Center 63, **161**
Emerald Bay State Park 263
emergency phone numbers 281
English in California 7
Esherick, Joseph 24
Esplanade Gardens 24, **70**
Ethnic Dance Festival 244
Euphemia 9
events *see* festivals & events
Exotic Erotic Ball 192
Exploratorium 98, **196**, 197

f

Fair, James 10
Fairmont Hotel & Tower **45-47**,
 84
Fall of the I-Hotel, The 12
Farnsworth, Philo T 64, 199
fashion
 accessory shops 175-177
 designer 170-171
 shops 168-175
Federal Building 25
Ferlinghetti, Lawrence 14, 28, 97
Fernet Branca 152
ferries 276-277
Ferry Building 23, **24**, 63
Ferry Plaza Farmers' Market 17,
 24, 55, 63, **65**, 65, **178**
Festival ¡Cine Latino! 201
festivals & events **188-194**
 best, the 189
 film 201-203
 foreign language 201
 schools & classes 203
 tickets & information 199
Finding Nemo 196
Fire Engine tour **54**, 196
fire of 1906 12, 22
First Thursdays 204
First Unitarian Universalist
 Church 212
Fish Alley 80
Fisher-Friedman's Oriental
 Warehouse 25
Fisherman's Wharf **80**, 161, 196
 cafés 145
 restaurants 128
 where to stay 44
fitness *see* sport & fitness
flea markets 163
Fleet Week 192

Flood, James 10, 22, 84
Flood Mansion 22
Flower Power Walking Tour 55
Folk Art International 23, **57**
Folsom Street Fair 71, **192**, 225
food delivery services 179
food & drink shops 178-179
football, American 236
Forbes Island 80
Ford, Gerald 48
foreign cinema 85, **134**
Forest of Nisene Marks 270
Fort Funston Beach 106
Fort Funston Reservation 110
Fort Mason 98, **100**
Fort Point 80, 98, **102**
'49ers *see* San Francisco 49ers
 or Gold Rush of 1849
49-Mile Scenic Drive 54
Foster, Jim 15
Fotheringham, Michael 56
Fourth of July celebrations 190
Fourth Street, Berkeley 113
Francis 'Lefty' O'Doul Bridge 72
Franklin, Benjamin 78
Free Love movement 224
Fremont, Captain John 7, 9, 101
French in San Francisco 10
Fringe Festival 191
fuel stations 277
Funston, General Frederick 12

g

galleries **204-208**
 see also museums & galleries
 in San Francisco
gay *see* queer San Francisco
Geary Boulevard 105
Geary, John White 9
Geary Station Post Office 92
George R Moscone Center 197
Getty, Gordon and Anne 96
Ghee Kung Tong Building 77
Ghirardelli Square **80**, 161
 Chocolate Festival 191
Giants *see* San Francisco Giants
gift shops 180
Gilroy Garlic Festival 191
Ginsberg, Allen 14, 15, **27**, 28, 78,
 97, 224
Glacier Point 266
Glass Key, The 27
Glen Ellen 27
Glide Memorial United Methodist
 Church 67, **68**, 287
Gloria Ferrer Champagne Caves
 257
Goggin, Brian 207
Gold Rush of 1849 **9**, 21, 26, 27, 73
'Golden Gate' 9, 101
Golden Gate Bridge 13, 20, 23, 55,
 96, **101**, 103
Golden Gate Bridge Beach 106
Golden Gate Fortune Cookie
 Factory 77
Golden Gate International
 Exposition of 1939 14, 64
Golden Gate National Recreation
 Area 106
Golden Gate Park 10, 22, 55, 92,
 104, **107-110**, 107, 108-109,
 198, 234, 240
Golden Gate Promenade 80
Golden Gate Theater 244
Golden State Warriors 234, **236**
golf 105, 110, **237-238**
gondolas 111
Gonzalez, Matt 19
Gorilla Sports Club 202
Gothic Revival houses 22
Gough, Charles 97
Gough Street 160
'Gourmet Ghetto' 113
Gouvela, Ricardo 207
Grace Cathedral **84**, 212, 287
Graham, Bill 92
Grant Avenue **74**, 159
Grateful Dead 15, 92, 94

Gray Whale Cove 269
Great American Music Hall 67, 209, **216**
Great Nave 24
Green Apple Books 164, **166**
Green Party 19
Grogan, Emmet 28
Grotto, the **28**, 29, 70
Grove Street 22
Guadalupe-Hidalgo Treaty 7
Gump's 160
gyms 238

Haas, William 22, **97**
Haas-Lilienthal House 22, 96, **97**
Haight-Ashbury 21, 22, 15, **91-95**
  bars 148, **154-156**
  cafés 146
  clubs 222-223
  jazz & blues 212-213
  literary scene 28
  restaurants 135-136
  rock, pop & hip hop 218
  shopping 160
  where to stay 49
Haight Street 160
Haight Street Fair 189
hair salons 181
Half Dome 266
Half Moon Bay 267-269
Hall, William Hammon 10, 110
Hallidie, Andrew 58
Halloween **192**, *194*, 225
Hammett, Dashiell 27, 57
handbag shops 175
Harbin Hot Springs 258
Harding, George F 48
Hardly Strictly Bluegrass Festival 192
Harold and Maude 105
Harte, Bret 9, 26
Harvey Milk Plaza 90
Hass, Robert 207
Hayes Street 95, 160, **167**
Hayes Valley **91-95**, 160, 163
  bars 154-156
  cafés 146
  clubs 222-223
  jazz & blues 212-213
  restaurants 135-136
  rock, pop & hip hop 218
health & beauty shops 180
health & medical resources 282
Hearst Castle 23
Hearst, Patty 15
Hearst, William Randolph 23
Heartbreaking Work of Staggering Genius, A 29
helplines 282
Henry Cowell Redwoods State Park 270
'Herb Caen Way' 63
Herbst Theatre 23, 68, 210, **244**
Herzog & de Meuron 18, 24
Hess Collection 261
Highway 1 250, 251, 267
hiking 238
  see also walks
Hindu Vedanta Society 22
hip hop 213-218
Hippie Hill 108
hippies 15, 91
Hirohito, Emperor 48
history **6-16**
HIV 16, 282
Holiday Lighting Festivities 194
holidays, public 291
Hollis, Doug 64
Holocaust Memorial 207
Holographic Museum and Camera Obscura **107**, 196
homelessness 16
Hongisto, Sheriff Richard 12
Hopkins, Mark 10, 22, 84
horseracing 236
horse-riding 238
hospitals 282

hostels *see* accommodation
Hotaling Street 62
hotels *see* accommodation
Hounds, the 9
House of Representatives Un-American Activities Committee (HUAC) 15
housing 20
Howl **27**, 28, **97**
Hufnagel, Keith 'Huff' 170
Hulk, The 199
Human Be-in 15, 94
Huntington, Collis P 10, 22, 84
Huntington Park 84
Hutton, Bobby 15
Hyde Street Pier 80, **81**, 81

ice hockey 236
ID 283
  student 288
immigration 283
Ina Coolbrith Park 82
Indian Springs Spa 258
Industrial Light & Magic (ILM) 199
information *see* tickets & information
in-line skating 238
Innercity-Home **207**, *207*
insurance 283
International Film Festival 199
International Hotel *see* I-Hotel
International Museum of Gay and Lesbian History 225
International Women's Museum 25
internet 20, 283
Introductions and Summer Art walk 204
Inverness 255
Irving Street 110
Italianate houses 22
Italians in San Francisco 10, 77

Jack London Museum 27, **257**
Jack London Square 111
Jack London State Historic Park 27, **257**
Jacks Peak Regional Park 271
Jackson Square Historical District 21, **61**, 163
Jackson Street 62
James C Hormel Gay & Lesbian Center **68**, 225
James V Fitzgerald Marine Reserve 269
Japan Center 95, **160**
Japanese American Community Center 95
Japanese in San Francisco 92
Japanese Tea Garden 108, 110
Japantown 92, **95**
jazz festivals *see* Fillmore Street Jazz Festival *and* San Francisco Jazz Festival
jazz music 78, **212-213**
Jefferson Airplane 15, 94
Jefferson Street 80
Jenkins, John 9
Jeremiah O'Brien Liberty Ship 196
jewellery shops 176
Jewish Film Festival 203
Jewish Holocaust Memorial 105
Jewish Museum of San Francisco 18, 24, **64**
  see also Judah L Magnes Museum
Jews in San Francisco 92
John McLaren Rhododendron Grove 108
Jolson, Al 48
Jones, Jim 92
Joplin, Janis 15, 94

JP Morgan Chase Building 25
Judah L Magnes Museum 64, **113**
Justin Herman Plaza 63

kayaking 240
Kearny Street Workshop 29
Kelham, George 24
Kenwood Winery 257
Kerouac, Jack 14, 15, 26, 27, 28, 78, 83, 97
Kesey, Ken 28
Kilgallen, Margaret 207
Kimber Group 19
King Jr, Martin Luther 70
Kong Chow Temple 74
Kos, Paul 207
Kronos Quartet 210

Labaudt, Lucien 105
Lafayette Park 96
Laguna Street 160
Lake Merced 110, 234
Lake Tahoe 263-265, *263*
Lamantia, Philip 97
Lamplighters Musical Theater 210
Lancaster, Burt 82
Land's End 105
Land's End Beach 106
Larkspur 253
Latinos in San Francisco 85
launderettes 182
Lawrence Hall of Science 113, **198**
leather goods & luggage 176
Leavenworth Federal Penitentiary 82
Lee, Wah 10
left luggage 283
legal help 283
Legorreta, Ricardo 18, 24
lesbian *see* queer San Francisco
Letterman Digital Arts Center 25
Libeskind, Daniel 24
libraries **68**, 69, 196, 281, 283
Lilienthal-Pratt House 22
Lily Pond 108
Lincoln Park 207
lingerie shops 173
Lisick, Beth 29
literary San Francisco **26-30**
Little Chile 9
Little House on the Prairie 82
Lloyd Wright, Frank 57
Lombard Street 82
London, Jack 26, 257
longshoremen's strike of 1934 13
Looff, Charles 70
Loma Prieta earthquake 16, 63, 95, 98
lost property 283
Lotta's Fountain 61
Louise M Davies Symphony Hall 68, **210-211**
Lower Haight 92
Lucas, George 25, 102, 199

Mabuhay Gardens 79
Mackay, John 10
Macmurtrie, Chico 70
Macondray Lane 29, **84**
Macy's 160
MadCat Women's International Film Festival 203
magazines 284
Maiden Lane 57
Main Library 23, **68**, 196
Main Post 102
Maki, Fumihiko 72
malls 161
Maltese Falcon, The **27**, 57
Manilatown 12
Manong, the 12
Manson, Charles 94

marathon **190**, 240
Marin Civic Center 23, *252*, **253**
Marin County 251
Marin Headlands 234, 237, **251**, *251*
Marina & the waterfront 96, **98-101**
  bars 148
  walk 197
  where to stay 51-52
Marina Green 98
Marine Mammal Center **198**, **251**
Market Street 207
markets 17, 65, 163
Mark Hopkins Inter-Continental Hotel 11, 22, **47**
Marshall, James 9
Marshall Plaza 24
Martini, invention of the 157
Martin Luther King Jr Birthday Celebration 194
Matrix, The 199
Mattachine Society 15
Maupin, Armistead **29**, 78, 84
Mavericks Beach 269
Mayback, Bernard 23, 100
Mayne, Thom 25
McClure, Michael 97
McGee, Barry 207
McLaren, John 105, 108, 110
McLaren Lodge 108, **110**
McSweeney's 29
Mechanics' Institute 57, **281**
media 284
Mendoza, Antonio de 7
Merced River 266
Merchant's Exchange 61
message services 280
Metreon Center 24, 70, **161**
Mexican-American War 7
Mexican Museum 18, 24, **70**
Mexicans in California 7
Milk, Harvey **15-16**, 29, 68, 90
Mill Valley 251, **253**
Mill Valley Film Festival & Videofest **203**, 253
Miller, Henry 28
Miller, Joaquin 28
Mills College 288
mime 247
Mime Troupe *see* San Francisco Mime Troupe
Mineta San Jose International Airport (SJC) 274
Misión San Francisco de Asis 7, **88**
Mission Adobe, Santa Cruz 269
Mission Bay 17
Mission Bay Residential Block 25
Mission Creek *17*
Mission Cultural Center 87
Mission Dolores 7, 21, 86, **88**
Mission Street **85**, 87
Mission, the 17, 21, **85-90**
  arts & entertainment, queer 231
  bars 148, **153-154**
  bars, queer 228-229
  cafés 145-146
  clubs 222
  jazz & blues 212
  restaurants 132-135
  rock, pop & hip hop 218
  shopping 159, 162
  walk 86
  where to stay 49
Mission Trail Park 271
Mist Trail 266
Mitchell, Artie and Jim 67
Mitchell Brothers O'Farrell Theatre 67
Miwok, the 6, 7
mobile phones 289
Modern Times Bookstore 86, 164, *165*, **166**
Moe's 113, 164, **166**
money 286
Monopoly on the Park, San Jose 267

Index

Monroe, Marilyn 68, 79
Montalvo, Garcia Ordóñez de 11
Monterey 7, 267, **270-272**
Monterey Bay Aquarium 271
Monterey Bay Blues Festival 270
Monterey Jazz Festival 270
Monterey State Historic Park 271
Montez, Lola 10
Montgomery, John B 74
Moon, Sunhee 170
Moore, Henry 207
Morgan, Julia 23, 61, 77
Morning Sun Trail 238
Morrow, Irwin F 101
Moscone Convention Center 24, **70**
Moscone, George 15, 70
Moscone West 24
Mount Davidson 110
Mount Diablo 234
Mount Livermore 252
Mount Tamalpais State Park 253
Mountain Lake Park 102
Muir Woods National Monument 254
Mulford, Prentice 28
Muni metro streetcars 276
Municipal Pier 80
murals 86, 87, **88**
Musée Mécanique **81**, 107, 196
Museo ItaloAmericano 100
Museum of the African Diaspora 18, **70**
Museum of the City of San Francisco 69
Museum of Colonial and Federal Decorative Arts 98
Museum of Craft Folk Art 100
Museum of the Money of the American West 61
museums & galleries in San Francisco
  art & design: Asian Art Museum 23, 24, 25, 56, **68**; Cartoon Art Museum 71; Design Museum 24; Cultural Heritage Museum 61, **63**; SFMOMA 13, 16, 24, 56, 70, *71*, **72**
  children: Bay Area Discovery Museum 196; Exploratorium 98, **196**, 197; Randall Museum 90, **195**; Zeum *195*, **196**, 198
  cable cars: Cable Car Museum 59, **84**, 196
  decorative arts & crafts: Museum of Colonial and Federal Decorative Arts 98; Museum of Craft Folk Art 100
  ethnic communities: African-American Historical and Cultural Society Museum 100; Chinese American National Museum & Learning Center 77; Mexican Museum 18, 24, **70**; Museo ItaloAmericano 100; Museum of the African Diaspora 18, **70**
  gay history: International Museum of Gay and Lesbian History 225
  history: California Historical Society 71; Fort Mason 98, **100**; Museum of the City of San Francisco 69; Museum of the Money of the American West 61; Presidio Museum 102; Society of California Pioneers Seymour Pioneer Museum 71, **72**; Wells Fargo History Museum 61, **63**
  Judaism: Jewish Museum of San Francisco 18, 24, **64**; Judas L Magnes Museum 64

maritime: National Maritime Museum **81**, 196; San Francisco Maritime National Historical Park Museum Building 80, **81**
miscellaneous: Musée Mécanique **81**, 107, 196; Ripley's Believe It Or Not! Museum 80; Wax Museum 80
performing arts: San Francisco Performing Arts Library & Museum 70
science: California Academy of Sciences 195; Chabot Space & Science Museum 196-198; Holographic Museum and Camera Obscura **107**, 196; Lawrence Hall of Science 198
women: International Women's Museum 25
music 209-218
  by San Francisco artists 293
  church venues 212
  classical & opera 210-212
  jazz & blues 212-213
  live 209
  rock, pop & hip hop 213-218
  shops 182
musical instrument and sheet music shops 185
Mystery Spot 269

Nagano, Ken 211
Napa 260-262
Napa Valley 256, **260-262**
National AIDS Memorial Grove 108
National Japanese American Historical Society 95
National Maritime Museum **81**, 196
navigation, street 54
neighbourhoods 47
Neiman Marcus 161
New Century Chamber Orchestra 210
New College of California 29, **86**
New Helvetia 9
Newmark, Craig 20, **62**, *62*
Newsom, Gavin 19
newspapers 284
Newton, Huey 15
New Year's Eve 194
Niebaum-Coppola Winery 260
nightlife **219-223**
  queer 230
Nihonmachi Street Fair 95
Nob Hill 10, **83-84**
  restaurants 128-131
  where to stay 45-49
Noe Valley 85, **90**
  restaurants 135
Nordstrom 161
North Beach **73-80**, 159
  bars 148, **152-153**
  cafés 55, **144-145**
  clubs 222
  jazz & blues 212
  restaurants 126-128
  rock, pop & hip hop 217-218
  walk 78
  where to stay 42-44
North Beach Festival 189
Northstar 264
'Nova Albion' 7
Nutcracker, The 194

Oakland Athletics **234**, 235
Oakland East Bay Symphony 211
Oakland International Airport 274
Oakland Museum of California 111, **112**
Oakland Raiders 234, **236**
Oakland Zoo 111, **198**
O'Brien, William 10

Ocean Beach **103**, 105, 106, 109, 110, 196
Octagon House 23, 96, **98**
O'Doul, 'Lefty' 72
office services 280
Officers' Club, the Presidio 21
Ohlone, the 6, 15
Old Faithful geyser 259
Old First Presbyterian Church 212
Old St Mary's Cathedral 74, **77**, 287
Oldenburg, Claes 63, 207
On The Road 27
opera 210-212
Opera House *see* War Memorial Opera House
Opera Plaza 68
opticians 185
Orlovsky, Peter 27
Orpheum 244-245
Osbourne, Fanny 26
Osento **182**, 225
Our Lady of Guadalupe **190**, *190*

Pac Bell Park *see* SBC Park
Pacific Coast Stock Exchange 23, 61, **62**
Pacific Film Archive 113, **200-201**
Pacific Grove 272
Pacific Grove Museum of Natural History 272
Pacific Heights **96-103**
  bars 156-157
  cafés 146-147
  restaurants 136-139
  shopping 160
  where to stay 50-51
Pacific Heights Walking Tour 55
Pacific Heritage Museum 61, **63**
Pacific Mail Steamship Company Warehouse 25
'Painted Ladies' 21
Palace Hotel 10, 22, **41-42**, 48, 61
Palace of Fine Arts 23, 98, **100**, 197
Palo Alto 267
Panama-Pacific Exposition of 1915 **13**, 23, 98
Panhandle 110
Panoramic Highway 254
paragliding 240
Parisian Beaux Arts style 23
parking 20, **277**
parks & gardens
  Alta Plaza Park 96
  Aquatic Park 80
  Crissy Field *96*, **98**, 197, *239*, 240
  Esplanade Gardens 24, **70**
  Golden Gate Park 22, 92, 104, **107-110**, *107*, 198, 234, 240
  Huntington Park 84
  Ina Coolbrith Park 82
  Lafayette Park 96
  Lincoln Park 207
  Marina Green 98
  Mission Dolores 86, **88**
  Mountain Lake Park 102
  Redwood Park 61
  Sutro Heights Park 105
  Yerba Buena Gardens **70**, 198
Parkway Theater 111, **201**
passenger vans
  to & from the airport 275
passports 275
Payer, Jeanine 171
Peace Pagoda 95
Pelli, Cesar 25
Pereira, Willaim 63
Pescadero 267
pet shops 185
Petrified Forest 259
Pflueger, Timothy L 56, 62, 90, 231
pharmacies 182
Phelan Building 57
Phelan, James 57

Philharmonia Baroque 210
Phillips, April 56
Philo TV 64
photography 185
  galleries 208
Piano, Renzo 25
Pier 39 80
PlumpJack 260
Pocket Opera 210
poetry 29, 292
Point Lobos State Reserve 271
Point Pinos Light Station 272
Point Reyes Lighthouse 255
Point Reyes National Seashore 254, **255**
police stations 286
politics 19
Polk Gulch 84
  cafés 144-145
  restaurants 128-131
Polk Street 163
Polk, Willis 23, 84, 105
pool 240
pop 213-218
Portals of the Past 109
Pórtola, Gaspar de 7
Portsmouth Square 21, **74**
Portuguese in California 7
postal services 286
'Postcard Row' 22, 93
Potrero Hill **88-89**
Powell Street 57
Prayer Book Cross 109
Precita Eyes Mural Arts & Visitors Center 87, **88**
prehistoric history 6
Presidio, the 7, 14, 16, 96, **101**
Presidio Heights 21
Presidio Museum 102
Pride 90, **189**, 225
prison *see* Alcatraz
public holidays 291
public transport 275-277
Purcell, Charles H 64

Quarry Beach 252
Queen Anne houses 22
Queen Elizabeth I 6, 112
Queen Elizabeth II 48
Queen Wilhelmina's Tulip Gardens 109
queer San Francisco 15-16, 84, 89-90, **224-233**
  arts & entertainment 230-231
  bars 227-230
  resources 287
  restaurants & cafés 231-233
  sport & fitness 233
  where to stay 225-227

radio 285
rafting 266
Raiders *see* Oakland Raiders
Railroad Grade 237
railways 10
Rainbow Falls 109
Ralston, William 10, 22, 48
Randall Museum 90, **195**
Rasselas Jazz **213**, 215
Reclining Figure in Four Pieces 207
record shops 184
Red Harvest 27
Redwood Park 61
reference, further 292-293
Refregier, Anton 23, 64
Reggae in the Park 192
religion 287
religious buildings *see* churches & other religious buildings
repair, shoe 176
Republic of California 7, 9, 256
RESFEST 201
resources A-Z 280-291
restaurants 17, **116-140**

best, the 118
budget 132-133
burritos 125
by cuisine
 American 118-119, 120,
  123-124, 126, 128,
  132-134, 135-138,
  140
 Asian 119, 120-123,
  124-125, 126-127,
  128-131, 134, 135,
  136, 138, 140
 Cuban 131
 European 116-118, 119-120,
  123, 125-126, 127-128,
  131, 134, 136, 138-139,
  140
 Latin American 134-135, 139
 seafood 119, 128, 131
 vegetarian 120, 139
 queer 231-233
restrooms 290
Rexroth, Kenneth 27, 79, 97
Richardson, Captain William 7
Richmond **104-110**
 bars 157-158
 cafés 147
 restaurants 140
 where to stay 52
Rigo *see* Gouvela, Richardo
Rigo, Pascal 121
Rincon Annex Post Office
 Building 23
Rincon Center 23, 63, **64**
Ringolevio 28
Ripley's Believe It Or Not!
 Museum 80
Rivera, Diego 23, 61, 80, 82, 83, 87
Roach, Mary 28
Robert Louis Stevenson Museum,
 St Helena 259
Robert Louis Stevenson State
 Park 26, **259**
Robert and Margrit Mondavi
 Center for Performing Arts 211
rock climbing *see* climbing
rock music 213-218
Rockaway Beach 269
Rodin Sculpture Garden, Palo
 Alto 267
Rolling Stone 15
Rolling Stones 15
Rolph, 'Sunny Jim' 23
Rosicrucian Egyptian Museum,
 San Jose 267
rowing 240
running 189, 240
Run to the Far Side 194
Russian Hill 29, **82-83**
 restaurants 128-131
Rustic Bridge 109

Sacramento Street 97
Safari West Wildlife Preserve and
 Tent Camp 259
safety 287
Sai Gai Yat Bo Company 74
sailing 240
St Boniface Catholic Church 67,
 68, 287
St Helena 26
St Mary's Cathedral 23, **95**, 212,
 287
St Maytag *see* St Mary's
 Cathedral
St Patrick's **71**, 212
St Patrick's Day Parade 188
St Regis Museum Tower 70
St Stupid's Day Parade 188
sake bars 150
Saks Fifth Avenue 161
sales tax 160
San Andreas Fault 11, 16
San Francisco Airport (SFO) 274
San Francisco Art Commission
 Gallery 68, **205**

San Francisco Art Institute 82,
 83, 203, 204, 288
San Francisco Arts Commission
 207
San Francisco Ballet 244, *246*, **248**
San Francisco Blues 27
San Francisco Centre 18, 57, **163**
San Francisco Chronicle 284
San Francisco Cinematheque 200
San Francisco Conservatory of
 Flowers 25, *104*, **108**
San Francisco Conservatory of
 Music 288
San Francisco Film Commission
 203
San Francisco 49ers 9, 234, **236**
San Francisco Giants 20, 234,
 235, **236**
San Francisco International Art
 Exposition 192
San Francisco International Asian
 American Film Festival 203
San Francisco International Film
 Festival 188, **203**
San Francisco International
 Lesbian & Gay Film Festival
 203
San Francisco Jazz Festival 192
San Francisco Main Library 68, **69**
San Francisco Marathon **190**, 240
San Francisco Maritime National
 Historical Park Museum
 Building 80, **81**
San Francisco Mime Troupe
 94, 191, **247**
San Francisco National Cemetery
 102
San Francisco Opera 210
San Francisco Peninsula 102
San Francisco Performing Arts
 Library & Museum 70
San Francisco Poetry Center 29
'San Francisco Poetry
 Renaissance' 27
San Francisco Reservations 33
San Francisco Seaplane Tours 55
San Francisco Silent Film Festival
 203
San Francisco State University
 203, 204, 288, **289**
San Francisco Symphony 210
San Francisco Today **17-20**
San Francisco Tribal, Folk &
 Textile Arts Show 194
San Francisco Writers' Guild
 28, 29
San Francisco Zoo 110, **195**
San Francisco-Oakland Bay
 Bridge *see* Bay Bridge
San Gregorio State Beach **267**, 269
San Jose 267
San Jose Airport 274
San Jose Earthquakes 234, **237**
San Jose Sharks 234, 236, **237**
San Pedro Point 269
San Quentin Prison 253
San Rafael 23
Sand Harbour 263
Santa Cruz 267, **269-270**
Santa Cruz Beach Boardwalk 269
Santa Cruz Mission State Historic
 Park 269
Santa Cruz Museum of Natural
 History 269
Sather Tower 112
saunas 182
Sausalito 252-253
Savio, Mario 15
Sawyer, Tom 61
SBC Park 16, 20, 72, **234**
Scharffen Berger 113
Schmitz, Mayor Eugene 12
Schrager, Ian 25
Schramsberg 261
Schwarzenegger, Arnold 19
Scofidio, Ricardo 24
scuba diving 241
Sea Wolf, The 27
Seale, Bobby 15

seaplane *see* San Francisco
 Seaplane Tours
second-hand
 bookshops 27
 clothes shops 175
security 287
Segal, George 105, 207
Serra, Father Junipero 7
services *see* shops & services
Seventeen-Mile Drive 272
Sex Pistols 92
sex shops 181
SF Bay Model Visitor Center 252
SFMOMA (San Francisco
 Museum of Modern Art) 13, 16,
 24, 55, 56, 70, 71, **72**
Shakespeare Festival 191
sharks 241
Sharks *see* San Jose Sharks
Sharon Meadow 108
Sharpsteen Museum, Calistoga
 259
Shilts, Randy 16, 29
shoe repair 176
shoe shops 176
shopping centres 161
shops & services 18, **159-186**
 areas 159-160
 best, the 159
Shuler, Dustin 207
Sia, Beau 29
sidewalk sales 163
sightseeing **53-114**
 best, the 55
Silicon Valley 16, **267-269**
Silver Rush, the 10
Silverado Squatters, The 26
Silverado Trail 260
Simon, Cathy 23
Sisters of Perpetual Indulgence
 226-227
Six Gallery reading 27, 28, **97**
16th Street 86
skateboarding 241
skating, in-line 240
skiing **242, 264**
slams, poetry 29
Small Traffic Press 29
Smith, Jedediah 7
smoking 287
Snicket, Lemony 29
snowboarding 242
Snyder, Gary 97
soccer 237
Society for Individual Rights 15
Society of California Pioneers
 Seymour Pioneer Museum
 71, **72**
SoMa 17, 24, 56, **56-72**
 art 207
 bars 149-152, 229
 cafés 143-144
 classical music & opera
  210-211
 clubs 221-222, 230
 jazz & blues 212
 restaurants 123-126
 where to stay 41-42
SoMarts Gallery **205**, 208
Sonoma 7-8, **256-260**, 257
Sonoma County 251
Sonoma County Wineries
 Association 256
Sonoma Mission 256
Sonoma Mission Inn & Spa 258
Sonoma State Historic Park 256
Sonoma Train Town 256
Sonoma Valley **256-260**
South Beach 72
South of Market Cultural Center
 29
South of Market *see* SoMa
South Park 72
Spade, Sam 27, 57
Spanish in California 6-7
spas 182, 258
'Specific Whites' 96
Spicer, Jack 28
Spider Pelt 207

Spike & Mike's Festival of
 Animation 203
Spinnaker Sailing (tours) 55
sport & fitness **234-243**
 queer 233
 shops 186
Spreckels, Adolph 22
Spreckels, Alma 107
Spreckels Lake 109
Spreckels Mansion 22, **96**
Sproul Plaza 113
Squaw Valley 264
Stackpole, Ralph 62, 63
stairways 84
Stanford, Leland 10, 22, 84
Stanford University 267, **288**
Stanley, Owsley 15
Star Wash **182**, 202
Starck, Philippe 25
Stateline 263
Steamer Lane 269
Steel, Danielle 22, 96
Stegner, Wallace 28
Stein, Gertrude 27, *29*
Steinbeck, John 15, 271
Steiner Street 22
Sterling Vineyards 261
Stern Grove 110
Stern Grove Festival 110, **191**
Stevenson, Robert Louis 9, **26**,
 57, 74, 259, 270
Stick-Eastlake houses 22
'Sticks' *see* Stick-Eastlake houses
Stinson Beach 254
Stockton Street 74
Stone, Robert 28
Storrs Winery 270
Strauss, Joseph 72, 101
Strauss, Levi 10
street numbering 54
Strike of 1934, General 13
Stroud, Robert 82
Strybing Arboretum & Botanical
 Gardens 108
study 287-288
Subterraneans, The 27
Sugar Bowl 264
Sugar Pine Point State Park 263
Sullivan, Fire Chief Dennis 12
Summer of Love *14*, 15, 94
Summer Solstice 189
Sun Mountain 10
Sunset 104, **104-110**
 bars 157-158
 cafés 147
 restaurants 140
surfing **242**, 269
Surfing Museum, Santa Cruz 269
Sutro, Adolph 10, 22, 105
Sutro Baths 22, 105, 106
Sutro Heights Park 105
Sutter, John 9
swimming 242
 see also beaches
Sydney Town 9
Symbionese Liberation Army 15

Tahoe Rim Trail 263
Tahoe *see* Lake Tahoe
Tales of the City 29, 84
taquerias 85
tattoos & body piercing 182
tax 289
 sales 160
taxis **277**
 to & from the airport 274
tea & coffee shops 179
Telegraph Avenue 164, **113**
Telegraph Hill 79
telephones 289
television 284
Tenderloin, the 56, **67**
 restaurants 119-120
 where to stay 38-41
tennis 243
Tet Festival 194
theatre **244-248**

Thomas, Dylan 78
thrift stores 162-163
Tiburon 251, **252-253**
tickets & information
  art 205
  clubs 219
  film 199
  music 209
  public transport 275
  queer 225
  sport 234
  theatre & dance 244
  tourist 290
Tien Hau Temple 77
Tilden Regional Park 113
time 289
Tioga Pass 266
tipping 290
tobacconists 186
toilets 290
Toklas, Alice B 27
Tomales Bay **254**, *254*, 255
topless clubs 76
tourism 18
tourist information 290
tours **54-55**
  Barbary Coast Trail 55
  Beats 28
  Black Panther 111
  Chinatown 55
  Cruisin' the Castro 55
  Dashiell Hammett 55
  Fire Engine **54**, 196
  Flower Power 55
  49-Mile Scenic Drive 54
  Pacific Heights (architecture) 55
  San Francisco Seaplane 55
  Spinnaker Sailing 55
Towering Inferno, The 61
toy shops 186
Toy Story 199
traffic 20
trains 276
Transamerica Pyramid 23, 61, **63**
Treasure Island 14, 64
trips out of town **250-272**
Trollope, Anthony 9
Truckee 264
Truman, Harry 74
Twain, Mark 9, 26, 61
24th Street 88, **90**
Twin Peaks 90

Union Square 25, **56-57**, 159
  clubs 219-221
  restaurants 116-118
  where to stay 37
Union Street **98**, 160
United Nations Charter 14
United Nations Plaza 68
University of California Berkeley 288
University of California San Francisco 288
Upper Fillmore Street 97
USS *Pampanito* 80, **81**
USS *Portsmouth* 74

Vaillancourt, Armand 63
Valencia Street **85**, 86
Vallejo, General Mariano G 256
Vallejo Street Stairway 82
Valley of the Moon 27
Van Bruggen, Coosje 63
Vedanta Temple 22, **98**
vehicle hire 279
Vertigo 199
Vesuvio 28
Veterans' Memorial Building 68
Viansa Winery and Italian Marketplace 257
Victorian terraces 21-22
Vida, Vendela 28
Vietnam War 15
vineyards 270

  see also Wine Country
vintage clothes shops 175
visas **275**, **291**
  work 288
Visitor Information Center 57, **291**
Vista Point 251
Visual Aid 208
ViV and a Movie 202
volleyball 243

W

walking **55**, **279**
walks
  Berkeley 112
  Golden Gate Park 108
  Introductions and Summer Art Walk 204
  Marina, the 197
  Mission, the 86
  murals 88
  North Beach 78
  organised and self-guided 55
  stairways 84
War Memorial Opera House 13, 23, 68, 209, **210**, **211**
Warriors *see* Golden State Warriors
Washington Square 78
waterfront, the *see* Marina & the waterfront
Watters, Ethan 28
Wattis Institute for Contemporary Arts 204
Wave Organ 98, 197
Waverly Place 77
Wax Museum 80
weather 290-291
websites about San Francisco 293
Wehrle, John 72
Wells Fargo History Museum 61, **63**
Wenner, Jann 15
Werepad 202
Westerfield House 93
Western Addition, the **91-95**
  bars 154-156
  cafés 146
  clubs 222-223
  jazz & blues 212-213
  restaurants 135-136
  rock, pop & hip hop 218
  where to stay 49-50
Westin St Francis Hotel 48, **57**, 198
whale watching 243
Whalen, Philip 97
Whipple, Diane 19
White, Dan **15-16**, 68
White Night Riot 16
Wi-Fi 285
Wilde, Oscar 9
Wilder, Laura Ingalls 82
Willis Polk substation 18, 24, **64**
windsurfing 243
Wine Country **256-262**
Wine Exchange of Sonoma 257
wineries 270
  see also Wine Country
wines, Californian 260
Winterland 92
Wolf House 27, **257**
Wolfe, Tom 28
Women's Building, The 86, **87**, **88**, 225
work permits 291
Works Progress Administration (WPA) 23
World War II 14
Wormser-Coleman House 22
Wrecker, The 26
Wright, Frank Lloyd 23

Y

Yerba Buena 6, 7, 9, 17, 18
Yerba Buena Center for the Arts 16, 70, **72**, 200, **247**

Yerba Buena Gardens **70**, 198
Yerba Buena Performing Arts Theater 210, **211**, *211*
Ying On Labor Association 74
yoga 234, **243**
Yosemite National Park 263, **265-266**, *265*
Yosemite Point 266
Yosemite Valley 266
Yoshi's at Jack London Square 111, 209, **213**, *213*, 215
Young, Henry 82
YouthSpeaks 29

Z

Zephyr Cove 263
Zeum 16, 70, *195*, **196**, 198
Zoetrope: All-Story Magazine 29
zoos
  Oakland 111, **198**
  San Francisco 195

Restaurants

A Sabella's 118, **128**
Absinthe 95, **136**
Acme Chop House 123-124
Acquerello 131
Alfred's Steak House 118, **126**
Alice's 135
Alioto's 128
Andalu 121, **134**
Aqua 119
Asia de Cuba *116*, 118, **119**
Asia SF 233
Azie 124
Bacar 124
Baker Street Bistro 138-139
Barney's 132
Bay Wolf 137
Beach Chalet **105**, 109, 140
Betelnut 118
Blue 133, **231**
Blue Mermaid 128
Boulevard 120
Butterfly Embarcadero 118, **120**
Caesar's 78
Catch 231-232
César 113
Chapeau! **140**, 142
Charm, Le 125
Cheese Board Pizza 113
Chez Nous 121, **139**
Chez Panisse **137**, 113
Chow 132, **135**, **232**
Cliff House Bar & Restaurant 105, **107**
Cortez Restaurant & Bar **119**, 121
Da Flora 233
Delfina 86, **132**
Dining Room, The 131
Dol Ho's 126
Ebisu 110, 118, **140**
Elite Café **136**, *138*, 142
Enrico's 28
Eos Restaurant 136
Farallon 116
Farolito, El 118, **134**
Fifth Floor 116-118
Firecracker 134
Firefly 135
500 Jackson 118
Fleur de Lys 120
Florio 139
Folie, La 131
Foreign Cinema **134**, 142, 202
French Laundry 261
Fresca 139
Fringale 125
Galette 121, **146**
Gary Danko 118, **128**, *129*
Globe Restaurant 118, **120**
Goat Hill Pizza 89
Good Luck Dim Sum 105
Greens 100, 118, **139**
Habana 131

Harbor Village 119
Harris' 118, **138**
Hay Street Grill 95
Helmand, The 118, **128**
Hermanos, Los 125, **139**
House 126-127
House of Nanking 126
Indigo 123
Jardinière 123
John's Grill 57
Kabuto 118, **140**
Khan Toke 140
Kokkari Estiatorio 119
Lark Creek Inn 137
Le Petit Robert 121
Loft 11 124-125
LuLu 125
Luna Park 85, **132-133**
Masa's 118
Mayflower 140
Mecca 135
Mediterranee 233
Memphis Minnie's BBQ 153
Mifune 136
Millenium 120
Moose's **126**, 142
Nuevo Frutilandia, El 134
Oliveto 137
One Market 120
Ozumo 118, **120**, 150
Paragon 124
Park Chow 110, **132**, *132*
Pauline's Pizza 133
Pesce 131
PJ's Oyster Bed 140
Plouf 119
PlumpJack Café 138
Pluto's 132, *133*
Postrio 116
Public, The 124
Q 133, **140**
R&G Lounge 126
Red's Java House 63
Restaurant Isa 139
Rivoli 137
RNM 121, **135-136**
Sam's Grill 118-119
Samovar 233
Sanppo 136
Scala's Bistro 118
Seoul Garden 136
Slanted Door 118, **123**
Slow Club 89, **134**, 132
Sodini's 127, *127*
Soluna 123
Spenger's 113
Suppenküche 95, **136**
Sushi Groove 118, **128-130**, 150
Swan Oyster Depot 118, **131**
Tablespoon 128
Taqueria, La 87, **135**
Taqueria Cancun 118, **135**
Taqueria La Cumbre 135
Thanh Long 110
Thep Phantom 118, **136**
Thirsty Bear Brewing Company 125
Ti Couz Creperie 134
Tommaso's Ristorante Italiano 127
Ton Kiang 140
Toro Taqueria, El 135
Town Hall Restaurant 124
Truly Mediterranean 88, **133**, **146**
2223 Restaurant & Bar 231
21st Amendment 124
Universal Café 89, **134**, 142
US Restaurant 127
Vivande Porta Via 97
Washington Square Bar & Grill 126
XYZ 125-126
Yank Sing 63, 118, **123**
Yuet Lee 126
Zante's Indian Cuisine & Pizza 89
Zarzuela 131
Zuni Café 95, **123**

Cafés

Arabi 141
Atlas Cafe 145
Bagdad Café 231
Blue Danube Coffee House 141, **147**
Bob's Donut Shop 144
Bombay Ice Creamery 145, **178**
Boudin Sourdough Bakery & Cafe 145
Boulange de Polk, La 144
Brain Wash Cafe & Laundromat 143
Butler & the Chef, The 143
Cafe Abir 92, 141, **146**
Café Claude 141
Cafe Commons 145
Café Niebaum-Coppola 29, **78**
Cafe de la Presse 141
Cafe de Stijl 141
Caffe Centro 143-144
Caffe Puccini 144
Caffe Roma 79
Caffe Trieste 79, **145**
Cavern on the Green 197
Cheesecake Factory 57, **141**
Chloe's Cafe 145
Citizen Cake 146
Cold Stone Creamery 113
Cup A Joe 233
Dottie's True Blue Cafe 142
Ella's 142, **146**
Firewood Café 232-233
French Hotel Café 113
Galette 146-147
Grind Café 146
Grove 98, **147**, *147*
Home 142
Imperial Tea Court 141, **144**
Japanese Tea Garden 108
Java Beach Cafe 110, **147**, 240
Just For You Bakery & Cafe 146

Kate's Kitchen 142, **146**
Kuleto's Cafe 142
Liberty Café 89
Louis 105
Lovejoy's Antiques & Tearoom 90, **146**
Mabel's Just for You Cafe 233
Mama's on Washington Square 142, **145**
Mario's Bohemian Cigar Store 141, *144*, **145**
Miss Millie's 90, 142, **146**
Mocca Café 57
Peet's 113
Perry's **142**, 157
Pier 23 143
Powell's Place 95
Primo Patio Cafe 143
Saigon Sandwich Cafe 142
Steps of Rome 145
Tart to Tart 147
Town's End Restaurant & Bakery 144
Truly Mediterranean 88, **133**, **146**
Zazie 92, 141, **143**, *143*
Zero Degrees 145

Bars

Albatross Pub 158
Alley, The 158
An Bodhrán 154
Argus Lounge, The 153
Aub Zam Zam 92, **156**
Aunt Charlie's Lounge 229
Badlands 227
Bar on Castro 227-228
Beach Chalet 105, 157
Beauty Bar San Francisco 85, **153**
Bix 72, **148**
Blondie's Bar & No Grill 157

Brennan's 113
Bubble Lounge 148
Butter 148
C Bobby's Owl Tree 149
Canvas Café Gallery 157
Capp's Corner 79
Castro Country Club 228
Cliff House **105**, 157
Club Mallard 158
Colonial, Le 150
Daddy's 228
Dalva 153
Detour 224, **228**
Doc's Clock 153
Edinburgh Castle 149
Esta Noche 229
First & Last Chance Saloon **158**, 111
Fly Bar 150
G Bar 156
Gino & Carlo's 28, **79**
Harvey's 228
Hayes & Vine 154
Heinold's First & Last Chance Saloon *see* First & Last Chance Saloon
Hobson's Choice 156
Hole in the Wall 229
Hotel Biron 154
Hotsy Totsy 158
Julip Cocktail Lounge *149*, 150
Lexington Club 229
Li Po 152
Lion Pub, The 229-230
Liverpool Lil's 157
Loading Dock 229
Lone Star Saloon 229
Lucky 13 154
Mad Dog in the Fog 156
Marlena's 229
Martuni's 157, **228**
Matrix 157
Mecca 154

Midnight Sun, The 228
Midori Mushi 150
Mix, The 228
Moby Dicks 228
Movida Lounge 150, **156**
Nickie's BBQ 92, **156**, 215, 219
Noc Noc 92, 93, **156**
North Star 79
Odeon Bar 154
Orbit Room 228
Persian Aub Zam Zam 156
Place Pigalle 156
Plough & Stars, The 157
Powerhouse 229
Ramp, The 151
Red Room 151
Redwood Room 151
Rio, El **212**, 228
Rohan 150
Rosewood 152
Ruby Room 158
Sadie's Flying Elephant 154
Sake Lab 150, **151**
Saloon 79, **212**
San Francisco Brewing Company 152
Spats 158
Spec's 78, **153**
Stud, The **229**, 230
Tonga Room 84, **153**
Top of the Mark 84, **153**
Toronado 92, **156**
Tosca Café 78, **153**, *155*
Trader Sam's 158
Treat Street Cocktails 154
Tsunami 151
Tunnel Top 152
Twin Peaks Bar **89**, 90
Vesuvio 78, **153**
W Hotel 152
Whiskey Lounge 228
Wildside West 89, **230**
Zeitgeist 154

Advertisers' Index

Please refer to the relevant sections for contact details

Time Out City Guides	IFC

In Context

Hertz	4
CityPass	4

Where to Stay

Hotel Nikko	30
Renoir Hotel	36
Lodging.com	40

Sightseeing

Golden Gate Jeep Tours	60

Restaurants

The Stinking Rose/ Calzone's/ Crab House	114
Ozumo	122

Shops & Services

Noe Valley Pet Company	174

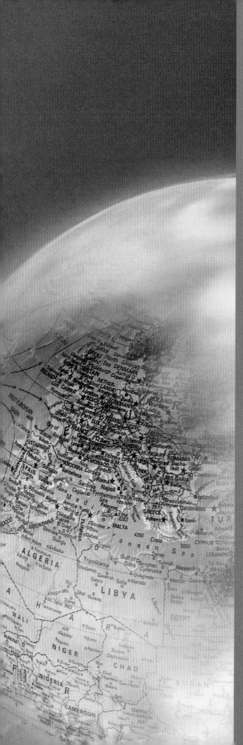

Points of interest	☐
Hospital or college	☐
Neighbourhoods	FILLMORE
Visitor Information Center	❶
Muni Metro BART station	⬤
Parks	☐
Cable car line	─ⓅⒽ─

Maps

BART & Muni Map	302
Trips Out of Town	304
City Overview	305
San Francisco by Area	306
San Francisco Street Maps	308
Street Index	316

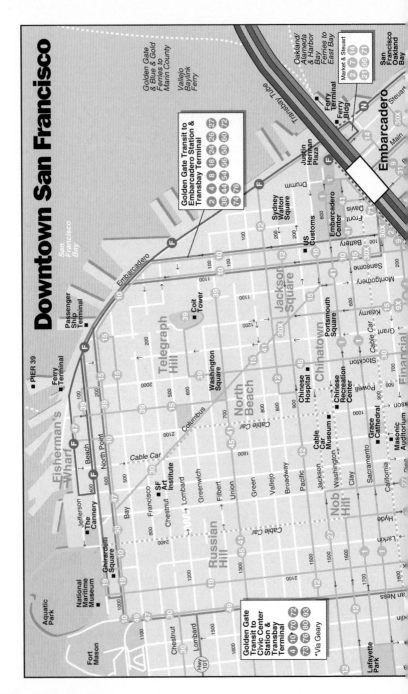

Downtown San Francisco

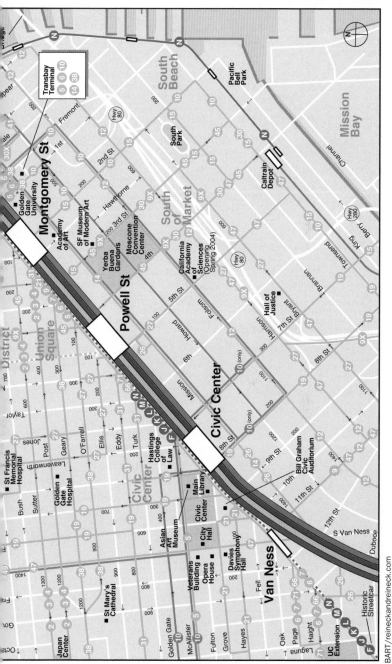

BART/reineckandreineck.com

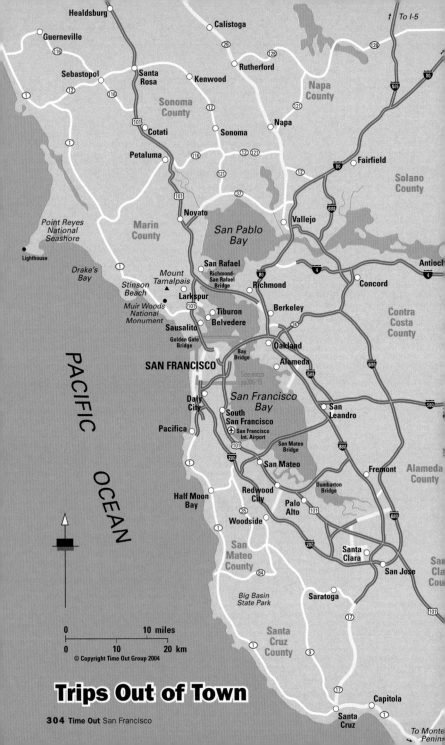

San Francisco by Area

San Francisco Bay

Crissy Field

Marina Green

Marina BOULEVARD

Palace of Fine Arts & Exploratorium

BAKER STREET

RICHARDSON AVENUE

101

MARINA

Moscone Playground

BAY STREET

DIVISADERO STREET

LOMBARD STREET

101

Cow Hollow Playground

LION STREET

COW HOLLOW

PRESIDIO

VALLEJO STREET

Presidio Golf Course

WEST PACIFIC AVENUE

PRESIDIO AVENUE

Alta Plaza Park

PACIFIC HEIGHTS

California Pacific Medical Center

PRESIDIO HEIGHTS

Mountain Lake Park

CALIFORNIA STREET

PINE STREET

BUSH STREET

CALIFORNIA STREET

ARGUELLO BOULEVARD

PARK PRESIDIO BOULEVARD

CLEMENT STREET

GEARY BOULEVARD

UCSF Medical Center

Kaiser Medical Center

GEARY EXPRESSWAY

Japan Center

GEARY BOULEVARD

RICHMOND

University of San Francisco

TURK STREET

GOLDEN GATE AVENUE

WESTERN ADDITION

BALBOA STREET

FULTON STREET

Alamo Square

Painted Ladies

MASONIC AVENUE

FULTON STREET

University of San Francisco

DIVISADERO STREET

FELL STREET

OAK STREET

FULTON STREET

St Mary's Medical Center

FELL STREET

OAK STREET

Panhandle

LOWER HAIGHT

Golden Gate Park

Sharon Meadow

STANYAN STREET

HAIGHT-ASHBURY

ASHBURY STREET

Buena Vista Park

BUENA VISTA TERR EAST

Duboce Park

DUBOCE AVENUE

UCSF Davies

Muni Metro Church S

LINCOLN WAY

Corona Heights Park

CASTRO STREET

MARKET STREET

PARNASSUS AVENUE

SUNSET

7th AVENUE

University of California San Francisco

17th STREET

Muni Metro Castro St

CASTRO

DIAMOND STREET

To Golden Gate Bridge

1

San Francisco
Bay

Aquatic
Park

JEFFERSON STREET
THE EMBARCADERO

FISHERMAN'S
WHARF

NORTH POINT STREET

BAY STREET

Russian
Hill Park

San Francisco
Art Institute

NORTH
BEACH

Lombard Street

Coit Tower

BATTERY STREET

COLUMBUS AVENUE

POWELL STREET

RUSSIAN
HILL

Washington
Square

THE EMBARCADERO

POLK STREET

LARKIN STREET

VALLEJO STREET

EMBARCADERO

BROADWAY

FRANKLIN STREET

BROADWAY

Jackson
Square

PACIFIC AVENUE

Transamerica
Pyramid

Ferry Building

JACKSON STREET

Portsmouth
Square

FINANCIAL
DISTRICT

101

POLK
GULCH

CHINATOWN

MONTGOMERY STREET

SANSOME STREET

BATTERY STREET

Muni
Metro BART
Embarcadero

STEUART STREET

VAN NESS AVENUE

NOB
HILL

Huntington
Park

KEARNY STREET

MARKET STREET

BEALE STREET

80

Lafayette
Park

St Francis Memorial
Hospital

PINE STREET

FREMONT STREET

1st STREET

Bay Bridge

BUSH STREET

TAYLOR STREET

SUTTER STREET

UNION
SQUARE

2nd STREET

Muni
Metro BART
Montgomery St

GEARY STREET

Union
Square

MASON STREET

GEARY STREET

GOUGH STREET

St Mary's
Cathedral

FRANKLIN STREET

TENDERLOIN

POLK STREET

LARKIN STREET

LEAVENWORTH STREET

HOWARD STREET

SFMOMA

Yerba
Buena
Gardens

FOLSOM STREET

HARRISON STREET

BRYANT STREET

South
Park

BRANNAN STREET

SOUTH
BEACH

BERRY STREET

Jefferson
Square

Muni
Metro BART
Powell St

5th STREET

SOMA

80

SBC
Park

China
Basin

GATE AVENUE

GOLDEN GATE AVENUE

Asian Art
Museum

6th STREET

Muni
Metro BART
Civic Center

7th STREET

3rd STREET

City Hall

CIVIC
CENTER

HAYES
VALLEY

OCTAVIA STREET

Muni
Metro
Van Ness Av

9th STREET

10th STREET

11th STREET

MARKET STREET

VAN NESS AVENUE

HOWARD STREET

FOLSOM STREET

BRYANT STREET

BRANNAN STREET

5th STREET

4th STREET

3rd STREET

101

UPPER
MARKET

14th STREET

16th STREET

280

Central
Basin

Mission
Dolores

GUERRERO STREET

16th STREET

SOUTH VAN NESS AVENUE

16th St
BART

Franklin
Square

POTRERO AVENUE

Jackson
Park

POTRERO HILL

3rd STREET

17th STREET

MISSION

101

Mission
Dolores
Park

A

Golden Gate
Bridge

1

Fort
Point

1

Golden Gate Promenade

*Pacific
Ocean*

101

View
Point

Golden Gate
National
Recreation
Area

B

*San Francisco
Bay*

Golden Gate Promenade

*Crissy
Field*

Golden Gate
National
Recreation
Area

*Baker
Beach*

2

GOLDEN GATE BRIDGE FREEWAY

101

LINCOLN BOULEVARD

LINCOLN BOULEVARD

LINCOLN

*San Francisco
National
Cemetery*

Visitor
Information
Center

MONTGOMERY STREET

*Main
Post*

MORAGA

AVENUE

FUNSTON AVENUE

ARGUELLO BOULEVARD

1

WASHINGTON BOULEVARD

WASHINGTON BOULEVARD

P r e s i d i o

3

WASHINGTON BOULEVARD

MacArthur
Tunnel

*Presidio
Golf Course*

WEST PACIFIC AVENUE

ARGUELLO BOULEVARD

CHERRY STREET

*Mountain Lake
Park*

LAKE STREET

LAKE STREET

4

*Richmond
Playground*

20th AVENUE

18th AVENUE

16th AVENUE

CALIFORNIA STREET

14th AVENUE

12th AVENUE

10th AVENUE

8th AVENUE

6th AVENUE

CALIFORNIA STREET

CORNWALL STREET

4th AVENUE

CALIFORNIA STREET

2nd AVENUE

PALM AVENUE

JORDAN AVENUE

COMMONWEALTH AVENUE

CLEMENT STREET

308 Time Out San Francisco

CLEMENT STREET

PARK

See
p312

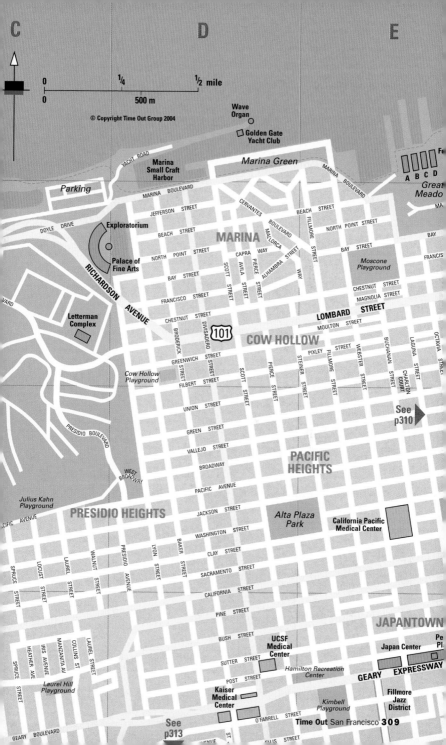

C   D   E

0   ¼   ½ mile
0   500 m

© Copyright Time Out Group 2004

Wave
Organ

Golden Gate
Yacht Club

Marina
Small Craft
Harbor

Marina Green

Parking

JEFFERSON STREET

CERVANTES

MARINA BOULEVARD

BEACH STREET

MARINA BOULEVARD

Great
Meado

A B C D

Fe

BOULEVARD

FILLMORE STREET

NORTH POINT STREET

BAY

MARINA

Exploratorium

BEACH STREET

CAPRA WAY

MALLORCA STREET

BAY STREET

FRANCIS

RICHARDSON AVENUE

Palace of
Fine Arts

NORTH POINT STREET

AVILA STREET

PIERCE STREET

ALHAMBRA STREET

WAY

*Moscone
Playground*

DOYLE DRIVE

BAY STREET

SCOTT STREET

CHESTNUT STREET

FRANCISCO STREET

MAGNOLIA STREET

Letterman
Complex

CHESTNUT STREET

DIVISADERO

101

LOMBARD STREET

VARD

BRODERICK STREET

MOULTON STREET

PIXLEY STREET

LAGUNA STREET

OCTAVIA STREET

*Cow Hollow
Playground*

GREENWICH STREET

COW HOLLOW

PIERCE STREET

STEINER STREET

FILLMORE STREET

WEBSTER STREET

BUCHANAN STREET

CHARLTON COURT

FILBERT STREET

SCOTT STREET

UNION STREET

See
p310

PRESIDIO BOULEVARD

GREEN STREET

VALLEJO STREET

PACIFIC
HEIGHTS

*Julius Kahn
Playground*

WEST BROADWAY

BROADWAY

PACIFIC AVENUE

PRESIDIO HEIGHTS

JACKSON STREET

*Alta Plaza
Park*

California Pacific
Medical Center

CIFIC AVENUE

WASHINGTON STREET

SPRUCE STREET

LOCUST STREET

LAUREL STREET

WALNUT STREET

PRESIDIO AVENUE

LYON STREET

BAKER STREET

CLAY STREET

SACRAMENTO STREET

CALIFORNIA STREET

PINE STREET

HEATHER AVE

IRIS AVENUE

MANZANITA AV

COLLINS ST

LAUREL STREET

BUSH STREET

JAPANTOWN

Pe
Pl

Japan Center

UCSF
Medical
Center

SUTTER STREET

*Hamilton Recreation
Center*

GEARY EXPRESSWAY

*Laurel Hill
Playground*

SPRUCE STREET

POST STREET

Kaiser
Medical
Center

*Kimbell
Playground*

Fillmore
Jazz
District

See
p313

O'FARRELL STREET

ST

GEARY BOULEVARD

AVENUE

ELLIS STREET

Time Out San Francisco 309

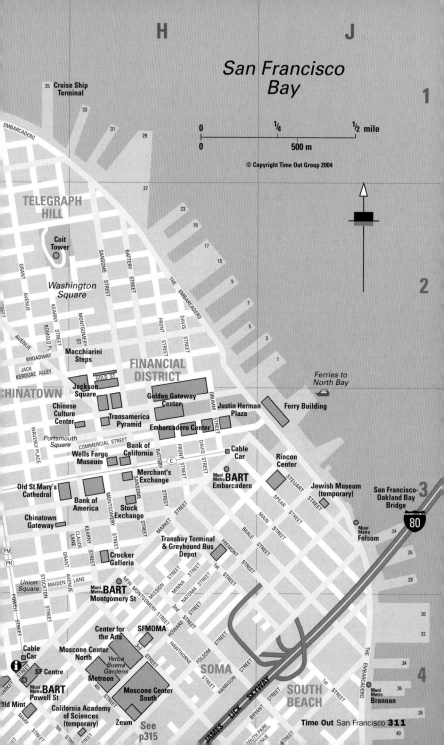

San Francisco Bay

35 Cruise Ship
Terminal

33

EMBARCADERO

31

29

27

0   ¼   ½ mile

0   500 m

© Copyright Time Out Group 2004

1

23

TELEGRAPH
HILL

19

Coit
Tower

17

15

9

7

Washington
Square

5

2

3

1

Ferries to
North Bay

Macchiarini
Steps

FINANCIAL
DISTRICT

Jackson
Square

Golden Gateway
Center

Justin Herman
Plaza

Ferry Building

CHINATOWN

Chinese
Culture
Center

Transamerica
Pyramid

Embarcadero Center

Portsmouth
Square

COMMERCIAL STREET

Bank of
California

Wells Fargo
Museum

Cable
Car

Rincon
Center

Merchant's
Exchange

Old St Mary's
Cathedral

C

Muni
Metro

BART
Embarcadero

Jewish Museum
(temporary)

San Francisco-
Oakland Bay
Bridge

3

Bank of
America

Stock
Exchange

Muni
Metro
Folsom

80

Chinatown
Gateway

24

26

PM
PH

Crocker
Galleria

Transbay Terminal
& Greyhound Bus
Depot

28

Union
Square

Muni
Metro

BART
Montgomery St

30

32

Center for
the Arts

SFMOMA

Cable
Car

Moscone Center
North

Yerba
Buena
Gardens

34

SF Centre

i

Metreon

SOMA

Muni
Metro

BART
Powell St

Moscone Center
South

SOUTH
BEACH

Brannan

36

Old Mint

California Academy
of Sciences
(temporary)

Zeum

See
p315

JAMES LICK SKYWAY

38

40

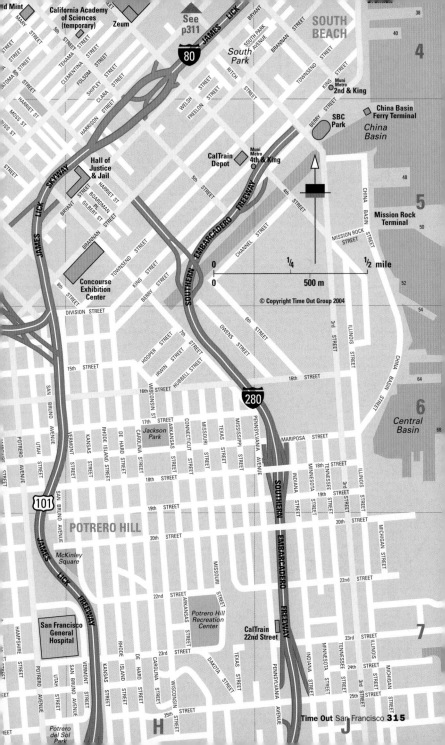

Street Index

1st Street – p311 H3/J4
2nd Avenue – p308 B4, p312 C6
2nd Street – p311 H4
3rd Avenue – p312 B5/6
3rd Street – p311 H4, p315 J7
4th Avenue – p308 B4, p312 B6
4th Street – p315 J5
5th Avenue – p312 B5/6
5th Street – p311 G4, p315 H5
6th Avenue – p308 B4, p312 B6
6th Street – p315 G4/H6
7th Avenue – p312 B5/7
7th Street – p314 G5, p315 H6
8th Avenue – p308 B4, p312 B6
8th Street – p314/15 G5
9th Avenue – p312 B5/7
9th Street – p314 G5
10th Avenue – p308 B4, p312 B6
10th Street – p314 G5
11th Avenue – p312 B5/7
11th Street – p314 G5
12th Avenue – p308 A4, p312 B6
12th Street – p314 F5
13th Avenue – p312 A5/B7
14th Avenue – p308 A4, p312 A7
14th Street – p313 E6, p314 F6
15th Avenue – p312 A5/7
15th Street – p313 D6, p314 F6, p315 H6
16th Avenue – p308 A4, p312 A7
16th Street – p314 F6, p315 J6
17th Avenue – p312 A5/7
17th Street – p313 C6, p315H6
18th Avenue – p308 A4, p312 A6
18th Street – p313 D7, p315 J6
19th Avenue – p312 A5/7
19th Street – p313 D7, p315 J6
20th Avenue – p308 A4, p312 A6
20th Street – p313 D7, p315 J7
21st Avenue – p312 A5/7
21st Street – p313 E7, p314 F/G7
22nd Avenue – p312 A6
22nd Street – p313 D7, p315 J7
23rd Street – p313 D7, p315 J7
24th Street – p313 D7, p315 J7
25th Street – p314 G7, p315 J7
Alabama Street – p314 G6/7
Alameda Street – p314 G6
Albion Street – p314 F6
Alhambra Street – p309 D2
Alvarado Street – p313 D7
Ames Street – p314 F7
Anza St – p312 A/B5, p313 C4
Anza Vista Avenue – p313 D4
Arguello Blvd – p308 B3, p312 C5
Arkansas Street – p315 H6/7
Ash Street – p314 E5
Ashbury Street – p313 D6
Austin Street – p310 F3
Baker Street – p309 D3, p313 D5
Balboa Street – p312 A/B5
Balmy Alley – p314 G7
Bartlett Street – p314 F7
Battery Street – p311 H2/3
Bay St – p309 D/E2, p310 E/G2
Beach St – p309 D/E2, p310 G1
Beale Street – p311 H3
Beaumont Avenue – p313 C4
Belvedere Street – p313 C6
Berry Street – p315 H/J5
Brady Street – p314 F5
Brannan St – p311 J4, p315 H5
Broadway – p309 D3, p310 F3, p311 G2
Broderick St – p309 D2, p313 D5
Brosnan Street – p314 F6
Bryant Street – p311 H4, p314 G6/7, p315 G/H4
Buchanan Street – p309 E2, p310 E2, p314 E4
Buena Vista Avenue – p313 D6
Burnett Avenue – p313 D7
Bush Street – p309 D4, p310 G3
Cabrillo Street – p312 A/B5
California Street – p308 A/B4, p309 D4, p310 G3
Capp Street – p314 F6/7
Capra Way – p309 D2
Carl Street – p313 C6

Carolina Street – p315 H6/7
Castro Street – p313 E6/7
Cedar Street – p310 F4
Central Avenue – p313 D5
Central Skyway – p314 G6
Cervantes Boulevard – p309 D2
Chattanooga Street – p314 E7
Chestnut Street – p309 D/E2, p310 E/G2
China Basin Street – p315 J5/6
Church Street – p314 E6/7
Clara Street – p315 H4
Clarendon Avenue – p312/13 C7
Claude Lane – p311 H3
Clay Street – p309 D3, p310 G3
Clayton Street – p313 D6
Clement St – p308/12 A/B4
Clementina Street – p315 H4
Clinton Street – p314 F6
Cole Street – p313 C6
Collingwood Street – p313 E7
Columbus Avenue – p310 G2
Commercial Street – p311 H3
Commonwealth Ave – p308 C4
Connecticut Street – p315 H6
Corbett Avenue – p313 D7
Cornwall Street – p308 B4
Corwin Street – p313 D7
Cumberland St – p313/14 E7
Davis Street – p311 H2/3
De Haro Street – p315 H6/7
Delbrook Avenue – p313 C7
Delmar Street – p313 D6
Diamond Street – p313 E7
Divisadero Street – p309 D2, p313 D5
Division Street – p315 H6
Dolores Street – p314 E6/F7
Dore Street – p314 G5
Douglass Street – p313 D7
Downey Street – p313 D6
Doyle Drive – p309 C2
Drumm Street – p311 H3
Duboce Avenue – p313/14 E6
Eddy Street – p310 G4, p313 D4
Ellis Street – p310 G4, p313 D4
Elm Street – p310/14 F4
Embarcadero – p310 G1, p311 J4
Eureka Street – p313 D7
Fair Oaks Street – p314 F7
Fell St – p313 C/E5, p314 E/F5
Fern Street – p310 F3
Filbert St – p309 D2, p310 G2
Fillmore Street – p309 E2, p313/14 E4
Florida Street – p314 G6/7
Folsom Street – p311/15 H4, p314 G5/7
Francisco Street – p309 D2, p310 E/G2
Franklin Street – p310/14 F2/4
Frederick Street – p313 C6
Fremont Street – p311 H3
Front Street – p311 H2/3
Fulton St – p312 A/B5, p313 C/D5
Funston Avenue – p308 C2
Geary Boulevard – p309 C4, p312 A/B4
Geary Expressway – p309/10 E4
Geary Street – p310 G4
Golden Gate Avenue – p310/14 F4, p313 C/D5
Golden Gate Bridge Freeway – p308 B2
Gough Street – p310 G2, p314 F5
Grace Street – p314 G5
Grand View Avenue – p313 D7
Grant Avenue – p311 G2/3
Green Street – p309 D3, p310 G2
Greenwich St – p309 D2, p310 G2
Grove St – p313 C/D5, p314 E5
Guerrero Street – p314 F6/7
Haight Street – p313 C6/E5, p314 E5
Hampshire Street – p315 G6/7
Hancock Street – p313/14 E7
Harriet Street – p315 G5
Harrison Street – p311 H4, p314 G5, p315 H5

Hartford Street – p313/14 E7
Hawthorne Street – p311 H4
Hayes St – p313 C/E5, p314 E5
Hemlock Street – p310 F4
Henry Street – p313/14 E6
Hermann Street – p314 E5
Hill Street – p313/14 E7
Hooper Street – p315 H6
Howard Street – p311 H4, p314 G5
Hubbell Street – p315 H6
Hugo Street – p312 B6
Hyde St – p310 F2/G4, p314 G4
Ilinois Street – p315 J6/7
Indiana Street – p315 J6/7
Irving Street – p312 A/B6
Irwin Street – p315 H6
Jack Kerouac Alley – p311 G2
Jackson St – p309 D3, p310 G3
James Lick Freeway – p315 G7
James Lick Skyway – p311 H4, p315 H4/G5
Jefferson St – p309 D2, p310 F1
Jersey Street – p314 E7
John F Kennedy Drive – p312 A/B5
Jones Street – p310 F2/G4
Jordan Avenue – p308 C4
Judah Street – p312 A/B6
Julian Street – p314 F6
Kansas Street – p315 H6/7
Kearny Street – p311 G2/H3
Kezar Drive – p312/13 C6
King Street – p315 H5/J4
Kirkham Street – p312 A/B7
Laguna Street – p309/10 E2, p314 E4
Lake Street – p308 A/B4
Langton Street – p314 G5
Larkin St – p310 F2/4, p314 F4
Laurel Street – p309 C3/4
Lawton Street – p312 A/B7
Leavenworth Street – p310 F2/G4, p314 G4
Lexington Street – p314 F6
Liberty Street – p313/14 E7
Lincoln Boulevard – p308 A/C2
Lincoln Way – p312 A/B6
Linden Street – p314 E5
Locust Street – p309 C3
Lombard St – p309 E2, p310 G2
Lyon Street – p309 D3, p313 D5
MacArthur Avenue – p310 E2
Magnolia Street – p309/10 E2
Maiden Lane – p311 G3
Main Street – p311 J3
Maple Street – p308 C3
Marina Boulevard – p309 D2/E1
Mariposa St – p314 G6, p315 J6
Market Street – p311 G4/H3, p313 D6/7, p314 E6/F5, F5, p315 G4
Martin Luther King Jr Drive – p312 A/B6
Mary Street – p311/15 G4
Mason Street – p310 G2/4
Masonic Avenue – p313 D4/5/6
McAllister Street – p312 C5, p313 D5, p314 F4
Minna Street – p311 H3, p314 F5, p315 G4
Minnesota Street – p315 J6/7
Mission Street – p311 H3, p314 F7/G4
Mission Rock Street – p315 J5
Mississippi St – p315 H6
Missouri Street – p315 H6/7
Montgomery Street – p311 H2/3
Montgomery Street (Presidio) – p308 B2
Moraga Avenue – p308 B2
Moraga Street – p312 A/B7
Moulton Street – p309 E2
Myrtle Street – p310 F4
Natoma Street – p311 H4, p314 F5, p315 G4
New Montgomery St – p311 H3
Noe St – p313/14 E6/7
Noriega Street – p312 A/B7
North Point Street – p309 D/E2, p310 F1
Oak Street – p313 C/E5, p314 E5

Octavia St – p310 E2, p314 F4
O'Farrell Street – p309/13 D4, p310 G4
Olive Street – p310 F4
Ortega Street – p312 A/B7
Owens Street – p315 H6
Pacheco Street – p312 B7
Pacific Ave – p309 D3, p310 G3
Page St – p313 C/E5, p314 E5
Palm Avenue – p308 C4
Panorama Drive – p313 C7
Park Presidio Boulevard – p312 A4
Parker Avenue – p309 C4
Parnassus Ave – p312/13 B6
Pennsylvania Avenue – p315 J6/7
Pierce Street – p309 D2, p313 E4
Pine Street – p309 D4, p310 G3
Pixley Street – p309 E2
Polk Street – p310 F2/4, p314 F4
Pond Street – p313/14 E6
Post Street – p309 D4, p310 G3
Potrero Avenue – p315 G6/7
Powell Street – p310 G2, p311 G4
Presidio Avenue – p309 D3
Presidio Boulevard – p309 C3
Quane Street – p314 F7
Rhode Island Street – p315 H6/7
Richardson Avenue – p309 C2
Ritch Street – p315 H4
Romain Street – p313 D7
Romolo Place – p311 G2
Roosevelt Way – p313 D6
Rose Street – p314 F5
Rossi Avenue – p312 C5
Sacramento Street – p309 D3, p310 G3
San Bruno Avenue – p315 G6/H7
San Carlos Street – p314 F6
San Jose Avenue – p314 F7
Sanchez St – p313 E6, p314 E6/7
Sansome Street – p311 H2/3
Scott Street – p309 D2, p313 E4
Shipley Street – p315 H4
Shotwell Street – p314 F6/G7
Shrader Street – p313 C6
Southern Embarcadero Freeway – p315 H5/J6
South Park Ave – p311/p315 H4
South Van Ness Ave – p314 F6/7
Spear Street – p311 J3
Spruce Street – p309 C3/4
St Joseph's Street – p313 D4
Stanyan Street – p313 C5/6
Steiner Street – p309 E2, p313/14 E4
Steuart Street – p311 J3
Stevenson Street – p310 G4, p314 F5/G4
Stockton Street – p311 G2/3
Sutter Street – p309 D4, p310 G3
Taylor Street – p310 G2/4
Tehama Street – p315 G4
Tennessee Street – p315 J6/7
Townsend Street – p315 H5/J5
Treat Avenue – p314 G6/7
Turk St – p310 G4, p313 C5/D4
Twin Peaks Boulevard – p313 D7
Union Street – p309 D3, p310 G2
Upper Terrace – p313 D6
Utah Street – p315 G6/7
Valencia Street – p314 F6/7
Vallejo Street – p309 D3, p310 G2
Van Ness Ave – p310 F3, p314 F3
Vermont Street – p315 H6/7
Vicksburg Street – p314 E7
Waller Street – p313 C6, p314 E5
Walnut Street – p309 D3
Washington Blvd – p308 A/B3
Washington Street – p309 D3, p310 G3
Waverly Place – p311 G3
Webster Street – p309/10 E2, p313/14 E4
West Pacific Avenue – p308 B3, p309 C3
Willow Street – p310 F4
Wisconsin Street – p315 H6/7
Yacht Road – p309 D1
York Street – p314 G6, p315 G7